I0120686

THE

LAW GLOSSARY:

BEING A SELECTION OF THE

GREEK, LATIN, SAXON, FRENCH, NORMAN AND ITALIAN

SENTENCES, PHRASES, AND MAXIMS,

FOUND IN THE LEADING

ENGLISH AND AMERICAN REPORTS, AND ELEMENTARY WORKS.

WITH HISTORICAL AND EXPLANATORY NOTES.

ALPHABETICALLY ARRANGED, AND TRANSLATED INTO ENGLISH, FOR THE USE
OF THE MEMBERS OF THE LEGAL PROFESSION, LAW STUDENTS,
SHERIFFS, JUSTICES OF THE PEACE, ETC. ETC.

DEDICATED, (BY PERMISSION,)

TO THE HONORABLE JOHN SAVAGE,
LATE CHIEF JUSTICE OF THE SUPREME COURT OF THE STATE OF NEW YORK.

BY THOMAS TAYLER,

AUTHOR OF "PRECEDENTS OF WILLS, DRAWN CONFORMABLY TO THE
REVISED STATUTES OF THE STATE OF NEW YORK."

FOURTH EDITION, REVISED, CORRECTED AND ENLARGED.

BY A MEMBER OF THE NEW YORK BAR.

THE LAWBOOK EXCHANGE, LTD.
Clark, New Jersey

ISBN 978-1-61619-608-0

Lawbook Exchange edition 1995, 2019

The quality of this reprint is equivalent to the quality of the original work.

THE LAWBOOK EXCHANGE, LTD.
33 Terminal Avenue
Clark, New Jersey 07066-1321

*Please see our website for a selection of our other publications
and fine facsimile reprints of classic works of legal history:*
www.lawbookexchange.com

Library of Congress Cataloging-in-Publication Data

Tayler, Thomas, fl. 1833-1843.
  The law glossary : being a selection of the Greek, Latin,
Saxon, French, Norman, and Italian sentences, phrases, and
maxims ... / by Thomas Tayler.
      p. cm.
Originally published: 4th ed., rev., corr. and enl. New York :
Lewis & Blood, Law Booksellers and Publishers, 1856.
Includes bibliographical references.
  ISBN 1-886363-12-9 (cloth : alk. paper)
  1. Law--Dictionaries--Polyglot. 2. Legal maxims. 3.
Dictionaries, Polyglot. I. Title.
  K54.T39 2000
  340'.1'4--dc21   99-047230

Printed in the United States of America on acid-free paper

THE

LAW GLOSSARY:

BEING A SELECTION OF THE

GREEK, LATIN, SAXON, FRENCH, NORMAN AND ITALIAN

SENTENCES, PHRASES, AND MAXIMS,

FOUND IN THE LEADING

ENGLISH AND AMERICAN REPORTS, AND ELEMENTARY WORKS.

WITH HISTORICAL AND EXPLANATORY NOTES.

ALPHABETICALLY ARRANGED, AND TRANSLATED INTO ENGLISH, FOR THE USE
OF THE MEMBERS OF THE LEGAL PROFESSION, LAW STUDENTS,
SHERIFFS, JUSTICES OF THE PEACE, ETC. ETC.

DEDICATED, (BY PERMISSION,)

TO THE HONORABLE JOHN SAVAGE,

LATE CHIEF JUSTICE OF THE SUPREME COURT OF THE STATE OF NEW YORK.

BY THOMAS TAYLER,

AUTHOR OF "PRECEDENTS OF WILLS, DRAWN CONFORMABLY TO THE
REVISED STATUTES OF THE STATE OF NEW YORK."

FOURTH EDITION, REVISED, CORRECTED AND ENLARGED.

BY A MEMBER OF THE NEW YORK BAR.

NEW YORK:
LEWIS & BLOOD, LAW BOOKSELLERS AND PUBLISHERS,
NO. 84 NASSAU STREET.
1856.

Northern District of New York, ss.:

[L. S.] BE IT REMEMBERED, That on the second day of November, in the fifty-eighth year of the Independence of the United States of America, A. D. 1833, JAMES HUNTER, of the said district, hath deposited in this Office, the title of a Book, the right whereof he claims as Proprietor, in the words following, to wit:

"The Law Glossary: being a Selection of the Greek, Latin, Saxon, French, Norman and Italian Sentences, Phrases and Maxims, found in the works of Lord Coke, Shower, Peere Williams, Sir William Blackstone, Sir Francis Buller, Vezey, Chancellor Kent, Reeves, Durnford and East, Taunton, Sellon, Johnson. Cowen, Sugden, Preston, Bosanquet, Starkie, Tidd, Phillips, Chitty, Moore, Wendell, and numerous other Law Writers: with Historical and Explanatory Notes: alphabetically arranged and translated into English, for the use of the members of the Legal Profession, Law Students, Sheriffs, Justices of the Peace, &c., &c. Dedicated (by permission) to the Honorable John Savage, Chief Justice of the Supreme Court of the State of New York."

The right whereof he claims as Proprietor, in conformity with an Act of Congress, entitled An Act to amend the several Acts respecting Copyrights.

RUTGER B. MILLER,
Clerk of the Northern District of New York.

Entered according to Act of Congress, in the year 1845, by JAMES J. STEWART, in the Clerk's office of the District Court of the United States, for the Southern District of New York.

Entered according to Act of Congress, in the year One thousand eight hundred and fifty-five,

BY LEWIS & BLOOD,

In the Clerk's office of the District Court of the United States, for the Southern District of New York.

JOHN W. AMERMAN, PRINTER,
No. 60 William-street, N. Y.

PREFACE TO THE FOURTH EDITION.

THE great utility of the following work, and its appreciation by a discerning public, are shown by the rapid exhaustion of three large editions, and the demand for a fourth. It is, indeed, extremely popular with the profession, and has become an almost indispensable adjunct of every law-library. Nor is its practical value confined to lawyers, for whom it was originally prepared and mainly designed. The intelligent of both sexes, and among all classes of our citizens, no less than the members of the other learned professions, cannot fail to derive profitable instruction from its pages. Its matter has been carefully gathered, with judgment and great good taste, from the ancient oracles and standard authorities of the law. It contains many phrases of classical beauty, and much curious learning, expressed in the rich, though quaint language, of the olden time. Nowhere else within the same compass, can be found such stores of rare and useful information.

Thus much have we felt at liberty to say in commendation of this work. All who are familiar with it will bear us witness that we have not over-estimated it, nor can we, as humble editors of the distinguished labors of another (now no more), be charged with egotism in thus frankly expressing our admiration of this his legacy to the generations to come after him.

A single word will dispose of what we have done. The work has been thoroughly revised with a view to its entire accuracy, and it is now placed in a permanent form. To the present edition have been added over one hundred pages of new matter, comprising upwards of eighteen hundred phrases, besides several notes. It is now complete in all respects, and we confidently look for a continuance of the patronage and favor it has hitherto received.

NEW YORK, March 1st 1855.

CERTIFICATES.

ALBANY, February 1st, 1830.

SIR—Yours of the 26th ult. is received. I have no doubt that your book will be found useful in every lawyer's library, and essentially aid the progress of the student. I have no possible objection to the honor you intend me, by dedicating it to me. I am, very respectfully, your obedient servant, JOHN SAVAGE.

Having been favored with a sight of "the Law Glossary," translated and alphabetically arranged, we consider it a work which does credit to the industry and talent of the author; and we fully concur in opinion with the Honorable Chief Justice Savage, that it will be found useful in every lawyer's library, and essentially aid the progress of the student. F. P. HUNN, (late District Attorney,) Monticello.
    G. O. BELDEN, same place.

I have perused the manuscript of "the Law Glossary," which appears to be a copious work and faithfully executed. I should suppose its publication will be useful to the profession.
    April 22, 1830. W. T. McCOUN, (V. Chancellor, N. York.)

I have perused "the Law Glossary;" it is replete with usefulness—the labor of the compilation must have been immense.
        JOHN VAN NESS YATES, (late Secretary of State.)
    Albany, April 16, 1832.

Having read the greater part of "the Law Glossary" with profit and much gratification, I can cheerfully recommend it as an elaborate, accurate, and useful book. It will be found valuable to all other literary and professional men, as well as to gentlemen of the bar.
    Albany, Oct. 28, 1833. JAS. R. WILSON, D.D.

LAW GLOSSARY.

A AVER ET TENER.——To have and to hold

AB ACTIS.——A person who has charge of *acta*, public records, registers, or journals; a notary or clerk. Chancellors also bore this title in the early history of that office.

ABACTOR.——Among the Romans, a stealer or driver away of cattle.

ABALIENATIO vel translatio dominii vel proprietatis.—— The alienation or transfer of the domain or property. *Vide note.*

AB aratro abductus est.——He was taken from the plough.

AB ardendo.——" By burning." Whence " arson."

ABAMITA.——The sister of one's great great grandfather.

ABARNARE, from *Sax. Abarian.*——To disclose to a magistrate any secret crime.

ABATAMENTUM.——An entry by intrusion.

ABBAS.——An Abbot. *Vide note.*

ABBATIS.——A steward of the stables; an ostler.

ABBATISSA.——An abbess.

ABBATTRE maison.——To ruin or throw down a house.

ABBETTAVIT, incitavit, et procuravit, &c.——He abetted, incited, and procured, &c.

ABBROCAMENTUM.——The forestalling of a market or fair.

ABBUTTALS.——Properly, the limits or boundary lines

of lands on the *ends,* as distinguished from those of the sides. *Vide note.*

ABCARIARE.——To take or carry away.

ABDITE latet.——He lurks privily.

ABDITORIUM.——An abditory or hiding place to conceal plate, goods, and money. It is also sometimes used for a place in which relics are preserved.

ABDUCERE.——To abduct, to take away by force.

ABEARANCE.——Deportment, bearing, or behavior

ABEGIT pecora.——He drove away the cattle.

ABEREMURDER.——Plain or manifest murder, as distinguished from the offence of manslaughter and chance-medley. The *Saxon* word for open, or manifest, is "*œbere,*" and "*morth,*" murder.

ABEYANCE.——Suspense, expectation. An estate is said to be *in abeyance,* that is, in expectation, where there is no person existing in whom it can be vested; the law considering it as always existing, and ready to vest when a proper owner appears.

ABIATICUS.——A grandson.

ABIGEATOR.——*See Abactor.*

ABIGEI.——Persons who stole cattle.

AB inconvenienti.——From the inconvenience.

AB ingressu ecclesiæ.——" From entering the church." These words composed part of the writ of excommunication.

AB initio.——From the beginning.

AB intestato.——From (or by) the intestate.

ABJECTIRE.——To lose a cause by default or neglect to prosecute.

ABJUDICARE.——To deprive of a thing by the decision of a court.

ABJURARE.——To forswear; to renounce or abandon upon oath.

ABMATERTERA.——A great great grandmother's sister.

ABNEPOS.——A great great grandson. ABNEPTIS a great great grand-daughter.

AB officio et beneficio.——From the office and benefice.

AB olim ordinatum.——Formerly constituted.

AB olim consensu.——By ancient consent.

ABPATRUUS.——A great great grandfather's brother.

ABRASIO.——An erasure.

ABROCEUR.——A broker.

ABROGATE.——To repeal.

ABSOILE.——To absolve, to pardon.

ABSOLUTE CONVEYANCE.—Conveying the right or property in a thing free from any condition or qualification.

ABSOLUTE RIGHTS.—The rights which belong to persons as individuals, viz., the right of personal security, personal liberty, and the right to acquire, hold, and dispose of property.

ABSOLUTE WARRANDICE.——A warranty against all incumbrances.

ABSOLUTUM dominium in omnibus licitis.——Absolute power in all things lawful.

ABSOLUTUM et directum dominium.——The absolute and direct ownership, (or fee simple.)

ABSONIARE.——To detest and shun.

ABSQUE abstractione, amissione, seu spoliatione, portare tenentur, ita quo pro defectu dictorum communium portatorum seu servientium suorum, hujusmodi bona et catalla eis sic ut prefertur deliberata, non sunt perdita, amissa, vel spoliata.——They are bound to carry the goods without abstraction, loss, or injury, for notwithstanding the neglect of the said common carriers or their servants, goods and chattels of this sort are to be delivered to them in the same manner as stated, not being injured, lost, or damaged.

ABSQUE aliqua probabili causa prosecutus fuit quoddam breve de privilegio.——Without any other probable cause he was sued by a certain writ of privilege.

ABSQUE aliquo inde reddendo.——Without yielding anything therefrom.

ABSQUE consensu majoris partis præfectorum collegiorum.——Without the consent of the major part of the prefects of the colleges.

ABSQUE generali senatu, et populi conventu et edicto. ——Without the general convention and order of the senate and people. *Vide note to "Is ordo."*

ABSQUE hoc, quod feoffavit in forma, &c.——Without this, that he enfeoffed in form, &c.

ABSQUE impetitione vasti.——Without impeachment of waste.

ABSQUE probabili causa.——Without a probable cause

ABSQUE purgatione facienda.——"Without purgation being made." Without clearing himself by oath. *Vide note to "Compurgatores."*

ABSURDUM etenim clericis est, imo etiam opprobriosum, si peritos se velint ostendere disceptationum esse forensium.——For it is absurd, nay, even disgraceful, if the clergy should boast of showing their skill in legal disputes.

ABUNDANS cautela non nocet.——Abundant caution does no injury.

ABUT.——To limit or bound.

ACATE, or ACHATE.——A purchase, contract, or bargain.

ACCAPITUM.——The money paid to the chief lord by a vassal upon his admission to the feud.

ACCEDAS ad curiam.——That you go to court.

ACCEDAS ad vice comitem.——That you go to the sheriff.

ACCEPTANCE au besoin.——To accept in case of need.

ACCEPTANCE supra protest.——An acceptance of a bill after protest. Such acceptance made by a third party for the honor of the drawer, or some particular endorser.

ACCEPTILATIO.——It is a mode of releasing a person from an obligation without payment, called an imaginary payment. But only verbal contracts could thus be dissolved, the form being verbal by question and answer.

ACCESSARY.——One who participates in the commission of an offence, either by advice, command, instigation, or concealment, before or after the offence is committed, though not present at the committal.

ACCESSORIUM non ducit, sed sequitur suum principalem. ——An accessory does not lead, but follows his principal.

ACCESSORIUS sequitur naturam sui principalis.——An accessory follows the nature of his principal.

ACCIDENS quod per custodiam, curam et diligentiam mentis humanæ evitari non potest.——An accident which cannot be prevented by the watchfulness, care, and diligence of the human mind.

ACCION sur le case.——An action on the case.

ACCO.——Abbreviated from *Actio*, an action.

ACCOLA.——A husbandman.

ACCOLADE. From the Fr. "*accoler*," "collum amplecti." ——A ceremony used in making a knight, the king putting his hand about the knight's neck.

ACCOMPLICE.——One who unites with others in the commission of a felony.

ACCREDULITARE.——To purge one's self of an offence by oath.

ACCRESCERE.——To grow to ; to accrue.

ACCUSARE debet nemo se ipsum.——No person should accuse himself.

AC etiam billæ.——And also to the bill, (or writ.)

ACQUIETATUS inde.——Therefore he is discharged (or acquitted).

ACQUIETATUS inde de præmissis.——Therefore he is acquitted of the matters.

ACTA exteriora indicant interiora secreta.——The outward acts show the secret intentions.

ACTIO accrevit.——An action has accrued.

ACTIO bonæ fidei.——Action of good faith.

ACTIO commodati directa.——An action brought to recover a thing loaned, and not returned.

ACTIO commodati contraria.——Action brought to compel the execution of a contract.

ACTIO de dolo malo.——Action of fraud.

ACTIO ex empto.——An action of purchase; brought
by the buyer to obtain possession of the thing sold.

ACTIO ex vendito.——An action of sale; brought by
the seller to recover the price of the article sold and delivered.

ACTIO furti.——Action of theft.

ACTIO finium regundorum.——An action to determine
boundaries between adjoining lands.

ACTIO in rem.——An action to recover a thing belonging to us in the possession of another.

ACTIO in simplum.——An action for the single value
of a thing.

ACTIO legis aquiliæ.——An action to recover damages
far maliciously injuring, killing or wounding anything belonging to another.

ACTIO quod jussu.——Action brought against a master
for business transacted by his slave, under his *order*.

ACTIO or interdictum quod vi aut clam.——An action
against one who has clandestinely erected or destroyed a
building, either on another's ground or his own, which has
thereby unlawfully injured him.

ACTIO redhibitoria.——To compel a seller to receive
back the thing sold and to return the price.

ACTIO quod metus causa.——An action granted to a
person who had been compelled unlawfully, either by
force or just fear to sell, promise or deliver a thing to another.

ACTIO, or interdictum unde vi.——To recover possession
of land taken by force; similar to the modern action of
ejectment.

ACTIO vi bonorum raptorum.——An action for goods

forcibly taken, and to recover a penalty of triple their value.

ACTIONARE.—i. e. *in jus vocare.*——To prosecute one in a suit at law.

ACTIONEM præcludere debet.——He ought to bar the action.

ACTIONES compositæ sunt, quibus inter se homines disceptarent; quas actiones ne populus prout vellet institueret, certas solennesque esse voluerunt.——Actions are so prepared (or adjusted) in which men litigate with each other, that they are made definite and established (or customary) lest the people proceed as each may think proper (in his own case). *Vide note.*

ACTIONES in personam, quæ adversus eum intenduntur, qui ex contractu, vel delicto, obligatus est aliquid dare, vel concedere.——Personal actions which are brought against him, who, either from contract or injury, is obliged to give, or allow something. *Vide note.*

ACTIONES legis.——Law suits. *Vide note.*

ACTIO non accrevit infra sex annos.——The action has not accrued within six years.

ACTIONEM non habere debet.——He ought not to have an action.

ACTIO personalis moritur cum persona.——A personal action dies with the person.

ACTIO sequitur.——" An action lies," (or is sustainable.)

ACTOR.——A plaintiff.

ACTOR sequitur formam rei.——" A plaintiff follows the course of proceeding"—i. e. according to the nature of the property to be recovered.

ACTUM agere.——" To labor in vain," alluding to a Roman judgment once pronounced which was in general irrevocable.   *Vide Cic. Amic.* 22.

ACTUS curiæ neminem gravabit.——An act of the court shall prejudice no one. As where a delay in an action is the act of the court, neither party shall suffer for it.

ACTUS legitimi non recipiunt modum.——Acts required by law admit of no qualification.

ACTUS Dei nemini facit injuriam.——The act of God injures no one.

ACTUS legis nemini facit injuriam.——The act (or proceeding) of the law injures no person. *Vide note.*

ACTUS me invito factus, non est meus factus.——" An act done involuntarily is not my deed:" as where a lighted squib was thrown, and warded off by another person, the injury arising therefrom is not the act of the latter person.

ACTUS non reum facit, nisi mens sit rea.——" An act does not make the person guilty, unless the intention be also guilty." There is not a maxim more true, nor one which should be more seriously considered than this; for by the various degrees of criminality in the offender, the punishment should be inflicted. There are more gradations in crime, even where attached to the *same* offence, than " colors in the bow."

AD admittendum clericum.——To admit a clerk (to holy office). A writ so called.

AD aliud examen.——To another trial (for jurisdiction).

AD annum vigessimum primum, et eousque juvenes sub tutela reponent.——To the twenty-first year, and until that period, they place youth under guardianship.

AD arma militare suscipienda.——Taking the arms from the knights.

AD assizam primam.——To the first assize.

AD assizas capiendas.——To hold the assizes.

AD audiendum, et faciendum, et consentiendum.——To hear, perform, and consent.

AD audiendum errores.——To hear errors.

AD colligendum defuncti.——To collect (the goods) of the deceased.

AD communem legem.——At common law.

AD commune nocumentum.——To the common nuisance (or grievance).

Ad compotem.——To account.

AD consulendem.——To counsel.

AD curiam.——At a court.

AD custagia.——Expenses of judicial proceedings.

AD custodiend' sub certis conditionibus, et quod ipso paratus est ad deliberand' cui vel quibus cur' consideravit, &c. Sed utrum conditiones illæ ex parte prædicti quærentis adimpletæ sunt ipse omnino ignorat et petit quod idem J. S. premuniatur.——For safe keeping under certain conditions, and which he is ready to deliver to him, or to those persons the court shall see fit, &c. But whether the conditions on the part of the said plaintiff are fulfilled he is altogether ignorant of, and he demands (or requires) that the said J. S. may be secured.

AD damnum ipsorum.——To their loss.

AD delinquendum.——In default.

AD ecclesiam, et ad amicos, pertinebit executio bonorum. ——The administration of the goods will belong to the church and to the friends (of the intestate).

AD effectum sequentem.——To the effect following.

ADEO recepta hodie sententia est, ut nemo ausit contra dicere.——The decree (or decision) was this day so received that no one dared to dispute it.

AD eversionem juris nostri.——To the overthrow of our right.

AD excambium.——To recompense.

ADEPRIMES.——For the first time.

ADERERE.——Behind.

ADESOUTH.——Beneath.

AD executionem decretorum judicii; ad estimationem pretii; damni; lucri, &c.——For the execution of the award of judgment; to the value of the price, loss, profit, &c.

AD exhæreditatem domini sui, vel dedecus corpori suo. ——To the disinheriting his lord, or the disgrace of his personal appearance.

AD exhæreditationem episcopi, vel ecclesiæ.——To the disinheriting the bishop or the church.

AD faciendum attornatum.——To appoint an attorney.

AD faciendum, subjiciendum, et recipiendum.——To do, submit and receive.

AD fidem bonam statuit pertinere notum esse emptori vitium quod noscet venditor. Ratio postulat ne quid insidiose, ne quid simulate.——It is a matter of good faith (in trade) that the buyer be made acquainted with the default (if any) which the seller knows. Reason demands that nothing be done treacherously, nor in a concealed manner.

AD fidem utriusque regis.——To the fealty of either king.

AD filum aquæ.——To the middle of the water (or stream,

AD filum medium aquæ.——To the middle line of the stream.

AD firman.——To farm.

AD finem litis.——To the conclusion of the suit.

AD gaolas deliberandas.——At the goal delivery.

AD hoc autem creatus est, et electus, ut justitiam faciat universis.——For he was made and chosen for this (office), that he may render justice to all.

AD hominem.——"To the person." This is used as meaning an argument touching the prejudice or qualities of the person addressed.

ADHUC existit.——It still remains.

ADHUC remanet quædam scintilla juris et tituli, quasi medium quid, inter utrosque status, scilicet illa possibilitas futuri usus emergentis, et sic interesse et titulus, et non tantum nuda auctoritas seu potestas remanet.——Hitherto there remains some spark of right and title, like some medium between both positions, to wit, the possibility of a future springing use, and this becomes an interest and a title, and not remains only as a naked authority or power.

ADHUC sub judice lis est.——As yet the dispute is be-fore the judge.

AD idem.——" To the same." To the like intent.

AD illud.——Thereunto.

AD imitationem pristini familiæ emptoris : quia hoc totum negotium testamenti ordinandi gratia, creditur hodie inter testatorem et hæredem agi.——Agreeably to the ancient law of family purchase, for the whole business of manag-ing the will is at this day entrusted to the testator and the heir. *See note to " Hæredes Successoresque.*

AD infinitum.——To the utmost.

AD informandum conscientiam.——To inform the mind, (to forewarn a person).

AD inquirendum.——To make inquiry.

AD inquirendum tam per sacrum proborum et legalium hominum com' n'ri *South'ton* quam per depositiones quorum-cunque testium, ac omnibus aliis viis mediis quibuscunque, "Si Prior aut Prioratus S'ci *Swithini Winton,* in jure domus, sive Prioratus, fuit seisitus in quibusdam terris vocat' *Wood-crofts,* &c. ut parcell' de manerio de *Hinton-Daubney :* Necnon " *Si Henricus* pater noster (in ejus vita) *Dominus Edwardus Sextus* Regina Maria, aut nos ipsi, a tempore dissolutionis Prioratus *S'ci Swithini,*" &c.——To inquire as well by the oath of good and lawful men of our county of Southampton, as well as by the depositions of all the witnesses, and by all manner of other means whatsoever, " Whether the Prior or Priory of *Saint Swithin* at *Winchester,* in right of the house (or monastery) or priory was seized of certain lands called Woodcrofts, &c., as parcel of the manor of *Hinton-Daubney :* or if Henry our Father (in his lifetime) our Lord Edward the Sixth, Queen Mary, or we ourselves (were seized) from the time of the dissolution of *Saint Swithin's* Priory," &c.

AD instructiones reparationesque itinerum, et pontium, nullum genus hominum nulliusque dignitatis ac venera-tionis meritis, cessare oportet.——That no description of

2

persons, of whatever dignity and consequence, should refuse assistance in the making and repairing roads and bridges.

ADIRATUS.——Strayed, lost.

ADITUS.——Public road.

ADJUDICABITUR reus ad legem suam duodecima manu. ——A defendant (or an accused person) shall be adjudged (to wage) his law by the hands of twelve compurgators. *Vide note to " Compurgatores."*

ADJUDICATIO.——" An adjudgment." One of the legal modes of obtaining property among the ancient Romans. *Vide note.*

AD jungendum auxilium.——To join in aid

AD jura legis.——A writ sued out by the king's clerk presented to a living, against those who endeavor to eject him to the prejudice of the king's title.

ADJUVAT hostem.——He assists the enemy.

AD Kalendas Græcas.——" At the *Greek* calends." The calends were a division of time among the *Romans,* but not so with the *Greeks*—consequently the phrase " *Ad Kalendas Græcas,*" was synonymous to stating what was impossible to happen. Thus we say of an unprincipled debtor, " he will pay *ad Kalendas Græcas.*"

ADLEGIARE—or *aleir,* Fr.——To purge himself of crime by oath.

AD legem Falcidiam.——According to the *Falcidian* law.

AD libitum.——At pleasure: at will.

AD litem.——To (or in) the suit or (controversy).

AD majus.——At the most.

ADMALLARE.——To sue.

AD matrimonium colendum.——To contract matrimony.

AD medium filum aquæ.——To the middle line of the water.

AD medium filum viæ.——To the middle line of the road.

ADMINICLE.——To aid or support.

ADMINICULATOR.——An official in the church of Rome,

who administers to the necessities of the indigent and infirm.

ADMINISTRATION cum testamento annexo.——This is granted when a testator has made a will without naming executors, or where those named fail to serve, either from refusing to act, incompetency to do so, or from death.

ADMINISTRATOR de son tort.——Administrator in his own wrong.

ADMINISTRATOR de bonis non.——When a part of an estate is left by the death of an executor, unadministered, the administrator appointed to carry into effect the will, is called by this name.

ADMINISTRATOR durante absentia.——One who administers to an estate during the absence of the executors.

ADMINISTRATOR durante minore ætate.——One who serves as administrator until the executor is of lawful age to act.

ADMINISTRATOR pendente lite.——One who serves as an administrator while a suit is pending to test the validity of the will.

AD nocumentum liberi tenementi sui.——To the damage of his free tenement or freehold.

AD omnes eorum violatores puniendos.——For the punishment of all such wrong doers.

AD omnia placita.——To all the pleas.

ADONQUES, Adonque, Adunque, Adoun.——Then.

AD ostium ecclesiæ.——"At the church door." Dower was formerly assigned at the door of the church. *Vide note to "Assignetur."*

AD perpetuam rei memoriam.——As a perpetual remembrance of the matter.

AD pios usus.——For pious purposes.

AD pios usus, causas, et personis descendentium, consanguineis, servitoribus, et propinquis, seu aliis pro defunctarum animarum salute.——For pious uses and purposes, and to the persons and relations of the deceased; to servitors and neighbors, or to others for the welfare of the souls of the departed.

AD pœnam, et restituendam.——For punishment and restitution.

AD ponendam loquelam coram justiciariis.——To lay the complaint before the judges.

AD prosequendum, testificandum, deliberandum.——To prosecute, give evidence, to advise.

AD proximum antecedentem fiat relatio, nisi impediatur sententia.——The relative may be reckoned next to the antecedent, unless the sentence restrains (or prevents such a construction.)

AD quædam specialia.——To certain special matters.

AD quæstionem juris respondent judices; ad quæstionem facti respondent juratores.——The judges answer as to the question of law; the jurors to the matter of fact.

AD quæstiones facti non respondent judices; ad questiones legis non respondent juratores.——The judges do not answer as to the fact; nor the jurors as to the questions of law.

AD quem diem (ss.) ad sessionem pais tent' apud U. die Jovis, &c. coram, &c. idem Vicecomes retornavit quod prædictus T. S. non fuit inventus in balliva sua, ideo præceptum fuit eidem Vicecomiti quod exigi faciat, &c.——At which day (to wit) at the sessions of the peace held at U. on Thursday, &c., before, &c., the same Sheriff returned that the aforesaid T. S. was not found in his bailiwick, therefore a writ was (directed) to such Sheriff that he should cause him to be summoned.

AD quod damnum ——To that injury.

AD rationem ponere.——To place to account.

ADRAHMARE.——To pledge solemnly.

ADRECTARE.——To make amends.

AD reparationem et sustentationem.——For the repairing and maintenance.

AD requisitionem defendentis.——At the defendant's request.

AD reson.——To call to account.

ADSALLIRE.——To assail

· ADSCRIPTUS glebæ.——Attached to the soil. *Vide note.*

AD sectam.——At the suit of.

AD studendum et orandum.——"To study and pray." The students of the several inns of court were particularly enjoined to perform *both* these duties.

AD synodos venientibus, sive summoniti sint, sive per se quid agendum habuerint, sit summa pax.——That the most peaceful conduct be observed toward those coming to the synods (or general councils) to transact their business, whether they be summoned, or attend voluntarily.

AD terminum annorum.——For a term of years.

AD terminum qui præteriit.——For an expired term.

AD tractandum et consilium impendendum.——To exercise and weigh advice.

ADTRACTUS.——A purchase.

AD tristem partem strenua est suspicio.——Suspicion strongly rests on the unfortunate side.

AD tunc et ibidem.——"Then and there being found."

AD tunc existens generosus et ultra ætatem sex decem annorum.——Then being a gentleman and more than sixteen years of age.

AD unguem.——(Accomplished) to a tittle. Finished.

AD usum et commodum.——For the use and benefit.

AD usum et commodum infantis.——For the use and benefit of the infant.

AD valorem.——According to the value.

AD veniendum coram justiciariis ad compotum suum reddendum.——To come before the judges to render his account.

ADVERSUS profugium ac solatium præbent; delectant domi; non impediunt foris; pernoctant nobiscum, peregrinantur, rusticantur.——They afford a refuge and a solace in adversity; cheer our fire-sides; obstruct not our business; pass the night with us; go abroad, and accompany us in our rural walks.

AD vigessimum primum, et eousque juvenes sub tutelam reponunt.——To the twenty-first year, until which time they place the youth under guardianship.

AD vitam aut culpam.——An office so held as to determine only by the death or delinquency of the possessor.

ADVOCATI fisci.——Fiscal advocates. Advocates of the revenue.

ADVOCATIO.——An advowson. A right of presentation to a church living.

AD voluntatem domini.——At the will of the lord.

AD voluntatem domini secundum consuetudinem, &c.—— At the will of the lord according to the custom, &c.

ADVOWSON.——A right of presentation to a church or benefice. *Vide note.*

ÆDIFICARE in tuo proprio solo non licet quod alteri noceat.——It is unlawful to build on thy own land, what may injure another.

ÆQUE bonis adnumerabitur etiam, si quid est in actionibus, petitionibus, persecutionibus; nam et hæc in bonis esse videntur.——Also if there be anything (left) in actions, petitions, or suits, they shall be accounted as chattels. For these seem also to be considered as the property (of the deceased).

ÆQUE pauperibus prodest, locupletibus æque.—— Equally profitable to rich and poor.

ÆQUITAS sequitur legem.——Equity follows the law.

ÆRIE; aeria accipitrum.——"An airy of goshawks." Airy is the proper term for that, which of other birds we call *a nest.* This word is generally said to come from the *Fr. aire,* a hawk's nest. *Spelman* derives it from the *Sax. eghe,* an egg, softened into *eye,* (used to express a brood of pheasants,) and thence *eyrie,* or *aerie,* a repository for eggs.

ÆS debitorem leve; graviorem inimicum facit.——A slight sum makes a debtor; a large one an enemy.

ÆSTIMATIO capitis.——The value of a man's head. Among the early Saxons the life of every man, including even the king himself, was valued at a certain price, which was called the *œstimatio capitis.*

ÆTAS infantiæ proxima.——The age next to infancy.

ÆTAS pubertati proxima.——The age next to manhood.

ÆTATE probanda.——A writ which lay to inquire whether the king's tenant, holding *in chief by chivalry,* was of full age to receive his lands into his own hands.

AFFEERE.——To assess an amercement.

AFFEERERS.——Those who in courts leet, upon oath, moderated and settled the fines and amercements.

AFFERUNT domino tres palfridos, et sex asterias narenses ad inquisitionem habendam per legales, &c.——They bring to the lord three state horses and six herons (or egrets), for (the privilege of) holding trial by legal men (or freemen), &c. *Vide note.*

AFFIDARE.——To plight one's faith, or give, or swear fealty, *i. e.* fidelity.

AFFIDATIO dominorum.——The oath taken by a lord in parliament.

AFFILARE.——To file.

AFFINES.——Connexions by marriage. *Kindred* are relations by blood; but *affinity* is the tie which exists between one of the married parties with the kindred of the other. The term affinity is, therefore, used in contradistinction to *consanguinity* or kindred.

AFFLICTIONEM afflictis addere.——To distress the distressed.

AFFORCIARE.——To add, to make stronger or increase.

AFFRAYER.——To terrify.

AFFRI.——Beasts of the plough.

A FORTIORI.——By so much the stronger; by a more powerful reason.

AGALMA.——The impression, or image on a seal.

AGARD.——An award.

AGENFRIDA.——The true owner.

AGENHINE.——A domestic; the name given by the Saxons to one belonging to the household.

AGENTES et consentientes pari pœna plectantur.——That the agents and abettors be punished alike.

AGE-prier: ætatem precare; or, ætatis precatio.—— " Aid-prayer." Is when an action being brought against a person under age, for lands which he hath by descent, he, by petition, or motion, shows the facts to the court, and prays that the action may stay until full age.

AGGREGATIO mentium.——A mutual agreement.

AGILD.——Free from the usual penalty for an offence.

AGILLER. From the *Sax. a gilt* (without fault).——An observer, an informer.

AGISTER.——A person who takes other men's cattle to feed upon his grounds at a certain compensation.

AGNATI.——Relations by the father's side.

AGNOMEN.——A surname.

AGNUS Dei.——A piece of white wax in a flat oval form, like a small cake, stamped with the figure of a lamb, and consecrated by the Pope.

A GRATIA.——From (or by) favor.

AGRI ab universis per vices occupantur; arva per annos mutant.——Fields are occupied by all in turn; arable lands change yearly.

AIEUL.——A grandfather.

AISNE.——Eldest or first born.

A LATERE.——By the side, or in attendance.

ALBA firma.——When quit rents, payable to the crown by freeholders of manors, &c., were reserved in silver or *white* money, they were anciently called white rents, "*redditus albi*," in contradistinction to rents reserved in work, grain, &c., which were called "*redditus nigri*," or black mail.

ALBANUS.——An Alien.

ALBUM breve.——A white, or blank precept. *Vide Hob.* 130.

AL comon ley, avant le stat. de *West.* 1, c. 12, si ascun ust estre appeal, et ust estre mute, il serra convict de felony.
——At common law before the statute of *Westminster*, 1, c. 12, if any one was charged with an offence, and remained mute, he was convicted of felony.

A LEGE suæ dignitatis.——By right of his own dignity.

ALIA enormia.——Other great offences.

ALIA lex Romæ; alia Athenis.——There is one law at Rome; another at Athens.

ALIAS ca. sa.——Another writ to take (the person) to make satisfaction.

ALIAS dictus.——Otherwise called (or named).

ALIAS scire facias.——" That you again cause to be informed." A second writ of *scire facias*.

ALIA tentanda via.——Another way must be tried.

ALIBI.——" In another place." This is very frequently the excuse made use of by hardened offenders who endeavor to prove they were in different places from those where crimes had been committed; and though this is a defence too common, yet prejudice should not prevent our giving it its due estimation.

ALIBI natus.——Born in another place.

ALICUI rei impedimentum offerre.——To oppose an impediment to another's business.

ALIENI appetens; sui profusus.——Greedy of another's property; wasting his own.

ALIENI generis.——Of a different sort or kind.

ALIENI juris.——Applied to persons subject to the authority of others. As an infant under father or guardian's authority, and a wife under her husband's control.

ALIENI solo.——In another's soil.

A l'impossible nul est tenu.——What is impossible no one is bound to perform.

ALIO intuitu.——On another (or different) view.

ALIQUIBUS de societate.——With others of the society.

ALIQUID possessionis et nihil juris.——Somewhat of possession and nothing of right.

ALIQUIS non debet esse judex in propria causa.——No one should be a judge in his own cause.

ALIQUO modo destruatur.——By any other manner destroyed. *Mag. Ch.*

ALITER non.——Otherwise not.

ALITER quam ad virum, ex causa regiminis et castagationis uxoris suæ, licite et rationabiliter pertinet.——Otherwise than what legally and reasonably belongs to the husband, on account of governing and chastising his wife. *Vide note.*

ALITER, vel in alio modo.——Otherwise, or in another way.

ALIUD est celare, aliud tacere ; neque enim id est celare quicquid retineas ; sed cum quod tu scias, id ignorare emolumenti tui causa velis eos, quorem interest id scire. ——It is one thing to conceal, and a different thing to be silent ; there is no concealment in withholding a matter, unless it be from those who ought to know it, and it be done purposely for your own advancement.

ALIUDVE quid simile si admisserint.——Or if they have admitted anything of a like sort.

ALIUNDE.——From another place, *or* from some other person.

ALLEGATA.——Matters alleged.

ALLEGATIO contra factum non est admittenda.——An allegation contrary to the deed is not to be admitted (as evidence).

ALLEGATIO contra interpretationem verborum.——An allegation against the meaning of the words.

ALLEGIARE.——To defend, or judge in due form of law.

ALLER sans jour.——" To go without day." To be finally dismissed the court.

ALLOCATUR.——It is allowed.

ALLODIUM est proprietas quæ a nullo recognoscitur.——

Allodium is that (kind of) property which is acknowledged (recognized or understood) by no person.

ALLODUM, or allodium, or allode.——Lands held in absolute dominion. *Vide note.*

ALLONGE.——When a bill of exchange or note is too small to receive the endorsements to be made on it, a piece of paper is annexed to it which is called *allonge.*

ALLUMINOR.——A painter; an illuminator. *Vide note.*

ALMESFESH.——A *Saxon* word for alms-money. It was also called *rome's-fesh, romescot,* and *hearth-money. Vide Seld. Hist. Tithes,* 217.

ALNAGE.——Ell measure. An *alnager* was a sworn public officer in England, required to look to measure of woollen cloths manufactured there, and put a special seal upon them.

A loco et domo.——From the place and habitation.

ALTA proditio.——" High Treason ;" the crime against the state government.

ALTA via.——A highway.

ALTERUM non lædere.——Not to injure another.

ALTIUS non tollendi.——Where the owner of a house is restrained from building beyond a particular height, the servitude due by him is thus called.

ALTUM mare.——The high sea.

A ma intent vous purres aver demurre sur luy que le obligation est void, ou que le condition est encountre common ley, et *per Dieu* si le plaintiff fuit icy, il irra al prison tanq; il ust fait fine au Roy.——On my action you could claim a demurrer, on the plea that the obligation is void, or that the contract is contrary to common law, and on *oath,* if the plaintiff were present, he would be put in close confinement, and must pay a fine to the king.

AMBIGUITAS latens.——A latent ambiguity ; concealed doubt or uncertainty.

AMBIGUITAS patens.——A manifest ambiguity or uncertainty : that kind of uncertainty of which there can be no reasonable doubt. These last two extracts are frequently applied to clauses in deeds or wills; but the inferences drawn from them are distinct in their principles.

AMBIGUITAS verborum latens verificatione suppletur; quam quod ex facto oritur ambiguum, verificatione facti tollitur.——A latent ambiguity of words is supplied by the verification (or plea); for that uncertainty which arises by the deed is removed by the truth of the fact itself.

AMBIGUUM pactum contra venditorem interpretandum est.——An ambiguous covenant (or contract) is to be expounded against the vendor.

AMBIGUUM placitum.——" An ambiguous (or doubtful) plea." A plea for delay.

AMBULATORIA voluntas.——As long as a man lives he has the power to alter his will or testament.

A MENSA et thoro.——"From bed and board." A divorce between husband and wife, which does not make the marriage void, *ab initio*, or from the beginning. *Vide note.*

AMERCEMENT.——A light or merciful penalty imposed by the court upon the officers of the court, sheriffs, coroners, &c., for trivial offences or neglect in the discharge of their official duties.

AMICI consilia credenda.——A friend's advice should be regarded.

AMICUS curiæ.——A friend of the court. *Vide note.*

AMITTERE legem terræ, or liberam legem.——To lose, or be deprived of the liberty of swearing in any court. To become infamous.

AMORTIZATIO—amortization—amortizement, Fr.——An alienation of lands or tenements in *mortmain*, viz., to any corporation or fraternity, and their successors, &c.

AMOVEAS manus.——That you remove your hands: give up the possession.

AMPLIARE jurisdictionem.——To increase the jurisdiction.

AMPLIARE justitiam.——To enlarge (or extend) the right.

ANATOCISM.——Compound interest.

ANCIENT demesne, or demain.——An ancient inherit-ance.——" *Vetus patrimonium domini.*" *Vide note.*

ANFELDTYHDE, Sax.——A simple accusation. *Vide note.*

ANGARIA.——The compulsory service required by a feudal lord from his tenant.

ANIMALIA feræ naturæ.——Animals of a wild nature.

ANIMO custodiendi.——With an intention of guarding (or watching).

ANIMO furandi.——With an intent to steal.

ANIMO possidendi.——With intent to possess.

ANIMO revertendi.——With intent to return.

ANIMO testandi.——With an intent to make a will.

ANIMO revocandi.——With an intention to revoke.

ANIMUS cancellandi.——The intention of cancelling.

ANIMUS furandi.——An intention of stealing.

ANIMUS manendi.——A determination of settling or re-maining.

ANIMUS morandi.——A purpose of delaying, (hindering, or disturbing.)

ANIMUS non deponendus ob iniquum judicium.——The mind is not to be cast down because of an unjust judgment.

ANIMUS revertendi.——An intent to return.

ANNATES.——First fruits.

ANNI nubiles.——The age at which a woman becomes marriageable by law, viz., twelve years.

ANNOTATIONE principis.——By the emperor's sign manual.

ANNUS et dies.——A year and a day.

ANNUS luctus.——" The year of mourning." The widow's year of lamentation for her deceased husband.

A NOTIORIBUS.——By (or from) those more known.

ANTE exhibitionem billæ.——Before the commencement of the bill, (or suit.)

ANTE litem contestatem.——Before the suit be contested.

ANTENATI.——Born before.

ANTE occasum solis.——Before sunset.

ANTICHRESIS.——A contract or mortgage by which the creditor receives the fruit or revenues of the thing pledged, instead of interest. It is recognized by the Louisiana Code, and the modern Welsh mortgage resembles it; but in general it is obsolete.

ANTIQUUM mollendinum.——An ancient mill.

ANTISTITIUM.——A monastery.

ANTITHETARIUS.——A term given to an accused person, who charges upon his accuser the crime of which he is accused, in order to discharge himself.

APANAGE.——In French law, the provision made for the support of the younger members of a royal family from the public revenues.

APERTA, vel patentes brevia.——Open writs.

APERTUM factum.——An overt act.

APEX juris.——Subtle point of law.

APICES juris non sunt jus.——"The utmost extremity of the law, is injustice." Straining the cords of the law in *some* cases to their greatest length, will produce as much oppression as if there were no law at all.

A PIRATIS et latronibus capta, dominium non mutant. ——Being taken by pirates and robbers, they do not change their ownership.

A POSTERIORI.——"From the latter." Words often referring to a mode of argument.

APPELLATIONE "fundi," omne ædificium et omnis ager continetur.——By the name of "land" ("fundum" among the ancient *Romans*) every field and building is comprised.

APPRENDRE.——To learn—from whence the word "apprentice."

APPUYE.——The point to lean on: the defence.

APRES ce, est tend le querelle a respondre; et aura congie, de soy conseiller, s'il le demande; et quan il sera conseille, il peut nyer le faict dont il est accuse.——After that, he is bound to answer the complaint; and shall have leave to imparle, if he require it; and when he has imparled, he may deny the act of which he is accused.

A PRIORI.——From the former. *Vide "A posteriori."*

APTUS et idoneus moribus et scientiis.——"Proper and sufficient in morality and learning." Words inserted in college certificates, on a student passing his examination.

AQUA cedit solo.——"The water yields to (or accompanies) the land." The grant of the land conveys the water.

AQUA currit et debet currere.——Water runs, and ought to run.

AQUAGIUM.——A ditch to draw off water.

AQUÆ haustus.——The right to draw water from the well or spring of another.

A QUA non deliberentur, sine speciali præcepto domini regis.——From which they cannot be delivered without the special writ (or license) of the king.

AQUITALIA alia sunt regalia; alia communia.——Some waterfowl are royal; some are common.

ARACE.——"To rase, or erase," from the Fr. *arracher.*

ARARE.——To plough. *Arator*, ploughman.

ARALIA—mis-spelled *arnalia* and *aratia.*——Arable lands.

ARATIA.——Arable lands.

ARATRUM terræ.——As much land as can be tilled with one plough.

ARATURA terræ.——This was an ancient service which the tenant performed for his lord by ploughing his lands.

ARBITER.——An arbitrator. *Vide note.*

ARBITRIO boni viri.——By the judgment of an honest man.

ARCA cyrographica, sive cyrographorum Judæorum.—— This was a common chest, with three locks and keys, kept by certain *Christians* and *Jews*, wherein by order of *Richard*

the First, all the contracts, mortgages and obligations be·
longing to the *Jews*, were kept to prevent fraud.

ARCANA imperii.——The secrets of the empire.

ARCTA et salva custodia.——In close and safe custody.

ARCUI meo non confido.——"I do not depend on my
own bow." I have taken a better opinion than mine own.

ARDENTIA verba, sed non vera.——Words of energy, but
destitute of fact.

ARENTARE.——"To rent out." To let at a rent certain.

ARGENTIFODINA.——A silver mine.

ARGENTUM album.——Silver coin.

ARGUMENTUM ad crumenam.——An argument, or appeal to the purse.

ARGUMENTUM ad hominem.——An argument (or appeal)
to the person : a personal application.

ARGUMENTUM ad ignorantiam.——Argument founded on
ignorance of the fact, (as shown by an opponent.)

ARGUMENTUM ad verecundiam.——An argument (or
appeal) to the modesty (of an opponent).

ARIERISMENT.——"Surprise—affright." To the great
"*arierisment*" and "*estenysment*" of the common law. *Vid.*
Rot. Parl. 21 *Edw.* 3d.

ARIMNANNI.——The title of a class of freemen in the
middle ages, who possessed some independent property of
their own, employing themselves in agriculture. They
rented lands, also, from the neighboring lords, paying be-
side the stipulated rent, certain services of labor for their
landlord, as at harvesting, or ploughing. *See Robertson's*
Charles 5., Appendix.

ARMA dare.——"To present with arms—to make a
knight." *Arma capere*, or *suscipere* to be made a knight.
Vide *Kennet's Paroch. Antiq.* 288, and *Walsingham, p.* 507.
The word "*arma*" in these places signifies only a *sword;*
but sometimes a knight was made, by giving him the whole
armour.

ARMA libera.——"Free arms." A sword and lance.

These were usually given to a servant when made free. Vide *Leg. Will. cap.* 65.

ARMA moluta.——Sharp weapons that *cut*, opposed to those which were *blunt*, which only break or bruise. Vide *Bract. lib.* 3.

ARMA reversata.——A punishment which took place when a knight was convicted of treason or felony. Thus the historian *Knighton* speaking of *Hugh Spencer* tells us, "*Primo vestierunt eum uno vestimento, cum armis suis reversatis.*" First they arrayed him in a robe with his arms reversed.

ARMIGER—"Esquire."——One who bears arms. A title of dignity belonging to such gentlemen as "*bear arms*," and these either by courtesy, as sons of noblemen, eldest sons of knights, &c., or by creation. The word "*Armiger*" was also formerly applied to the higher servants in convents. Vide *Paroch. Antiq.* 576. Ancient writers and chronologers make mention of some who were called *Armigeri*, whose office was to carry the shield of some noblemen. *Camden* calls them *Scutiferi* (which seems to import as much), and *homines ad arma dicti.* These are accounted next in order to knights.

ARMISCARIA.——This was anciently a punishment decreed, or imposed on an offender by the judge. Vide *Malmesb. lib.* 3, 97. *Walsingham*, 340. At first it was to carry a saddle on his back in token of subjection. *Brampton* says that in the year 1176, the king of the *Scots* promised *Henry* the Second—"*Lanceam et sellam suam super altâre Sancti Petri ad perpetuam hujus subjectionis memoriam offerre*—to offer up his lance and saddle upon the altar of St. Peter, in perpetual token of his subjection. Vide *Spelm.* It may not, however, be improper to observe, that these loose *dicta* should be taken very cautiously.

ARPEN, or ARPENT.——An acre or furlong of ground; and according to the old *Fr.* account in *Domesday Book*, one hundred perches make one "*arpent.*"

ARRAMEUR.——Title given by the Normans to officers employed to load vessels.

ARRENTARE.——To rent.

ARRESTER.——To stay : to arrest.

ARRHA.——A proof of a purchase and sale. Earnest money.

ARRIERBAN.——The proclamation which the sovereign issued in feudal times to his vassals, to summon them to military service.

ARSÆ et pensatæ.——"Burnt and weighed." Applied to the melting of coin to test the purity.

ARTICULI super chartas.——"Articles (made) upon the charters ;" *i. e.* upon the great charter, and charter of the forest, &c.

ASPORTARE.—To carry away.

ASSARTUM.——Land cleared and cultivated.

ASSECURATOR, qui jam solvit æstimationem mercium deperditarum, si postea dictæ sint, an possit cogere dominum accipiendas illas, et ad reddendam sibi æstimationem quam dedit? Distingue! Aut merces, vel aliqua pars ipsarum appareant, et restitui possint, ante solutionem æstimationis ; et tunc tenetur dominus mercium illas recipere, et pro illa parte mercium apparentium liberabitur assecurator ; nam qui tenetur ad certam quantitatem respectu certæ speciei dando illum, liberatur ; ut ubi probatur. Et etiam quia contractus assecurationis est conditionalis, scilicet si merces deperdantur ; non autem dicuntur perditæ, si postea recuperantur. Verum si merces non appareant in illa pristina bonitate, aliter fit æstimatio ; non in tantum, sed prout hic valent. Aut vero post solutam æstimationem ab assecuratore, compareant merces ; et hinc est in electione mercium assecurati, vel recipere merces, vel retinere pretium.——Can the assurer who has already paid the value of the lost merchandise, if afterwards they should become visible and be recovered, oblige the owner to receive them, and return him the value which he has paid? Mark!

Either the merchandise or some part thereof should be visible and restored before payment of the valuation, and then the owner of the goods is bound to receive them, and for that which is forthcoming the assurer shall be discharged; for he who is bound to a certain quantity in respect of a particular thing given, shall be exonerated; as is everywhere proved. And therefore because the assurer's contract is conditional, to wit, if the goods are lost; but they do not consider them destroyed when they are afterwards recovered. But if the merchandise be not forthcoming in its original value, there is another valuation made, not at so high a rate, but for what they are now worth. But if the goods shall be seen after the payment of the valuation by the assurer, it is in that case at the election of the insurer of the goods either to receive them, or to retain the price.

ASSEDATION.——A Scotch name for lease.

ASSEZ.——Enough.

ASSIDERE, or ASSEDARE.——To tax.

ASSIGNETUR autem ei pro dote sua, tertia pars totius terræ mariti sui, quæ sua fuit in vita sua, nisi de minori dotata fuerit ad ostium ecclesiæ.——But there may be assigned to her for her dower the third part of the whole land which belonged to the husband in his life-time, unless she were endowed of a less quantity at the church door. *Vide note.*

ASSIZE.——A species of jury or inquest; a certain number of persons summoned to try a cause, and who sat together for that purpose. This term was applied to a species of writ, or real action. It also signified a court;—an ordinance, statute;—a *fixed* time, number, quantity, weight, measure.

ASSIZORS.—Sunt qui assizas condunt, aut taxationes imponunt.——"Those who hold the assizes, or lay on the taxes." In *Scotland* (according to *Skene*), they were the same with jurors, and their oath is this:

" We shall leil suith say,

And *na suith* conceal for *nothing* we may,

As far as we are charged upon the *assize*,

Be (by) God himself, and be (by) our own paradise.

As we will answer to God upon the dreadful day of Dome."

ASSISTERE, maintainare et consolare, et e converso, et sic de similibus, in quibus est professio legis, et naturæ.——To assist, maintain, and comfort (the father), and do the same (for the son) ; and so in similar cases, for this is nature's law and profession.

ASSIZA et recognitio.——The assize and recognizance.

A SOCIETATE nomen sumpserunt, reges enim tales sibi associant.——They take the name from a society, for kings attach such persons to themselves.

ASSOILE.——" To absolve." " To deliver from excommunication." In one of the *English* statutes mention being made of *Edward* the First, it is said, " whom God *assoile.*"

ASSUMPSERUNT super se.——They took upon themselves.

ASSUMPSIT.——He undertook (or promised).

ASSUMPSIT pro rata.——He undertook agreeably to the proportion.

ASSYTHEMENT.——The indemnification which in Scotch law a person is bound to make for killing or injuring another.

ASTRICT.——To bind. *Vide note.*

AT si intestatus moritur cui suus hæres nec extabit, agnatus proximus familiam habeto.——But if a person die intestate leaving no heir, then let the next of kin possess the property.

As usuarius.——A pound lent upon usury (or interest).

ATAVUS.——The male ancestor in the fifth degree.

A TEMPORE cujus.——" From the time of which." Where these words appear, they frequently intimate " from the time of which the memory of man is not to the contrary," which extends as far back (in the *legal* acceptation of the words) as the Crusades.

ATRIUM.——A court before a house; and sometimes a church yard.

ATTACAR——To tie or bind.

ATTACHIAMENTA bonorum.——A distress taken upon goods, where a man is sued for personal estate, or debt.

ATTINCTUS.——"Attainted." A person is said to be attainted, when convicted of murder, treason, &c.

ATTORNARE.——To transfer.

AU bout de compte.——At the end of the account; after all.

AUDI alteram partem.——Hear the other side.

AUDITA querelâ.——The complaint having been heard.

AUDITOR compotæ.——The auditor of the account.

AUGUSTA legibus soluta non est. The queen is not freed from the laws.

AULA regis.——The king's hall (of justice).

AUSIS talibis istis non jura subserviunt.——The laws will not assist in such daring purposes.

AUT re, aut nomine.——Either really or nominally.

AUTRE action pendante.——Another action pending.

AUTRE droit.——Another's right.

AUTREFOIS acquit.——Formerly acquitted.

AUTREFOIS convict.——Formerly convicted.

AUTREFOITS attaint.——Formerly attained.

AUTREFOITS *or* autrefois acquit.——"Formerly acquitted." The name of a plea used by a prisoner, who had been tried and acquitted of the offence for which he was a second time indicted.

AUXILIA fiunt de gratia, et non de jure; cum dependeant ex gratia tenentium, et non ad voluntatem dominorum.——Aids are made of favor, and not of right; as they depend on the affection of the tenants, and not upon the will of the lords (of the fee). *Vide note.*

AUXILIOR vassallum in lege.——" I assist my vassal in his suit." Something as the *Patron* did his *Client* under the *Roman* law.

A VERBIS legis non est recedendum.——"There is no deviating from the words of the law." No interpretation can be made contrary to the express words of a statute.

AVERIÆ carucæ.——Beasts of the plough.

AVERIA elongata.——Cattle eloigned.

AVERSIO periculi.——The fear of danger.

A VINCULO matrimonii.——From the bond of marriage. *Vide note.*

AVUNCULUS.——An uncle by the mother's side.

AVUS.——A grandfather.

AXIS.——A board or table such as *Solon's* laws were written upon at Athens.

NOTES TO A.

ABALIENATIO, VEL TRANSLATIO DOMINII, &c.—The transferring of the property of the *res mancipi* among the ancient *Romans*, was made by a certain act, called *Mancipatio* or *Mancipium*, vid. Cic. Off. iii. 16, de Orat. i. 39, in which the same formalities were observed as in emancipating a son, only that it was done but *once*. This *Cicero* calls "*traditio altori nexu*," i. e. a transfer into another connection (or possession). *Topic.* 5, s. 28. Thus, *Dare mancipio*, i. e. *ex forma* vel *lege* mancipii, to convey the property of a thing in that manner; "*accipere*," to receive it. *Plaut. Curc.* iv. 2, 8. *Trin.* ii. 419. *Pont.* iv. 5, 39. *Sui mancipii esse*, to be one's own master; to be subject to the dominion of no one. *Cic. ad Brut.* 16. So, *mancipare agrum alicui*, to sell an estate to any one. Plin. Ep. vii. 18. *Emancipare fundos*, to divest one self of the estate, and convey it to another. *Id. x.* 3.

Cicero commonly uses mancipium, and *nexum* or *nexus*, as of the same import, pro *Muren.* 2—pro *Flacc.* 32. *Cæcin.* 16, but sometimes he distinguishes them, as *de Harusp.* 7, where *mancipium* implies complete property, and *nexus* only the right of obligation, as when a person receives anything by way of a pledge. Thus a creditor had his insolvent debtor, *jure nexi ;* but not *jure mancipii*, as he possessed his slave.

There were various other modes of acquiring legal property, as *jure cessio*, or *cessio in jure*, i. e. a giving up by law or in law. *Cic. Top.* 5. This was the case when a person gave up his effects to any one before the *Prætor*, or President of a province, who adjudged them to the person who made good his claim legally (*vindicanti addicebat*), which chiefly took place in the case of debtors, who, when they were insolvent, gave up their goods (*bona cedant*) to their creditors. Another method of acquiring property among the *Romans*, was by *Usucaptio*, when a person obtained the property of a thing by possessing it for a certain time, without interruption,—*Emptio sub corona*, i. e. purchasing captives in war; who wore a crown when sold. *Auctio*, where things were exposed to sale, a spear being set up, and a public crier calling out the price; *Adjudicatio, Donatio*, &c. These will be mentioned in subsequent notes.

ABBAS.—It appears that monasteries were originally founded in retired places, and the religious had little or no concern with secular affairs, being entirely subject to the prelates. But the abbots possessing most of the learning, in ages of ignorance, were called from their seclusion to aid the churches in opposing heresies. Monasteries were subsequently founded in the vicinity of cities: the abbots became ambitious, and set themselves to acquire wealth and honors; some of them assumed the mitre; threw off their dependence on the bishops, and obtained seats in Parliament. For many centuries, princes and noblemen bore the title of abbots. At present, in Catholic countries, abbots are *regular*, or such as take the vow, and wear the habit of the order; and *commendatory*, such as are secular, but obliged, when of suitable age, to take orders. The title is borne, also, by some persons who have not the government of a monastery: as bishops, whose sees were formerly abbeys. *Encyc.*

ACTIONES COMPOSITÆ SUNT, &c.—Amongst the *Romans*, if the parties could make no private agreement, they both went before the *Prætor.* Then the plaintiff *proposed* the action which he intended to bring against the defendant, and demanded a writ (*actionem postulabat*), from the *Prætor* for that purpose. For there were certain forms (*formulæ*), or set words (*verba concepta*) necessary to be used in every cause—(*Formulæ de omnibus rebus constitutæ. Cic. Rosc. Com.* 8)—i. e. forms (of writs) were settled for all things. At the same time the defendant requested that an advocate or lawyer should assist with his counsel. There were several actions for the same thing. The prosecutor chose which he pleased, and the *Prætor* usually granted it, (*actionem vel judicium dabat vel reddebat*,) i. e. giving or rendering him a suit or judgment. *Cic. pro Cæcin*, &c.; but he might also refuse it. The plaintiff, having obtained his writ, offered it to the defendant, or dictated to him the words. This writ it was unlawful to change, (*mutare formulam non licebat*,) i. e. it was unlawful to change its form. *Senec. de Ep.* 117. The greatest caution was necessary in drawing up the writ (*in actione vel formula concipienda*), i. e. in devising the form of the writ or action; for if there was a mistake in *one* word, the whole cause was lost. (*Cic. de invent.* ii. 19., &c.) A person skilled only in the framing of writs, and the like, is called by Cicero, "*Leguleius:*" he attended on the advocates to suggest to them the laws and forms; as those called "*Pragmatici*" did among the *Greeks.*

ACTIONES IN PERSONAM, &c.—Personal actions among the *Romans* were very numerous. They arose from some contract, or injury done; and required that a person should do, or give certain things, or suffer a certain punishment. Actions from contracts or obligations, were about buying and selling (*de emptione et venditione*); about letting and hiring; about commissions, partnerships, deposits, loans, pledges, dowries and stipulations, which took place almost in all bargains, and was made in this form, —"*An spondes?*"—"Do you promise?" "*Spondeo*,"—"I do promise." "*An dabis?*"—"Will you give?" "*Dabo*,"—"I will give." "*An promittis?*"—"Do you promise?" "*Promitto, vel repromitto*,"—"I do promise or engage."

ACTIONES LEGIS.—Certain rites and forms necessary to be observed in prosecuting suits under the *Roman* laws, were composed from the Twelve Tables, called "*actiones legis*," (*quibus inter se homines disceptarent*,) concerning which persons could litigate (or dispute). The forms used in making bargains, in transferring property, &c., were called "*actus legitimi.*" There were also certain days on which a law suit could be instituted, or justice lawfully administered—these were called "*dies fasti,*" lucky days, and others, on which that could not be done, called "*nefasti,*" unlucky days—and some on which it could be done for some part of the day, and not for another part; (*intercisi.*) The knowledge of all these things appears to have been confined to the *Patricians,* and chiefly to the *Pontifices* for many years, until one *Cn. Flavius,* the son of a freedman, the scribe or clerk of *Appius Claudius Cæcus,* a lawyer, who had arranged these actions and days, stole (or perhaps more probably copied) the book which *Appius* had composed; and published it A. U. 440. (*Fastos publicavit, et actiones primum edidit*); he first published the law days and showed the nature of actions. In return for which favor he was made *Curule Ædile* by the people, and afterwards *Prætor.* From him the book was called, "*Jus civile Flavianum,*" vide Liv. ix. 46. Cic. de Orat. i. 41, &c.

ACTUS LEGIS, &c.—If land, &c., out of which a rent charge, or annuity be granted, is recovered by an elder title, the grantee shall have a writ of annuity, because the rent charge is become void *by course of law.*

ADJUDICATIO.—This mode of acquiring legal property took place, as it appears, only in three cases, i. e. *hæreditate dividenda,* in dividing an inheritance among co-heirs, vid. Cic. Orat. i. 58. Cæcin. 3. *In communi dividendo,* in dividing joint stock among partners, vid. Cic. Ep. vii. 12. Or in settling boundaries among neighbors, vid. Cic. Legg. i. 21; when the judge determined anything to any of the heirs, partners or neighbors, of which they got immediate property; but *arbiters* were commonly appointed in settling bounds.

ADSCRIPTUS GLEBÆ.—Slaves passed in the feudal ages on the transfer of the soil, the same as any other appendant or appurtenant.

ADVOWSON.—This is the name given in English ecclesiastical law to the right of presentation to a vacant church or benefice. Sometimes this right is vested in the bishop of the diocese, sometimes in the manor to which the church belongs. The person possessing this right is called Patron or Advocate, or Advowee, and has the privilege, whenever the benefice becomes vacant by the death of the incumbent, to select and present a suitable candidate for the vacancy, to the bishop by whom he is instituted. When the bishop himself is the patron, he does by the act of *collation,* or conferring the benefice, what is otherwise done by the separate acts of *presentation* and *institution.* The right is called an *advowson,* because the patron is bound to protect and advocate the rights of the church and its incumbent.

AFFERUNT DOMINO, &c.—Fines payable to the King, on suing by special original writ, were formerly of several sorts; some in nature of an exaction by the King, on giving leave to a subject to prosecute a writ in his superior courts; others, in nature of a penalty, set upon offenders after conviction; and on plaintiffs failing in their suits; or parties making false claims; or for fraud and deceit to the court; for vexation under color of law; for contempt of the King's writs or statutes; others, again, in nature of an imposition set by the court on the suitors, with a view to enforce plainness and perspicuity in pleading. The latter were imposed, even in the superior courts, till the statute of *Marlbridge* provided "that neither in the circuit of justices, nor in counties, hundreds, and courts baron, any fines should be taken of any man *pro pulchre placitando,* or beau-pleading."

which statute was further enforced; and made to extend to the superior courts by stat. *Westminster*, the first 3d Edward 1. c. 8. But the former species of fines were suffered to continue; and they were formerly of money, or other things, as money was scarce.

ALITER.—The ancient common law of England justified a proper chastisement of the wife by the husband; and about sixty years since, a judge at the assizes at Gloucester stated on the trial of a cause that this was still the law, provided the husband used a cane no larger than his little finger. It is said that the ladies of the city sent to the judge on the next morning, the following note: "The ladies of Gloucester present their compliments to Mr. Justice—and request to have the exact admeasurement of his little finger, in order that they may know whether their husbands chastise them *legally* or not."

ALLODUM.—The history of the establishment, and progress of the feudal system, is an interesting subject to the historian, and particularly to the lawyer. In some countries the jurisprudence and laws are even now in a great measure *feudal.* In others, where the feudal system has long since been abolished (as in England), many forms and practices established by custom, or founded on statutes, take their rise from the feudal laws; and for this reason, the student cannot well understand some of the present laws, customs and forms, without attending to the ideas peculiarly attaching themselves to the feudal system. Several of the Notes interspersed throughout this Glossary, it is hoped may be, in this respect, not only serviceable, but entertaining. *Allodum* is the free and entire right of property and dominion in the land. However, to understand more clearly the difference between land held *allodially*, and that held "*ut feudam,*" it will be first necessary to state a few particulars. Property in land seems to have gone through four successive changes, among the barbarous nations who settled upon the extensive possessions of the *Roman* empire, and who brought with them manners and customs, and used those tenures unknown to those they conquered.

1st. While the barbarous nations remained in their original countries, their possession of land was generally *temporary*, and seldom had any distinct limits: but they were not, in consequence of this imperfect species of tenure, brought under any positive or formal obligation to serve the community. After tending their flocks in *one* great district, they removed with them, their wives and families, into *another*. Every individual was at liberty to choose how far he would contribute to carry on any military enterprise. If he followed a leader in any expedition, it was from attachment, or with a view to obtain a more prolific soil, or plunder; and not from any sense of obligation. The state of society among them was of a very rude, and simple form: they subsisted entirely by hunting, or by pasturage. *Cæs. lib.* vi. c. 21. They neglected (and perhaps despised) agriculture; and lived chiefly on milk, cheese, and such animal food as they caught in hunting. *Ibid. c.* 22. Tacitus agrees with Cæsar in most of these particulars. *Vide Tacit. de moribus Germ. c.* 14, 15, 23. The *Goths* were equally negligent of agriculture. *Prisc. Rhet. ap. Byz. scrip. vol.* i. *p.* 31. *B.* Society was in the same state among the *Huns*, who disdained to cultivate the earth, or to touch a plough. *Amm. Marcel. lib.* xxxi. *p.* 475. The same manners subsisted among the *Alans. ib.* 477. Whilst property continued in this state, we can discover nothing that can bear any resemblance to a *feudal tenure;* or to the subordination and military services, with the long train of grievances, which so heavily oppressed the tenure of lands for so many ages afterwards, upon the introduction of the feudal system.

2d. Upon settling in the countries which they had subdued, the vic-

torious troops divided the conquered lands. Whatever portion of them
fell to a soldier, he seized as the recompense due to his valor; as a settlement acquired by his *own* sword. He took possession of it as a freeman,
in *full property.* He enjoyed it during his own life, and could dispose of
it at pleasure, or transmit it, as an inheritance to his children. Thus
property in land became fixed : it was at the same time *allodial,* i. e. the
possessor had the *entire right* of property and dominion: he held of no
sovereign, or superior lord, to whom he was bound to do homage, or perform service. It was, it would appear, the reward of service *done;* not
duties *to be* performed ; a tenure retrospective, not prospective, in its
nature.

3d. When property in land became fixed, and subject to military service, another change was introduced, though slowly, and step by step.
We learn from *Tacitus,* that the chief men among the *Germans* endeavored to attach to their ranks certain adherents. whom he calls *Comites.*
These fought under their standards, and followed them in all their inter-
prises. The same custom continued among them in their new settlements, and those attached or devoted followers were called *Fideles, An-
trustiones homines in truste Dominica ; Leudes.* Tacitus informs us that
the rank of a *Comes* was deemed honorable. *De morb. Germ. c.* 13. The
composition, which is the standard by which we must judge of the rank
and condition of persons in the middle ages, paid for the murder of one
in truste Dominica, was triple to that paid for the murder of a freeman.
Vid. Leg. tit. 44, § 1 & 2.

While the *Germans* remained in their country, they courted the favor
of these *Comites* by presents of arms, and horses, and by hospitality. As
long as they had no fixed property in land, they were the only gifts that
they could bestow ; and the only rewards which their followers desired;
but on settling in the countries which they conquered, they bestowed on
these *Comites* a more substantial recompense in land. What were the
services originally exacted in return for these *beneficia* cannot be determined with absolute precision. *M. de Montesquieu* considers these *beneficia* as fiefs, which originally subjected those who held them to military
service. *L'Esprit des Louis, l.* xxx. *c.* 3. and 16. M. l'Abbe de Mably contends that such as held these were, at first, subjected to no other service,
than what was incumbent on every freeman. But comparing proofs and
reasonings and conjectures, it seems to be evident, that as every freeman,
in consequence of his allodial property, was bound to serve the community
under a severe penalty, no good reason can be assigned for conferring
these *beneficia,* if they did not subject such as received them to some new
obligation. Why should a king have stripped himself of his domain, if
he had not expected that by parcelling it out, he might acquire a right to
services, to which he had formerly no title?

We may then warrantably conclude, that as ALLODIAL property subjected those who possessed it to serve the *community,* so *beneficia* subjected
those who held them to personal service and fidelity to him, from whom
they received these lands.

4th. But the possession of benefices did not continue long in this state.
A precarious tenure during pleasure, was not sufficient to satisfy such as
held lands, and by various means they gradually obtained a confirmation
of their benefices during life. Du Cange produces several quotations
from ancient charters and chronicles in proof of this. *Gloss. voc. beneficium.* After this it was very easy to obtain or extort charters, rendering *beneficia* hereditary, first in the direct line, then in the collateral, and
at last in the female line. *Leg. Longob. lib.* iii. *tit.* 8. *Du Cange voc.
beneficium.*

It is no easy matter to fix the precise time when each of these changes
took place. *M. l'Ab. Mably* conjectures, with some probability, that

Charles Martel introduced the practice of granting *beneficia* for life; *Observat. tom.* i. *p.* 103, 160; and it is said, that *Louis le Debonnaire* was among the first who rendered them hereditary, from the authority to which he refers; *ib.* 429. *Mabillon*, however, has published a *Placitum* of *Louis le Debonnaire*, by which it appears that he still continued to grant some *beneficia* only during life. *De Re Diplomatica lib.* vi. *p.* 358. In the year 889, *Odo*, king of *France*, granted lands to *Ricabodo fideli suo, jure beneficiario et fructuario :* i. e. to Ricabodo, his faithful (friend) the right, benefit and enjoyment for life, and if he should die, and a son were born to him, that right was to continue during the life of his son. *Mabillon*, 556. This was an intermediate step between fiefs merely during *life*, and fiefs *hereditary*, in perpetuity. While *beneficia* continued under their *first* form, and were held only during *pleasure*, he who granted them not only exercised the *dominium* or prerogative of superior lord, but he retained the property, giving his vassal only the *usufruct*. But under the latter form, when they became hereditary, although feudal lawyers continued to define a *beneficium* agreeably to its *original* nature, the property was, *in effect*, taken out of the hands of the superior lords, and lodged in those of the vassal. As soon as the reciprocal advantages of the feudal mode of tenure came to be understood by superiors as well as vassals, that species of holding became agreeable to both, that not only lands, but casual rents, such as the profits of a toll, the fare paid at ferries, &c., the salaries or perquisites of offices, and even pensions themselves, were, it is said, granted, and held as fiefs; and military service was promised and exacted on account of these. *Vide Hist. Bretagne tom.* ii. 78. 690. How absurd soever it may seem to grant or to hold such precarious property as a *fief*, it was properly an ecclesiastical revenue, belonging to the clergy of the church, or monastery, who performed that duty; but these were sometimes seized by the powerful barons. In order to ascertain their right to them, they held as fiefs of the church, and parcelled them out in the same manner as other property to their sub-vassals. *Boquet recueil des Hist. vol.* x. 238, 480. The same spirit of encroachment which rendered *fiefs* hereditary, led the nobles to extort from their sovereigns hereditary grants of office.

ALLUMINOR—A person so called who anciently illuminated, or painted upon paper or parchment, particularly the latter, the initial letters of charters and deeds—the initial letters of the chapters of the Bible were formerly often beautifully gilt and colored; and at this day we sometimes see old MSS. exhibited for sale in the windows of large cities, with the initial letters elegantly illuminated, and many are to be found in the different *Museums* of Europe.

A MENSA ET THORO—A divorce from bed and board does not *dissolve* the marriage; for the cause of it is subsequent to the marriage, and supposes the marriage to have been *lawful*—this divorce may be by reason of adultery in either of the parties; for cruelty of the husband; and for other reasons. And as a divorce *a mensa et thoro* does not dissolve the marriage, so it doth not debar the woman of her dower; or bastardize the issue ; or make void any estate for the life of the husband and wife. Vide *Co. Litt.* 235. 3. *Inst.* 89. 7. *Rep.* 43.

AMICUS CURRIÆ—If a judge be doubtful, or mistaken in a matter of law a stander-by may inform the court as "*amicus curiæ*," i. e. a friend of the court, *Co. Inst.* 178. In some cases a thing is to be made apparent by suggestion on the roll, by motion; and sometimes by pleading; and sometimes as "*amicus curiæ*." Vide 2 *Keb.* 548. Any one as "*amicus curiæ*," may move to quash a vicious indictment, for in such case, if there were a trial, and verdict, judgment must be arrested. *Comb.* 13. In 2 *Show. Rep.*, a counsel urged that he might, as *"amicus curiæ,"* inform the court of an error in proceedings, to prevent giving false judgment: but this was denied, unless the party was *present.* There does not seem to be any good reason for this distinction.

AMITTERE LIBEREM LEGEM—That is, that he should *"lose his protection in law,"* as *"liber homo,"* or a freeman; and be subject to the same laws as the *"servi,"* or *"adscriptitii glebæ."* See notes to both.

ANCIENT DEMESNE—These words are frequently found in the *English* law books. It means a tenure, whereby all the manors belonging to the crown in the days of Saint *Edward* and *William* the Conqueror were held. The number and names of all the manors were, after the great survey made in the last-mentioned king's reign, written in the book of *Domesday:* and those which by that book appear, at *that* time, to have belonged to the crown, and are contained in the title *"Terra Regis,"* are called *"ancient demesne."* *Vide Kitch.* 98. It appears that those lands only are *"ancient demesne"* at this day, which are written down in the book of *Domesday*—and whether they are *"ancient demesne"* or not, is to be tried *only* by that book. Vide i. *Salk* 57. 4 *Inst.* 269. *Hob.* 188.

ANFELDTYHDE—A simple accusation. The *Saxons* had two sorts of accusations, viz. *simplex* and *triplex:* that was called *single,* when the oath of the criminal, and *two* men were sufficient to discharge him—but his own oath, and the oaths of *five* persons were required to free him *"a triplici accusatione,"* (from a triple accusation.) Blount. *Vide leg. Adelstani.*

ARBITER—An arbitrator was frequently made use of among the *Romans:* this *"arbiter"* judged in those cases which were called *"bonæ fidei,"* and arbitrary, and was not restricted by any law or form; (*totius rei arbitrium habuit et potestatem;*) i. e. he had the arbitrament and power over the whole cause; he determined what seemed equitably in a thing not sufficiently defined by law. *Festus. Vid. Cic. pro. Rosc. Com.* 4. 5. *Off.* iii. 16. *Topic* 10. *Senec. de Benef.* iii. 3. 7. Hence he is called *"Honorarius."* Cic. Tusc. v. 41. de Fato 17. *Ad arbitrium vel judicem ire, adire, confugere;* i. e. to come, to go, to hasten to arbitrament, or judgment. *Cic. pro Rosc. Com.* 4. *Arbitrium sumere, capere;* i. e. to receive or take an award. *Arbitrium adigere;* i. e. *ad arbitrium agere, vel cogere;* i. e. to force one to submit to an arbitration. Cic. Off. iii. 16. Top. 10.— *Ad arbitrium vocare, vel appellare;* to call one, or compel him to arbitrate. Plaut. Rud. iv. 3. 99, 104.—*Ad, vel apud judicem, agere, experiri, litegare, petere;* to require, to seek, to try, to sue, and request judgment. But *arbiter,* and *judex arbitrium,* and *judicium,* are sometimes confounded. *Vide Cic. Rosc. Com.* 4. 9, *Am.* 39. *Mur.* 12. *Quint.* 3. Arbiter is also sometimes put for *testis. Vide Flacc.* 36. *Sallust. Cat.* 20. *Liv.* ii. 4. Horace used the word as the master, or director of the feast. Vid. Od. ii. 7. 23.—(*Arbiter bibendi.*)—A person chosen by two parties by compromise (*ex compromisso*), to determine a difference, without the appointment of the *Prætor,* was also called *"arbiter,"* but more properly *"compromissarius."*

ASSIGNETUR, &c.—No doubt marriages were, for some considerable time, formerly celebrated at the *door of the church,* where, it appears, *verbal* settlements were made by way of dower, out of the husband's lands, in the presence of sufficient witnesses.

ASTRICT—In old Scotch law, the cultivators of the land in each barony, whether temporal or spiritual, were bound to bring their corn or other grain to be ground at the particular mill of the territory. This service was a very vexatious one, for they were charged a heavy duty or toll upon their grain. This duty was termed a *multure*, and those lands which required this service were said to be *astricted*. If they evaded this service or *thirlage*, as it was called, and carried their grain to another mill, they were liable to a fine or dry multure. See Sir W. Scott's note to the Monastery.

AUXILIA FIUNT, &c.—The feudal landlords were sometimes called upon to assist the chief lord of the fee, on the marriage of his eldest daughter, and for other purposes, when required. As these aids were *voluntary*, the sums obtained depended on the good will the tenants retained towards their lords.

A VINCULO MATRIMONII.—A divorce of this kind absolutely *dissolves* the marriage, and makes it *void* from the *beginning*, the cause or causes of it being *precedent* to the marriage. On *this* divorce dower is gone. But it is said, the wife shall receive all again that she brought with her, because the nullity of the marriage arises through some impediment *prior* to the marriage; and the goods of the wife were given for *her* advancement in marriage, which now ceaseth; but this is mentioned to be the case, where the goods are not *spent;* but if the husband give them away, during the coverture, without any collusion, it shall bind her. If she *knows* her goods which are unspent, she may, it is said, bring an action of detinue for them; and as for money, &c., which cannot be identified, she would probably obtain relief in a court of equity. *Vide Dyer.* 62. *Nels. Abr.* 575. This divorce enables the party to marry again. Where lands were formerly given to the husband and wife, and the heirs of their bodies in *frank marriage*, if they were afterwards divorced the wife was to have her whole lands. After a sentence of divorce in the spiritual court of England (*causa præcontractus*), the issue of that marriage shall be bastards, so long as the sentence stands unrepealed; and no proof shall be admitted at common law to the contrary. *Vid. Co. Lit.* 235. 1 *Nels.* 674. In such case, the issue of a second marriage may inherit, until the sentence be repealed. 2 *Leon.* 207. A divorce for adultery was anciently *a vinculo matrimonii;* and therefore in the reign of *Queen Eliz.* the opinion of the church of *England* was, that after a divorce for adultery, the parties might marry again; but in *Foliambe's* case, 44 *Eliz.* that opinion was changed, and Archbishop *Bancroft*, by advice of the divines, held that adultery was *only* a cause of divorce, "*a mensa et thoro.*" Vide 3 *Salk.* 138.

B.

BACBEREND.——Applied to a thief caught with the stolen article on his back.

BACULO et annulo.——"With staff and ring." The *insignia* of the *Roman* Catholic bishops.

BACULUS nunciatorius.——"The proclaiming wand or staff." Also a rod frequently used by the criers of courts.

BAILIWICK.——The jurisdiction of a bailiff.

BAILLER.——" To deliver" over to bail.

BALNEARI fures.——These were idle thieves, who frequently visited the public baths at Rome, and stole the clothes of the persons who bathed there. *Vide note.*

BANCO.——"In Bench." As "*dies in banco,*" or days in which the court sits.

BANCUS regis.——The king's bench.

BANCUS ruptus.——"A broken bank." From which the word "Bankrupt."

BANLEUCA.——A space or district surrounding certain towns, cities, or religious houses protected by peculiar privileges.

BARCARIA.——A house or shed to keep bark for tanning purposes.

BARON et feme.——The husband and wife.

BARRATTA.——A contention; a quarrel.

BARRATTRY.——It appears that the etymology of this word is doubtful. It is probably from the Italian *barratrare,* to cheat; it appears to be any act of the master or mariners of a criminal nature, or which is grossly negligent, tending to their own benefit, to the prejudice of the owners of the ship, and without their privity or consent. *Vide* 1 *Stra.* 581, 2 *Stra.* 1173, *Cowp.* 143, 1 *Term Rep.* 323.

BASILEUS.——A king: a governor.

BASTARD eigne.——The eldest son born in concubinage, where the father and mother afterwards married.

BASTARDUS nullius est filius; aut filius populi.——"A bastard is no man's son; or the son of the people." He is *legally* no man's issue.

BASTART.——One born out of lawful wedlock.

BATTEL *or* bataille.——Single combat.

BATTELLUS.——A small boat or skiff.

BEATUS qui leges, juraque servat.——That man is blessed who keeps the laws and ordinances.

BEAUPLEADER.——Fair pleading.

BEDEFORDSHIRE Maner. Lestone redd' per annum XXII lib., &c.; ad opus reginæ ii uncias auri.——Bedfordshire Manor. That *Leyton* pay annually twenty-two pounds, &c.; and two ounces of gold for the queen's use.

BELLO parta, cedunt reipublicæ.——Being obtained in war, they are given up to the state.

BELLUINAS atque ferinas immanesque Longobardorum leges accipit.——(Italy) received the savage, wild, and monstrous laws of the Lombards. *Vide note.*

BELLUM intestinum.——A civil war.

BENE advocat captionem.——He rightly advises the taking.

BENE cognovit actionem.——He fairly confessed the action.

BENE cognovit captionem.——He rightly acknowledges the taking.

BENEFICIA.——Benefices: Gifts: also church livings. *Vide note to Allodum.*

BENEFICIUM competentiæ.——In Roman law, the right which an insolvent debtor had, when he made over his property for the benefit of his creditors, to keep what was honestly requisite for him to live according to his condition.

BENEFICIUM non datur nisi propter officium.——A benefice is not bestowed unless it be because of some service or duty.

BENEPLACITUM.——Good pleasure.

BENIGNÆ faciendæ sunt interpretationes chartarum, ut magis valeat, quam pereat.——The interpretation of writings (or deeds) are construed favorably in order that more may prevail than be lost.

BENIGNE interpretamur chartas, propter simplicitatem laicorum.——We explain deeds favorably because of the simplicity (or ignorance) of laymen.

BEREAFODON.——They bereaved.

BEREWICA.——A village belonging to some town or manor.

BESAYEL.——Great grandfather.

BESTES.——"Beasts;" often meaning in the law books, "*game.*"

BIBLIOTHECA.——A library. *Vide note.*

BIELBRIEF.——In maritime law a statement furnished by the builder of a vessel of her length, breadth, and dimensions in every part. Sometimes the terms of the bargain between the builder and owner are included in this document. It corresponds with the English, French, and American *register*, and is equally necessary to the lawful ownership of a vessel.

BIENS.——Goods : chattels : wealth.

BIENS meubles et immeubles.——Goods moveable and immoveable.

BIGAMUS.——One guilty of bigamy.

BILLA cassetur.——That the bill be quashed.

BILLA excambii.——A bill of exchange.

BILLA vera.——The indorsement made by a grand jury in old times upon a bill of indictment, if they found evidence sufficient to sustain it.

BILLÆ nundinales.——Fair (or market) bills.

BINOS, trinos, vel etiam senos, ex singulis territorii quadrantibus.——(They were summoned) by two, three, and even by six, from every part of the district (or country.)

BIRAUBAN.——To rob.

BIRAUBODEDUN.——They robbed.

BIS petitum.——Twice asked.

BLADA crescentia.——The growing grass (or grain.)

BONA.——Goods: personal estate. Lord *Coke* says this word includes all chattles, as well real as personal. *Co. Lit.* 118, 6. It is however generally used to designate moveable property.

Bona civium.——The citizens' goods.

Bona felonum, &c. ideo plene prout abbas habuit. The chattles of felons, &c. and that as fully as the abbot enjoyed.

Bona fide asportavit. He carried off (the chattels) in good faith (or with a good intent).

Bona fide; et clausula inconsuet' semper inducunt suspicionem.——In good faith; and unusual clauses always create suspicion.

Bonæ fidei venditorem, nec commodorum spem augere nec incommodorum conditionem obscurare oportet.——It behoves a vendor of integrity neither to increase the expectation of profits, nor conceal the state of the disadvantages.

Bona gestura.——Good behavior.

Bona gratia matrimonium dissolvitur.——Mutual agreement dissolves the marriage.

Bona immobilia.——Immoveable effects; as lands, houses, &c.

Bona mobilia.——Moveable things; as mortgages, bonds, &c.

Bona notabilia.——"Extraordinary (or notable) goods;" as bonds, mortgages, specialties, bills of exchange, &c.

Bona paraphernalia.——Goods which the wife has for her own separate use; as rings for her fingers, ear-rings, &c.

Bona patria.——"An assize of countrymen, or good neighbors;" sometimes called "assiza bona patriæ," otherwise "juratores."

Bona peritura.——Perishable goods.

Bona vacantia.——"Goods left (or having no owner:) goods lost;" those liable to be taken by the first finder.

Bona waiviata.——"Goods waived." Goods which had been stolen, and thrown away, or relinquished.

Bon brevato.——A happy suggestion: a good hint.

Bones gents.——Good men.

4

BONI et legales homines.——Good and lawful men.

BONI judicis est ampliare jurisdictionem.——It is the province of a good judge to increase the jurisdiction (or power).

BONIS non amovendis.——"That the goods be not taken away." A precept issued where a writ of error has been brought, in order that the goods be not removed until the error be tried, or determined.

BONITAS tota æstimabitur cum pars evincitur.——The goodness (or value) of the whole may be estimated when a part is proved.

BONO et malo.——"For good and evil." The name of a special writ of gaol delivery.

BONUS.——A consideration given for what is received: a premium paid to a grantor or vendor.

BORDLANDS.——The lands which the old lords particularly reserved to furnish food for their table or board.

BORGE.——A pledge.

BOSCAGE.——That food which trees yield for cattle.

BOTES.——Wood cut off a farm by the tenant for the purpose of repairing dwelling-houses, barns, fencing, &c., which the common law allows him, without any prior agreement made for that purpose.

BOVATA terræ.——An ancient measure of land; as much as one ox can plough.

BRACHIUM maris, in quo unusquisque subjectus domini regis habet, et habere debet liberam piscariam.——An arm of the sea, in which every subject of the lord the king, hath, and ought to have, free fishery.

BREPHOTROPHI.——Persons charged with the care of houses for foundlings.

BREVE de extento.——A writ of extent.

BREVE de recto.——A writ of right.

BREVIA domini regis non currunt.——The king's writs do not run; (are inoperative).

BREVIA formata.——"Special writs." Writs made to suit particular cases.

BREVIA formata super certis casibus de cursu, et de commune consilio totius regni concessa et approbata.——Writs usually framed on special cases, and allowed, and approved of by the general advice of the whole kingdom.

BREVIA judicialia.——Judicial writs.

BREVIA magistralia.——Magisterial writs.

BREVIA originales.——Original writs.

BREVIA testata.——Attested writs.

BREVIARIUM.——The name of a code of laws, compiled under the direction of Alaric II. king of the Visigoths, for the use of his Roman subjects.

BREVIBUS et rotulis liberandis.——A writ or mandate to the sheriff to deliver to his successor, the county, and the appurtenances; with the rolls, briefs, remembrances, and all other things belonging to the office of sheriff.

BRIEFE de recto clauso.——Writ of right close.

BRUTUM fulmen.——A harmless thunderbolt; a noisy but ineffectual menace: a law neither respected nor obeyed.

BURGA.——House-breaking.

BURGI latrocinium.——Burglary: the robbery from a castle or mansion-house.

BURSA.——A purse.

BUTTS.——The short pieces of land at the *ends* of fields which are necessarily left unploughed when the plough is turned around. They are sometimes termed *headlands,* and the same pieces on the sides, *sidelings.*

BUTTS and BOUNDS.——Words used in describing the boundaries of land. Properly speaking, *butts* are the lines at the *ends,* and *bounds* are those on the sides if the land is of rectangular shape. But in irregular shaped land, *butts* are the points or corners, where the boundary lines change their direction.

NOTES TO B.

BALNEARI FURES.—As the public baths of the *Romans* are so frequently·
noticed in the Classics, it may not be improper to say a few words concerning them.　In later times of the *Roman* empire, the *Romans* before supper,
used always to bathe, (for using little or no linen, this custom was very
necessary.)　Vide *Plaut. Stich.* v. 2. 19.　The wealthy had their baths for
the family, both cold and hot, (at their own houses.)　*Cic. de Orat.* ii. 55.
There were also public baths for the use of the citizens at large (*Hor. Ep.* i.),
where there were several apartments for men and women.　These *balneari
fures* used to steal the clothes, leaving the bathers in no very agreeable situation, when they wished to return home.　Each bather paid to the keeper
(or overseer) of the bath a small coin (*quadrans*).　Hor. Sat. i. 3. 137.　The
usual time for bathing was two o'clock (*octava hora*) in summer; and three
in winter.　The *Romans*, before bathing took various kinds of exercise (*exer-
citationes campestres, post decisa negotia, campo*),—i. e. field exercises in the
camp after business was ended; as the ball or tennis, throwing the javelin,
or *discus*, quoit, &c., (vide *Hor. Od.* i. 8. 11,) riding, running, leaping, &c.;
from this it appears that the *Romans* bathed when warm with exercise.

BELLUINAS, &c.—Italy, it is true, accepted, or was rather *compelled* to accept, laws of the Barbarians, who laid her waste; and the state in which
she appears to have been for several ages, after the barbarous nations settled
there, is the most decisive proof of their cruelty, as well as the extent of their
depredations.　Vide *Muratori Antiquitates Italicæ medii ævi, dissert.* 21. v. 2.
p. 149. *et sub.*　The state of desolation in other countries of *Europe* was very
similar.　In some of the most early charters now extant, the lands granted
to the monasteries, or to private persons, are distinguished by such as were
cultivated, or inhabited, and such as were "*eremi,*" desolate.　In many instances, lands were granted to persons, *because* they had taken them from the
desert (*ab eremo*), and had cultivated and planted them with inhabitants.
Muratori adds that during the eighth and ninth centuries *Italy* was greatly
infested with wolves, and other wild beasts; another mark of want of population.　Thus *Italy*, once the pride of the ancient world, for its learning,
science, prowess, fertility, and cultivation, was reduced to the state of a
country, *newly* peopled, and lately rendered habitable, leaving an *awful* example and warning to avoid the luxury, effeminacy, pride, cruelty, and oppression of the inhabitants of that once imperial country.

BIBLIOTHECA.—A Library.　*Festus.*—A great number of books, or the
place where they were kept, was by the Romans called "*Bibliotheca.*"　The
first famous library was collected by *Ptolemy Philadelphus*, at *Alexandria* in
Egypt, B. C. 284; and contained, it is said, 700,000 volumes.　Vide *Gell.* vi. 17.
The next by *Attalus* or *Eumenes*, king of *Pergamus*.　Plin. xiii. 12.　Adjoining the *Alexandrian* library was a building called "*Museum,*" vide *Plin. Ep.*
i. 9., for the accommodation of a college or society of learned men, who were
supported there at the public expense, with a covered walk and seats, where
they might dispute.　*Strab.* 17.—but the word *Museum* is used by us as meaning a repository of curiosities; as it also seems to be by *Pliny* xxvii. 2. s. b.
A great part of the *Alexandrian* library was burnt by the flames of *Cæsar's*
fleet.　Vide *Plutarch in Cæs.* and *Dio.* 43. 38.　It was again restored by
Cleopatra, who, for that purpose, received from *Antony*, the library of *Pergamus*, then consisting, it is said, of 200,000 volumes.　*Plutarch in Anton.*　It
was totally destroyed by the *Saracens*, A. D. 642.　The first public library
at *Rome*, and in the world, as *Pliny* observes, was erected by *Asinius Pollio*,
(Plin. vii. 30. &c.,) in the *Atrium*, or Temple of Liberty (*Ovid. Trist.*), on Mount
Aventine, Mart. xii. 3. 5.　Many private persons had good libraries.　*Cic.* Libraries were adorned with statues and pictures, particularly of ingenious and
learned men.　The books were put in presses, or cases, along the walls, which
were sometimes numbered.

C.

CABELLERIA.——Spanish measure for a lot of land one hundred feet front, and two hundred deep.

CADERI.——To fall or come to an end.

CADIT assiza, et vertitur in juratum.——The assize ceases, and it is turned into a jury.

CADIT in perambulationem.——It falls by the way.

CADIT quæstio.——" The question falls": i. e. if matters are as represented, " *quæstio cadit*," the point at issue admits of no farther discussion.

CADUCARY.——Relates to forfeiture or confiscation.

CÆTERA desunt.——The rest is wanting.

CALENDS.——The first day of the month in the Roman calendar.

CAMERA scaccarii.——The chamber of the exchequer.

CAMERA stellata.——" The Star Chamber." An odious court once held in England, but many years since abolished.

CAMPANA.——A bell.

CAMPI partitio.——"Champerty—a division of the land." This is an offence mentioned in the law books—it is the purchasing a right, or pretended right to property, under a condition, that part when obtained by suit shall belong to the purchaser. *Vide note.*

CAMPUM partire.——To divide the field.

CANCELLARIA.——The court of chancery.

CANCELLARIUS.——The chancellor.

CANDIDATI.——" Candidates." Those who sought for office under the Roman government. *Vide note.*

CANTRED. The Welsh counties were divided into districts called *cantreds*, as in England into *hundreds.* See *Hundred.*

CAPAX doli.——" Capable of committing crime:" of sufficient understanding to be liable to punishment for an offence.

CAPE.——A judicial writ touching a plea of lands or tenements. This writ is divided into "*cape magnum*" (great), and "*cape parvum*" (little).

CAPE ad valentiam.——Take to the value.

CAPE de terra in bailiva sua tantæ terræ, quod B. clamat ut jus suum.——Take of the land in your bailiwick to (the value) of so much land which B. claims as his right.

CAPELLA.——A chapel.

CAPERE, et habere potuisset.——He ought to take, and to hold.

CAPIAS.——"You may take." A writ authorizing the defendant's arrest. *Vide note.*

CAPIAS ad audiendum judicium.——A writ to summon a defendant found guilty of a misdemeanor, but who is not then present, although he has previously appeared. The writ is to bring him to receive his judgment.

CAPIAS ad computandum.——That you take (defendant) to make account.

CAPIAS ad respondendum.——That you take (defendant) to make answer.

CAPIAS ad satisfaciendum.——That you take (defendant) to make satisfaction.

CAPIAS ad satisfaciendum, ita quod habeas corpus ejus, &c.——That you take (defendant) to satisfy, so that you may have his body, &c. *Vide note.*

CAPIAS ad valentiam.——That you take to the value.

CAPIAS in withernam.——That you take a reprisal. *Vide "Withernam."*

CAPIAS qui capere possit.——Let him catch who can.

CAPIAS si laicus.——That you take (defendant) if he be a layman.

CAPIAS utlagatum.——That you take the outlaw.

CAPIATUR pro fine.——A writ to levy a fine due to the king.

CAPITA distributio, *i. e.*——To every person an equal

share, when all the parties claim in their own right, and not "*jure representationis*," by right of representation.

CAPITALES, generales, perpetui, et majores; a latere regis residentes, qui omnium aliorum corrigere tenentur injurias et errores.——They (the judges of the king's bench) are principal, general, perpetual, and superior, sitting with the king, who are bound to correct the wrongs and errors of all others.

CAPITALES inimicitiæ.——Deadly hatred. This was formerly held sufficient to dissolve the *espousals* of marriage.

CAPITALIS baro.——Chief baron.

CAPITALIS justiciarius in itinere.——The chief judge in eyre; or itinerant judge.

CAPITALIS justiciarius totius *Angliæ*.——The chief justice of all *England*.

CAPITALIS plegius.——The principal pledge.

CAPITANEUS.——In feudal law, a chief lord or baron of the king; a leader, a captain.

CAPITARE.——In surveying, to *head* or *abut*.

CAPITILITIUM.——Poll money.

CAPITIS æstimatio.——A fine paid by the *Saxons* for murder, &c. *Vide note*.

CAPITIS diminutio.——The loss of civil qualification.

CAPITULA.——A collection of laws or regulations arranged under particular heads or divisions.

CAPITULA de Judæis.——The chapters (or heads) of an ancient book or register for the starrs, or mortgages, made to the *Hebrews*.

CAPITULA itineris.——Articles or heads of inquiry upon all the various crimes or misdemeanors, which, in old practice, the itinerant justices delivered to the juries from the various hundreds at the opening of their *eyre* or court.

CAPITULARIA.——Collection of laws promulgated by the early French kings.

CAPTIO.——Taking or seizing of a person or thing.

CAPTURAM avium per totam Angliam interdixit.——He forbade the catching of birds throughout all England.

CAPUT lupinum.——Anciently an outlawed felon was said to have "*caput lupinum;* that is, he was proscribed as the wolf of the forest.

CAPUT, principium, et finis.——The principal, the beginning, and the end.

CAPUTIUM.——A headland

CARCANNUM.——A prison or a workhouse.

CARCERE mancipenter in ferris.——That they be kept in prison in irons.

CARECTA.——A cart. *Carreta.*——A carriage or cartload.

CARENA.——Forty days; quarantine.

• CARNALIS copula.——This was formerly considered a lawful impediment to marriage; for if any one, during the life of his wife, contracted matrimony or espousals with another, and a "*carnalis copula*" (carnal knowledge) ensued, and the woman knew the man had another wife, such marriage could not afterwards be established: but if she were ignorant of that fact, and no *carnalis copula* had taken place, the marriage might be solemnized *after* the death of the first wife.

CARET periculo, qui etiam tutus, cavit.——He is most free from danger who, even when safe, is on his guard.

CAR tel est notre plaisir.——"For such is our pleasure." This was a form of a regal ordinance under the *Norman* line. It is now, happily, used only ironically, to note some arbitary act.

CARRUM.——A four-wheeled vehicle

CARUA, or Caruca.——A plough. The tax which was formerly imposed upon every plough was called *carucage,* or *carvage.*

CASA.——A house. When land was added to it sufficient for one family's support, it was called *Casata.*

CASSETUR billa.——That the bill be quashed.

CASSETUR processus.——That the process be quashed (or abated).

CASTELLANUS.——A castellain; keeper of a castle.

CASTELLORUM operatio.——Castle work.

CASTER, CHESTER, CESTER.——Signify *fort* or camp.

CASTRUM.——A castle.

CASUS.——A casualty.

CASUALITER, et per infortunium, contra voluntatem suam.——Casually, and by misfortune, against his will.

CASUS Fœderis.——The matter of the treaty.

CASUS fortuitus.——An accidental case.

CASUS fortuitus; magis est improvisus proveniens ex alterius culpa, quam fortuitus.——A chance case; this is the more unexpected as arising from the fault of another person, than as happening accidentally.

CASUS omissus.——An omitted case; an opportunity neglected.

CATALLA.——"Chattels: things moveable." It primarily signified beasts of husbandry.

CATALLA otiosa.——Cattle which are not worked; as sheep, swine, &c.

CATANEUS.——A chief tenant or Captain.

CATCHPOLE.——An officer who made arrests.

CATEUX sont meubles et immeubles; si comme vrais meubles sont qui transporter se peuvent, et ensuiver le corps; immeubles sont choses qui ne peuvent ensuiver le corps, niester transportees, et tout ce qui n' est point en heritage.——Chattels are moveable and immoveable; if they are really moveable chattels they are those which may be taken away and follow the person; immoveable (chattels) are those things which cannot follow the person, nor be carried away; and all that is not in heritage.

CAULCEIS.——Causeways.

CAUPO.——An inn-keeper.

CAURSINES.——Money lenders from Italy, who came into England in Henry 3d's reign.

CAUSA adulterii.——On account of adultery.

CAUSA impotentiæ.——On account of incapacity.

CAUSA latet, vis est notissima.——The cause is unknown, but the effect is most evident.

CAUSA matrimonii prælocuti.——By reason of the said marriage.

CAUSA mortis.——On account of death : In prospect of death.

CAUSA præcontractus, causa metus, causa impotentiæ seu frigiditatis, causa affinitatis, causa consanguinitatis.——On account of precontract, fear, impotence or frigidity, affinity or consanguinity.

CAUSA proxima, et non remota, spectatur.——The nearest cause, and not a remote one should be attended to.

CAUSATOR.——One who litigates another's cause.

CAUSA venationis.——For the sake of hunting.

CAUSA venditionis.——On account of a sale.

CAUSE de remover plea.——Cause to remove a plea.

CAUSIDICUS.——A pleader.

CAVEAT actor.——" Let the actor be cautious." Let him beware of his own conduct.

CAVEAT emptor.——" Let the purchaser take heed." Let the person buying see that the title be good.

CAVEAT vicecomes.——Let the sheriff beware.

CAVENDUM tamen est ne convellantur res judicatæ, ubi leges cum justitia retrospicieri possint.——It is however to be guarded against that adjudged cases be not reversed, where the laws on a review appear to have had respect to justice.

CAYA.——A quay.

CAYAGIUM.——The duty paid on goods landed at a quay.

CEAPGELD.——The forfeiture of a beast.

CE beau contrat est le noble produit du génie de l'homme, et le premier garant du commerce maritime. Il a consulté les saisons ; il a porté ses regards sur la mer ; il a interrogé ce terrible élément ; il en a jugé l'inconstance ; il en a presenti les orages; il a épié la politique; il a reconnu les portes et les côtes des deux mondes; il a tout soumis à des calculs savans, à des theories approximatives, et il a dit au commerçant habile; au navigateur intrepide; certes il y a des desastres sur lesquels l'humanitie ne peut que gemir; mais quant à votre fortune, allez francissez les mers, déployez votre activité et votre industrié, je moi charge de vos risques.——This excellent contract is the able production of the genius of man, and is the first security to naval commerce. He has consulted the seasons; he has made his observations on the sea, and has, as it were, interrogated this formidable element; he is a judge of its inconstancy; he personally experienced the effects of storms; he possesses the political acumen; he, in fine, possesses a knowledge of the harbors and coasts of the two worlds; he is in possession of the most difficult researches of the learned, and of their parallel theories; and he is acknowledged to be well skilled in commercial affairs; he is also a most intrepid navigator—that is to say, one well experienced in those dangers at which humanity shudders; but when your fortunes, your activity, and industry are employed on the sea, I become responsible for the results.

CEDENT.——One who transfers or assigns.

CELDRA.——A chaldron, a measure.

CELEBERRIMO huic conventu episcopus, aldermanus inter sunto; quorum alter jura divina: alter humana populum edoceto.——At this renowned assembly, let a bishop and an alderman be present; let one instruct the people in divine, the other in human laws.

CELERARIUS.——The steward of a monastic institution.

CELLES que ne recognoissent superieure en Feidalité. ——Those who acknowledge no superior in fidelity.

CELLES que trusts.——Those persons entitled to the purchase money, or the residue of any other property, after discharging debts, &c.

CELTÆ.——A brave and warlike nation, or tribe, who
formerly possessed old *Gaul;* and afterwards the whole,
. or a considerable part of *Scotland. Vide note.*

CELUI dont cette eau l'heritage, peut meme est user
dans l'intervalle qu'elle y parevent, mais a la charge de la
rendre a la sortee, de des sords a son course ordinarie.——
He who owns waters can use them along all the course or
space through which they run, with the obligation of re-
ducing them again within their ordinary banks.

CELUI dont la pur priett bord un eau courante autre que
celle qui est declarée dependance du domaine publique par
l'article, &c.—peut a en saver a son passage pour l'irriga-
tion de ses propriettes.——He whose property is bounded
on a stream of water which is not by the deed, &c., declared
to belong to the domain for public use, may yet use sufficient to irrigate his lands.

CELUI qui a parte dans une fonds peut an user a .sa vo-
lante, saufle droit que la proprietaire du fonds superieur
pourait avoir acquis, par litre, ou par prescription.——He
who has a part in a freehold property, can dispose of it at
his own will and pleasure, saving the right which the principal proprietor thereof might have acquired, by virtue of
contract, or of prescription.

CENEGILD.-——Among the Saxons the *fine* which was
paid by a *murderer* to the relatives of the deceased, by way
of compensation or expiation.

CENELLÆ.——Acorns.

CENNINGA.——Where one party purchases an article
of another, and afterwards the thing sold is claimed by
a third party, the buyer gives notice or *cenninga* to the
seller, that he may appear and justify the sale. *Saxon
law.*

CENSARII.——Farmers subject to a tax.

CENSUALES.——Persons who subjected themselves voluntarily to a church or monastery, in order to procure protection.

CENSUMORTHIDUS.——A dead rent.

CENSUS regalis.——The ancient royal revenue.

CENTENA.——A hundred weight.

CENTENARIUS.——A petty judge under the sheriff (and deputy to the principal governor of the county), who had rule of a hundred; and was a judge in small concerns among the inhabitants of the hundred.

CENTENI.——The hundred men from each district among the old Germans, who were enrolled for military service.

CENTENI ex singulis pagis sunt, idque ipsum inter suos vocantur; et quod primo numeris fuit, jam nomen et honor est.——The hundredors are (electors) from the several counties, and are so called among themselves; and that which was at first a number, is now a name and honor.

CENTESSIMÆ.——Interest at twelve per cent. per annum.

CENTUMVIRI.——Judges among the Romans. *Vide note.*

CEO est le serement que le roy jurre a soun coronement: Que il gardera et meintenera lez droitez et lez franchisez de seynt esglisé grauntez auncienment des droitez roys christiens d'Engleterre, et quil guardera toruez sez terrez, honoures et dignitez droiturelx et franks del coron du roilme d'Engleterre, en tout maner dentierte sanz null maner damenusement, et lez droitez dispergez dilapidez ou perdez de la corone a soun poiair, reappeller en l'auncien estate, et quil guardera le peas de seynt esglise, et al clergie, et al people de bon accorde, et quil facc faire entontez sez judgementez owel et droit justice, oue discrecion et misericorde, et quil grantera a tenure lez leyes et custmez du roialme, et a soun poiair lez face garder et affirmer, que lez gentez du people avont faitez et esliez, et les malveys leyz et custumes de tout oustera, et ferme peas et establie al people de soun realme, en ceo garde esgardera a son poiair ; come Dieu luy aide.——This is the oath which the King swears at his coronation: That he will keep and maintain the rights and franchises of the holy church, formerly granted by the rightful christian kings of England; and that he will keep all his lands, honors and dignities of royal and free right, pertaining to the crown of the kingdom of England, in all manner without diminution; and that the rights of the crown, scattered, dilapidated or lost, he shall recall to the best of his power, to their ancient estate; and that he will keep the peace of the holy church, both to the clergy and the people with good accord: and that he will dispense in all his judgments, equal and impartial justice, with discretion and mercy: and that he will adhere to the laws and customs of the kingdom: and to the best of his power cause them to be kept, and maintained, which the people have made and agreed to: and that he will abolish the bad laws and customs altogether; and preserve firm and lasting peace to the subjects of his kingdom, in this regard he will keep to the utmost of his power. So help him God.

CEORL, CARL, CHURL.——A Saxon name for a freeman employed in husbandry.

CEO n'est que un restitution en lour ley pur que a ceo n'avemus regard, &c.——This is but a restitution in their law, to which we pay no attention, &c.

CEPI corpus, et est in custodia.——I have taken the body, and it is in custody.

CEPI corpus, et est languidus.——I have taken the body, and it is sick.

CEPI corpus et paratum habeo.——I have taken the body, and have it ready.

CEPI corpus in custodia.——"I have taken the body in custody."

These were several returns to writs, formerly made when the proceedings were in Latin.

CEPIT et asportavit.——He took and carried away.

CEPIT et asportavit centum cuniculos.——He took and carried away a hundred rabbits.

CEPIT et asportavit captivum et ipsum in salva sua custodia adtunc et ibidem habuit et custodivit, quosque defensores ipsum e custod' prædict' felonice ceperunt et recusser', &c.——He took and carried away the prisoner, and then and there held and kept him in safe custody, until the defendants feloniously took him out of his said custody, and refused, &c.

CEPIT in alio loco.——He took in another place.

"CE qui manque aux orateurs en profondeur,
Ils vous la donne en longueur."

——What orators want in depth, they give you in length.

CEREVISIA.——Ale or beer.

CERTA et utilia agendo.——By doing things sure and useful.

CERTE, altero huic seculo, nominatissimus in patriâ juris consultus, ætate provectior, etiam munere gaudens publico et prædiis amplissimis, generosi titulo bene se habuit; forte quod togatæ genti magis tunc conveniret civilis illa appellatio, quam castrensis altera.——Certainly in the last age the most eminent counsellor in the country, advanced in life, who enjoyed a public gift (or pension) and most ample estates, and was well (satisfied) that he obtained the title of a gentleman; perhaps, because this civil term, better suited a gownsman at that period, than a military title.

CERTIFICATIO assisæ novæ disseisinæ.——A writ formerly granted for the review of any matter passed by assize, where some points had been overlooked or neglected.

CERTIORARI.——"To be certified of: to be informed of." A writ directing the proceedings, or record of a cause, to be brought before a superior court.

CERTIORARI, ad informandum conscientiam.——To certify, to inform the conscience.

CERTIORARI ex debito justitiæ.——To be informed of a debt (or what is due) on account of justice.

CERTIORARI quare executionem non.——To certify why execution (has not been issued).

CERTIORARI quare improvide emanavit.——To be certified wherefore it improperly issued.

CERTMONEY.——Head money or fine.

CERTUM est quod certum reddi potest.——"That is fixed or determined which can be reduced to a certainty;" as where a person covenants to pay as much money as a given quantity of a particular stock will be worth on a certain day; this can be reduced to a certainty by a calculation, and is therefore a sum *certain* for which an action lies.

CERVISARII.——Those tenants who were obliged to provide *ale* or *cervisia* for the lord or his steward.

CERVISIARIUS.——A brewer.

CE sont des choses que faut pensir.——These are things which must be considered.

CESSANTE causa, cesset effectus.——"Remove the cause, and the effect will cease."

CESSANTE ratione, cessat et ipsa lex.——"The reason ceasing, that law is (then) superseded." Many statutes have been made on pressing occasions to meet the exigencies of the moment; as where some crime is peculiarly predominant, and nothing can check it but a most sanguinary law; yet when that vice is at an end, it would be cruelty to give those laws a permanent duration.

CESSANTE statu primitivo cessat derivativus.——The original or first condition ceasing, that which is derived from it also ceases.

CESSAT executio.——"The execution ceases." These words are often applied in case trespass be brought against two or more persons, and if it be tried, and found against one only, and the plaintiff take execution against him, the writ will abate as to the others: then there ought to be a "*cessat executio*" till it be tried against the other defendants.

CESSAVIT.——An obsolete writ which could formerly be sued out when a tenant had *ceased* for two years to pay his rent and services, and had not sufficient goods upon the premises to be distrained.

Cesse.——An assessment.

Cessio bonorum.——"A surrender of effects." This was in use among the *Romans* where a debtor became insolvent. It is also a process in the law of *Scotland*, very similar to that under the statutes relating to bankruptcy in *England*.

Cessit processus.——The proceeding has ceased.

Cessor.——One who is liable to have a writ of *cessavit* served against him for the long neglect of some duty devolving upon him.

Cessure.——A bailiff.

C' est une autre chose.——"It is another thing." The proof is at variance with the statement of the case.

C'est le crime qui faite la honte, et non pas l'echafaud.——It is the guilt, not the scaffold, makes the crime.

Cestuy que trust.——A person for whose use another is seized of lands, &c.

Cestuy que use.——A person for whose use land, &c., be given or granted.

Cestuy que doit enheriter al pere, doit enheriter al fils.——He who should inherit to the father, should inherit to the son.

C' est un beau spectacle que celui des lois feodales; un chêne antique s'éleve il faut percer la terre pour les racines trouver.——Feudal laws are an excellent subject for observation: in order to ascertain the growth of an ancient oak, we must penetrate the earth to find its roots.

Cestuy que vie.——One for whose life a gift or grant is made.

C' est une espece de jeu, qui exige beaucoup de prudence de la part de ceux qui s'y addonent. Il faut faire l'annalyse des hazards, et possider la science du calcul des probabilities; prévoir les ecueils de la mer, et seu de la marivaise foi; ne pas perdre de vue les cas insolites et extraordinaires; combiner le tout, le comparer avec le taux des

5

primes, et juger quel sera le resultat de l'ensemble.——This is a species of game which requires much prudence on the part of those who engage therein; persons must examine with scrutiny all its hazards, and possess the science of calculating probabilities; they must previously know the effects of sea storms; nor are they to lose sight of isolated or rare occurrences: those must be well combined and compared together: nor let the result of the whole be considered despicable or unworthy of notice.

CETTE interdiction de commerce avec les ennemis comprehend aussi de plein droite, le defense d'assurer les effets, qui leur apartieñnent, qu'ils soient chargés sur leur propres vaisseaux, ou sur des navires amis, allies, ou neutres, &c. ——This interdict on commerce with the enemy, comprehends, of course, the prohibition to insure the effects which belong to them, whether (loaded) in their own vessels, those of their friends, allies or neutrals.

CHAFEWAX.——An officer in English chancery who melts or fits the wax used in sealing writs, commissions, etc.

CHAFFERS.——Wares, merchandise.

CHALUNGE.——A claim.

CHAMBIUM.——Change or exchange.

CHAMPART.——Champarty. Vide "*Campi partitio.*"

CHARGEANT.——Weighty; heavy.

CHARGE des affaires.——A person in charge of the embassy.

CHARE.——A plough. CHARETTE.——A cart.

CHARTA cyrographata.——A written charter which is executed in two parts, and cut through the middle.

CHARTA de foresta.——The charter of the forest.

CHARTÆ, folia, vel plagulæ, liber.——Papers or writings, leaves, sheets (of paper) a book. *Vide note.*

CHARTA libertatum regni.——The charta of the nation's liberties, usually called "*Magna Charta*" (the great charter).

CHARTA per legem terræ.——The charter by the law of the land.

CHARTA sua manifeste expressa.——Clearly expressed by her deed (or writing).

CHARTEL.——A letter of challenge to single combat.

CHARTIS reddendis.——Writ for re-delivering a charter.

CHASEA.——A chase.

CHASTELL.——A castle.

CHATEAUX.——Chattels.

CHAUD-MEDLEY.——Chance-medley: death by accident.

CHAUX.——Those.

CHAYE.——Fallen.

CHEAUNCE.——An accident.

CHEF de la societe.——The chief (or president) of the company (or firm).

CHEIR, Checir.——To fall; to abate.

CHESEUN.——Every one.

CHEVAGE.——A tribute formerly paid by bondmen to their lord.

CHEVANCE.——Goods; money.

CHEVERES.——Goats.

CHEVISANCE.——Signifies, in the French language, agreement, compact. Legally, it means an unlawful bargain or contract.

CHEVITIÆ.——The *heads* at the end of ploughed lands.

CHI apres.——Hereinafter.

CHIPPINGAVEL.——A tax upon wares or merchandise brought to a place to be sold.

CHIRGEMOT.——An ecclesiastical assembly or court.

CHIROGRAPHA.——Writings under hand.

CHOSE in action.——A thing in action.

CHRISTIANI-JUDAIZANTES.——" Judaizing-Christians." Jews converted to Christianity, but retaining a regard for the Mosaic ceremonies.

CHURCHESSET.——An ancient annual tribute paid to the church in grain on St. Martin's day.

CHURCH reeve.——Church warden.

CIBATUS.——Victualled.

CINQUE ports.——Formerly five, but now seven ports on the southeast coast of England.

CIPPI.——The stocks.

CIRCA ardua regni.——Concerning the weighty affairs of the realm.

CIRCADA.——An ancient tribute paid to the bishop or archdeacon upon visiting the churches.

CIRCUMSPECTE agatis.——"That you act cautiously." The title of an act of 13th of *Edward* the First, (or rather 9th *Edward* Second) prescribing certain cases to the judges concerning which the king's prohibition was of no avail.

CIVILITER mortuus.——"Dead civilly—or dead in law." Thus if a man be sentenced to die—he is said to be " *civiliter mortuus,*" or dead in the eye of the law.

CIVITAS ea autem in libertate est posita, quæ suis stat viribus non ex alieno arbitrio pendet.——That state is free, which depends upon its own strength, and not upon the arbitrary will of another.

CLAIA.——A hurdle.

CLAMANTEM et auditum infra quatuor parietes.——"Crying and being heard within the four walls." This was applied to cases where a man married a woman, seized in fee, and a child was born, which *had been heard to cry*, the husband was then called tenant by the curtesy. Vide " *Tamen clamorem.*"

CLANDESTINO copulati fuerunt.——"They were united by stealth": the marriage was solemnized secretly.

CLARE constat.——A precept to give possession of lands to an heir.

CLAUSE ROLLS or CLOSE ROLLS.——Rolls containing the records of writs, close and other documents, which are preserved in the English public records.

CLAUSTURA.——An enclosure.

CLAUSUM fregit.——He broke the close, or field.

CLAUSUM paschæ.——The eighth day after Easter, or the close of that feast.

CLAVES insulæ.——The title of twelve persons in the Isle of Man, to whom all doubtful cases were referred. Literally, the keys of the island.

CLAVIA.——A club.

CLEMENTIA principis, de consilio procerum indulta.—— The indulgence of the prince, allowed from the council of nobles.

CLERICI de cancellaria.——Clerks of the Chancery.

CLERICI prænotarii.——The six clerks in Chancery.

CLERICO capto per statutum mercatorum.——Writ to deliver a clerk out of prison, who had been arrested upon the breach of a statute merchant.

CLERICUS mercati.——Clerk of the market.

CLERIMONIA.——Privilege of clergy.

CLERONIMUS.——An heir.

CLITO—Sax.——The son of a king.

CNAFA—Sax.——A knave. Vide note.

CNYT—Sax.——A knight. Lat. Miles; and Eques au· ratus. Vide note.

COCKET.——A custom-house seal.

CODEX Justinianus.——Justinian's code of laws. Vide note.

CODICILLUS.——A little book: a codicil to a will. Vide note.

COEMPTIO.——A mutual purchase. Vide note.

COGNATI.——Cousins; kinsmen.

COGNATIO legalis; est personarum proximitas ex adoptione vel arrogatione, solemni ritu facta perveniens.—— "A legal relationship is a proximity (or near degree of affinity) of persons, either from adoption or assumption (as belonging to the family) established by a solemn act." This was formerly by the canon law an impediment to marriage.

Cognitio.——Roman law. The judicial hearing of a cause.

Cognoscit.——He confesses; he acknowledges.

Cognovit actionem.——"He has acknowledged the action." After suit brought, the defendant frequently confesses the action; judgment is then entered on the record without trial: or the defendant signs an instrument called a *cognovit.*

Cognovit actionem, relicta verificatione.——He confessed the action, having abandoned his plea.

Collatio bonorum.——An assessment of goods: also an assessment or impost upon the people.

Collectum ex senibus desperatis, ex agresti luxuria, ex rusticis decoctoribus, ex iis, qui vadimonia deserere quam illum exercitum maluerunt.——A mob collected from desperate veterans, and rustic spendthrifts, in servile (or clownish) luxury, and from those who would rather desert their bail than that army.

Collegium si nullo speciali privilegio subnixum sit hereditatem capere non posse, dubium non est.——If a corporation be erected without any special privilege (or grant) it is certain it cannot take an inheritance.

Collistrigium.——"A pillory." This was formerly used in *England* to punish many offences. *Vide note.*

Collobrium.——A covering worn by sergeants-at-law upon their shoulders, with the *coif* upon the head.

Colloquium.——"A discourse: a conference." A talking together, or affirming a thing laid in a declaration for words in an action for slander.

Colore officii.——Under color (or pretence) of office (or duty).

Colne.——A calculation.

Colpare.——To lop off—as to cut off the tops or boughs of trees.

Colpicium.——The Latin form for *coppice* or young wood closely cut or lopped.

COLUNT discreti et diversi, ut fons, ut campus, ut nemus placuit.——Their habitations were severed and distinct, as a fountain, a field, or a grove pleased them.

COMBE.——A valley.

COMBUSTIO domorum.——The burning of houses: arson.

COME ceux qui refusent etre a la commune loy de la terre.——Those who refuse to abide by the common law of the land.

COMES.——An earl: the governor of a county.

COME semble.——As it appears.

COMITAS inter gentes.——Courtesy between nations.

COMITATUS.——A county.

COMITIA centuriata.——These were courts held by the *Romans*, where the people voted by Centuries.

COMITIA majora, et comitia minora.——The greater and lesser courts among the *Romans*.

COMITIA tributa.——In the *Comitia* tributa the *Romans* voted, divided into tribes according to their regions or wards, (ex regionibus et locis.) Vide *A. Gell.* xv. 27. *Vide note.*

COMITISSA.——A countess.

COMMENDA.—A commendam.——A recommendation to elect a bishop.

COMMERCIA belli.——War contracts.

COMMITTITUR piece.——A written instrument by which a defendant already in custody, is charged in execution at the suit of the person who arrested him.

COMMORANCY.——The staying or living in a place as an inhabitant.

COMMODATUM.——A loan: a thing trusted to a bailee.

COMMON pur cause de vicinage.——Common by reason of neighborhood.

COMMOTE.——Half of a cantred in Wales, numbering fifty villages.

COMMUNE concilium regni, magnum concilium regis curia, magna conventus magnatum, vel procerum, assiza generalis.——The general council of the realm, the king's great council, the great court, the assembly of the great men or nobles, the general assize (or array).

COMMUNE piscarium.——Common fishery; a right of fishing without restriction.

COMMUNE vinculum.——The common bond: the common stock (of consanguinity).

COMMUNIA pasturæ.——"Common of pasture." The major part of the farms in *England* have a right of feeding certain cattle at different seasons of the year, as an appurtenant; which right passes on sale or lease of the land; and when an act is passed for inclosing the commonable lands in the parish, &c., where the farm is situate, the commonable lands are then generally divided between the persons entitled to the tithes, and the freeholders, in proportion to their respective interests in the land, in the parish, &c.

COMMUNIA piscariæ.——The right or liberty of fishing in another man's water.

COMMUNIA placita non sequantur curiam regis, sed teneantur in aliquo loco certo.——"The Common Pleas cannot follow the king's court (or household) but be held in some certain (or fixed) place. Formerly, the Common Pleas court was held at the place where the king resided; but that being found inconvenient, it has been for many years disused, and for ages held at *Westminster Hall. Vide note.*

COMMUNIA turbariæ.——The liberty of digging turf on another man's ground.

COMMUNIBUS annis.——In ordinary years: one year with another.

COMMUNIS error facit jus.——" Common error (or wrong) gives a law or right." This may be sometimes the case, as what was illegal at *first*, may in the course of years become an incontrovertible right. Lord *Kenyon*, in the case of *Rex* v. The inhabitants of *Eriswell, Durnf. & East's Rep.* said,

"I perfectly well recollect Mr. Justice *Foster* say, that he had heard that '*communis error facit jus*,' but I hope I shall never hear that rule insisted on, setting up a *misconstruction* of the law, a *destruction* of the law."

COMMUNIS rixatrix.——"A common female brawler or scold." Formerly, a woman guilty of this offence, was liable to be immersed in a pool of water.

COMMUNIS strata via.——The common paved way.

COMMUNITAS regni Angliæ.——An ancient name for the English parliament.

COMMUNITER usitata et approbata.——Generally used and approved.

COMPASCUUM.——Belongs to commonage.

COMPELLATIVUM.——An adversary.

COMPENSATIO criminis.——A compensation for crime.

COMPENSATIO necessaria est, quia interest nostra potius non solvere, quam solvere.——Compensation is necessary, because it is rather for our benefit not to pay, than to pay.

COMPERTORIUM.——A judicial inquest to find out the truth of a cause.

COMPERUIT ad diem.——He appeared at the day.

COMPESTER.——To manure.

COMPONERE lites.——To settle disputes.

COMPOSITIO mensarum.——The composition of measures.

COMPOS mentis.——"Of sound mind." A man in such a state of mind as to be qualified legally to sign a will, or deed, &c.

COMPURGATORES.——Compurgators. *Vide note.*

CONCESSIMUS etiam pro nobis et hæredibus nostris ex certa scientia nostra et de assensu prædicto eidem majori, ballivis, et burgensibus ac eorum hæredibus, et successoribus quod ipsi se appropriare et commodum suum facere possint de omnibus purpresturis, tam in terris, quam in aquis, factis vel faciendis, et de omnibus vastis ipsa limites et bundas villæ prædictæ in supportationem onerum infra villam prædictam in dies emergentium.——Also we grant for ourselves and our heirs, by reason of our certain knowl-edge, and by the aforesaid consent to the same mayor, bailiffs and burgesses, and to their heirs and successors, that they appropriate and take (money) for their own ben-efit, on account of all the purprestures (or obstructions) as well in the lands as in the waters, made or to be made, and from all the wastes, the limits and bounds of the aforesaid village to support the charges within the said village for the time to come. Vide *Dicitur purprestura.*

CONCESSIONES.——Grants.

CONCESSISSE.——To have granted or yielded up.

CONCESSIT, et demisit.——He has granted, and demised.

CONCESSIT secundum consuetudinem manerii.——He granted (or demised) according to the custom of the manor.

CONCILIABULUM.——A council-house.

CONCORDIA discordantium canonum.——"The agree-ment of the undigested (or jarring) church laws." Gener-ally known by the name of "*Decretum Gratiani.*" One *Gratian*, an *Italian* monk, about the year 1150, reduced the ecclesiastical constitutions into some method in three books, which are called "*Concordantia discordantia decretum.*"

CONCUBITU prohibere vago.——To forbid an indiscrimi-nate connection.

CONCULCARE.——To trample upon.

CONCURRENTIBUS iis quidem jure requiruntur.——By the concurrence of those things which the law requires.

CONDITIO est melior possidentis.——The condition of the possessor is preferable.

CONDITIONEM testium tunc inspicere debemus cum sig-narent, non mortis tempore.——We ought to consider the condition (or respectability) of witnesses *when* they sign, not *when* they die.

CONDITIO scripti obligatorii prædicti.——The condition of the said writing obligatory.

CONDITIO testium.——The condition (or appearance) of the witnesses.

CONDONATIO injuriæ.——A remitting of injury.

CONDUCTIO.——A hiring.

CONDUXISTI vehenda mancipia : mancipium unum in navi mortuum est; quæritur num vectura debeatur? Si de mancipiis vehendis inita conventus est non debetur, si de mancipiis tantum navi imponendo debetur.——You have bargained to carry slaves : one died on board the ship, it was asked if any thing be due for the carriage. If the agreement was for carrying the slaves, it is not due, but if only for those put on board the ship, it is payable.

CONE and KEY.——An old English phrase used for *accounts* and *keys* which were put in a woman's possession when she commenced housekeeping.

CONFECCION.——The making a charter, deed or other instrument in writing.

CONFIRMATIO chartarum.——" The confirmation of the charters." After *Magna Charta* was signed by king *John*, in *Runnymede* meadow, near *Windsor ;* and after the signing of *Charta foresta*, the barons frequently required subsequent kings to confirm these charters; this was called " *Confirmatio chartarum.*"

CONFLICTUS legum.——A contradiction of laws.

CONGEABLE.——Lawful.

CONGE d' elire.——"Leave to elect."—The king's permission to a dean and chapter to elect a bishop.

CONGIUS.——A measure containing a gallon and a pint.

CONJUDEX.——An associate judge.

CONJUNCTIM, aut separatim.——Jointly or severally.

CONJURATION.——A sworn plot formed by persons to do any public harm. (*Old English law*).

CONNOISSEMENT.——A bill of lading.

CONNUBIUM.——Matrimony between citizens. *Vide note.*

CONQUAESTOR.——Conqueror

CONQUISITIO.——Acquisition.

CONSANGUINEI.——Relations.

CONSCIENTIA boni viri.——The conscience of an hon-est man.

CONSENSUS facit legem.——" Consent makes the law." Where persons of sane mind enter into contract with each other, and their consent to the bargain be obtained without deceit, there must be a considerable inadequacy in the value given or received to rescind the contract.

CONSENSUS, non concubitus facit nuptias.——Consent, not consummation, makes the marriage (valid).

CONSENSUS tollit errorem.——Consent removes the error.

CONSENTIO modum dat donationi.——Consent gives the form to the gift.

CONSENTIRE videtur, qui tacet.——" He appears to con-sent, who remains silent ;" or, as the old adage expresses it, " silence gives consent."

CONSERVATORES pacis.——Keepers of the peace.

CONSIDERATUM est per curiam.——It is considered by the court.

CONSILIARIUS.——A counsellor.

CONSILIARIUS natus.——Sometimes said of a nobleman : one who sits by hereditary right in the house of peers.

CONSILII fraudulenti nulla obligatio est, cæterum si do-lus et caliditas intercessit, de dolo actio competit.——We are not bound by dishonest counsel ; but it is otherwise, if deceit and craft have been used (there) the action lies. because of the deceit.

CONSIMILI casu. In a like case.

CONSISTATORIO et collegio suo perpetuo excludatur, et universitate exulabit.——That he may be forever excluded from the consistory, and from his college, and exiled from the university.

CONSISTORY.——A council of ecclesiastics

CONSOBRINI.——Cousin germans.

CONSOLATO del mare.——The title of the most ancient collection of European sea laws extant.

CONSTAT feudorum originem a septentrionalibus gentibus fluxisse.——It is agreed that the origin of feuds descended from the northern nations.

CONSTRUCTIO generalis.——A general construction.

CONSUETUDINARIUS.——An old book, containing the customs of abbies and monasteries.

CONSUETUDINES.——Customs; usages.

CONSUETUDO est altera lex.——Custom is another law; custom is equivalent to law.

CONSUETUDO et lex Angliæ.——The custom and law of *England.*

CONSUETUDO loci observanda est.——The custom of the place is to be observed.

CONSUETUDO manerii et loci est observanda.——The custom of the manor and place is to be considered.

CONSUETUDO pro lege servatur.——Custom is to be held as law.

CONSULES, (a consulando ;) reges enim tales sibi associant ad consulendum.——Consuls (deriving their name from consulting), for kings associate with such persons to be advised.

CONTEMPORANEA consuetudo optimus interpres.——Cotemporary custom is the best interpreter.

CONTEMPORANEA expositio est fortissima in lege.——A contemporaneous interpretation (exposition or declaration) is strongest in the law.

CONSULTI periti.——Lawyers. *Cic.*

CONTENEMENTUM, est æstimatio et conditionis forma, qua quis in republica subsistit.——Contenement, (countenance or credit,) is that estimation and manner of rank or value which any persons sustains in the commonwealth.

CONTESTATIO litis.——The contesting a suit.

CONTINETUR ad tenorem, et ad effectum sequentem.—— It comprised to the tenor and effect following.

CONTINUANDO prædictam transgressionem.——By continuing the said trespass.

CONTINUO voce.——With a continual cry (or claim).

CONTRA bonos mores. Against good morals.

CONTRAFACERE.——To counterfeit.

CONTRA fictionem non admittitur probatio; quid enim efficeret probatio veritatis, ubi fictio adversus veritatem fingit? Nam fictio nihil aliud est, quam legis adversus veritatem in re possibili ex justa causa dispositio.——Proof is not admitted against fiction, for what could the evidence of truth effect, where fiction supposes against truth? For fiction is no other than an arrangement of the law against truth, in a possible matter, arising from a just cause.

CONTRA jus belli.——Against the law of war.

CONTRAMANDARE.——To countermand.

CONTRA morem et statuta.——Against the custom and the statutes.

CONTRA officii sui debitum.——Contrary to the duty of his office.

CONTRA omnes homines fidelitatem fecit.——He performed fealty (or homage) in opposition to all men.

CONTRA pacem. Against the peace. *Vide note.*

CONTRA pacem bailivorum.——Against the peace of the bailiffs.

CONTRA pacem domini regis.——Against the king's peace.

CONTRA pacem domini regis et contra formam statut' in hoc casu nuper edit' et provis'.——Against the king's peace, and contrary to the form of the statute in this case lately enacted and provided.

CONTRAPLACITUM.——A counterplea.

CONTRA proferentem.——Against him who offers (or produces).

CONTRAROTULATOR.——A controller.

CONTRAROTULUS.——A counter roll.

CONTRA vadium et plegium.——Against gage and pledge.

CONTRAXISSE unusquisque in eo loco intelligitur, in quo

solveret se obligavit.——Every one is understood to have contracted in that place where he has bound himself to pay.

CONTROVER.——A false newsmonger.

CONTUBERNIUM.——The cohabitation of slaves among the *Romans* was so called. *Vide note.*

CONUSANCI.——Cognizance.

CONVENÌRE.——To covenant.

CONVENTIO vincit legem.——A covenant governs (or rules) the law.

CONVENTIO vincit et dat legem.——The agreement prevails and gives the law.

CONVENTIO vincit et dat modum donationi.——The agreement prevails and establishes the manner of the gift (or grant).

CONVENTUS privatorum non potest publico juri derogare. ——The agreement of individuals cannot abridge the public right.

CONVICTUS est, et satisfaciet juxta formam statuti.—— He is convicted, and should make satisfaction according to the form of the statute.

COOPERTIO.——An outer coat or covering, as the bark of a tree.

COOPERTUM.——A covert; a hiding place or shelter for beasts in a forest.

COPE.——A hill.

CORAAGIUM.——A tribute of a certain measure of corn.

CORAM Domino Rege, &c., ad respondendum *Asley* de placito transgressionis.——Before the lord the king to answer *Asley* of a plea of trespass.

CORAM Domino Rege ubicunque tunc fuerit Angliæ.—— Before the lord the king wheresover he shall then be in *England.*

CORAM justiciariis ad hoc specialiter assignatis.——Before justices specially assigned for this purpose.

CORAM me vel justiciariis meis.——Before me or my justices.

CORAM nobis ubicunque fuerimus in Angliæ.——Before us wheresoever we shall be in *England.*

CORAM non judice.——Not before a judge : at an improper tribunal.

CORAM non judice, quod omnes concesserunt.——All have agreed that there is no jurisdiction.

CORAM paribus.——In presence of (his) peers (or equals).

CORAM paribus curiæ.——In presence of (his) peers (or equals) of the court.

CORAM paribus de viceneto.——In presence of (his) peers (or equals) of the neighborhood.

CORAM vobis.——A writ of error, on judgments of the court of Common Pleas or other courts than the King's or Queen's Bench; the writs to correct the judgments of this latter court are styled CORAM NOBIS.

CORNAGE.——A tenure, the service of which was to *blow a horn* in case the enemy was perceived.

CORODY.——A right of sustenance.

CORPORA cepi.——I have taken the bodies.

CORPORA corporata.——Bodies corporate.

CORPORE nullis contagiosis, aut incurabilibus morbis vitioso, aliasve deformi aut mutilo.——"Not having a diseased body, afflicted with any contagious or incurable disease, or deformed or mutilated." These were objections to fellowships in some colleges.

CORPUS delicti.——"The body of the offence;" or the very nature and essence thereof.

CORPUS humanum non recipit æstimationem.——The human body is above all price.

CORPUS juris canonici.——The body of the canon law.

CORPUS juris civilis.——The body of the civil law.

CORSEPRESENT.——The present given to the minister of a parish upon the death of a parishioner, was anciently thus called, because it was brought to the church at the time of the burial along with the corpse.

CORSNED.——"The mouthful of execration." The piece

of bread by which some suspected criminals were tried under the *Saxon* laws.

CORT.——Short.

CORTULARIUM.——A yard adjoining a farm.

COSENING.——An offence mentioned in old English law, where deceit is practised.

COSHERING.——A feudal practice for lords to entertain themselves at their tenants' houses.

COSINAGE de consanguineo.——Relationship concerning kindred.

COSTAGES.——Costs.

COSTS de incremento.——Costs of increase.

COTA, cotagium.——A cottage.

COTARIUS, cotarellus.——A cottager.

COTEMPORANEA expositio.——A cotemporaneous interpretation.

COTLAND, cotselhland.——Land held by a cottager.

COTURE.——An enclosure.

COUCHANT.——Lying down.

COUNTER-ROLL.——In old practice, a roll kept by one officer as a check upon another's roll.

COUPE.——Fault.

COURT of Star Chamber.——A court of very ancient origin in England having jurisdiction over riots, and other notorious misdemeanors, without any jury. In the progress of time, its powers were much abused, so that it was abolished in the reign of Charles I.

COUSTUMIER.——A book of customs and usages in the old law of France.

COVERT.——Married.

COVERT Baron.——Under the protection of a husband.

COVINOUS.——Fraudulent.

CRASSA negligentia.——" Gross negligence." Sometimes applied to professional persons and others who have managed matters, for which they were retained, in a very careless manner, or with " gross negligence;" such persons are

6

liable to actions on the case at the suit of the party injured.

CRASTINUM animarum.——"The morrow of all Souls." One of the ancient returns of original writs.

CREAMUS, erigimus, fundamus, incorporamus.——"We create, erect, found and incorporate." Words used on incorporating a college.

CREANCI.——Belief, faith.

CREMENTUM comitas.——The increase of the county.

CREPARE occulum.——To put out an eye.

CREPUSCULUM.——Twilight.

CRIEZ la peez.——Rehearse the concord or peace.

CRIMEN animo felleo perpretratum.——A crime committed with an evil intent.

CRIMEN falsi.——Forgery.

CRIMEN imponere.——To impute a crime or offence.

CRIMEN incendii.——Arson.

CRIMEN læsæ majestatis.——High Treason.

CRIMEN Raptus.——Rape.

CROCKARDS.——An ancient foreign coin prohibited in England in Edward 1st reign.

CROFT.——A small piece of land adjoining a dwelling, and enclosed for cultivation.

CROISES.——Pilgrims.

CRUCE judicium.——The trial of the cross.

CRUCE signati.——Signed or marked with the cross.

CRY de pais.——A cry of the country.

CUI ante divortium.——To whom, before a divorce.

CUI bono?——"To what end?" For what good purpose?

CUICUMQUE aliquis quid concedit, concedere videtur et id sine quo res ipsa esse non potest.——"To whomsoever any person grants a thing, he appears to grant that without which it cannot be enjoyed." Thus, if a man grant the trees standing in his field, a right of way is also tacitly granted for the purpose of felling and carrying them away.

Cui de jure pertinet.——To whom by right it belonged.

Cui in vita sua, vel cui ante divortium, ipsa contradicere non potuit.——What in her lifetime, or previous to divorce, she could not contradict.

Cuilibet in arte sua credendum est.——"Every person should be believed in his own art or mystery." Persons skilled in any particular science are entitled to have credit given them as to those matters which they have made their peculiar study, especially when on oath.

Cui licet quod majoris, non debet quod minus est non licere.——He to whom the greater thing is lawful, has certainly a right to do the less thing.

Cui malo?——To what evil? What injury will result from the act proposed?

Cuique enim in proprio fundo quamlibet feram quoque modo venari permissum.——For it is permitted to every person to hunt a wild beast on his own land, in any manner he pleases.

Cujus commodum ejus debet esse incommodum.—— He who has the benefit should also bear the disadvantage.

Cujus est dare ejus est disponere.——He who has the power to give has the right to designate the mode of its application.

Cujus est divisio, alterius est electio.——"Who makes the division, the other has the election." Thus, where a division of an estate is made, if one party apportion, the other shall take which share he pleases.

Cujus est solum ejus est usque ad cœlum, et ad inferos. ——He who owns the soil, has it even to the sky, and to the lowest depths.

Cujusque rei potissima pars et principium.——The most important of every thing is the beginning.

Cujus quidem tenor.——Also of this purport.

Cujus regis temporibus hoc ordinatum sit, non reperio. ——I do not find in what king's reign this was ordained.

Cujus tenor sequitur.——Whose import follows.

CUL'.——This is an abbreviation of "*culpabilis*," guilty.

CULPÆ adnumerantæ: veluti si medicus curationem dere-linquerit, male quempiam secuerit, aut puerperam ei medi-camentum dederit.——These are reckoned offences: if a Physician has neglected a cure; performed an operation improperly on any person, or given a woman in childbirth medicine unskilfully.

CULPA lata æquiparatur dolo.——"A concealed fault is equal to deceit." Morally speaking this maxim is true, but a purchaser should have the words "*caveat emptor*," (let the purchaser beware,) continually in his mind.

CULVERTAGE.——Confiscation.

CUM acciderit.——When it may happen.

CUM assensu præfectorum ædium.——With the consent of the governors of the houses (or colleges).

CUM autem emptio et venditio contracta sit, periculum rei venditæ statim ad emptorem pertinet, tametsi adhuc ea res emptori radita non sit. Itaque si, aut ædes totæ, vel aliqua ex parte incendio consumptæ fuerint, emptoris damnum est, cui necesse est, licet rem non fuerit nactus pretium solvere.——For when a purchase and sale be made, the risk of the thing sold immediately belongs to the pur-chaser, although the property be not as yet delivered to him. Therefore, if either a whole house, or any part of it be destroyed by fire the loss is the purchaser's, who must pay the price, although he has not obtained the property.

CUM capitemus, retento semper primo proposito, et desti-natione, in accessoriis totaliter illam non sequitur, mutando viam de recta, in indirectam; vel plures scalas, plures portus attingendo, animo tamen et intentione prosequendi viagium ad metam destinationem.——When a captain, continually bearing in mind his first purpose and destination, does not entirely follow it with the insurers, by changing his direct course for an indirect one; or touching at more landing places or harbors, but still with the intent of proceeding on his voyage to the intended destination.

CUM domorum subversione, et arborum extirpatione.——
"By pulling down the houses and rooting up the trees."
This was formerly the punishment inflicted on the jury for
giving a corrupt verdict.

CUM in partes illas venerint.——When they come into
those parts.

CUM in tali casu possit, eadem res pluribus aliis creditoribus, tum prius, tum posterius, invadiari.——As in such
case the same property may be pledged to many other creditors, as well before as afterwards.

CUM lex abrogatur, illud ipsum abrogatur, quo non eam
abrogari oporteat.——"When a law is repealed that (clause)
is abolished by which (it declares) that it should not be repealed." Laws have been made containing clauses against
their repeal, but these cannot prevent a subsequent, or even
the then present legislature from exercising their right to
repeal at any time.

CUM licet fugere, ne quære litem.——"Enter not into
law, if you can avoid it."

CUM lites potius restringendæ sunt quam laxandæ.——
That law-suits may rather be restrained than increased.

CUM litore maris eidem adjacente.——With the sea shore
adjoining the same.

CUM multis aliis illicite, et riotose assemblaverunt, &c.
——With many others, lawlessly and riotously, they assembled.

CUM multis aliis, quæ nunc præscribere longum est.——
With many other matters which it would now be tedious
to enumerate.

CUM olim in usu fuisset, alterius nomine agi non posse,
sed quia hoc non minimam incommodatem habebat, cœpe-
runt homines per procurationes litigare.——As formerly it
was a custom not to transact business in the name of another, but because this was inconvenient, men began to sue
by their proctors (or attorneys).

CUM onere.——With the charge (or burthen.)

CUM pertinentiis.——With the appurtenances.

CUM quod ago non valet ut ago, valeat quantum valere potest.——When that which I do is not efficacious in the way I perform it, (still) let it avail as far as it can.

CUM sit contra præceptum Domini, "Non tentabis Dominum Deum tuum."——As it is against the command of the Lord, "Thou shalt not tempt the Lord thy God."

CUM tali filia mea, &c. tenendum sibi, et hæredibus suis de carne talis uxoris.——"With this my daughter, &c. to hold to him and the heirs of the body of such wife." Words often found in ancient settlements of land.

CUM testamento annexo.——With the will annexed.

CUNA.—Coin. CUNEARE.——To coin.

CUNCTANDO restituit rem.——He restored his cause by delay.

CUNCTAS nationes, et urbes populus, aut primores, aut singuli regunt: delecta ex his et constituta republicæ forma laudari facilius quam eveniri, vel, si evenit, haud diuturna esse potest.——The people, or chiefs, or individuals, govern all nations and cities; and the constituted form of a commonwealth chosen from them is more easily praised than practised; or if it be so (constituted) it cannot long exist.

CURA animarum.——Care of souls.

CURATOR ad hoc.——A special guardian.

CURATORES viarum.——Surveyors or guardians of the public roads.

CURFEW.——A bell which was rung by law at eight o'clock in the evening in England, from the time of the Norman conquest till the reign of Henry First. When this bell rang every householder was compelled to *cover* his *fire* and put out his light. The object of this practice originally was to prevent the Saxons or any other persons from meeting together in parties by night for seditious purposes or to plot against their conquerors.

CURIA advisare vult.——The court will consider (the matter).

CURIA advisare vult post, &c.——The court will advise afterwards, &c.

CURIA comitatus.——The county court. *Vide note.*

CURIÆ christianitates.——Ecclesiastical courts. *Vide note.*

CURIÆ speciales.——Special courts. *Vide note.*

CURIALITAS.——The tenure by courtesy.

CURIA palatii.——The palace court.

CURIA publica.——A public court (of law). *Vide note.*

CURIA regis.——The court of the king.

CURIARUM: habet unam propriam, sicut aulam regiam, et justiciarius capitalis, qui proprias causas adjudicat, &c. ——Of courts: he has one peculiar court, as a royal court; a chief justice who tries the proper actions, &c.

CUR omnium fit culpa, paucorum scelus?——Why should the iniquity of a few, be laid to the account of all?

CURRIT quatuor pedibus.——" It runs upon four feet."

CURRUS.——A chariot.

CURSITOR.——A clerk belonging to the English Court of Chancery, whose office is to make out original writs.

CURSUS.——A course or practice.

CURTILES terræ.——Court lands.

CUSTODES pacis.——Justices of the peace.

CUSTODES placitorum in plenu comitatu.——The keepers of pleas in full county court.

CUSTODES pœnam sibi commissorum non augeant, nec eos torqueant; sed omni sævitia remota, pietatique adhibita judicia debite exequantur.——That the keepers do not increase the punishment of those prisoners committed to their custody; nor torture them; but all cruelty being removed, and compassion adhered to, that they duly execute the judgments.

CUSTODIA, Lat.—*Garde,* Fr.——" A custody; or care of defence." Sometimes used for such as have the care and guardianship of infants; sometimes for a writ to sue by wardship, as *droit de garde,* right of wardship; *ejectione de garde,* ejectment of ward : and *ravishment de garde.* Vide *Fitz. Nat. Br.* 139.

CUSTODIA legis.——Legal custody.

CUSTOS brevium.——The keeper of the writs.

CUSTOS ferarum.——A game keeper.

CUSTOS horrei regii.——Keeper of the royal granary.

CUSTOS Rotulorum.——The keeper of the Rolls, one of whom is appointed in each of the *English* counties.

CUSTOS spiritualium.——A keeper of spiritual or Ecclesiastical matters.

CUSTOS temporalium.——In ecclesiastical law the person who was appointed by the king to the custody of a vacant see or abbey, and who, acting as the steward of its revenues, rendered his account of the same to the escheator.

CUSTUMA.——Customs : duties.

CUSTUMA antiqua, et magna.——The ancient and great customs (or duties).

CUSTUMA parva et nova.——The small and new customs (or duties).

CUTH.—*Sax.* Known. UNCUTH.——Unknown.

CY.——Here.

CY apres.——Hereafter. CY pres.——so near; as near.

CYMETER.——A burial place.

CYNEBOTE.——See *Cenegild.*

CYNSOUR de burse.——A pickpocket.

CYRIC.——A church. (*Saxon*).

CYRICBRYCE.——Saxon name for breaking into a church.

CYRICSCEAT.——A tribute due to the church.

CYROGRAFFE.——A chirograph.

CYROGRAPHUM.——*Vide note.*

NOTES TO C.

CAMPI PARTITIO.—Champerty. Before the passing of the statute to prevent this, men in power and affluence, frequently made such bargains with persons (who were unable to maintain a protracted suit) to recover possession of their estates. Many landholders died in the crusades, and persons had wrongfully taken possession of lands, and assumed the ownership, to the injury of the heirs of the deceased.

CANDIDATI.—When men sought for office or preferment among the *Romans*, they were called "*Candidati*," from a *white* robe (*toga*) worn by them, which was rendered shining, (*cadens vel candida*) by the art of the fuller; for all the wealthy *Romans* wore a gown naturally white (*toga alba*). This was, however, anciently forbidden by law (*ne cui album, i. e. cretam in vestimentum addere, petitionis causa licet*). Liv. iv. 25. These *candidates* did not wear tunics or waistcoats, either that they might appear more humble ; or might the more easily show the scars they had received on the breast, or forepart of the body. In the latter ages of the republic, no one could stand candidate, who was not *present*, and did not declare himself within the *legal* days, i. e. before the *comitia* were summoned, and whose name was not received by the magistrates: for it seems they might refuse to admit any one they pleased, but not without assigning a just cause. Vide *Liv.* viii. 15, xxiv. 7, 8. *Val. Max.* iii. 8 3. *Vell.* ii. 92. The opinion of the *Consuls*, however, might be overruled by the Senate, *Liv.* iii. 21.

For a long time before the election, the *candidati* endeavored to gain the favor of the people ·by every popular art; *Cic. Attic.* i. ; by going round their houses (*ambiendo*); by shaking hands with those they met; by addressing them in a kindly manner, and naming them, &c., on which account they commonly had with them a *monitor*, or *nomenclator*, who whispered in their ears every person's name. Vide *Hor. Ep.* i. 6, 50. Hence *Cicero* calls candidates "*natio officiosissima*," i. e. an over officious class. On the market days, they used anciently to come into the assembly of the people, and take their station on a rising ground (*in colle consistere*), i. e. to stand upon a hill, where they might be seen by all. *Macrob. Sat.* i. 16. When they went down to the *Campus Martius*, at certain times, they were attended by their friends and dependents. They had likewise friends to divide money among the people (*divisores*). Cic. Att. i. 17. For this, although forbidden by law, was often done openly, and once it is said, against *Cæsar*, even with the approbation of *Cato.* Vide *Suet. Jul.* 19. There were also persons to *bargain* with the people for their votes called "*Interpretes*"; and others in whose hands the money promised was deposited. Vide *Cic. Att. in Verr.* i. 8, 12. Sometimes the candidates formed combinations (*coitiones*) to disappoint (*ut dejecerent*), i. e. that they might prostrate the other competitors. *Cic. Att.* ii. *Liv.* iii. 35. So that it would appear, that even these ancient and stern republicans understood *management* in this respect, as well as they do at the present day.

CAPIAS.—Formerly, when a defendant was arrested, and brought into court upon the process, it was the duty of the plaintiff to deliver in his charge, to which the defendant answered; and the plaintiff replied *viva voce* in person, in open court. The pleadings were then carried on by word of mouth, and the parties obliged personally to attend. But the stat. 13. *Edw.* the First, authorised the appointment of *attorneys*, who had full power in all pleas moved during the circuit, until the same were determined, or such attorney was removed. After that time, it appears that the personal attendance of parties being dispensed with, they carried on the pleadings in the court by their attorneys; still, however, there were *parol* pleadings delivered *viva voce ;* and it has been said, that these *viva voce* proceedings continued till after the Reformation; though others think they were reduced to writing at a much earlier period. It is said, by some, so early as the reign of *Edward* the Third, and there is good reason to conclude, from the alterations in the pleadings about that time, that they were not hastily spoken, but rather deliberately penned. It is clear, however, that the practice of delivering pleading, *ore tenus*, continued longer in the Common Pleas, than in the Court of King's Bench. When the mode of pleading was discontinued in the King's Bench, the practice was, that if the defendant appeared personally at the return of the writ, the plaintiff was to declare within three days. If he appeared by attorney, he was to declare within the term.

CAPIAS AD SATISFACIENDUM, &c.—Whilst society remained in its rudest and most simple form, debt seems to have been considered as an obligation merely *personal*. Men had made some progress towards refinement before creditors acquired the right of seizing the property of the debtors in order to recover payment. The expedients for this purpose were all introduced originally into communities; and we can trace their gradual progress. First, the simplest, and most obvious security was, that the person who sold any commodity, should receive a pledge from him who bought it, which he restored upon making payment. Of this custom, there are vestiges in several charters of community. D'Ach. ix. 185. xi. 377. Secondly, when a pledge was given, and the debtor became refractory or insolvent, the creditor was allowed to seize his effects, with a strong hand, and by his private authority. The citizens of *Paris* are warranted by the royal mandate "*et ubicumque, et quocumque modo poterunt tantum plenarie habeant, et inde sibi invicem adjutores existant.*" Ordon. &c. tom. i. p. 6.

This rude practice, suitable only to the violence of that which has been called a state of nature, was tolerated longer than one can reasonably conceive to be possible in any society where laws and order were at all known. The ordinance authorizing it was issued A. D. 1134, and that which corrects the law, and prohibits creditors from seizing the effects of their debtors, unless by a warrant from a magistrate, and under his inspection, was not published till 1351. Thirdly. As soon as the interposition of a magistrate became requisite, regular provision was made for attaching or distraining the movable effects of a debtor: and if his movables were insufficient to discharge the debt, his immovable property or estate in land, was liable to the same distress, and was sold for the benefit of the creditor. *D'Ach.* ix. *p.* 184, 185. xi. *p.* 348, 380. As this regulation afforded the most complete security to the creditor, it was considered as so severe, that humanity pointed out several limitations in the execution of it. Creditors were prohibited from seizing the wearing apparel of their debtors, the beds, the door of their house, their instruments of husbandry, &c. *D'Ach.* ix. 184, xi. 377. Upon the same principle, when the power of distraining effects became more general, the horse and arms of a gentleman could not be seized. *ib.* ix. 185. And as hunting was the favorite amusement of martial nobles, the Emperor *Ludovicus Pius,* prohibited the seizing of a hawk, on account of any debt; but if the debtor had no other moveables, even these privileged articles might be seized.

CAPITIS ÆSTIMATIO.—This means the payment of a *fine,* by the way of *satisfaction* to the person or family injured; and was one of the first devices of a rude people, to check the career of *private* resentment, and to extinguish those deadly feuds which were prosecuted among them with the utmost violence. This custom may be traced back to the ancient Germans. *Vide Tac. de mor. Ger.* c. 21; and prevailed among other civilized nations. Many examples of this are collected by the ingenious and learned author of *Historical Law Tracts,* vol. i. p. 41. These fines were ascertained and levied in *three* different manners. At first they were settled by voluntary agreement between the parties at variance. When their rage began to subside, and they felt the bad effects of their continuing enmity, they came generally to terms of concord, and the satisfaction made was called "*a composition*," implying that it was fixed by mutual consent. Vide *De l'Esprit des lois, lib.* xxx. *c.* 19. It is apparent from some of the more ancient code of laws, that at the time these were compiled, matters still remained in that simple state. In certain cases, the person who had committed an offence was left to the resentment of those whom he had injured, until he should recover their favor, "*quoque modo potuerit,*" (in what way he could.) *Lex. Frision tit.* 11, *sec.* 1. The next mode of levying this fine was by the sentence of *arbiters*—an *arbiter* was called in the *Regiam Majestatem,* "amicabilis compositor," *Liv.* xi. *c.* 4.; i. e. a friendly adjuster or arbitrator. He could estimate the degree of offence with more impartiality than the parties interested; and determine with greater equity what satisfaction ought to be demanded. It is difficult to bring an authentic proof of this custom previous to the law records of the fierce northern nations of *Europe.* But one of the *Formulæ Andevagenses,* compiled in the sixth century, seems to allude to a transaction carried on, not by the authority of the judge, but by the mediation of *arbiters* chosen by mutual consent. Vide *Bouquet Recueil des Histor. tom.* 4, *p.* 566. But an *arbiter* wanted authority to enforce his decisions, judges were appointed with compulsive powers of authority to oblige *both* parties to acquiesce in their decisions. Previously to this last act, the expedient of paying compositions was an imperfect remedy against the pernicious effects of private resentment. So soon, however, as this important change was introduced, the magistrate, putting himself in the place of the party injured, ascertained the *composition,* with which he ought to remain satisfied. Every possible injury that could occur in the intercourse of civil society was considered and estimated, and the compositions due to the persons aggrieved, were fixed with such minute attention, as to discover in *most* cases, amazing discernment and delicacy; but in some instances unaccountable caprice. Besides the *composition,* payable to the private party, a certain sum called "*Fredum,*" was paid to the king or state, (as *Tacitus* expresses it,) or to the "*Fiscus,*" in the language of the barbarous laws. Some authors, blending the ideas of modern policy with their reasonings concerning ancient transactions, have imagined that the "*Fredum,*" was a compensation due to the community, on account of the violations of the public peace; but it would appear to be manifestly nothing more than the *price* paid to the magistrate for the *protection* which he afforded against the violence of resentment; the enacting of which was a considerable step, in those rude ages, towards improvement in criminal jurisprudence. In some of the more ancient codes of laws, the "*freda*" are altogether omitted, or so seldom mentioned, that it is evident they were but little known. In the latter codes the "*fredum*" was as *precisely* specified, as the composition. In common cases it was equal to the *third* part of the composition. *Vide Capitul. vol.* i. *p.* 52. In some extraordinary cases, where it was difficult to protect the person, who had committed violence, the "*fredum*" was augmented. *Idem. vol.* i. *p.* 515. These "*freda*" made a considerable branch in the revenue of the barons; and in whatever district territorial jurisdiction was granted, the royal judges were prohibited from levying any "*freda.*" In explaining the nature of the "*fredum,*" the opinion of *M. de Montesquieu* is followed in a great measure; though several learned antiquarians have taken the word in a different sense. Vide *De l'Esprit des Lois, liv.* xxx. *c.* 20, &c. The great object of the judges was to *compel* the party to *give,* and the other to *accept,* the satisfaction prescribed. They multiplied regulations for this purpose, and enforced them by grievous penalties. *Leg. Longob. lib.* i. *tit.* 9. *sec.* 34. *Ibid. tit.* 37, *sec.* 1, 2. *Capitul. vol.* i. *p.* 371, § 22. The person who received a composition was *obliged* to cease from all further hostility; and confirm his reconciliation to the adverse party by an oath. *Leg. Longob. lib.* i. *tit.* 9, *sec.* 8. As an additional, and more perfect evidence of reconciliation, he was required to give a bond of security to the person from whom he received the composition, absolving him from all further prosecution. *Marcelfus*, and other writers of ancient writs, have presented several forms of such bonds, vide *Marc. lib. ix. sec.* 18. *Append.* 23. *Form. Surmondica* § 39. The *Letters of Slanes*, known in the laws of *Scotland*, are similar to these bonds of security. By the *Letters of Slanes*, the heirs and relations of a person who had been murdered, *bound* themselves in consideration of "*an assythment,*" or compensation paid to them, "to forgive, pass over, and forever forget, and in oblivion inter all rancour, malice, revenge, grudge and resentment, that they have, or may conceive against the aggressor or his posterity, for the crime which he had committed, and discharge him from all actions civil or criminal, against him or his estate, for now and ever." Vide *System of Stiles by Dallas of St. Martins, p.* 862. In the ancient form of *Letters of Slanes*, the *private* party not only "*forgives and forgets,*" but "*pardons and grants* remission of the crime." This practice, *Dallas*, reasoning according to the principles of his own age, considers as an encroachment on the rights of sovereignty; as none he says could *pardon* a criminal but the king. *ibid.* But it appears that in early times, the prosecution, the punishment and the *pardon* of criminals, were all deeds of the *private* person who was injured. *Madox* has published two writs, one in the time of *Edward* the First; the other in the time of *Edward* the Third, by which *private* persons grant a release, or *pardon* of all trespasses, felonies, robberies and murders committed. *Fromul. Anglican. nos.* 702, 705. In the last, however, of these instruments, some regard seems to be paid to the *rights* of the sovereign, for the principal is pardoned, "*en quant que in nous est,*" (in as much as in us lies). Even after the authority of the magistrate was interposed in preventing crimes, the punishment of criminals was long considered *chiefly* as a gratification to the resentment of the persons who had been injured. It is remarkable how similar this is to the *aborigines* of North America; and perhaps to the custom of all nations in a rude state of society. In *Persia*, a murderer is still *delivered* to the relations of a person whom he has slain, who often put him to death *with their own hands.* If they refuse to accept a sum of money as a compensation, the sovereign, absolute as he is, cannot, it is said, pardon the murderer. Vide *Voyages de Chardin,* iii. *p.* 417, *edit.* 1735, *4to.* also *Voyages de Travenier, liv.* v. *c.* 5, 10. Among the *Arabians,* the same custom still subsists. Vide *Description De l'Arabie par M. Niebuhr, p.* 28. By a law of the kingdom of *Aragon,* as late as the year 1564, the punishment of one condemned to death cannot be mitigated, but by the *consent* of the parties who have been injured. *Fueros, and Observancias del Reyne de Aragon, p.* 204, 6. Lady *Montague* in her letters says that "murder is never prosecuted by the officers of government. It is the business of the next relations, and these *only* to revenge the murder of their kinsman, and if they rather choose, as they generally do, to compound the matter for money, nothing more is said about it."

CELTÆ.—Of all the *Celtic* nations, that which possessed old *Gaul* is perhaps the most renowned; not, probably, on account of worth superior to the others, but from the circumstance of warring with a people, who had historians to transmit the fame of occurring events to posterity. *Britain* was peopled with them, according to the testimony of respectable authors. Vide *Cæs. lib.* i. *Tac. Agric. c.* 2. Its situation, with respect to *Gaul,* makes the opinion probable; but that which apparently puts it beyond dispute, is, that the same customs and languages prevailed among the inhabitants of both in the time of *Julius Cæsar.* Vide *Cæs. Pomp. Nel. Tacit.* That the ancient *Scots* were of *Celtic* original, is past all doubt. Their conformity with the *Celtic* nations, in language, manners and religion, proves it to a full demonstration. The *Celtæ* were a great and mighty people, altogether distinct from the *Goths* and *Teutones,* and they at once extended their dominion over all or greatest part of the west of Europe; but they

seem to have had their most full and complete establishment in *Gaul.*
Wherever the *Celtæ* or *Gauls* are mentioned by ancient writers, we seldom
fail to hear of their *Druids* and their *Bards;* the institution of which two
orders was the capital distinction of their manners and policy. The *Druids*
were their philosophers and priests; the *Bards,* their poets and recorders of
heroic actions: and both these orders of men seem to have subsisted among
them, as *chief* members of the state from time immemorial. We must not,
therefore, imagine the *Celtæ* to have been altogether a gross and rude nation.
They possessed, from very remote ages, a formed system of discipline and
manners, which appear to have had a lasting influence, and although the
antiquarian has scarcely, if ever, informed us, that many of their principles
and maxims became incorporated, and made part and still continue to be the
common law of *England,* yet it is more than *probable* that such was the case,
and that tradition has handed down some of the wise maxims and doctrines
of their jurisprudence between man and man, as established by their *Druids*
and *Philosophers.* Ammianus Marcellinus gives them this express testimony,
that there flourished among them the most laudable arts, introduced by the
Bards and by the *Druids,* who lived in retired places in societies, after the
Pythagorean manner, and philosophizing upon the highest subjects, asserted
the immortality of the soul. "*Per hæc loca,*" (speaking of Gaul,) "*hominibus
paulatim excultis viguere studia laudabilium doctrinarum; inchoata per Bar-
dos et Euhages et Druidas. Et Bardi quidem fortia virorum illustrium facta
heroicis composita versibus cum dulcibus lyræ modulis cantitärunt. Euhages
vero scrutantes serium et sublimia naturæ pandere conabantur. Inter hos,
Druidæ ingeniis celsiores, ut auctoritas Pythagoræ decrevit, sodalitiis adstricti
consortiis, quæstionibus altarum occultarumque rerum erecti sunt; et despanctes
humana pronuntiärunt animas immortales.*" Amm. Marc. lib. xv. c. 9. "In
these parts, the study of commendable science flourished by easy degrees
among the educated men; these things originated with the Bards, Orators
and Druids. The Bards also sung suitable songs respecting the illustrious
deeds of their heroes, accompanied with the delightful notes of the lyre.
And the Orators endeavored to show the secrets of creation, and the sublime
things of nature. Among those the Druids were the most eminent in literature (or science) according to the authority of *Pythagoras,* and were bound
by mutual sympathies closely with each other—they encouraged the knowledge of high science, and despising human things, asserted the immortality
of the soul." Though *Julius Cæsar,* in his account of *Gaul,* does not *ex-
pressly* mention the *Bards,* yet it is tolerably plain that under the title of
Druids he comprehended that whole order; of which the *Bards,* who, it is
probable, were the disciples of the *Druids,* undoubtedly made a part. According to his account, the Druidical institution first took its rise in *Britain.*
He adds, too, that such as were to be initiated among the *Druids* were obliged to commit to their *memory* a great number of verses, inasmuch that
some employed *twenty* years in this course of education; and that they did
not think it lawful to *record* their poems in writing, but sacredly handed
them down by *tradition* from race to race. Vide *Cæsar de bello Gall. lib.* vi.
It is not too much, therefore, to suppose that many maxims and principles
now composing part of the common law of England owe their origin to the
Celtæ. The *Bards* were held in high estimation by this warlike nation; and
it may not even here be unentertaining to mention a circumstance related
by *Priscus,* in his history of the embassy to Attila, King of the *Huns,* which
gives a striking view of the enthusiastic passion for war, which prevailed
among the fierce barbarians of the north, who swept away as it were with
"the besom of destruction" the *Roman* nation, their laws, religion and institutions. When the entertainment, to which that brave conqueror admitted the *Roman* ambassador, was ended, two *Scythians* advanced towards
Attila, and recited a poem, in which they celebrated his victories and military virtues. "All the *Huns* fixed their eyes with attention on the *Bards;*

some seemed to be delighted with the verses, thus remembering their own battle exploits, exulted with joy; while such who were become feeble through age, burst out into tears, bewailing the decay of their vigor, and the state of mortality to which they were rapidly hastening." *Excerpta ex Hist. Prisci.* It is supposed that among the ancient inhabitants of *Scotland* and *Ireland*, not only the Kings, but every petty chief had their *Bards* attending them in the field. *Ossian*, in his epic poem, entitled "*Temora*," says, "Like waves, blown back by sudden winds, *Erin* retired at the voice of the King. Deep-rolled into the field of night, they spread their humming tribes. Beneath his own tree at intervals each *Bard* sat down with his harp. They raised the song, and touched the string each to the chief he loved." Those *Bards* in proportion to the power of the chiefs who retained them, had a number of inferior *Bards* in their train. Upon solemn occasions all the Bards in the army would join in *one chorus;* either when they celebrated their victories, or lamented the death of a person, worthy and renowned, slain in the war. The words were of the composition of the *Arch-Bard*, retained by the King himself, who generally attained that high office on account of his superior genius for poetry.

CENTUMVIRI.—These were judges among the *Romans*, chosen from the thirty-five tribes, three from each tribe, so that properly there were *one hundred and five;* but they were always named by a round number *one hundred* (" centumviri.") Vide *Festus.* The causes which came before them, (*causæ centumvirales*) are enumerated by Cicero de Orat. i. 38. They seem to have been first instituted soon after the creation of the Prætor, *Peregrinus.* They judged chiefly concerning testaments and inheritances. *Cic. ibid. pro Cæcin.* 18. *Val. Max.* vii. 7. After the time of *Augustus*, they formed the council of the *Prætor*, and judged in the most important causes, *Tac. de Orat.* 38; whence trials before them (*judicia centumvirilia*) are sometimes distinguished from private trials. *Plin. Ep.* i. 18, vi. 4, 33—*Quinctil.* iv. 1, v. 10; but these were not criminal trials, as some have thought, vide *Suet. Vesp.* 10; for in a certain sense all trials were public (*judicia publica*). Cic. pro. Arch. 2. The number of the *Centumviri* was increased to one hundred and eighty; and they were divided into four councils. *Plin. Ep.* i. 18, iv. 24, vi. 33, *Quintil.* xii. 5. Hence, where we find the words "*quadruplex judicium*," they mean the same as "*centumvirale.*" Ibid. Sometimes they were only divided into two. *Quinct.* v. 2, xi. 1: and sometimes in important cases they judged altogether. *Val. Max.* viii. 8. A cause before the *Centumviri* could not be adjourned. *Plin. Ep.* i. 18. Ten men called "*Decemviri*" were appointed; *five* senators, and *five* equites, to assemble these counsels, and preside in them, in the absence of the *Prætor. Suet. Aug.* 36.

Trials before the *Centumviri* were usually held in the *Basilica Julia.* Plin. Ep. ii. 24; but sometimes in the *Forum.* They had a spear set upright before them. *Quinct.* v. 2. Hence the term we sometimes find of "*judicium hastæ*," i. e. the judgment of the spear, for "*centumvirale.*" *Val. Max.* vii. 8, 4. "*Centumviralem hastam cogere*," i. e. to assemble the courts of the *Centumviri*, and preside in them. *Suet. Aug.* 36. So "*centum gravis hasta virorum*," i. e. the solemn sentence of the Centumviri. Mart. Ep. vii. 62. "*Cessat centeni moderatrix judicis hasta*," the spear government of the Centumvir's ceases. *Stat. Salv.* iv. 4, 43. The Centumviri continued to act as judges for a whole year. The *Decemviri* also judged in certain cases, *Cic. Cæcin.* 33; and it is thought that, in particular cases, they previously took cognizance of the causes which were to come before the *Centumviri;* and their decisions were called "*præjudicia.*" Vide *Signonius de Judic.*

CHARTÆ-FOLIA, VEL PLAGULÆ.—When in the writings of various authors we find either of these words, we are apt to consider the *substance* of the matter somewhat similar to the *paper* now in use; but if we take the trouble to trace the *progress of writing*, and the *materials* used, in the different ages of the world, we shall obtain some curious and entertaining information, as well in respect of the *writing*, as of the *matter* upon which, from time to time, letters have been made. It has been well observed that the knowledge of writing is a constant mark of civilization. Before the invention of this art, men employed various methods to preserve the memory of important events; and to communicate their thoughts to those from whom they were separated. The memory of important events was probably, in the *first* ages of the world, preserved by raising altars, or heaps of stones, vide *Genesis*, c. xxviii. v. 18, and iv. *Joshua* from 3 to 9; planting groves, and instituting names and festivals; and was afterwards more universally transmitted to posterity by historical songs (*Ex.* c. xv.¹, &c., as was also the custom of the *Druids.* Vide *Tacit. de mor. Germ.*, and see note to *Cellæ.* One of the first attempts towards the representation of thought was the painting of objects: Thus to represent a murder, the figure of one man was drawn, stretched on the ground, and another with a deadly weapon standing over him. When the *Spaniards* first arrived in *Mexico*, it is said that the inhabitants gave notice of it to their Emperor, *Montezuma*, by sending him a large cloth, on which was *painted* what they had just seen. The *Egyptians* contrived certain signs, or symbols, called *Hieroglyphics*, whereby they represented several things by one figure; and two or three gentlemen of curiosity and learning, it is reported, have lately been, to some extent, successful with a few of these Hieroglyphics, in establishing their true meaning; and perhaps it is not too much to hope, that the time is not very distant, when many material facts will be illustrated by a farther acquaintance with them, which must tend very much to assist our knowledge of some ancient authors; and be a great *desideratum*, particularly to the biblical critic. The *Egyptians* and *Phœnicians* both contended about the honor of having invented letters. *Tac. Ann.* xi. 14. *Plin.* vii. 56. Luan. iii. 220. Cadmus, the *Phœnician*, first introduced letters into *Greece*, nearly fifteen hundred years before Christ. Vide *Herodot.* v. 58. They were then only sixteen in number. To these, four were added by *Palamedes*, in the time of the *Trojan* war; and four afterwards by *Simonides.* Vide *Plin.* vii. 56, s. 57. *Hygin. fab.* 277. Letters were brought into *Latium*, by *Evander*, from *Greece. Ibid. et Liv.* i. 7. The Latin letters, at first, were nearly of the same form with the Greek. *Tacit. Plin.* vii. 58. Some nations ranged their letters perpendicularly from the top to the bottom of the page; but most of them horizontally. Some from the right to the left, as the *Hebrews* and *Assyrians.* Some from right to left and *vice versâ*, alternately, like cattle ploughing; as the ancient *Greeks.* But most adopt the form we use, from left to right.

The most ancient materials for writing were stones, and bricks. Vide *Josephus' Antiq. Jud. Tac. Ann.* ii. 60. *Lucan*, iii. 223. Thus the decalogue, vide *Exod.* xxiv. v. 12, and the laws of *Moses*, in all probability. Vide also *Deut.* xxvii. v. 2, where the people were commanded to set up great stones, and plaster them with *plaster*, and write upon them all the words of the law. Then plates of brass were used. Vide *Liv.* iii. 57. *Tacit. Amm.* iv. 43; or of lead; vide *Plin.* xiii. 11, s. 21, also *Job*, xix. 24; and wooden tables. Vide *Isaiah*, xxx. 8. *Hor. Art. Poet. Gell.* ii. 12. On these, public acts and monuments were preserved. Vide *Cic. Font* 14. *Liv.* vii. 20. As the art of writing was little known, and rarely practiced, it behoved that the materials should be durable. Capital letters only were used, as appears from ancient marbles and coins. The materials first used in common for writing, were the leaves or inner bark (*liber*) of trees, whence *leaves* of paper (*chartæ, folia, vel plagulæ*), and LIBER, a book. The leaves of trees are still used for writing by several nations of *India ;* and bark may be obtained of that size and quality in *America*, well adapted for writing upon. Afterwards, *linen*, vide *Liv.* iv. 7, 13, 20; and tables covered with wax, were used. About the time of *Alexander* the Great, *paper* first began to be manufactured from an *Egyptian* plant, or reed, called *papyrus*, whence our word *paper*. The *papyrus* was about 10 cubits high; and had *several* coats or skins above one another, like an onion, which were separated with a needle, or some such instrument. One of these membranes was spread on a table lengthwise, and another placed above it *across*. The one was called a *stamen;* and the other *substamen*, as the warp and the woof in a web. Being moistened with the muddy waters of the *Nile*, which served instead of glue, they were put into a press, and afterwards dried in the sun. Then these sheets (*plagulæ* or *s*ᵇ*edæ*) thus prepared were joined together end to end; but (it is said) never more than twenty in what was called one *scapus*, or roll. Vide *Plin.* xiii. 11. s. 21. The sheets were of different sizes and quality.

Paper was smoothed with a shell, or the tooth of a boar, or some other wild animal. Hence we read of *charta dentata*, i. e. smoothed or polished. Vide *Cic. Q. fr.* ii. 15. The finest paper was called at *Rome* after Augustus, "*Augusta regia;*" the next *Livinia;* the third *Hieratica*, which used anciently to be the name of the finest kind, being appropriated to the sacred volumes. The Emperor *Claudius* introduced some alteration, so that the finest paper after him was called *Claudia*. The inferior kinds were called *Amphitheatrica, Saitica Leneotica*, from places in *Egypt*, where paper was made; and *Fanniana*, from *Fannius*, who had a noted manufactory for dressing *Egyptian* paper at Rome. Vide *Plin.* Papers which served only for wrappers was called *Emporetica*, because chiefly used by merchants for packing goods. Fine paper of the largest size, was called *Macrocolla* (as we call some paper imperial or royal paper), and anything written on it, *Macrocollum*.

The exportation of paper having been prohibited by one of the *Ptolomies*, out of envy against *Eumenes*, King of *Pergamus*, who endeavored to rival him in the magnificence of his library, the use of parchment, or the art of preparing *skins* for writing, was discovered at *Pergamus*, hence called *Pergamenta*, sc. *Charta* vel *Membrana* parchment. Hence, also, Cæsar calls his four books of Academics, "*quatuor libri e membranis facti*," i. e. the four books made out of skins. Att. xiii. 24. Dipthera Jovis is the register book of Jupiter, made of the skin of the goat Amalthea, (by whose milk he was nursed,) on which he is supposed by the poets to have written down the actions of men; whence the proverb, "*Diptheram sero Jupiter inspexit*," i. e. Jupiter too late looked into the register. And "*Antiquiora dipthera*," i. e. more ancient registers. *Erasm.* in *Chiliad.* vide *Poiluc.* vii. 15. *Aelian* ix. 3. To this Plautus beautifully alludes. *Rud. prol.* 21. The skins of sheep are properly called *parchment;* of calves, *vellum*. Most of the ancient MSS. which have escaped the ravages of time are written on parchment—few on papyrus. It is said that lately an ingenious method has been discovered of unfolding the rolls.

Egypt having fallen under the dominion of the *Arabs*, in the seventh century, and its commerce with *Europe*, and the *Constantinopolitan* empire being stopped, the manufacture of paper from the *papyrus* ceased. The art of making paper from cotton, or silk, was invented in the East about the beginning of the tenth century; and in imitation of it, from *linen* rags in the fourteenth century.

The instrument used for writing on waxen tables, the bark of trees, plates of brass or lead, &c., was an iron pencil, with a sharp point, called *stylus*, or *graphum*. Hence "*stylo abstinco*," i. e. I forbear writing. *Plin. Ep.* vii. 21. On paper or parchment, a *reed* sharpened and split in the point like our pens, called *calamus, arundo, fistula*, vel *canna*, which they dipt in ink, (*atramento intingebant*,) as we do our pens. *Cic. Att.* vi. 8, &c.

Sepia, the cuttle fish, is sometimes put for ink, (*Pers.*) because when afraid of being caught it emits a black matter to conceal itself, which, it is said, the *Romans* used for ink. *Cic. de nat. D.* ii. 20.

The ordinary writing materials of the *Romans* were tablets covered with *wax, paper* and *parchment.* Their *stylus* was broad at one end; so that when they wished to correct anything, they turned the *stylus,* and smoothed the wax with the broad end, that they might write on it anew. Hence "*sæpe stilum vertas,*" i. e. to make frequent corrections, or change the manner of composition. *Vid. Hor. Sat.* i. 10, 72.

An author while composing, usually wrote first on these tablets for the convenience of making alterations; and when anything appeared sufficiently correct, it was generally transcribed on paper, or parchment, and published. *Vide Hor. Sat.* ii. 3, 2. It seems one could write more quickly on waxen tablets than on paper, where the hand was retarded by frequently dipping the reed in ink. *Quinct.* x. 3, 30.

The labor of correcting was compared to that of working with a file. (*limæ labor,*) hence "*opus limare,*" to polish. (Cic. Orat. i. 25 :) "*limare de aliquo,*" to lop off redundancies. *Ibid.* iii. 9. "*Supremam limam operiri,*" i. e. to wait the last polish. Plin. Ep. viii. 5. "*Lima mordacius uti,*" to correct more carefully. Ov. Pont. i. 5, 19. "*Liber rasus lima amici,*" polished by the correction of a friend. Ib. ii. 4, 17. "*Ultima lima defuit meis scriptis.*" Ov. Trist. i. 6, 30, i. e. *summa manus operi defuit, vel non imposita est;* i. e. the last polish was not put to the work—it was not finished.

The Romans also used a kind of blotting, or coarse paper, or parchment, (*charta deletitia,*) i. e. blotting paper called *palemsestos,* on which they might easily erase what was written and write it anew. *Mart.* xiv. 7. But it seems this might have been done on any parchment. *Vide. Hor. Art.* p. 389.

Very many of the writings of the classic age were, in the former centuries of the Christian era, erased to make room for the rude, undigested and often ridiculous composition of the Monkish clergy. The Romans commonly wrote on one side only of the paper or parchment, and joined ("*agglutinebant,*") i. e. glued one sheet (*Scheda*) to the end of another, till they finished what they had to write; and then rolled it up on a cylinder or staff, (hence *volumen*—a volume or scroll.) *Vid. Isaiah,* xxix. 11. An author generally included one *book* in a volume, so that generally in a work there was usually the same number of volumes as of books. Thus Ovid calls his fifteen books of Metamorphoses "*mutatæ ter quinque volumina formæ.*" When a book was long, it was sometimes divided into two volumes. When a book, or volume was finished, a ball, or boss of wood, bone, horn, or the like was affixed to it, on the outside, for ornament and security, called "*umbilicus*"—hence the expression "*ad umbilicum adducere,*" to finish. The Romans, it is said, frequently carried with them wherever they went small writing tables, called "*pugillares,*" on which they marked down anything that occurred. (Plin. Ep. i. 6,) either with their own hands, or by means of a slave, called from his office "*Notarius,*" or *Tabularius.* These *pugillares* were of an oblong form, made of citron, boxwood, or ivory; also of parchment, covered with colored or white wax. (*Ov. Am.* i. 12, 7,) containing two leaves, three, four, five, or more, (*Mart.*) with a small margin, raised all round, as may be seen in the models of them which still remain. They wrote on them with a *stilus,* hence "*ceris et stylo incumbere,*" (to apply with wax and stile,) for *in pugillaribus scribere,* (to write on the note books or tables.) Vide Plin. Ep. vii. 27. "*Remittere stilum,*" i. e. to give over writing. Ib.

As the Romans never wore a sword or dagger in the city, (*Plin.* xxxiv. 14. s. 39,) they often upon a sudden provocation used the *graphum,* or *stilus,* as a weapon, (*Suet. Cæs. C.* 28, &c.,) which they carried in a case. Hence probably the *stiletto* of the modern *Italians.*

When a book was sent anywhere the roll was tied with a thread, and was placed on the knot and sealed; hence "*signata volumina,*" i. e. sealed volumes. *Vid.* Hor. Ep. i. 13. So letters, *Cic. Cat.* iii. 5. The roll was usually wrapt around with a coarser paper or parchment, *Plin.* xiii.; or with part of an old book, to which *Hor.* is supposed to allude, *vid. Ep.* i. 20.

Julius Cæsar, in his letters to the senate, introduced the custom of dividing them into pages, (*paginæ*,) and folding them into the form of a pocket book, or account book, with distinct pages, like our books, whereas formerly Consuls and Generals when they wrote to the senate used to continue the line quite across the sheet, (*transverâ chartâ*,) i. e. athwart the paper, without any distinction of pages, and roll them up in a volume. *Suet. Cæs.* 56. Hence, after this, all applications and requests to the Emperors, and messages from them to the senate, or public orders to the people, used to be written, and folded in this form, and were called "Libelli." *Suet. Aug. Mart. &c.*

CHIROGRAPHUM.—*Cirographum,* Cyrographum. This word signifies *hand writing,* or writing with one's own hand. It is of Greek origin, in use among the Romans to denote a bond or obligation, written or subscribed with a person's own hand. The Saxons borrowed it of the Latins, to apply to public instruments of gift or conveyance, attested by the signatures and crosses of the witnesses present.

The Normans altered the form of executing these instruments and their name also; which they termed *charta.* But in time a practice arose of executing these charters or deeds in *two parts;* that is a part and a counterpart. They wrote the whole of the instrument *twice* on the same sheet of paper, or skin of parchment, leaving a space in the middle between the parts where the word CHIROGRAPHUM was written in capital letters. Then the parchment was divided by cutting it across through these letters, so that when the two parts were separated, one would exhibit one half of the capital letters, and one the other half; thus, when joined, the words would appear entire. At first this cut was made in a straight line. Afterwards they cut through the word in acute angles, passing between the letters alternately like the teeth of a saw, which gave these deeds the name of *indentures.* See Reeves Hist. Eng. Law.

CNAFA.—*Sax.* A knave.—This old Saxon word had at first a sense of *simplicity and innocence,* for it signified *"a boy."* The *Sax.* ("*Cnafa*") distinguished a boy from a girl, in several ancient writers. Thus, the poet says, "a *knave* child between them two they gate." *Gower's Poem.* And *Wickliffe,* in his old translation, *Exod.* i. 16, says, "if it be a *knave* child," alluding to *Pharaoh* and the *Hebrew* children, *vid. Exod.* i. v. 16. Afterwards the word was taken for a *servant boy.* At length, however, it was applied for any servant man; also to a member or officer who. bore the weapon, or shield of his superiors, as "*scild knapa,*" whom the Latins call "*armiger,*" and the French "*escuyer,*" whence the English word "*esquire,*"—we find at games with cards that the one immediately inferior to the *queen* in each suit is called "the *knave;*" a word, probably, at the time cards were first introduced into England, signifying an officer or servant who bore the shield of, or waited upon his superior. It was sometimes of old made use of as a titular addition, as "*Johannes C. filius Williehelmi C. de Derby,* knave, *i. e.* John C. the son of William C. of Derby, a knave. In the vision of *Piers Plowman* are these words, "*Cokes, and thierre knaves cryden holes pyes,*" *i. e.* "Cooks, and their *boys* cried hot pies." This word *knave,* however, with many others in the English language, has now another and a different signification. The reader will, perhaps, pardon one digression, elucidatory *how a living language* can not only vary its signification, but how some words in process of time completely alter in their signification. In *Psalms* xxi. v. 3, are these words, "For thou *preventest* him with the blessings of goodness." At the present day this is mystery to many readers, but if we revert to the original meaning of the word "*prevent,*" derived from the Latin "*prævenio*" to go before, the sense is very obvious. So the words of the collect, "prevent us, O Lord, in all our doings with thy most gracious favor," &c. A curious instance of the old use of this word occurs in *Weller's* "Angler," where one of the characters says, "I mean to be up early to-morrow morning to *prevent* the sun rising," that is, to be up before the sun. Numerous other instances might be added to prove, if necessary, that words are *continually* and gradually changing their original significations; and some have obtained *totally* different ones—this proves how very cautious authors should be to adhere to the strict *etymology* of words.

CNYT.—Sax. *knight*—Lat. *miles*, and *eques auratus*, from the guilt spurs he usually wore.—*Blackstone* remarks that it is observable that almost all na-tions call their knights by some appellation derived from a *horse*. Mr. Chris-tian, however, in his notes on *Blackstone*, says that it does not appear that the English word *knight* has any reference to a horse, for *cniht*, in the Saxon, signified *puer*, *servus*, or attendant, vide also *Spelm. in v. v. knight, miles.* There is now probably only one instance where it is taken in that sense, and that is "*knight of the shire*," who properly serves in parliament for a county; but in all other instances it is supposed to signify one who "*bears arms*," who for his virtue and natural prowess is exalted to the rank of knighthood. *Camden,* in his *Britannia,* thus shortly expresses the manner of making a knight: "*Nostris vero temporibus, qui equestrem dignitatem sus-cipit, flexis genibus, leviter in humero percutitur, princeps his verbis gallice affa-tur,*" i. e. in our time he who would receive knighthood being on his bended knees, is gently touched on the shoulder, the prince speaking to him in these words, "Arise, or be thou a knight, in the name of God." "*Soiyez vel sois, Chevalier, au nom de Dieu.*" This is meant of *Knights Bachelors,* the lowest, but a very ancient degree of knighthood in *England,* for we have an instance of king Alfred conferring this order on his son *Athelstan.* Knights, *Black-stone* says, were called "*Milites,*" because they formed part of the royal army in virtue of their tenures under the feudal system.

COMITIA TRIBUTA.—The names of *tribes* was probably derived either from their original number three (*a numero ternario*), or from paying tribute, *vide Liv.* i. 43.

The first tribe was named from *Romulus,* and included the *Roman* citi-zens who occupied the *Palatine* hill; the second from *Titus Tatius,* and in-cluded the *Sabines,* who possessed the *Capitoline* hill; and the third from one *Lucumo,* a *Tuscan,* or rather from the grove (*a luco*), which *Romulus* turned into a sanctuary, *vid. Virg. Æn.* viii. 342, and included all foreign-ers, except the *Sabines.* Each of these tribes had at first its own tribune or commander (*tribunus vel præfectus*), vid. *Dionys.* iv. and its own Augur, vid. *Liv.* x. 6.

Tarquinus Priscus doubled the number of tribes, retaining the same names; so that they were called *Ramnenses primi, et Ramnenses secundi,* or *pos-teriores, &c.*

But as the *Luceres* in a short time greatly exceeded the rest in num-ber, *Servius Tullius* introduced a new arrangement; and distributed the citi-zens into tribes, not according to their extraction, but from their local sit-uation.

He divided the city into four regions or wards, the inhabitants of which constituted as many tribes, and had their names from the wards which they inhabited. No one was permitted to remove from one ward to another, that the tribes might not be confounded, vid. *Dionys.* iv. 14; on which account certain persons were appointed to take an account where every one dwelt; also of their age, fortune, &c. These were called city tribes, and their num-ber always remained the same.

Servius at the same time divided the Roman territory into fifteen parts, (some say sixteen, others seventeen,) which were called country tribes (*Tribus Rusticæ*) Vid. *Dionys.* iv. 15.

In the year of the city 258, the number of tribes was made twenty-one. Vid. *Liv.* ii. 21. Here, for the first time, *Livy* directly takes notice of the number of tribes; although he alludes to the original institution of three tribes. *Vide* x. 6. Dyonysius says that *Servius* instituted thirty-one tribes. *Vide* iv. 15. But in the trial of *Coriolanus*, he only mentions twenty-one as having voted. *Vid.* vii. 64.

The number of tribes was afterwards increased, on account of the addition of new citizens at different times, (*Liv.* vi. 5, &c.,) to thirty-five, (*Liv.* xxiii. 13), which number continued to the end of the republic. (*Liv.* i. 43.)

After the admission of the *Italian* states to the freedom of the city, eight or ten new tribes are said to have been added; but this appears but to have been of short continuance; for they were soon all distributed among the thirty-five old tribes.

The *Comitia Tributa* were held to create magistrates, to elect certain priests, to make laws, and to hold trials. At the *Comitia Tributa* were created all the *inferior city magistrates*, as *Ædiles*, both Curule and Plebeian; the tribunes of the commons; questors, &c., all the *provincial magistrates*; as the proconsuls, proprætors, &c.; also commissioners for settling colonies, &c.; the *Pontifex Maximus*; and after the year 650 the other *Pontifices, Augures feciales, &c.*

The laws passed at these *Comitia*, were called *Plebiscita*, which at first only bound the *Plebeians;* but after the year 306 the whole *Roman* people. *Vide Liv.* iii. 55.

These *Plebiscita* were made about various things; as about making peace, *Liv.* xxxiii. 10; about granting the freedom of the city; about ordering a triumph when it was refused by the Senate, *Liv.* iii. 63; about bestowing commands on Generals on the day of their triumph, *Liv.* xxvi. 21; about absolving him from the laws, which in latter times the Senate assumed as its prerogative.

There were no *capital* trials at the *Comitia Tributa;* these were only held at the *Centuriata:* but about imposing a fine, *Liv.* iv. 41: and if any one accused of a capital crime did not appear on the day of trial, the *Comitia Tributa* were sufficient to decree banishment against him. *Liv.* xxvi. 3.—xxv. 6. In the *Forum,* there were separate places for each tribe marked out with ropes. Vide *Dionys.* vii. 59. In the *Campus Martius,* Cicero proposed building in *Cæsar's* name, marble enclosures for holding the *Comitia Tributa,* Cic. Att. iv. 16, which work was prevented by various causes; and at last entirely dropped upon the breaking out of the civil wars; but it was afterwards executed by *Agrippa.* If there had been thunder or lightning, (*si tonuisset aut fulgurasset,*) the *Comitia Tributa* could not be held on that day. For it was a constant rule from the beginning of the republic, *Jove fulgente, cum populo agi nefas esse,* i. e. when it lightened it was unlawful to transact public affairs.

CODEX JUSTITIANUS.—*Justitian* first published a collection of the imperial constitutions, A. D. 529, called "*Codex Justitianus.*" This was the Emperor who first reduced the *Roman* law into certain order. For this purpose he employed the assistance of the most eminent lawyers in the empire, at the head of whom was *Tribonian.* He ordered a collection to be made of everything that was useful in the writings of the lawyers before his time, which are said to have amounted to *two thousand* volumes. This work was executed by *Tribonian,* and sixteen associates, in three years, although they had been allowed ten years to finish it. It was published A. D. 533, under the title of "*Digest,*" or "*Pandects*" (*Pandectæ vel Digesta*). It is sometimes called in the singular "*The Digest,*" or "*Pandect.*"

The same year were published the *Elements,* or first principles of the *Roman* Law, composed by three persons, *Tribonian, Theophilus* and *Dorotheus,* and called "The Institutes" (*Instituta*). This book was published before the *Pandects*, although it was composed after them. As the first code did not appear sufficiently complete, and contained several things inconsistent with the *Pandects*, *Tribonian* and four other men were employed to correct it. A new code, therefore, was published A. D. 534, called "*Codex repetitæ prelectionis*," i. e. the book of a renewed Lecture, and the former code declared to be of no further authority. Thus in *six* years was completed what is called "*Corpus juris*"—the body of (*Roman*) law, to which we are indebted for much of our civil jurisprudence.

But when new questions arose, not contained in any of the above-mentioned books, new decisions became necessary to supply what was wanting, or correct what was erroneous. These were afterwards published, under the title of "Novels," (*Novellæ*) sc. *Constitutiones*, not only by *Justinian*, but also by some of the succeeding Emperors. So that the "*Corpus juris Romani civilis*," i. e. the body of the Roman civil law, is made up of these books, the *Institutes*, *Pandects*, or *Digests*, *Code* and *Novels*.

The *Pandects* are divided into fifty books, each book into several titles; each title into several laws, which are distinguished by numbers, and sometimes one law into beginning (*princ. for principium*) and paragraphs thus, *D.* 1, 1, 5, i. e. *Digest, first book, first title, fifth law.* If the law be divided into paragraphs, a fourth number will be added thus, *D.* 48, 5, 13, *pr.* or 48, 5, 13, 1. Sometimes the first word of the law, not the number, is cited. The *Pandects* are often marked by a double *f*, thus *ff.* The code is cited in the same manner as the Pandects, by book, title and law. The Novels by their number, the chapters of that number, and the paragraphs, if any, as Nov. 115, c. 6.

The Institutes are divided into four books, each book into several titles or chapters, and each title into paragraphs, of which the *first* is not numbered, thus *Inst. lib.* 1, *tit.* 10, *princip.*, or more shortly, *Inst. lib.* 1, 10, *pr.*, so *Inst. l.* 1, 10, 2. The student will notice this.

The *Justinian* code of law was universally received through the *Roman* world. It flourished in the East, until the taking of *Constantinople* by the *Turks*, A. D. 1453. In the West it was, in a great measure, suppressed by the irruptions of the barbarous northern nations, till it was revived in *Italy*, in the twelfth century, by *Irnerius*, who had studied at *Constantinople*, and opened a school at *Bologna*, under the auspices of *Frederick* the First, Emperor of Germany. He was attended by an innumerable number of students from all parts, who propagated the knowledge of the "*Roman Civil Law*" through most countries of Europe, where in a great measure it still continues, and will continue for ages, to be of great authority in courts of judicature, and seems to promise, at least in point of *legislation*, the fulfilment of the famous prediction of the ancient Romans concerning the "ETERNITY OF THEIR EMPIRE."

CODICILLUS.—When additions were made by the Romans to a will, they were called *Codicilli*, and were, it is said, expressed in the form of a Letter, addressed to the heirs; sometimes also to the trustees, (*ad fide commissarios.*) After the testator's death, his will was opened, vide *Hor. Ep.* i. 7, in the presence of the witnesses who had sealed it, or a majority of them. Vide *Suet. Tib.* 23. And if they were absent or dead, a copy of the will was taken in the presence of other respectable persons; and the authentic testament was laid up in the public archives, that if the copy were lost, another might be taken from it. Horace ridiculed a miser who ordered his heirs to inscribe on his tomb the sum he left. Vide *Sat.* ii. 3. 84. It was esteemed honorable to be named in the testament of a friend or relation; and considered as a mark of disrespect to be passed over.

COEMPTIO.—This word signified, among the Romans, a kind of mutual purchase (*emptio; venditio;*) when a man and woman were married, by delivering to one another a small piece of money, and repeating certain words. Vide *Cic. Orat.* i. 57. The man asked the woman "*an sibi mater familias esse vellet*"—whether she would be the mother of the family; she answered "*se velle,*" i. e. that she was willing. In the same manner the woman asked the man, and he made a similar answer. *Boeth. in Cic. Topic.* 3. The woman was to the husband in the place of a daughter, and he to her as a father. *Serv. in Virg. G.* She assumed his name, together with her own, as *Antonia Drusi, Domitia Bibuli,* &c. She resigned to him all her goods. *Ter. Andr.* i. 5, 61: and acknowledged him as her lord and master. (*Dominus.*) Vide *Virg. En.* iv. 103, 214. The goods which a woman brought to her husband, besides her portion, were called "*Parapherna.*" In the first days of the republic, dowries were very small—that given by the Senate to the daughter of Scipio, was only eleven thousand *asses* of brass, £35 10s. 5d. and one *Meguillia* was surnamed "*Dotata,*" or the great fortune, who had fifty thousand *asses,* i. e. £161 7s. 6d. sterling. Vide *Val. Max.* iv. 10. But afterwards, upon the increase of wealth, the marriage portions of some women became greater, *Decies centena* sc. *sestercia,* £8072 18s. 4d. sterling. *Mart.* ii. 65. *Juv.* vi. 136. The usual portion of a lady of a Senatorian rank. *Juv.* x. 355.

Sometimes the wife reserved to herself part of the money, and a slave, who was not subject to the power of the husband. Some think that "*coemptio*" was used as an accessory rite to "*consecratio,*" and retained when the primary rite was dropped, from *Cic. Flacc.* 34.

The right of purchase in marriage was not peculiar to the *Romans,* but prevailed also among other nations; as the Hebrews, *Genesis,* xxix. 18, 1 *Samuel,* xviii. 25, the *Thracians. Xenoph. Anab.* vii. &c., &c. So in the days of Homer. Vide *Odyss.* viii. 317, to which Virgil alludes. *G.* i. 31.

Some say a yoke used anciently to be put on a man and woman about to be married, whence they were called "*Conjuges,*"—others think this expression merely metaphorical. Vid. *Hor. Od.* ii. 5.

COLLISTRIGIUM.—A pillory. *Collum stringens; Pilloria,* Fr. *Pilleur.* This was an engine made of wood to punish offenders by exposing them to public view, and rendering them infamous. By 51 *Hen.* 3, *stat.* 6, it is appointed for bakers, forestallers, and those who use false weights, perjury, forgery, &c. Vide 3 *Inst.* 219. Lords of leets are to have a pillory and tumbril, or, it is said, it will be a cause of forfeiture of their leet, and a vill may be bound by prescription to provide a pillory, &c. 2 *Hawk. P. C.* c. 11, § 5.

COMMUNIA PLACITA.—It was the ancient custom for the feudal monarchs to preside themselves in their courts, and to administer justice in person. Vide *Marculf, lib.* i. § 25. *Murat. Dissert.* xxxi. Charlemagne, whilst he was dressing, used to call parties into his presence; and having heard and considered the subject of litigation gave judgment concerning it. Vide *Eginhartus Vita Carolomagni,* cited by *Madox,* Hist. Excheqr. vol. i. p. 91. The trial and decision of causes by the sovereigns themselves, could not fail of rendering their courts respectable. *St. Louis,* who encouraged the practice of appeals, revived the ancient custom, and administered justice in person, with all the ancient simplicity: "I have often seen the Saint," says *Joinville,* "sit under the shade of an oak, in the wood of *Vincennes,* when all who had any complaint freely approached him. At other times he gave orders to spread a carpet in a garden, and seating himself upon it, heard the causes which were brought before him." Vide *Hist. de St. Louis, p.* 13. *Edit.* 1761. Princes of inferior rank, who possessed the right of sitting in judgment, dispensed it in person, and presided in their tribunals. Two instances of this occur, with respect to the *Dauphines of Vienne.* Vide *Hist. de Dauphine, tom.* i. *p.* 18, *tom.* ii. 257. It appears, however, probable, that prior to the law or regulation contained in the text, the courts of justice of all the feudal monarchs, were originally ambulatory, and followed their persons, and were held during some of the great festivals. *Philip Augustus,* A. D. 1305, rendered it stationary at Paris, and continued its terms during the greater part of the year. William, the Conqueror, established a constant court in the hall of his palace, from which the four courts now intrusted with the administration of justice in England, took their rise; and as the king used to sit in ancient times upon the bench, it is a probable reason why a blow given in the Court of *King's Bench* upon any provocation whatever, was punished with the loss of the offender's hand, as it was done in the king's presence. Henry the Second divided his kingdom into six circuits, and sent itinerant judges to hold their seats in them, at stated seasons. Justices of the peace were appointed in every county by subsequent monarchs, to whose jurisdiction the people had recourse in very many cases.

COMPURGATORES.—Formerly, in most cases, where the notoriety of the fact did not furnish the most clear and direct evidence, the person accused, or he against whom an action was brought, was called upon legally, or voluntarily offered to purge himself *by oath;* and upon his thus supporting his evidence, he was immediately acquitted. The pernicious effects of this mode of trial were sensibly felt; and in order to guard against them, the laws ordained that the oath should be administered with the greatest solemnity; and accompanied with every circumstance which could inspire religious reverence, or superstitious terror. Vide *Du Cange Gloss. voc.* "Juramentum." This, however, after a time, proved but a feeble remedy; the rites and ceremonies became *familiar;* and when men found "that sentence against a perjurer was not executed speedily," the impression on the imagination gradually diminished. Men who could venture to disregard truth, were not startled at the *solemnities* of an oath, nor the "pomp and circumstance" with which it was taken. This put the legislators upon devising a new expedient for rendering the purgation by oath more safe and satisfactory. They required the person accused to appear with a certain number of *freemen,* his neighbors, or relations, who *corroborated* the oath which he took, by swearing that *they* believed all that he uttered to be *true.* These persons produced were called "*Compurgatores,*" and their number varied according to the importance of the subject in dispute; or the nature of the case with which a person was charged. In some important cases, it is said, that no less than the concurrence of *three hundred* witnesses was necessary to acquit the person accused. Vide *Spelman's Gloss. voc.* "*Assarth.*"

CONNUBIUM.—This word is often found in the Roman law. No *Roman* citizen was permitted to marry a slave, a barbarian, or a foreigner, unless by permission of the people. Vid. *Livy,* xxxviii. 36. By the laws of the *Decemviri,* intermarriages between the Patricians and Plebeians were prohibited. But this restriction was abolished. *Vid. Liv.* iv. 6. Afterwards, however, when a Patrician lady married a Plebeian she was excluded from the rights of Patrician ladies. *Vide Liv.* x. 23. When any woman married out of her own tribe it was called *Enuptio Gentis,* which likewise seems anciently to have been forbidden. Vide *Liv.* xxxix. 19.

CONTRA PACEM.—At several times during the year, the church formerly imposed an interdiction on the Barons against all private wars: the Sovereign also insisted upon this *when* the Barons were required for the defence of the kingdom, and on other occasions; the offence of waging *private* wars at those times was considered highly criminal, and was said to be committed, "*contra pacem Domini Regis*," i. e. against the king's peace: from this circumstance it is probable the custom arose of inserting the words ."*contra pacem*" in indictments for offences at the Common Law.

CONTUBERNIUM.—With the ancient *Romans* there was no regular marriage among slaves, but their connection was called *Contubernium*, and themselves *Contubernales.* The whole company of slaves in one house was called familia, (hence our word *family*,) and the slaves *Familiares.*
The proprietor of slaves was called *Dominus. Terent. Eun.* iii. 2, 23, whence the word was put for tyrant. *Liv.* ii. 60. On this account, *it is said,* Augustus refused the name. *Suet. Aug.* 53.
Slaves employed to accompany boys to and from school were called *Pædagogi;* and the part of the house where these young slaves staid, who were instructed in literature (*literæ serviles*), was called *Pædagogium.* Vid. *Plin. Ep.* vii. 27.

CURIÆ CHISTIANITATES.—Du Cange, in his Glossary, *voc. Curiæ Christianitates,* has collected most of the causes with respect to which the clergy arrogated an exclusive jurisdiction. *Giannone,* in his civil history of *Naples,* has ranged these under proper heads. *M. Fleury* observes that the clergy multiplied the pretexts for extending the authority of the spiritual courts with so much boldness that it was soon in their power to withdraw almost every person and every cause from the jurisdiction of the civil magistrate. *Hist. Eccl. tom.* xix. It has been said that the origin of Ecclesiastical jurisdiction had its source in that advice of St. Paul, who reproves the scandalizing of Christianity, by carrying on law suits against others before heathen judges, and recommends the leaving all matters in dispute between Christians to the church, or the congregation of the faithful. 1 *Cor.* vi. 1, 8.

CURIA COMITATUS.—Anciently the principal causes came into the Great County Court held by the sheriff, who was assisted by the bishop and earl. This court had cognizance of offences against religion; of temporal offences which concerned the public, as felonies, breaches of the peace, nuisances, and the like; of civil actions, as titles to land, and suits upon debt or contract: it also held the view of *frankpledge,* which was an inquest impannelled by the sheriff to see that every male above the age of twelve years had entered into some tything, and taken the oath of allegiance. From the time of king *Edgar,* the Great County Court was divided into two; the one a *Criminal,* the other a *Civil* Court. The Criminal was called the sheriff's *Tourn,* and was held by the sheriff and bishop twice in the year, viz.: in the months following *Easter* and *Michaelmas,* for the purpose of trying all criminal matters whatever: from this, it is said, was derived the *Court Leet.* The Civil Court retained the name of the County Court (from which came the *Court Baron*), and in it all the civil pleas of consequence arising in the county were tried. In the *Criminal* Court offences were punished according to the superstition of the times, if they did not purge themselves of the matter wherewith they were charged by the *ordeal,* by the *corsned* or morsel of execration, or by wager of law with Compurgators. In the *Civil* Court, parties complained against might purge themselves by their sureties, by wager of law. Trials by jury were also frequently used; for that mode of trial is generally considered to have been of *Saxon* origin; though whether that jury was composed of twelve men, or whether they were bound to a strict unanimity, does not appear to be precisely known at this period of time.

CURIA PUBLICA.—A public (or open court) more generally with some particular word, or addition to the word "*Curia,*" to denote whether of the King's Bench, Common Pleas, or Exchequer, &c. There have also been from a very early period a multiplicity of inferior courts, many of them established in the feudal times, whose services are extremely peculiar, nay, sometimes to us, ludicrous; and the tenures by which estates are held in several of them, are very remarkable, and denote the simplicity and rude customs of our ancestors. There is a court held on *King's Hill, Rochford,* in *Essex,* called *"Lawless Court,"* on the Wednesday morning next after *Michaelmas* day, yearly, at *cock-crowing;* at which court they *whisper,* and have *no candle,* nor *other light,* nor have they any pen and ink; but only a piece of charcoal, and he that owes suit or service, and does not appear, forfeits *double* his rent. This court is mentioned by *Camden,* who informs us that this *servile* attendance was imposed on the tenants for conspiring, at the like unseasonable time, to raise a commotion. Vide CAMDEN'S BRITAN. The title is in rhyme, and as it may be amusing to the reader, it is inserted. The Court roll runs thus:

" King's Hill in
   Rochford.

      Curia de domino rege,
      Dicta sino lege,
      Tenta est ibidem,
      Per ejus consuetudinem
      Ante ortum solis,
      Luceat nisi polus,
      Senescallus solus
      Nil scribit nisi colis,
      Toties voluerit.
      Gallus ut cantaverit,
      Per cujus soli sonitus,
      Curia est summonitus;
      Clamat clam pro rege,
      In curia sine lege.
      Et nisi cito venerint,
      Citius pœnituerint,
      Et nisi clam accedant,
      Curia non attendat;
   Qui venerit cum lumine, erat in regimine,
   Et dum sunt sine lumine, capti sunt in crimine;
      Curia sine cura,
      Jurata de injuria;
Tenta ibidem die Mercurii (ante diem) proxime, post festum Sancti Michaelis, anno, &c., &c.

"The Court of our Lord the King, held without law, is kept there by custom before the rising of the sun, unless the north pole may emit a glimmering light. The steward himself, when decrees are to be entered, writes the same with charcoal. At the crowing of the cock, by whose clarion the court is summoned, the steward proclaims the opening of this lawless court in the King's name; and that unless they forthwith come, they shall quickly repent, and unless in secrecy they attend, the court will not give audience to their business, and he who shall come with light is under a penalty, for whilst they associated in darkness, they were caught in crime. This lawless court was sworn to try offences, and held on Wednesday, next after Michaelmas day (before daylight), in the year, &c., &c."

Another singular ceremony is performed as an ancient tenure for lands, held in the parish of *Broughton.* On Palm Sunday, a person from *Broughton,* brings a very large whip, which is called a *gad,* into the church at *Caister,* the stock of which whip is made of wood, tapering towards the top, having a large thong of white leather, and being wrapped towards the top with the same. He comes towards the north porch about the conclusion of the first lesson, and cracks the whip as loud as possible three times, the thong reaching within the porch; after which he wraps the thong round the stock, having four twigs of mountain ash placed within the same. He then ties the whole together with whip cord, and suspends a leathern bag to the top of the stock, with two shillings in it, (originally twenty-four silver pennies;) he then takes the whole on his shoulder, marches into the church, and stands till the commencement of the second lesson. He next goes to the reading desk, and kneeling down upon a cushion, holds the purse suspended over the priest's head till the end of the lesson. He then retires into the choir, and, after the service is concluded, carries all to the manor house of *Hundon*, where they are left.

D.

DA.——Yes.

DA gratiam loquendi.——Give the liberty of speech.

DAMAGE feasant.——Doing damage.

DAMAIOUSE.——Causing damage.

DAMNANDA res.——A condemned estate, or thing.

DAMNI injuriæ actio.——An action given against a person who has intentionally injured the property of another.

DAMNOSA hæreditas.——A disadvantageous inheritance.

DAMNUM absque injuria.——"A loss without injury." A loss for which no recompense can be obtained.

DAMNUM fatale.——Damages arising from inevitable events, such as loss by shipwreck, lightning, &c.

DAMNUM sine injuria.——A loss without injury.

DANE-LAGE.——"Danish custom, or law." The *Danish* laws were at one time in force in particular parts of *England* which the *Danes* had taken from the *Saxons*.

DANGER de la terre.——Land-risk.

DANS un pays libre, on crie beaucoup, quiqu'on souffre peu; dans un pays de tyrannie, on se plaint peu quoiqu'on souffre beaucoup.——In a free country there is much clamor, with little suffering; in a despotic state, there is little complaint but much grievance.

DARE aliquam evidentiam.——"To give some evidence." Thus it may be necessary to give *some* evidence in the county to which the venue is changed.

DARE autem non possunt tenementa sua, nec ex causa donationis ad alios transferre, non magis quam villani puri; et unde si transferre debeant, restituunt domino vel baillivo; et ipsi ea tradunt aliis in villenagium tenenda.——But they cannot give away their tenements nor transfer them to others on account (of the mode) of the donation, no more than as though they were simple villains; and therefore, if they are to be transferred, they render them back to the lord or his bailiff; and they deliver them to others to be held in villainage.

DARE judicium.——To give judgment; to decide the cause. *Vide note.*

DARIEN presentment.——The last presentation.

DATA.——"Things granted." We must proceed on certain "*data*," that is, on matters previously admitted to be correct.

DATIO tutoris.——The appointment of a guardian or tutor by a magistrate, where the will had not provided one.

DATUM.——A thing granted: a point fixed upon: a first principle.

DAYSMAN.——An arbitrator.

DE acquirenda possessione.——Of obtaining possession.

DE admensuratione dotis.——A writ which lies where the heir or guardian assigns to the widow more land than rightly belongs to her.

DE admensuratione pasturæ.——"Of the admeasurement of pasture." A writ so called.

DE advisamente consilii nostri.——By the advice of our council. An expression used in the old writs of summons to parliament.

DE æquitate et lege conjuncta.——Of equity and law conjoined.

DE ætate probanda.——A writ to summon a jury to inquire whether the heir to an estate is of age or not.

DE aliquibus tenuris intrinsecis et transgressionibus, aut

contractibus, intra eundem burgum factis.——Concerning other domestic tenures, and trespasses, or contracts, performed within the same borough.

DE allocatione faciendo.——A writ for making an allowance.

DE´ alto et basso.——An expression used in ancient times to signify the absolute submission of all differences to arbitration.

DE ambiguis et obscuris interpretandis.——As to doubtful and obscure translations.

DE ambitu.——The *Romans* had a law (*de ambitu*) against bribery and corruption in elections, with the infliction of new, severer, and, perhaps, just punishments for this offence, which strikes at the root of all good government. *Vid. Dio.* xxxix., 37. They had also a law (*de ambitu*), Suet. 34, against forestalling the market; also another called *de ambitu*, limiting the pleadings in criminal cases to one day's duration, allowing two hours to the prosecutor, and three to the accused.

DE ampliori gratia.——Of more abundant or special grace.

DE anno bissextili.——Of the bissextile or leap year.

DE annua pensione.——Writ of annual pension.

DE annua redditu.——A writ for recovering an annuity, payable either in money or goods.

DE apibus. Apium quoque fera natura est; itaque apes, quæ in arbore tua constituerunt, antequam a te alveo includantur, non magis tuæ intelliguntur esse, quam volucres quæ in arbore tuo nidum fecerint; adeoque si alius eas incluserit, is earum dominus erit.——Of Bees. The nature of bees is also wild; therefore, bees which have swarmed in your tree, before they are inclosed by you in the hive, are not understood to be yours, any more than birds which have made their nest in your tree; and therefore, if any other person has inclosed them he shall be their owner.

DE apostata capendo.——Writ for taking an apostate.

DE arrestandis bonis ne dissipentur.——A writ *to seize goods to prevent their being made way with* during the pending of a suit.

DE arrestando ipsum qui pecuniam recepit.——A writ to seize one who had taken the king's *prest money* to serve in war, and secreted himself when the time came for him to go.

DE asportatis religiosorum.——Of taking away of (the property) of religious persons.

DE assiza novæ disseysinæ.——Of the assize of novel disseisin.

DE assiza proroganda.——Writ for proroguing an assize.

DE attornato recipiendo.——Writ to receive an attorney.

DE audiendo et terminando.——A writ for hearing and determining.

DE averagiis mercium 6 navibus projectarum, distribuendis, vetus habetur non impressum, cujus exemplar apud me extat.——With respect to the average of merchandise thrown from vessels, and to be divided, there is an ancient statute, not in print, of which I have a remembrance.

DE averiis captis in withernamium.——Writ for taking cattle or goods in withernam.

DE averiis replegiandis.——Writ for replevying beasts.

DE averiis retornandis.——Writ for returning the cattle.

DE avo.——Writ of ayle.

DE banco.——Of the bench.

DE bene esse.——Conditionally.

DEBET esse facta bona fide, et tempestative.——The thing should be done fairly, and seasonably.

DEBET et detinet.——He owes and detains.

DEBET sui cuique domus esse perfugium tutissimum.—— "Every person's house should be his most safe refuge." Every man's house is his castle.

DE bien et de mal.——For good and evil.

DEBITA fundi.——Debts secured upon land.

DEBITA laicorum.——Debts of the laity.

DEBITO aut legitimo modo.——In a due or legal form.

DEBITO justitiæ.——By a debt of justice: by a claim justly established.

DEBITO modo electus.——Elected in a legal manner.

DEBITOR non præsumitur donare.——A debtor is not presumed to make a gift (to his creditor by will).

DEBITUM et contractus sunt nullius loci.——Debt and contract have no locality.

DEBITUM in præsenti.——A debt due at the present time.

DEBITUM in præsenti, solvendum in futuro.——A debt contracted (or due) at present, payable at a future day.

DEBITUM recuperatum.——A debt recovered.

DE bone memorie.——Of good memory.

DE bonis asportatis.——Of goods carried away.

DE bonis defuncti primo deducenda sunt ea quæ sunt necessitatis; et postea, quæ sunt utilitatis; et ultimo, quæ sunt voluntatis.——From the goods of a deceased person, those which are of necessity are first to be deducted; and afterwards those of utility, and lastly, those of bequest.

DE bonis ecclesiasticis levari.——To be levied from the goods of the church.

DE bonis et catallis debitoris.——Of (or concerning) the debtor's goods and chattels.

DE bonis et catallis testatoris, et quæ ad manus testatoris devenirent administrand'.——Of the goods and chattels of the testator; and whatsoever came to the testator's hands to be administered.

DE bonis intestatoris.——Concerning the goods of an intestate.

DE bonis non.——Of goods not (administered).

DE bonis non administrandis.——Of goods unadministered.

DE bonis non amovendis.——A writ to prevent the removing of goods.

DE bonis propriis.——Of his own goods.

DE bonis propriis, si non, de bonis testatoris.——Of his own goods, (if he have any,) if not, of the goods of the testator.

DE bonis testatoris.——Of the goods of the testator.

DE bonis testatoris cum acciderint.——Of the testator's effects, when they come to hand.

DE bonis testatoris si, &c., et si non, tunc de bonis, propriis.——Of the testator's goods if, &c., and if not, then of his own proper goods.

DE bonis testatoris, si tantum in manibus habeant unadministrand'.——Of the goods of the testator, if they have so much in their hands unadministered.

DE bono gestu.——For his good behavior.

DEBUIT reparare.——He ought to repair.

DE cætero non recedant quærentes à curia domino regis, pro eo quod tenementum transfertur de uno in alium.—— From henceforth that plaintiffs do not withdraw from the court of the lord the king, because the tenement is transferred from one to another.

DE calceto reparando.——Writ for repairing a causeway.

DE capitalibus dominis feodi.——Of the chief lords of the fee.

DE capitalibus feodis.——Of the chief fees.

DE castro, villa et terris.——Concerning a castle, vill, and lands.

DE catallis reddendis.——Writ for rendering goods.

DE cartis reddendis.——Writ for re-delivering charters or deeds.

DE causis criminalibus, vel capitalibus, nemo quærat consilium quin implacitatus statim pernegat, sine omne petitione consilii. In aliis omnibus, potest, et debet uti consilio.——In criminal or capital cases that no one obtain traverse; but if arraigned, that he plead immediately, without any request for a traverse. In all other cases he may and ought to have traverse.

DE cautione admittenda.——Writ to take caution or security.

DECEMVIRI.——"Ten men." They were appointed to compose the twelve tables of the laws for the *Roman* people. *Vide note.*

DECENNARIES.——The division of persons by tens. *Vide note.*

DE certificando.——A writ for certifying.

DECET tamen principem servare leges, quibus ipse salutus est.——For it becomes the prince to keep the laws, by which he himself is preserved in security.

DE champertia.——The unlawful purchase of an interest in a thing in dispute with the object of maintaining the litigation.

DE chimino.——A writ to enforce a right of way.

DECIMÆ.——Tithes—or Tenths. *Vide note.*

DECLARA hoc dictum, "Ubi nauta munere vehendi in parte sit functus, quia tunc pro parte itineris quo merces inventæ sint vecturam deberi æquitas suadet, et pro ea rata mercedis solutio fieri debet."——Show forth this, "That where the mariner having partly discharged his business of transporting the goods, consequently for that part of the voyage to which the merchandise has arrived, equity recommends that the freight should be paid, and for that part of the merchandise, payment ought to be made."

DE clerico admittendo.——Writ directed to the bishop, commanding him to admit the plaintiff's clerk.

DE clerico capto per statutum mercatorium deliberando.——Writ for delivering a clerk arrested on a statute merchant.

DE clerico infra sacros ordines constituto non eligendo in officium.——Writ directed to a bailiff, commanding him to release a person in holy orders who has been compelled to accept the office of bailiff or beadle.

DE clero.——Concerning the clergy.

DE coctoribus.——"Concerning spendthrifts." By the *Roman* law, a certain place in the theatre was allotted to *spendthrifts;* vide *Cic. Phil.* ii. 18. The passing of this law occasioned considerable tumult, which was allayed by the eloquence of *Cicero,* the Consul; vide *Cic. Att.* ii. To this it is probable *Virgil* alludes: vide. *Æn.* i. 125.

DE comitibus legatorum.——Of the courts of bequests.

DE communi consilio super negotiis quibusdam, arduis et urgentibus regem, statum, defensionem regni Angliæ, ecclesiæ Anglicanæ concernentibus.——Of the general council upon certain important and urgent concerns, relating to the king, the state, defence of the kingdom of *England* and the church of *England.*

DE comon droit.——Of common right.

DE compoto.——Of accounting.

DE concionibus.——Relating to the assemblies (or public orations).

DE confes.——Canon law in France. Such persons who died without confession were so called in former times.

DE cònflictu legum.——Of the contradiction of the laws.

DE conjecturis ultimarum voluntatum.——Concerning the interpretation (or meaning) of last wills (or testaments).

DE conjunctim feoffatis.—— Concerning individuals jointly seized.

DE consanguinitate.——Concerning relationship by blood.

DE consilio curiæ.——By the direction of the court.

DE consuetudine Angliæ, et super consensu regis et suorum procerum in talibus ab antiquo concesso.——According to the custom of *England,* and by the assent of the king and his nobles anciently conceded in like matters.

DE consuetudinibus et servitiis.——Concerning customs and services.

DE continuando assisam.——Writ to continue an assize.

DE contributione facienda.——Writ for making contribution.

DE contumace capiendo.——Writ for the arrest of certain vicious persons.

DE copia libelli deliberando.——A writ for delivering the copy of a libel.

DE cornes et de bouche.——"With horns and with mouth or voice."

DE coronatore eligendo.——Concerning the election of a coroner.

DE coronatore exonerando.——Of discharging a coroner.

DE corpore comitatus.——From the body of the county.

DE corpore delicti constare opertebat; id est, non tam fuisse aliquem in territorio isto mortuum, inventum, quam vulneratum et cæsum. Potest enim homo etiam exalia causa subito mori.——The substantial part of the offence should be manifest; that is, not only that a person was found dead in that district, but (whether) wounded and slain. For a man may also die suddenly from some other cause.

DE corpore suo.——Of his own body.

DE corrodio habendo.——Writ to exact from a religious house a corody.

DE credulitate.——From belief.

DECRETA juris, justitia, veritate quæ funduntur.——The decisions of the law, which are founded in justice and truth.

DE cursu.——Of course.

DE custode amovendo.——Writ for removing a guardian.

DE custodia terræ, et hæredis.——Of the custody of the land, and the heir.

DE cy en avant.——From now henceforth.

DE damnis.——Concerning damages.

DE défaute de droit.——Of a defect of right. *Vide note.*

DE defensione juris.——Of defending the right.

DE defensione ripariæ.——Concerning the defence of the banks of rivers.

DE die in diem.——From day to day.

DEDI et concessi.——I have given and granted.

DEDIMUS potestatem.——We have given authority.

DE disseisina super dissieisinam.——Of disseisin (or intrusion) upon intrusion; or one intrusion upon another.

DEDITIO.——A surrender: a giving up.

DE dolo malo.——Of, or founded upon fraud.

DE domo reprando.——Writ to compel a man to repair his house when it was in danger of injuring the property of another.

DE donis.——"Concerning gifts, or grants." A statute so called.

DE donis conditionalibus.——Concerning conditional gifts.

DE dote assignanda.——Writ for assigning dower.

DE dote, unde nihil habet.——Concerning dower, in relation to which she has no interest.

DE ejectione firmæ.——Of ejection of the farm.

DE eo, quod quis post mortem fieri velit.——Concerning that which any one desired to be performed after his decease.

DE escæta.——A writ to recover land from a tenant who has died without an heir.

DE escambio monetæ.——Anciently a writ authorizing a merchant to make a bill of exchange.

DE esse in peregrinatione.——Of being on a journey.

DE essendo quietum de theolonio.——A writ of being quit of toll.

DE estoveriis habendis.——Of having estovers.

DE estrepamento.——An ancient writ to stop or prevent a waste in lands by a tenant, while a suit was pending against him to recover them.

DE et super præmissis.——Of and upon the premises.

DE excommunicate capiendo.——Of arresting an excommunicated person.

DE excommunicato deliberando.——Of discharging an excommunicated person.

DE excommunicato recapiendo.——Writ for retaking

an excommunicated person who had recovered his liberty without giving security to the church.

DE executione judicii.——Concerning execution of the judgment.

DE exitibus terræ.——Of the rents (or issues) of the land.

DE exoneratione sectæ.——Writ for exoneration of suit.

DE expensis militum.——"Of the expenses of knights." The name of a writ commanding the sheriff to levy the expenses of a knight of a shire, for attendance in Parliament. His allowance was four shillings per day by statute. And there is also a similar writ called "*De expensis civium et burgensium,*" or for the expenses of the citizens and burgesses, to levy for each of these two shillings *per diem.*

DE exportatis bonis.——Concerning exported goods.

DE facto jus oritur.——The law arises from the fact.

DE falso moneta.——The name of an ancient statute ordaining that persons importing false coins should forfeit their lives and goods.

DEFEAZANCE.——A conditional undertaking to annul the effect of a bond, &c.

DEFECTUS jurisdictionis.——A want of jurisdiction.

DEFENDENS tam negligenter et improvide custodivit, et carriavit.——The defendant so negligently and carelessly kept and carried (the goods).

DE feodo.——Of fee.

DE fide et officio.——Of (his) faith (or integrity) and his office.

DE fide et officio judicis non recipitur quæstio.——"No question can be entertained as to the duty and integrity of a judge." No presumption can be entertained against him, in the first instance; there must be strong and full proof of malversation.

DE fidei læsione.——Of breaking his faith (or fealty).

DE fidelitate.——Concerning fealty.

DE fide privata bello.——"Of private faith in war." In case one of the hostile parties send a flag of truce to the other, or sailors are shipwrecked; in these cases *private* faith or the law of nature must be observed.'

DE fine capiendo pro terris.——Writ for a juror who had been convicted of giving a false verdict, to obtain the release of his person and property on paying to the crown a fine.

DE fine non capiendo pro pulchre placitando.——Writ forbidding the taking of fines for beau pleader.

DE fine pro redisseisina capiendo.——Writ for the release of one in prison for a re-disseisin, on paying a reasonable fine.

DE formulis et impetrationibus actionis sublatis.——As to producing the forms and petitions of the suit.

DE foro legatorum.——Of the court of bequests.

DE frangentibus prisonam.——Of those breaking prison.

DE furto.——Of theft. A criminal appeal formerly made use of in England.

DE gestu et fama.——Of behavior and reputation.

DE gratia justiciorum.——By favor of the judges.

DE hærede deliberando illi qui habet custodiam terræ. ——Writ for delivering an heir to him who has wardship of the land.

DE hæretico comburendo.——Concerning the burning of a heretic.

DE homine replegiando.——Of replevying a man (out of custody).

DEHORS.——Out of: abroad.

DE hujusmodi malifactoribus, qui hujusmodi inquisitionibus sigilla sua apponant, et sicut dictum est de vicecomitibus, observetur de quolibet bailivo libertatis.——And it is also commanded the sheriffs to warn each bailiff of the liberty of those wicked persons who set their seals to such inquisitions.

DE idemplitate nominis.——Writ relating to identity of name.

DE idiota inquirendo.——Of making inquisition as to an idiot.

DEI, et sanctæ ecclesiasiæ.——Of God and the Holy Church.   •

DE iis qui ponendi sunt in assisis.——Of those who are to be put on assises.

DE incendio, ruina, naufragio, rate, (nave expugnata.) ——For the ·burning, loss, damage by shipwreck, for the vessel (the ship being taken by force).

DE incremento.——Of increase.

DE ingressu.——Of entry.

DE injuria sua.——Of his own wrong.

DE injuria sua propria, absque residua causa.——Of his own wrong (or injury) without any other cause.

DE injuria, vel de son tort demesne.——Of his own injury or first wrong.

DE inofficioso testamento.——Concerning an inofficious will, *i. e.* one made contrary to natural duty.

DE jactis in mare levandæ navis causa.——Concerning goods thrown into the ocean, for the object of lightening a vessel.

DE judaismo.——A statute prohibiting usury.

DE judicio sisti.——For appearance in court.

DE jure belli et pacis.——Of the law of war and peace.

DE jure communi.——Of common right.

DE jure—de facto.——"From the law : from the fact." Sometimes an offender is guilty the moment the wrong is committed—then he may be said to be guilty "*de facto.*" In other cases he is not·guilty until he be·convicted *by law,* then he is guilty "*de jure.*"

DE jure et judicio feciali.——Concerning the law (or right) and trial by heraldry.

DE jure maris.——Of the maritime law.

DE jure maris, et brachiorum ejusdem.——Of the law of the sea, and its branches (arms or rivers).

DE jure naturæ cogitare per nos, atque dicere debemus: de jure populi *Romani,* quæ relicta sunt et tradita.——By the law of nature, we ought to consider and pronounce of ourselves: by the law of the *Roman* people we should (think) of what has been left and handed down to us.

DE jure principis circa commerciorum libertatem tuendam.——Of the right of the prince as to defending the freedom of commerce.

DE la pluis beale (or belle).——An old term applied to a species of dower which was given out of the best of the husband's property.

DEL credere.——Of trust.

DELEGATA potestas non potest delegari.——A power given cannot be transferred (or assigned).

DELEGATUS non potest delegare.——A deputy cannot transfer his trust.

DE lege Rhodia de jactu.——In respect to the *Rhodian* law as to jettison (or throwing goods overboard).

DE legitimo mercatu suo.——Concerning his lawful merchandise.

DE leproso amovendo.——"As to removing a leper." An ancient writ so called.

DE levi culpa.——As to a trifling offence (or fault).

DE libera falda.——Writ of freehold.

DELIBERANDUM est diu, quod statuendum semel.—— That should be maturely considered, which can be decided but once.

DE libero tenemento.——Concerning a free tenement, or (tenure).

DE libertate probanda.——Of proving (their) freedom.

DE libertatibus allocandis.——Writ for allowing liberties.

DE licentia transfretandi.——Writ directed to the warden of a seaport, authorizing him to permit the person named in the writ to leave that port, and cross the sea upon certain conditions.

DELICTUM.——A fault, offence, or crime.

DELICTUS pro modo pœnarum, equorum, pecorumque, numero convicti mulctantur. Pars mulctæ regi, vel civitati; pars ipsi qui vindicatur, vel propinquis ejus, exsolvitur.——By way of punishment for their offences, those persons who are convicted are fined in a number of horses, and other cattle. Part (of the fine) is paid to the king, or to the state, part to him who is injured, or to his relations. *Vide note to Weregild.*

DE lunatico inquirendo.——A commission for inquiring whether a party be a lunatic or not.

DE magna assiza eligenda.——Of appointing the grand assize.

DE malo lecto.——Of being sick in bed.

DE malo veniendi.——Of being sick on his way.

DE malo villæ.——Of being ill in the town.

DE manucaptione.——Writ of mainprise.

[These were returns formerly made to writs when such cases occurred.]

DE mediatate.——Of a moiety.

DE mediatate linguæ.——"As to a moiety of the language." If an alien be tried on a criminal charge, the jury are to be "*de mediatate linguæ*," one half foreigners.

DE medio.——Writ of mesne.

DE melioribus damnis.——Of better (or greater) damages.

DEMENTIA naturalis.——Idiocy: permanent, or natural madness.

DE mercatoribus.——Relating to merchants.

DE militibus.——"Concerning knights." A statute so called.

DE minimis non curat lex.——The law regards not mere trifles.

DE minis.——Writ to compel an offender to keep the peace, where he had threatened another with either personal violence or destruction to his property.

DE minoribus rebus principes consultant; de majoribus omnes.——Concerning minor affairs, the princes (or chieftains) consult; on important matters, all deliberate. *Vide note.*

DEMISI.——I have demised (or granted).

DEMISSIO regis, vel coronæ.——The demise of the king, or the crown.

DE modo decimandi.——Of the manner of taking tithes.

DE modo procedendi contra magistrum.——As to proceeding against the master (or principal).

DE modo procedendi contra socios, scholares et discipulos, in majoribus criminibus.——As to the manner of proceeding against the fellows, scholars and learners in respect to higher offences.

DE monticollis Walliæ, duodeni legales homines, quorum sex Walli, sex Angli erunt, Anglis et Wallis jus dicunto.——Concerning the Welch inhabitants, let there be twelve lawful men (appointed) six of whom shall be Welchmen, and six Englishmen, and let them expound the law in English and Welch.

DEMORARI.——To demur.

DEMORATUR.——"He demurs: he abides." A demurrer, whilst the law proceedings were in Latin was synonymous to a *resting place*.

DE morte antecessoris.——Of the death of the ancestor.

DE morte hominis.——Of the death of a man.

DE morum honestate servanda, et dissentionibus sedandis.——Of preserving probity of morals, and appeasing disputes.

DE mot en mot.——From word to word.

DE muliere abducta cum bonis viri.——Concerning a woman taken away with her husband's goods.

DE nativo habendo.——Writ to apprehend a fugitive villain, and restore him with all his goods to his lord.

DE nautico fœnore.——Of nautical interest, usury or bottomry.

DENIQUE, cum lex *Mosaica*, quanquam inclemens et aspera, tamen pecunia furtum, haud morte mulctavit, ne putemus Deum, in nova lege clementiæ, quâ pater imperat filiis, majorem induisse nobis invicem sæviendi licentiam. Hæc sunt cur non licere putem, quam vero sit absurdum, atque etiam perniciosum reipublicæ furem, atque homicidam, ex æquo puniri, nemo est (opinor) qui nesciat.——Lastly, seeing that the *Mosaic* law, although rigorous and severe, punished theft, not by death, but only by a pecuniary penalty, we cannot suppose that God, in the new law of mercy, by which as a father he governs his children, has given us a greater license of severity against one another. These are (the reasons) why I do not consider it to be lawful—no man (I think) exists who does not know how truly absurd, and even injurious to the public (it must be) that a *thief* and a *murderer* should be punished in the *same* manner.

[This was the opinion of a philanthropist, expressed in very forcible language. For ages past penal laws have become less sanguinary; and to the honor of the United States, crimes only of the greatest turpitude are punished with death.]

DE non apparentibus, et non existentibus eadem est ratio. ——The reason is the same respecting things which do not appear, as to those which do not exist.

[This rule is applicable, as well to the arguments of counsel, as to a jury deliberating on their verdict; and although there *may* be a very strong probability that many circumstances exist, which, if proved, would give a different complexion to the case, yet, if they are not in evidence, agreeably to the rules of testimony, it would be too much for a jury to say that they were *facts.*]

DE non capiendo.——Of not taking (or arresting).

DE non decimando.——Of not being subject to tithes.

DE non ponendis in assisis, et juratis.——Of not being liable to serve on the jury, and at the assizes.

DE notitia nummi.——Of the knowledge of pecuniary affairs.

DE novo.——Anew: afresh.

DENTER omnes decimæ primariæ ecclesiæ, ad quam

parochia pertinet.——That all tithes be given to the Mother Church, to which the parish belongs. *Vide note.*

DENT operam consules, ne quid respublica detrimenti capiat.——That the Consuls use their exertions, lest the commonwealth should be injured.

DE occupatione ferarum. Feræ igitur bestiæ, et volucres, et pisces, et omnia animalia, quæ mari, cœlo, et terra nascuntur simul atque ab alio capta fuerint, jure gentium statim illius esse incipiunt: quod enim ante nullius est, id naturali ratione occupanti conceditur; nec interest, feras bestias, et volucres utrum in suo fundo quis capiat, an in alieno. Plane qui alienum fundum ingreditur venandi, aut aucupandi gratia, potest a domino, si præviderit, prohiberi ne ingrediatur.——Concerning the possession of wild animals. Therefore wild beasts, and birds, and fish, and all animals existing in the sea, the air, and on the land, when they are taken by any person, become immediately, by the law of nations, his property; for that which by natural reason was no person's property, is allowed to him who first obtains it; nor is it material whether a person take wild beasts and birds on his own soil, or on that of another. It is evident that he who enters into another's land, for the purpose of hunting, or fowling, may be prevented from doing so by the owner, if he has foreseen (his intention).

DEODANDUM.——" A gift of God." It is also a forfeiture to the king or the lord of a manor of that beast or chattel which is the cause of a person's death; and appears formerly to have been applied to pious uses and distributed in alms by the High-Almoner. Vide 1. *H. P. C.* 419. *Fleta, lib.* 1 *c.* 25. *Vide note.*

DE odio et atia.——Of hatred and malice.

DE officio coronatoris.——Concerning the office of the coroner.

DE omnibus oneribus ordinariis et extraordinariis necessitate rei.——Concerning all ordinary and extraordinary burthens or expenses (arising out) of the necessity of the case.

DE omnibus quidem cognoscit, non tamen de omnibus judicat.——It certainly takes cognizance, but does not judge of all actions.

DE pace, de plagis, et roberia.——Of (breaking) the peace, injuries and robbery. *Vide note.*

DE pace, et imprisonamentis.——As to (breaking) the peace, and imprisonments.

DE pace, et legalitate tuenda.——Of keeping the peace and for good behavior.

DE pace infracta.——Of breaking the peace.

DE pannagio.——" Of food for swine ;" the mast. Sometimes it means the sum paid for the mast of the forest.

DE parco fracto.——Concerning pound breach.

DE parendo mandatis ecclesiæ, in forma juris.——Of obeying the decrees (or orders) of the church in form of law.

DE parte domus.——Of part of the house.

DE parte sororum.——Of the sisters' share.

DE partitione facienda.——" Of making a division." The name of an ancient writ directing the sheriff to make a partition of the lands.

DE pertinentiis.——Of the appurtenances.

DE pignore surrepto furti actio.——An action to recover a pledge stolen.

DE placito transgressionis.——Of a plea of trespass.

DE placito transgressionis et contemptus, contra formam statuti.——Of a plea of trespass and contempt against the form of the statute.

DE plagis et mahemio.——" Of wounds and maihems." Maihem is the injuring a limb, or other member of the body, which would incapacitate a person in fight ; and a greater punishment than for a common wound, was inflicted, by the old law, for this offence.

DE pleine age.——Of full age.

DE ponendo sigillum ad exceptionem.——Writ for putting a seal to an exception.

DE ponte reparando.——Of repairing a bridge.

DEPOPULATIO agrorum.——The depopulating (or laying waste) of fields.

DE portibus maris.——Concerning seaports.

DEPOSITUM.——"A deposit." A thing laid down: part of the price paid by way of earnest: a simple bailment.

DE præfato Qu. hæc verba dixit.——He spoke these words concerning the said plaintiff.

DE præfato querente existente fratre suo naturali.——Of the said plaintiff being his natural brother.

DE præsenti.——Of the present time.

DE probioribus, et potentioribus comitatus sui custodes pacis.——Concerning the more worthy, and capable persons of his county (to be) keepers of the peace.

DE probioribus juratoribus.——Of a better jury.

DE proprietate probanda.——Of proving the right (to the property).

DE quadam portione decimarum.——Of a certain portion of the tithes.

DE ques en ca.——From which time until now.

DE questo suo.——Of his own acquiring.

DE quodam ignoto.——Of a certain person unknown.

DE quo jure?——By what right?

DE quo, vel quibus, tenementa prædicta tenentur ignorant.——They know not by what, or by whom the said tenements are held.

DE rationabile parte bonorem.——Of a reasonable part of the goods.

DE rationabilibus divisis.——Writ for settling reasonable boundaries between lands belonging to individuals of different townships, where a complaint of encroachment by one of the parties had been against the other.

DE receptamento.——Of harboring.

DE recordo et processu mittendis.——Writ of error.

Dᴇ re coronatore.——Of the coroner's business.

Dᴇ re corporali, in personam, de propria manu, vel aliena, in alterius manum gratuita translatio.——" A free transfer of a corporeal thing, from person to person, by his own hand, or that of his attorney, into the hand (or possession) of another."

[Alluding to the granting lands by feoffment, which was at one time the general mode of transferring real estate ; and this has its peculiar advantages. In *some* cases, by the *English* law, it bars an entail.]   Vide *Preston, &c.*

Dᴇ recto clauso.——Concerning (a writ) of right close.

Dᴇ recto de advocatione.——Writ of right of advowson.

Dᴇ recto de dote.——Writ of right of dower.

Dᴇ recto deficisse.——To be defective in right.

Dᴇ religiosis.——" Of religious persons." The name of an ancient statute.

Dᴇ reparatione facienda.——Of making reparation.

Dᴇ rescussu.——A writ which lay where persons or cattle having been arrested or distrained, were recovered from those who took them.

Dᴇ retorno habendo.——Of having a return (of cattle, &c., taken in distress.)

Dᴇʀɪᴠᴀᴛɪᴠᴀ potestas non potest esse major primativâ. ——" A delegated (or derived power) cannot be greater than the original one." Thus, a person acting under a power of attorney, can exercise no further authority than his principal could have done had he been present.

Dᴇ salva gardia.——Writ of safe guard.

Dᴇ sa vie.——Of his or her life.

Dᴇ scaccario.——Relating to the exchequer.

Dᴇ scandalis magnatum.——" Of the defamation of great men."

[An ancient statute so called, which enacted severe punishment on the offenders.]

Dᴇsᴄᴇɴᴅɪᴛ itaque jus, quasi ponderosum, quid cadens deorsum recta linea, et nunquam reascendit.——Therefore a right (or title) descends, like a heavy weight, falling downwards in a direct line, and never reascends.

[This alludes to a man's dying intestate, whose grandfather or father could not succeed to the inheritance.]

DESCENDIT itaque jus quasi ponderosum quid cadens deorsum recta linea vel transversali, et nunquam reascendit ea via qua descendit: a latere tamen ascendit alicui propter defectum hæredum provenientium.——Therefore a right (or title) descends like a heavy weight falling downwards in a direct or transverse line, and never reascends in a like manner; yet collaterally it ascends to a person for want of succeeding heirs.

DESCRIPTIO personarum.——A description of persons.

DE se bene gerendo.——For his good behavior.

DE secta ad furnam, ad torale, et ad omnia alia hujusmodi.——"Concerning suit to the oven (or bakehouse); to the malt-house; and to all other matters of this kind."

[These were services often obliged to be made by certain tenants of lords of the fee, in order that the profits might augment their rents.]

DE secta et ad molendinam, quam ad illam facere debet et solet.——Concerning suit (or service) to the mill, which he owed, and was accustomed to perform there.

DE secunda superoneratione.——Concerning surcharging a second time.

DE seisina super disseisinam.——"Of a seisin upon a disseisin, (or intrusion upon intrusion.")

[This is when a person intrudes upon land, where the tenant *himself* was trespasser.]

DE servitiis et consuetudinibus.——Of services and customs.

DE servitio regis.——Concerning the king's service.

DE scutagio habendo.——An old writ which lay against tenants to compel them to serve in the king's army, or furnish a substitute, or pay escuage, that is money.

DESIGNATIO personæ vel personarum.——A description of the person or persons.

DESIGNATIO unius personæ est exclusio alterius.——The nomination (or appointment) of one person is an exclusion of another.

DESIIT esse miles seculi, qui factus est miles Christi; nec beneficium pertinet ad eum qui non debet gerere officium.——He ceased to be a knight (or a soldier) of this world, who was made a soldier of Christ; nor does any benefit belong to him who was not obliged to perform a duty. *Vide note.*

DE similibus idem est judicandum.——" Of like things, (in like cases) the judgment is to be the same."

DE sociorum qualitatibus.——Of the qualifications of the Fellows.

DE son don.——Of his gift.

DE son tort.——" Of his own wrong." This was part of a plea very similar to *son assault demesne.*

DE son tort demesne, sans telle cause.——Of his own wrong, without such cause.

DE sormes.——From henceforth.

DESOUBS, dessous.——Under.

DESOUTH le petit seale; ne issera desormes nul briefe que touch le comon ley.——Respecting the petit seal; no writ or process shall henceforward be issued which concerns the common law.

DE speciali gratia.——Of special favor.

DE sturgione observetur, quod Rex illum habebit integrum: de balæna vero sufficit si Rex habeat caput, et regina caudam.——"As to the sturgeon, it may be observed that the king shall have it whole; but of the whale it is sufficient, if the king have the head and the queen the tail."

[The sturgeon, when chanced to be caught in the *English* rivers, belongs to the king, who gives the fisherman a fee for his trouble, often more than its value.]

DE successionibus apud Hebræos.——Concerning the right of succession among the Jews.

DE superonoratione forestariorum, et aliorum ministrorum forestæ; et de eorum oppressionibus populo regis illatis.—— Concerning the overburthening the foresters, and other servants of the forest, and of their oppressions brought on the king's subjects.

DE sylva cædua.——"Of cuttable underwood." *Sylva cædua*, means underwood, or wood cut at certain short periods of years; and therefore subject to tithe.

DE tallagio non concedendo.——Of refusing a talliage (or subsidy).

DE tempore cujus contrarium memoria hominum non existit.——"From time whereof the memory of man does not exist to the contrary."

DE tempore in tempus.——From time to time.

DE termino Hilarii.——Of Hilary term.

DE termino Sancti Michaelis.——Of Michaelmas term.

DE termino Trinitatis.——Of Trinity term.

DE terra sancta.——Of the Holy land.

DE terris acquisitis, et acquirendis.——Of lands acquired, and to be acquired.

DE terris mensurandis.——Of lands to be admeasured.

DE theolonio.——Writ of toll.

DETINET.——He keeps; he detains.

DETINUIT.——He has detained.

DE transverso.——On the other side.

DETRIMENTUM quod vehendis mercibus accidit, ut fluxus vini, frumenti corruptio, mercium in tempestatibus ejectio; quia adduntur vecturæ sumptus, et necessariæ aliæ impensæ.——Which is an injury happening to the carrying of merchandise, as the leakage of wine, the spoilage of grain, or throwing out goods in a storm; because these things increase the expense of the carriage, and other necessary charges.

DE trois puissances, dont nous avons parlé, celle des

9

juges est en quelque facon mille.——Of the three powers of which we have spoken, that of the judiciary is in some respects the greatest.

DE ulterioribus damnis.——Of further damages.

DE ultima presentatione.——Of the last presentation (to a Church Living).

DE ultra mare.——Of (the matter) beyond sea.

DE una domo, et de uno pomario.——Of one house and one orchard.

DE una mediatate.——Of one moiety.

DE uno messuagio, sive tenemento.——Of one messuage or tenement.

DE uxore abducta, cum bonis viri.——Of the wife taken away, with the husband's property.

DEVASTAVIT.——He wasted.

DEVASTAVIT, nolens volens.——He wantonly committed waste.

DE vasto facto.——Of waste committed.

DE vasto facto, et quod vastum prædict' A. fecit.——Of waste committed, and which was done by the said A.

DE verbo in verbum.——Word for word.

DEVENIO vester homo.——"I become your man." Part of the ancient homage.

DE ventre inspiciendo.——"Of examining the abdomen."

[This is the name of a writ sometimes issued by the presumptive heir at law, requiring the sheriff to summon a jury of matrons, and a jury of men (twelve of each) to inquire if the widow is pregnant or not. The matrons examine the widow, and report to the male part of the jury—the inquisition is then signed by the sheriff and the twelve male jurors, and returned to the Court of Chancery.] Vide "*Ventre inspiciendo.*"

DE veritate ponunt se super patriam pro defectu sectæ, vel alterius probationis quam ad manum non habuerint. ——"Of the truth of which they put themselves upon the country for want of suit, or other proof, which they have not at hand." The words of *Bracton* when *neither* party had proof in the suit.

De vicineto.——From the neighborhood.

De viridi et venatione.——"Of vert and hunting." Or of the green herbage or foliage, and of hunting (deer).

Devisavit vel non.——Whether he devised or not.

De vita hominis nulla cunctatio longa est.——No delay is too long when a man's life is in jeopardy.

De warrantia chartæ.——"Concerning the warranty of the deed (or grant)." There was formerly a writ so called.

De advocare.——To abandon the advocacy of a cause.

De afforest.——To discharge from the forest law.

Dealbare.——To whiten. A term used in old English law to express the converting of base money in which rents were paid into silver (while money).

Debassa.——Downwards.

Deca, decea, decha.——On this side.

Decanatus.——A deanery.

Decanus.——A dean. An officer having charge over ten. A term applied to civil and military officers as well as to ecclesiastical.

Decanus friborgi.——An officer among the Saxons having supervision over a friborg or association of ten inhabitants.

Decanus in majori ecclesiæ.——Dean of a cathedral church.

Decies tantum.——Ten times as much.

Decoctor.——A term in Roman law for bankrupt, spendthrift.

Decreet absolvitor.——In Scotch law. The decree acquitting a defendant.

Decreet arbitral.——In Scotch law. The award of arbitrators.

Decuria, or decenna.——In Saxon law. A tithing: consisting of ten freeholders and their families.

DECURIÆ.——In old European law. Marks made upon trees to designate the boundary lines.

DECURIO.——A provincial senator.

DEDI et concessi.——I have given and granted. Words of conveyance made use of in old charters and deeds of grant.

DEEMSTER.——An officer in the Isle of Man who acted as judge.

DEFENSA.——In old English law. A place fenced in for deer, and defended for that peculiar use.

DESFONTAINES.——The name of the oldest law writer in France. Pierre Desfontaines published, in 1253, his work on the French law of custom.

DEFORCE.——To keep from another, unlawfully, his freehold.

DEFUER.——To run away.

DEFUSTARE.——To beat with a club.

DEGUERPYS.——Abandoned.

DEI judicium.——The judgment of God.

DEINS.——Within.

DELICT.——A misdemeanor.

DEMENS.——One who has lost his mind.

DEMESNE.——Lands which a man held of himself, and had immediate control of, as distinguished from that held of a superior lord.

DEMI-MARK.——An old English coin of the value of six shillings and eightpence.

DEMI-VILL.——One of the smallest of the ancient divisions of England, comprising only five freemen, with their families.

DEMOLLIRE.——To demolish.

DENARII.——Any kind of ready money.

DENARIUS dei.——(In old English law) God's penny. A small coin given by parties to bind a contract between them; and so called, because it was *given* to God, that is, to the church.

DENARIUS tertius comitatus.——The third part of the fines of the county courts, and which belonged to the earl as his official due.

DERCHIEF, derechief, derichefs.——Again, moreover.

DESBLEMY.——Unblemished.

DESTRUERE.——To destroy.

DETAINER.——The withholding from another the possession of his lands or goods.

DEVISAVIT vel non?——Did he devise or not?

DEXTRAM dare.——"To give the right hand:" to close a bargain.

DICA.——In old English law. Marks or notches for accounts.

DICEBATUR fregisse juramentum regis juratum.——He was said to have broken the king's oath, (or the oath which the king had sworn to.)

DICITUR purprestura quando aliquid super dominum regem injuste occupatur ut, &c., vel viis publicis obstructis. ——"It is called a purpresture when anything is unjustly held against the king, as, &c., or by obstructions in the highways."

[The word purpresture is derived from the Fr. *pour-pris*, and means anything done to the injury of the king's demesne, or the highways, &c., by inclosures or buildings, by endeavoring to make that *private* which ought to be *public*.] Vide *Glanv.*, *lib.* 9. *c.* 11, i. *Inst.* 38. 272.

DICOLONNA.——A term used in Italian law. It is a contract made between the owner of a vessel and the captain and sailors, that the voyage shall be for their mutual benefit. The whaling ships of New England are regulated by this species of contract.

DICUNTUR liberi.——They are called freemen.

DIE intromissionis de collectione et levatione.——On the day of entry, collection and levying.

DIEM clausit extremum.——"He closed the last day."

The name of a writ which precluded the defendant from redeeming his property.

DIES amoris.——The days of grace : the Essoin days.

DIES communis in banco.——The common (or usual) day in bank.

DIES consilii.——" The day of Imparlance ;" also a day appointed to argue a demurrer.

DIES datus.——" The given day." The day or time for the defendant or tenant's answer.

DIES datus prece partium.——A day given at the request of the parties.

DIES Dominicus non est dies juridicus.——The Lord's Day is not a day for legal proceedings. *Vide note.*

DIES fasti et nefasti.——" Lucky and unlucky days."

[The *Romans* accounted certain days inauspicious, wherein no law matters were heard, nor any assemblies of the people held.] *Vide note.*

DIES fasti, in quibus licebat *Prætori* fari tria verba, "DO, DICO, ADDICO."——Lucky (or propitious) days,.in which it was lawful for the Prætor to speak three words, " I GIVE JUDGMENT, I PRONOUNCE THE LAW, I CONDEMN."

DIES in banco.——" Days in bank." Days on which the courts sit to hear motions in arrest of judgment; for new trials, &c.

DIES juridicus.——A Court Day.

DIES marchiæ.——In old English law. A day appointed by the English and Scotch to meet on the *marches* or borders to settle all disagreements and to preserve the contract of peace.

DIES non juridicus.——" Not a Court Day." Sometimes meaning a day on which business is transacted by the Judges at Chambers.

DIETA.——A day's journey. A day's work.

DIEU son acte.——God's act.

DIGNITATEM istam nacta sunt ut villis sylvis et ædibus

aliisque prædiis comparentur; quod solidiora mobilia ipsis ædibus ex destinatione patrisfamilias cohærere videantur, ex pro parte ipsarum ædium æstimentur.——They have obtained that dignity which may be imparted to villages, woods, and houses, and to other estates; but the more solid movables seem to belong to the house itself, according to the determination of the householder, and are considered as part of the edifice.

DILATIONES in lege sunt odiosæ.——Delays in law are odious.

DIMIDIETAS.——In old English law. One half.

DIMISI, concessi, et ad firmam tradidi.——I have demised, granted, and to farm let.

DIPTYCHA.——Tablets of metal, wood or other substances, in use among the Romans for writing purposes, and folded like a book of two leaves. They were more particularly used for public and church registers.

DISBOCATIO.——Anciently a conversion of wood lands into pastures.

DISCONTINUANCE nihil aliud quam intermittere, desenescere, interrumpere.——Discontinuance is nothing else than to intermit, to abate, to interrupt.

DISCOOPERTA.——Uncovered.

DISGAVEL.——(See *Gavelkind.*)

DISMES.——Another name for tithes.

DISPARATA non debent jungi.——Things unlike ought not to be joined.

DISPUTARE de principali judicio non oportet; sacrilegii enim instar est, dubitare an is dignus sit quem elegerit Imperator.——It is improper to dispute the chief judgment; for it is like sacrilege to doubt his capability, whom the Emperor has chosen.

DISRATIONARE.——To prove; to establish a charge.

[Bracton employs it in this sense. Example: et quod fecit hoc—offert se disrationare versus eum;—and that he did this—he offers himself to deraign (or prove) against him.]

DISSEIZIN.——The ouster of a tenant from possession.

DISSEIZOR.——A Disseizor: an Intruder or Trespasser: one who turns the tenant out of possession.

DISTINGUE; aut merces fuerunt æstimatæ pro certa quantitate tempore contractus assecurationis, et tunc non sumus in dubio, quia dicta quantitas æstimata solvenda est; aut assecuratio fuit facta pro asportandis mercibus salvis *Roman*, et tunc æstimatio inspicienda est *Romæ*. Aut assecuratio fuit facta *simpliciter*, de solvendo æstimationem seu valorum mercium, in casu periculi, si navis perierit, et tunc inspici debet tempus obligationis; et prout tunc valebant, debet fieri æstimatio, et *sic damnum* quod assecuratus patitur in amissione rei, non *lucrum* faciendum consideratur; lucrum non spectatur.——Mark; either the goods were estimated at a certain quantity at the time of the assurer's contract, and in such case we are in no doubt, because the said estimated quantity is to be paid for; either the insurance was made for the carriage of goods safely to *Rome*, and then the valuation should be inquired into at *Rome;* or the assurance was made *simply* as to payment of the valuation or worth of the goods, in case of danger, if the vessel be lost, and then the time of the obligation (or contract) is to be inquired into; and as the goods may be *then* valued, the estimation should be made, and *thus the injury* which the assured suffers for the loss of the commodity, not the profit which is made, should be considered, nor regard had to the advantage (which arises).

DISTRAIN.——To bind or coerce.

DISTRICTIO.——A distress: a distraint.

DISTRINGAS.——That you distrain.

DISTRINGAS ad infinitum.——That you distrain without limit.

DISTRINGAS juratorum corpora.——That you distrain the bodies of the jurors.

DISTRINGAS nuper vice comitem.——That you distrain the late sheriff.

DISTRINGAS per acras et catalla.——That you distrain by his acres (or lands) and cattle.

DISTRINGAS tenere curiam.——That you distrain to hold the court.

DISTRINXERUNT abbatum et homines suos, &c.——They bound the Abbot and his servants (by recognizance).

DIU amisimus vera vocabula rerum.——We have a long time lost the true names of things.

DIVERSA bona et catalla ipsius querentis ibidem inventæ.——Divers goods and chattels of the plaintiff there found.

DIVERSIBILIS in semper divisibilia.——A thing divisible may be forever divided.

DIVERSIE des courtes.——The difference of the courts.

DIVERSIS diebus ac vicibus.——On several days and times.

DIVERSO intuitu.——By a retrospective view.

DIVINA providentia, Terram *Walliæ*, prius nobis jure feodali subjectam, jam in proprietatis nostræ dominium convertit, et coronam Regni Angliæ, tanquam partem corporis ejusdem, annexuit et univit.——At this period by Divine permission, he appropriated *Wales*, which before was subject to us by the law of fealty, into a seigniory belonging to us, and as a part of our possession, and annexed it to the crown of the King of *England*.

DIVISIORES.——Persons among the *Romans*, who divided money among the people at elections, were called "*Divisiores.*"

DIVISUM imperium.——A divided empire: an alternate jurisdiction.

DIVORTIUM sine causa, vel sine ulla querela.——A divorce without cause, or any complaint.

DIVUS Hardrianus rescripsit eum, qui stuprum sibi, vel suis inferentem, occidit, dimittendum.——The divine *Hadrian* discharged him who killed a person attempting to violate the chastity of himself, or any of his family.

DOARIUM.——In the early law of France signifies dower, or a widow's portion of her husband's property.

DOCTOR legum mox a doctoratu dabit operam legibus *Angliæ;* ut non sit imperitus earum legum quas habet sua patria; et differentias exteri patriique juris noscat. ——A Doctor of Laws, after his degree, shall apply himself to the laws of *England;* that he be skilled in those laws, which appertain to his own country; and may know the distinction between the foreign and the national law.

DOG-DRAW.——Pursuing or *drawing* after a deer with a dog.

DOIGNE.——I give.

DOITKIN, DOTKIN, DODKIN.——A foreign coin of small value.

DOLI capax.——" Capable of mischief." Having knowledge of right and wrong.

DOLI incapax.——Incapable of fraud.

DOLIUM.——A tun, or ton.

DOLUS.——A trick used to deceive some one.

DOLUS versatus in generalibus.——Fraud lurks in loose generalities.

DOMBEC—or Domebec.——A book of local *English* customs, &c. *Vide note.*

DOMESCHE.——Domestic.

DOMESDAY—or Domesday Book.——A Book, showing the tenures, &c., of most of the lands in *England*, in the time of *William* the Conqueror. *Vide note.*

DOMESMEN.——Persons appointed to *doom*, to pronounce judgment in differences.

DOMINA.——A lady.

DOMINICUM.——The demesne: the absolute ownership or inheritance. *Vide Allodum.*

DOMINIUM a possessione cepisse dicitur.——Right is said to have its beginning from possession.

DOMINIUM directum et absolutum.——" The direct and

absolute dominion." The Seigniory or Lordship in the land. *Vide note to Allodum.*

DOMINIUM utile.——The beneficial ownership, or property in the land.

DOMINUS capitalis feodi, loco hæredis habetur, quoties per defectum vel delictum extinguitur sanguis tenentis.—— The Chief Lord of the fee stands in the place of the heir, when the blood of the tenant becomes extinct by death or offence.

DOMINUS ligius.——Liege lord.

DOMINUS non concessit.——The Lord did not grant, or demise.

DOMINUS pro tempore.——The temporary owner.

DOMINUS rerum non apparet.——The owner of the goods does not appear.

DOMITÆ naturæ.——Of a tame nature.

DOM.' proc.'——An abbreviation of Domo Procerum. "In the House of Lords."

DOMUS conversorum.——Anciently, a house established by Henry 3d., for the benefit of converted Jews.

DOMUS mansionalis Dei.——The mansion-house of God.

DONA clandestina sunt semper suspiciosa.——"Clandestine (or private) gifts are always suspicious."

" *Timeo Danaos et dona ferentes.*"

I fear the *Greeks* with presents in their hands.

DONATIO.——A gift; a donation. *Vide note.*

DONATIO feudi.——The donation (or grant) of a fee.

DONATIO inter vivos.——A gift among living persons.

DONATIO mortis causa.——A gift in prospect of death.

DONATIONES sint stricti juris, ne quis plus donasse presumatur, quam in donatione expresserit.——"Donations are of strict right, that no one be presumed to have given more than he expressed in the gift." With respect to grants the case is different.

DONATIO perficitur possessione accipientis.——A gift is rendered complete by the possession of the receiver.

Donatio stricta.——"A precise or peculiar gift." One which passes no more than is plainly expressed.

Donatio stricta et coarctata, sicut certis hæredibus, quibusdam a successione exclusis.——A donation exact and restrained respecting certain heirs, some being excluded from succession.

Donec terræ fuerint commune.——Whilst lands were in common.

Doni rationabilis.——Of a reasonable gift.

Donum gratuitum.——A free gift.

Dormit aliquando jus moritur nunquam.——A right sometimes sleeps, but never dies.

Dos.——Dower: Money or other property given or settled on a marriage. *Vide note.*

Dos de dote peti non debet.——Dower ought not to be sought for out of dower.

Dos rationabilis.——A reasonable (fair) dower.

Do tali tantam terram in villâ tali, pro homagio, et servitio suo, habendum et tenendum eidem tali et hæredibus suis, de me et hæredibus meis, tantum, pro omni servitio, et consuetudine seculari, et demanda; et ego, et hæredes mei warrantizabimus, acquietabimus, et defendemus in perpetuam predictam, tali, et hæredes suos versus omnes gentes per prædictum servitium, &c.——I give to such a person so much land, in such a village, for his homage and service, to have and to hold to him and his heirs, of me and my heirs, only, for all service, worldly custom and demands; and I and my heirs will warrant, acquit, and forever defend the same estate to him and his heirs against all persons for the aforesaid service, &c.

[These were part of the words used in deeds made during the feudal system.]

Dotalitii; et trientis ex bonis mobilibus viri.——Of dower; and a third part of the husband's goods.

Dotem non uxor marito, sed uxori maritus affert: intersunt parentes et propinqui, et munera probant.——"A wife does not bring dower to the husband; but the husband to the wife: the parents and relations are present and approve the gifts."

[Sir *Martin Wright* informs us that "dower was probably introduced into *England* by the *Normans* as a branch of their doctrines of fiefs or tenures;" but how dower could assist the feudal system of tenures of land is a little mysterious.]

DOTEM unde nihil habet.——From which she has no dower.

Do tibi terram si *Titius* voluerit: si navis venerit ex *Asia:* si *Titius* venerit ex *Jerusalem:* si mihi decem aureos dederit: si cœlum digito tetigeris.——"I give you the land if *Titius* please: if the ship arrive from *Asia:* if *Titius* come from *Jerusalem:* if he give me ten pieces of gold: if you touch the sky with your finger."

[Such words as these constituted what were called *conditional* grants: wherein the fee was in abeyance till the event happened.]

DOTISSA.——A dowager.

DOUNT.——From whence.

Do ut des, do ut facias, facio ut des, facio ut facias.—— I give that you may give—I give that you may perform—I perform that you may give—I do that you may perform.

DOWER ad ostium ecclesiæ.——Anciently, a species of dower, where a man, after being affianced to his wife, endowed her with the whole or part of his lands.

DOWRY.——The property a wife brings her husband in marriage.

DOZ., dozime, dozine.——Twelve.

DRAWLATCHES.——Anciently, thieves.

DRIFT-WAY.——Path used for driving cattle.

DRINCLEAN.——Saxon word. Offerings from the tenants to provide ale, etc., for the entertainment of the lord or his steward.

DROFDENE.——From the Saxon. A grove in which cattle were kept.

DROIT d' aubaine.——The King's right of escheat of an alien's property. *Vide note.*

DROIT de bris.——In ancient times. A right which the lords living on the coast of France claimed to persons and property shipwrecked, and which were confiscated to their benefit.

DROIT des gens.——The law of nations.

DROIT—droit.——A twofold, or double right.

DROIT patent.——A patent right.

DRQITURE.——Justice.

DRUNGARIUS.——A military commander.

DRY exchange.——An expression formerly in use in English law intended to conceal the act of usury.

DRY multures.——In Scotch law. A supply of corn paid to a mill, no matter whether the one who pays grind or not.

DUAS uxores eadem tempore habere non licet.——It is not lawful to have two wives at the same time.

DUCES ex virtute sumunt.——Dukes (or leaders) receive (their honors) from their virtue (or renown).

DUCES tecum.——"That you bring with you."

[A subpœna so called when the person is commanded to produce books, papers, &c., to the court and jury.]

DUCES tecum languidum.——That you bring the sick person with you.

"DULCIA defectâ modulatur carmina lingâ,
Cantator cygnus, funeris ipse sui."
"The dying swan will with his latest breath,
Chaunt sweetest strains, and sing himself to death."

DUM bene se gesserit.——As long as he conducted himself well.

DUM deliberamus quando incipiendum, incipere jam serum fit.——Whilst we consider when to begin, it is too late to act.

DUM fervet opus.——While the business is in agitation.

DUM fuit infra ætatem.——Whilst (he or she) was under age.

DUM fuit in prisona.——"While he was in prison."

DUM fuit non compus mentis.——Whilst he (or she) was of unsound mind.

DUMMODA.——A term in ancient conveyances signifying limitation.

DUM recens fuit maleficium.——Whilst the injury was fresh.

DUM sola et casta.——Whilst she was single and chaste.

DUM sola et casta vixerit.——Whilst she may have lived chaste and unmarried.

DUM tacet, clamat.——He claims though he be silent.

DUN.——A small hill.

DUODENI legales homines, quorum, sex *Walli*, et sex *Angli* erunt; *Anglis* et *Wallis* jus dicunto.——Let twelve lawful men, of whom six shall be *Welch*, and six *English*, declare the law to the *English* and *Welch*.

DUO pene millia liborum esse conscripta, et plus quam tricentena decem millia versuum a veteribus effusa.—— "It was written in nearly two thousand volumes, and diffused in more than three millions of ancient fragments."

[*Tribonian* complained to *Justinian* of the multiplicity of law books, when directed to compose his great work on *Roman* jurisprudence, and it would appear from this extract that he had good reason.]

DUPLEX querula.——A double plea or plaint.

DUPLICEM valorem maritagii.——Double the value of the marriage. Vide *Maritagium*.

DUPONDIUS.——Two pounds.

DURANTE absentia. During absence.

DURANTE bene placito.——"During our good pleasure."

[By this tenure the *English* judges once held their seats, at the will of the Sovereign—they now hold them " *Quamdiu bene se gesserint.*"

DURANTE itinere.——During the voyage, or journey.

DURANTE minori ætate.——During minority.

DURANTE viduitate.——During widowhood.

DURANTE vita.——During life.

DURESS per minas.——Imprisonment (or compulsion) by threats.

DURSLEGI.——In ancient European law. Blows without any blood or wounds, otherwise called *dry blows.*

DUSCENS.——From the French. Two hundred.

DUSKES a chou qe.——Until that.

DUZ.——One who leads.

DY.——Just.

DYENT.——They say.

DYSNOMY.——The making of bad laws.

NOTES TO D.

DARE JUDICIUM.—The manner and circumstances of giving judgment among the *Romans* were peculiar. The pleadings being ended, (*causâ utrinque peroratâ,*) judgment was given after mid-day, according to the law of the Twelve Tables, although only one of the parties might be in court. Vide *Gell.* xvii. 2. If there were any difficulty in the case the judge sometimes took time to consider it, *diem diffindi,* i. e. *differri jussit, ut amplius deliberaret,* i. e. he commanded it to be postponed, that he might more particularly deliberate. If, after all, he remained uncertain, he said (*dixit vel juravit,* i. e. he said or swore) "*Mihi non liquet,*" i. e. I am not clear. Vide *Gell.* xiv. 2. And thus the affair was either left undetermined, (*injudicata,*) or the cause was again resumed, (*secunda actio instituta est,*) i. e. a second action was commenced. *Cic. Cæcin.* 2. If there were several judges, judgment was given according to the opinion of the majority; but it is said to have been necessary that they should be all present. If their opinions were equal, it was left to the *Prætor* to determine. The judge commonly retired, (*secessit,*) with his assessors, to deliberate on the case, and pronounced judgment according to their opinion, *ex consilii sententia,* i. e. by sentence agreeably to the opinion. *Plin. Ep.* v. *et* vi.

The sentence was variously expressed: in an action for freedom thus, "*videri hunc hominem liberum,*" i. e. it appears to me that this man is free: in an action for injuries, "*videri jure fecisse, vel non fecisse,*" i. e. it appears to have been done lawfully, or unlawfully: in an action of contract, if the cause was given in the plaintiff's favor, "*Titium Seio centum* CONDEMNO," i. e. I adjudge *Titius* (to pay) one hundred (asses) to Seius; if in favor of the defendant, "*Secundum illum litem* DO," i. e. I pronounce for the defendant. *Val. Max.* ii. 8, 2.

DECEMVIRI.—The laws of *Rome,* as of all other ancient nations, were, at first, very few and simple. Vide *Tac. Ann.* iii. 26. As luxury and wealth increased, penal laws multiplied. It has been remarked that among the citizens of a refined community, penal laws which are in the hands of the rich, are too apt to be laid on the poor; and as nations grow in years, they seem to acquire the moroseness of old age. The depraved will continually discover new modes of evading every law, and thus the multiplication of laws produces new vices, and new vices call for fresh restraints: it were to be wished, that instead of contriving new laws to punish vice; instead of drawing hard the cords of society till a convulsion comes to burst them; instead of converting correction into vengeance, that legislators would always endeavor to make laws the protector, and not the tyrant of the people. By the extension of education and morality, we should then find that many thousands of miserable souls, at present the subject of the law's *vengeance*, only wanted the hands of the *refiner*, and that many a youth, cut off in the spring of life, might, by the laws of *prevention*, have become a useful member of society. Experience has incontestably proved that early morals and education prevent more crimes than the ingenuity of man can devise. These reflections may not appear misplaced if we consider the many oppressions exercised by the *Roman* magistrates under the sanction of *multiplied* penal laws, which, in fact, are getting into fashion with us, and some of them restrict the amusements of the community, often when they are harmless and inoffensive; and youth being deprived of these, are led into secret vices and follies.

It is supposed that there was not for some time at *Rome* any written law, (*nihil scripti juris;*) differences were determined by the pleasure of the kings, (*regum arbitrio;*) according to the principles of natural equity, (*ex æquo et bono,*) i. e. agreeably to what is right and just. *Senec. Ep.* 90. And their decisions were held as laws. *Dion.* x. The kings used to publish their commands either by placing them up in public, or on a white wall or tablet, (*in album relata proponere in publico,*) i. e. placed in a public situation and reported on a tablet or white wall, *Liv.* i. 32, or by a herald. *Ib.* 44. Hence, they were said *omnia manu gubernare*, i. e. to govern all things at their pleasure. *Pompon. lib.* 2, § 3, &c. The king, however, in everything of importance, consulted the senate, and likewise the people. Hence we read of the "*Leges curiatæ,*" i. e. the court laws, of *Romulus* and of the other kings, which were also called " *Leges regiæ,*" i. e. royal laws. *Liv.* vi. But the chief legislator was *Servius Tullius*, Tac. Ann. iii. 26, all of whose laws, however, were abolished at once, (*uno edicto sublatæ,*) i. e. removed by one act, by *Tarquinus Superbus*. Vide *Dionys.* iv. 43. After the expulsion of *Tarquin*, the institutions of the kings were observed, not as written laws, but as customs, (*tanquam mores majorum,*) i. e. according to the customs of their ancestors; and the *Consuls* determined most causes, as the kings had done, according to their pleasure. But justice being thus extremely *uncertain*, as depending upon the *will* of an individual, (*in unius voluntate positum,*) i. e. placed in the power of a single person, *Cic. Fam.* xi. 16. *C. Terentius Arsa*, a *tribune* of the Commons, proposed to the people that a body of laws should be drawn up, to which all should be obliged to conform, (*quo omnes uti deberent,*) i. e. which all should use. But this was violently opposed by the *Patricians*, in whom the whole justiciary power was vested; and to whom the knowledge of the few laws which then existed were confined. *Liv.* iii. 9. At last, however, it was determined, *A. U.* 299, by a decree of the senate, and by the order of the people, that three ambassadors should be sent to *Athens* to copy the famous laws of *Solon;* and to examine the customs, institutions and laws of the other states of Greece. *Liv.* iii. 31. *Plin. Ep.* viii. 24. Upon their return, ten men (*Decemviri*) were created from the *Patricians*, with supreme power, and without the liberty of appeal, to draw up a body of laws, (*legibus scribendis,*) all the other magistrates having first abdicated their office. *Liv.* iii. 32, 33. The *Decemviri* at first behaved with great moderation. They administered justice to the people, each, every *tenth* day. The twelve *fasces* were carried before him who was to preside; and his nine colleagues were attended by a *single* officer called "*Accensus*." *Liv.* iii. 33. They proposed ten tables of the laws, which were ratified by the people at the *Comitia Centuriata*. In composing them they are said to have used the assistance of one *Hermodorus*, an *Ephesian* exile, who served them as an interpreter. *Cic. Tusc.* v. 36. As two other tables seemed to be wanting, the *Decemviri* were again created for another year, to make them. But these new magistrates acting tyrannically, and wishing to retain their command beyond the legal time, were at last forced to resign, chiefly on account of the base passion of *Appius Claudius*, one of their number, for *Virginia*, a virgin of Plebeian rank, who was slain by her father to prevent her falling into the *Decemvir's* hands. A most affecting tragedy has been written on this subject. The *Decemviri* all perished, either in prison, or in banishment.

The Law of the Twelve Tables (called *leges duodecem tabularum*) continued ever after to be the rule and foundation of public and private right, through the Roman world. "*Fons universi publici privatique juris*," i. e. the fountain of general, public, and private right. *Finis æqui juris*, i. e. the end of equal right (or law). *Tac. Ann.* They were engraven on brass, and fixed up in public, (*Leges decemvirales quibus talibus duodecem est nomen, in æs incisas in publico proposuerunt, sc. consules,*) i. e. the decemviral laws, such as are called the Twelve Tables, are engraven on brass and placed in public like counsellors. *Liv.* iii. 57. And even in the time of *Cicero*, the noble youth who used to apply to the study of jurisprudence, were obliged to get them by heart, as a necessary rhyme, (*tanquam carmen necessarium*,) vid. *Cic. de leg.* ii. 23—not that they were written in verse, as some have thought: for any set form of words, even in prose, was called "*Carmen*." *Liv.* i. 24, or "*Carmen compositum*."

It may not be irrelevant here to mention a few of the laws of the Twelve Tables: those students who wish further information are referred to the invaluable Commentaries of Chancellor *Kent*.

By the Twelve Tables the husband was allowed, with the consent of his wife's relations, to put her to death when taken in adultery or drunkenness. A pecuniary fine of three hundred pounds of brass was the punishment for dislocating a bone; and twenty-five asses of brass for a common blow with the fist. One *Lucius Neratius*, when *Rome* became rich, amused himself by striking persons in the street, and then ordering his servant who followed him with a bag of money, to pay the person assaulted.

It was declared that slanderers by words or verses should be beaten with a club. *Horace* wittily alludes to this law somewhere in his admirable poems.

The *Prætor* was to decide cases promptly by *day light;* and, if the accuser wanted witnesses, he was allowed to go before his adversary's house, and repeat his demand for *three days* together by loud out-cry.

The *Romans* had power of life and death over their children; and the right to kill a child immediately, who was born deformed; but if the father neglected to teach his son a trade, he was not obliged to maintain his father —nor was an illegitimate child bound to support the father.

Guardians and Patrons who acted fraudulently in their trusts were fined and held odious. *Fragments* of the Twelve Tables have been collected from various authors, many of them from *Cicero*, and, as they are frequently referred to by *Roman* authors, it is thought proper to subjoin some of them. They were very briefly expressed: thus,

SI IN JUS VOCET, ATQUE, (i. e. *statim*) EAT. If he summon you to court, go immediately.

SI MEMBRUM RUPSIT (*ruperit*) NI CUM EO PACIT (*paciscatur*) TALIO ESTO. If a person break a limb, unless he make satisfaction, let there be a retaliation (i. e. limb for limb).

SI FALSUM TESTIMONIUM DICASSIT (*dixerit*) SAXO DEJICITOR. If a person give false testimony, let him be thrown from the Rock. (Meaning the Tarpeian Rock.)

PRIVILEGIA NE IRROGANTO (sc. magistratus). Do not arrogate to yourself the rights of magistracy.

DE CAPITE (de vitâ libertate, et jure) CIVIS ROMANI, NISI PER MAXIMUM CENTURIATUM (per comitia centuriata) NE FERUNTO. Concerning things capital (of life, liberty and law) of a Roman citizen, nothing shall be done except by the great assembly of the Comitia Centuriata.

QUOD POSTREMUM POPULUS JUSSIT, ID JUS RATUM ESTO. That which the people enacted last, let that be accounted the law.

HOMINEM MORTUUM IN URBE NE SEPELITO, NEVE URITO. Do not bury nor burn a dead body in the city.

AD DIVOS ADEUNTO CASTE: PIETATEM ADHIBENTO, OPES AMOVENTO. QUI SECUS FAXIT, DEUS IPSE VINDEX ERIT. Go before the Gods devoutly (or with purity), not considering thy riches. He who acts contrary, God himself will be the avenger.

FERIIS JURGIA AMOVENTO. EX PATRIIS RITIBUS OPTIMA COLUNTO. Refrain from lawsuits on the holidays. Let them follow the most excellent examples (found) in the customs of their country.

PERJURII PŒNA DIVINA, EXITIUM; HUMANA, DEDECUS. The divine punishment of perjury is destruction; the human punishment is disgrace.

IMPIUS, NE AUDETO PLACARE DONIS IRAM DEORUM. Let not the impious man dare to appease the wrath of the Gods with offerings.

Several authors have endeavored to collect and arrange the fragments of the Twelve Tables. Of these the most eminent is *Jacobus Gothofredus.* According to his account, the first table is supposed to have treated of *lawsuits.* The second of *thefts and robberies.* The third of *loans* and the right of *creditors* over their *debtors.* The fourth of the right of *fathers of families.* The fifth of *inheritance and guardianship.* The sixth of *property and possession.* The seventh of *trespasses and damages.* The eighth of *estates in the country.* The ninth of the *common rights of the people.* The tenth of *funerals,* and *all ceremonies* relating to the dead. The eleventh of the worship of the Gods, and of *religion.* The twelfth of *marriages* and the rights of *husbands.*

Several ancient lawyers are said to have commented on these laws, vide *Cic. de legg.* ii. 23.—*Plin.* xiv. 13, but their works are lost.

After the publication of the Twelve Tables, every one understood what was his right, but did not know the way to obtain it; for this they depended on the assistance of their *patrons.* The origin of lawyers at *Rome* was derived from the institution of patronage; it was one of the offices of a *patron* to explain the law to his clients, and to manage their lawsuits. Hence, a wealthy and generous *Roman* took on himself a very considerable trouble, and was often waited upon by his clients at unreasonable times. *Horace* alludes to this in one of his elegant compositions.

See Sat i. on this subject, part of which *Francis* has translated as follows:

When early clients thunder at the gate,
The barrister applauds the rustic's fate;
While, by subpœnas dragged from home, the clown
Thinks the supremely happy dwell in town.

DECENNARIES.—In the reign of *Alfred,* the constitution of England appears to have undergone a considerable change; the kingdom being reduced into one regular and gradual subordination of government: one man was answerable to his immediate superior, not only for his own conduct, but for that of his neighbors: the people were classed in *Decennaries,* who were reciprocally the pledges and conservators of each other. What was called a *Hundred* appears to have consisted of ten of these *Decennaries,* and a county composed an indefinite number of these *Hundreds.* Such a legislation was a wise step for the prevention of crime.

DECIMÆ.—Tithes: from the *Sax.* "*Tvetha,*" i. e. *Tenth.*—Some law books define tithes to be an ecclesiastical *inheritance,* or property of the church, *collateral* to the estate of the lands thereof. But in others, they are more fully defined to be a *certain* part of the fruit of the lawful increase of the earth, beast and man's labor, which, *by law,* hath been given to ministers of the gospel in recompense of their attending their office. Vide 11 *Rep.* 13.— *Dyer,* 84.

Bishop *Barlow, Selden, Father Paul,* and others, have observed that neither tithes nor ecclesiastical benefices were ever heard of for many ages in the Christian Church, or pretended to be due to the Christian priesthood; and as that bishop affirms, no mention is made of tithes in the Grand Code of Canons (ending in the year 451), which is reputed to be a most authentic work; and that it thereby appears that during all that time both churches and churchmen were maintained by *free* gifts and oblations only. Vide *Barlow's Remains,* 169. *Selden on Tithes,* 82; *and Watson's complete Incumbent.*

Selden contends that tithes were not introduced into *England* till towards the end of the *eighth* century, *i. e.* about the year 786, when parishes and ecclesiastical benefices came to be settled; for it is said that tithes and ecclesiastical benefices being correlative, the one could not exist without the other; for when an ecclesiastical person had any tithes granted out of certain lands, this naturally constituted the *benefice:* the granting of the tithes of such a manor, or parish, being, in fact, a grant of the benefice, as the grant of the benefice did imply a grant of the tithes; and thus the relation between patrons and incumbents was nearly analagous to that of lord and tenant by the feudal law.

About the year 794, *Offa,* king of *Mercia,* (the most potent of all the *Saxon* kings then in *Britain,*) made a law whereby he gave unto the church the tithes of all his kingdom; which the historians tell us was done as an expiation for the death of *Ethelbert,* king of the *East Angles,* whom, in the year preceding, he had basely caused to be murdered. But that tithes were before paid in *England, by* way of *offerings,* according to the ancient usage and decrees of the church, appear from the canons of *Egbert,* Archbishop of *York,* about the year 750, and from an epistle of *Boniface,* Archbishop of *Mentz,* which he wrote to *Cuthbert,* Archbishop of *Canterbury,* about the same time; and from the seventeenth Canon of the General Council, held for the whole kingdom, at *Chalcuth,* in the year 787. But this law of *Offa* was that which first gave the church a civil right to the tithes in *England,* by way of property and inheritance; and enabled the clergy to gather and receive them as their *legal* dues by the coercion of the civil power: yet this establishment of *Offa* reached no farther than the kingdoms of *Mercia* (over which *Offa* reigned), and *Northumberland,* until *Ethelwolf,* about sixty years after, enlarged it for the *whole* kingdom of *England.* Vide *Prideaux* on *Tithes,* 166, 167. The reader will observe that those persons entitled to benefices and tithes, insist that they claim by a title as *ancient* as almost any of the Nobles' or Commoners' title to their estates. And they contend that it is as independently good and valid—that very many *laymen* have purchased tithes and advowsons in "market overt" as they would any other property at sale, and paid, perhaps, twenty-five or thirty years' purchase for them; and that, consequently, any statute, tending to injure their rights, would be most iniquitous and arbitrary. They further allege that tithes bear not so heavily on the public, as most persons on first consideration are apt to imagine; because lands which have formerly been exonerated from tithes (having been purchased from religious houses or monasteries), cannot be *now* purchased except for a much larger sum than is paid for those estates which are titheable; they further contend that if tithes were altogether abolished, and some other provision made for the clergy, and to compensate those who have *bona fide* laid out their money in the purchase of advowsons, &c., that the public, *in general,* would not be materially benefited, as the great landed proprietors would *then* lay on additional rents for their lands, and the commercial and manufacturing part of the community would be unfairly taxed to pay a remuneration to the tithe proprietors.

DE DEFAUTE DE DROIT.—This was the name of an ancient appeal brought on account of the refusal of justice. According to the maxim of the feudal law, if a baron had not as many vassals as enabled him to try by his peers, the parties who offered to plead in his court; or if he delayed, or refused to proceed in the trial, the cause might be carried by appeal to the court of the superior lord of whom the baron held, and tried there. Vide *De l'Esprit des Loix, liv.* xxviii. *c.* 28. *Du Cange voc. Defectus Justitiæ.* The number of peers or assessors in the courts of barons was frequently very considerable. It appears from a criminal trial in the Court of the *Viscount de Lautree, A. D.* 1299, that upwards of two hundred persons were present, and assisted at the trial, and voted in passing judgment. *Hist. de Langued., par D. D. de Vic. et Vaisette, tom.* iv. *Preuves, p.* 114. But as the right of jurisdiction had been usurped by many inconsiderable barons, they were often unable to hold courts. Hence arose one of the reasons for the appeal, *De défaute de droit.*

DE MINORIBUS REBUS, &c.—If we consider that the ancient tribes who overran the Roman Empire lived in an abject state, under their chiefs, we are much mistaken. It is not improbable that when the honor of a tribe was concerned, the commands of a chief were willingly obeyed—but when an expedition of any magnitude was proposed, or law about to be made, a general council was held, in which they all deliberated; the vestige of this may be seen in the *Wittenagemot* of the ancient *Saxons*—and there was, probably, among those nations, whom we are too apt to call "Barbarians," a greater degree of liberty than it is reasonable to suppose could have existed among nations almost totally destitute of literary acquirements.

DENTUR OMNES, &c.—It appears that when the Popish clergy had such an unbounded power in *England,* Laymen sometimes paid their tithes to churches *out* of the jurisdiction in which they resided; sometimes that a greater number of *masses* might be sung for their souls; at other times from private favor. This practice some of the principal prelates endeavored to abolish; and ordained that tithes, tenths and offerings should be paid to a church *near* the residence of the person paying them.

DEODANDUM.—The Deodand seems to have been *originally* designed as an expiation for the sins of such as were snatched away by *sudden* death; and, for that purpose, it is probable was intended to have been given to "*Holy Church,*" in the same manner as the apparel of a stranger, who was formerly found dead, was applied to purchase *masses, pro animæ salute,* for the welfare of his soul. And this may account for that rule of law that no *Deodand* is due where an *infant,* under age of discretion, is killed by a fall from a cart, horse or the like, *not being in motion,* whereas if an adult person fall from thence, and be killed, the thing is certainly forfeited, (vide 3 *Inst.* 57, 1 *H. P. Cor.* 422,) such infant being presumed incapable of actual sin, and *therefore* not needing a *Deodand* to purchase propitiatory masses, 1 *Comm.* 300. But if an ox, horse, or other animal, of his *own* motion, kill an infant, or an adult, or a cart run over him, they shall be forfeited as a *Deodand;* which is grounded upon this additional reason, that such misfortunes are, in fact, to be attributed to the *negligence* of the owners, and therefore they are properly punished by the forfeiture. *Bract., lib.* 3, *c.* 5. Where a thing not in motion is the occasion of a person's death, *that part* only which is the *immediate* cause is forfeited: as if a man be climbing up the wheel of a cart, and is killed by falling from it, the *wheel alone* is a Deodand. 1 *H. P. c.* 422. But where the thing is in motion, *all things* which move with it, and tend to make the wound more dangerous, are forfeited. *Hawk. P. C. c.* 26. No Deodands, however, are to be paid for accidents arising on the *high seas*; but if a person fall from a ship, or boat in *fresh* water, and be drowned, it hath been said that the vessel and cargo shall be *Deodands*. Vide 3 *Inst.* 58. 1 *H. P. C. c.* 423. Juries, however, *greatly* mitigate these oppressive forfeitures under the old law; and usually find some trifling thing, as *part* of the entire thing, the cause of the death.

DE PACE, DE PLAGIS, ET DE ROBERIA.—Mention is frequently made by historians of the Robberies and Murders committed in the middle ages. It appears from a letter of *Lupus*, abbot of *Ferrieres*, in the ninth century, that it was necessary for travellers to form themselves into companies, or caravans, that they might be safe from the assaults of robbers. Vide *Bouquet Recueil des Hist., vol.* vii. p. 515. The numerous regulations, published by *Charles* the Bald, in the same century, discover the frequency of these disorders; and such acts of violence were become so *common*, that by many they were scarcely considered criminal; for this reason the inferior judges, called *Centenarii*, were required to take an oath, that *they* would not commit any robbery *themselves*, nor protect such as were guilty of that crime. Vide *Capitul. Edit. Baluz., vol.* ii. *p.* 63, 68. The historians of the ninth and tenth centuries give pathetic descriptions of these disorders. Some remarkable passages are collected by *Matt. Jo. Beehr. Rer Mecleb., lib.* 8, 603. Indeed, they became so frequent and audacious, that the civil magistrate was unable to suppress them. The ecclesiastical jurisdiction was called in to assist. Councils were held with great solemnity; the bodies of the Saints were brought thither, and in the presence of their sacred reliques, *Anathemas* were denounced against *Robbers* and other violators of the public peace. One of these forms of excommunication, issued *A. D.* 988, is still preserved. After the usual introduction, and mentioning the outrage which gave occasion to the *Anathema*, it runs thus: "*Obtenebrescant oculi vestri; arescant manus, quæ rapuerunt; debilitentur omnia membra, quæ adjuverunt. Semper laboretis, nec requiem inveniatis fructuque vestri laboris privemini. Formidetis et paveatis, a facie persequentis, et non persequentis hostis, ut tabescendo deficiatis. Sit portio vestra cum Juda traditore Domini, in terra mortis, et tenebrarum; donec corda vestra ad satisfactionem plenam convertantur. Ne cessant a vobis hæ maledictiones, scelerum vestrorum persecutrices, quamdiu permanebitis in peccato pervasionis. Amen. Fiat. Fiat.*" Vide *Bouquet Recueil des Hist., tom.* 10, *p.* 517, *i. e.* "May your eyes be blinded, your hands withered, which committed the plunder: may all your members which assisted you become enfeebled: may you always labor and find no rest, and may you be despoiled of the fruit of your toil. May you fear and be in dismay before the face of the pursuing foe, and when no man hunteth after you; so that wasting may consume you. Let your portion be with *Judas*, the betrayer of our Lord, in the land of death and darkness, until your hearts be converted to make a full restitution. May these curses never depart from you, but follow as avengers of your crimes as long as you shall remain in the commission of your sins. Amen. So be it. So be it."

DESIIT ESSE MILES SECULI, &c.—When so many Barons and great Proprietors of Estates entered upon the Crusades, or Holy War, as it was termed, they enjoyed several immunities on that account. 1st. They were exempted from prosecution on account of *Debts*, during the time they were engaged in the holy service. Vide *Du Cange voc.* "*Crucis privilegium.*" 2dly. They were exempted from paying *Interest* for the money which they had borrowed, in order to fit them out for the sacred warfare. *Ibid.* 3dly.

They were exempted, either entirely, or during a certain time, from the payment of their *Taxes.* 4thly. They might alienate their *Lands,* without the consent of the superior Lord from whom they held. 5thly. Their *persons and effects* were taken under the protection of *St. Peter,* and Anathemas of the Church were denounced against all who should molest them, or carry on any quarrel, or hostility against them, during their absence, on account of the holy war. They enjoyed all the *Privileges* of Ecclesiastics, (being considered *"Milites Christi,"* or soldiers of Christ;) and were not bound to plead in any *civil* court; but were declared subject to the *spiritual* jurisdiction alone. Vide *Du Cange—Ordon. des rois, tom.* 1, *pp.* 34, 174, 7. They also obtained a *plenary remission* of all their sins ; and the gates of heaven were set open to them, without requiring any other proof of their penitence than by their engaging in this expedition. When we read this, we cannot refrain from deploring how far it is possible for superstition and fanaticism to triumph over reason and justice.

DIES DOMINICUS, &c.—It appears that, anciently, courts of justice sat on *Sundays.* Vide *Burrows,* 3*d vol. and Tidd,* 44. Sir *Henry Spelman* says "The Christians, at first, used all days alike for hearing of causes, not sparing, as it seemeth, *Sunday* itself." Possibly they had, at that time, two reasons for it, one was in opposition to the *Jews and Heathen,* who were superstitious about observing days and times, conceiving some to be ominous and unlucky, and others to be fortunate; and therefore *it is said* that the early Christians were more remiss in the observance of *Sunday* than is commonly supposed. A second reason probably was, that by keeping their own courts *always open,* to prevent Christian Suitors resorting to Heathen Courts of Judicature.

But in the year 517 a Canon was made. "*Quod nullus Episcopus, vel infra positus, die Dominico causas judicare præsumat,*" i. e. that no bishop or any under him should presume to try causes on the Lord's Day. And the canon for exempting *Sundays* was ratified in the time of *Theodosius,* who fortified it with an imperial constitution. "*Solis Die (quem dominicum recte dixere majores) omnium omnino litium et negotiorum quiescat intentio,*" i. e. that on the Lord's Day, (which the Elders rightly call Sunday,) it was his wish that all law suits and business should entirely cease. Vid. *Capit. Car. et Ludov.*

There are likewise several other canons taken notice of in *Spelman's* origin of terms. One of them was in the council of *Tilbury* about the year 895. "*Nullus comes, nullusque omnino secularis, diebus dominicis, vel sanctorum in festis, seu quadragessimmæ aut jejuniorum, placitum habere, sed nec populum illo præsumat coercere,*" i. e. that no Earl or other secular person shall presume on Sundays or on the feast days of Saints, or on the Quadragessima days, or on fast days, to hold pleas, nor to force persons for that purpose to come to him. Another of them was made in the council of *Erpfurd,* in the year 932, and afterwards became general, upon being taken into the body of the canon law, by *Gratian.* "*Placita secularia dominices vel alijs festis diebus, seu etiam in quibus legitima jejunia celebrantur secundum canonicam institutionem minime fieri volumus,*" i. e. we ordain that, on no account, any secular pleas be held on the Lord's Days, or on any other days, in which the lawful fasts be celebrated agreeably to canonical institution. It goes on and appoints vacations; but these were enlarged by the council of St. Medard. "*Decrevit sancta synodus, ut a quadragessima usque ad octavam Epiphaniæ, necnon in jejuniis quatuor temporum, et in litaniis majoribus, et in diebus Dominicis, et in diebus rogationum (nisi de concordia et pacificatione) nullus supra sacra Evangelia jurare præsumat,*" i. e. "The Holy Synod has decreed that from Quadragessima to the octave of the Epiphany, and also in the four times of the fasts, and in the greater Litanies, and on the Lord's days, and on Rogation days, (unless of consent and concord,) no one

152

presume to swear upon the Holy Evangelists." By which expression is meant, that no causes should be tried or pleas holden on these days. These Canons were received and adopted by the *Saxon* Kings.

DIES FASTI ET NEFASTI.—The *Pontifex Maximus* and his college had the care of regulating the year, and the public calendars (*Suet. Jul.* 40, &c.) called "*Fasti kalendares*," because the days of each month, from kalends to kalends, or from the beginning to the end, were marked in them through the whole year, and what days were "*fasti*," and what "*nefasti*," &c., vid. *Festus.* The knowledge of which was confined to the *Pontifices* and *Patricians*, Liv. iv. 3, till *C. Flavius* divulged them (*fastos circa forum in albo proposuit.*) Liv. ix. 46. In the *fasti* of each year were also marked the names of all the magistrates, particularly of the *Consuls.* A list of the *Consuls* engraved on marble, in the time of *Constantius*, son of *Constantine* (as it is thought), and found accidentally by some person digging in the *Forum* in 1545, is called "*Fasti consulares*," or the "*Capitoline Marbles*," because beautified, and placed in the *Capitol* by Cardinal *Alexander Farnese.* In later times it became customary to add, on particular days, after the name of the Festival, some remarkable occurrence. Thus, on the "*Lupercalia*," it was marked (*adscriptum est*) that "*Antony* had offered the crown to *Cæsar.*" To have one's name thus marked in the "*Fasti*," was reckoned the highest honor. *Cic. Ep. ad Brut.* 15. *Ovid. Fast.* i. 9, (whence, probably, the origin of canonization in the Church of *Rome;* and possibly of inserting the names of eminent men in the *Almanacs.*) It was the greatest disgrace to have one's name erased from the *Fasti*—Cic. Sext. 14, &c.

DOM-BEC, or DOME-BOOK. *Liber judicalis.*—This was a book composed under the direction of *Alfred*, for the general use of the whole kingdom of *England*, containing the local customs of the provinces of the kingdom. This book is said to have been extant so late as the reign of *Edward* the Fourth ; but is now lost. It probably contained the principal maxims of the common law; the penalties for misdemeanors; and the forms of judicial proceedings. This much, at least, may be said from the injunction to preserve it in the laws of *Edward* the Elder son of *Alfred*, c. 1.

DOMESDAY, or DOMESDAY BOOK.—This is a most ancient record, frequently referred to in the law books, made in the time of *William* the First, called the Conqueror, and now, or lately, remaining in the *Chapter House*, at Westminster, where it may be consulted; it is fair and legible, consisting of two volumes, a greater and a lesser; the greater containing a survey of all the lands in *England*, except the counties of *Northumberland*, *Cumberland*, *Westmoreland*, *Durham*, and part of *Lancashire*, which are said to have been never surveyed, and excepting *Essex*, *Suffolk*, and *Norfolk*, which three last are comprehended in the lesser volume. There is also a *third* book, which differs from the others in form, more than matter, made by command of the same King; the design of these books was to serve as a *register*, by which sentence might be given in the tenure of estates; and from which the noted question whether lands are held in *ancient demesne* or not, is *still decided.* It was begun in the year 1081, but not completed till 1087. For the execution of this great survey, some of the *King's Barons* were sent as *Commissioners* into the country; and juries summoned in the hundreds where the lands were situated, out of all orders of freemen, from Barons, down to the lowest Farmers, who were sworn to inform the *Commissioners* what was the *name* of each manor; who held it in the time of *Edward* the Confessor; and who held it then; how many *hides* of land; how much *wood;* and how much *pasture land* it contained; how many *ploughs* were in the *demesne* part of it; and how many in the *tenanted* part; how many *mills;* how many *fish-ponds*, or *fisheries* belonged to it; what had been added to it, or taken away from it; what was the value of the whole together in the time of King *Edward*, and when granted by *William;* what at the *time* of the survey; and whether it might be improved or advanced in its value. They were likewise required to mention the *tenants of every degree;* and how much of them each *held*, at that time, and what was the number of the slaves. Nay, they were even required to return a particular account of the *live stock* on each manor. These inquisitions, or verdicts, were first methodized in the country, and afterwards sent up into the King's Exchequer. The lesser *Domesday Book*, containing the originals so returned from the counties of *Essex, Norfolk* and *Suffolk*, includes the *live stock.* The greater book was compiled by the officers of the Exchequer, from the other returns, with more brevity, and a total omission of this article, which gave much offence to the people; probably, because they apprehended that the *designs* of the King in requiring such an account, was to make it a foundation for some new imposition; and the apprehension seems to have extended itself to the *whole* survey at that time. But whatever jealousy it might have excited it certainly was a work of very great labor, and was of considerable benefit to the public; the knowledge that it imparted to the government of the state of the kingdom, being a most necessary ground work for the many improvements in relation to agriculture, trade, and the increase of the population in different parts of the country; as well as a rule to proceed by in the levying of taxes. It was also of no small utility for the ascertaining of the right to property; and for the speedy decision, and prevention of law suits. In this light it is considered by the author of the dialogue "*De Scaccario*," as the perfection of good policy, and royal care for the advantage of the realm, and done to the intent that every man should be satisfied with his own right, and not usurp with impunity what belonged to another. He likewise adds that it was called, "*Domesday Book*," by the *English*, because a sentence arising from the evidence therein contained, could no more be appealed from, or eluded, than the final *Doom* of the Day of Judgment. This book was formerly kept under three different locks and keys; one in the custody of the *Treasurer*, and the others in the keeping of the two *Chamberlains* of the *Exchequer*. Sir *Henry Spelman* calls this book, "if not the most ancient, yet, without controversy, the most valuable monument of literature in *Great Britain*." Reference is made so frequently to this book, by the ancient law writers, that it is considered that a particular description of it would not only be entertaining but instructive. Vide *Spelman in verb.* "*Domesdei*," *et Ree's Encyclopædia*, vol. 12. A fine copy is in the State Library, at Albany, N. Y., and may be inspected on applying to John Tillinghast, Esq., the polite Librarian at the Capitol.

DONATIO.—Donations among the *Romans,* which were made *for* some cause, were called "*Munera*," as from some client, or freedman to his patron, on occasion of a birth or marriage, *Ter. Phorm.* i. Things given *without* any obligation were called "*Dona;*" but it seems these words are often confounded. At first, presents were rarely given among the *Romans;* but afterwards, upon the increase of luxury, they became more frequent and costly. Clients and freedmen sent presents to their patrons; (*Plin. Ep.* v. 14;) slaves to their masters; citizens to the Emperors and magistrates; friends and relations to one another; and that on various occasions, particularly on the *Kalends of January,* called *Strenæ;* at the feasts of *Saturn;* and at public entertainments, (*Apothoreta;*) to guests, (*Xenia;*) on birth days, at marriages, &c. *Plin. et Mart. passim.*

DOS.—Some idea may be had of the wealth of the *Flemish* and *Italian* commercial states in the middle ages. The Duke of *Brabant* contracted his daughter to the Black Prince, son of *Edward* the Third, A. D. 1339, and gave her a portion, which we may reckon of the value of three hundred thousand pounds sterling. Vide *Rymer's Fœdera*, vol. v. 113. John Galeaz-zo Visconte, Duke of Milan, concluded a treaty of marriage between his daughter and *Lionel*, Duke of *Clarence*, Edward's third son, A. D. 1367, and granted him a portion, now equal to two hundred thousand pounds sterling.

DROIT DE AUBAINE.—In many places, during the middle ages, a stranger dying, could not dispose of his effects by will; and all his real as well as personal estate fell to the King, or to the Lord of the Barony, to the exclu-sion of his natural heirs.

This practice of confiscating the effects of strangers upon their death, was very ancient. It is mentioned, though very obscurely, in a law of *Charle-magne*, A. D. 813. Not only persons, who were born in a foreign country, were subject to the *Droit de Aubaine*, but in some other countries, such as removed from *one* diocese to *another*, or from the lands of one Baron to those of another. Vide *Brussel* vol. ii. p. 947, 949. It is hardly possible to con-ceive any law more unfavorable to the intercourse between nations. Some-thing similar, however, may be found in the ancient laws of every kingdom in *Europe*. As nations advanced in improvement, this cruel practice was gradually abolished.

E.

EADEM auctoritate.——By the same authority.

EADEM curia apud *Westmonasterium* adtunct tenta exis-tente.——At the same court then holden and being at *Westminster*.

EADEM persona cum defuncto.——The same person as the deceased.

EA est in re prava pervicacia, ipsi fidem vocant.——That which is obstinacy in a depraved matter, they call honor.

EALDERMANN.——Elder man. Sax.

EANE.——Water.

EA sunt animadvertenda peccata maxime, quæ difficilime præcaventur.——Those crimes are to be particularly pun-ished, which are with difficulty guarded against.

EAT inde quietus.——" That he go thence discharged."

EAT inde sine die.——" That he go thence without day :" *i. e.* that he be discharged :

EAT sine die.——Let him go without day (or be dis-charged).

EBEREMORD.——Sax. Manifest murder.

ECCE modo mirum, quod fœmina fert breve regis, non nominando virum conjunctim roboro legis.——What new thing is this, that a woman brings the King's writ, without her husband being joined (therein) according to law!

ECCLESIA decimas non solvit ecclesiæ.——"The church does not pay tithes to herself." Thus, where lands have been granted by religious houses to laymen, tithes are not payable. These lands are called "*tithe free*."

ECCLESIÆ de feudo domini regis non possunt in perpetuum dari, absque assenu, et consensione ejus.——The churches which belong to the King in fee, cannot be disposed of in perpetuity, without his assent and concurrence.

ECCLESIA non moritur.——The church does not die.

ECDICUS.——Gr. The attorney of a corporation.

E CONSENSU patris.——By the father's consent.

E CONVERSO.——On the other hand; on the contrary.

E CONTRARIO parte.——On the other hand.

E DEBITO justitiæ.——By a debt of justice.

E DELICTO.——From (or by) the crime, or offence.

EDICTA magistratum, constitutio principis.——The ordinance of the magistracy (or civil government) is the constitution (or decree) of the Emperor.

EES.——Bees.

EFFORCER.——To aid or assist.

EFFRACTORES.——Burglars.

EFFUSIO sanguinus.——The shedding of blood.

EGO, *Stephanus* Dei gratia, assensu cleri et populi, in regem Anglorum electus, &c.——I, *Stephen*, by the grace of God, and by the consent of the clergy and people, elected to the realm of *England*.

EGREDIENS et exeuns.——Going out of the land.

EIA or EY.——Sax. An island.

EIGNE.——The first born. Sometimes Eisne or Aisne.

EI incumbit probatio qui dicit, non qui negat; cum per rerum naturum factum negantis probatio nulla sit.——The proof lies upon him who accuses, not on him who denies, as in the nature of things, the fact of the denial is no proof.

EIK.——Scotch. An addition.

EI legitur in hæc verba.——And it is read in these words.

EINECIA. Esnecia.——The right of the first born.

EINS ces que.——Inasmuch as.

EIRE, Eyre, Eyer.——The journey which the justices itinerant anciently made from one place to another to administer justice.

EJECTIONE de gardino.——In ejectment for a garden.

EJECTIONE firmæ.——"In trespass for a farm:" trespass in ejectment.

EJECTIONE firmæ n'est que un action de trespass en sa nature, et le pleyntife ne recovera son terme que est à venir, nient plus que en trespass l'homme recovera les dommages pur trespass nient fait, mes a feser; mes il convient a suer par action de covenant al comon ley a recoverer son terme; quod tota curia concessit. Et per *Belknap*, la comon ley est lou homme est ouste de son terme par estranger il avera ejectione firmæ versus cestuy que luy ouste; et sil soit ouste par son lessor, briefe de covenant; et sil par lessee ou grantée de reversion briefe de covenant versus son lessor, et countera especial count, &c.——Ejectment of farm is only an action of trespass in its nature; and the plaintiff shall not recover his term, which is to come, any more than in trespass a man shall recover damages for a trespass not committed, but to be committed; but then he must sue by action of covenant at the common law to recover his term: which the whole court agreed to. And according to *Belknap*, the common law is, that where a man is ejected of his term by a stranger, he shall have ejectment of farm (or an action of trespass) against him who ejected him; and if he be ousted by his lessor, (he shall have) a writ of covenant; and if by the lessee or grantee of the reversion, (he shall have) his writ of covenant against his lessor; and he shall count a special count, &c.

 EJECTMENT de garde.——Ejectment of ward.

EJURARE.——To abjure.

EJUSDEM generis.——Of the same kind (or nature).

ELEEMOSYNARIUM.——An almoner.

ELEGIT.——"He has chosen." A judicial writ directed to the sheriff, empowering him to seize one moiety of the defendant's lands for damages recovered.

ELEMENTA juris civili.——The elements of the civil law.

ELEMENTA juris privata *Germanici.*——The private elements of the *German* law.

ELIDERE.——To defeat the pleading of an opponent.

ELIGENDI, nominandi et appunctuandi.——Elected, nominated, and appointed.

ELIGUNTUR in conciliis et principes, qui jura per pagos, vicosque reddunt: centeni singuli, ex plebe comites, consilium simul et auctoritas adsunt.——And the principal persons (or chiefs) who declare the law in the districts and villages, are chosen in the councils: the hundredors are present at these (meetings) as Counts for the people, to advise, and also to authorize.

ELISORS.——"Chosen persons." Those appointed by the court to try a challenge.

ELOIGNED.——To remove afar off.

ELONGAVIT.——He has eloigned.

EMANARE.——To issue.

EMANCIPATIO et adoptio.——Emancipation and adoption. *Vide note.*

EMBRACERY.——The attempting to corrupt a jury.

EMENDALS.——An old word used in accounts to signify so much in bank; to supply emergencies.

EMENDATIO.——The correction of an error. *Vide note.*

EMENDATIO panis et cerevisiæ.——The assizing of bread and beer.

E MERA gratia.——From mere favor.

EMPHYTEUSIS.——A lease by which houses or lands are given to be possessed for a long period, upon condition that the land shall be *improved*, and a small yearly rent paid to the proprietor.

EMPTIONES, vel acquisitiones suas, det cui magis velit. Terram autem quam ei parentes dederunt non mittat extra cognationem suam.——A person may give his purchased or acquired property to whom he please. But the land given him by his parents, he cannot dispose of that to the exclusion of his kindred.

[This was the law of *England* for many years, until commerce and the general diffusion of learning made way for an alteration in this respect.]

EMPTIONIS, venditionis contractæ argumentum.——The proof of a purchase and sale being made.

EMPTIO sub corona.——A purchase made under a crown (chaplet or garland). *Vide note.*

EMPTOR emit quam minimo potest; venditor vendit quam maximo potest.——A purchaser buys as low as he .can; a vender sells for as much as he is able.

EN affrayer de la pees.——A breach of the peace. ·

EN autre droit.——In another's right.

EN ce cas le ley entend le properté de bestes en moy.—— In this case the law intends the ownership of the game to be in me.

EN cest court de Chauncerie, home ne serra prejudice par son mispleading ou per defaut de forme, mes solonque le veryte del mater; car il droit agarder solonque consciens, et nemi ex rigore juris.——In this Court of Chancery no man shall be prejudiced for his mispleading, or for default of form; but according to the truth of the matter; for it ought to be decided by conscience, and not by the rigor of the law. *Vide note.*

ENCHESON.——Cause; reason.

ENDITER.——To indict.

EN especes au cours de se jour.——In the coin or currency of the present day.

ENFEOFF.——To give or convey a fee or fief.

ENGETTER.——To eject.

ENGLECERY.——The fact of being an Englishman.

ENGYN.——Fraud; deceit.

ENITIA pars.——The part of the eldest.

ENKE.——Ink.

EN la defence sont iij choses entendantz: pertant quil defende tort et force, home doyt entendre quil se excuse de tort luy surmys per counte; et fait se partie al ple; et per tant quil defende les dommages, il affirm le parte able destre respondu; et per tant quil defende ou et quant il devera, il accepte la poiar de court de counustre, ou trier lour ple.——In a defence, these three things are understood: if he defends the injury and force, a man ought to consider that he excuses himself of the wrongs imputed to him by the count, and makes himself a party to the plea; and if he defends the damages, he admits that the party is able to answer; and if he defends when and where he ought, he acknowledges the power of the court to acknowledge, or try the plea.

ENLARGER l' estate.——To enlarge the estate, or interest.

EN le per.——In the post.

EN pleyn vie.——In full life.

EN poigne.——In hand.

EN primes.——In the first place.

ENPROUER.——To improve.

ENS.——Existence.

ENSEMENT.——Likewise.

ENSENSES.——Instructed.

ENSIENT per A.——Pregnant by A.

ENSY, ensi.——Thus; so.

ENTENCION.——A plaintiff's declaration.

ENTERLESSE.——Omitted

ENTRE.——Entry.

Entrebat.——An interloper.

Entrelignure.——Interlining.

Enure.——To take effect.

Enveer.——To send.

En ventre sa mere.——In the womb.

Eo instanti.——At this instant; immediately.

Eo intuito.——With that view (or intent).

Eo ligamine quo ligatur.——By that tie by which he (or it) is bound.

Eo maxime præstandum est, ne dubium reddatur jus domini, et vetustate temporis obscuretur.——That is principally to appear, lest the right of the lord be rendered doubtful and obscured by the antiquity of time.

Eo nomine et numero.——Under that name and number (or amount).

Eo quod desiit esse miles seculi qui factus est miles Christi: nec beneficium pertinet ad eum qui non debet gerere officium.——Because he declined to be a soldier of this world who was made a champion of Christ; nor should he receive any advantage who ought not to do the duty.

Eo quod tenens in faciendis servitiis per biennium jam cessavit.——Because the tenant has ceased to perform service for two years.

Eorum enim merces non possunt videri servandæ, navi jactæ esse, quæ periit.——For their goods cannot be understood to be preserved, which were thrown out of the vessel, which was lost.

Eos qui negligenter ignem apud se habuerint, fustibus, vel flagellis cædi.——That those who negligently carry fire with them, be beaten with clubs or sticks.

Eos qui opibus valebant multos habuisse devotos quos secum ducerunt in bello, soldurios sua lingua nuncupatos; quorum hæc est conditio, ut omnibus invita commodis una cum his fruantur, quorum se amicitiæ dediderint, si quid iis per vim accedat, aut eundem casum, una ferant, aut sibi mortem consiscant.——That those who were rich had many devoted to them, whom they took with them to the war, called in their own language, soldiers, whose condition was such, that they could enjoy all advantages in life, in company with those to whom they had pledged their friendship; and that if anything happened to them from violence, or any other cause, that they might suffer together, even if it led to their death.

EOTH.——The *Saxon* word for an oath.

EPISCOPI, sicut cæteri barones, debent interesse judiciis cum baronibus, quosque præveniantur ad diminutionem membrorem vel ad mortem.——The Bishops, as well as the other barons, ought to be present at judgment with the Lords, unless prevented on account of loss of limb or death. *Vide note.*

EQUES.——A Knight. *Vide note.*

EQUITAS sequitur legem.——Equity follows the law.

EQUITES aurati.——Knights with gilt spurs.

EQUITES Garterii.——Knights of the order of the Garter. *Vide note.*

ERANT in Angliæ quodammodo tot reges, vel potius tyranni, quot domini castellorum.——There were in *England*, in a certain degree, as many kings or rather tyrants, as lords of castles. *Vide note.*

ERANT omnia communia, et indivisa omnibus, veluti unum cunctis patrimonium esset.——All things were common and undivided to all, as if it were one inheritance for the whole.

ERAT autem hæc inter utrosque officiorum vicissitudo, ut clientes ad colocandas senatorum filias de suo conferrent; in æris alieni dissolutionem gratuitam pecuniam darent; et ab hostibus in bella captos redimerent.——For there was this interchange of (good) offices between them, that the clients should contribute from their property, to portion the daughters of the senators: that they would give a voluntary sum for the payment of their debts: and

11

redeem captives from the enemy when taken in war.   *Vide note.*

ERCISCERE.——To divide.

E RE nata.——Arising from that business.

ERGO ita existimo hanc rem manifeste pertinere ad eversionem juris nostri, ac ideo non esse magistratus hæc obligatos é jure gentium ejusmodi nuptias agnoscere, et ratas habere.   Multoque magis statuendem est eos contra jus gentium facere videri, qui civibus alieni imperii sua facilitate jus patriis legibus contrarium scienter violenter impertiunt.——Therefore I consider that this thing clearly tends to the overthrow of our law, and on that account the magistrates are not to acknowledge by the law of nations the obligations of such marriages, and to confirm them.   And much more is it to be resolved, that those who appear to do these things, act contrary to the law of nations, as knowingly and rashly bestowing (marriage ceremonies) with such facility on the citizens of another dominion, contrary to the laws of their own country.

ERIACH.——In Irish law, the pecuniary satisfaction which a murderer was obliged to make to the friends of the murdered.

ERIGIMUS.——We erect.

ERROR fucatus nuda veritate in multis est probabilior; et sæpenumero rationibus vincit veritatem error.——Error artfully disguised is, in many cases, more probable than naked truth; and frequently error overwhelms truth by its show of reasons.

ERROR qui non resistitur approbatur.——An error which is not resisted, is approved.

ERUDITUS in lege.——" Learned in the law." A counsel.

ESBRANCATURA.——A cutting off the branches of trees.

ESCÆTA.——An escheat.

ESCAMBIUM.——Exchange.

ESCHAPER.——To escape.

ESCHEAT.——The reverting of lands to the state upon the death of the owner without heirs. *American law. Kent's Commentaries.*

ESCHIER.——To fall to.

ESCHUER.——To eschew.

ESCOTER.——To pay.

ESCRIE.——Notorious.

ESCROW.——A deed or writing left with another, to be delivered on the performance of something specified.

ESCU.——A shield or buckler.

ESCUAGE.——" Scutage—Knight's service." One of the ancient tenures of land.

ESKIPPAMENTUM.——In old English law, tackle of ships.

ESKIPPER.——To ship.

ESLISOR.——Elector.

ESPLEES.——Full profits of land.

ESSART.——Woodland turned to tillage.

ESSE optime constitutam rempublicam, quæ ex tribus generibus illis, regali, optimo, et populari, sit modice confusa. ——That government is best constituted, which is moderately blended with these three general things, the regal, aristocratic, and the democratic (orders).

ESSENDI quietum de theolonio.——A writ of exemption from toll.

ESSOINER.——To excuse.

ESSOINDAY.——The first general day of the term when the courts anciently sat to receive *essoins* or excuses, for parties not present, who had been summoned to appear.

EST autem magna assiza regale quoddam beneficium, clementia principis, de concilio procerum, populis indultum; quo vitæ hominum, et status integritatis tam salubriter consulitur, ut, retinendo quod quis possidet in libero tenemento suo, duelli casum declinare possint homines ambiguum. Ac per hoc continget, insperatæ et prematuræ mortis ultimum evadere supplicium, vel saltem perennis infamiæ opprobrium illius infesti et inverecundi *verbi*, quod

in ore victi turpiter sonat consecutivum.   Ex equitate item
maxima prodita est legalis ista institutio.   Jus enim, quod
post multas et longas dilationes vix evincitur per duellum,
per beneficium istius constitutionis commodius et accelera-
tius expeditur.——" For the great assize is a certain royal
benefit granted to the people by the clemency of the
prince, with the advice of the great men; by which the
lives of persons, and the state of their condition, are so
wholesomely consulted, that, retaining what each possesses
in his own freehold, men may decline the doubtful chance
of single combat.   And in this manner it happens that
they may avoid the ultimate punishment of an unexpected
and premature death; or, at least, the disgrace of the enduring reproach of that odious and. shameful *word*, which
sounds dishonorably upon the lips of the vanquished.
Therefore, from the greatest equity was that legal institution framed.   For the right, which, after many long delays,
could scarcely be shown by single combat, by the benefit
of this institution, is more advantageously and speedily decided."

[The author of this extract is here speaking of the horrible trial of the right to land, by *Single Combat*, the particulars of which are found in *Black. Comm.*   The odious
word above referred to, which the vanquished uttered, was
" *Craven*," upon which it was decided that he had lost his
cause.   The word *Craven* is even now used in many parts
of *England*, and means " *a Coward*."]   *Vide note.*

Est boni judicis ampliare jurisdictionem.——It is the
part of a good judge to extend the jurisdiction.

Est enim ad vindicanda furta nimis atrox, nec tamen ad
refrenanda sufficiens; quippe neque furtum simplex tam
ingens facinus est, ut capite debeat plecti; neque ulla pœna
est tanta, ut ab latrociniis cohibeat eos qui nullam aliam
artem quærendi victus habent.——(The law) is certainly
too severe in punishing thefts, nor yet is it sufficient to restrain them, for surely a simple theft is not so heinous an

offence as to merit a capital punishment ; nor is any punishment so great that it can restrain those persons from
committing robberies, who have no other mode of seeking
a livelihood.

ESTENDRE.——To extend.

ESTENTE.——Extent.

ESTERLING, STERLING.——English silver penny.

ESTOPPEL.——" A stop :" a preventive plea.

ESTOVERIA ædificandi, ardendi, arandi, et claudendi.——
Estovers for building, burning, ploughing, and for inclosing.

ESTOVERS.——Wood cut from a farm by the tenant,
which by the common law he has a right to use on the estate for necessary purposes.

EST quidem alia præstatio, quæ nominatur *Heriettum ;*
ubi tenens, liber, vel servus, in morte sua, dominum suum,
de quo tenuerit respicit, de meliori averio suo, vel de secundo meliori, secundem diversum locorum consuetudinem.
Magis fit de gratia, quam de jure.——" There is, however,
another service, called *Herriot* service, where the tenant
(whether) a freeman or vassal, considers that on his decease, the lord of whom he holds is entitled to the best
beast, or the second best, according to the custom of different places. It is done more out of favor than of right."

[These Herriots are due, in many places in *England*, and
are now generally compounded for by a pecuniary fine.]

ESTREITE.——Straitened.

ESTREPAMENTUM.——Injury done by a tenant for life
upon lands or woods.

EST senatori necessarium novi rempublicam ; isque late
patet ; genus hoc omne scientiæ, diligentiæ, memoriæ est ;
sine quo paratus esse senator nullo pacto potest.——It is
necessary for a senator to be acquainted with the constitution ; and this is a knowledge of an extensive nature ; one
of science, diligence and reflection, without which a senator cannot possibly be fit for his office. *Vide note.*

ET ad ea quæ frequentius occurrunt.——And respecting those things which more frequently happen.

ET adhuc detinet.——And he still retains.

ET ad omnia al' statut' contra decoctor' edit, et sic idem *Johannes* et *Eleanora*, vigore stat' prædict' parliament' dict' dom' Reginæ nunc edit', dicunt quod causa action' prædict' accrevit præfat' *Miles*, antequam idem *Johannes Williams* devenit decoctor'; et hoc parat' sunt verificare; unde pet' jud' si prædict' *Miles* action', &c.——And against all the other statutes made against bankrupts, and therefore the same *John* and *Eleanor* by force of the aforesaid statutes now passed in the said Parliament of our said lady the Queen, say that the cause of the said action accrued to the aforesaid *Miles*, before the said *John Williams* became a bankrupt; and this they are ready to prove, wherefore they pray judgment of the said *Miles* (should maintain) his action, &c.

ET alii non venerunt, ideo respectuentur.——And the others do not appear, therefore they are respited.

ET cum duo jura in una persona concurr', æquam est ac si essent in diversis.——And when two rights blend together in one person, this is equitable, although they were (derived) from several sources.

ET curia consentiente.——And the court agreeing.

ET damna, et quicquid quod ipse defendere debet, et dicit, &c.——And the damages, and whatever he should defend, and says, &c.

ET de hoc ponit se super patriam.——And of this he puts himself upon the country.

ET de jure hospitalis.——And concerning the law of the hospital.

ET dona claud' sunt semp' suspiciosa.——And private gifts are always suspicious.

ET ego, et hæredes mei, &c., warrantizabimus.——And I, and my heirs, &c., will warrant. *Vide note.*

ET ejectione firmæ.——And in ejectment of farm.

ET fuit dit que le contraire avait estre fait devant ces heures.——And it was said that the contrary had been done in former times.

ET gist touts temps deins l'an et jour.——And it always lies within a year and a day.

ET hæredibus de carne sua.——And to the heirs of her body.

ET hæredibus eorum communibus (vel) hæredibus ipsius uxoris tantum.——And to their general heirs (or) to the heirs of the wife only.

ET hoc paratus est verificare per recordum.——" And this he is ready to verify by the record."

[This was part of an ancient plea, where in support thereof the defendant appealed to the record.]

ET hoc petit quod inquiratur per patriam.——And this he prays may be inquired of by the country.

ET hoc sequitur.——And this follows.

ETIAM consentientibus.——Likewise to those who agree.

ETIAMSI ad illa, personæ consueverint, et debuerint per electionem, aut quem vis alium modum, assumi.——Although as to those matters, persons had been used, and ought to take them by election, or (by) some other mode.

ET ideo dicuntur liberi.——And therefore they are called (or declared to be) freemen.

ET impotentia excusat legem.——" And inability excuses (or avoids) the law."

[Thus, if a man enter into a bond that a ship shall sail to the *East Indies* on a specified day, and the ship be destroyed before that day by lightning, &c., the bond is void; *et sic de similibus.*]

ET inde producit sectam.——And thereupon he produces suit.

ET in majore summa continetur minus.——And in the greater sum the less is included.

ET issint.——And so.

ET legitimo modo acquietatus.——And in a legal manner discharged.

ET lex plus laudatur, quando ratione probatur.——And law is the more praiseworthy when it is approved by reason.

Et modo ad hunc diem venit.——And in this manner he came to the day (or to the end).

ET non alibi.——And in no other place.

ET omnes comites et barones *una voce* responderunt "Quod nolunt leges *Angliæ* mutare, quæ hucusque usitatæ sunt et approbatæ."——And all the Earls and Barons *unanimously* shouted "That they would not change the laws of *England*, which heretofore have been used and approved."

ET personaliter, libere, et debito modo resignavit.——And he resigned in person, freely, and in due manner (or form).

ET petit judicium de narratione illa et quod narratio illa cassetur.——And he prays judgment of that declaration (or count), and that the same may be quashed.

ET petunt judicium de breve, et quod breve illud cassetur.——And they crave judgment concerning the writ, and that the same may be quashed.

ET prædictos cives a tempore prædicti mandati Regis eis directi majoribus districtionibus graverunt, &c.——From the time of the said command of the King to them directed, they burthened the said citizens with heavy fines (or distresses).

ET prædictus *A. B.* similiter.——"And the said *A. B.* (doth) the like.

ET prædictus quærens in propria persona sua, venit, et dicit, quod ipse placitum suum præd' versus præd' defenden, ulterius prosequi non vult; sed ab inde omnino se retraxit.——And the said plaintiff in his proper person comes and says, that he will not farther prosecute his said suit against the said defendant; but from thence has altogether withdrawn himself.

ET probat *Johannes de Evia*, &c., quod hoc extendet in casu, quo merces fuerint deperditæ, una cum navi, et certa pars ipsarum mercium postea salvata et recuperata; tunc naulum deberi pro rata mercium, recuparatarum, et pro ·rata itineris usque ad locum, in quo casus adversus accide-rat, fundat, &c.——And *John of Evia* proves that this ex·tends to a case in which the goods were lost, together with the vessel, and that a certain part of these goods were sub-sequently recovered and saved; then he proves that the .freight is due, according to the proportion of the goods recovered, and the proportion of the journey (made) to-wards the place where the accident happened, &c.

ET quia, per veredictum juratorum, invenitur quod præ-dictus *Robertus* non habuit accessum ad predictam *Beretri-cem* per unam mensem ante mortem suam, per quod *magis* præsumitur contra prædictum *Henricum.*——And because, by the verdict of the jury it is found that the said *Robert* had no access to the said *Beretrice* for one month prior to her death, by which it is the *more* fully presumed against the said *Henry.*

ET quia prædictus *Johannes* cognoscit dictam literam per se scriptam *Roberto de Ferrers*, &c.——And because the said *John* knows that the said letter written by him to *Roberto de Ferrers*, &c.

ET quod hujusmodi deputatus, &c.——And for which purpose he was deputed, &c.

ET quod non habet principium, non habet finem.—— And what hath not a beginning, hath no end.

ET regali dignitate coronæ regni *Angliæ* perpetuis tem-poribus annexa, unita, et incorporata.——And by the royal dignity, at· all times, annexed to the crown, and the king-dom of *England,* sole and incorporate.

ET respondere debet quousque, &c.——And that he should answer until, &c.

ET sciendum quod possessionum, quædam nuda pedum positio, quæ dicitur intrusio, et dicitur nuda, eo quod non vallatur aliquo vestimento, et minimum habet possessionis, et omnino nihil juris, et in parte habet naturam disseisinæ, et in quibusdam sunt dissimiles ; quia ubicunque est disseisina ibi quodammoda est intrusio, quantum ad dissertorem, sed non e contrario, quia ubicunque est intrusio, ibi non est disseisina, propter vacuam possessionem. Et in utroque casu possessio est nuda, donec ex tempore et seisina pacifica acquiratur vestimentum.——And be it known, that as to possessions, some being a (mere) naked foothold, which is called an intrusion, and said to be naked, because it is not clothed with any investiture, and has the least (kind) of possession, and altogether devoid of right, and has in part the nature of a disseisin, though in certain respects, dissimilar ; because wherever there is a disseisin, there is, after a certain manner, an intrusion, so far as relates to the disseisor ; but not on the contrary, for wherever there is an intrusion, there is no disseisin, on account of the vacant possession. And in either case, the possession is naked, until, by time, and a peaceable possession, an investiture be acquired.

ET scire feci *W. H.* filio hæredi predict' *M.* le Cognizor. ——And I have warned *W. H.* the son and heir of the aforesaid *M.* the Cognizor.

ET semble.——And it seems.

ET sequitur aliquando pœna capitalis ; aliquando perpetuum exilium, cum omnium bonorum ademptione.—— And sometimes a capital punishment follows ; sometimes perpetual exile, with confiscation of all the goods.

ET sic de similibus.——And so of the like (matters).

ET sic ultra.——And so on the other part : or on the contrary.

ET sic vide que livery dun fait dun enfant nest semple al livery de terre ou biens per luy.——And thus see that the delivery, which a person makes on the part of an infant, is not a simple delivery of lands or goods made by himself.

ET si forte exceperint, quod non tenentur, sine brevi originali, respondere.——And if by chance they be taken, that they are not bound to answer without an original writ.

ET si homo prist certain aubres, et puis el fait boards de eux, uncore le owner port eux reprender; quia major pars substantiæ remanet.——And if a man takes certain trees, and converts them into boards, the owner may take them again, because the principal part of the substance remains.

ET si la nef etoit preste au fair voyage, elle ne doit pourt demeurrer pour ley; et s'il querit, il doit avoir son loyer tout comptant, en rabutant les frais, si le maitre luy en afait. Et s'il meurt, sa femme et se prochains le doivent avour pour luy.——And if the vessel be ready to proceed on the voyage, she should not wait for him; and if he require he should have all his wages paid him, after deducting the expenses, if the master has been put to any; and if he die, his wife and children should receive them instead of him.

ET si navis in causa prædicta mutaverit iter, vel cepit secundum viagium; vel convenit asportare alias merces in alium locum; vel alias assecurationes fecerit pro dicto secundo viagio, tunc in casibus prædictis assecuratores pro primo viagio amplius non tenentur. Ita probat.——And if a ship, in the case before mentioned, shall have changed her voyage; or taken a second voyage; or agreed to carry other goods to another place; or made other insurances for the said second voyage, then, in the cases aforesaid, the assurers for the first voyage are no longer bound.—So it is proved.

ETSI non prosunt singula, juncta juvant.——Although individually the effect is wanting, yet collectively it is powerful.

ET si super totum, &c.——And if upon the whole, &c.

ET stet nomen universitatis.——And the name of the corporation may stand.

ET suis, post ipsum, jure hæreditario perpetue possidendum.——And to them, after his decease, to be forever possessed by hereditary right.

ET, traditio libro, legit ut clericus.——"The book being delivered him, he reads like a clerk (or clergyman)."

[This was a test formerly used when a criminal claimed the benefit of clergy, the book was delivered him, and if he could read in it, he was entitled to the privilege of clergy.]

ET ubi eadem est ratio, idem est jus.——And where the same is reason it is also law.

EUANGELIES.——The evangelists.

EUM qui noscentum infamat, non est æquum et bonum ob eam rem condemnari; delicta enim nocentium nota esse oportet et expedit.——It is not just and right, on that account, to condemn him who slanders a bad man; for it is proper and expedient that the delinquencies of wicked men should be exposed.

EUNDO, redeundo, et morando.——In going, returning, and staying.

EVERWYK.——York.

EVESCHE.——Diocese. EVESQUE.——A bishop.

EVICTUM perpetuum.——A perpetual eviction; or ouster of possession.

EVIDENTISSIMIS probationibus ostenditur testatorem multiplicasse legatum voluisse.——By the most evident proofs it was shown that the testator was desirous to increase the legacy.

EW.——Marriage. EWBRICE.——Marriage breach. *Sax.*

EWA.——Law.   Old German and Saxon law.

EWAGE.——Toll paid for water passage.

EWE.——Water.

Ex abundanti cautela.——From great (or abundant) caution.

Ex abusu non arguitur ad usum.——No argument can be drawn from the abuse (of a thing) against its use.

EXADONIARE.——To manumit.

Ex æquo et bono.——In justice and honesty.

Ex antecedentibus et consequentibus fit optima interpretatio.——By what precedes and follows the surest interpretation is obtained.

. Ex arbitrio judicis.——At the will of the judge.

Ex assensu omnium tenentium.——By the consent of all the tenants.

Ex assensu patris.——With the father's consent.

Ex assensu suo.——Of his own accord (or assent).

EXCADENTIÆ.——Escheats.

Ex causa furtiva.——From a secret cause.

Ex causa metus.——On account of fear.

EXCEPTA dignitate regali.——Saving the royal dignity.

EXCEPTIO ad breve prosternendum.——A plea in abatement.

EXCEPTIO doli mali.——A plea of fraud.

EXCEPTIO ejusdem rei cujus petitur dissolutio.——An exception of the same thing which is sought to be dissolved.

EXCEPTIO jurisjurandi.——An exception, or plea of oath.

EXCEPTIO probat regulam.——The exception proves the rule.

EXCEPTIO rei adjudicatæ.——An exception to the matter adjudged.

EXCEPTIO rei venditæ et traditæ.——A plea that the article claimed was sold and delivered to the defendant.

EXCEPTIO semper ultima ponenda est.——The exception is always to be placed the last.

EXCEPTIO pecuniæ non numeratæ.——An exception of money not paid.

EXCEPTIS viris religiosis.——Clergymen excepted.

EXCEPTO eo solo quod damno fatali, aut vi majore,

veluti naufragio, aut piratarum injuria perisse constat.——
That only excepted, which by an irremediable loss, or by
a greater fury, as by shipwreck, or injury received from
pirates, is destroyed.

Ex certa scientia, et mero motu.——From positive knowledge (or information), and from mere will (or pleasure).

Excessus in jure reprobatur.——Excess in the law is
condemned.

Exclusa.——A sluice for carrying off water.

Excommunicato capiendo.——" Of arresting an excommunicated person :" a writ so called.

Ex concessis.——From matters conceded.

Ex contractu, multis modis; sicut ex conventione, &c.;
sicut sunt pacta conventa quæ nuda sunt aliquando, aliquando vestitæ, &c.——In several modes, by way of contract; as well as by agreement; as also by way of covenants agreed upon, which are sometimes without, and
sometimes with a consideration, &c.

Ex contractu, vel ex delicto.——From, or by, a contract,
or from an injury (or offence).

Ex debito justitiæ.——By (or on account of) a debt to
justice.

Ex debito vel merito justitiæ, vel ex gratia.——From a
debt or reward of justice, or from favor.

Ex delicto, quasi ex contractu.——From (or by) an offence (or crime) as though it were by way of contract.

Ex demissione.——From, or on the demise.

Ex dicto majori.——From (or by) the more important
expression.

Ex dicto majoris partis juratorum.——By the verdict
of the major part of the jury.

[In ancient times, if the jury (in civil causes) were not
unanimous, the majority might give a verdict, and judgment was given *Ex dicto majoris partis juratorum;* nay,
jurors might even bring in a verdict upon their *belief* only.
Vide *Reeve's Hist.,* ii. 268.]

Ex directo.——By a direct course.

Ex dolo malo non oritur actio.——No action can be founded on a deceit.

Ex donatione regis.——By the king's gift.

Ex donationibus, servitia militaria vel magnæ serjentiæ non continentibus, oritur nobis quoddam nomen generale, quod est "Soccagium."——From grants, not containing Knight's services, or grand Serjeantries, a certain general name arises for us, which is "Socage."

[This was the name of a certain tenure of land in the feudal times, now extinct, or nearly so.]

Ex eadem lege descendit, quod dominus sine voluntate vassalli feudum alienare non potest.——It follows that by the same law, the lord cannot alienate the fee without the vassal's consent.

EXEANT seniores duodecim thani, et præfectus cum eis, et jurent super sanctuarium quod eis in manus datur, quod nolint ullum innocentum accusare, nec aliquem noxium celare.——That twelve chief landholders (or thanes) and the sheriff with them, go and swear upon the holy testament, which is delivered into their hands, that they will not accuse any innocent person, nor screen the guilty.

EXEAT aula qui vult esse pius.——Let him who would be a good man retire from court.

EXECRABILE illud statutum.——That abominable statute.

EXECUTIO est fructus, finis et effectus legis.——Execution is the fruit, the end and effect of the law.

EXECUTIO juris non habet injuriam.——The execution of the law does no injury.

EXECUTOR de son tort.——"An executor of his own wrong:" one who acts illegally under a will.

Ex empto.——Founded on purchase.

" EXEGI monumentum, ære perennius,
    Regalique situ pyramidum altius:
    Non omnis moriar; multaque pars mei
    Vitabit libitinam."

"To my own name this monument I raise,
High as the Pyramids, and strong as brass,
Which neither storms, nor tempests shall deface;
This shall remain whilst time glides nimbly by,
And the swift years in measured stages fly;
For I 'll not perish; not entirely die."

Oldsworth.

Ex facto.——From (or by) the deed.

Ex facto oritur jus.——The law arises from the fact.

Ex fructibus prædiorum, ut blada, fœnum, &c., seu ex fructibus arborum, ut poma, pyra, &c.——From the profits of the estates, as the grass, hay, &c., or from the fruits of the trees, as apples, pears, &c.

Ex furto, rapina, damna, injuria.——By theft, robbery, damage, and (personal) violence. *Vide note.*

Ex gratia curiæ.——By favor of the court.

Ex gravi querela.——From or on the grevious complaint.

Ex hæreditate.——From the inheritance.

Ex hoc jure gentium, omnes pene contractus introducti sunt.——According to this law of nations, almost all contracts are introduced.

Ex hypothesi.——By way of supposition (or argument).

EXIGENT.——A writ preceding excommunication.

EXIGI facias.——That you cause to be exacted (or demanded).

Ex industria.——On purpose.

Ex institutione legis.——By the institution of the law.

Ex integro.——Anew.

EXISTENS.——Being: remaining.

Ex justa causa.——For a good reason (or cause).

Ex legibus.——According to the laws.

EXLEX.——An out-law.

Ex locato.——From situation.

Ex maleficio non oritur contractus; et, in pariter delicto, potior est conditio defendentis.——From turpitude no contract arises; and, when both are alike depraved, the defendant is in the better situation.

Ex maleficio.——By malice (by fraudulent intent).

Ex mandato.——By command.

Ex mensa et thoro.——"From bed and board."
[A term applied to divorce, where parties are divorced not from any sufficient cause to invalidate the marriage, *ab initio;* where *that* is the case the parties are frequently divorced " *a vinculo matrimonii,*" or from the bonds of marriage altogether, in which case *no* relation of husband and wife subsists. Vide notes to " *A mensa et thoro,*" and " *A vinculo matrimonii.*]

Ex mero motu.——"From mere motion." From a person's own will, without any suggestion or restraint.

Ex natura rei.——From the nature of the thing.

Ex necessitate legis.——From the necessity of the law.

Ex necessitate rei.——"From the necessity of the matter." Arising from the urgency of the circumstances.

Ex nudo pacto non. oritur actio.——"No action arises from a bare, or naked agreement." There must be some consideration expressed, or implied.

Ex officio.——Officially: by virtue of the office.

Ex officio, et debito justitiæ.——Officially, and as in justice due.

Ex officio judicis.——By the office of the judge.

Exoneretur.——That he, she, or it, be discharged.

Exoneretur nunc pro-tunc.——Let him (or it) be now discharged, instead of at some past time.

Exonier.——"To excuse." The word *Essoin* is probably derived from this word. An Essoin was an excuse allowed by law, in order that no person might be surprised or prejudiced by his absence from court, provided he had a just cause to be excused, by anything that was not owing to his own default. It is not improbable but that it was originally allowed to give opportunity to the litigating parties to settle their disputes, in conformity to the precept " Agree with thine adversary quickly." Essoins, however, were anciently divided into five kinds. 1st. *De servitio Regis*—being in the king's service. 2d. *In terram sanctam*—being absent in the Crusades. 3d. *Ultra mare*—being beyond sea. 4th. *De malo lecti*—being sick in bed. 5th. *De malo veniendi*—being seized with sickness on the way.

Ex parte materna.——On the part of the mother.

Ex parte paterna.——On the part of the father.

Ex parte quærentis.——On the part of the plaintiff.

Ex parte talis.——The name of a writ in old English practice. It signifies "on the behalf of such an one."

Ex paucis.——From a few things or words.

EXPEDITIO contra hostem; arcium constructio; et pontium reparatio.——An expedition against the enemy; the building of forts, and repairing of bridges.

EXPENSA vero totius operis.——Certainly the cost of the whole work.

EXPERTO crede.——Give credit to an experienced person.

Ex post facto.——From (or by) an after act.

Ex præcogitata malicia.——Of malice aforethought.

EXPRESSIO eorum quæ tacite insunt.——"The expression of those things which are therein tacitly comprised;" (*i. e.* those things which are implied.)

EXPRESSIO eorum quæ tacite insunt nihil operatur.——The expression of those things which are therein implied has no force.

EXPRESSIO unius est exclusio alterius.——The naming of one person is an exclusion of the other.

EXPRESSUM facit cessare tacitum.——The meaning of this law phrase is, that a thing which is expressed invalidates that which otherwise might have been implied by intendment of law.

Ex principiis nascitur probabilitas; ex factis vero veritas.——Probability arises from principles; but certainly is obtained (only) from facts.

Ex proprio vigore.——By their own force.

Ex provisione hominis.——By a provision of the person.

Ex provisione legis.——By a provision of the law.

Ex provisione mariti.——By a provision of the husband.

Ex quasi contractu.——As of agreement.

Ex relatione.——"By, or from, relation." Sometimes the words mean "*by the information*."

Ex rigore juris.——In strictness (or severity) of law.

Ex scriptis olim visis.——From writings formerly seen.

Ex speciali gratia, certa scientia, et mero motu regis.—— By special favor, positive knowledge, and the mere will of the king.

Ex suo moto.——By his own will.

Ex tempore.——Out of hand (without delay or premeditation).

EXTENDI ad valentiam.——To be extended to the value.

EXTENDI facias.——That you cause to be extended.

EXTENDITUR hæc pax et securitas ad quatuordecem dies, convocato regni senatu.——This peace and security is extended to fourteen days, the Parliament of the realm being assembled.

EXTENSORES.——Appraisers. (Old English law).

EXTRAHURA.——A stray animal.

EXTRA quatuor maria.——"Beyond the four seas:" out of the realm.

EXTRA territorium.——Without the territory.

EXTRA viam.——Beyond (or out of) the way.

EXTRA villenagium.——Out of villenage: or servitude.

EXTUMÆ.——Reliques.

Ex turpi causa non oritur actio.——No action arises out of a wicked cause.

Ex turpi contractu non oritur actio.——No action arises from an immoral contract.

EXULARE.——To banish.

Ex visceribus testamenti.——From the body of the will.

Ex visitatione Dei.——By the visitation of God.

Ex vi termini.——By force (or virtue) of the term. Vide *Rex.* v. *Shepherds & Agnew—East. Rep.* 44, *Geo.* 3.

EYDE.——Aid; help.

EYRE.——Scotch *Ayre.* The court of the justices itinerant.

NOTES TO E.

EMANCIPATIO ET ADOPTIO.—It was the custom among the *Romans,* when a father wished to free his son from his authority, (*emancipare,*) to bring him before the *Prætor,* or some magistrate, (*apud quem actio erat,*)—i. e. who had authority in the case—and there sell him *three* times, *per æs et libram,* i. e. by money and balance, (as it was termed,) to some friend, who was called *Pater Fiduciarius,* (a kind of trustee,) because he was bound after the third sale to sell him back (*remancipare*) to the natural father. There were present, besides a *Libripens,* who held a *brazen* balance, five witnesses. *Roman* citizens, past the age of puberty, and an *Antetestatus,* who is supposed to be so named, because he summoned the witnesses, by touching the tip of their ears. Vide *Hor. Sat.* i. 9. 76. In the presence of these, the natural father gave over *mancipabat* (i. e. *manu tradebat*)—i. e. delivered out of his hand his son to the purchaser, adding these words, "MANCIPO TIBI HUNC FILIUM, QUI MEUS EST," *i. e.* I deliver you this son, who is my property. Then the person holding a brazen coin (*Sestertius*) said, "HUNC EGO HOMINEM EX JURE QUIRITIUM MEUM ESSE AIO, ISQUE MIHI EMPTUS EST HOC ÆRE ANEAQUE LIBRA," *i. e.* "I affirm that this man is mine by the law of the *Romans,* and is purchased by me with this money and by the brazen balance:" and having struck the balance with the coin, gave it to the natural father by way of price. Then he *manumitted* his son in the usual form. But, as by the principles of the *Roman* law, a son, after being manumitted once and again, fell back into the power of his father, this imaginary (or at least fictitious) sale was *thrice* to be repeated, either on the same day, and before the same witnesses, or on different days, and before different witnesses; and then the purchaser (or friend) instead of manumitting him, which would have conferred a *Jus patronatûs* on himself, sold him back to the natural father, who immediately manumitted him, by the same formalities as those used on the emancipation of a slave, (*Librâ et ære libera emittebat,* i. e. "he discharged him by free money and balance.") *Liv.* vi. 14. Thus the son became his own master, (*sui juris factus est.*) *Liv.* vi. 16. The student frequently reads of the ceremony of making wills among the *Romans,* at one time *per æs, vel assem et libram.* Vide note to "*Hæredes successoresque, &c.*"

The custom of selling *per æs et libram* took its rise from this: that the ancient *Romans,* when they had no coined money, (*Liv.* iv. 60,) and afterwards, when they had *asses* of a pound weight, *weighed* their money, and did not count it. The same custom of weighing money is mentioned in

Genesis, c. xxiii. 15, 16. "My Lord, Hearken unto me, the land is worth four hundred shekels of silver, what is that betwixt thee and me? Bury therefore thy dead. And Abraham hearkened unto Ephron, and Abraham weighed unto Ephron the silver which he had named in the audience of the Sons of Heth, four hundred shekels of silver current money with the merchant."

In emancipating a daughter or grand children, the same formalities were used, but only once, (*unica emancipatio sufficiebat,*) i. e. "one sale was sufficient." But these formalities, in process of time, began to be thought troublesome. *Athanasius*, therefore, and *Justinian*, invented new modes of emancipation. *Athanasius* appointed, that it should be sufficient, if a father showed to a judge the Rescript of the Emperor for emancipating his son; and *Justinian*, that a father should go to any magistrate competent, and before him, with the consent of his son, signify that he freed his son from his power, by saying "HUNC SUI JURIS ESSE PATIOR, MEAQUE MANU MITTO," *i. e.* "I permit him to become his own master, and discharge him from my control."

When a man had no children of his own, lest his sacred name and rites should be lost, he might assume strangers (*extraneos*) as his children by ADOPTION.

If the person adopted was his own master, (*sui juris*) it was called ARROGATIO, because it was made at the *Comitia Curiata*, by proposing a Bill to the people, (*per populi rogationem,*) i. e. "by request of the people." *Gell.* v. 19. If he was the son of another, it was properly called "*Adoptio*," and was performed before the *Prætor*, or President of a Province, or any other magistrate, (*apud quem legis actio erat,*) i. e. "who in such case had authority." The same formalities were used as in emancipation. It might be done in any place. *Suet. Aug.* 64. The adopted passed into the family and name, and assumed the sacred rites of the adopted, and also frequently succeeded to his fortune. *Cicero* makes no distinction between these two forms of adoption, but calls both by the general name of "*Adoptio*."

EMENDATIO.—The correction of an error committed in any process, which might be amended after judgment; but if there were any error in giving the judgment, the party was driven to his writ of error; though where the fault appeared to be in the *Clerk* who wrote the record, it might be amended. At *Common* Law, there was anciently but little room for amendments, which appears by the several statutes of *amendment* and *jeofails*, and likewise by the constitution of the courts; for, says *Bracton*, "the judges are to record the *parols* (or pleas) deduced before them in judgment." Also, he says, "*Edward* the First granted to the Justices to record the pleas pleaded before them; but they are not to *erase* the records, nor amend them: nor record against their inrolment." This ordinance of *Edward* the First was so rigidly observed, that when Justice *Hengham*, in his reign, (moved with compassion for the circumstances of a poor man, who was fined thirteen shillings and fourpence,) *erased* the record, and made it six shillings and eight pence, he was fined eight hundred marks; with which, *it is said*, a Clock-house at *Westminster* was built, and furnished with a clock—*sed qu de hoc?* for it does not appear that clocks were then in use; but it is probable the fine was inflicted on the Judge, "*gratia exempli.*"

EMPTIO SUB CORONA.—Those prisoners made captives in war by the *Romans*, either in the field, or in the storming of cities, were sometimes sold by auction *sub corona*, (vide *Liv.* v. 22, &c.,) because they wore a *crown* when sold. There was also a sale of slaves, *sub hasta*, because a *spear* was set up where the crier or auctioneer stood.

EN CEST COURT, &c.—At the present time, it is astonishing to reflect

what nicety was formerly required in the pleadings and · entries of the
Courts of Law. Those who have made a point of investigating this subject,
have noticed how extremely difficult the practice of the common law must
have been in those days—not only *every word*, but *every letter* was examined with the greatest caution—the burthen of this became at length
absolutely *insupportable*. Many statutes were made, and enlightened
judges did *all they could* to render justice to the suitors; and they succeeded
to a very considerable extent: the Student will, however, perceive, that
too many of the *vestiges* now remain, which it is hoped a few succeeding
years will clear away—vestiges as ridiculous as they are derogatory to the
human intellect. The ancient records, kept in the Tower of London, and
in some of the Courts of *Westminster*, present astonishing pieces of penman-
ship, not only remarkable for their extreme correctness, (which the law rendered *absolutely* necessary,) but for the beauty of the engrossing. Indeed,
the writing was of such a superior quality, when *Magna Charta* was obtained,
that it surprises us, if we take into consideration the time it was penned.
A fine copy is to be seen *gratis* in the *British Museum*.

EPISCOPI SICUT CÆTERI BARONES, &c.—When the Barbarians, who overran the *Roman* empire, first embraced the Christian faith, they found the
Clergy possessed of considerable power; and they naturally transferred to
these new guides that profound submission and reverence which they
were accustomed to yield to the priests of that religion which they had
forsaken. They deemed their persons to be equally sacred with their
function; and would have considered it as impious to subject them to the
profane jurisdiction of the Laity. The Clergy were not blind to these advantages, and established courts, in which every question relating to their
own character, their functions, or their property, was tried; and were generally present with the Barons, at the trials, or at the judgments given, in
other cases. They pleaded, and almost obtained, a total exemption from
the authority of the *Civil Judges*. Upon different pretexts, and by a multiplicity of artifices, they communicated these privileges to so many persons,
and extended their jurisdiction to such a variety of cases, that a considerable, if not the greater part of those offences, which gave rise to contest and
litigation, were, at one period, drawn under the cognizance of *spiritual*
Judges. Vide *Du Gange Gloss.*, voc. " *Curia Christianitatis.*"
It appears that Ecclesiastics scarcely, if ever, submitted, during any period
of the middle ages, to the laws contained in the codes of the barbarous
nations, but were governed by the *Roman* Law. They regulated all their
transactions by such of its maxims as were preserved by tradition; or were
contained in the *Theodosian* code, and other books then extant among them.
This we learn from a custom, which prevailed universally in those ages.
Every person was permitted to choose among the various Codes of Law
then in force, that to which he was willing to conform. In any transaction
of importance, it was usual for the person contracting to mention the law
to which he submitted, that it might be known how any dispute, that
might arise between them, was to be decided. Innumerable proofs of this
occur in the Charters of the middle ages. But the clergy-considered it such
a valuable privilege of their order to be governed by the *Roman* law, that
when any person entered into Holy Orders, it was usual for him to renounce
the Code of Laws to which he had been formerly subject, and to declare
that he now submitted to the *Roman* law. Vide *Houard, Anciennes Loix
des Francois*, &c., vol. i, p. 203.

EQUES.—The *Equites*, among the ancient *Romans*, did not, at first, form
a distinct order in the State. When *Romulus* divided the people into three
tribes, he chose from each tribe one hundred young men, the most distinguished for their rank, wealth, and other accomplishments, who should

serve on horse-back, and whose assistance he might use for guarding his person. These three hundred horsemen were called *Celeres*, and were divided into three companies. The number was, at several times afterwards, increased.

Servius Tullius made eighteen centuries of *Equites*; he chose twelve new centuries from the chief men of the State, and made six others out of the three instituted by *Romulus*. Ten thousand pounds of brass were given to each of them to purchase horses; and a tax was laid on widows, who were exempt from other contributions, for maintaining their horses. Vide *Liv.* i. 43. Hence the origin of the Equestrian order, which was of the greatest utility in the State, as an intermediate bond between the Patriciáns and Plebeians.

The *Equites* were chosen promiscuously from the Patricians and Plebeians. Those descended from ancient families were called *Illustres, Speciosi*, and *Splendidi.* The age requisite was about eighteen years, and the fortune, at least towards the end of the republic, and under the Emperors, was four hundred *sestertia*, that is, something more than fifteen thousand dollars. Vide *Hor. Ep.* i., *Plin. Ep.* i. 19.

The badges of the *Equites* were, 1st. A horse given them by the public; hence called *Legitimus.* Vide *Ovid. Fast.* iii. 130. 2d. A golden ring, whence "*Annulo aureo donari,*" for *inter Equites legi.* 3d. *Augustus Clavus.* 4th. A separate place at the public spectacles. Vide *Dio.* xxxvi. 25. *Juv.* iii. 159.

If any *Eques* was corrupt in his morals, or had diminished his fortune, or even had not taken proper care of his horse, (*Gell.* iv. 20,) the Censor ordered him to sell the horse, vide *Liv.* xxix. 37, and thus he was reckoned to be removed from the Equestrian order.

EQUITES GARTERII.—"Knights of the Garter." This order was founded by *Edward* the Third, who (after obtaining many splendid victories), for furnishing this order, made choice in his own realm, and in all *Europe*, of *twenty-five* excellent and renowned persons for virtue and honor, and ordained himself and his successors to be the *Sovereign* thereof, and the rest to be *Fellows* and *Brethren,* bestowing this dignity on them, and giving them a *Blue Garter,* ornamented with gold, pearl, and precious stones, and a buckle of gold to wear on the left leg only; a kirtle, crown, cloak, chaperon, a collar, and other magnificent apparel. *Camden,* and others, inform us, that this order was instituted by *Edward* the Third, upon his having obtained great success in a battle, wherein the King's *Garter* was used as a token.

But *Polydore Virgil* gives it another original, and says that this King, in the height of his glory, (the Kings of *France* and *Scotland* being both prisoners in the Tower of *London at one time,*) first erected this order of the Garter, A. D. 1350, from the circumstance of the Countess of *Salisbury* having dropped her garter in a dance before the King, which he took up, and seeing some of his Nobles smile, he said, "*Honi soit qui mal y pense,*" i. e. "Evil (or shame) be to him that evil thinks," (which has ever since been the motto of the order of the Garter, and indeed is now the motto of the Royal Arms of England,) declaring that such veneration should *thereafter* be done to that silken tie, that the best of them should be proud of enjoying its honors.

ERANT IN ANGLIÆ.—The feudal policy, which seemed for so many successive ages, to be so admirably calculated against the assaults of any *foreign* power, yet its provisions for the *interior* order and tranquillity of society was extremely defective, and led to anarchy, confusion, tyranny and bloodshed. The principles of disorder and corruption are discernible in that constitution, under its best and most perfect form. They soon unfolded themselves, and, spreading with rapidity through every part of the system, produced the most baneful effects upon society. The fierce and powerful vassals of the Crown soon extorted a confirmation *for life* of those grants of land, which being *at first* purely gratuitous, had been bestowed during pleasure. They also obtained the power of supreme jurisdiction, both civil and military, within their own territories; the right of coining money; together with the privilege of carrying on war against their own *private* enemies. Such a state of society must have been *terrible*. A thousand causes of jealousy and discord subsisted among them, which gave rise to numerous petty wars, and cruel resentments. Sudden, unexpected and indiscriminate slaughter often followed the transmission of property. The Nobles were superior to restraint, and harassed each other with every oppression. Incursions were made with ferocity, on slight, or supposed provocations: their respective vassals were dragged into the field to fight against their own countrymen, often their immediate friends and neighbors; and their lands seized and desolated by the victorious party. Well, indeed, might it be said, in the language of the text, "*Erant in Angliæ, quodammodo tot reges, vel potius tyranni, quot domini castellorum.*" What a horrid picture of society! and how happy should we feel that property is protected by good laws, and that we have a general diffusion of the benign doctrines of Christianity and education; for the extension of the latter blessing, in particular, the *American* nation deserves the thanks of the civilized world.

ERAT AUTEM HÆC, &c.—That the *Patricians* and *Plebeians* might be connected together by the strongest ties, *Romulus* ordained that every *Plebeian* should choose from the *Patricians* any one, as his *Patron*, or protector, whose *Client* he was (*quod eum colebat*). It was the part of the *Patron* to advise and defend his *Client*, to assist him with his interest and substance; and serve him with his life and fortune in any extremity. Vide *Dionys*. ii. 10. It was unlawful for *Patrons* and *Clients* to accuse, or bear witness against *each* other, and whoever was found to offend in this respect, might be slain by any one with impunity, as a victim devoted to Pluto, and the. infernal Gods. Hence both *Patrons* and *Clients* vied with each other in fidelity; and for more than *six hundred years*, we find no dissensions between them. *Ibid.* It was esteemed highly honorable for a *Patrician* to have numerous Clients, both hereditary and acquired by his own merit. Vide *Hor. Ep.* ii., *Juv.* x. 44.

EST AUTEM MAGNA, &c.—Whilst the trial by *Judicial Combat* subsisted, proofs by charters, contracts, or other deeds, were rendered nearly ineffectual. When a charter, or other evidence was produced by *one* of the parties, his opponent might challenge it, and affirm that it was *false*, or *forged*, and offer to *prove* this by *Combat* Vide *Leg. Longob.*, lib. 2, sec. 34. It is true, that among the reasons enumerated by *Beaumonoir*, on account of which judges might *refuse* to permit a trial by combat, one is, "If the point in contest could be *clearly* proved, or ascertained by *other* evidence." But this regulation only removed the evil a single step. For, if the party *suspected* that a witness was about to depose in a manner unfavorably to his cause, he might accuse him of being *suborned;* give him the *lie;* and challenge him to *Single Combat;* if the witness was vanquished in battle, no other evidence could be admitted, and the party, by whom he was summoned to appear, lost his cause. Vide *Leg. Baivar.*, tit. 16, sec. 2. *Leg. Burgund.*, tit. 45. *Beaumon.*, c. 61, 315. The reason given for obliging a witness to accept of a defiance, and to defend himself by Combat, is remarkable, and contains the *same* idea, which is *still* the foundation of what is called "*the point of honor*," "for it is just, that if any one affirms that he publicly knows the truth of anything, and offers to give oath upon it, he should not hesitate to *maintain* the veracity of his affirmation in *Combat*." Vide *Leg. Burg.*, tit. 45. That the trial by judicial combat was established in every country of *Europe*, is a fact well known, and requires no proof. That this mode of decision was *frequent*, appears not only from the Codes of ancient laws, which established it, but from the earliest writers concerning the practice of the law in the different nations of *Europe*. It appears from *Madox* that trials by Single Combat, were so frequent in *England*, that the *fines* paid on these occasions, made no inconsiderable branch of the king's revenue. ' *Hist. of the Excheq.*, *vol. i. p.* 349. A very curious account of a Judicial Combat between *Mesire Robert de Beaumonoir* and *Mesire Pierre Tournemine*, in the presence of the *Duke of Burgundy*, *A. D.* 1383, is published by *Maurice*, *Mem. pour servir de preuves, a la Hist. de Bretagne, tom.* 2, *p.* 498. All the formalities observed in these extraordinary proceedings are there minutely described. *Tournemine* was accused by *Beaumonoir* of having murdered his brother. The former was vanquished; but was saved from being hanged, on the spot, by the generous intercession of his antagonist. This mode of trial was at one time so acceptable, that *Ecclesiastics*, notwithstanding the prohibitions of the Church, were constrained not only to *connive* at the practice, but to *authorize* it. A remarkable instance of this is found in *Pasquier's Researches, lib.* 4, *cap.* 1, *p.* 350. The Abbot *Willikindus* considered the determination of a point of law *by combat*, as the *best*, and most *honorable*, mode of decision. In the year 978, a Judicial Combat was fought in the presence of the Emperor. The *Archbishop of Aldebert* advised him to terminate a contest, which had arisen between two noblemen of his court, by this mode of decision. The vanquished combatant, though a person of high rank, was beheaded on the spot. Vide *Chronic. Ditmari, Episc. Mersb. des Hist., tom.* 9, 729, *and* 612, *&c.* The Emperor *Henry* the First declares that this law authorizing the practice of Judicial Combats was enacted with the *consent* and *applause* of many *faithful* Bishops. *Ib., p.* 231. "So remarkably did the *martial* ideas of those ages prevail over the genius and maxims of the Canon Law, which, in other instances, was of the highest credit and authority with Ecclesiastics." The author would here suggest that it might probably be adduced as a better reason, that the prevailing superstition of those ages consisted in the idea of a *particular* prevailing Providence, watching over the rights of the individual accused; and rescuing him from the consequences of an unjust sentence by the signal interposition of Heaven itself. Such an idea was common to both Christian and Heathen philosophy, and is not (with many persons) foreign to the refined theories of the present day. To suppose it a *general* rule, is an unwarrantable assumption, that the moral exemplified government of nature does not justify, nor the just and reverenced estimation of an Omniscient Being, warrant; but, notwithstanding this, the idea appears to have been implanted in the mind of man, in every age, from the most reflecting philosopher to the rudest savage; nor has it been implanted in vain, nor failed of its innumerable and incalculable advantages. A Judicial Combat was appointed in Spain by *Charles* the Fifth, A. D. 1522. The combatants fought in the Emperor's presence; and the battle was conducted with all the rights prescribed by the ancient laws of Chivalry. The whole transaction is described at great length by *Pontus Heuterus Rer. Austriac.*, lib. 8, c. 17, 205. A trial by combat was appointed in England, *A. D.* 1571, under the inspection of the Judges of the Common Pleas; and, although it was not carried to that extremity with the former, (Queen *Elizabeth* having interposed her authority, and enjoined the persons to compound the matter,) yet, in order to preserve their honor, the lists were marked out, and all forms *previous* to the combat, were observed with much ceremony. Vide *Spelm Gloss., voc.* " *Campus,*" 103. And even so late as the year 1631, a Judicial Combat was appointed between *Donald, Lord Rea*, and *David Ramsey*, Esquire, by authority of the *Lord High Constable* and *Earl Marshal* of England; but that quarrel likewise terminated without bloodshed, being accommodated by King *Charles* the First. Another instance also occurs seven years later. Vide *Rushworth's Observ. on Statutes*, 266.

EST SENATORI, &c.—The Senate was instituted by *Romulus* to be "the perpetual Council of the Republic." (*Concilium Reipublicæ sempiternum.* Vide
Cic. pro. Sextio, 65.) It consisted, at first, of only one hundred; they were
chosen from among the *Patricians.* The *Senators* were called "PATRES,"
either on account of their age, or out of their *paternal* care of the state; and
their offspring, "PATRICII." After the *Sabines* were taken into the city,
another hundred were chosen from them by the suffrages of the *Curiæ.*
Vide *Dionys.* ii. 47.   But, according to *Livy*, there were only one hundred
senators at the death of *Romulus;* and their number was increased by *Tullius Hostilius*, after the destruction of *Alba.   Tarquinius Priscus*, the fifth
king of Rome, added one hundred more, who were called "PATRES MINORUM
GENTIUM," *i. e.* Senators of the lower tribes.   Those created by *Romulus*
were called "PATRES MAJORUM GENTIUM," *i. e.* Senators of the higher tribes.
This number of three hundred continued, with small variation, to the time
of *Sylla*, who increased it; but how many he added is uncertain.   It appears there were, at least, above four hundred.   In the time of *Julius Cæsar*,
the number of senators were increased to *nine hundred;* and after his death,
to *a thousand;* but many worthless persons having been admitted into the
senate, during the civil wars, one of them is called by *Cicero*, "*lectus ipse
a se*," (elected by himself;) *Augustus* reduced the number to *six* hundred.   *Suet. Aug.* 35.   The powers and duties of the Senate were as
follows:

1st. They assumed to themselves the guardianship of the public religion;
so that no *new God* could be introduced, nor altar erected, nor the *Sybilline*
books consulted, without their order.   *Liv.* ix. 45.

2d. The senate had the direction of the treasury, and distributed the public money at pleasure.   *Cic. in Vatin.* 15, &c.   They appointed stipends to
their generals and officers; and provisions and clothing to their armies.
Polyb. vi. 11.

3d. They settled the provinces which were annually assigned to the *Consuls* and *Prætors;* and, when it seemed fit, they prolonged their command.
Cic. pro. Dom. 9.

4th. They nominated, out of their own body, all ambassadors sent from
Rome, (*Liv.* ii. 15, &c.,) and gave to foreign ambassadors what answers they
thought proper.   *Cic. in Vatin.* 15, &c.

5th. They decreed all public thanksgivings for victories obtained; and conferred the honor of an *ovation* or triumph, with the title of "IMPERATOR,"
on their victorious generals.   *Cic. Phil.* xiv. 4, 5, &c.

6th. They could decree the title of a king to any prince whom they
pleased; and declare any one to be an enemy by a vote.   *Cæs. Liv. et Cic.
passim.*

7th. They inquired into public crimes, or treasons, either in *Rome* or the
other parts of *Italy*, *Liv.* xxx. 26, and heard and determined all disputes
among the allied and dependent cities. · *Cic. Off.* i. 10, &c.

8th. They exercised a power, not only of interpreting the laws, but of
absolving men from the obligation of them; and even of abrogating them.
Cic. pro. dom. 16, 27, *pro lege Manil.* 21, *de Legg.* ii. 6, &c.

9th. They could postpone the assemblies of the people, *Cic. pro. Mur.* 25.
Att. iv. 16; and prescribe a change of habit to the city, in case of any im-
minent danger or calamity.   *Cic. pro. Sext.* 12.   But the power of the Senate was chiefly conspicuous in *civil* dissensions, or dangerous tumults within
the city, in which that solemn decree used to be passed, "UT CONSULES
DARENT OPERAM NE QUID DETRIMENTI RESPUBLICA CAPERET."   That the Consuls should make it their study (or toil) that the republic receive no injury;
by which decree an absolute power was granted to the *Consuls* to punish,
and put to death, whom they pleased, without a trial; to raise forces; and
carry on war without the order of the people.   *Sallust de bello Cat.* 29.

ET EGO ET HÆREDES MEI, &c.—The verb *warrantizo*, used in the law, is only appropriated to make a *warranty*. Littleton, in his chapter of Warranty, saith that this word *warrantizo* maketh the warranty, and is the cause of warranty, and no other word in our law; and the argument to prove his assertion is produced from the form and words used in a fine; as if he had said, because the word *defendo* is not contained in fines to create a warranty, but the word *warrantizo* only; *ergo*, &c., which argument deduced and drawn, *à majore ad minus*, is very forcible. But it appears that *Littleton* is to be understood only of an express warranty in deed, and of a warranty annexed to lands; for there may be, and are, other words which will extend and enure sufficiently to warrant chattels, &c., and which imply a warranty in law, as *dedi*, &c.

EX FURTO, RAPINA, &c.—The different punishments of thefts among the Romans were borrowed from the *Athenians*. By the laws of the Twelve Tables, a thief in the *night* time might be put to death, "*Si nox (noctu) furtum faxit, sim (si eum) aliquis occisit (occiderit) jure cœsus esto*," i. e. "If a theft be committed in the night, and a person kill him, (the thief,) let him be (accounted) slain by the *law*;" and also in the *day* time, *if* he defended himself with a weapon, but not without having first called out for assistance. The punishment of slaves was severe; they were scourged, and thrown from the *Tarpeian Rock*. Slaves, it is said, were so addicted to the crime of theft, that they were anciently called "*Fures*." "*Quid domini faciant, audent cum talia fures!*" See *Virg.* Eccl. iii. 16, and *Hor.* Ep. i. 46. But afterwards, those punishments were mitigated by various laws, and by the edicts of the *Prætors*. One caught in manifest theft (*in furto manifesto*) was obliged to restore four-fold, besides the thing stolen. If a person was not caught in the fact, but so *evidently guilty* that he could not deny it, he was called "*Fur nec manifestus*," and was punished by restoring double. *Gell.* xi. 18. When a thing stolen was, after much search, found in the possession of any person, it was called "*furtum conceptum*," a discovered theft; and by the law of the Twelve Tables was punished as manifest theft, *Gell. ibid.*, but afterwards as *furtum nec manifestum*. If a thief, to avoid detection, offered things stolen (*res furtivas vel furto ablatas*) to any one to keep, and they were found in his possession, he had an action, called *actio furti oblati*, i. e. an action of manifest theft, against the person who gave him the things, whether he were the thief or another, for the triple of the value. *Ibid.* If any one hindered a person to search for stolen goods, or did not exhibit them when found, actions were granted by the *Prætor*. And in whatever manner theft was punished, it was always with infamy.

Robbery (*Rapina*) took place only in movable things, (*in rebus mobilibus*.) Immovable things were said to be *invaded*, and the possession of them was recovered by an interdict of the *Prætor*. Although the crime of robbery (*crimen raptûs*) was much more pernicious than that of theft, it was, however, less severely punished. An action (*actio vi bonorum raptorum*) was granted by the *Prætor* against the robber only for *four-fold*, including what he had robbed.

If any one slew the beast of another it was called "*damnum injuria datum*," i. e. *dolo vel culpa nocentis admissum*—i. e. "a loss given for the injury (or wrong) admitted to have arisen from the guile or negligence of the wrong doer;" whence *actio vel judicium damni injuria, sc, data;* (Cic. Rosc.) *i. e.* he had an action or judgment for the loss and injury, whereby he was obliged to repair the damages by the *Aquillian* law.

Personal injuries or affronts (*injuriæ*) respected either the body, the dignity or character of individuals. They were variously punished at different periods of the republic.

By the Twelve Tables, smaller injuries, (*injuriæ leviores*,) were punished by a fine of twenty-five *asses*, or pounds of brass. But if the injury was more atrocious, as, for instance, if any one deprived another of the use of a limb, (*si membrum rapsit*, i. e. *ruperit*,) he was punished by retaliation, (*talione*,) if the person injured would not accept of any other satisfaction. If he only dislocated or broke a bone, he paid three hundred *asses*, if the sufferer was a freeman; and one hundred and fifty, if a slave. *Gell.* xx. If any one slandered another by defamatory verses, (*si quis aliquem publicè diffamasset, eique adversus bonos mores convicium fecissit*)—i. e. "if any one defamed another, or cast reproach on him contrary to good manners or morality;" affronted him (*vel carmen famosum in eum condidisset*)—i. e. "made an infamous libel upon him," he was beaten with a club, vid. *Hor. Sat.* ii. which alludes to the law for this species of libel.

But these laws gradually fell into disuse, *Gell.* xx.; and by the edicts of the *Prætor*, an action was granted on account of *all* personal injuries and affronts only, for a *fine*, which was proportioned according to the dignity of the person, and the nature of the injury. This, however, being found insufficient to check licentiousness and insolence, *Sulla* made a new law concerning injuries, by which, not only a *civil* action, but also a criminal prosecution, was appointed for certain offences, with the punishment of exile, or working in the mines. *Tiberius* ordered one, who had written defamatory verses against him, to be thrown from the *Tarpeian* Rock. *Dio.* lvii. 22. An action might also be instituted against a person for an injury done by those under his control, which was called "*actio noxalis*," as if a slave committed theft, or did any damage without the master's knowledge, he was to be given up to the injured person. And so, if a beast did any damage, the owner was obliged to offer a compensation, or give up the beast. There was no action for ingratitude, (*actio ingrati*,) as among the *Macedonians*, or rather *Persians*; because, says *Seneca*, "*all the courts at Rome* would scarcely have been sufficient for trying it." These are some few of the remedies given by the *Roman* laws for injuries, &c.; by the spirit of these the reader will judge how far that powerful nation was advanced in jurisprudence.

F.

FACERE cum aliquo.——To be on this side.

FACIAS habere rationabilem dotem.——That you cause (her) to have a reasonable dower.

FACIET jurare duodecim legales homines de viceneto, seu de villa, quod inde veritatem secundum conscientiam suam manifestabant.——That he should cause to swear twelve lawful men of the neighborhood, or vill, whereby they may show the truth, according to their conscience.

FACIO, ut des.——I perform, that you may give.

FACIO, ut facias.——I perform, in order that you may.

FAC ita esse.——Suppose it to be so.

FACTA armorum.——Tournaments: Feats of arms.

FACTA potentissima.——Facts (or deeds) are most powerful.

FACTOR armorum regalium.——The king's armorer. *Vide note.*

FACTUM præclarum, atque divinum.——A noble and divine act.

FACULTAS ejus quod cuique facere libet, nisi quid vi, aut jure prohibetur.——The power of doing what every one pleases, unless what is forbidden by authority, or by law.

FACULTAS secreta certis in rebus.——There is a secret efficacy in certain things.

FACULTATES in plurali.——Wealth: means: abilities.

FADERFIUM.——Sax. A gift made to a woman by her father or brother upon her marriage.

FAIDA.——Malice: deadly fued.

FAITE enrolle.——A deed of bargain and sale.

FAITOURS.——In *Stat.* 7, *Rich.* 2d, *c.* 5, this word is used for "*evil doers;*" and may be interpreted, "*idle livers,*" from "*faitardise*"—which signifies a kind of sleepy disease.

FALCATURA.——"A day's mowing of grass." Formerly one of the feudal services performed for the superior lord of the fee.

FALLONIA.——Felony.

FALDA.——A sheepfold. FALDATA.——A flock of sheep.

FALDÆCURSUS.——A fold course.

FALDFEY.——Sax. The fee paid by a tenant for leave to fold his sheep on his own ground.

FALERIÆ.——The furniture and tackle of a cart.

FALSA demonstratio non nocet.——A false description does not vitiate (the deed).

FALSA fit pœnitentia laici, cum penitus ab officio curiali vel negotiali non recedit, quæ sine peccatis agi ulla ratione non prævalet.——"The repentance of a layman will be inefficacious, unless he withdraw entirely from professional and mercantile pursuits, which cannot, on any account, be transacted without (committing) sin." The false logic of Monkish superstition. *Vide note to " Homo mercator."*

FALSARE curiam.——To deceive the court.

FALSE, fraudulente et maliciose.——Falsely, fraudulently and maliciously.

FALSONARIOUS.——A counterfeiter.

FALSO retorno brevium.——A writ which might have been sued out against a sheriff for returning writs falsely.

FALSUS in uno, falsus in omnibus.——False in one matter, deceitful in everything.

FAMÆ damna majora quam quæ possint æstimari.—— The injury done to character is so great that it cannot be estimated.

FAMA tantum modo publico accusat.——Public opinion only accuses him.

FAMOSI libelli.——Infamous books, or writings.

FAMOSIS libellis si quis scripserit quod pertineat ad injuriam alterius, de quo est publica accusatio pœnæ capitalis; non tantum in auctorem famosi libelli, sed etiam eum qui invenit, nec combussit, sed evulgavit; quia iste auctor præsumitur esse libelli, qui eum sparsit in vulgos, non prodito auctore.——If any person has written notorious libels, which may tend to the injury of another, who is publicly accused of meriting a capital punishment, not only the au-thor of such libel, but he also who has found it, and has not burnt it, but given it publicity, is to be considered the author, because he hath published it among the common people, without having produced the author.

FAMOSOS latrones in his locis ubi grassati sunt, furca figendos placuit, ut conspectu detereantur alii, et sit consolatio cognatis, ut eodem loco pœna redditur, in quo latrones homicidia fecissent.——It pleased him that infamous rob-bers should be fixed on a gibbet in the same place where they committed their crimes, that others might be deterred by the sight, inasmuch as the punishment being inflicted in the same place where the robbers committed the murders, it might be some consolation to the relations (of those who were killed).

FANG, fangen.——Sax. To take.

FARANDMAN.——Scotch.——A merchant traveller, or stranger.

FARDEL.——A fourth part.

FARDINGDEAL.——The fourth part of an acre.

FARINARIUM.——A mill.

FARISTEL.——Sax. Stopping of way.

FARRAGO legum nauticarum.——The absurd collection of maritime laws.

FAS.——Right.

FASTERMANS.——Sax. Bondsmen.

FASTI.——Lawful.

FATETUR facinus is qui judicum fugit.——He confesses his guilt who flies from trial.

FATUUS.——An idiot.

FAUCES terræ.——"The mouth or chops of a channel;" (where a person may see from land to land.)

FAUSENERIE.——Forgery.

FEARME.——Food; a feast.

FEE.——The land or estate held of a superior by service.

FEFELLIT.——He has deceived, or betrayed.

FELAGUS.——Among the Saxons, a friend bound for another's good behavior.

" FELICES ter, et amplius
Quos irrupta tenet copula; nec malis
  Divulsis querimoniis,
Suprema citius solvet amor die."

"Happy, thrice happy they, whose friendships prove
One constant scene of unmolested love;
Whose hearts, right tempered, feel no various turns,
No coolness chills them, and no madness burns;
But, free from anger, doubts, and jealous fear,
Die as they live, united and sincere.——*Orrery.*

FELO de se.——A suicide; a self-murderer.

FELONIA.——Felony. *Vide note.*

FELONIA per quam vassallus amitteret feudum.——A felony by which a vassal would lose his fee.

FELONICE cepit, et asportavit.——He feloniously took, and carried away.

FEME covert.——A married woman.

FEME sole.——An unmarried woman.

FEME sole sub modo.——A single woman to a certain extent.

FEODA propria, et impropria.——Proper and improper feuds or fees.

FEODUM.——An estate in fee. *Feodum* appears to be compounded of "OD," possession, and "FEO," wages, or pay; intimating that it was stipendiary, and granted as a recompense for services. Vide *Wachter voce "Feodum."*

FEODUM est quod quis tenet sibi et hæredibus suis, sive tenementum sit, sive redditus, &c.——A fee is that which a person holds to himself and his heirs, whether it be a tenement, or a rent, &c.

FEODUM laicum.——A lay fee. *Vide note.*

FEODUM militare.——A Knight's fee. *Vide note.*

FEODUM militare, or. Feudum militis.——A Knight's fee. Vide *note to Feudum.*

FEODUM novum, ut antiquum.——A new fee (given or granted), as an ancient fee.

FEODUM restituit ejusdem estimationis quod erat tempore rei judicatæ.——"He restored a fee of the same value as it was at the time of the judgment." That is, that the lord give or grant to the tenant, or feoffee, when he shall be ejected, land of the same value.

FEODUM simplex.——A fee simple: an unconditional fee.

FEODUM, sine investitura, nullo modo constitui potest.——"A fee cannot, in any way, be made without an investiture." This was the ancient law relating to freeholds.

FEODUM talliatum.——An entailed estate.

FEOFFAMENTUM.——A feoffment: the donation of a fee; or a feoffment giving possession by livery of seizin. *Vide note.*

. FEOFFARE.——To enfeoff: or grant in fee.

FEOFFAVIT et demisit.——He enfeoffed and demised.

FEORME.——A farm: a provision: rent.

FERÆ.——Wild beasts.

FERÆ campestres.——"Beasts of chase." These are five; the buck, doe, fox, martin and roe.

FERÆ igitur bestiæ, et volucres et omnia animalia, quæ mari, cœlo, et terra nascuntur, simul atque ab aliquo captæ fuerint, jure gentium statim illius esse incipiunt.——Quod enim nullius est, id naturali ratione occupanti conceditur. ——Therefore, wild beasts, and birds, and all animals which are produced in the sea, air, or earth, as soon as they are taken by any one, immediately, by the law of nations, begin to be his property. For that which is not the property of any person, by natural reason is conceded to be the property of the possessor.

FERÆ igitur bestiæ, simul atque ab aliquo captæ fuerint jure gentium statim illius esse incipiunt.——Therefore, wild beasts, as soon as they are taken by another, become the property of the captor by the law of nations.

FERÆ naturæ.——Of a wild nature.

FERÆ naturæ, et nullius in bonis.——Beasts of a wild nature, and not belonging to any (particular) person.

FERÆ naturæ per industriam hominis.——Animals of a wild nature (tamed by man's industry).

FERÆ naturæ propter privilegium.——Animals of a wild nature on account of privilege.

FERÆ naturæ ratione impotentiæ.——Animals of a wild nature for want of power.

FERÆ sylvestres.——"Beasts of the forest." Frequently called beasts of venary. These are the hart, hind, boar and wolf: the beasts and fowl of the Warren, are the hare, coney, partridge and the pheasant. A reward was anciently given for the destruction of wolves in England; they have all long since been destroyed.

FERITA.——A wound.

FERLINGUS.——A furlong.

FERNIGO.——Where fern grows.

FERIÆ.——Certain days on which marriage could not formerly be performed, and celebrated; which were from Advent to the Epiphany; from Septuagessima to the Octave of Easter; and from the first Rogation day to the Octave of Pentecost.

FERIÆ Nundinæ.——Holidays, Fairs, or great markets. These are frequently held on some holiday of the Roman Church.

FERRA electio : destre whipt, ou de paier costs.——A hard choice; he shall be whipt, or pay costs. *Vide note.*

FERRAMENTUM.——The iron instruments about a mill.

FERRIFODINA.——An iron mine.

FESTINUM remedium.——A speedy remedy.

FESTIS diebus omnibus et legitimis jejuniis, ordalium nullus ingreditor, neve ad jusjurandum addicitor.——That upon holidays and the regular fasts, no man should be subjected to the ordeal, or called to judgment.

FEUDIS antiquis.——By fees of ancestry.

FEUDORUM libri.——A book of feudal law.

FEUDUM.——A fee : land held in fee simple. *Vide note.*

FEUDUM apertum.——An open fee.

FEUDUM avitum.——A fee derived from the grandfather.

FEUDUM ligeum.——A fee held by fealty.

FEUDUM maternum.——A fee descended from the mother.

FEUDUM novum.——A new (or acquired) fee.

FEUDUM paternum.——A fee, or inheritance acquired from the father.

FEY.——Faith; a deed.

FEYN.——A fine.

FEYRE.——A fair.

FIAT nisi prius per proviso si querens fecet defaultam. ——Let it be done, unless first (performed) by proviso, if the defendant has made default.

FICTIO cedit veritati.——Fiction yields to truth.

FIDEI commissa.——Trusted in confidence: trust settlements. *Vide note.*

FIDEI commissarius.——A trustee: a factor.

FIDEI jussores.——Persons who appeared as sureties for others among the ancient *Romans.*

FIDELITAS.——Fealty.

FIDEM adhibens.——Showing confidence.

FIDES nuptialis contractus.——A promise (or obligation) of a marriage contract.

FIDES semper servanda est.——Integrity is always to be kept.

FIDES servanda est; simplicitas juris gentium prævalet. ——Faith must be kept; the honesty of the law of nations must prevail.

FIEF.——"A fee." What we call a fee is, in other countries, the contrary to *chattels.* In *Germany,* certain districts or territories are called "*Fiefs,*" where there are *Fiefs* of the Empire.

FIEF d'haubert.——A tenure by knight's service.

FIERI facias.——That you cause to be made, or done; or levied. A writ of execution so called.

FIERI facias ad valentiam.——That you cause (a levy) to be made to the value.

FIERI facias de bonis ecclesiasticis.——"That you cause to be levied of the ecclesiastical goods." A judicial writ to the sheriff to levy damages and costs.

FIERI facias de bonis propriis.——That you cause to be levied of his (or her) own goods.

FIERI facias de bonis testatoris si, &c., et si non, de bonis propriis.——That you cause to be levied of the testator's goods, if, &c., and if he has none of those, then of his own goods.

FIERI feci.——I have caused to be made, or levied.

FIERI feci sequestrari.——I have caused sequestration to be made.

FIERI non debet, sed factum, valet.——It ought not to be done; but being done, it is valid.

FI: fa: de bonis testatoris, &c., et si constare poterit quod devastavit, tunc de bonis propriis.——That you cause to be levied of the testator's goods, &c., and if it can be shown that he wasted them, then of his own proper goods.

FIGHTWITE.——Sax. A fine put upon one who fights or quarrels to the disturbance of the peace.

FILARE.——To file.

FILAZER, Filacer, or Filizer.——An officer of the Court of Common Pleas, who issues writs.

FILCTALE.——In ancient times, an entertainment given by bailiffs of hundreds, at which they extorted money from the guests.

FILII nobilium.——Noblemen's sons.

FILIUS hæres legitimus est.——A son is the legitimate heir.

FILIUS hæres legitimus est quem nuptiæ demonstrant. ——He is the lawful heir whom marriage designates.

FILIUS mulieratus.——The eldest son of a woman, born before the father married her.

FILIUS nullius.——No person's son; a bastard; who at common law cannot succeed to an inheritance.

FILIUS populi.——A son of the people; a bastard.

FILUM aquæ.——The middle of the water (or stream).

FILUM forestæ.——The line, or boundary of the forest.

FINALIS concordia.——The final agreement.

FINIS, fructus, exitus et effectus legis.——A fine (levied of lands) is the profit, the end and effect of the law.

FINIUM regundorum actio.——Action for regulating boundaries.

FIRDFARE.——Sax. A going forth to a military expedition.

FIRDSOCNE.——Sax. Exemption from military duty.

FIRDWITE.——A fine for refusing to do military service.

FIREBARE.——Sax. A seaside tower or beacon with lights for the guidance of mariners.

FIREBOTE.——An allowance of fuel.

FIRMA.——From the *Sax.* "Feorme," *i. e.* food (there is also a word "*feorman,*" to feed, or yield victuals). Also a messuage and land taken by lease under a certain rent—from "*Firma*" comes the word "*Farm.*" *Vide note.*

FIRMA ipsius quærentis.——The plaintiff's farm.

FIRMARIUM.——A word used in old records for infirmary.

FIRMARIUS, vel Proprietarius.——The farmer, or proprietor.

FIRMITAS.——An assurance of some privilege by deed or charter.

FISC.——The treasury of a prince or state.

FISK.——The right of the King, in Scotch law, to the moveable estate of a rebel.

FISTUCA.——A staff or wand which, anciently, was delivered when any property was transferred.

FIT autem disseisina, non solum cum quis præsens, vel procurator vel familia, qui nomine suo fuerit in seisina violenter, injuste, et sine judicio, ex libero tenemento suo, qualicunque ejecti fuerunt—verum erit disseisina, cum quis ad nundinas, vel peregre profectus fuerit, nemine in domo relicto, vel possessione, alius in possessionem ingrediatur, et ipsum reversum non admittat, vel eum ingredi voluerit, per se vel assumptis viribus, violenter repellat. Item non solum fit disseisina, secundum quod prædictum est, sed etiam si quis præpotens uti voluerit in alterum tenementum, contra ipsius tenentis voluntatem, arando, falcando, asportando, et contrahendo, tenementum esse suum, quod est alterius, si autem nihil clamaverit in tenemento aliud erit,

quæ tunc erit transgressio, non disseisina, in libero tenemento.——But it becomes a disseisin, not only when any
one being present, or his agent, or family, who, in his
name, were in possession, have been violently, unjustly,
and without any judgment, in any manner ejected from
the freehold—but it will be a disseisin when any person
shall be gone to a market (or a fair) or shall have gone
from home, and no one being left in the house or in possession, another shall take possession, and not admit the
owner to enter on his return : or when he would enter re-
pels him, either by himself, or with the assistance of others.
And it not only becomes a disseisin, according to what
has been said, but also if any powerful person insists upon
using the land of another, contrary to the tenant's will,
by ploughing, digging, cutting up, carrying away, and
wasting the same, as though it were his own, which is another's property ; but if he claim no interest in the land,
it will be otherwise, for then there will be a trespass, not a
disseisin, in the free tenement.

FIT juris, et seisinæ conjunctio.——It becomes a joinder
of right and possession.

FLAGELLIS et fustibus acriter verberare uxorem.——Severely to beat his wife with whips and clubs.

FLAGRANTE bello.——Whilst the war rages.

FLAGRANTE delicto.——In the commission of the crime.

FLEM.——Sax. A fugitive.

FLEMENESFIRINTHE, or Flemenfirma.——The sustenance
and relieving of fugitives or outlaws.

FLEMENESWITE, or Flemeswite.——A fine imposed upon
a fugitive.

FLETA.——In old English law, an estuary.

FLETA.——This is the title of an excellent law book,
supposed to have been written by a Judge, confined in the
Fleet prison, *temp. Edward* 1st.

FLETH.——Sax. Land (given by some authorities)
a house (by others).

FLIEDWITE, or Flightwite, from *Sax.* "*Flyth.*" *i. e.* fuga, and, "*wite,*" mulcta.——This word, in ancient law, signifies the discharge of a person from amerciaments, where, having been a *fugitive*, he comes to the king's peace of his own accord, or with license.

FLODEMARK.——High-water mark.

FLOTSAM.——Goods floating on the sea.

FLUMINA autem omnia et portus publica sunt, ideoque jus piscandi omnibus commune est, in portu, fluminibusque.——Also all rivers and harbors are common, together with the right of fishing in all rivers and in port.

FOCALE.——Firewood.

FOELLAN.——To offend.

FOELNISSE.——An offence; felony.

FŒMINA presenti marito feloniam agens, non rea est constructione legis, quia per ejus coercionem instigari cogitur.——A married woman, committing felony in her husband's presence, is not guilty in the eye of the law, she being supposed to have been instigated to the commission of the act by the coercion of her husband.

FŒMINA viro coöperta.——A married woman.

FOENUS nauticum.——Nautical usury.

FOLC-LANDS.——Sax. Copyhold lands, so called in the time of the *Saxons:* as charter lands are called *Book-lands* —vide *Kitchen,* 174. Folc-land was *terra vulgi,* or *popularis,* the land of the common people who had no *certain* estate therein, but held the same under the rents and services accustomed or agreed; and was therefore not put into writing, but accounted "*prædum rusticum et ignobile.*" Vide *Spelm. on Feuds.*

FOLC-MOTE.——Sax. A general Council, or Assembly. *Vide note.*

FOLGARE.——From Saxon *folgan,* to follow or serve.

FOLGARII, FOLGHERES.——Followers or servants.

FORANEUS.——A foreigner.

FORATHE.——Sax. One who could swear for another.

FORBALCA.——A piece of unploughed land lying next the highway.

FORBANNITUS.——Banished. (*Old Europ. law.*)

FORBATUDO.——He who struck the first blow. (*Old Europ. law.*)

FORCELET.——A fortress.

FORCERIUM.——A strong box for the safe-keeping of papers.

FORCLORRER.——To foreclose; to shut out.

FORDANNO.——The first assailant in a fight. (*Old Europ. law.*)

FORDIKA.——The grass growing on the banks of ditches.

FORECHEAPUM.——Pre-emption.

FORERA.——Foreland.

FORESCHOKE.——Forsaken.

FORESTALLAN.——Forestalling.

FORFANG, FORFENG.——Sax. A previous taking.

FORFEITURE de terre.——A forfeiture of the land.

FORGABULUM.——A quit rent.

FORGAVEL.——Sax. A small reserved rent in money.

FORI disputationes.——Arguments in the Law Courts.

FORISFACERE.——To outlaw.

FORISFACTURA.——Forfeiture.

FORMA essentialis.——A substantial form.

FORMA et figura judicii.——The form and manner of the judgment.

FORMEDON. (*Breve de forma donationis.*)——"The form, or manner of a gift." A writ formerly issued to recover entailed property.

FORMEDON in descender.——Formedon in descent. *Vide note.*

FORMEDON in remainder.——Formedon in the remainder.

FORMEDON in reverter.——Formedon in the reversion.

FORO domestico.——"In the court at home." Perhaps the Lord's Court of the Manor.

Foro ecclesiæ.——In the Spiritual Court.

Forprise.——Taken beforehand. An exception.

Forschet.——The forepart of a furlong, that which skirts the highway.

Forsprise.——Except.

Forsque.——But; only.

Fortior et potentior est dispositio legis quam hominis. ——The disposition of the law is stronger and more powerful than that (effected) by man.

Fortuitus casus providendus.——A chance case is to be regarded.

Forum domesticum.——A Court held at home, or in the vicinity.

Forum plebiæ justitiæ, et theatrum comitivæ potestatis. ——The court of justice for the common people, and public place of meeting for the power of the county.

Forum rei.——The Court held where the defendant resides.

Fossa.——A ditch full of water where formerly women convicted of felony were drowned. Fosse.——A dyke or ditch.

Fourcher.——To divide or *fork*. A term used respecting an old practice of casting essoins or excuses by two tenants *alternately*, in order to delay the proceedings. See *Reeves' Hist. Eng. Law.*

Fovea.——A grave.

Franc-aleu or alleu.——Allodial land.

Franchiare.——To enfranchise.

Franchilanus.——A freeman.

Franchise.——A privilege, or exemption. *Vide note.*

Francigena.——A Frenchman.

Franclaine, Franclein, Frankleyne.——A freeholder or gentleman; a freeman.

Francus.——Free.

Francus bancus.——*Free-bench—Sedes libera.* That estate in copyhold lands, which the wife acquires on the death of her husband, for her dower, according to the custom of the manor. Freebench also means the widow's estate in such lands as her husband died seized of: there is a distinction between *freebench* and *dower;* which last is the estate of the widow in *all* lands of which her husband was seized during the coverture. The custom of freebench prevails in the manor of *East* and *West Enborne*, and *Chaddleworth*, in the county of *Berks;* at *Torr*, in Devonshire, and other places in the West of England. There is a curious custom in the manor of West and East Enborne, to be found in the "*Spectator*," No. 623, Nov. 22, 1714.

FRANCUS plegiws.——A frank or free pledge; a tithing decennary or friborg, so called because every freeman belonging to it was a *pledge* for the good conduct of the others; the chief of whom was called *friborgesheofod* or *freoborhesheofod*.

FRANK-ALMOIGN.——A free gift. *Vide note.*

FRANK-FEE.——Freehold lands, held exempt from all services, except the homage.

FRASSETUM.——Woody ground.

FRATER consanguineus.——A half-brother by the father's side.

FRATER fratri sine legitimo hærede defuncto in beneficio, quod eorum patris fuit succedat; sin autem unus e fratribus a domino feudum acceperit, eo defuncto sine legitimo hærede, frater ejus in feudum non succedit.——One brother may succeed to another brother, dying without a lawful heir, in respect to the estate which was their father's; but if one of them receive his fee from the lord, and die without a lawful heir, the other brother shall not succeed thereto.

FRATER fratri uterino non succedit in hæreditate paterna. ——A brother does not succeed to a maternal brother in a paternal inheritance.

FRATER uterinus.——A brother by the mother's side.

FRAUDEM facere legi.——To commit a fraud in the law.

FRAUNKE-FERME.——Free-farm.

FRAUS, dolus, qui fit in contractibus et venditionibus. ——Fraud, deceit, which is made in contracts and sales.

FRAUS dolus vel deceptio.——A fraud, trick or deception.

FRAXINETUM.——From *fraxinus*, an ash. A place where ashes grow.

FREA.——A female ward.

FREDUM.——A sum paid to the magistrate by a person who had injured another in order to secure his protection. It was usually about one-third as much as he had previously paid to the injured party for a satisfaction.

FREDWITE.——Frithwite. Sax. See FREDUM.

FRENDLESMAN.——Sax. An outlaw; to whom all persons were forbidden to give food or shelter.

FRENDWITE.——Sax. A fine imposed upon one who protected or assisted an outlawed friend.

FRENTIKE.——Frantic.

FREOBORGH.——A free pledge. Sometimes Friborgh.

FREOBORHESHEOFED.——In Saxon law, a chief pledge. The title of the chief of a friborgh or decennary. See FRANCUS PLEGIUS.

FRIDHBURGUS.——A species of frank pledge by which the lords or chiefs bound themselves for the good behavior of their dependents.

FRIDSTOLL.——A chair of peace.

FRILAZIN.——One freed from bondage.

FRISCA disseisina.——"Fresh disseisin"—from Fr."*fresche*," late, and "*disseiser*," to eject. That disseisin which a man might formerly seek to defeat of himself, and by his own power, without resorting to the king, or the law: as where it was not above fifteen days old, or of some other short continuance. Vide *Britton*, c. 5.

FRITHBOTE.——A fine for breach of the peace.

FRITHSOKE.——Frithsoken: from *Sax.* "Frith," *pax* and " socne," *libertas.*——" Surety of defence:" a jurisdiction for the purpose of preserving the peace. According to Fleta, "*libertas habendi franci plegii, seu immunitas loci,*" (the liberty of frank pledge, or the immunity of the place.) Vide *Cowell. Blount.*

FRUCTUS industriales.——Profits, or fruits of industry: as corn growing, fixtures, &c.

FRUMGYLD.——Sax. The first payment made to the kindred of a person slain, towards the recompense for his murder. Vide *Ll. Edmund.*

FRUMSTOLL.——A chief seat or residence.

FRUSTRA fit per plura, quod fieri potest per pauciora. ——It is useless to do that by many things, which may be accomplished by few.

FRUSTRA legis auxilium invocat, qui in legem committit. ——"He seeks the aid of the law in vain, who offends against it." He must come into court with clean hands.

FRYDERINGA, *Frithing, Fridung,* and *Friderung,* i. e. expeditionis apparatus.——"The fitting out of an expedition:" "Going out to war:" or a military expedition at the king's command: the refusal to do which was punished by fine at his pleasure. Vide *Leg. Hen.* 1, c. 10.

FRYMTH.——The receiving a person into one's dwelling and harboring him. Sax.

FUAGE.——In the reign of *Edward,* the Third, the *Black Prince* having *Acquitain* granted to him, laid an imposition of "*fuage*" upon the subjects of that dukedom, *i. e.* twelve pence for every fire. *Rot. Par.* 25 *Edw.* 3. It is not improbable that the *hearth-money* imposed (16 *Car.* 2) took its rise from hence.

FUER.——Fr. *fuir*—Lat. *fugere.* "Flight"; is used substantively, though it be a verb; and is two-fold, *fuer in* "fait," and *fuer in* "ley," *lege:* when being called to the court he appeareth not, which is flight in law. *Staunf. Pl. Cor.,* lib. 3, c. 22.

FUERUNT in conquestu liberi homines, qui libere tenerunt tenementa sua per libera servitia, vel per liberas consuetudines.——There were freemen at the Conquest, who held their tenures by free services, or free customs.

FUGACIO.——The chase or hunting of wild animals.

FUGAM fecit.——"He made flight." Used when it is found, by inquisition, that a person has fled, for felony, &c.

FUIT resolve per totam, curiam que action sur le case. ——It was resolved by the whole court that it was an action on the case.

FULFREA.——Entirely free.

FULLUM aquæ.——A stream of water.

FUNCTUS officio.——Having discharged the office: or *officially* dead.

FUNDAMUS.——We found (or establish); often used in charters for establishing colleges.

FUNDATOR perficiens.——The endower (or founder).

FUNDI patrimonales.——Lands of inheritance.

FURCA et flagellum.——This was the meanest of all servile tenures, where the bondman was at the disposal of his lord for life or limb. *Plac. Term. Mich.* 2 *John, Rot.* 7.

FUR.——A thief. FUR MANIFESTUS.——A thief caught in the act of stealing.

FURCHE.——A gallows.

FUREM, si aliter capi non potest, occidere permittunt. ——They suffer a thief to be killed if he cannot otherwise be taken.

FURIGELDUM.——A fine paid for theft.

FURIOSUS solo furore punitur.——"A madman is punished by his own insanity." The law considers that a madman suffers sufficiently by his dreadful malady, without inflicting punishment for those acts committed when deprived of his reasoning powers.

FURTUM lege naturali prohibitum est.——Theft is forbidden by the law of nature.

FURTUM non est casus fortuitus.——Theft is not a chance case, (accidental or unpremeditated.)

Furtum non manifestum.——"The theft does not appear." It is not discovered.

Futuros casus providendos.——That future causes be provided for.

Futyf.——A fugitive from justice.

Fyrd.——An army.

NOTES TO F.

FACTOR ARMORUM REGALIUM.—One of the *English* Historians observes, that immediately preceding the Conquest, the art of working in iron and steel had arrived at such a state of improvement, that even the horses of some of the Chief Knights and Barons were covered with steel and iron armor. Artificers, who wrought in iron, were so highly regarded, in those warlike times, that every officer had his *Smith*, who constantly attended his person to keep armor in order. The Chief Smith was, it is said, an officer of considerable dignity in the court of the *Anglo-Saxon* and *Welch Kings*, where he enjoyed many privileges; and his *Waregild* or *Weregild*, i. e. a fine payable by any person who murdered him, was much higher than that of any other artificer. In the *Welch* court the King's *Smith* sat next to the Domestic Chaplain, and was entitled to a draught of *every* kind of liquor which was brought into the Hall—a privilege which many of our artificers of the present day would not think lightly of. Vide *Lardner's Encyclopædia.* See, also, note to "*Hindeni Homines.*"

FELONIA.—A Law Term, including generally all capital crimes *below* that of treason. Vide 4 *Comm.* 98. This word appears to be of *Feudal* origin; but authors differ as to its derivation; some derive it, fancifully enough, from "*felos,*" Gr., an impostor; from *fallo,* Lat., to deceive; and *Coke* says it is *crimen felleo animo perpetratum,* a crime done with a malicious intent. All, however, agree, that it is *such* a crime as occasions a *forfeiture* of the offender's lands or goods: this, therefore, gives great probability to *Spelman's* derivation from the *Teutonic,* or German, "*Fee,*" that is, a *feud,* or *fief,* and "*lon,*" price, or value.

FEOFFAMENTUM.—Among the Romans, if the question was about a farm, a house, or the like, the Prætor anciently went with the parties (*cum litigantibus*) to the place, and gave possession to which he thought proper. But, from the increase of business, this soon became impracticable; and then the parties called one another from court (*ex jure*) to the spot, (*in locum, vel rem presentem,*) to a farm for instance, and brought from thence a turf, (*glebam,*) vide *Festus;* and contested about that, as though it were the whole farm. It was delivered to the person to whom the *Prætor* adjudged the possession.

But this custom was also dropped, and the lawyers devised a new form of process for suing for possession, which *Cicero* pleasantly ridicules. Vide *Cic. pro Mur.* 12. The plaintiff thus addressed the defendant, "*Fundus qui est in agro, qui Sabinus vocatur, eum ego ex jure Quiritium meum esse aio, inde ego te ex jure manu consertum,*" i. e. "the land situated in the country, called *Sabinus,* that, I affirm, belongs to me by the *Roman* laws; for this reason, therefore, I contest the matter according to law." If the defendant yielded, the *Prætor* adjudged possession to the plaintiff. If not, the defendant thus answered the plaintiff, "*Unde tu me ex jure manum consertum vocasti, inde ibi te revoco.*" "Why do you call me into law; from this situation and place I refer the matter." Then the *Prætor* repeated his set form, "*Utriusque superstitibus præsentibus,*" (i. e. *testibus præsentibus,*) i. e. "the witnesses on both sides being present." "*Istam viam dico; Inite viam.*" "I say this way. Go your way." Immediately they both set out, as if to go to the farm to fetch a turf, accompanied by a lawyer to direct them. Then the Prætor said, "*Reddite viam,*" Return; upon which they returned. If it appeared that one of the parties had been dispossessed by the other through force, the *Prætor* thus decreed, "*Unde tu illum dejecisti, cum nec vi, nec clam, nec præcario possideret eo illum. Restituas jubeo,*" i. e. "why have you ejected him; for he has not possessed the estate by force nor fraud, nor by petition. I ordain that you restore it." If not, he thus decreed, *Uti nunc possidetis, &c,* i. e. retain (the possession) as you now enjoy, &c. The possessor being thus ascertained, the action about the right of property (*de jure dominii*) commenced. The person ousted first asked the defendant if he were the lawful possessor. Then he claimed his right, and in the meantime required that the possessor should give security not to do any damage to the subject in question (*ne nihil deterius in possessione facturum*) by cutting down trees, demolishing houses, &c.

Thus the student will perceive that the practice of livery and seisin clearly appears to be a relic of *Roman* jurisprudence. Vide 2 *Black. Comm.* 315, 316.

The giving of a glove was, in the middle ages, one of the tokens of investiture in bestowing lands and dignities. In A. D. 1002, two Bishops were put in possession of their sees, each by receiving a glove. So in England, in the reign of *Edward* the Second, the deprivation of gloves was a ceremony of degradation. With regard to the shoe, as a token of investiture, Castell. *Lex. Polyg.,* col. 2342, mentions that the Emperor of the *Abyssinians* used the casting of a shoe as a sign of dominion; see, also, Psalm 60. To these instances the following may be added: *Childebert* the Second, was fifteen years old when his uncle declared he was of age, and capable of governing himself. "I have put," says he, "a Javelin in thy hand. as a token that I have given thee my kingdom," and then, turning towards the assembly, added, "You see that my son *Childebert* has become a man. Obey him." Vide *Montesquieu's Spirit of the Laws, vol.* i. 361.

FERRA ELECTION.—This is still the law in *England,* where a person sues "*in forma pauperis;*" but the last time it was requested to be put in execution by a defendant, or his counsel, the Judge who tried the cause very humanly, but laconically, replied, "*I have no officer to do the duty.*"

FEUDUM.—Feuds, or Fees, were enjoyed in *England* by the followers of the Conqueror; but as these new proprietors were in danger of being disturbed by the remainder of the ancient inhabitants, and in still greater danger of being attacked by other invaders, or petty Lords, they saw the necessity of coming under strong obligations to protect the community, for their *mutual* preservation. We can trace back this obligation on the proprietors of land to a very early period in the history of the *Franks.* Childeric, who began his reign *A. D.* 562, exacted a Fine, "*bannos jussit exegi,*" (i. e. he ordered fines to be levied,) from certain persons who had refused to accompany him in an expedition. Vide *Gregor. Turon. lib.* 5, *c.* 26, *p.* 211. Childebert, who began his reign A. D. 576, proceeded in the same manner against others, who had been guilty of a like offence. *Ibid., lib.* 7, *c.* 42, *p.* 342. Such a fine would not have been exacted whilst property remained in its first state, or as *allodial* property, when military service was entirely voluntary. Notwithstanding the almost general prevalence of these *Feuds*, no doubt many estates were *allodial* in every respect.—The clearest proof of the distinction between *allodial* and *beneficiary* possessions is contained in two charters published by *Muratori*, by which it appears that a person might possess *one* part of his estate as *allodial*, which he could dispose of at pleasure; and the other as a *beneficiary*, or a *feud*, of which he had only the *usufruct;* the property returning to his superior lord on his demise. Vice *Antiq. Ital. medii ævi*, vol. i. *p.* 559, 565. The same distinction is pointed out in a *Capitulaire* of *Charlemagne*, A. D. 812. *Edit. Bal.*, vol. i. *p.* 491. Count *Everard*, who married a daughter of *Louis le Debonaire*, in the will, by which he disposes of his vast estates among his children, distinguishes between what he called *"proprietate,"* or *allodial*, and what he held "*beneficio*," or as *a feud;* and it appears, that the greater part was allodial, *A. D.* 837. Vide *Aul. Miræi opera Diplomatica, Lovan.* 1723, vol. 1, *p.* 19.

When allodial possessions were *first* rendered feudal, they were not at *once* subjected to all the feudal services. The transition here, as in all other things of importance, was *gradual*, as the great object of a feudal vassal was to obtain protection. When allodial proprietors first consented to become vassals of any powerful leader, they continued to retain so much of their ancient independence as was consistent with that new relation. The homage they did to the superior of whom they chose to hold, was called "*Homagium planum*," (*Simple Homage*,) and bound them to nothing more than Fidelity, but without any obligation either of military service, or attendance in the courts of their superior. Of this "*Homagium planum*," some traces, though obscure, may still be discovered. *Brussel, tom.* 1, *p.* 97. Among the ancient writs, published by *D. D. De Vie*, and *Vaisette, Hist. de Langued.* are a great many which they call "*Homaga.*" They seem to be an intermediate step between the "*Homagium planum*," mentioned by *Brussel*, and the engagement to perform certain *feudal* services. The one party promises *protection*, and grants certain lands; the other engages to defend the person of the grantor, and to assist him likewise in defending *his* property, as often as he shall be summoned to do so. But *these* engagements were accompanied with none of the *feudal* formalities; and no mention is made of any of the other feudal services. They appear rather to possess the nature of a *mutual* contract between equals, than the agreement of a vassal to perform services to his superior lord. Vide *Preuves de l'Hist. de Long., tom.* 2, 173, *et passim.* As soon as men became, *by degrees*, accustomed to these, the other feudal services were (perhaps gradually) introduced. We may, from the whole, therefore conclude, that as *allodial* property often subjected those who possessed it to serve the *community*, so *Feuds, Fiefs,* or *Beneficia*, subjected such as held them to *personal* services and fidelity to *him* from whom they received their land, or from whom they held it, to be *protected* as before mentioned.

FIDEI COMMISSA.—Sometimes, among the *Romans*, a man left his property in trust (*fidei committebat*) to a friend, on certain conditions; particularly, that he should give it up (*ut restitueret*, vel *redderet*) to some person or persons. Whatever was left in this manner, whether the whole estate, or any one thing, as a farm, &c., was called *fidei commissum* (like a trust estate with us); and a person to whom it was left was called *Hæres fiduciarius*, who might either be a citizen or a foreigner.

It is probable that from this custom originated the devising of estates in Trust, and upon Uses, which has been so *minutely* described, in volume upon volume, by some of the *English* conveyancers. Vide *Preston, Sugden, Fearne, &c., &c.* The *minutia* of uses, trusts, contingent remainders and executory devises, necessary to be learned by the *English* conveyancers, appear, on the first view, to require abilities of no ordinary description to comprehend them.

A testament of the kind above referred to, was in the form of request or entreaty (*verbis precativis*); thus *Rogo, Peto, Volo, Mando, Fidei tuo committo,* Ter. And. ii. 5, and not by way of command, as other testaments usually were (*verbis imperativis*). These kind of testaments, it is said, might be written in any language.

FIRMA.—About the time of *William* the Conqueror, Rents for Lands were reserved to the lords, or great landed proprietors, in victuals, and other necessaries for their use; but afterwards, (perhaps about the reign of *Henry* the First,) these Rents were generally altered, and commuted to monied payments.

FŒDUM LAICUM.—A Lay-Fee. Lands held in fee of a *Lay* Lord, as distinguished from the *Ecclesiastical* holding in *Frank-almoign.* Vide *Kennet's Gloss.*

FŒDUM MILITARE.—A Knight's Fee.—This is said to have been so much inheritance as was enough to maintain a *Knight,* with sufficient retinue: which in *Henry* the Third's day was fifteen pounds sterling. *Stowe,* in his Annals, says, there were found in *England,* in the time of the *Conqueror,* 60,211 *Knights' fees,* whereof the *Religious* houses, before their suppression, possessed 28,015.

FOLCMOTE, or FOLKMOTE.—*Spelman* says the *Folkmote* was a sort of annual parliament, or convention of the *Bishops, Thanes, Aldermen,* and *Freemen,* upon every *May Day* yearly. But *Doctor Brady* infers from the laws of the *Saxon* Kings, that it was an inferior Court, held before the *King's Reeve* or *Steward,* every month, to do "*Folk-right,*" or compose smaller differences, from whence there lay an appeal to the superior courts. Vide *Brady's Gloss.* 48. Squire seems to think the *Folkmote* not distinct from the *Shiremote,* or common general meeting of the county. According to *Kennet,* the *Folkmote* was a Common Council of all the inhabitants of a city, town or borough, convened often by sound of bell to the *Mote-Hall,* or house; or it was applied to a large congress of all the freemen, within a county, where, formerly, all Knights and military Tenants did *Fealty* to the King, and elected the annual Sheriff on October the first. After which the City *Folkmote* was swallowed up by the Select Committee, or Common Council; and the County *Folkmote,* in the *Sheriff's Tourn* and *Assizes.*

FORMEDON in the *Descender;* Formedon in the *Remainder;* and Formedon in the *Reverter.*—These are *three* species of writs, frequently mentioned in the law books. 1st. Formedon in the *descender* lies, where a gift in tail is made, and the tenant in tail aliens the lands entailed; or is disseised of them and dies; in this case the heir in tail shall have his writ of "*Formedon in the descender,*" to recover the lands so given in tail, against him who is then the actual tenant of the freehold. 2d. A *formedon in remainder* lies, where a man gives lands to another for life, or in tail, with remainder to a third person in tail, or in fee; and he who hath the particular estate, dieth without issue inheritable, and a stranger intrudes upon him in remainder, and keeps him out of possession: in this case the remainder man shall have his writ of "*Formedon in the remainder,*" wherein the whole form of the gift is stated, and the happening of the event upon which the remainder depended. This writ is not given in express words by the statute *De donis;* but is founded upon the *equity* of the statute, and upon this *maxim* in law, "that if any one hath a right to land, he ought also to have an action to recover it." Vide *Fitz. N. B.* 217. 3d. A "*Formedon in the reverter*" lies, where there is a gift in tail, and afterwards, by the death of the donee, or his heirs, without issue of his body, the reversion falls in upon the

14

donor, his heirs or assigns; in such case the reversioner shall have this writ to recover the lands, wherein he shall suggest this gift, his own title to the reversion minutely derived from the donor, and the failure of issue upon which his reversion takes place. Vide *Fitz. N. B.* 219. 8 *Rep.* 88.

FRANCHISE.—This means a privilege or exemption from ordinary jurisdiction, as for a corporation to hold pleas, &c., &c. And sometimes it is an immunity from tribute: it is either *personal* or *real,* i. e. belonging to the person *immediately,* or by means of *this* or *that* place. Franchises are a species of incorporeal hereditaments. Franchise, and Liberty, are frequently used as *synonymous* terms.

FRANK-ALMOIGN—or Free Gift. This often means a tenure by a Spiritual service, where an ecclesiastical corporation, sole or aggregate, holds lands to them, and their heirs in free and perpetual alms; and *perpetual,* supposes to be a *fee simple;* though it may pass without the word successors. Vide *Litt.* § 133. *Co. Litt.* 94.

G.

GABELLA.——A tax on merchandise or personal property.

GAFOL, GAFEL.——Rent; tax; interest.

GAIGNONT son terre.——Tilling his land.

GAINAGE or GAIGNAGE.——Implements of husbandry; also profits from land.

GAINOR.——One who cultivated arable lands.

GAJUM.——A dense wood.

GALES.——Wales.

GALLIA causidicos docuit facunda Brittannos.——France, elegant in its oratory, taught the British lawyers.

GAMACTA.——A stroke.

GARANDIA, GARANTIA, GARANTUM.——A warranty.

GARATHINX.——An absolute gift.

GARRENA.——A warren.

GARSUMME.——A fine.

GARTH.——A yard; a small homestead.

GASACHIO.——An adversary.

GASINDUS.——A house servant.

GASTALDUS.——A steward.

GAUDENS hæreditate sua.——Rejoicing in his inheritance.

GAVELKIND.——A peculiar tenure of land. *Vide note.*

GAVELET.——A process to recover rent or service.

GEBOCIAN.——A written conveyance. Sax.

GEBURUS.——A neighbor; one who dwelt in a *geburscip* or village.

GELD, GILD.——A fine; payment; the value.

GEMOTE.——An assembly.

GENERALIA comitatuum placita certis locis et vicibus teneanter. Intersunt autem Episcopi, Comites, &c., et agantur primo debita veræ Christianitatis jura: secundo, Regis placita: postremo, causæ singulorum dignis satisfactionibus expleanter.——That the general pleas (or suits) of the counties, be held in certain places, and courses. Also that the Bishops, Earls, &c., be present, and that in the first place, the just rights of the true Christian religion be determined; secondly, the pleas (or suits) of the king; and lastly, that the causes of all persons be determined with due satisfaction. *Vide note.*

GENERALIS clausula non porrigitur ad ea quæ ante specialiter sunt comprehensa.——A general clause does not extend to those matters which have been before specially provided for.

GENEROSUS.——A gentleman. *Vide note.*

GENUS generalissimum.——The most general kind.

GEREFA, or REEVE.——A public officer. Sax. This title was attached to various grades of officers. Sheriff or shire-reeve comes from it.

GERERE bellum.——To wage war.

GERMANUS.——Descended from the same ancestors.

GERONTOCOMI.——The name of officers (in Roman law) who managed hospitals for the indigent and infirm.

GERSUMA.——A price for a thing.

GESTIO pro hærede.——Acting as heir. *Pro hærede*

gerere est pro domino gerere.——To act as heir is to act as owner.

GETTER.——To cast.

GEWINEDA.——Sax.　The public convention of the people to decide a cause—"*Et pax quam aldermanus regis in quinque burgorum* 'Gewineda' *dabit emendatur* 12 *libres.*" *El. Etheldred, cap.* 1.

GEWITNESSA.——Sax.　The giving of evidence.

GIFTOMAN.——The person who has a right to dispose of a woman in marriage.　*Swedish Law.*

GILDA mercatoria.——"A gild of merchants."　A mercantile meeting, or assembly; hence the word "*Guild.*"

GILOUR.——One who cheats in merchandise.

GISARMES.——An axe.

GIST of action.——From Fr. *gist.*　The cause for which the action is brought: the *very* point in question, without which the action is not maintainable.　Vide 5 *Mod.* 305.

GIT.——The foundation, or ground: the point.

GLADIIS, baculis et cultellis.——With swords, staves, and knives.

GLEANING.——*Leasing,* or *Lesing,* from "*glanier,*" i. e. gathering loose corn in the fields after reaping.　*Vide note.*

GLEBA.——"Church lands."　Generally taken for the lands belonging to the parish church.

GLYN.——A valley.

GODBOTE.——A fine for a religious offence.　Sax.

GOOLE.——A breakage in a sea wall.

GORS.——A place where fish are kept.

GRADUS habitudo distantium personarum, qua propinquitates distantia inter personas duas vel diversas discernitur. ——The state, or degree of different persons, by which is distinguished the affinity between two or more.

GRÆCA leguntur in omnibus fere gentibus; Latina suis finibus sane continetur.——The Greek language is read in almost all nations.　The Latin, indeed, is confined within their own territories.

GRAFIO.——Used in European law as *gerefa* in Anglo-Saxon, and supposed to have a similar signification; viz., a chief magistrate; one who collected public dues.

GRAFFER or GREFFIER.——A clerk or notary.

GRAND cape.——A writ whereby the king takes possession of land by the tenant's default. *Vide Cape.*

GRAND Serjeanty per magnum servitium.——"Grand Serjeanty by a superior service." One of the ancient tenures of land.

GRANGIA.——A farm house: a farm. *Vide note.*

GRASS-HEARTH.——A service of one day's ploughing done by inferior tenants.

GRATA superveniet quæ non sperabitur hora.——That hour will prove the most pleasing, which is not anticipated.

GRATIS dictum.——A free saying: a transitory observation.

GRATIS litigans.——Suing as a pauper.

GRAVA.——A small grove.

GRAVIUS.——Chief magistrate.

GRAVIORIS injuriæ species est quæ scripta fit quia diutius in conspectu hominum perseverat. Vocis enim facile obliviscimur, at litera scripta manet; et per manus multorum longe, lateque vagatur.——Writing is a species of more serious injury, because it remains longer in public sight, for we easily forget words; but what is written remains, and passes through the hands of many, far and near.

GRITHBRECH.——Sax. Breach of the peace.

GRITHSTOLE. A chair of peace; a sanctuary.

GROSSE bois.——"Great wood." Such wood, as by the common law, or custom, is reputed timber. 2 *Inst.* 642.

GUADAGIUM.——The price given for safe conduct through another person's province or lands.

GUARDIAN ad litem.——A guardian in the suit.

GUBERNATOR.——A pilot or steersman of a ship.

GUILD.——From *Sax.* " gildan," to pay.　A fraternity, or company, each of whom was "*gildare*," to pay something.　*Vide note.*

GULE OF AUGUST.——The first of August.

GWALSTOW.——Sax.　A place of execution.　" *Omnia gwalstowa, i. e. occidendorum loca, totaliter Regis sunt in soca sua.*"—i. e. all the places where murderers are executed wholly belong to the king in soccage.　*Leg. Hen.* 1, c. 11.

GYLTWITE.——Sax.　A compensation, or amends for trespass, "*mulcta pro transgressione.*"　Ll. Edgari Regis anno, 964.

GYVN.——A Jew.

NOTES TO G.

GAVELKIND.—This is a common tenure of landed property in *Kent,* in *England,* whereby the estate of the father is equally divided at his decease among all his sons; or the land of the brother among all his brethren, if he has no issue of his own.

It is said that all the lands of *England* were of a *Gavelkind* nature before the Conquest (A. D. 1066), and descended to all the issue equally ; but that after the Conquest, when Knight's Service was introduced, the descent was restrained to the eldest son for the preservation of the tenure (vide *Lamb.* 167, 3 *Salk.* 129), except in *Kent;* for the supposed reason of which see *Blount,* in v. " *Gavelkind,*" who relates the story of the *Kentish* men surrounding *William* the First, with a moving wood of boughs, and thus obtaining a confirmation of their ancient rights.　It has been said, that in the reign of *Henry* the Sixth, there was not above thirty or forty persons in all *Kent* that held by any other tenure than that of *Gavelkind.*　It appears that the tenure of a considerable part of the lands of that county was altered by the petition of diverse *Kentish* gentlemen, so as to descend to the *eldest* son, according to the course of the common law.　Vide *Hen.* viii., c. 3.

Blackstone relies on the nature of the tenure in *Gavelkind* as a pregnant proof that tenure in free *Soccage* was a remnant of *Saxon* liberty.　It is well known what struggles the sturdy *Kentish* men made to preserve their ancient liberties, and the success with which they were attended.　And it is principally here that we meet with this good and equitable custom, (at least in preference to the unreasonable, if not unjust law of primogeniture,) and we may reasonably conclude that this was a part of those liberties, agreeably to the opinion of *Selden,* who considered that Gavelkind, before the *Norman* Conquest, was the general custom of *England.*

GENERALIA COMITATUM, &c.—There is good reason to believe that the powerful leaders, who seized by force, or who obtained for their services from the Conquerors of the *Roman* Empire different districts of the countries which they acquired, kept possession of them, with all the rights of criminal and civil jurisdiction.　The privilege of judging his own vassals appears to have been a right inherent in every Baron, who had a *Fief*, and no doubt was often used as a privilege for the most oppressive cruelty. As far back as the *Archives* of the Northern nations can conduct us with any certainty, the *Jurisdiction* and *Fief* were united. One of the earliest charters is that of *Ludovicus Pius*, A. D. 814, and it contains the right of territorial jurisdiction in the most express and extensive terms. Vide *Capitul.*, vol. ii. 1405. It appears from a charter in the thirteenth century, that the Barons, who had the right of holding Courts of Justice, received the *fifth* part of the value of the thing sued for, from every subject whose property was the cause of a trial determined in their courts. If, after the *commencement* of a lawsuit, the parties *terminated* it in an amicable manner, or by arbitration, they were (it seems) nevertheless bound to pay the *fifth* part of the subject contested for to the court before which the action had been brought. Vide *Historie de Dauphine, Geneve.* 1722, *tom.* 1, p. 22. What was the extent of the jurisdiction which those who held *Fiefs* originally possessed, we cannot now determine with certainty. It is evident that during the disorders, which in the middle ages prevailed in every kingdom of *Europe*, the great Barons took the advantage of the feebleness of the monarchs, and greatly enlarged their criminal, as well as civil jurisdictions. As early as the tenth century, the more powerful Barons had usurped the right of deciding all causes, civil or criminal, "*The High Justice*," as well as "*The Low.*" Vide *Establ. de St. Louis, lib.* 1, c. 24, 25. Their sentences were final; and there lay no appeal from them to a superior court. Not satisfied with this, the more powerful Barons procured their territories to be erected into *Regalities*, with almost every royal prerogative and jurisdiction.

GENEROSUS.—Gentleman. From the Fr. "*Gentil.*" i. e. *honestus, vel honesto loco natus,—i. e.* honorable, or born of an honorable family; and the *Sax. Mon*, a man, thus meaning a *man well born.* The *Italians* call those "*Gentil homini*," whom we style "*Gentlemen.*" The *French*, under their ancient monarchy, distinguished such by the name of "*Gentil homme;*" and the *Spaniards* adhere to the meaning, by using the word "*Hidalgo*," or "*Hijo d'alga*," who is the son of a man of *account.*

According to some, under the denomination of "*Gentlemen*," are comprised all above *Yeomen.* Vide *Smith de Rep. Ang., lib.* 1, c. 20, 21. A Gentleman has been defined to be one who, without any title, "*bears a coat of arms,*" or whose ancestors have been freemen; and "by the coat of arms which a Gentleman giveth, he is known to be, or not to be, descended from those of his name that lived many hundred years since." There are also said to be "Gentlemen" *by office* and *reputation*, as well as those which are born such. Vide 2 *Inst.* 668; and we read that *Kingston* was *made* a "*Gentleman*" by King *Richard* the Second. *Pat.* 13, *Richd.* 2d, *par.* 1. "*Gentilis Homo*," when the law proceedings were in Latin, was adjudged a *good* addition. *Hil.* 27, *Edw.* 3d. But the addition of "*Esquire*," or "*Gentleman*," was rare before the 1st *Hen.* the Fifth, though that of "*Knight*" is very ancient. 2 *Inst.* 595, 667. Some suppose the word "*Gentleman*" is derived from "*gentle*" man, in opposition to fierce, rude, brutal, &c., but this does not appear to have been the case, for we find the word "*gentle*" in the meaning we *now* generally use it, to have very materially changed its ancient signification: formerly the word "*gentle*" seems to have been synonymous with *spirited, high-bred, courageous*, &c. Thus one of the old poets says:

"A GENTLE Knight came pricking o'er the plain,
Who nought did *fear*, nor ever was *ydrad.*"

And again:

"He is *gentle*, and not *simple.*"

GLEANING, LEASING, OR LESING—(from *Glainer.*) Gathering loose corn in the fields. It has been often said, that by the Common Law and Custom of *England* the poor are allowed to enter and *glean* upon another's ground after the harvest without being guilty of trespass, which humane provision appears borrowed from the *Mosaic* Law. Vide also *trials per Pais.* c. 15, pp. 438, 534. But it now appears to have been settled, by a solemn judgment, that a *right* to glean in the harvest field cannot be legally claimed by any person at Common Law. Vide 1 *H. Black. Rep.* 51, 63. *Burr. Rep. Rex* v. *Price,* 1926.

GRANGIA.—A house, or farm, where corn is laid up in barns, *granaries,* &c., and provided with stables for horses, stalls for oxen, and other things necessary for husbandry. This definition is agreeable to *Spelman.* According to *Wharton,* " *Grange*" is strictly, and properly, the farm of a monastery where the religious deposited their corn. Dr. *Johnson* derives the word from *Grange,* Fr., and defines it to be a farm, generally—a farm, with a house, distant from neighbors. In *Lincolnshire,* and in other northern counties of *England,* a *lone* house, or farm, is called a " *Grange.*" Vide *Stevens's Shakspeare.*

GUILD.—The original of the *Guilds* is said to be from the old *Saxon* law, by which neighbors entered into an *association,* and became bound to each other, to bring forth any person who committed a crime, or make satisfaction to the party injured; for which purpose they raised a sum of money themselves, and put it in a *common* stock, whereout a pecuniary compensation was made, according to the nature of the offence committed. In those rude times, this obligation was of great service to the community, as it excited the householder to be watchful of the conduct of every new sojourner in his vicinity.

H.

HABEAS corpora.——That you have the bodies.

HABEAS corpora juratorum.——"That you have the bodies of the jurors." A writ so called.

HABEAS corpora quatuor militum.——That you have the bodies of four knights.

HABEAS corpora recognitorum.——That you have the bodies of the recognitors.

HABEAS corpus.——"That you have the body." The great writ of the people's liberty.

HABEAS corpus ad recipiendum.——That you have the body to receive.

HABEAS corpus ad respondendum.——That you have the body to answer.

HABEAS corpus ad satisfaciendum.——That you have the body to make satisfaction.

HABEAS corpus ad satisfaciendum, et ad recipiendum.—— That you have the body to satisfy, and to receive.

HABEAS corpus ad subjiciendum.——That you have the body to submit (or answer).

HABEAS corpus ad testificandum.——That you have the body to give evidence. .

HABEAS corpus cum causa.——That you have the body with the cause (why he is arrested).

HABEAS corpus cum causa, ad faciendum, et recipiendum.——That you have the body, with the cause (of the arrest) to do, and to receive.

HABEAT et habebit tam plenam potestatem, &c.—— He may have and shall enjoy as full power (or authority) &c.

HABENDUM et tenendum sibi et hæredibus.——To have and to hold to him and his heirs.

HABENDUM per liberum servitium.——To hold by free service.

HABENTEM hæreditatem in maritagio—vel aliquam ter- ram ex causa donationis.——Having an inheritance in marriage, or some other gift of land.

HABENTIA.——"Riches." In some ancient charters, the term "*habentes homines*," is taken for rich men.

HABENT legibus sancitum, si quis quid de republica, si- nistris, rumore, aut fama acceperit, ut ad magistratum de- ferat neve cum alio communicet; quod sæpe homines temerarios atque imperitos falsis rumoribus terreri, et ad facinus impelli, et de summis rebus consilium capere cog- nitum est.——They have it ordained by law, that if a per- son hear anything affecting the republic, by omens, rumor, or report, that he lay it before the magistrate, and not communicate with any other person; because it is known that thoughtless and illiterate men are frequently fright- ened by false rumors, and driven to commit crimes, and conceive (bad) intentions in affairs of the greatest importance.

HABENT recognitiones.——They have their recognizances.

HABERE.——To have.

HABERE cognitionem placitorum.——To hold cognizance of pleas.

HABERE facias possessionem.——That you cause to take possession.

HABERE facias seisinam.——That you cause to have the possession.

HABERE facias visum.——" That you cause a view to be taken." Also a writ which lay in divers cases, in real actions, as in *formedon*, &c., where a view was required to be taken of the lands in controversy. Vide *Fitz. N. B.*

HABERE in procinctu.——To have in a state of readiness.

HABERE non debet.——He ought not to have.

HABERET, occuparet et gauderet.——He might have, held and enjoyed.

HABET aliquid ex iniquo omne magnum exemplum, quod contra singulos, utilitate publica rependitur.——Every great example of punishment has in it something of injustice; but the sufferings of individuals are compensated by the service rendered to the public.

HABET nulla bona.——He has no goods.

HABETO tibi res tuas.——Have your goods to yourself.

HABET Rex plures curias in quibus diversæ actiones terminantur, et illarum curiam habet unam propriam, sicut aulam regiam, et judices capitales, qui proprias causas regis terminant, et aliorum omnium per querulam, vel per privilegium, seu libertatem.——The King holds more courts in which various actions are terminated, and among these he has one proper court, as a Royal Hall, and Chief Justices, who decide the king's own causes, and those of all others (brought) by complaint, privilege or license.

HABILES ad matrimonium.——Fit for marriage.

HABILIS et inhabilis diversis temporibus.——Capable and incapable, at different times.

HABITATIO dicitur ab habendo.——A dwelling house is (so) called from holding (or possessing).

HABITUM et tonsuram clericalem.——A clerical gown, and shaving of the head.

HÆC falsa, ficta, malitiosa verba.——These false, feigned and malicious words.

HÆC est finalis concordia.——This is the last agreement.

HÆC in fœdera non venimus.——We have not entered into these agreements.

HÆC quæ nullius in bonis sunt, et olim fuerunt inventoris, de jure naturali, jam efficiuntur principis de jure gentium.——Those things which have no owner, and heretofore were the property of the finder, are now made the right of the sovereign by the law of nations.

HÆC sunt institutæ quæ *Edgarus* Rex, consilio sapientium suorum, instituit.——These are the institutes which King *Edgar* enacted, by the advice of his learned counsellors.

HÆC sunt institutiones quæ Rex *Edmundus* et Episcopi sui, cum sapientibus suis instituerunt.——These are the ordinances which King *Edmund* and his Bishops, with their council, enacted.

HÆC sunt judicia quæ sapientes in rebus arduis instituerunt.——These are the rules enacted, by the learned in difficult matters.

HÆ nugæ in seria mala ducunt.——These trifles lead to serious mischiefs.

HÆREDA de omnibus quidem cognoscit, non tamen de omnibus judicat.——The Court Leet, indeed, takes cognizance of all things, but does not give judgment in all.

HÆREDEM deus facit, non homo.——God makes the heir, ot man.

Hæredes extranei.——Extraneous heirs, such as were not within the power of the testator.

Hæredes maritentur absque disparagatione.——That heiresses be not improperly married, (meaning not married to persons of low estate.)

Hæredes proximi.——Children of the deceased.

Hæredes successoresque sui cuique liberi, et nullum testamentum—si liberi non sunt, proximus gradus, in possessione, fratres, patrii, avunculi.——The children of every man are his heirs and successors, if there be no will—if there be no children, the next of kin, as brothers, paternal or maternal uncles succeed to the possession. *Vide note.*

Hæredi facti.——Heirs made (by will or testament).

Hæredipeta.——One who seeks to become heir to another.

Hæreditas jacens.——An estate lying vacant between the demise of the last occupant and the entry of the successor.

Hæreditas luctuosa.——An inheritance opposed to the natural order of humanity,—such as a parent to succeed to the estate of a child.

Hæreditas naturaliter decendit, nunquam naturaliter ascendit.——An inheritance naturally descends, never naturally ascends.

Hæreditas nunquam ascendit.——An inheritance never ascends.

Hæreditatem augendo.——By increasing the inheritance.

Hæres astrarius.——The heir in actual possession of the estate he is to inherit.

Hæres est nomen juris; filius est nomen naturæ.—— Heir is a term of law; son, a term of nature.

Hæres factus.——A person who becomes the heir by gift or devise.

Hæres fideicommissarius.——The person for whose benefit the estate was given in trust to another.

HÆRES fiduciarius.——An heir to whom the estate is given in trust for another person.

HÆRES jure representationis.——The heir by right of representation.

HÆRES legitimus est quem nuptiæ demonstrant.——He is the lawful heir whom the marriage shows to be so.

HÆRES natus.——"A person born the heir:" in opposition to *hœres factus* (a person made heir by will).

HÆRES non redimet terram suam sicut faciebat tempore fratris mei, sed legitima et justa revelatione relevabit eam.——The heir shall not redeem his land as he did in the time (or reign) of my brother; but by a lawful and just fine he shall relieve it.

HÆRETICO comburendo.——By burning the heretic. *Vide note.*

HÆRETICUS est qui dubitat de fide Catholica; et qui negligit servare ea quæ *Romana* Ecclesia statuit.——A heretic is one who doubts the Catholic faith; and neglects to observe those things which the *Roman* church has ordained.

HAFNE courts.——Courts held in certain havens or ports in ancient times.

HAGA.——An enclosure or hedge.

HALFKINEG.——The title given to the aldermen of England.

HALIGEMOT.——A Saxon word. A meeting of citizens in their public hall, or tenants in the hall of their baron.

HALLAGE.——(In old English law.) A fee due for such commodities as were sold in the public hall of the town.

HALLYWERCFOLK.——Persons among the Saxons who had charge of land for the benefit of the church, or to repair or defend sepulchres.

HAMALLARE.——To summon.

HAMESECKEN.——Robbery from a dwelling: burglary.

HAMSOCA.——From *ham*, Sax., and *scone*, liberty. *Vide note.*

HANAPER.——A large bag or basket used in the English chancery court for keeping the fees or money received.

HANC veniam damus, petimusque vicissim.——We give and ask leave in return.

HANDGRITH.——Protection given by the king with his own hand.

HANDBABEND.——Having in hand.

HANDSALE.——Anciently it was the custom among northern nations to confirm a sale by the parties shaking hands.

HANTELOD.——(From the German.) An attachment.

HARMISCARA, harniscara.——A species of fine.

HARO.——Hue and cry.

HARTH penny.——In ancient law a tax laid upon every hearth—similar to Peter-pence.

HAUBER.——A great lord.

HAUD inscia, et non incauta futuri.——Neither ignorant, nor careless, with respect to the future.

HEALFANG, or Halsfang, from *Sax.* "Hals," *collum,* and "fang," *capere.*——That punishment " qua alicui collum stringatur," i. e. Collistrigium, the Pillory. Sometimes the word means, " a pecuniary mulct," to commute for standing in the pillory. *Leg. Hen.* 1, c. 11.

HEDAGIUM.——The toll paid at a wharf for landing goods.

HENCHMAN, from the Ger. "*Hengst,*" a war horse.—— It signifies one who runs on foot, attending upon a person of honor. Vide *Stat.* 3, *Edw.* 4.

HE ne es othes worthes that es enes gylty of oth broken. ——This was the old English proverb, spoken of a person who had been convicted of perjury.

HERBAGIUM anterius.——The first crop of grass or hay, in opposition to the aftermath. Vide *Paroch. Antiq.* 459.

HERBAGIUM terræ.——The herbage of the Land: the crop.

HERBERGARE.——To harbor—from " heribergum,"

"heriberga;" *Sax.* "hæreberg," a house of entertainment.

HERCISCERE.——To divide. The word Erciscere is frequently used instead.

HEREDITAMENT.——Anything whatever capable of being inherited, be it real, personal or mixed property.

HEREGELD.——Sax. A tribute or tax for the maintenance of an army : "*Heregeld*" or "*Herezeld*" is also sometimes synonymous with Heriot.

HERETOCHE.——From Sax. "*here*," army, and "*togen*," to lead. The General of an army. *Leg. Edw. Confess.* Ducange says the "*Heretochii*" were the Barons of the realm.

HERETOCHII.——Dukes: Generals: Leaders.

HERI.——Landholders, or proprietors.

HERIREITA.——From Sax. "here," army, and "ryt," a band, a military band.

HERRIETTUM.——A "Herriot." The giving of the best beast, or second best to the Lord of the soil, upon the death of the tenant.

HERUS dat, ut servus faciat.——The master pays, that the servant may do his work.

HERISCHILD.——Army service, or knight's fee.

HETAERIA.——Fraternity, brotherhood.

HEYLODE.——A tax upon the lower tenants, to mend or repair hedges.

HIATUS maxime deflendus.——A chasm greatly to be deplored.

HIC contractus (scilicet feudalis) proprius est *Germanicarum Gentium;* neque usquam invenitur nisi ubi *Germani* sedes posuerunt.——This contract (to wit the feudal one) is peculiar to the *German* nations, nor is it found any where else, except where the *Germans* were located.

> " HIC est qui leges regni cancellat iniquas,
>   Et mandata pii principis æquua facit."

" It is he who expunges the unjust laws of the realm ;

and performs the equitable commands of a pious King." The words of *Johannis Sarisburiens*, speaking of the office of Chancellor—he died in the 12th century.

HIC finis fandi.——Here was an end of the discourse.

HIDARE.——(In old English law.) A tax upon land payable by hides.

HIJS testibus, *Johanne Moore, Jacobo Smith*, et aliis, ad hanc rem convocatis.——"These witnesses *John Moore, James Smith*, and others, being called together for the purpose."

[When lands, during the middle ages, were transferred by writings, the scribe usually wrote the *names* of the witnesses himself. Vide note to "*In cujus rei testimonium*."]

HINC petenda ratio, cur posthumo præterito placeat testamentum ab initio valere; nimirum quia fieii potest, ut non nascatur abortum muliere, ex qua sperabatur, atque hactenus ergo nec pro nata habetur; frustraque objicitur eum qui in utero est, quoties de commodo ejus agitur, pro eo qui in rebus humanis sit, non haberi. Nullum enim hic incommodum sentit, cum statim ut editus est testamentum rumpat; et regula ista sic temporanda est, si modo postea nascatur, tunc enim fictione juris nativitas retro trahitur. ——On this account the reason is to be demanded, why a will may, from its commencement, be efficient in benefiting a posthumous child; certainly it is because it may so happen that it may be born alive by the expecting parent, but as hitherto it cannot be considered *in esse;* and it is unreasonably objected that an unborn child, as often as a thing is done for its benefit, is not to be esteemed as already in existence. For he is sensible of (doing) no injury who destroys the will (itself) as soon as he is born; and in this manner the rule is regulated, that if a child be afterwards born, then, by a fiction of law, the birth has a retrospective application.

HINDENI homines.——From Sax. "*hindene*," i. e. *societas*. A society of men. *Vide note.*

HINE.——A servant. *Vide note.*

HIS damnare reos, illis absolvere culpa.——By these the guilty are condemned, by those the innocent are acquitted. *Vide note.*

HIS perfectis, jurabant in leges judices, ut obstricti religione judicarent.——This being accomplished, the judges swore upon the laws, that they would judge under the obligation of their religion.

HOC audi, homo, quem per manum teneo, &c.——Hear this, O man, whom I hold by the hand, &c.

HOC facias alteri, quod tibi vis fieri.——Do to another, as you would he should do to you.

HOC paratus est verificare per recordum.——This he is ready to verify by the record.

HOC quidem perquam durum est, sed *ita* lex scripta est.——This truly is somewhat severe, but *so* the law is written.

HOC te uno, quo possum, modo, filia, in libertatem vindico.——My daughter, I set you at liberty, by the only method of which I am capable.

HOC vobis ostendit.——This shows to you.

HOC volo, sic jubeo : stet pro ratione voluntas.——This I will; this I command : let my will stand in the place of reason.

HOKETIDE, Hockday or Hocktide (*Cædes*) diem observatum tradunt in memoriam omnium Danorum, ea die clanculo et simul a mulieribus fere occisum : *Hoketide.*——(The day of slaughter). They hand down this transaction as one to be observed in memory of the *Danes*, who were almost totally and secretly murdered on that day by the women. Vide *Spelm. Gloss. verb. " Hoc Day."*

HOLOGRAPH.——A will in the testator's own hand-writing.

HOMAGE ancestral.——Homage by ancestry.

HOMAGIUM.——Homage.

HOMESOKEN, Homsoken, or Hamsoken, or Hamsoca.—— From " *Ham,*" Sax. a house, and " *scone,*" liberty.

HOMICIDIA vulgaria, quæ aut casu, aut etiam sponte

15

committuntur; sed in subitaneo quodam iracundiæ colore et impetu.——Common homicides, which are committed by chance, or even by design; but in some sudden heat and violence of passion.

HOMICIDIUM quod nullo vidente, nullo sciente, clam perpetratur.——Homicide, which, no one seeing or knowing, is done privately.

HOMINE replegiando.——"By replevying (or redeeming) a person." A writ so called.

HOMINES liberi.——Lawful men: liege men. *Vide note.*

HOMINES ligii, Homines de fief, Hommes feodaux.—— Feudal tenants.

HOMO alta mente præditus.——A man endowed with a lofty mind.

HOMO casutus.——One who served within a house.

HOMO chartularius.——A slave freed by charter.

HOMO commendatus.——One who delivered himself into the power of another for protection or maintenance.

HOMO consiliarius.——A counsellor.

HOMOLOGARE.——To confirm or approve.

HOMO mercator vix aut nunquam potest Deo placere; et ideonullus christianus debet esse mercator; aut si voluerit esse, projiciatur de ecclesiæ Dei.——A merchant can scarcely, if at all, please God, and therefore no Christian should be a merchant; and if he wishes to be one, let him be expelled the church of God. *Vide note.*

HONESTE vivere; alterum non lædere; suum cuique tribuere.——To live honorably, not to injure another, and to give to every one his own.

HONORUM luce conspicuos et patrimonii ditioris.——Conspicuous from the splendor of rank, and richer from (the inheritance of) patrimony.

HORAL juridicæ.——Hours during which judges preside in court.

HORS de son fee.——Out of his fee.

HOSPITIA curiæ——Inns of court.

HOSPITILARII.——Hospitallers: or Knights of a religious order. *Vide note.*

HOSTELAGIUM.——A right reserved in ancient times by lords to receive lodging and entertainment in the houses of their tenants.

HOSTEM adjuvat.——He abets the enemy.

HOSTES hi sunt qui nobis, aut quibus nos publice bellum decrevimus; cæteri latrones, aut prædones sunt.——They are enemies against whom we have publicly declared war; others (are considered) as spoilers and robbers.

HOSTIS humani generis.——An enemy of the human race: a Pirate.

HOTCHPOT.——This word alludes to a custom that the property given to a child in the father's life-time shall, upon his decease, be reckoned with the remainder of the effects of the person dying; and then a division be *equally* made. *Vide note.*

H. P. captus per querimoniam mercatorum *Flandriæ,* et imprisonatus offert domino regi *hus* et *haut* in plegio ad standum recto, et ad respondendum prædictis mercatoribus et omnibus aliis qui versus eum loqui voluerint, &c.—— H. P., arrested on complaint of the merchants of *Flanders* and imprisoned, offers to the King an elder-tree, and a halbert's staff, as a pledge, to stand (or appear in court) and to answer to the said merchants and to all others who shall be desirous to allege anything against him.

HUNDRED.——(In English law.) A subdivision of a county, so named because originally composed of ten tilings, or consisting of one hundred freemen. It is said that Alfred instituted this territorial division.

HUSSIER.——Doorkeeper.

HUTESIUM et Clamor.——Hue and cry. *Vide note.*

HYDE Lands.——From "*hyden,*" Sax., to *cover.* A plough land. *Vide note.*

HYPOTHECA.——A Gage or Mortgage. *Vide note to Mortgagium.*

NOTES TO H.

HÆREDES, SUCCESSORESQUE, &c.—That estates should descend to the heirs of the body, and, in case of the default of such representatives, to the next in proximity of blood, if not a law of nature, seems to correspond with its dictates. History hardly carries us back to a time, when the admission of this claim did not prevail among mankind. This appears to have been the universal rule of transmission of property, and to have been established in communities *widely* separated by time and place. Thus, the representation in the channel of blood and proximity, seems to have had its foundation higher than any *positive* institutions, though to *positive* institutions we must, of course, refer the, *modifications* of this rule of succession, which, indeed, has been so variously ordered, that perhaps no two nations *exactly* resemble each other in their institutions regarding it.

That the right of controlling this succession by the private will of the possessor, was an *improved* age of legislation, there is much concurrent testimony to show. Until the legislation of *Solon*, the *Athenians* did not possess this privilege; as it appears from many authors, particularly from *Plutarch*, in his life of *Solon;* nor, according to *Selden* " *de success. de bonis Hebr.*," c. 24, did it exist among the ancient *Jews;* nor, as we learn from *Tacit. de mor. Ger.*, c. 20, among the *Germans* in his day.

The tenderness which continued to prevail among the ancient *Romans* for the legal heir, is strongly displayed in their provisions by the laws, *Furia, Vocania,* and *Falcidia;* and more pointedly, perhaps, by their remedy of " *Querula inofficiosi testamenti*"—i. e. "the complaint or suit as to a disinheriting will." This suit often, or perhaps generally, arose, wherever a will was made against the order of *natural* affection, without *reasonable* cause.

With respect to the question, how far the *right* of disposition by *will* existed among the *Romans, before* the law of the Twelve Tables, there seems to be much variety of opinion. *Justinian* proposed the order in which the form of the " *testamenti factio* "—i. e. " the making of a testament," proceeded, which the student will consult with much satisfaction, in the commentary of *Vinnius,* edited with notes by *Heineccius,* in the title "*De testamentis ordinandis.*" It appears that the most ancient mode of making a testament among the *Romans,* was by converting a man's *private* will into a public law; for such seems to have been the object and intention of the promulgation of a testament " *in calatis comitus,*" i. e. " in the presence of the *Roman* people," summoned before the sacerdotal college, "*per curias.*" And, according to *Heineccius,* these assemblies were not convened specially for the giving sanction to wills, *sed legum ferendarum magistratum, qui creandorum causa immo, et ob alia negotia publica bellum, pacem, judicia,*" &c.—i. e. " but rather for the making magisterial laws, for those about to be created, and for other public affairs, such as war, peace, judgments," &c.

Thus, was the *private* disposition by testament of the property of an individual promulged and ratified, in the same manner as a *public* law; and for this reason, the " *testamenti factio* " has, in the text of the imperial law, been said to be *non privati, sed publici juris*—i. e. "not of private, but of public right." And again, by *Ulpian,* it is said, " *legatum est, quod legis modo testamento relinquitur.*" *Ulp., tit.* 24, § 1—i. e. "it is appointed, that, in this form of a will, he gives up what is required by the law."

Another form of testament which existed antecedently to the law of the Twelve Tables, was that called " *testamentum procinctum,*" which was the privilege of those who were on *the eve of going to battle,* or " *girt* " for war, with the uncertainty on their minds of their ever returning; and was among the *immunities,* in regard to property, conferred by the *Romans* on the defenders of their country.

.But, as the *Comitia* was held but twice a year, and as a man might be surprised by sickness, without having the opportunity of thus solemnizing his last will; and the attendance upon their public assemblies was often difficult, or impossible to the aged and infirm; and, furthermore, as women were, by their forms, precluded from making any testament, as not having any communion with these " *Comitia,*" (according to *Gellius, lib.* 5. c. 19,) a third method was struck out, which might facilitate the ultimate disposal of private property to *all* descriptions of persons; and this last method was called the " *testamentum per œs et libram*—i. e. "the testament made by money and balance," which was a *fictitious* purchase of the family inheritance, or heirship, by *money weighed in a balance,* and tendered to the intended inheritor of the testator, before witnesses. [The weighing of the purchase money appears to be very ancient. Vide *Gen.* xxiii. 16.]

Thus, it is said to be " *Imago vetusti moris in venditione atque alienatione rerum mancipi, quæ uno verbo, mancipatio dicitur, nimirum ut is in quem hæ res transferebantur, eas emeret domino ære et libro appenso ei numma uno*"— i. e. "the form of ancient usage in the sale and alienation of disposable property, which is termed in one word ' conveyancing,' to wit, that he to whom the property is transferred, should buy the same from the owner by brass, weighed out for him by balance, in moneys only." And, it seems, that this fictitious proceeding was still retained after the promulgation of the law of the Twelve Tables had authorized the making of wills by the clause of " *Paterfam, uti legassit, &c., ita jus esto*"—i. e. "as the master of the family chooses to do, &c., let that be the law ;" for it was still considered as necessary to raise the will of a private man to a level with the laws of the state, that it should take the shape of a strict legal transaction " *inter vivos ;*" for *testandi de pecunia sua legibus certis facultas est permissa, non autem juris dictionis mutare formam, vel juri publico derogare cuiquam permissum est ;*" c. 6. 23, 13—i. e. "the power of disposing of his property is permitted by certain laws, not, however, to alter the form of the language of the law, nor is it permitted to subtract anything from a public right (or law.") The two former methods were thrown into total disuse by the " *testamentum per œs et libram ;*" but this last mode of *willing,* again made way for others of a more convenient description.

The methods above mentioned were referable to the " *Jus Civile,*" or, as we express it, the law of the land; but, from the edict of the *Prætor,* other forms, at length, were brought into practice, by virtue of which "*jus honorarium,*" the " *mancipatio,*" and the weighing and delivering of money was dispensed with; and, in their stead, the solemnity of *signing by seven witnesses,* was introduced, the *presence* only, and not the signature of the witnesses, being necessary by the " *Jus Civile.*"

At length, however, by gradual use, and progressive alterations, as the text of *Justinian* informs us, the " *Lex Prætoria,*" and the " *Jus Civile,*" were, in some degree, incorporated ; and a compounded regulation took place, whereby it became requisite to the valid constitution of a will, that the witnesses should be *present* (the presence of witnesses being the rule of the " *Jus Civile,*") that *they,* and also the *testator,* should *sign,* according to the superadded institutions of positive law ; and, lastly, that in virtue of the *Prætorian* edict, their *seals* should be affixed; and that the number of witnesses should be *seven.* Afterwards, the further ceremony of *naming* the heir in the testament was added by *Justinian,* and again taken away by the same Emperor, and, at length, the excess of testimony was corrected by the *Canon* law, in the *Pontificate* of *Alexander* the Third, by which it was declared sufficient to prove a testament by *two* or *three* witnesses, the parochial minister being added, " *improbata constitutione juris civilis de septem testibus adhibendis et nimis longe recedente ab eo quod scriptum est, in ore duorum vel trium testium stet omne verbum.*" Vide *Swinb.* 64, *Duet.* c. 18, *Matt.* c. 18— i. e. "that is very far removed from the constitution of the civil law as to the producing of several witnesses according to that which is written, in the mouth of two or three witnesses every word shall be established," which information obtained the sanction of general usage. *Swinburn* says that "this institution had also been reformed by the general custom of the realm, which distinctly required no more than *two* witnesses, so they were free from any just cause of exception," which observation he repeats in several places of his treatise on wills. *Bracton* has also the following passage—"*Fieri autem debet testamentum liberi hominis ad minus coram duobus vel pluribus viris legalibus et honestis, clericis vel laicis ad hoc specialiter convocatis, ad probandum testamentum defuncti si opus fuerit, si de testamento dubitatas.*" Bracton, *lib.* 32, fol. 61,—i. e. "the testament of every freeman should, at least, be made before two or three good and honorable men, assembling with them, for this special purpose, some of the clergy and laity, to prove, if there be necessity, the will of the deceased, if there be any doubt relating thereto." But these words import a recommendation, and not an imperative rule. Until of late years, however, wills of personalty were made without the requisites anciently observed. Students, who require particular information on this point, may consult the valuable works of *Roper, Swinburn, Roberts,* and *Powell.*

HÆRETICO COMBURENDO.—This writ formerly lay against a *Heretic,* who had been convicted of *Heresy,* by the *Bishop,* and afterwards abjured it, fell into the same again, or some other heresy; and was thereupon delivered over to the *Secular* power. Vide *Fitz.* N. B. 69. By this writ, grantable out of Chancery, *Heretics were burnt;* and so were, likewise, witches, sorcerers, &c. Thanks to the general intelligence of the present day, this writ "*hæretico comburendo,*" is only known in name. We can only say "such things were." However, it now appears to us a matter of astonishment, that human reason could ever have been so far degraded, especially under the mild precepts of Christianity.

HAMSOCA, &c.—This means the privilege or liberty which every one has in his own house; and he who *invades* it is properly said to commit "*Homesoken.*" This we take to be what is now called *Burglary.* Vid. *Bract., lib.* 3, *Du Cange Leg. Canuti, c.* 39. It is also *sometimes* taken for an impunity to those who commit burglary. Vide *W. Thorn., p.* 2030. In the *Scotch* law, "*Haimsucken*" is defined to be the crime of beating or assaulting a person in his *own* house, and was anciently punished with death. Vide *Bele's Scotch Law Dict.*

HINDENI HOMINES.—In the time of the *Saxons* all men (among them) were ranked into *three* classes, and valued as to satisfaction for injuries, &c., according to the class they were in: the highest class were valued at *twelve* hundred shillings, and were called *Twelfth hind;* the middle class were valued at *six* hundred shillings, and were called *Sex hind men;* and the lowest at *two* hundred shillings, and called *Twy hind men;* their wives were termed *Hindas.* Vide *Brompt. Leg. Alf., cap.* 12, 30, 31.

HINE—or, rather, perhaps, "HIND." A servant, or one of the family; but is properly a term for a servant in *husbandry;* and he that oversees the rest was called the "*Master Hine.*"

HIS DAMNARI REOS, &c.—It was anciently the custom with the *Romans* to use *white* and *black* pebbles (*lapilli, vel calculi*), in voting at trials, "*mos erat antiquis niveis atrisque lapillis*"—i. e. "it was a custom (to vote) with white and black pebbles." "*His damnare reos, illis absolvere culpa*"—i. e. "by these the accused are condemned, by these they are acquitted." *Ov. Met.* xv. 41. Hence the expression, "*Causa paucorum calculorum,*" a cause of small importance; where there were few judges to vote. *Quinct.* viii. 3, 14. " *Om-nis calculus immittem demittitur ater in urnam*," meaning "he is condemned by all the judges." Ov. Met. xv. 44. " *Reportare calculum deteriorem*," to be condemned; " *meliorem*," to be acquitted. *Corp. Juris*—" *Errori album calculum adjicere*," meaning to pardon or excuse. Vide *Plin. Ep.* i. 2. To this *Horace* is thought to allude. *Sat.* ii. 3, 246. " *Cretâ an carbone notandi?*" i. e. "are they to be acquitted, or condemned?" and *Pers. Sat.* v. 108; but more probably to the *Roman* custom of marking in their calendar unlucky days with black (*carbone*), with charcoal, whence " *dies atri*," for " *infausti*," i. e. unlucky days, and lucky days, marked with white (*cretâ vel cressâ notâ*), with chalk. Hence, " *notare*, vel *signare diem lacteâ gemmâ* vel *albâ melioribus lapillis; vel albis calculis*," meaning to mark a day as fortunate. *Mart.* viii. 45, ix. 53, xi. 37. This custom is said to have been borrowed from the *Thracians*, or *Scythians*, who, every evening before they slept, threw into an urn, or quiver, a *white* pebble *if* the day had passed agreeably; but if not, a *black* one: and at their death, by counting the pebbles, their lives were judged to have been happy, or otherwise. Vide *Plin.* vii. 40. To this *Martial* beautifully alludes, xii. 34. The *Athenians*, in voting about the banishment of a citizen who was suspected to be too powerful, used *shells*, on which those who were for banishing him wrote his *name;* and threw each his shell into an urn. This was done in a popular assembly; and if the number of shells amounted to six thousand, he was banished for *ten* years by an *Ostracism*. *Nep. in Themist.* 8, *Arrist*. Diodorus says the banishment was for *five* years only, xi. 55. When the number of judges who condemned and those who acquitted were *equal*, the criminal was dis. charged, (vide *Cic. Cluent.* 27. *Plut. in mario*) calculo *Minervæ;* by the vote of *Minerva*, as it was called; because when *Orestes* was tried before the *Areopagus* at *Athens* for the murder of his mother, he was acquitted by the determination (*sententiâ*) of that goddess. Vide *Cic. pro Mil.* 3, &c. In allusion to this, a privilege was granted to *Augustus*, if the number of the *judices* was but *one* more than those who acquitted, of adding *his* vote to make an equality; and thus of *acquitting* the criminal. Vide *Dio.* li. 19. While the *judices* were putting the ballots in the urn, the criminal and his friends threw themselves at their *feet*, and used every method to move their compassion; and very frequently the greater the degree of turpitude with which the criminal was tainted, the more *abject* and earnest were his supplications; while the man of stern inflexibility scorned to act so meanly *;* and was, on that account, the more liable to condemnation by his undiscerning judges.

When there was any obscurity in the case, and the *judices* were uncertain whether to condemn or acquit the criminal, they expressed this by giving in tablets, on which the letters N. L. were written, and the *Prætor*, by pronouncing " *Amplius*,"—i. e. "a longer time," the cause was then deferred to any other day the *Prætor* chose to name. This was called " *Ampliatio*,"— i. e. "an adjournment," and the criminal, or cause, was said " *ampliari*"—i. e. "adjourned," which sometimes was done several times, and the cause pleaded each time anew. *Cic. Brut.* 22. " *Bis ampliatus, tertia, absolutus est reus.*" Liv. xliii. 2.—i. e. "Twice and thrice adjourned, the accused is discharged." *Causa L. Cottæ, septies ampliata, et ad ultimum octavo judicio absoluta est.* Val. Max. viii.—i. e. "The cause of L. Cotta was adjourned seven times, and, at length, on the *eighth verdict, he was discharged.*" Sometimes the *Prætor*, to gratify the criminal, or his friends, put off the trial, till he should resign his office; and thus not have it in his power to pass sentence against him. *Liv.* xli. 22. If the criminal was acquitted, he went home and resumed his usual dress (*sordido habitu posito, albam togam resumebat*)—i. c. "throwing off his mean garb, he put on the white gown or robe." If there was ground for it, he might bring his accuser to a trial for false accusation (*calumnia*), i. o. for detraction, or for what was called " *prevaricatio*," i. e. betraying the cause of one's client, and by neglect or collusion in assisting his opponent, (*Cic. Topic,* 36. *Plin. Ep.* i. 20, iii. 9, *Quinctil.* ix. 2,) which were considered among the *Romans* most odious crimes; but to the *immortal* honor of that nation, the offence was not even mentioned to have arisen for *several hundreds of years!*

HOMINES LIBERI.—These were persons employed, it is said, chiefly in agriculture, and were distinguished by various names among the writers of the middle ages. *Arimanni; Conditionales; Originarii; Tributales, &c.* These seemed to have been persons who possessed some small *allodial* property of their own; and besides that, frequently cultivated some farm belonging to their more wealthy neighbors, for which they paid a fixed rent, and likewise bound themselves to perform several small services "*in prato, vel in messe, in aratura, vel in vinea,*" such as ploughing a certain quantity of their lord's ground, assisting him in the harvest, and vintage work, &c. The clearest proof of this may be found in *Murat.* vol. i. p. 712, and in *Du Cange,* under the respective words above mentioned. Whether these *Arimanni, &c.,* were removable at pleasure, or held their lands by way of lease for a certain number of years, it is difficult to ascertain; the former, if we may judge from the genius and maxims of the age, seems to be the most probable. These persons were, however, considered as "*homines liberi,*" or freemen, in the most honorable sense of the word: they enjoyed all the privileges of that condition; and were even called to serve in war, an honor to which no slave was admitted. Vide *Murat. Antiq.* vol. i. 743, *et* vol. ii. 446. This account of the condition of these different classes of persons will enable the student to comprehend the wretched state of the *majority* of the people in the middle ages. Notwithstanding the immense difference between the "*Servi,*" or slaves, and these *Arimanni, &c.,* such was the spirit of tyranny which prevailed among the great proprietors of land, and so various their opportunities of oppressing with impunity those who were settled on their estates, and of rendering their condition almost intolerable, that many *freemen* in despair renounced their liberty, and *voluntarily* surrendered themselves as slaves to their powerful masters, This they did in order that these masters might become, in those warlike times, more immediately interested to afford them *protection,* together with the means of subsistence for themselves and their families. The forms of such a surrender (or " *Obnoxiatio,*" as it was then called) are preserved by *Marculphus, lib.* ii., c. 28; and in the collection of *Formulæ* compiled by him, c. 16. The reason given for the " *Obnoxiatio,*" is the wretched and indigent condition of the person who gave up his liberty. It was still more common for freemen to surrender their liberty to *Bishops* and *Abbots,* that they might partake of that security which the vassals and slaves of churches and monasteries enjoyed, in consequence of the superstitious veneration paid to the Saint, under whose immediate protection they were supposed to be taken. Vide *Du Cange,* voc. " *Oblatus,*" *vol.* iv. 1286. That condition must have been miserable, indeed, which could have induced a Freeman *voluntarily* to renounce his liberty, and give up himself as a *slave* to the disposal of another. The number of slaves in every nation of *Europe* was immense. The greater part of the inferior class of the people in *England,* and also in *France,* was at one time reduced to this state. Vide *Brady's Preface to Gen. Hist.;* also *L'Espr. des loix, liv.* 30, *c.* 11.

HOMO MERCATOR, &c.—The *odium* with which the Monkish Clergy looked upon those engaged in traffic was the cause of this illiberal sentence. Ignorant of almost all the social and endearing duties of life, and interpreting the greater part of the scriptures by their own narrow prejudices, and frequently from isolated passages, they condemned mercantile pursuits *altogether;* and considered it *impossible* that any one could be honest, who was so engaged; and much is it to be regretted that the least *spark* of this odium should, even at the present day, exist among many of those whose only merit consists in their primogeniture to great landed proprietors, or the accidental circumstance of being born of opulent parents.

HOSPITILARII—HOSPITALLERS.—These were Knights of a Religious order, so called, because they built an Hospital at. *Jerusalem*, wherein pilgrims were received. To these Pope *Clement* transported the *Templars;* which order he afterwards repressed for their many great offences. The institution of this order was first allowed by *Gelasus* the Second, *Anno* 1118. Their chief abode was afterwards in *Malta*, an Island given them by the Emperor *Charles* the Fifth, after they were driven from *Rhodes* by *Solyman* the Magnificent, Emperor of the *Turks;* and for that they were called "*Knights of Malta.*" Vide *Mon. Ang.*, 2 *par.* 489, *et Stowe's Ann.*

HOTCHPOT.—This word comes from the Fr. "*Hotchepot,*" used for a confused mingling of divers things, and, among the *Dutch*, it seems flesh cut into pieces, and sodden with herbs and roots; but, by a metaphor, *it is a blending, or mixing of lands given in marriage with other lands in fee, falling by descent;* as if a man seised of thirty acres of land in fee, hath issue only two daughters, and he gives with one of them *ten* acres in marriage, and dies seised of the other *twenty* acres: now she that is thus married, to gain her share of the *rest* of the land, must put her part given in marriage into *Hotchpot*, i. e. she must refuse to take. the sole profits thereof, and cause her land to be *mingled* with the other, so that an *equal* division may be made of the *whole* between her and her sister, as if *none* had been given to her; and thus, for her *ten* acres, she will have *fifteen;* otherwise the sister will have the *twenty* acres of which her father died seised. Vide *Co. Litt.* 3, *cap.* 12.

HUTESIUM ET CLAMOR.—Hue and Cry. Shouting aloud. The *Normans* had such a pursuit, with a *Cry* after offenders, which was called "*Clamor de haro.*" Vide *Grand Custumary*, c. 54. But the *Clamor de haro* seems not to have been a *pursuit* after offenders, but rather a challenge by a person of anything to be his *own;* after this manner, viz.: he who demanded the thing, did, "*with a loud voice,*" before many witnesses, affirm it to be his property, and demanded restitution. This the *Scots* called "*Hutesium,*" and *Skene* says it is deduced from the French "*Oyer*," i. e. *Audire*, to hear, (or rather *Oyez*,) being a cry used before a proclamation. The manner of their *Hue and Cry* he thus describes: "If a robbery be committed, a *horn* is blown, and an *outcry* made; after which, if the party flee away, and doth not yield himself to the King's *Bailiff*, he may be lawfully slain, and hanged upon the next gallows. Vide *Skene in verb.* "Hutesium." In *Rot. Claus.* 30, *Hen.* 3, 5, we find a command to the King's Treasurer to take the City of *London* into his own hands, because the Citizens did not, *secundum legem et consuetudinem regni*," according to the law and custom of the realm, raise the "*Hue and Cry*" for the death of *Guido de Aretto*, and others who were slain. *Hue and Cry* is likewise defined to be the pursuit of an offender from town to town, without any delay, until he be arrested.

HYDE LANDS.—The Hyde of Land is often used in ancient MSS.; and in one old MS. it is said to be one hundred and twenty acres. *Bede* calls it "*Familiam*," and says it is as much as will maintain a *Family*. Others call it *Mansum, Causatam, Carucallam, Sullingham*, &c. Crompton, in his Jurisdiction, says a *Hyde* of land contains one hundred acres; and eight hides make a *Knight's Fee*. But Sir *Edward Coke* holds that a Knight's fee, a hide, or plough land, a yard land, or an ox-gang of land, do not contain any *certain* number of acres. *Co. Litt., fo.* 69. The distribution of *England* by *Hides* of land is very ancient, for there is mention of them in the Laws of King *Ina*.

I.

IBI esse pœna, ubi et noxia est.——Where the offence exists, let there be the punishment.

ICTUM avertere.——To ward off the blow.

ICTUS fulminis.——A stroke of lightning.

ID certum est, quod certum reddi potest.——"That is certain which can be rendered so."——Thus, where a man borrows the cash which a certain quantity of stock realizes on the day he receives the money; and covenants to replace the same quantity of stock on a defined future day—this is a contract *certain;* because it can be ascertained to a demonstration on the day the money becomes payable.

IDEO allegatur per judicium coronatorum.——Therefore it is alleged by the coroner's inquest.

IDEO committitur.——Therefore he is committed.

IDEO consideratum est quod computet; et defendens in misericordia, &c.——Therefore it is considered that he account; and that the defendant be in mercy, &c.

IDEO consideratum est quod convictus sit.——Therefore it is considered that he be convicted.

IDEO consideratum est quod in manu sua læva cauterizetur.——Therefore it is considered that he be burnt in his left hand.

IDEO consideratum est quod prædict' quæren' et pleg' sui de prosequend' sint inde in misericordia.——Therefore it is considered that the said plaintiff and his pledges to prosecute be from thenceforth in mercy.

IDEO consideratum est quod prædictus *W. G.* de utlagaria prædicta exoneretur, et ea occasione non molestatur in aliquo, nec gravetur; sed sit et eat quietus.——Therefore it is considered that the aforesaid *W. G.* be exonerated from the said outlawry; and on that account that he be not in any manner molested nor aggrieved, but that therefore he be and go discharged.

IDEO immediaté veniat inde jurata.——Upon which therefore the jury may immediately come.

IDEO mihi restat dubitandum.——Therefore I must remain in doubt.

IDEO præceptum est vic' quod per probos homines, &c., sc. fa. quod sit hic, &c.——Therefore it is commanded that the sheriff, by good (or lawful) men, &c., make known that he be here, &c.

IDEO præceptum fuit Vicecomiti quod exegi faciat eundem *T. G.* de comitatu in comitatum, &c.——Therefore the sheriff was commanded that he cause the same *T. G.* to be exacted (or demanded) from county to county.

IDEOQUE si mulier, ex qua posthumus, aut posthuma sperabatur, abortum fecerit, nihil impedimentum est scriptis hæredibus ad hæreditatem adeundam.——Therefore if the woman from whom a posthumous son or daughter was expected, produce an abortion, that is no impediment to the heirs (appointed) in writing from succeeding to the inheritance.

IDEOTA a casu, et infirmitate.——An idiot from chance and infirmity.

IDEO utlagatur.——Therefore he may be outlawed.

IDONEI atque integri homines.——Substantial and honest men.

IDONEUS testis.——A good (or sufficient) witness.

ID quod nostrum est, sine nostro facto, ad alterum transferri non potest. Facti, autem nominis, vel consensus, vel etiam delicti intelligitur.——That which is our own property cannot be transferred to another except by our own act. But it is considered this may be done by deed, title, consent, or even by (the commission of) a crime.

ID tenementum dici potest "Socagium."——That tenure may be called "Socage."

IGNITEGIUM.——The curfew bell.

IGNORAMUS.——"We are ignorant." A word written on a bill of indictment when the evidence is insufficient to put the accused on his trial.

IGNORANTIA facti excusat.——"Ignorance of the fact excuses." As if an illiterate man sign a deed which is read to him falsely, the same shall be void.

IGNORANTIA juris non excusat.——Ignorance of the law excuses no person.

IGNORANTIA juris, quod quisque tenetur scire, neminem excusat.——Ignorance of the law, which every one is bound to know, excuseth no one.

IGNORANTIA legis non excusat.——Ignorance of the law does not excuse.

IGNORANTI assecuratore.——The assurer being ignorant.

IGNOSCITUR ei qui sanguinem suum qualiter redemptum voluit.——"He is pardoned who would in such a manner ransom his own blood,"—*i. e.* That person who kills another in defence of his *own* life shall be acquitted.

IGNOTUM per ignotius.——A thing unknown by something more unknown.

IGNOTUM tibi tu noli præponere notis.——Do not give the preference to what is unknown to you, to that which you are satisfied of.

IL conviendroit quil fust non mouable, et de durie a toujours.——It was proper that it should be immovable, and of long duration.

IL' covint aver' avec luy xi maynz de jurer avec luy, sc' que ils entendre en lour conciens que il disoyt voier.—— It was necessary to have with him eleven compurgators, to swear with him that they conscientiously believed he spoke the truth. *Vide note to Compurgatores.*

IL est impossibile de concevoir un contrat sans le consentement de toutes les parties. Mais il n'est pas nécessaire que les volentés des parties concurrent dans le même instant; pourou que le volenté soit déclarée avant que l'autre ait révoqué la sienne, la convention est valablement formée.——It is impossible to conceive of a contract without the consent of all the parties. But it is not necessary that the consent of the parties should be simultaneous; provided that the consent be declared before the other party has made his revocation, the agreement is valid.

IL fuit juge par le parlament de *Paris*, que l'ordonnance n'avoit point liens d'autant qu'elle ou ad litis decisionem. ——It was decided by the parliament of *Paris*, that an ordinance should be of no effect, unless it tended to the decision of the suit.

ILLA sit, ut difficilis sit ejus prosecutio.——That may be, as its prosecution may be difficult.

ILLE honore dignus est, qui se, suæ legibus patriæ, et non sine magno labore et industria, reddidit versatum.—— He deserves reverence, who with much labor and industry has rendered himself conversant with the laws of his country.

ILLE qui tenet in villenagio, faciet quicquid ei præceptum fuerit, nec scire debet sero quid facere debet in crastino; et semper tenebitur ad incerta.——He who holds in villenage shall perform what he shall be commanded; nor is it necessary that he should know in the evening what he should perform on the morrow; and he shall be always held (to perform) uncertain services.

ILLICITE, diabolice, nequiter, et malitiose conspiraverunt. ——They conspired devilishly, wickedly and maliciously.

ILLICKES.——There. ILLONQUES.——There.

ILLIS autem qui communiam tantum habent in fundo alicujus, aliud remedium non competet, nisi admensuratio. ——No other remedy is proper, but an admeasurement for those who have a commonalty in the land of another person.

ILLUD dici poterit fœdum militare.——That may be called a Knight's fee.

ILLUD enim nimiæ libertatis indicium, concessa toties impunitas non parendi; nec enim trinis judicii consessibus pœnam perditæ causæ contumax meruit.——For it is a sign of too much liberty, when disobedience to appear (in court) so frequently passes with impunity; nor did the contumacious party deserve the penalty (only) of a lost cause, three days for judgment being allowed.

ILLUD ex libertate vitium, quod non simul nec jussi conveniunt, sed et alter, et tertius dies cunctatione coeuntium absumiter.——That vice arising from liberty, because they do not meet together when commanded; for both the second and the third day is consumed by the delay of the members.

ILLUMINARE.——To illuminate. To draw in gold and silver the initial letters and the occasional pictures in MSS. Vid. *Brompton sub Anno.* 1076. Those persons who practiced this art were called "*Illuminatores,*" whence our word "*Limners.*" Vide note to "*Alluminor.*"

IL n' pas permis decouferer, ou de negocier avec les enemis del etat.——It is not permitted to disclose (secrets) or to negotiate with the enemies of the state.

IL peut cependant être laissè d' l'arbitrage d'untiers, si le tiers ne veut ou ne peut fair l'estimation il n'y a point de vente.——It may, however, be left to the arbitration of a third person; but if the third person will not, or cannot, make the valuation, it is no sale.

IMBLADER.——To sow grain.

IMMENSUS aliarum super alias acerbatarum legum cumulus.——A huge pile of severe laws upon laws heaped one upon another.

IMMISCERE.——To mingle or meddle with a thing.

IMMODERATE suo jure utatur, tunc reus homicidii sit.——He who excessively uses his own right may be guilty of homicide.

IMPARCARE.——To shut up.

IMPARLANCE.——A time granted by the court for the defendant to plead.

IMPARLANCE est quando ipse defendens petit licentiam

interloquendi, sc. quant le defendant desir le cour de douer
à luy temps de pleader al suit ou action que est commence
vers luy.——Imparlance is when the defendant asks leave
for interlocution, that is to say, when the defendant requests the court to grant him time to plead to the suit or
action which is commenced against him. *Vide note.*

IMPARSONEE.——He who is inducted into a benefice.

IMPEDIENS.——A defendant, or deforciant.

IMPENSÆ.——Expenses.

IMPERATOR solus et conditor et interpres legis existima-
tur.——The Emperor alone is considered the founder and
interpreter of the law.

IMPERIUM in imperio.——" One government within
another ;" which has been wittily expressed, " A power behind the throne." Some power acting irresponsibly within
the government, but not always discernible.

IMPETERE.——To impeach—to sue—to attach.

IMPIERMENT.——Injuring or prejudicing.

IMPLACITASSET quendam, &c.——He should have im-
pleaded a certain, &c.

IMPONERE.——To impose.

IMPOTENTIA excusat legem.——Inability avoids the law.

IMPRIMATUR.——(Let it be printed.) A permission to
print a book which it was necessary at one period to obtain.

IMPRIMIS autem debet quilibet, qui testamentum fecerit,
dominum suum de meliori re quam habuerit recognoscere ;
et postea ecclesiam de alia meliori.——For, in the first place,
each person in making his will should acknowledge his
lord entitled to the best chattel which he had ; and the
church to the next best. Vide *Herriettum.*

IMPRUIAMENTUM.——The improvement of land.

IMPURIS manibus nemo accedat curiam.——Let no one
come to court with unclean hands.

IN adjudicatione executionis.——In adjudging of the
execution.

IN adjudicatione executionis judicii.——In the adjudging execution of the judgment (or decree).

IN adjudicatione executionis super recognitionem.——In adjudging execution upon the recognizance.

IN æquali jure, vel injuria, potior est conditio defendentis.——In equal right, or wrong, the defendant's situation is preferable.

IN æquilibrio.——In equal balance: of equal weight or importance.

IN alieno solo.——In the land of another.

IN antea.——Henceforward.

IN aperta luce.——In open day.

IN arcta et salva custodia.——In close and safe custody.

IN articulo mortis.——At the point of death.

IN autre droit.——In right of another.

IN banco Regis.——In the King's Bench.

IN bonis, in terris, vel persona.——In goods, lands, or body.

IN Britannia tertia pars bonorum decedentium ab intestato in opus ecclesiæ, et pauperum dispensanda est.——In *England*, a third part of the goods of persons dying intestate shall be applied for the use of the church and poor.

IN capita, propter honoris respectum; defectum: propter affectum; vel propter delictum.——Challenges to the polls of a jury, either on account of respect (as to a nobleman), or from a defect of birth (as an alien, &c.), or from partiality, or on account of crime.

IN capite.——In chief. Lands held "*in capite*" are those held of the chief lord of the fee.

IN casu proviso.——In the case provided.

IN causa honesta et necessaria.——In a just and necessary cause.

INCENDIT et combussit.——He sat on fire and burnt up.

INCERTAM et caducam hæreditatem relevebat.——He raised up an uncertain and falling inheritance.

INCESTUS, Uxorcidium, Raptus, Susceptio proprii filii de

fonte, Presbytericidium, pœnitentia solennis.——"Incest, murder of the wife, rape, the taking his own child from the (baptismal) font, murder of a Presbyter, annual penance." Either of these was formerly considered an impediment to marriage.

INCHOATE.——Begun.

INCIPIENTIBUS nobis exponere jura populi Romani, ita videntur tradi posse commodissime, si primo levi ac simplici via singula tradantur; alioqui, si statim ab initio rudem adhuc et infirmum animum studiosi multitudine ac varietate rerum oneravimus, duorum alterum, aut desertorem studiorum efficiemus, aut cum magno labore, sæpe etiam cum diffidentia, quæ plerumque juvenes avertit, serius ad id perducemus ad quod, leviore via ductus, sine magno labore, et sine ulla diffidentia maturius perduci potuisset.——To expound to us scholars the Roman Laws, it appears therefore that they may be most easily taught us if they are treated of in a light and simple manner at first—but it is otherwise, if directly from the beginning, we students have loaded our minds, as yet unskilled and weak, with a great store and variety of matter; (then) we do one of these two things, either desert our studies, or, with greater labor, oftentimes with diffidence, which chiefly impedes young students, arrive at that knowledge later, which, if conducted by a more simple method, would have been acquired in less time, without any great labor and without discouragement. *Vide note.*

INCIPITUR.——It is begun.

INCLAMARE.——To cry out, or proclaim, as in court.

IN clientelam recipere.——To receive under protection.

INCLUSIO unius est exclusio alterius.——The name of one person being included, is a (tacit) exclusion of the other.

INCOLA.——A resident in a place, not a native of it.

IN colloquio.——In a discourse.

IN communibus placitis.——In the Common Pleas.

IN consimili casu.——In a like case.

16

IN constantem virum.——Upon a courageous man.

IN continuando flagrante disseizina, et maleficio.——By persevering in a wicked and malicious dispossession.

IN contractibus veniunt ea quæ sunt moris et consuetudinis in regione in qua contrahitur.——These things occur in agreements which are of usage and custom in that place where the contract is made.

IN conventionibus.——In agreements : or covenants.

IN conventionibus contrahentium voluntas potius quam verba.——In the agreements of contracting parties, the intention (is to be regarded) rather than the words.

IN crastino animarum.——On the morrow of all souls.

INCREMENTUM.——Increase : improvement.

INCROCARE.——To hang from a hook.

IN cujus rei testimonium apposui sigillum meum, &c.—— In testimony whereof, I have set my seal, &c. *Vide note.*

IN curia domini regis ipse in propria persona jura discernit.——"In the Court of our Lord, the King, he personally considers the law." *Vide note.*

IN curia wardorum.——In the court of wards.

INDEBITATUS assumpsit.——Indebted, he undertook.

IN delicto.——In an offence : or in default.

INDEPENDENTER se habet assecuratio a viagio navis.—— The insurance clears itself by the voyage of the ship.

INDE producit sectam.——"Therefore he brings suit." Formerly the plaintiff was obliged to bring pledges, (called *suit*,) that he would prosecute his claim. John Doe and Richard Roe are now generally used as the persons on whom this obligation devolves.

INDICAVIT.——He proclaimed.

INDICIUM.——A hint: a sign: a mark.

INDICTARE.——To indict.

IN descender.——In descent.

IN dominicis terris.——In the lord's lands.

IN dominico suo ut de feodo.——In his demesne, as of fee.

IN dominico suo ut de feodo et de jure ad voluntatem domini, secundum consuetudinem manerii.——In his demesne, as of fee, and of right, at the will of the lord, according to the custom of the manor.

IN dominico suo ut de feodo talliato.——In his demesne, as of fee tail.

IN dominio suo.——In his demesne; or lordship.

IN domo procerum.——In the House of Lords.

IN dorso.——On the back.

INDOSSANS.——An indorser.

INDOSSATARIUS.——An indorsee.

IN dubiis.——In doubtful cases.

INDUCIÆ.——A stopping or suspension of proceedings.

IN Eire.——This means in the ancient court of the judges in " *Eyre*," who went the circuit of England.

IN ejus unius persona veteris reipublicæ vis atque majestas per cumulatas magistratuum potestates exprimebatur. ——The power and dignity of the ancient Republic was represented in his person alone by the authority of the magistrates collected together.

IN equilibrio.——In even balance. Equal.

IN esse.——In being.

IN eum statum qui providentia humana reparari non potest.——In that situation which in all human foresight cannot be restored.

IN eventu.——In the end, or event.

IN executione sententiæ, alibi latæ, servare jus loci in quo fit executio; non ubi res judicata.——In the execution of a judgment, otherwise extensive, the law of the place shall prevail where the execution takes effect; not where the matter was adjudged.

IN extenso.——At large: to the extent.

IN extremis.——In the last moments: near death.

IN facie ecclesiæ.——In the presence of the church. *Vide note to* " *Assignetur*."

IN facie ecclesiæ, et ad ostium ecclesiæ, non enim valent

facta in lecto mortali, nec in camera, aut alibi ubi clandestina fuere conjugia.——In the presence and at the door of the church, for marriages are of no validity when performed in a man's bed, nor in his chamber, nor elsewhere where they were secretly made.

INFANGTHIEF.——A thief taken with a Lord's fee.

INFANTLÆ proxima.——Next to infancy.

IN favorem prolis.——In favor of the issue.

IN favorem vitæ, et privilegii clericalis.——In favor of life, and of benefit of clergy.

INFECTUM reddere.——To render void or defective.

IN felicitate viri.——For the husband's happiness.

INFEUDARE.——To enfeoff: grant in fee.

IN feudis antiquis.——In ancient fees.

IN feudis novis.——In fees newly acquired.

IN feudis vere antiquis.——In fees truly ancient.

IN fictione semper subsistit æquitas.——In fiction of law equity always subsists.

IN flagranti delicto.——In the commission of crime.

IN forma pauperis.——"In the form of (suing) as a pauper."

[By a statute of Hen. VIII., any one not able to pay the costs of a suit at law or in equity, making affidavit that he is not worth more than five pounds, after payment of all his debts, sues "*in forma pauperis*," and pays no Counsel or Attorney's fees.]

IN foro conscientiæ.——Conscientiously: in the court of conscience: in a man's own conviction of what is equitable.

IN foro seculari.——In a lay court.

INFRA ætatem.——Within age.

INFRA annum luctus.——Within the year of mourning: the "widow's year." *Vide note.*

INFRA corpus comitatus.——Within the body of a county.

INFRA hospitium.——Within an inn.

INFRA dignitatem curiæ.——Below the dignity of the court.

INFRA intention' seperal' statut' contra decoctor' edit' et provis'.——Within the meaning of the several statutes made and provided against Bankrupts.

INFRA præsidia.——Under the garrison, guard or convoy.

INFRA præsidia hostium.——Under the enemy's protection.

INFRA quatuor maria.——Within the four seas: (meaning within the realm of *England.*)

INFRA sex annos.——Within six years.

INFRA summonitium Justiciorum.——Within the summons of the Justices.

INFRA tempus semestre.——Within half a year.

IN fraudem legis.——Contrary to law.

INFREGIT conventionem.——He broke the agreement.

IN furto, vel latrocinio.——In theft or larceny.

IN hac parte.——In this behalf.

IN his, quæ respiciunt litis decisionem, servanda est consuetudo loci contracti. At in his quæ respiciunt litis ordinationem, attenditur consuetudo loci ubi causa agitur.—— In these matters, affecting the decision of a controversy, the custom of the place where the contract is made is to be observed. But in those which concern the form of the process, the custom of the place where the cause is tried is to be attended to.

IN iisdem terminis.——In the same bounds.

IN infinitum.——To infinity—time without end.

IN initio.——In the beginning.

IN invitum.—Unwillingly.

IN ipso concilio, vel principium aliquis, vel pater, vel propinquus scuto, frameaque, juvenem ornant. Hæc apud illos ut toga, hic primus juventæ honos: ante hoc domus pars videtur; mox reipublicæ.——In the council itself, some one of the chiefs, or the father, or a near relation, adorns the youth with a shield and a short spear. These are (prized) as much as the robe, being the first honor conferred on youth; before this time he is considered one of the family; afterwards of the republic.

INIQUUM.——Unequal.

INITIA magistratuum nostrorum meliora firma; finis inclinat.——Our public offices are more vigorous at their commencement; they weaken at their conclusion.

IN judicium adesto.——Come to hear judgment.

IN jus vocando.——In calling to the court: suing another at law.

[These were phrases used by the ancient *Romans*.]

INJURIA illata in corpus non potest remitti.——Personal injuries cannot be remitted.

INJURIAM sibi illatam probis hominibus ostendere et sanguinem, si quis fecerit, et vestium scissiones.——" To show her ostensible injury to men of probity; and also the blood, if any, which she shed; and the laceration of her clothes." Requisites formerly shown by those who complained of rape.

INLAGATION.——Sax. "*in lagian.*" A restitution of one outlawed to the protection of the laws; and benefit of a subject.

INLEGIARE.——This word was used where a delinquent satisfied the law, and is again "*rectus in curia,*" untainted in court.

IN libera eleemosyna.——Frankalmoign: or in free alms.

IN liberam puram et perpetuam eleemosynam.——In (or as of) free, pure and perpetual alms.

IN libero maritagio.——In free marriage.

IN limine.——In, or at the beginning: at the threshold.

IN loco hæredis.——In the place of the heir.

IN loco parentis et liberorum.——In the place of the parent and children.

IN majoram cautelam.——In or for greater safety.

IN maleficio.——In wickedness.

IN manu.——In possession.

IN misericordia domini regis pro falso clamore.——In the mercy of the King for (making) a false claim (or suit).

IN mitiori sensu.——In the milder sense : in a more kind manner.

IN modum juratæ, et non in modum assizæ.——After the manner of a (common) jury (or inquest), and not by way of an assize.

IN mortua manu.——In mortmain: in a dead hand or possession.

IN naufragorum miseria et calamitate tanquam vultures ad prædam currere.——In the misery and misfortune of the shipwrecked they run like vultures to their prey.

IN nomine dei, amen.——In the name of God, Amen.

IN non decimando.——Not being titheable.

IN nostra lege una comma evertit totum placitum.——In our law, one comma upsets the whole plea. *Vide note to* " *En cest court, &c.*"

INNOTESCIMUS.——(We make known.) A title formerly given to letters-patent.

IN nubibus, in mare, in terra, vel in custodia legis.—— In the air, earth and sea, or in the custody of the law.

INNUENDO.——" By signifying : thereby intimating." A word much used in declarations for slander and libel, to ascertain the application to a person or thing previously named. An oblique hint.

IN nullo est erratum.——It is in no respect erroneous.

IN numero impiorum ac sceleratorum habentur. Ab iis omnes decedunt, additum eorum sermonemque defugiunt, ne quid ex contagione, incommodi accipiant ; neque iis petentibus jus redditur ; neque honos ullus communicatur. ——They are reckoned in the class of impious and wicked men. All persons shun them, and fly from their approach, and discourse ; lest they receive an injury from contagion ; neither is any law afforded them when seeking it ; nor is any honor conferred upon them.

IN obsequio domini regis, vel alicujus episcopi.——In the service of the King, or of some Bishop.

IN odium spoliatoris.——In hatred towards the despoiler.

INOFFICIOSUM testamentum.——An unkind will. *Vide note.*

IN omnibus contractibus, sive nominatis, sive innominatis, permutatio continetur.——In all agreements, whether it is named or not, an exchange is comprised.

IN omnibus fere minori ætati succurritur.——In almost all cases relief is given to minors.

IN omnibus imperatoris excipitur fortuna, cui ipsas leges Deus subjecit.——In all things the fortune (or lot) of the Emperor is excepted, to whom God has subjected those laws.

IN omnibus placitis de felonia, solet accusatio per plegios dimitti, præterquam in placito de homicidio, ubi ad terrorem aliter statutum est.——In all charges of felony, the accused has been accustomed to be dismissed, on giving sureties, except when charged with homicide, where it is otherwise appointed by way of terror.

IN omnibus quidem, maxime tamen in jure, æquitas est.——There is equity in all things, but particularly in the law.

IN omni scientia, et de qualibet arte.——In every science, and of every art.

IN omni transgressione quæ fit contra pacem.——In every trespass which is done against the peace.

INOPS consilii.——Devoid of counsel: wanting advice.

IN pais.——In the country.

IN pari delicto.——In a like offence (or crime).

IN pari delicto, melior est conditio possidentis.——In equal fault the possessor's case is the better.

IN pari materia.——In a like matter: similarly.

IN perpetuum rei testimonium.——In perpetual testimony of the fact.

IN personam.——To, or against, the person.

In pios usus.——For pious purposes.

In pleno comitatu.——In full assembly of the county: in full county court.

In potentia viri.——In the husband's power.

In potestate hostium.——In the enemy's possession.

In potestate parentis.——In the power of the parent.

In potestate viri.——In the husband's power.

In propria persona accedat ad tenementum, et coram eos per primos juratores, et alios legales homines, faciat inquisitionem.——He should go personally to the tenement and before them by the first jury, and other lawful men, make an inquisition.

In propria persona sedente curia.——In his own person while the court is sitting.

In proprio jure.——In his own right.

In puram et perpetuam eleemosynam.——"In pure and perpetual charity."

[Part of the language on the endowment of charitable foundations.]

In puris naturalibus.——In a state of nature.

In quibusdam locis habet ecclesia melius animal de consuetudine; in quibusdam secundum, vel tertium melius; et in quibusdam nihil; et ideo consideranda est consuetudo loci.——In some places the church hath the best beast by custom; in some the second, or third best; and in some nothing; and in this manner the custom of the place is to be regarded.

Inquiratur super possessionem et usum.——Let inquiry be made respecting the tenure and the custom.

Inquisitio post mortem.——An inquisition (or inquest) after death.

In quodam loco vocat'.——In a certain place called.

In rebus.——In things, matters, or cases.

In rei exemplum.——By way of example.

In rei exemplum et infamam.——By way of example and disgrace.

IN rem.——To, or against, the property. To the point.

IN rem et personam.——Against the body and goods.

IN rem judicatam.——In the matter adjudged.

IN remuneratione servi.——In rewarding the servant.

IN re pari potiorem causam esse præbentis constat.—— In a similar matter the person offering (or showing) his complaint (or action) has the more preferable side.

IN re potiorem causam esse prohibentis constare.——A better cause in the matter is found to exist on the part of the person defending.

IN rerum naturâ.——In the nature (or order) of things.

IN re submissa agere cautus.——To act with caution in the business submitted.

IN retallia.——In or by retail.

IN rigore juris.——In strictness of law.

IN salva et arcta custodia.——In safe and close keeping.

IN scaccario.——In the exchequer.

INSETENA.——A ditch dug within another for the greater protection.

INSIDIATIO viarum.——Infesting, or laying in wait on the highways.

INSIDIATORES viarum.——Way-layers: highway robbers.

INSILIARIUS.——An evil adviser.

INSIMUL computassent.——They accounted together.

IN solido.——In coin: in substance.

INSTAR dentium.——"Like teeth"—similar to the top of an ancient *Indenture*, that word being, as supposed, derived from "*instar dentium*."

INSTAR omnium.——One example may suffice for all.

IN statu quo ante bellum.——In the state it was before the war.

INSTAURUM.——The whole stock of a farm, including cattle and implements.

INSTIRPARE.——To plant, or establish.

In stirpes.——To the stock or lineage.

INSTITUTION au droit François.——An institution of French right.

IN stricto jure.——In strict right.

INSTRUMENTA domestica seu adnotatio, si non aliis quoque adminiculis adjuventur, ad probationem sola non sufficiunt.——Private, or family documents, or a memorandum, if not supported by other evidence, are not of themselves sufficient proof.

IN subsidio.——In aid of subsidy.

——————————————"INSULA portum
Efficit objectu laterum, quibus omnis ab alto
Frangitur inque sinus, scindit sese unda redactos
Deportibus maris."

"Within a long recess there lies a bay,
An island shades it from the rolling sea,
And forms a port secure for ships to ride,
Broke by the jetting land on either side :
In double stream the briny waters glide."

INSULTUS.——An assault.

IN summo jure.——In the rigor of the law.

In suo jure.——In his own right.

IN tam amplo modo.——In such an ample manner (or form).

IN tam amplo modo habere non potuit, sed proficuum suum inde per totum tempus amisit, &c.——He had not been able to enjoy (the land, &c.,) in so ample a manner, but, on that account, lost his profit for the whole time, &c.

INTENDERE.——To claim in an action; also to apply one's self earnestly to any duty.

INTENTARE.——To prosecute.

INTENTIO cæca.——A secret purpose.

INTENTIO mutita, nec manca.   The intention being changed, not becoming impotent.

INTER.——Among.

INTER alia promisit.——He promised among other things.

INTER alios acta.——Things done between other parties.

INTER amicos.——Among friends.

Inter apices juris.——Among the extremes or (hardships) of the law.

INTER arma leges silent.——The laws are silent (or disregarded) in the heat of hostility.

INTER canem et lupum.——" Twilight." Words formerly used to signify an act done between night and day —or betwixt the time the dog slept and the wolf roamed.

INTERESSE damni.——To participate in the loss (or damage).

INTERESSE lucri.——To participate in the profit.

INTERESSE termino, vel terminis.——To be interested for a term or terms of years (in an estate).

INTEREST reipublicæ quod carcere sint in tuto.——It concerns the commonwealth that they be safely (kept) in prison.

INTEREST reipublicæ ut sit finis litium.——The commonwealth is interested, that there be an end of contention.

INTER hæredes masculos.——Among the heirs male.

INTER leges *Gulielmi* Primi.——Among the laws of *William* the First.

INTERLOCUTIO.——Imparlance, *vel licentia inter loquendi.* From Fr. "*parler*," to speak. In the common law this word was taken for a petition in court of a day to consider, or advise what answer the defendant should make to the plaintiff's action, being a continuance of the cause till another day, or longer time given by the court. But now the more common signification of imparlance is *time to plead.*

INTER minora crimina.——Amongst lesser crimes (or misdemeanors).

INTER mœnia.——Within the walls: within the domicile.

INTER nubilia caput.——The origin (of this) is among the clouds (or unknown).

INTER pares non est potestas.——Among equals their power is alike.

INTER præsidia.——Within the fortifications: or in safe shelter.

INTERREGNUM.——A space between two reigns.

INTERREGNUM quare clausum fregit?——In the meantime why did he break the close?

IN terrorem.——By way of terror (or warning).

INTER SESE.——Among themselves.

INTERTIARE.——To sequester.

INTERVENIRE.——To come between.

INTER veteres satis abunde hoc dubitatur, constaret ne venditio, aut non.——It is more fully doubted among the ancients whether the sale should stand or not.

INTER vivos, ante nuptias, et post nuptias.——Among those living before and after the marriage.

INTOL and UTTOL.——Custom on things imported and exported.

IN totidem verbis.——In so many words.

IN toto regno ante ducis adventum, frequens et usitata fuit; postea cæteris adempta; sed privatis quorundam locorum consuetudinibus alibi postea regerminans: *Cantianis* solum integra et inviolata remansit.——This (custom) was frequent and usual, throughout the kingdom, before the arrival of the Duke (called the Conqueror); afterwards it was abolished; but among the private customs of some other places, it was again springing up: it remained whole and incorrupted among the *Kentish* people only. *Vide note.*

IN toto se attingunt.——They agree all together: it is all in point.

INTRA mænia.——A term given to domestic servants because they are *within the walls.*

IN transitu.——"In the passage." Merchandise is said to be "*in transitu,*" while on its way to the consignee.

INTRA parietes.——Between friends.

INTRARE.——To enter.

INTROMISSION.——(In Scotch law.) The taking possession of property belonging to an heir, either with or without authority.

INTROMITTERE.——To intermeddle with.

INTRUSIO dicitur *nuda* eo quod non vallatur aliquo vestimento, et minimum habet possessionem; et omnino nihil
juris, et in parte habet naturam cum disseisina, et in quisbusdam sunt dissimiles, quia ubicunque est disseisina ibi
quodammodo est intrusio, quantam ad dissertorem; sed
non a contrario, quia ubicunque est intrusio ibi non est
disseisina, propter vacuam possessionem; et in utroque
casu possessio est nuda donec ex tempore et seisina pacifica
acquiratur vestimentum.——Intrusion is called *naked*, because it is not clothed with any investiture, and has the
least possession, and altogether no right, and has in part
the nature of a disseisin, and in certain respects they are
dissimilar; because wherever there is a disseisin there is,
in a certain manner, an intrusion to that extent against the
disseisor. But not on the contrary, because wherever there
is an intrusion, there is not a disseisin, on account of the
empty possession; and in either case the possession is
naked, until by time and a peaceable possession an investiture be acquired.

IN ultima voluntate.——In the last will.

IN uno quorum continetur inter alia juxta tenorem.——
In one of which is contained among other things nearly
to the effect following, &c.

IN urnam sortito mittuntur, ut de pluribus necessarius
numerus confici posset.——They are thrown casually into
an urn, that from many (names) the requisite number may
be completed.

IN vacuum venire.——To enter on an empty possession.

INVADIARE.——In feudal law, to pledge or mortgage
lands. Sometimes written *invadiare*.

INVENIENDO.——Finding. INVENTUS.——Found.

IN ventre sa mere.——In the mother's womb.

INVERSO ordine.——By an inverted order.

INVESTITURA propria dicatur possessio.——A proper investiture may be called a seisin.

IN via re uti pace.——"Settle the matter amicably by the way."

[The plaintiff and defendant, among the *Romans*, generally went to the *Prætor* together. Vide *note to* " *Vocatio in jus.*"]

IN villis, et territoriis.——In the vills and territories (or adjacent lands).

IN vita testatoris.——In the testator's lifetime.

INVITO domino.——Without the owner's consent.

IPSE advocatus cum tot libros perlegere et vincere non possit, compendia sectatur.——The lawyer, when he is unable to peruse and digest so many books, has recourse to abridgments.

IPSE illorum stipendia resarcienda curabit.——He shall be careful to make good their salaries.

IPSE tamen Feoffator in vita sua, ratione proprii doni sui, tenetur warrantizare.——Nevertheless, the Feoffor himself, in his lifetime, on account of its being a proper gift (or grant) of his own, is bound to warranty.

IPSI regali institutioni eleganter inserta.——Elegantly introduced for that royal institution.

IPSIUS patris bene placito.——By the favor of his father.

IPSO facto, et ab initio.——By the deed itself, and from the beginning.

IPSO facto, et constructione legis.——By the fact itself, and in construction of law.

IPSO facto, et eo instanti.——In fact, and immediately.

IPSO jure.——By the law itself—or by that right.

IRE ad largum.——To go at large.

IRREPLEGIABILIS.——Cannot be bailed.

ITER facere.——To travel or journey.

IRRITUS.——Invalid.

IRROTULARE.——To enrol.

Is cui cognoscitur.——He to whom it is acknowledged —the Cognizee in a fine : the recognizee.

ISH.——Scotch. The period of the ending of a lease.

Is ordo vitio careto cæteris specimen esto.——Let that rank be immaculate ; and an example to others. *Vide note.*

Is qui cognoscit.——"He who acknowledges." The Cognizor in a fine : the Recognizor.

ISSINT.——So : thus. *Norman French.*

ISTÆ conditiones sunt plenæ tristissimi eventus, et possunt invitare ad delinquendum.——These stipulations are pregnant with sorrowful consequences, and may instigate to some offence (or failure of duty).

ISTA ratio nullius pretii, nam et alieno signare licet.—— That reason is of no avail, for it is lawful for any other person to sign.

ISTE sccundus assecurator tenetur ad solvendum omne totum quod primus assecurator solverit.——The second assurer is bound to pay everything which the first assurer should have paid.

ISTI vero viri eliguntur per commune concilium, pro communi utilitati regni, per provincias, et patrias universas, et per singulos comitatus in pleno *Folkmote,* sicut et vicecomites provinciarum, et comitatum eligi debent.——These men are elected by the general council for the common benefit of the kingdom, through the provinces, and the whole country, and by all the counties in full *Folkmote* (or general assembly of the people), as the sheriffs of the provinces and counties should be elected.

ISTUD homicidium, si fit ex livore, vel delectatione effundendi humanum sanguinem, licet juste occidatur iste, tamen occisor peccat mortaliter, propter intentionem corruptam.——That is homicide, if it be done from malice, or a delight in shedding human blood, (and) although he be killed lawfully, yet the person who killed him commits a mortal sin on account of his depraved intention.

ITA lex scripta.——So the law is written.

ITA maritentur, ne disparagentur, et per consilium pro-pinquorum de consanguinitate sua.——So that they be married without disparagement; and with the advice of their nearest relations.

ITA quod hospitalibus nullum eveniet damnum.——So that no injury may happen to the guests.

ITA te Deus adjuvet.——So help you God.

ITE, et inter vos causas vestras discutite, quia dignum non est ut nos judicemus Deos.——Go, and discuss your affairs among yourselves, for it is improper that we should judge the Gods.

ITEM, declara, quod si dominus, seu magister navis sol-verit mercatori pretium deperditarum, tunc tenetur merca-tor ad solutionem nauli, quia merces habenter ac si salvatæ fuissent.——Also state, that if the owner or master of the vessel pay the merchant the price of the lost merchandise, then the merchant is bound to pay the freight, because the goods are then considered as though they had not been lost.

ITEM facit disseysinam, cum quis in seysina fuerit ut de libero tenemento, et ad vitam vel ad terminum annorum, vel nomine custodia, vel aliquo alio modo, alium feoffaverit in præjudicium veri domini; et fecerit alteri liberum tene-mentum, cum *duo* simul et semel, de eodem tenemento et in solidum, esse non possunt in seizina.——This also causes a disseisin, where any one shall be in possession, as of a freehold or for life, or for a term of years, or being in nominal possession, or in (possession) in any other manner, (and) enfeoff another to the injury of the rightful owner; and make it the freehold of another, because *both* at the same time cannot be substantially seised of the same tene-ment.

ITEM justiciariorum quidam sunt capitales, generales, perpetui, et majores, a latere regis residentes, qui omnium aliorum corrigere tenentur injurias et errores.——So some

17

of the judges are chief, general, permanent and important, abiding with the king, and who are obliged to correct the wrongs and errors of all the other (judges).

ITEM non solum fit disseisina secundum quod prædictum est, sed etiam si quis præpotens uti voluerit in alterius tenemento, contra ipsius tenentis voluntatem, arando, fodiendo, falcando, et asportando, contrahendo, tenementum esse suum quod est alterius; si autem nihil clamaverit in tenemento aliud erit, quia tunc erit transgressio, et non disseisina de libero tenemento.——Also it not only becomes a disseisin, according to what has been stated; but also if any very powerful person shall use the lands of another contrary to the tenant's will, by ploughing, digging, cutting up and taking away the tenement as his own, which is the property of another. But if he do not claim anything in the tenement, it will be otherwise, for then there will be a trespass and no disseisin of the freehold.

ITEM possessiones, alia nuda, alia vestita; nuda, ubi quis nil juris habet in re, nec aliquis juris scintillam, sed tantam nudam pedis possessionem; vestita, jure, titulo vel tempore.——So respecting possessions, some are naked, others are clothed; naked, is where a person has no right to the land, nor even a shadow of right; but only a naked foothold (as a squatter): a clothed possession is where there is right, title or time.

ITEM potuerit quis communiam cum alio, et jus fodiendi sicut jus pascendi, et jus venandi, piscandi, potandi, hauriendi, et alia plura quæ infinita sunt facienda, cum libero accessu et recessu, secundum quod ad dictam communiam pasturæ pertinent.——Also any person may have right of common with another, and the right of digging, as well as the right of depasturing, and the right of hunting, fishing, drinking, drawing water, and of using many other privileges which are unlimited, with free access and recess, according to that which belongs to the said common of pasture.

ITEM quæ ex hostibus capiuntur, jure gentium statim capientium fuere.———Also those things which are taken from
the enemy become immediately, by the law of nations, the
property of the captors.

ITEM quand il arrive qu' aucun maladie attaque un des
mariners de la nef, en rendant service en la dite nef, le
maitre le doit mettre hors de la dite nef, et luy doit trouvir
legis, &c.; et si la nef etoit preste a fair voyage, elle ne
doit point demourer pour luy; et s'il querit, il doit avoir
sou loyer, tout comptant, en rabutant les frais, si le maitre
luy en a fait. Et s'il meurt sa femme et se prochains le
doivent avoir pour luy.———Also, whenever it happens that
any sickness attacks one of the seamen of the vessel, doing
duty therein, the master should cause him to be removed
from the said vessel, and should procure him lodgings,
&c.; and if the vessel be ready to make her voyage, she
ought not to remain for him; and if demanded, he should
have his wages entirely paid, deducting the expenses, if the
master has incurred any. And if he die, his wife and his
nearest relations should receive his wages for him.

NOTES TO I.

IMPARLANCE.—It appears that the doctrine of *Imparlances* arose in the
early ages, from a desire that the parties might adjust their differences,
without proceedings at law; and arose from the mild practice of the
civil law, sanctioned by that precept of the Gospel, "*Agree with thine
adversary by the way.*" It appears to have been the custom with the
Romans, and probably with the *Jews,* for the plaintiff to take the defendant *with him* before the *Prætor* or Magistrate. Vide note to "*Vocatio
in jus.*"

INCIPIENTIBUS, &c.—The Civil Laws were, at one time, such a *Novelty,*
and, no doubt, loaded with such innumerable comments, that young students
found them extremely difficult. The *feudal* laws were comparatively few;
and had no very nice distinction of right and wrong.

IN CUJUS REI TESTIMONIUM, &c.—This is the last clause generally found
in ancient deeds of Feoffment of lands. Sealing has been for many ages
essentially requisite to the perfection thereof, because it deliberately and
clearly shows the Feoffor's consent and approbation of what the deed contains, and particularly so, as being sealed with the Grantor's own seal, at

least by the heads of ancient families. Some authors inform us, that the *Saxons*, in their time, (before the Conquest,) subscribed their names to their deeds, adding the sign of the cross; and setting down in the end, the names of certain witnesses, without any kind of sealing at all. But, when the *Normans* obtained a footing in *England*, they (loving their own country customs) changed that mode, with many others which they found in *England*. And *Ingulphus*, who was made Abbot of *Croyland*, A. D. 1075, appears to confirm this opinion in these words, "*Normanni chirographorum confectionem cum crucibus aureis, et aliis signaculis sacris in Anglia firmari solitam, in cera impressa mutant*"—i. e. "The *Normans* change the making up of chirographs (or deeds) with golden crosses or other sacred marks or signs, which were formerly established in *England*, into a wax impression." Yet we read of a *sealed* charter in *England* before the Conquest, viz., of *St. Ed.* made to the Abbey of *Westminster*, yet this does not impugn what is before stated; for we find in *Fabian's* Chronicle, and elsewhere, that *St. Ed.* was educated in *Normandy*, and it is very probable that he might, in some cases, incline to the fashion of that country. The *French* have a proverb, "*Rome n'a este bastie tout un jour*," and we use the same, "Rome was not built in a day;" so that it cannot be conceived that the *Normans* suddenly altered the *Saxon* custom *wholly*, in this particular, but that it changed by degrees; and, perhaps, at the first, the King had some about his person, who first used the impression of a seal to deeds, which is probable, from a story concerning *Richard de Lucy*, Chief Justice of *England*, who, in the time of *Henry* the Second, is said to have chidden a person because he had sealed a deed with a *private* seal, "*quant ceo pertain al Roy et Nobilite solement.*"

However, in the time of *Edward* the Third, sealing and seals were very common; which appears from many deeds now extant. But Sir *Edward Coke*, in the first part of his *Institutes*, seems to overthrow the former opinions about the first using of seals in *England*: "the sealing of charters and deeds," he observes, "is much more ancient than some have imagined; for the Charter of King *Edwin*, brother of King *Edgar*, dated A. D. 956, made of some land in the Isle of *Ely*, was *sealed* with his *own seal*, (which appears by these words,) "*Ego* Edwindus *gratiâ Dei totius Britannicæ telluris Rex meum donum* proprio sigillo *confirmavi*"—i. e. "I, *Edwin*, by the grace of God, King of the whole land of *Britain*, have confirmed my gift (or grant) with *my own* seal." And the Charter of King *Offa*, whereby he gave the *Peter pence*, was under *seal*. Either of which two charters are much more ancient than that of *St. Ed.* before mentioned.

IN CURIA DOMINI, &c.—After the dissolution of the *Aula Regis*, the *English* kings frequently sat in the Court of King's Bench. Vide 2 *Burr*. 851, &c. And, in later times, *James* the First is said to have sat there in person, but was informed by the Judge that he could not deliver any opinion. The first time the King sat in Court, after the plaintiff's counsel had finished his address to the jury, the King remarked (privately) to the Judge, that the *plaintiff* ought *certainly* to obtain a verdict—but, on hearing a very eloquent reply from the *defendant's* counsel, he became so extremely puzzled, that he declared it was impossible he could say which of the contending parties was right.

INFRA ANNUM, &c.—The civil law ordained that no widow should marry "*infra annum luctus*," a rule which obtained so early as the reign of *Augustus*, if not of *Romulus*; and the same constitution was probably handed down to our early ancestors from the *Romans*; for we find it established under the *Saxon* and *Danish* governments. In the reign of *Augustus*, however, the year was only *ten* months. Vide *Ov. Fast.*, i. 27.

INOFFICIOSUM TESTAMENTUM.—Among the *Romans*, (at least at one time of the Republic,) a man might disinherit his own children, and appoint what other persons he pleased, to be his heirs: he was then said to have made "*inofficiosum testamentum.*" Thus, "*Titius filius meus exhæres esto*"—i. e. "Titius, my son, be thou disinherited." Vide *Plin., Ep.* v. Hence, *Juvenal, Sat.* 10. "*Codice sævo hæredes vetat esse suos*"—i. e. "By a severe will he forbade them to be his heirs." When children brought an action (which was frequently the case) for rescinding such a will as this, it was said to be done, "*per querulam inofficiosi.*"

In TOTO REGNO, &c.—This *Saxon* custom, so completely opposed to the Feudal law, still remains in the county of *Kent*, in *England*, where, to a considerable part of the lands in that county, on the death of a person seised of a freehold estate, all the sons inherit alike. This is called *Gavelkind.* Among other private customs referred to in the text, is the law, or rather custom, of *Borough English*, where the *youngest* son inherits the freehold. *Blackstone* gives a very *curious* reason for this custom: it is not improbable, however, that it might have originated from a desire that the *youngest* son (who may be supposed to be left most destitute on his father's decease) should have some provision for his maintenance.

Is ORDO VITIO CARETO, &c.—*Augustus*, when he became master of the *Roman* Empire, retained the forms of the ancient Republic, and the names of the magistrates, but left very little of the ancient virtue (*prisci et integri mores. Tacit. Ann.* i. 3.) While he pretended always to act by the *authority* of the Senate, he artfully drew everything to himself. *Tiberius* apparently increased the power of the Senate, by transferring the power of creating magistrates and enacting laws from the *Comitia* to the Senate. In consequence of which, the decrees of the Senate obtained the force of laws; and were more frequently published. But this was only "a *shadow of power*," for the Senators, in giving their opinions, depended entirely on the will of the Prince; and it was necessary that their decrees should be confirmed by him. An oration of the Emperor was usually prefixed to them, which was not always delivered by himself, but generally read by one of the *Quæstors*, who were called "*Candidati.*" Vide *Suet., Tit.* 6, *Aug.* 65. Hence, what was appointed by the decrees of the Senate, was said to be "*oratione principis cautum*"—i. e. "provided for by the declaration of the Emperor;" and these orations are sometimes put for the "*Decrees*" of the Senate. To such a height did the flattery of these Senators proceed, that they used to receive these speeches with *loud acclamation.* Vide *Plin. Paneg.* 75, and never failed to assent to them, which they did, crying out "*Omnes! Omnes!*" all! all! Vide *Vopisc. in Tacit.* 7.

The messages of the Emperors to the Senate were called "*Epistolæ*," or "*Libelli;*" because they were folded in the form of a letter, or little book. *Julius Cæsar* is said to have first invented these "*Libelli*," which afterwards came to be used almost on every occasion. After this, the Emperors gradually began to order what they thought proper, without consulting the Senate; to abrogate *old* laws, and introduce *new* ones; and, in short, to determine everything according to their own pleasure; by their answers to the supplications or petitions presented to them, (*per rescripta ad libellos,*) by their mandates and laws, (*per edicta et constitutiones,*) &c. Vespasian appears to have been the first who made use of these rescripts and edicts. They became more frequent under *Hadrian*, from which time the decrees of the Senate concerning private right began to be more rare; and, at length, under *Caracalla*, were entirely discontinued.

The various laws and decrees of the Senate, whereby supreme power was conferred on *Augustus*, used to be repeated to succeeding Emperors, upon their succession to the throne. "*Tum Senatus omnia, principibus solita, Vespasiano decrevit*"—i. e. "Then the Senate decreed to

Vespasian all things usual to Emperors." *Tacit. Hist.* iv. 3. When taken together are called the Royal Law, ("*Lex regia*, vel *Lex imperii*, et *Augusti privilegium*,")—i. e. "The Royal Law, *or* law of the Empire, *and* privilege of the Emperor," probably in allusion to the law by which supreme power was granted to *Romulus*. *Liv.* xxiv. 5.

J.

JACERE.——To lie; to be prostrate.

JACTITARE.——To boast; to throw out.

JACTITATIO matrimonii.——Where a party gives out that either he or she is married to another, from which an impression may arise in the world that they are married.

JACTURA, JACTUS.——See JETTISON.

JADEMAINS.——Nevertheless.

JALEMEINS.——Always; still; yet.

JAM illis promissis non esse standum, quis non videt, quæ coactus quis metu et deceptus dolo promisserit? Quæ quidem plerumque jure prætorio liberantur, nonnulla legibus.——Now these promises cannot be supported, for who is there that does not perceive what a man, when compelled by fear, or deceived by stratagem, may have promised? These promises are, for the most part, discharged by the *Prætorian* law, and some by (other) laws.

JAMUNLINGUS.——One who put himself and his property under the protection of a powerful neighbor in order to avoid military service, and other state burdens.

JANUIS clausis.——With closed doors.

JATARDE.——Lately.

JEO doy.——I ought.

JEO done.——I give.

JEOFAILE.——"I have failed, or erred." This is the name of a statute to correct errors. The word is often used when an oversight has been made in the pleadings, or other law proceedings.

JE riens ne celari, ne sufferai estre celé, ne murdré.——
I will not conceal anything, nor suffer it to be concealed,
nor stifled.

JE suis prét.——I am ready.

JETTISON, JETSAM.——The throwing overboard part of
the goods or lading of a vessel, when it is in danger of
wreck; such goods sinking to the bottom of the sea.

JE vous dirai un fable. En ascun temps fuit un Pape,
et avoit fait un grand offence, et le Cardinals, vindrent a
luy et disoyent a luy "*peccasti,*" et il dit, "*judica me,*" et ils
disoyent "*non possumus quia caput es Ecclesiæ—judica te
ipsum;*" et l'apostol dit "*judico me cremari;*" et fuit com-
bustus, et apres fuit un saint. Et in ceo cas il fuit son
juge dememe, et issint n'est pas inconvenient que un home
soit juge dememe.——I will tell you a story. Some time
ago a Pope had committed a great offence, and the Cardinals came and said to him, "*thou hast sinned,*" and he replied, "*judge me,*" and they answered, "*we cannot judge
thee, because thou art the head of the church; judge thyself;*"
and the apostle said, "*I adjudge myself to be burnt;*" and he
was burnt, and afterwards became a Saint. And in this
case he was his own judge; therefore on such occasions it
is not improper that a man should be his own judge.

JOCALE, JOCALIA, JOIALX.——Jewels.

JOCARIUS.——"A Jester." In an ancient deed of *Richard* Abbot of *Bernay,* to *Henry Lovet,* among the witnesses
to it was *Willielmo tunc* Jocario "*Domini Abbati,*" i. e. *William* then the Lord Abbot's *Jester.* And in *Domesday,* it is
said that one *Berdic* was "*Joculator regis,*" the King's Jester.

JOCUS.——A game of chance.

JOCUS partitus.——It was so called when two proposals
were made, and a man had liberty to choose which he
pleased. *Bract.*

JONCARIA.——Where rushes grow.

JORNALE.——The land which might be ploughed in a
day.

JOURNAUNTE.——Break of day.

JUBEMUS honesta ; prohibens contraria.——Commanding what is honorable (or just), and forbidding the contrary.

JUCHUS.——As much land as might be ploughed in one
day by a joke of oxen.

JUDEX a quo.——An inferior judge.

JUDEX ad quem.——A superior judge.

JUDEX de ea re cognoscet.——The judge will take cognizance of the matter.

JUDEX de pace civium constituitur.——A judge is appointed for the peace of the citizens.

JUDEX non potest esse testis in propria causa.——A
judge cannot be a witness in his own cause.

JUDEX non reddat plus quam quod petens ipse requirat.
——The judge does not allow more than the plaintiff demands.

JUDEX qui injustum judicium judicabit alicui, det regi
cxx s., nisi jurare audeat, quod rectum judicare nescivit.
Leg. Edgar.——The judge who shall render an unjust sentence against a person, shall pay the king one hundred and
twenty shillings, unless he be bold enough to swear that
he knew not how to judge correctly. *Laws of King
Edgar.*

JUDICANDUM est legibus, non exemplis.——It is to be
adjudged by the laws, not by precedents.

JUDICATUM solvere.——To pay what is adjudged.

JUDICES delegati.——Chosen Judges : a court of dele-
gates.

JUDICES Quiritium.——The Roman Judges. *Vide note.*

JUDICIA ad populum.——Trials before the people. *Vide
note.*

JUDICIA odiosa.——Abominable decrees (or judgments).

JUDICIA perverterunt ; et in aliis erraverunt.——(In
some cases) they have perverted the judgments; and have
erred in others.

JUDICIUM a non suo judice dictum, nullius est momenti.
——Judgment, if not pronounced by the proper judge, is
of no effect.

JUDICIUM Dei.——" The judgment of God." The ordeal
of our *Saxon* ancestors, walking blindfold over (or rather
among) red-hot plough shares. Vide note to " *Tenetur se
purgare.*"

JUDICIUM ferri, aquæ et ignis.——The ordeal of fire, iron
and water. Vide note to " *Tenetur se purgare*," &c.

JUDICIUM intrare.——To enter into judgment.

JUDICIUM parium, aut lege terræ.——" The judgment
of the peers (or equals), or by the law of the land." It is
only by these, according to *Magna Charta*, that an Englishman can be condemned. *Vide note.*

JUDICIUM redditur in invitum.——Judgment is given
against an unwilling person.

JUGULATOR.——A cut-throat: a murderer.

JUGUM terræ.——A yoke of land. Vide " *Domesday.*"

JUNCARE.——" To strew with rushes." This was an
ancient custom for accommodating the parochial churches ;
and even the bedchambers of princes. Vide *Pat.* 14,
Edwd. 1st—also note to " *Litera.*"

JURA.——" Laws : rights : privileges." Often used for
laws in general thus " *Nova jura condere.*" Liv. iii. 33.

JURABIT duodecima manu.——He shall swear by twelve
compurgators. Vide note to " *Compurgatores.*"

JURA cognationis.——The laws (or rights) of relationship.

JURA enim nostra dolum præsumunt si una non pereant.
——For our laws presume it to be a fraud unless (the
goods) of both are lost.

JURA fiscalia.——" Fiscal rights." Those of the Exchequer or Revenue.

JURA in re.——Rights in the matter, or thing.

JURAMENTUM calumniæ.——" The oath of calumny."
By which parties swore that the cause was commenced, or
defended for the *sake of justice.*

JURAMENTUM fidelitatis.——The oath of fealty.

JURA naturæ sunt immutabila.——"Nature's laws are unchangeable." Chief Justice *Hobart* says, "an act of parliament made against natural justice is void."

JURA personarum.——The rights of persons.

JURA regalia.——Royal or crown rights (or privileges).

JURA rerum.——The rights of things.

JURA sanguinis.——The rights (or laws) of consanguinity.

JURA summi imperii.——The rights of supreme empire (or dominion).

JURATA.——A jury.

JURATORES.——"The jury." The persons impannelled to try a cause, civil or criminal.

JURE belli.——By the law of war.

JURE civili.——By the civil law.

JURE coronæ.——By the right of the crown.

JURE devolutionis.——By right of descent.

JURE divino et jure humano.——By divine and human right. *Vide note.*

JURE ecclesiæ.——In right of the church.

JURE et legibus.——By common and statute law—vide *Cic. Verr.* i, 42, 44. So Horace " *Vir bonus est quis? Qui consulta patrum, qui leges, juraque servat, &c.*" Vide *Ep.* i. xvi. 40. So Virg. *Æn.* i. 508, who says "*Jura dabat legesque viris.*"

JURE gentium.——By the law of nations.

JURE hæreditario.——By hereditary right.

JURE humano.——By human law (or right).

JURE mariti.——In right of the husband.

JURE naturæ.——By the law of nature.

JURE naturæ æquum est, neminem cum alterius detrimento et injuria fieri locupletiorem.——By the law of nature it is equitable, since no one can be made richer to the damage and wrong of another person.

JURE patronatus.——By the right of patronage.

JURE representationis.——By right of representation. *Vide note.*

JURE uxoris.——In right of the wife.

JURE vetusto obtinuit, quievisse omniá inferiora judicia, dicente jure rege.——He showed by ancient authority, that all inferior judgments ceased when the king declared the law.

JURIS disciplina.——The knowledge of law. *Vide Cic. Legg.* i. 5.

JURIS, et de jure.——Of right, and by law.

JURIS et seisinæ conjunctio.——The joinder of right and possession.

JURIS naturalis, aut divini.——Of natural or divine law (or right).

JURIS positivi.——Of positive law (or absolute right).

JURIS præcepta sunt hæc, honeste vivere, alterum non lædere, suum cuique tribuere.——These are the rules of law : to live honestly : not to injure another : and to render to every man his due.

JURIS privati.——Of private right or law.

JURIS procuratio omnibus prodest.——The administration of the law benefits every one.

JURISPRUDENCE des arrets.——The law of arrests.

JURISPRUDENTIA est divinarum atque humanarum rerum notitia.——Jurisprudence is the knowledge of things divine and human.

JURIS publici.——Of the public or people's right.

JURIS utrum.——Whether of right.

JURNEDUM.——A journey, or one day's travelling. Vide *Cowell.*

JUS.——"Law: Right." It is frequently, with the *Roman* writers, also put for the *place* where justice is administered ; thus—"*In jus eamus,*" i. e. "*ad prætoris sellam,*" (to the prætor's chair.) Vide *Donat. in Ter. Phorm.* v. 7, 43 et 88.

JUS accrescendi.——The right of accruer: benefit of survivorship.

Jus accrescendi inter mercatores.——The right of accruership among merchants.

Jus accrescendi inter mercatores pro beneficio commercii locum non habet.——For the advantage of commerce, there is no right of accruership among merchants.

Jus accrescendi præfertur ultimæ voluntati.——The right of accruership is preferred to the last will and testament.

Jus ad rem.——A right to the property.

Jus albinatus.——Right of escheat in the property of an alien.

Jus alluvionis.——"The right of the wash:" or to the lands thrown up by the sea or rivers.

Jus bellicum vel belli.——"The law of war." That which may be justly done to a state at war with us, and which may be done to the conquered. Vide *Cæs. de bell. G.* i. 27, *et Cic. Off.* i. 11, iii. 29.

Jus canonicum.——The canon law.

Jus civile.——The civil (or municipal law).

Jus civile est quod quisque sibi populus constituit.—— Civil law is what each nation has established for itself. *Vide note.*

Jus civitatis.——The law of the state.

Jus civium vel civile.——The law of the citizens, or the civil law.

Jus commune, et quasi gentium.——The common law, and, as it were, the law of nations.

Jus consuetudinis.——"The law of custom." That which hath been long established: opposed to "*lege jus*," or "*jus scriptum.*" Vide *Cic. de Invent.* ii. 22, 54.

Jus descendit ad primogenitum.——The right descends to the first born.

Jus dicere.——"To declare the law." To administer justice.

Jus dicere, et non dare.——To expound, not give the law.

Jus disponendi.——The right of disposal.

Jus domesticæ emendationis.——The law (or right) or domestic amendment.

Jus duplicatum.——A twofold, or double right.

Jus et æquitas.——Law and equity. *Vide note.*

Jus et fraus nunquam cohabitant.——Right and fraud never dwell together.

Jus et lex.——The right and the law. *Vide note.*

Jus et norma loquendi.——The right and form (or order) of speaking.

Jus et seisinæ conjunctio.——The right and conjunction of possession.

Jus feciale.——The law of arms or heraldry, *vide Cic. Off.* i. 11; or the form of proclaiming war; *vide* also Liv. i. 32.

Jus fiduciarum.——A right held in trust.

Jus fodiendi.——The right of digging.

Jus gentium.——The law (or right) of nations.

Jus gladii.——" The right of the Sword—Sword Law :" the arbitrary power of governing. *Vide note.*

Jus Hanseaticum maritimum.——The Hanseatic maritime law.

Jus hæreditarium, et dominicum.——Hereditary right and dominion.

Jus honorarium.——The honorary law. *Vide note.*

Jus humanum et divinum.——What is right with respect to things divine and human. Vide *Liv.* i. 18, 16. Hence "*fas et jura sinunt*," vide *Virg. G.* i. 269.

Jus imaginum.——The right of ancestry. *Vide note.*

Jus in re.——The right in the property.

Jus in res inferioris naturæ Deus humano generi indivisum contulit, hinc factum, quod quisque hominum ad suos usus arripere posset, quod vellet; et quæ consumi poterant, consumere.——God has conferred upon each individual of the human race the right to things of an inferior nature (or quality) for this reason, that every one may take for his own use what he pleases, and consume those things which may be eaten.

Jus judicium.——A judicial right.

Jus jurandum.——An oath.

Jus legitimum.——" A legal right." The common or ordinary law; the same with "*Jus civile.*" Vid. *Cic. pro Dom.* 13, 14. Thus "*jus legitimum exigere,*" to demand one's legal right, or what is legally due. Vid. *Fam.* viii. 6.

Jus libertatis.——The right of liberty. *Vide note.*

Jus matrimonii.——The right or law of marriage.

Jus municipale.——A municipal (or civil) right.

Jus naturæ.——The right (or law) of nature.

Jus naturæ propriè est dictamen rectæ rationis, quo scimus quid turpe, quid honestum, quid faciendum, quid fugiendum.——The law of nature is properly the dictate of right reason, by which we know what is dishonorable and what is honorable; what should be done, and what should be avoided.

Jus naturæ, vel naturale.——These words mean that law which nature or right reason teaches to be right; and "*jus gentium,*" what all nations esteem to be right. Vid. *Cic. Sext.* 42, *Harusp. resp.* 14.

Jus necessitudinis.——The law of necessity. *Suet Calig.* 26.

Jus non scriptum tacito et illiterato hominum consensu, et moribus expressum.——The unwritten law declared by the tacit and unlearned consent and customs of the people.

Jus pascendi.——The right of grazing.

Jus patris.——The father's right. *Vide note.*

Jus patronatus.——The right of patronage: the right of advowson.

Jus pontificum, vel sacrum.——" The Pontificial, or sacred law." That which is right with regard to religion and sacred things; much the same with what was after-

wards called "*Ecclesiastical Laws.*" Vide *Cic. pro Dom.*
12, 13, 14; *de legibus,* ii. 18, &c.

Jus positivum.——An absolute law (or right).

Jus postliminii.——The right of reprisal.

Jus possessionis.——The right of possession (or occupancy).

Jus prædicti *S.* et seisinam ipsius.——The right of the
said *S.* and his possession.

Jus Prætorium.——"The law (or discretion) of the
Prætor."—This was *distinct* from the "*Leges,*" or standing
laws. Vide note to *Prætor.*

Jus primogenituræ.——The right of primogeniture.

Jus projiciendi.——The right which a builder has to
project a part of his building towards an adjoining one.

Jus proprietatis et possessionis.——The right of property and possession.

Jus prosequendi in judicio, quod alicui debetur.——
The right of proceeding to judgment for what is due to
any one.

Jus protegendi. The right to extend the tilling of one
house over the adjoining one.

Jus publicum.——A public right or law.

Jus publicum et privatum.——A public and private
right or law. *Vide note.*

Jus quæsitum.——A right to recover.

Jus Quiritium.——The right of *Roman* citizens. *Vide
note.*

Jus regni.——The right of the crown.

Jus relictæ.——The right of a relict or widow.

Jus sanguinis.——The right of blood (or of kindred).

Jus sanguinis, quod in legitimis successionibus spectatur, ipso nativitatis tempore quæsitum est.——The right
of blood, which is regarded in all lawful inheritances, is
sought after in the very time (of our) nativity.

Jus scriptum aut non scriptam.——The written or the
unwritten law. *Vide note.*

JUSSU Cancellarii.——By the Chancellor's order.

JUSSU Cancellarii, cum assensu majoris partis præfec‑
torum collegorium.——By the command of the Chancel‑
lor, with the consent of the majority of the governors of
the colleges.

JUS summum sæpe summa est malitia.——"Strict law
is often the greatest mischief:" or "Right too rigid hard‑
ens into wrong."

JUS suum.——His own right.

JUSTA libertas.——A term anciently used on the eman‑
cipation of a slave. *Vide note.*

JUSTE rem judicato.——Weigh the matter correctly.

JUSTICIARII ad custodian *Judæorum* assignati.——Jus‑
tices appointed to take cognizance of the *Jews. Vide
note.*

JUSTICIARII ad omnia placita.——Judges of all pleas.

JUSTICIARII domini regis faciant fieri recognitionem de
disseisinis factis super assizam, a tempore quo Dominus
Rex venit in *Angliam* proxime post pacem factam inter ip‑
sum et regem filium suum.——That the judges of our lord
the King cause recognition to be made concerning the
disseisins done upon the assize from the time when our
lord the King arrived in *England,* next after the peace
concluded between him and the King his son.

JUSTICIARII in itinere.——"Judges in Eyre:" those who
went the circuit.

JUSTICIARII itinerantes venerunt apud *Virgorniam* in
octavis *S. Johannis Baptistæ;* et totius comitatus eos ad‑
mittere recusavit; quod septem anni nondum erant elapsi
postquam justiciarii ibidem ultimo sederunt.——The
judges in Eyre came to *Worcester* on the octave of *Saint
John the Baptist;* and the whole county refused to admit
them, because seven years had not elapsed since the judges
had sat in the same place. *Vide note.*

JUSTITIA nemini neganda est.——Justice is to be denied
to none.

JUSTITIA non est neganda, non differenda.——Justice is not to be denied nor delayed.

JUSTITIAR, vel Justicier.——"A Judge, or Justice;" or, as he was sometimes termed, *Justiciary*. *Shakspeare* uses the term "*Justicier*."

JUSTITIA virtutum regina.——Justice is the Queen of the virtues.

JUSTITIUM.——A suspension in judicial proceedings; a vacation of the courts.

JUS trium liberorum.——The right belonging to him who had three children. *Vide note.*

JUS utendi et fruendi.——The right of using and enjoying.

JUS venandi et piscandi.——The right of hunting and fishing.

JUVENES.——Chancery clerks of an inferior degree.

JUXTA formam statuti.——According to the form of the statute.

JUXTA tenorem sequentum.——According to the tenor following.

NOTES TO J.

JUDICES QUIRITIUM.—The student will be gratified to learn the manner of conducting a trial among the ancient *Romans*. When the day appointed came, the trial proceeded, unless the Judge, or some of the parties, were absent from a necessary cause, (*ex morbo, vel causa sontica. Fest.*)—i. e. "from disease, or some just impediment;" in which case the day was put off (*diffisus est*, i. e. *prolatus*). *Gell.* xiv. 2.

If the judge were present, he first took an oath, according to the best of his judgment, (*ex animi sententiâ*,) vide *Cic. Acad.*, Q. 47, at the altar, (*aram tenens*,) i. e. holding the altar, (*Cic. Flacc.* 36,) called "*Puteal Libonis*," or "*Scribonianum*," because that place being struck with thunder (*fulmine attactus*) had been expiated by *Scribonius Libo*, who raised over it a stone covering, (*suggestum lapideum cavum*,) open at the top, in the *Forum;* near which the tribunal of the *Prætor* used to be. Vide *Hor., Sat.* ii. 6, v. 35, *Ep.* i. 19, 8, and where the usurers met. Vide *Cic. Sext.* 8. *Ovid. de Rem. Am.* 561. The *Romans*, in their solemn oaths, used to hold a *flint stone* in their right hand, saying, "*Si sciens fallo, tum me Diespiter (salva urbe arceque) bonis ejiciat, ut ego hunc lapidem*"—i. e. "If knowingly I use deceit, then may Jupiter, (saving the City and Capitol) cast me out from good men, as I cast this stone." Vide *Fest. in lapis.* Hence the term, "*Jovem lap idem*

jurure," for *"per Jovem et lapidem."*—i. e. "by Jupiter and the stone."
Vide *Cic. Fam.* vii. 1, 12. *Liv.* xxi. 45, xxii. 53. *Gell.* i. 21.

The author understands there is a mode of swearing, something similar to
this, in use among the *Chinese.* The witness takes into his hand some
vessel that will readily break, and throws it up with the imprecation, *"May
God so dash me to pieces, if I swear not the truth."* The present mode of
swearing among the *Mahometan Arabs,* that live in tents, as the Patriarchs
did, according to *De La Roque,* (*Voy. dans la Pal., p.* 152,) is by laying their
hands on the *Koran.* They cause those who swear to *wash* their hands, before they give them the book; they then put their left hand underneath,
and their right over it. Whether, among the Patriarchs, one hand was
under, and the other upon . the thigh, is not certain : possibly *Abraham's*
servant might swear with one hand upon his master's thigh, and the other
stretched out to Heaven. As the posterity of the Patriarchs are described
as coming out of the thigh, it has been supposed this ceremony had some
relation to their believing the promise of God, to bless all the nations of the
earth, by means of one that was to descend from Abraham. Vide *Burder's
notes to Josephus.*

The *formula,* among the *Romans,* of taking an oath, we have in *Plaut.
Rud.* v. 2, 45, &c., and an account of different forms. *Cic. Acad.* iv. 47.
The most solemn oath among the *Romans,* was by *faith* or *honor.* Vide
Dionys. ix. 8, 10, 48, xi. 54.

The *judex* or *judices,* after having sworn, took their seats (in the *subsellia
quasi ad pedes Prætoris*)—i. e. "seats nearly at the Prætor's feet ; " whence
they were called, "*Judices pedanei*"—i. e. inferior judges, and "*sedere,*" (to
sit,) is often put for *cognoscere*—to examine, or to judge. Vide *Plin., Ep.* v.
Sedere is also applied to an advocate, while not pleading. *Plin., Ep.* iii. 9.
The *judex,* especially if there were but one, assumed some lawyers to assist
him with their counsel, (*sibi advocavit, ut in concilio adessent.*) Vide *Cic.
Quinct.* 2, (*in consilium rogavit,*)—i. e. desired his advice. Vide *Gell.*
xiv. 2,) whence they were called "*Consiliarii.*" Vide *Suet. Tib.* 33.
Claud. 12.

If any one of the parties were absent without a just excuse, he was summoned by an edict, or lost his cause. Vide *Cic. Quinct.* 6. If the *Prætor*
pronounced an unjust decree, in the absence of any one, the assistance of
the *Tribunes* might be implored. *Ibid.* 20.

If both parties were present, they were obliged to swear that they did not
carry on the lawsuit from a desire of litigation, (*calumniam jurare,* vel *de
calumnia.* Vide *Liv.* xxx. 49. *Cic. Fam.* viii. 8.) If this were the case at
the present day, causes for trifling matters would probably be less numerous.
By one of the *Roman* laws, called *Lex Memnia vel Remnia,* it was ordained
that if any one was convicted of false accusation (*calumniæ*) he should be
branded on the forehead with a letter, vide *Cic. pro Rosc. Am.* 19, 20, probably with the letter K, as *anciently* the name of this odious and cowardly
crime, was written *Kalumnia.*

Then the advocates were ordered to plead, which they did *twice,* one after
another, in two different methods. Vide *Appian. de Bell. Civ.* i. p. 663, first,
briefly, which was called "*causæ conjectio,*"—conjecturing, or *briefly* considering of the case ; and then in a *formal* oration (*justa oratione perorabant*) i. e.
arguing in a complete speech. Vide *Gell.* xvii. 2. They explained the state
of the case, and proved their own charge, or defence, *testibus et tabulis* (i. e.
by witnesses and writings), and by arguments drawn from the case itself
(*ex ipsa re deductis*). Vide *Cic. pro P. Quinct. et Rosc. Orat.* ii. 42, 43, 44,
79, 82. To prevent them, however, from being too tedious, (*ne in immensum
evagarentur*—i. e. lest they should greatly wander from the case,) it was ordained by the *Pompeian* law, in imitation of the *Greeks,* that they speak by
an hour-glass (*ut ad Clepsydram dicerent,* i. e. *vas vitreum graciliter fistulatum,
in fundo cujus erat foramen, unde aqua guttatim efflueret, atque ita tempus me-*

tiretur"—i. e. "that they should argue by the hour-glass, viz., a glass vase which had a small neck, in the bottom of which was a hole, from which the water trickled out, and in this manner the time was measured." [This water glass appears to have been something like our sand glasses formerly in use.] Vidé *Cic. de Orat.* iii. 34. How many hours were allowed to each advocate was left to the *Judices* to determine. Vide *Cic. Quinct.* 9; *Plin. Ep.* i. 20, iv. 9. Hence "*dare,* vel *petere pluras clepsydras*"—i. e. to ask more time to speak. "*Quoties judico, quantum quis plurimum postulat æquæ do*"—i. e. "I give the advocates as much time as they request." Vide *Plin. Ep.* vi. ii. The "*Clepsydræ*" were of different lengths—sometimes three of them in an hour. Vide *Plin. Ep.* ii.

The advocate sometimes had a person with him to suggest (*qui subjiceret*) what he should say, who was called "*Ministrator.*" Vide *Cic. de Orat.* ii. 75. *Flacc.* 22. A forward, noisy speaker was called "*Rabula*" (*a rabie, quasi Latrator*) vel "*Proclamator,*" a brawler, a wrangler. *Cic. de Orat.* i. 46. The *Romans,* it appears, considered noisy lawyers as men of inferior abilities. In many cases, these "*Clepsydræ*" would not be altogether useless at the present day.

Under the Emperors, advocates used to keep persons *in pay,* to procure for them an audience, or to collect hearers who attended them from court to court (*ex judicio in judicium*), and applauded them while they were pleading, as a man, who stood in the middle of them, gave the word or sign (*quam dedit signum*). Each of them for his services received his dole (*sportula*), or a certain hire (*par merces*), usually three *dernarii,* hence they were called "*Laudicœni,*" i. e. *qui ob cœnam laudabant*—i. e. "who applauded for their supper." This custom was introduced by one *Largius Licinius,* who flourished under *Nero* and *Vespasian,* and is greatly ridiculed by *Pliny.* Vide *Ep.* 214: see also vi. 2. When a client gained his cause, he used to fix a garland of green palm (*viridis palmæ*) at his lawyer's door. Vide *Juv.* vii. 118.

When the judges heard the parties, they were said "*iis operam dare*"—i. e. to give them their attention. How inattentive, however, they sometimes were, we learn from *Macrobius, Saturnal.* ii. 12.

JUDICIA AD POPULUM.—Trials before the *Roman* people were called "*Judicia ad populum,*" and were first held in the *Comitia Curiata.* Vide *Cic. pro Mil.* 3. Of this, however, we have only the example of *Horatius. Ibid.* After the institution of the *Comitia Centuriata,* and *Tributa,* all trials before the people were held in them; capital trials in the *Comitia Centuriata,* and concerning a fine, in the *Tributa.* Those trials were called "*capital*" which respected the life or *liberty* of a *Roman* citizen. There was one trial of this kind, held in the *Comitia* by tribes, namely that of *Coriolanus.* Vide *Liv.* ii. 35, but that appears to have been irregular, and conducted with violence. Vide *Dionys.* vii. 38, &c. Sometimes a person was said to undergo a *capital* trial, "*periculum capitis adire; causam capitis;* vel *pro capite dicere*"—i. e. to undergo a suit relating to his life; or to plead for life,—in a *civil* cause, *when,* besides his loss of fortune, his *character* was at stake, "*cum judicium esset de fama, fortunisque*"—i. e. "when the sentence affected his character and fortune." Vide *Cic. pro. Quinct.* 9, 13, 15. *Off.* i. 12. The method of proceeding in both *Comitia* was the same; and it was requisite that some *magistrate* should be the accuser. In the *Comitia Tributa,* the inferior magistrates were generally the accusers; as the *Tribunes,* or *Ædiles.* Vide *Liv.* iii. 55. iv. 21. &c. In the *Comitia Centuriata,* the superior magistrates, as the *Consuls,* or *Prætors;* sometimes also the inferior, as the *Questors,* or *Tribunes.* Vide *Liv.* ii. 41, iii. 24, 25, vi. 20. But they are supposed to have acted by the authority of the *Consuls.* No person could be brought to a trial, unless he was in a *private* station. But sometimes this rule was violated. Vide *Cic. pro. Flacc.* 3, *Liv.* xliii. 16.

The magistrate who was to accuse any one, having called an assembly, and mounted the *Rostra*, declared that he would, against a certain day, accuse a particular person of a certain crime; and ordered that the person accused (*reus*) should then be present. This was called *dicere diem sc. accusationis* vel *diei dictio*—i. e. "to state the day, or declaring the day of accusation." In the meantime the accused was kept in custody, unless he found persons to give security for his appearance (*sponsores eum in judicio ad diem dictam, sistendi aut mulctum, qua damnatus esset, solvendi*)—i. e. "Sureties that he should be forthcoming at the day appointed, or pay the fine for which he should be condemned," who, in a capital trial were called "*vades*," i. e. "sureties." *Liv.* iii. 13. xxv. 4; and for a fine "*prædes*," (perhaps freeholders.) *Gell.* vii. 19.

When the day arrived, the magistrate ordered the accused to be cited from the *Rostra* by a herald. Vide *Liv.* xxxviii. 51. If the criminal was absent, without a valid reason (*sine causa sontica*), he was condemned. If he was detained by indisposition, or any other necessary cause, he was said to be excused; and the day of trial was put off. An equal, or superior magistrate, might, by his negative, hinder the trial from proceeding. Vide *Liv.* xxxviii. 52. If the criminal appeared and no magistrate interceded, the accused entered upon his charge, which was repeated *three* times, with the intervention of a day between each, and supported his cause by witnesses, writings and other proofs. In each charge the punishment, or fine, was annexed, which was called "*anquisitio*." Sometimes the punishment first proposed was afterwards mitigated, or increased. The accused usually stood under the *Rostra*, in a mean garb, where he was frequently subject to the scoffs and railleries (*probis et conviciis*) of the people. This appears strange, if we consider the excellent method of the *Roman* people generally adopted in other parts of their jurisprudence. After the accusation of the third day was finished a bill (*Rogatio*) was published for three market days, concerning the law, in which the crime, and the proposed punishment, or fine, was expressed. This was called "*mulctæ, pœnæve, irrogatio*;" and the judgment of the people concerning it, "*mulctæ, pœnæve, certatio*," vide *Cic. de leg.* iii. 3; for it was ordained that capital punishment and a fine should never be joined together, (*ne pœna capitis cum pecunia conjungeretur.*) On the third market day, the accuser again repeated his charge, and the accused, or an advocate (*patronus*) for him, was permitted to make his defence, in which everything was introduced which could serve to gain the favor of the people, or move their compassion. Vide *Cic. pro Rabir.*, *liv.* iii. 12. 58. Then the *Comitia* were summoned against a certain day, in which the people, by their suffrages, should determine the fate of the accused. If the punishment proposed was only a fine, and a *Tribune* the accuser, he could summon the *Comitia Tributa* himself; but if the trial was capital, he asked a day for the *Comitia Centuriata* from the Consul, or in his absence from the *Prætor.* Vide *Liv.* xxxvi. 3. xliii. 16. In a capital trial, the people were called to the *Comitia* by a trumpet.

JUDICIUM PARIUM.—Among the *Romans*, the *Judices*, or Jury, were at first chosen only from the Senators: then by the *Sempronian* law of *C. Gracchus*, only from the *Equites;* afterwards, by the *Servilian* law of *Cœpio*, from both orders; then by the *Glaucian* law, only from the *Equites ;* and by the *Livinian* law of *Drusus*, from the Senators and *Equites.* But the laws of the *Drusus* being afterwards set aside by a decree of the Senate, the right, of judging was again restored to the *Equites*, alone. Then by the *Plautian* law of *Silvanus*, the *Judices* were chosen from the *Senators* and *Equites;* and some of them also from the *Plebeians;* then by the *Cornelian* law of *Sylla*, only from the *Senators;* by the *Aurelian* law of *Cotta* from the *Senators*, the *Equites*, and *Tribunes ærarii;* by the *Julian* law of *Cæsar*, only from the *Senators* and *Equites ;* and by the law of *Antony*, also from the *officers* of the army. Vide *Manutius de leg.* The number of these *Judices* were different at different times. By the law of *Gracchus*, 300; of *Servilius*, 450; of *Drusus*, 650; of *Plautius*, 525; of *Sylla* and *Cotta*, 300, (as it is thought,) from *Cic. Fam.* viii. 8; of *Pompey*, 360, *Paterc.* ii. 76. Under the Emperors, the number of the *Judices* was greatly increased. *Pl'n.* By the *Servilian* law, the age of the *Judices* must be above thirty, and below sixty years. By other laws it was required, that they should be at least twenty-five; but *Augustus* ordered that *Judices* might be chosen from the age of twenty. *Suet. Aug.* 32; as the best commentators read the passage. Certain persons could *not* be chosen *Judices*, either from some natural defect, as the deaf, dumb, &c., or by custom, as women and slaves; or by law, as those condemned upon trial of some infamous crime, (*turpi et famoso judicio*, e. g. *calumniæ, prævaricationis, furti, vi bonorum raptorum; injuriam, de dolo malo, pro socio, mandati, tutelæ, depositi, &c.*)—i. e. adjudged in a base and infamous judgment, e. g. for calumny, prevarication (or injuring his client by bribery, &c.), robbery of goods with violence; injuries of deceit, partnership, commission, guardianship and deposit, (or bailment,) &c. And by the *Julian* law, those degraded from being Senators; which was not the case formerly. *Cic. Cluent.* 43. By the *Pompeian* law, the *Judices* were chosen from persons of the highest fortune. *Judices* were annually chosen by the *Prætor Urbanus*, or *Peregrinus:* according to *Dio. Cassius*, by the Questors, xxxix. 7; and their names written down in a list (*in album relata, vel albo descripta*,) Suet. Tib. 51. Claud. 16, &c. They swore to the laws; and that they would judge uprightly, according to the best of their knowledge, (*de animi sententia.*) The *Judices* were prohibited by *Augustus* from entering the house of any one. *Dio.* liv. 18. That they sat by the *Prætor* on benches; whence they were sometimes called his *Assessors* or "*Consilium.*" The office of a *Judex* was attended with trouble, *Cic. in Verr.* i. 8; and, therefore, in the time of *Augustus* people declined it; but not so afterwards, when the number was greatly increased. *Suet. et Plin.*

JURE DIVINO, ET JURE HUMANO.—Among the *Romans*, things with respect to property were divided. Some things were said to be of "*divine right*"—others of "*human right*"—the former were called "sacred" (*res sacræ*) as altars, temples, or anything publicly consecrated to the Gods, by the authority of the Pontiffs—or "*religious*," (*religiosæ*) as sepulchres, &c. or inviolable "*sanctæ*," i. e. *aliqua sanctione munitæ*—i. e. defended by some sanction, as the walls and gates of a city. *Macrob. Sat.* iii. 3.

These things were subject to the law of the Pontiffs; and the property of them could not be transferred. Temples were rendered sacred by inauguration, or dedication, that is, by being consecrated by the Augurs, (*consecrata inaugurataque*). Whatever was legally consecrated, was ever afterwards inapplicable to profane uses. Vide *Plin. Ep.* ix. 39, &c. Temples were supposed to belong to the Gods; and could not be the property of a private person. Things ceased to be sacred, by being unhallowed (*exauguratione*). Vide *Liv.* i. 55. Any place became religious by interring a dead body in it. Sepulchres were held religious, because they were dedicated to the infernal Gods.

Things of *human* right were called profane, (*res profanæ,*) and were either public and common; as the air, running water, the sea and its shores, &c. *Virg. Æneid*, vii. 229, or private, which might be the property of individuals.

Things which properly belonged to nobody, were called "*res nullius,*" (i. e. the property of no one,) as parts of the world not discovered; animals not claimed, &c. To this class was referred "*hereditas jacens,*" or an estate in the interval of time betwixt the demise of the last occupier, and the entry of the successor.

Things were either movable, or immovable. The movable things of a farm were "*ruta cæsa*," (i. e. things dug, or thrown down) as sand, coals, stones, &c., which were commonly excepted "*recepta*" (or retained) by the seller. Vide *Cic. Top.* 26. *Orat.* ii. 55.

Things were also divided into corporeal and incorporeal, (such as rights, servitudes, &c.) The former *Cicero* calls "*res quæ sunt*," (things which are.) The latter "*res quæ intelliguntur*," (things which are understood.) Vide *Topic.* 5. But others, perhaps more properly, call the former "*Res*," (things,) and the latter "*Jura*," (rights.) Vide *Quinct.* v. 10, 116. The division of this, *Horace* briefly divides thus:

—————"*Fuit hæc sapientia quondam,*
Publica privatis secernere, sacra profanis." de Art. Poet. 396.

i. e. "This was the (rule of) wisdom, in ancient times, to draw a line of discrimination between public and private rights; between what was sacred and profane (or common)."

JURE REPRESENTATIONIS.—A question arose in the tenth century respecting the right of representation, which was not then fixed, though now universally established in *Europe* and *America*. "It was a matter of dispute," (saith the historian,) "whether the sons of a son ought to be reckoned among the children of the family, and succeed equally with their uncles, if their father happened to die while their grand-father was alive. An assembly was called to deliberate on the point, and it was the general opinion that it ought to be remitted to the examination and decision of the judges. But the Emperor, following a better course, and desirous of dealing honorably with his people and nobles, appointed the matter to be decided by battle between two champions. He who appeared in behalf of the right of the children to represent their deceased father, was victorious; and it was established by a perpetual decree, that they should thereafter share in the inheritance together with their uncles." Vide *Wittikundus Corbiensis lib. Annal. ap. M. de Lauriere, Pref. Ordon,* vol. i. p. 33. If we can suppose the caprice of folly to lead men to any action more extravagant than this (of settling a point in law by combat) it must be that of referring the truth or falsehood of a *religious* opinion to be decided in the same manner. To the disgrace of human reason it has been capable *even* of this extravagance. A question was agitated in *Spain* in the eleventh century, whether the *Musarabic* Liturgy and Ritual, which had been used in the churches of *Spain*, or that approved of by the See of *Rome*, which differed in many particulars from the other, contained the form of worship most acceptable by the Deity. The *Spaniards* contended most zealously for the Ritual of their ancestors. The *Popes* urged them to receive that to which *they* had given their sanction. A violent contest arose. The nobles proposed to decide the controversy by the sword. The King approved of this mode of decision. Two Knights, in complete armor, entered the list. *John Ruys de Mantanca*, the champion of the *Musarabic* Liturgy, was victorious. But the Queen and the Archbishop of *Toledo*, who favored the other form, insisted on having the matter submitted to *another* trial; and had interest enough to prevail in this request, inconsistent with the laws of Combat, which ought to have been acquiesced in as final. A great fire was kindled, and a copy of each Liturgy was cast into the flames. It was agreed that the book, which stood this proof and remained untouched, should be received in all the churches of *Spain*. The *Musarabic* Liturgy triumphed also in that trial; and *if* we may believe *Roderigo de Toledo*, remained unhurt by the fire, when the other was reduced to ashes.

JUS CIVILE, &c.—Among the calamities which the devastation of the Barbarians, who broke into the *Roman* Empire, brought upon mankind, one of the greatest was their overturning the system of *Roman* jurisprudence, the noblest monument of the wisdom of that great people, formed to subdue and govern the world. But the laws and regulations of a civilized community were altogether repugnant to the manners and ideas of the fierce northern invaders. The *Romans* had respect to objects of which a rude people had no conception; and *their* laws were adapted to a state of society, with which they (the invaders) were totally unacquainted. For this reason, wherever the northern conquerors settled, the *Roman* jurisprudence soon sank into oblivion; and lay buried for some centuries under the load of those institutions, which the inhabitants of *Europe* dignified with the name of "*Laws.*" About the middle of the twelfth century, a copy of *Justinian's Pandects* was accidentally discovered in *Italy;* and at *that* time the state of society was so far advanced, and the ideas of men so much enlarged and improved, by the occurrences of several centuries, that they were struck with admiration of a system which their ancestors could not comprehend. Men of letters studied this new body of laws with eagerness; and within a few years after the discovery of the *Pandects,* professors of the Civil Law were appointed, who taught it publicly in most countries of *Europe.*

Jus et æquitas, are distinguished, *Cic Off.* iii. 16. *Virg.* ii. 426; *jus et justitia;* i. e. right and justice—*jus civile;* the civil law—*et leges;* and the laws. *Phil.* ix. 5. So *æquum et bonum,* i. e. just and good—is opposed to *callidum versatumque jus,* i. e. an artful interpretation of a (written) law. *Cæcin.* 23. *Summum jus,* (the rigor of the law,) *summa injuria,* (the greatest injury.) *Off.* i. 11. *Summo jure agere; contendere; experiri;* &c., i. e. to try to the *utmost* stretch of the law. It would appear from these words, and other sentences found in the ancient classics, and law writers, that as unmerciful and oppressive a spirit, or *love* of litigation, possessed some persons' minds in ancient times, as is found in many litigating parties of the present day, who are really a bane to society.

Jus et Lex—Right and Law. The words "*Jus,*" and "*Lex,*" are used in various senses, though sometimes confounded. They are both expressed by the *English* word "Law." *Jus* seems to imply what is *just, and right in itself;* or what from *any* cause is binding on us. Vide *Cic. de Offic.* iii. 21. *Lex* is a written statute, or ordinance, (*lex quæ scripto sancit quod vult, aut jubendo aut vetando. Cic. de leg.* 1, 6.—i. e. a law established by writing, which is efficacious, either in commanding or forbidding. "*A legendo, quod legi solet, ut innotescat*"—i. e. "from reading, because it is wont to be read, that it might be notorious." *Varr de Lat. ling.* v. 7, *a justo et jure legendo,* i. e. *eligendo,* "from a just and select law," *Cic. de Leg.* ii. 5, *justorum injustorum quæ distinctio.* ibid.—i. e. "the law, which distinguishes the just and unjust." *Jus* is properly what the law ordains, or the obligation which it imposes; (*est enim Jus quod Lex constituit*)—i. e. that is right; (or that is binding) which the law ordains. *Cic. de Leg.* i. 15, *ad Herenn.* ii. 13—or according to the Twelve Tables, "*Quodcumque populus jussit, id jus esto*—i. e. whatever the people ordain, that is the law. *Liv.* vii. 17, ix. 33. *Quod major pars judicarit, id jus ratumque esto. Cic.*—i. e. that what the major part shall adjudge, let that be the law."

But *Jus* and *Lex* have a different meaning, according to the words with which they are joined—thus *jus naturæ,* vel *naturale*—i. e. "the law of nature, or natural law," is what nature, or right reason teacheth to be *right:* and *jus gentium,* i. e., "the law of nations," what all nations esteem to be *right:* both commonly reckoned the same. *Cic. Sext.* 42. *Harusp. resp.* 14. *Jus civium,* vel *civile,* i. e. "the law of citizens, or the civil law," is what the inhabitants of a particular country esteem to be right, either by nature, custom, or statute. *Cic. Top.* 5, *Off.* iii. 16, 17. *De Orat.* i. 48. Hence *constituere jus quo omnes retantur (pro Dom)*—i. e. "to establish the law in which all are conversant." *Cui subjecti sint (pro Cæcin)*—i. e. "to which all are subject." So *jus Romanorum, Anglicum, &c.* When no word is added to restrict it, *Jus Civile* is put for the civil law of the *Romans. Cicero* sometimes opposes *Jus Civile* to *Jus naturale*. *Sext.* 42; and sometimes to what we call *criminal* law, (*Jus publicum*)—i. e. public law. *Verr.* i. 42, &c. *Jus commune*, i. e. the common law, what is held to be right among men in general, or among the inhabitants of any country, (*Cic. Cæcin*). *Jus publicum, et privatum*—i. e. "the public and private law;" what is right with respect to the people (*quasi jus publicum*), or the public at large; and with respect to individuals, political and civil law. *Liv.* iii. 34, &c. But *Jus publicum* is also put for the *right*, which the citizens in common enjoyed. (*Jus commune.*) *Jus divinum et humanam*—i. e. "the divine and human law;" what is right with respect to things divine and human. *Liv.* i. 18, xxxix. 16. Hence, *fas et jura sinunt* (i. e. laws divine and human permit). *Virg.* G. i. 269. *Contra jus, fasque*—i. e. against law and justice. *Sall. Cat.* 15. *Jus fasque exure*—i. e. "to depart from law and justice." *Tacit. Hist.* iii. 5.

Jus GLADII.—Sword law is mentioned by our *Latin* authors, and by the *Norman* laws, and means *Supreme Jurisdiction*, or that kept by force of arms. Vide *Camden*. And it is said, that from hence, at the creation of an Earl, he is "*gladio accinctus*"—i. e. "girt with a sword," to signify that he has jurisdiction over the county of which he is made an Earl.

Jus HONORARIUM.—By order of the Emperor *Hadrian*, the various Edicts of the *Prætors* were collected into one, and properly arranged by the Lawyer, *Salvius Julian*, the great-grand-father of the Emperor *Didius Julian;* which was afterwards called *Edictum perpetuum*, or *Jus honorarium*, and no doubt was of the greatest service in forming that famous code of the *Roman* laws called CORPUS JURIS, compiled by order of the Emperor *Justinian*.

Jus IMAGINUM.—Among the *Romans*, those whose ancestors or themselves had borne any *Curule* magistracy, that is, had been *Consul, Prætor, Censor*, or *Curule, Ædile*, were called NOBILES; and had the right of making images of themselves (JUS IMAGINUM), which were kept with great care by their posterity, and carried before them at funerals. Vide *Plin.* xxxv. 2.

These images were nothing else but the busts or the *effigies* of persons down to the shoulders, made of wax, and painted; which they used to place in the courts of their houses (*atria*), inclosed in wooden cases; and which they seem not to have brought out except on solemn occasions. Vide *Polyb.* vi. 51. There were titles or inscriptions written below them, pointing out the honors they had enjoyed, and the exploits they had performed. *Juv. Sat.* viii. 69. *Plin.* xxxv. 2. Hence *Imagines* is often put for *Nobilitas*. Vide *Sallust. Jug.* 85, *Liv.* iii. 58; and *Cera* for *Imagines*. Vide *Ov. Amor.* i. 8, 65. Anciently, the right of images was peculiar to the Patricians; but afterwards the Plebeians also acquired it when admitted to Curule offices.

Those who were the *first* of their family that had raised themselves to any Curule office were called HOMINES NOVI, new men or upstarts. Hence, *Cicero* honestly calls himself "*Homo per se cognitus*," i. e. a person reported by himself (or indebted to his own abilities only). *Cic. in Cat.* i. 11.

Those who had no images of their own, or of their ancestors, were called *Ignobiles*, i. e. (lowly born, meanly descended).

Jus LIBERTATIS.—The right of liberty. This, among the *Romans*, comprehended freedom, not only from the power of the masters (*dominorum*), but also from the dominion of tyrants, the severity of magistrates, the cruelty of creditors, and the insolence of the more powerful citizens.

After the expulsion of *Tarquin*, a law was made by *Brutus* that no one should be King at *Rome;* and that whoever should form a design of making himself King. might be slain with impunity. At the same time, the people were bound by an oath that they would never suffer a King to be created.

Roman Citizens were secured against the tyrannical treatment of magistrates; first, by the right of appealing from them to the people, and that the person so appealing should in no manner be punished till the *people* decided the matter; but chiefly by the assistance of the *Tribunes*.

None but the whole *Roman* people in the *Comitia Centuriata* could pass sentence on the life of a *Roman* citizen No magistrate was allowed to punish him by stripes, or capitally. The single expression, "SUM ROMANUS CIVIS"—i. e. "I AM A ROMAN CITIZEN," checked their severest decrees, and stayed the Lictor's hand. *Cic. in Verr.* v. 54, and 57, &c. Hence, " *Quirtare dicitur," qui Quiritium fidem clamans implorat*"—i. e. one who implored the Roman protection. Vide *Varro de Lat. Ling.* v. 7. *Cic. ad Fam.* x. 32. *Liv.* xxix. *Acts Apost.* xxii. 25.

JUS PATRIS.—The right of the father. A father among the *Romans* had the power of life and death over his children. He could not only expose them when infants; which cruel custom prevailed at *Rome* for many ages, as among other nations. *Cic. de Leg.* iii. 8, &c., and a *new* born infant was not held *legitimate*, unless the father, or in his absence, some person for him lifted it from the ground (*terra levâsset*), and placed it on his bosom; hence called "*tollere filium*," i. e. "to raise or educate; "*non tollere*," "to expose;" but even when his children were grown up, he had the right to imprison, scourge, send them bound to work in the country; and also put them to death, by any punishment he pleased, if they deserved it. Vide *Sall. Cal.* 39. *Liv.* ii. 41, &c. Hence a father is called a "*domestic Judge*," or magistrate, by *Seneca;* and a *Censor* of his own son, by *Sueton. Claud.* 16. Romulus, however, at first, permitted this right only in certain cases. A son could acquire no property but with his father's consent, and what he *did* thus acquire was called his "*Peculium*," i. e. "his private property," as that of a slave. Vide *Liv.* ii. 41. If he acquired it in *war*, it was called "*peculium castrense.*" The condition of a son was in some respects harder than that of a slave: a slave when sold *once* became free from that master who sold him, but a son not so, until sold *three* times. The power of the father was suspended, when the son was promoted to any *public* office, but not extinguished. Vide *Liv. ibid.*, for it continued not only during the life of the children, but likewise extended to grandchildren, and great grandchildren. None of them became their own masters (*sui juris*) until the death of their father and grandfather. A daughter, however, by *marriage*, passed from the power of the father to that of her husband. And although the *Roman* laws in respect of children have been branded as very cruel and oppressive, yet, taking it in *all its bearings*, as a system of *patriarchal* authority, it has been a question whether it was not in the *aggregate* productive of *general* good to the Republic. It is but seldom that any *father* is cruel—and disobedience to parents was in the earlier stages of the world a crime, only to be atoned for *by death*, particularly by the *Mosaic* law.

JUS PUBLICUM ET PRIVATUM.—These words meant among the *Romans*, what is right with respect to the people (*quasi jus populicum*), as if popular law, with the public at large; and, in respect to individuals, political and civil law. Vide *Liv.* iii. 34. But *jus publicum* is also put for the right which the citizens in common enjoyed. Vide *Terent. Phorn.* ii. 2, 65.

JUS QUIRITIUM.—The right of *Roman Citizens*. These words were used abstractedly, and comprehended *all their rights*, which were different at different times. These rights were either private or public: the former were, perhaps, more properly called "*Jus Quiritium*," i. e. the right of citizens; and the latter "*Jus Civitatis*," i. e. the right of the state. *Plin. Ep.* x. 4, 6, 22; as there is a distinction between denization and naturalization. Those who did not enjoy the rights of citizens were anciently called " *Hostes*," but afterwards "*Peregrini.*" Vide *Cic. Off.* i. 12. After *Rome* had extended her empire, first over *Latium*, then over *Italy*, and afterwards over the greatest part of the then known world, the rights which the subjects of that Empire enjoyed came to be divided into four kinds, which may be called *Jus Quiritium; Jus Latii; Jus Italicum;* and *Jus Provinciarum,* vel *Provinciale.*

JUS SCRIPTUM, &c.—The *Roman* law (as with us) was either written, or unwritten (*jus scriptum, aut non scriptum*). The several species which constituted the *jus scriptum,* were laws, properly so called, the decrees of the Senate, the edicts or decisions of magistrates, and the opinions or writings of eminent lawyers. Unwritten law (*jus non scriptum*) comprehended natural equity and custom. Though, it is said, anciently, *jus scriptum* only comprehended laws properly so called. Vide *Digest de orig. jur.* All these the studious reader may find frequently enumerated, or at least alluded to by *Cicero,* who calls them *Fontes æquitatis*—i. e. the fountains of equity. Vide *Topic.* 5, &c., *ad Herenn.* ii. 13.

JUSTA LIBERTAS.—In the latter times of the *Roman* Empire, slaves used to be freed in various ways, as well as those which had been customary, which was called "*Justa libertas,*" and included their being emancipated. 1st. "*Per Censum;*" 2d. "*Per vindictam;*" and 3d. "*Per testamentum.*" In addition to these modes, they were also freed by letter (*per Epistolam*); among friends (*inter amicos*); or by table (*per mensam*); if a master bid his slave *eat* at his table. Vide *Plin. Ep.* vii. 16; for it was thought disgraceful to eat with slaves, or mean persons, and benches (*subsellia*) were assigned them, not couches, as generally used by the *Romans;* at least those of the more wealthy sort, at their meals. Hence, *imi subselli,* viz. "a person of the lowest rank." *Plaut.* Slaves made free, used to shave their heads in the temple of *Feronia;* and received a cap or hat as a badge of liberty. Hence, "*ad pileum servum vocare*"—i. e. "to call the slave to the cap," for, *ad libertatem* (to liberty). Vide *Liv.* xix. 44. They were also presented with a white robe, and a ring by their master. They then assumed a *prænomen,* and prefixed the name of their patron to their own. Thus, *Marcus Tullius Tiro,* (the freedman of *Cicero.*)

JUSTICIARII AD CUSTODIAM JUDÆORUM ASSIGNATI.—Called "Justices of the *Jews.*" King *Richard,* after his return from the Crusades, A. D. 1194, appointed particular justices, laws and orders, for preventing the frauds, and regulating the contracts and usury of the Jews.

JUSTICIARII ITINERANTES, &c.—Justice in Eyre—so termed from the old *Fr.* word "*erre.*" These were Justices, who were, in ancient times, sent into divers counties to hear causes, especially such as were termed "*Pleas of the Crown.*" These Justices, according to *Gwin,* were sent but *once* in *seven* years; but this may be doubtful. Vide *Hoveden.*

JUS TRIUM LIBERORUM.—This law is frequently mentioned by Pliny, Martial, &c. It was granted sometimes to women. Vide *Dio.* iv. 2. The privileges of having *three* children were an exemption from the trouble of guardianship, a priority in bearing offices (*Plin. Ep.* viii. 16), and a treble proportion of corn. Those who lived in celibacy could not succeed to an inheritance, except of their nearest relation, unless they married within one hundred days after the death of the testator; nor receive an entire legacy (*legatum omne,* vel *solidum capere*), to take all, or the entire legacy, and what they were thus deprived of, in certain cases, fell as an escheat (*caducum*) into the Exchequer (*fisco*), or prince's private purse. Vide *Juvenal,* ix. 88.

K.

KAIA.——A key, or wharf: a place to land and take in merchandise.

KALENDA.——The calends of a month.

Καλλε και δεσιαισυνες δογματα νομου.——The decisions of the law are those of equity and justice.

KARAXARE.——To make characters; to mark.

KARLE.——"A man." The *Saxons* called a domestic servant a *huskarle;* from whence, perhaps, the modern word *churl.*

KARRATA.——A cart-load.

KERCHE, Kirche, Kerchia, Kurk.——A Church.

KERNELLARE.——To fortify.

KIDDLE.——A dam in a river with a cut in it arranged to catch fish.

KILLIAGIUM, Keelage.——A privilege to demand money for the bottom of ships resting in a port or harbor.

KINSBOTE.——The fine or satisfaction paid for killing a kinsman.

KNIGHTEN-GYLD.——An ancient corporation in London, consisting of nineteen knights.

Κοινος——Common: public.

Κομπρομισσον.——A bond or engagement.

L.

LABEFACERE fidem suam.——To destroy his credit.

LACERTA.——A fathom.

LACHES.——Neglect: supineness.

LÆSIWERP.——To surrender; deliver up.

LÆSTUM.——See LATHE.

LAFORDSWIE.——Sax. Treachery against a lord or master.

LACTA.——" A defect in the weight of money" ; whence probably comes the word "*Lack.*"

LA chose recoit encore mains de difficulté si le capitaine parvenu au lien destiné, dissipé la pacotille chargé á sa consignation l'est alors un risque de terre, dont le assureurs ne respond en aucune maniere.——The matter is attended with still less difficulty, if the captain, after having arrived at his destination, injures or damages the vessel committed to his care; it is then a land risk for which the insurers are in no manner responsible.

LÆSÆ majestatis crimen.——High treason.

LAGA.——" Law." Hence we derive the *Saxon lage, Mercen-lage, Dane-lage*, &c.

LAGAN.——Sax. Goods found in the sea.

LAGE-DAY. A law-day.

LAGEMAN.——*Homo habens legem* i. e. *homo legalis :* such as we now call a good man of the jury.

LAHMAN.——A lawyer.

LAHSLIT.——Saxon or Danish. A breaking of the law.

LAICOS privilegio universitatis gaudentes.——"Laymen enjoying the privilege of the university :" matriculated laymen.

LAIEL.——French. Lawful. LAI.——Law.

LAIRWITE—Lecherwite, Legergeldum.——Sax. "*legan,*" i. e. to lie with; and "*wite,*" a fine; "Pœna vel mulcta offendentium in adulterio, et fornicatione." The punishment or fine (inflicted) on those caught in adultery and fornication. *Vide note.*

LA loy de *Mahomet* confonde l'usance avec le pret à interet. L'usure augmente dans les pais *Mahometans* a proportion de la severite de la defence : le pretuer s'indemnise du peril de la contravention.——The law of *Mahomet* confounds usance with the loan at interest. Usury increases in the *Mahometan* countries in proportion to the severity of its prohibition. The lender indemnifies himself against the danger of the risk.

LA mandant qui ne respond point la lettre per la quil seo commissionaries luy expliquent qu'ils on fait, est censi approver leur conducte quoiqu'ils agents excédé le mandat, cette reception de la lettre, non contradite, est, parmi les negocians un acte positif d'approbation.——The consignor who returns no answer to a letter from his consignees, explaining the transaction, is held to have approved their conduct, although they may have exceeded their commission (or instructions): the receipt of such a letter, not being denied, is considered among merchants as a conclusive act of approval.

LANCETA.——A kind of farming tenant. (Old English Law.)

LANDBOC.——A Saxon deed for land or house.

LANDEA.——A trench for draining lands.

LANDEGANDMAN.——An inferior tenant.

LANDGABLE.——Land rent.

LANDIMER.——Land boundary.

LANDSLAGH.——A Swedish compilation of *common* law.

LANGEMANNI.——Lords of estates.

LANGUEBAT usque ad decimum nonum diem mensis Decembris anno 1628, quo quidem decimo nono die, &c., obiit, &c.——He languished until the nineteenth day of the month of December in the year 1628, on whic hnineteenth day of, &c., he died, &c.

LANGUIDUS in prisona.——He is sick in prison: an ancient return to a writ.

LANGUIDUS vel mortuus est.——He is sick or dead.

LANO NIGER.——An inferior coin.

LA propriete des choses mobliares est acquisi â l'enemi, moment qu'elles sont en puissance: et si il leo vend chez nation neutres, le premisre proprietater n'est point endroit de les re eprendre.——Property in things personal is acquired by the enemy at the moment they are in his power; and if he sell them among neutrals, then the first proprietor has no right to retake them.

LARON.——A thief.

LAS partidas.——A code of Spanish laws.

LASIER.——To leave out.

LATA culpa dolo æquiparatur.——A concealed fault is equal to a deceit.

LATHE.——A division of a county, including sometimes two or three *hundreds* or more.

LATHEREVE.——He who exercised authority over a *lathe*.

LATITAT.——"He lies hid." The name of a writ.

LATITAT et discurrit.——He lurks, and runs about.

LATROCINIUM.——Larceny. *Vide note.*

LATRONI cum similem habuit, qui furtum celare vellet, et occulte sine judice compositionem ejus admittere.—— (The law) accounted that person as bad as the thief, who endeavored to conceal the larceny, and privately to receive a composition, without bringing the offender to justice.

LAUGHLESMAN. ——Sax. An outlaw.

LE defaut de transcriptionem ne pourraê etre suppléé ni regardé, comme convert par lar connaissance que les creanciers ou les tiers aquereurs pourraient avoir eue de la disposition par d' autres voies que celle de la transcription. ——A fault in the translation cannot be supplied, nor even regarded as truth, by the belief or testimony of those concerned (in the disposition); it must be decided by the other words of the translation.

LE defendant malitiose dit, que ceo fuit false affidavit; et que 40 voilent jure al contrarie.——The defendant maliciously says, that it is a false affidavit; and that he can produce forty witnesses who will swear to the contrary.

LEDO—Ledona.——The rising water, or increase of the sea.

LE don fuit bon et leal.——The present was good and lawful.

LE droit ecrit.——Statute right.

LEGABILIS.——Signifies what is not entailed, as hereditary; but may be bequeathed by a will or testament.

LEGATUM.——A legacy: bequest, or˙ gift of goods or money, by will.

LEGATUS.——A legate. *Vide note.*

LEGEM facere.——To make law.

LEGEM promulgare.——To publish the law.

LEGES autem *Anglicanas,* licet non scriptas leges appellari non est absurdum, cum hoc ipsum lex sit, quod principi placet, et legis habet vigorem, eas scilicet, quas super dubiis in consilio, diffindendis, procerum quidem consilio, et principis auctoritate accordante vel antecedente constat esse promulgatas, si enim ob solum scripturæ defectum leges minime conferenter, majoris proculdubio auctoritatis robur ipsis legibus videretur accommodare scripturâ, quam judices æquitate, aut ratione statuentis.——It is not, however, improper to bestow the name of *laws* upon the *English* laws, though they may not be written, inasmuch as that very thing may be *law,* which pleaseth the king, and hath the force of law; that is to say, those (laws) which are known to have been promulgated for the resolving of difficult questions, by the advice of the great men of the kingdom, upon the previous motion, or with the subsequent assent of the king; for if they were not to be holden for laws, by reason of their not being reduced into writing, it would seem that the law derived its weight and authority rather from the (bare) writing, than from the discretion of the judge, or the reasons which moved the lawgiver (for its enactment).

LEGES et constitutiones futuris certum est dare formam negotiis, non ad facta præterita revocari, nisi nominatim, et de præterito tempore, adhuc pendentibus negotiis cautum est.——It is certain that the laws and constitutions are to prescribe a form to future transactions, and not to be referred to matters already finished, unless specially named, and (as) of a preceding time, as a caution to those which are yet pending.

LEGES figendi et refigendi consuetudo est periculos issima.——The practice of making and re-making the laws is most dangerous.

LEGES non scriptæ.——The unwritten, traditional, or common law.—— *Vide note to* " *Traditione,*" &c.

LEGES posteriores priores contrarias abrogant.——Subsequent laws repeal those before enacted to the contrary.

LEGES quæ retrospiciunt raro, et magna cum cautione sunt adhibendæ; neque enim *Janus* locaretur in legibus. ——Laws which are retrospective are rare, and to be received with great caution, for *Janus* should have no situation among the laws. *Vide note.*

LEGES Quiritium.——The Roman Laws. *Vide note.*

LEGES Salicæ.——The Salic Laws. *Vide note.*

LEGES scriptæ.——The statute, or written law.

LEGES solâ memoriâ et usû retinebant.——" They retained their laws solely by memory and usage." This is what is called the Common law—the " *Leges non scriptæ,*" unwritten laws. Vide *note to Traditione,* &c.

LEGES sub graviori lege.——Laws subordinate to a superior law.

LEGES tabellariæ.——Laws respecting the vote by ballot.

LEGES vigilantibus, non dormientibus subveniunt.—— The laws relieve the vigilant, not those who sleep (over their rights).

LEGIBUS patriæ optime instituti.——Those best instructed in the laws of the country.

LEGIBUS solutus.——Freed from the laws.

LEGIS actiones.——Law suits.

LEGIS constructio non facit injuriam.——The construction of law does no injury.

LEGITIMA mariti et uxoris separatio apud competentem judicem cum causæ cognitione, et sufficiente ejus probatione factæ.——"A lawful separation of husband and wife, by a competent judge, with knowledge of the cause, and sufficient proof of the fact." This was the definition of a divorce by the ancient Canon law.

LEGITIME acquiatus.——Legally discharged or acquitted.

LEGITIMI.——The issue of a lawful marriage. *Vide note.*

LEGITIMO maritagio.——By a lawful marriage.

LEGITIMO matrimonio copulati.——Joined in lawful wedlock.

LEGITIMUM maritagium, et non ratum.——"A lawful marriage, and not confirmed." This applied to marriages formerly solemnized between *Jews*, or others, not professing Christianity.

LEGITIMUM maritagium ratum.——"A lawful, confirmed marriage." This was said of a marriage attended with due canonical solemnization.

LEGIT vel non?——Reads he or not? LEGIT ut clericus.——He reads like a clerk. This was the question and answer where the person on trial claimed the benefit of clergy.

LEGULEIUS quidam cautus et acutus præco actionum, cantor fabularum, auceps syllabarum.——A certain lawyer, wary and keen in declamation, a chatterer of idle stories, a captious (or pettifogging) fellow.

LEGUM Anglicanarum Conditor.——The founder of the *English* laws.

LEGUM Anglicanarum Restitutor.——The restorer of the *English* laws.

LEGUM denique idcirco omnes servi sumus, ut liberi esse possumus.——Wherefore, finally, we are slaves to the laws, that we may become free.

LEIPA.——"A departure from service." "*Si quis a domino suo sine licentia discedat ut "Leipa" emendatur, et redire cognatur.*" If any person leave his master without his consent, he shall be punished for such departure and compelled to return. Vide *Leg. Hen.* 1, c. 43. *Blount.*

19

LE loix extrems dans le bien font moitifs le mal extremes. ——Rigid laws, although made from good motives, produce bad effects.

LE reason est, quia le keeping del cheval est un charge, quia il mange; mes le keeping del apparel n'est aucun charge. The reason is, because the keeping a horse is an expense, because he eats; but there is no expense in keeping of clothes.

LE Roy le veut.——The king wills it.

LE Roy remercie ses loyal sujets, accepte leur benevolence, et aussi le veut.——The King thanks his loyal subjects, accepts their benevolence, and wills it to be so.

LE Roy s'avisera.——The king will consider. *Vide note.*

LES assureurs, qui se sont renders garans de la barraterie du patron (ils) sont responsable de la perte de la pacotille assureé, si cette perte arrivè par la faute du capitaine, charge de la commission.——The insurers, who have insured against the barratry of the commander, are responsible for the loss of the vessel insured, if this loss be occasioned by the fault of the captain charged with the care of it.

LESCHEIVES.——Trees fallen by chance.

LES juges sont sages personnes et autentiques si comme les archevesques, evesques, les chanoines des eglises cathedraulx et les autres personnes qui ont dignitez in saincte eglise; les abbes, les prieurs conventraulx, et les Gouverneurs des eglises, &c.——The Judges are wise persons, and of high authority, such as the Archbishops, Bishops, the Monks of the Cathedral Churches, and the other persons who hold dignities in the Holy Church; the Abbots, Priors of Convents, and the Governors of Churches, &c. *Vide note.*

LES loix extremes dans le bien font naitre le mal extreme; il falut payer pour la pret de l'argent et pour le danger despeines de la loi.——Laws extremely good produce the greatest evil. We must pay for the loan of money, and for the danger of the penalties of the law.

LESPEGEND.——Sax. An inferior thane.

LES prelats seigneurs, et commons en ce present parliament assembleés au nom de touts vous autres sujets, re-
mercient tres humblement votre Majeste, et prient à Dieu
vous donner en santé bonne vie et longue.——"The Prelates, Lords, and Commons, in this present parliament assembled, in the name of all your other subjects, most
humbly thank your Majesty, and pray to God to grant you
good health and a long life."

[This was an ancient address of the *British* Parliament
to the King.]

LESQUE l'changer a chez novo luis de la declaration du
guerre subsistent ou leur entir. S'il est forcè de si retirer,
il lui est eviseable de laisser sa procuration a un ami pour
exiger ce qui lui est du, et pour actioner ceo debitinero en
justice.——Those who, on a declaration of war, are obliged
to change their place of residence, must dwell in the latter
entirely; and if a person be compelled to retire, it is proper that he should authorize a friend to receive what is due
to him, and to prosecute those who are justly indebted.

LE subpœna ne serroit cy souventement usé come il est
ore, si nous attendemus tiels actions sur les cases, et main-
tenans le jurisdiction de ces court, et d'autre courts.——
The subpœna would not be so often used as it is, if we
bring such actions upon the case and maintain the jurisdiction of this and of the other courts.

LES usages et coutumes de la mer.——Marine usages and
customs.

LESWES.——Pasture lands.

LE tien et le mein.——Of thine and mine.

LETTEREURE.——Learning.

LEUCA, LEUGA.——A league.

LEUDIS.——A feudal tenant.

LEVANDÆ navis causa.——In order to lighten the
vessel.

LEVANT et couchant.——Lying down and resting.

LEVANTES et cubantes.——Easing themselves; rising up and lying down.

LEVARI facias.——That you cause to be levied.

LEVARI facias de bonis.——That you cause to be levied of the goods.

LEVARI facias de bonis ecclesiasticis.——That you cause to be levied of the church goods.

LEVIS culpa.——Slight fault.

LEX.——"The Law." This word, among the ancient *Romans*, was often taken in the same general sense as *Jus* (Right). When we find *Lex* put *absolutely*, the law of the Twelve Tables is meant. Vide *Cic. Verr.* i. 45.

LEX agraria.——The Agrarian law for distributing lands. *Vide note.*

LEX amissa: or *legem amittere.*——One who is an infamous, perjured, or outlawed person. *Bract.*

LEX angliæ nunquam sine parliamento mutari potest.——The law of England can never be changed without parliament.

LEX apparens.——A term applied in English and Norman law to the trial by duel and the trial by ordeal.

LEX apostata: or *legem apostare.*——To do anything contrary to the law.

LEX aquilia.——The Roman law concerning the compensation to be paid for injuring or killing another's slave or beast.

LEX atilia.——A law concerning guardianships.

LEX atinia.——A law respecting things stolen.

LEX Bainvariorum.——The law of the Bavarians.

LEX Barbara.——A term given by the Romans to the law of those nations not subject to their empire.

LEX Brehona.——The early law of Ireland before its conquest by Henry II.

LEX Burgundionum.——The Burgundian law.

LEX canonica.——The Canon law. *Vide note.*

LEX comitatus.——The county law.

LEX communis.——The common law, as opposed to statute law. *Vide note.*

LEX citius tolerare vult privatum damnum quam publicum malum.——The law will rather permit a private loss (or damage) than a public evil.

LEX Cornelia de sicariis.——The Cornelian law concerning assassins.

LEX Danorum.——The law of Denmark.

LEX deficere non debet in justitia exhibenda.——The law ought not to fail in showing justice.

LEX deraisina.——An ancient Norman law, by which the party sued denies that he committed the act with which he is charged.

LEX de maritandis ordinibus.——The law of marriage rites. *Vide note.*

LEX domicilii.——The law of domicile.

LEX est ab æterno.——Law is from everlasting.

LEX est sanctio sancta, jubens honestu et prohibens contraria.——Law is a sacred sanction commanding the right, and forbidding the wrong action.

LEX et consuetudo parliamenti ab omnibus quærenda; a multis ignota; a paucis cognita.——The law and custom of parliament, sought after by all, unknown by many, and understood by few.

LEX fori.——The law of the court.

LEX Falcidia.——A Roman law respecting a testator's disposal of his property.

LEX Francorum.——The law of the Franks.

LEX Frisionum.——The law of the Frisians.

LEX Fusia Canina.——Roman law respecting the manumission of slaves.

LEX Hostilia de furtis.——The *Hostilian* law concerning thefts.

LEX judicat de rebus necessario faciendis, quasi re ipsa factis.——The law judges of things that must of necessity be done, as if they were actually done.

Lex Julia magistratis.——The *Julian* law as to treason.

Lex loci contracti.——The law of the place where the agreement was made.

Lex Longobardorum.——The law of the Lombards; they were of Saxon origin, so that their laws are analogous to the English.

Lex mercatoria.——The law merchant; mercantile law.

Lex mercatoria est lex terræ.——The mercantile law is the law of the land.

Lex necessitatis est lex temporis.——The law of necessity is the law of the time or present moment.

Lex neminem cogit ad vana seu impossibilia.——The law compels no one to (perform things) vain or impossible.

Lex nemini facit injuriam.——The law does no injury

Lex nil frusta facit.——The law does nothing in vain.

Lex non cogit ad impossibilia.——The law does not oblige (a person) to do impossibilities.

Lex non curat de minimis.——The law does not regard trifles.

Lex non exacte definit, sed arbitrio boni viri permittit. ——The law does not exactly define (this), but leaves it to the judgment of an honest man.

Lex non requirit verificari quod apparet curiæ.——The law does not require to be proved what is apparent to the court.

Lex non scripta.——The unwritten, or common law: that which has been received from time immemorial by tradition. *Vide note to "Traditiones,"* &c.

Lex plus laudatur, quando ratione probatur.——Law is most commendable when approved by reason.

Lex Prætoria.——The Prætorian law.

Lex pure pœnalis, obligat tantum ad pœnam, non item ad culpam; lex pœnalis mixta, et ad culpam obligat, et ad pœnam.——The law, merely penal, binds only as to penalty, not as to fault; the mixed penal law binds both to fault and penalty.

Lex Salica.——" The *Salique* Law." A law by which males only are allowed to inherit. It was an ancient law made by *Pharamond*, King of the *Franks*. It is somewhat singular that a nation like the French, which prides itself on its gallantry, should be almost the only one to exclude females from the throne.

Lex scripta.——The written or statute law.

Lex talionis.——The law of requital in kind : "An eye for an eye," &c., as in the Mosaic law. *Vide note.*

Lex terræ.——The law of the land : generally taken in contradistinction to the civil law, or code of *Justinian.*

Lex Wallensica.——The law of Wales.

Lex Wisigothorum.——The law of the Western Goths who settled in Spain.

Lez.——Lands.

Libelli famosi.——Libels : infamous writings.

Libellus sine scriptis.——A unwritten libel.

Libera a prisona.——Discharge out of prison.

Libera batella.——A free boat.

Libera eleemosyna.——Free alms : charity.

Libera et pura donatio.——A free and pure gift (not clogged with conditions).

Libera lex.——Frank or free law.

Libera piscaria.——A free fishery.

Liber Assisarum.——The Book of Assizes.

Liber et legalis homo.——A free and lawful man.

Liber homo.——A free man. *Vide note.*

Liber homo non amercietur pro parvo delicto, nisi secundum modum ipsius delicti ; et pro magno delicto, secundum magnitudinem delicti, salvo contenemento suo ; mercator eodem modo, salva merchandiza sua ; et villanus eodem modo amercietur, salvo wainageo suo.——" That a free man be not fined for a trifling offence, but according to the extent of his crime ; and for a great offence according to the magnitude thereof, saving his freehold ; and the merchant, in the same manner, his merchandise being preserved; and the farmer in like manner, his wainage also being preserved." [Part of "*Magna Charta.*"]

LIBERI et legales homines de viceneto.——Free and lawful men (freeholders) of the vicinage, or neighborhood. Vide note to "*Non Numero,*" &c.

LIBERI sokemanni.——Tenants in free soccage.

LIBER judicalis.——The "*Dom-bec,*" or "*Dome-book,*" compiled soon after conquest of *England* by the *Normans.* *Vide Dom-bec and note.*

LIBER nigir scaccarii.——Black Book of the Exchequer.

LIBER ruber scaccarii.——Red Book of the Exchequer.

LIBEROS et legales homines juratos.——Free and lawful men sworn.

LIBERTAS est potestas faciendi id quod jure liceat.—— Liberty is the power of doing what is sanctioned by law.

LIBERTAS loquendi.——The liberty or freedom of speech. *Vide note.*

LIBERUM animum testandi.——A free (or uncontrolled) intention of bequeathing.

LIBERUM corpus æstimationem non recipit.——The life of a freeman is above all computation.

LIBERUM est cuique apud se explorare; aut expediat sibi consilium.——It is free for every one to weigh the matter in his own mind; or to have resort to counsel.

LIBERUM et commune soccagium.——Free and common soccage.

LIBERUM maritagium.——A free marriage. *Vide note.*

LIBERUM soccagium.——Free soccage.

LIBERUM tenementum.——"Frank tenure or freehold." Anciently an estate held by a freeman, independently of the mere will and caprice of the feudal lord.

LIBRÆ arsæ, et pensatæ, et ad numerum.——Money burnt and weighed, and counted. *Vide note.*

LIBRIPENS.——In Roman Law, the person who weighed or held the balances.

LICEAT eos exhæredare quos occidere licebat.——It may be lawful to disinherit those whom it is lawful to deprive of life.

LICEBAT palam excipere, et semper ex probabili causa tres repudiari; etiam plures ex causa pregnanti et manifesta.——It was lawful openly to except, and three for a probable cause were always rejected; and even more for a cause which was important and clear.

LICENTIA concordandi.——Leave to settle (a suit).

LICENTIA loquendi.——Liberty of speech.

LICENTIA surgendi.——Leave to arise.

LICET apud consilium accusare; quoque et discrimen capitis intendere.——It is likewise lawful to impeach at the (general) council; and to try capital offences.

LICET in ambiguis capere consilium.——He has liberty to have counsel in doubtful cases.

· LICET meretrix fuerit antea, certe tunc temporis non fuit, cum reclamando nequitiæ ejus consentire noluit.——Although she were a harlot before, she certainly was not so at that time, when, crying aloud, she would not consent to his lust.

LICET sæpe requisitus.——Although often requested.

LICITARE.——To bid at a sale.

LIEGE.——In feudal law, to bind; the subject thus bound in fealty to his lord was called *liege-man*, and the superior, *liege-lord*. It also signifies full; perfect; pure.

LIEGE-POUSTIE.——Scotch law. Lawful power.

LIEU eonus.——Known place.

LIGAN, or Lagan.——Goods sunk under water, fastened to a buoy, to prevent their being lost.

LIGEANCE—Ligiantia.——Old Norman, English and Scotch law. Allegiance.

LIGNAGIUM.——"The right of cutting fuel in woods." Sometimes it is taken for a tribute or payment due for the same.

LIGULA.——Old Eng. law. A copy or transcript of a deed or court paper.

LI. LO.——Abbreviated from licentia loquendi.

LINARIUM.——Where flax is grown.

LINEA collectio personarum ab eodem stipite descendentium.——The collected line of persons descending from the same stock.

LINGUA peregrina.——A foreign language. *Vide note.*

LIQUET.——It appears.

LIS mota.——A suit moved in court.

LIS pendens.——A suit depending.

LITE dijudicata.——A term used by the *Roman* lawyers when a law suit was determined. *Vide note.*

LITEM lite resolvere.——To remove one difficulty by introducing another.

LITEM suam facere.——To favor one of the contending parties. *Vide note.*

LITERA.——Litter: Straw. *Vide note.*

LITERÆ.——Letters. Writings. *Vide note.*

LITERA cambii.——A letter of Exchange.

LITERÆ absolutoriæ.——"Letters of absolution." Letters of absolution were given in former times, when an *Abbot* released any of his brethren "*ab omni subjectione, et obedientia*" (from all subjection and obedience), and this made them capable of entering into some other order of religion.

LITERÆ clausæ.——"Writs close." Those which are recorded in the *close* rolls.

LITERÆ patentes.——Letters patent, so called because they are not sealed up, but exposed to open view, with the Great Seal thereto pendant.

LITERÆ procuratoriæ.——A letter of attorney.

LITERÆ recognitionis.——A bill of lading.

LITERA scripta manet.——"The writing endures." This is often quoted in opposition to verbal slander. One endures perhaps for years or ages; the other is evanescent.

LITIS contestatio.——The trial of the cause.

LITTUS maris.——The sea shore.

LIVERER.——To deliver.

LIVORARE.——To beat.

LOBIUM.——A parlor.

LOCARIUM.——The price paid for the hire of a thing.

LOCATIO operis.——The hire to do the work.

LOCATIO operis faciendi.——The hire of performing the work.

LOCATIO operis mercium vehendarum.——A bargain for the transportation of merchandise.

LOCATIO rei.——The hire of the thing.

LOCO hæredis.——In place of the heir.

LOCO parentis.——In the place of the parent.

LOCUM tenens.——A Lieutenant Governor, or Deputy.

LOCUM tenens vicecomitis.——A Deputy Sheriff.

LOCUS delicti.——The place where the offence was committed.

LOCUS in quo.——The place in which.

LOCUS partitus.——A division made between two towns, or counties, to make trial where the land or place in question lies. *Fleta, lib.* 4.

LOCUS pœnitentiæ.——The place (or opportunity) for repentance (or of retracting).

LOCUS rei sitæ.——The place where a thing is situated.

LOCUS sigilli.——The place of the seal.

LOCUS vastatus.——The place laid waste.

LODEMANAGE.——A pilot's wages for guiding a vessel from one place to another.

LOIAL.——Lawful.

LOIER.——Fee; recompense.

LONGTEYNE.——Distant.

LOQUENDUM ut vulgus, sentiendum ut docti.——Speak as the common people, think as the learned.

LOWER.——Reward: a bribe.

LUAT in corpore si non habet in loculo.——If he has no cash in his purse, he must suffer in his person.

LUCRI causa.——For the sake of profit or gain.

LUCTUOSA hæreditas, vel tristis successio.——A mournful inheritance, or sad succession.

LUITUR homicidium certo armentorum ac pecorum numero, recipitque satisfactionem universa domus.—— Homicide is atoned for by a certain number of herds and flocks, and the whole family accept such satisfaction. Vide note to " *Capitis æstimatio.*"

LUNDRESS.——An ancient London silver penny.

LUPULICETUM.——Old English law. A hop-yard.

LUPUM caput gerere.——"To bear a *wolf's head.*" It signifies to be outlawed; and have one's head exposed like a *wolf's,* with a reward to him who should bring it in. *Plac. Cor.* 4, *Johan. Rot.* 2.

LUSHBOROW.——Inferior foreign coin; an imitation of the English.

LUXURIA.——Luxury: voluptuousness. *Vide note.*

LYEF-YELD.——Leave-money.

NOTES TO L.

LAIRWITE, &c.—This was the term for the punishment and fine of offenders committing adultery and fornication. The privilege of punishing these offences, anciently, belonged to the lords of manors in respect to their own tenants. Vide *Fleta, lib.* 1, c. 47.

LATROCINIUM.—A theft, or robbery of another's goods in his absence. It is divided into *Grand* Larceny and *Petit* Larceny. The ancient *Saxon* laws punished theft with death, if above the value of *twelve* pence; but the criminal was permitted to redeem his life by a pecuniary ransom.

LEGATUS.—A Legate. An ambassador, or *Pope's nuncio.* There are two sorts of Legates;—a Legate, *a latere,* and *Legatus natus*—the difference between which is this; *Legatus a latere* was usually one of the Pope's family, vested with the greatest authority, in all ecclesiastical affairs, over the whole family where he was sent; and, during the time of his legislation, he might determine even those appeals which had been moved from thence to Rome. *Legatus natus* had a more limited jurisdiction, but was exempted from the authority of the *Legate a latere;* and he could exercise his jurisdiction in his own province. The popes of *Rome* had formerly in *England* the Archbishop of *Canterbury* their "*Legatus natus;*" and upon extraordinary occasions they sent over a "*Legatus a latere.*"

LEGES QUÆ, &c.—The temple of Janus was built by *Numa (index belli et pacis*), with two brazen gates, one on each side, to be open in war, and shut in time of peace. Vide *Liv.* i. 19. *Vel.* ii. 38. It was shut only once during the Republic, at the end of the first Punic war, A. U. 529; thrice by *Augustus;* first, after the battle of *Actium,* and the death of *Antony* and *Cleopatra,* A. U. 725. *Dio.* li. 20: a second time after the *Cantabrian* war, A. U. 729. *Dio.* liii. 26: about the third time, authors are not agreed. Some suppose this temple to have been built by *Romulus,* and only enlarged by *Numa;* hence they take *Janus Quirini* for the temple of Janus, built by *Romulus.* Vide *Macrob. Sat.* i. 9.

LEGES QUIRITIUM.—The great foundation of *Roman* law or jurisprudence (*Romani juris*) was that collection of laws called the Law, (LIV. xxxiv. 6,) or Laws of the Twelve Tables, compiled by the *Decemviri,* and ratified by the people: a work, in the opinion of *Cicero,* superior to all the libraries of philosophers, "*omnibus omnium philosophorum bibliothecis anteponendum,*" "a work to be valued more than all the books of every philosopher." Vide *Cic. de Orat.* 1, 44. Nothing now remains of these laws but scattered fragments.

The unsettled state of the *Roman* government; the extension of the empire; the increase of riches and luxury, and, consequently, of the number of crimes, with various other circumstances, gave occasion to many new laws (*corruptissimâ republica, plurimæ leges*), i. e. "the more corrupt the republic, the more the laws." *Tacit Annal.* iii. 27.

At first, those ordinances only obtained the name of laws which were made by the *Comitia Centuriata* (*Populiscita*), (i. e. made where the people were summoned to enact them.) *Tacit Annal.* iii. 58; but afterwards, those also which were made by the *Comitia Tributa* (*Plebiscita*), when they were made binding on the whole *Roman* people; first, by the Horatian law (*ut quod tributim plebes jussisset, populum teneret*). *Liv.* iii. 55, i. e. "that which they voted by tribes should bind the people;" and afterwards more precisely by the *Publilian* and *Hortensian* laws (*ut plebiscita omnes Quirites tenerent*), i. e. "the Plebeian laws should bind all the Romans." Vide *Liv.* viii. 12. *Epit.* xi. *Plin.* xvi. 10, *s.* 15.

Any order of the people was called "Lex," whether it respected the public (*jus publicum* vel *sacrum*), the right of private persons (*jus privatum* vel *civile*), or the particular interest of an individual. But this last was properly called "PRIVILEGIUM." Vide *Gell.* x. 20.

The laws proposed by a Consul were called "*Consulares.*" Cic. Sext. 64. By a Tribune, *Tribunitiæ,* Cic. in Rull. ii. 8. By the "Decemviri," *Decemvirales.* Liv. iii. 55, 56, 57.

LEGES SALICÆ.—The *Leges Burgundiorum,* i. e. "The Laws of Burgundy," and other codes, published by the several tribes which settled in *Gaul,* were *general* laws extending to every person, province and district, where the authority of those tribes was acknowledged. But they seem to have become obsolete; and the reason of their falling into disuse is very obvious. Almost the whole property of the nation was *allodial* when those laws were framed. But when the *feudal* institutions became general, and gave rise to an infinite variety of questions, peculiar to that species of tenure, the ancient codes were of no use in deciding with regard to them, because they could not contain regulations applicable to cases which did not exist at the time they were compiled.

LEGITIMI.—The children of a lawful marriage were called by the Romans "*Legitimi;*" all others "*Illegitimi;*" of the latter there were four kinds: *Naturales, ex concubina; Spurii, ex meretrice,* vel *scorto, et incerto patre;* (*Plutarch Q. Rome,* 101.) *Adulterini* et *incestuosi*—i. e. "natural born from concubinage; basely born from a harlot, or a lewd woman, by an unknown father; adulterous and incestuous." There were certain degrees of consanguinity within which marriages were prohibited, as between a brother and sister, an uncle and niece, &c. Such connection was called "*Incestus.*" (Suet. Ct. 26;) or with a vestal virgin. Vide *Suet. Domit.* 8. These degrees were more or less extended or contracted at different times. *Plut. Quœst. Rom.* 6. *Tacit. Ann.* xii. 6, 7, &c.

LE ROY S'AVISERA.—This is a phrase, derived from the ancient *Normans,* by which the Kings of *England* were accustomed to dissent to bills which had passed the Legislature. By this mode of expression, the indelicacy of a *positive* refusal to give assent was avoided.

LES JUGES.—When the *English* laws were first dispensed according to the present mode of practice in the higher courts, the Judges in the Courts of Law and Equity were generally (or, perhaps, altogether) selected from the order of clergy mentioned in the text—they engrossed the greatest part of the learning of those days; and were considered the most proper persons for the offices of Judges and Chancellors. They, by degrees, softened the rigor of the Feudal and Common law, by introducing great part of the milder jurisprudence of the *Roman* code.

LEX AGRARIA.—The *Agrarian* law (among the *Romans*) for distributing the lands of *Campania* and *Stella* to twenty thousand poor citizens who had each three or more children. Vide *Cic. pro Planc.* 5, *Att.* ii. 16, &c. When *Bibulus,* Cœsar's colleague, gave his negative to this law, he was driven from the *Forum* by force. And next day, having complained in the Senate, but not being supported, he was so discouraged, that, during his continuance in office for eight months, he shut himself up at home, without doing anything but interposing by his edicts, vide *Suet. Jul.* 20; by which means, while he wished to injure his colleague, he increased his power.

LEX CANONICA.—The forms and maxims of the *Canon Law* had become respectable from their authority, and contributed not a little towards the improvement of jurisprudence. If the Canon Law be considered *politically,* and viewed either as a system to assist the clergy in usurping power and jurisdiction, no less repugnant to the nature of their function than inconsistent with the order of government; or as a chief instrument in establishing the dominion of the Popes, which shook the thrones and endangered the liberties of every kingdom of *Europe,* we must pronounce it one of the *most formidable* engines ever used against the happiness of civil society. But, if we contemplate it *merely* as a code of laws, touching the rights and properties of *individuals,* and attend only to the *civil* effect of its decisions concerning them, it will appear in a different and more favorable light. The code of the *Canon* law began to be completed early in the *ninth* century. It was more than two centuries after that before any collection was made of those customs which were the rule of judgments in the Courts of the Barons. Spiritual judges decided, of course, according to written and known laws. Lay judges, left without any *fixed* guide, were directed by loose traditionary customs. But besides this general advantage of the Canon law, its forms and principles were more consonant to reason, and more favorable to the equitable decision of every point in controversy, than those which prevailed in the Lay Courts. The whole spirit of ecclesiastical jurisprudence was adverse to those sanguinary customs which were destructive of justice; and the whole force of ecclesiastical authority was exerted to abolish them, and to substitute trials by law and evidence in their stead. Almost all the forms in Lay Courts, which contribute to establish, and continue to preserve *order* in judicial proceedings, are borrowed from the Canon Law. Vide *Fleury's Instit. de droit Canon, part* iii. c. 6, p. 52.

St. *Louis* confirmed many of his new regulations respecting property, and the administration of justice, by the authority of the Canon Law, from which he borrowed them. Thus, for instance, the first hint for attaching movables for the recovery of a debt was taken from the Canon Law. Vide *Estab. liv.* ii. c. 21 and 40. And likewise the *Cessio bonorum*, by a person who was insolvent. *Ibid.* In like manner he established new regulations with respect to persons dying intestate. *Liv.* i. *c.* 89. These, and many other salutary regulations, the Canonists had borrowed from the *Roman* Law. Many other examples might be produced of more perfect jurisprudence in the Canon Law than were known in Lay Courts. For that reason, it was deemed a high privilege to be subject to ecclesiastical jurisdiction. Among the many immunities by which men were allured to engage in the dangerous expedition for the recovery of the Holy Land, one of the most considerable was the declaring such as took the *Cross* to be subject only to the *spiritual* courts, and to the rules of decision observed in them.

LEX COMMUNIS.—The COMMON LAW. The law which is used by general consent, and has been so from time immemorial—*that* which we enjoy as "*Heir-looms*," and which *is* the law before any act of Parliament alters the same. This is the law almost in every constitution, grounded on long immemorial custom, reason, and general usage; and includes in it the LAW OF NATURE, the LAW OF GOD, and the PRINCIPLES and AXIOMS OF SOUND RATIOCINATION. It is founded upon reason, and said to be the PERFECTION of reason, acquired by long study, observation and experience; and refined by wise and learned men in all ages. And it is also the COMMON BIRTH-RIGHT that every person hath for the safeguard and defence, not only of his lands and goods, but of his wife and children, body, fame and life. Vide *Co. Litt.* 97, 142. As to the rise of the *Common Law*, this account is given by some ancient writers. After the decay of the *Roman* Empire, three sorts of the *German* people invaded the *Britons;* and having had *different* customs, they inclined to the *different* laws by which their respective ancestors were governed; but the customs of the *West Saxons*, and *Mercians*, who dwelt on the midland counties, being preferred before the rest, were, for that reason, called "*Jus Anglorum*," and, by these laws, those people were governed for many ages; but the *East Saxons*, having afterwards been subdued by the *Danes*, their customs were introduced, and other laws were substituted, called "*Dane-Lage*," as the other was then styled "*West Saxon-Lage.*" At length the *Danes* being overcome by the *Normans*, William the Conqueror, upon a consideration of all those laws and customs, abrogated some, and established others, to which he added some of his own country laws, which he considered most conducive to the preservation of the peace, and this is what is generally called "THE COMMON LAW."

But, though we usually date our *Common Law* from hence, this was not its *origin;* for it is said that *Ethelbert*, the first Christian King of *England*, made the first *Saxon* laws, which were published by the advice of some wise men of his council. And King *Alfred*, who lived three hundred years afterwards, collected all the old *Saxon* laws into one book; and commanded them to be observed throughout the *whole of England;* which before only affected certain parts thereof; and it was, therefore, properly called the *Common Law;* because it was *common* to the *whole* nation; and soon after it was called in *Saxon* "THE FOLC RIGHT," i. e. the people's right. *Alfred* was styled "*Anglicarum legum conditor*," (the founder of the English laws;) and when the *Danes*, on the conquest of the kingdom, had introduced their laws, they were afterwards destroyed; and *Edward* the Confessor, out of the former laws, composed a body of the *Common Law;* wherefore he is called by historians "*Anglicarum legum restitutor*," (the restorer of the English laws.) Vide *Blount.*

In the reign of *Edward* the First, *Britton* wrote his learned book of the

Common Law of *England*, which was done by the King's command, and runs in his name, answerable to the Institutions of the *Civil Law*, which *Justinian* assumed to himself, though made by others. Vide *Staundf. Prerog.* 6, 21. But *Justinian*, perhaps, ought to be entitled to the honor, as the Institutes were compiled by his direction. This *Britton* is mentioned by *Gwyn* to have been Bishop of *Hereford.* In those days ecclesiastical persons were the most learned, and had the highest offices in the law.

Bracton was a great lawyer in the time of *Henry* the Third; and wrote a learned treatise on the Common Law of *England*, held in high and deserved estimation; he is said to have been Lord Chief Justice of the Kingdom.

Also the famous and learned *Glanville*, Lord Chief Justice, in the reign of *Henry* the Second, wrote a book of the Common Law, which is said to be the most ancient composition on that subject extant. Besides those, in the reign of *Edward* the Fourth, the renowned lawyer, *Littleton*, wrote his excellent book of *English* tenures.

In the reign of King *James* the First, that great oracle of the Law, Sir *Edward Coke*, published his learned and laborious Institute of the *English* laws and Commentary on *Littleton*. About the same time, likewise, Doctor *Cowel*, a Civilian, wrote a short Institute on the *English* laws. In the reign of *George* the First, Doctor *Thomas Wood*, a Civilian, and common Lawyer, and at last a Divine, wrote an Institute of the Laws of *England*, which is something after the manner of the Institutes of the Civil Law.

To conclude the whole on this head, the learned and systematic *Blackstone*, published his well-known Commentaries on the laws of *England*, probably the best analectic and methodic system of the *English* Laws which ever was published; his work abounds with numerous maxims, quotations and sentences, chiefly extracted from the dead languages; all of which, or nearly so, are translated in this Glossary. The Commentaries of *Blackstone* are equally adapted for the use of the Student, and for those Gentlemen who wish to acquire that *general* knowledge of the Laws, which it is almost essentially necessary every person should be acquainted with. There is scarcely a doubt but that these Commentaries have been of more utility than any other law book ever published. The excellent Commentaries of Chancellor *Kent* have obtained high estimation

LEX DE MARITANDIS ORDINIBUS.—This was a *Roman* law, proposed by the Consuls, *Pappius* and *Popæus*, at the desire of *Augustus*, A. U. 762, enforcing and enlarging the *Julian* Law. *Tacit. Ann.* iii. 25, 28. The intent of it was to promote population, and repair the desolation occasioned by the civil wars. It met with great opposition from the nobility; and consisted of several distinct particulars, (*Lex satura.*) It proposed certain rewards to marriage; and penalties against celibacy, which had been always (and justly so) much discouraged in the *Roman* state, vid. *Val. Max.* ii. 9. *Liv.* xiv. 15, and, strange to say, still it greatly prevailed, for reasons enumerated. Vide *Plaut. Mil.* iii. 185, 111, &c. Whoever in the *city* had *three* children, in the other parts of *Italy*, *four*, and in the provinces *five*, became entitled to certain immunities. Hence the famous "JUS TRIUM LIBERORUM," so often mentioned by *Plin. Mart. &c.* Vide *note to* "*Jus trium liberorum.*"

LEX TALIONIS.—In the laws of King *Ethelbert*, we find the following laws. "*Gif on Earl's tune man mannan of sleath* xii. *scill. gebete,*" i. e. If one man slay another in an Earl's town, let him pay 12s. as a compensation. "*Gif in Cyninges tune man manna of sleagh L. scill. gebete,*" i. e. If one man slay another in the King's town, let him pay 50s. as a compensation. "*Gif man thone man of slœth* xx. *scill. gebete,*" i. e. If any man slay another let him compensate with twenty shillings. If the thumb should be cut off twenty shillings was to be paid. If the thumb nail should be cut off three shillings should be paid as a compensation. If any one cut off another's fore finger, he was to pay eight shillings: for the middle finger four shillings: for the gold finger (where the ring was worn) six shillings: for the little finger eleven shillings. There appears to have been considerable caprice in the apportionment of these penalties; and every murder appears to have been commutable for money in the time of our Saxon ancestors ! !

LIBER HOMO.—These words are commonly opposed to "VASSUS," or "VASSALUS." *Liber homo* generally denotes an ALLODIAL proprietor. *Vassus* one who holds of a *superior.* The words "*Liber Homo,*" in process of time, it is believed, meant those who were under no vassalage, servitude or bondage, although they might *not* own allodial lands. These freemen were bound to serve the state; and this duty was considered as so sacred, that freemen were prevented from entering into Holy Orders, unless they had obtained the consent of the sovereign. The reason given for this in the statute, or ordinance, is remarkable, viz.: "For we are informed that some do so, not so much out of devotion, as in order to avoid that military service they are bound to perform." Vide *Capitul. lib.* 1, § 114. If, upon being summoned into the field, any person refused to obey, a full "*Herebannum,*" i. e. a fine of sixty crowns, was to be exacted from him according to the law of the *Franks.* This expression, agreeably to the law, seems to imply that both the *obligation* to serve, and the *penalty* on those who disregarded it, were coëval with the laws made by the *Franks,* at their first settlement in *Gaul.* This fine was levied with such rigor, "that if any person convicted of this crime was insolvent, he was reduced to servitude, and continued in that state, until such time as his labor should amount to the value of the Herebannum." Vide *Capit. Car. Magn. ap. Leg. Longob. lib.* 1. The Emperor, *Lotharius,* rendered the penalty still more severe; and if any person, possessing such an extent of property, as made it incumbent on him to take the field in person, refused to obey the summons, all his goods were declared to be forfeited, and he, himself, might be punished with banishment. Vide *Murat. Script. Ital. vol.* 1, *pars* 2, *p.* 153.

LIBERTAS LOQUENDI.—Among the *Romans,* the speeches of the senators were sometimes received with shouts of applause; thus "*Consurgenti ad censendum acclamatum est, quod solet residentibus.*" *Plin. Ep.* iv. 9, i. e. "Applause was given to the person who arose to give his opinion as well as to those sitting down." And sometimes the most extravagant expressions of approbation were bestowed on the speakers; "*non fere quisquam in senatu fuit, qui non me complecteretur, exoscularetur, certatimque laude cumularet,*" Idem ix. 13, i. e. "there was scarcely a person in the senate who did not embrace, kiss, and eagerly applaud me." When *Cato* one day, to prevent a decree from being passed, attempted to waste the whole day in speaking, *Cæsar,* then Consul, ordered him to be led to prison; whereupon the house rose to follow him, which made *Cæsar* recall his order. Vide *Gell.* iv. 10.

When different opinions were delivered, the senators expressed their assent, some to one, and some to another, variously, by their looks, by nodding with their heads, by stretching out their hands, &c. Vide *Tacit. Hist.* iv. 4.

LIBERUM MARITAGIUM.—Frank marriage. A Tenure in tail special; where a man seized of land in fee-simple, gives it to another with his daughter, sister, &c., in marriage, to hold to them, and their heirs. This tenure groweth from the *words* in the gift, "*Sciant me* A. B. *dedisse, concessisse, &c.,* L. M. *filio meo, et* Annæ *uxori ejus, filiæ, &c., in liberum maritagium unum messuagium, &c.* Litt. § 17, i. e. "Know all men that I, *A. B.,* have given and granted, &c., unto *L. M.,* my son, and *Anne* his wife, daughter of, &c., in *Frank-marriage* one messuage, &c." The effect of which words is, that they shall have the land to them, and the heirs of their bodies; and shall do no service to the donor, except *fealty,* until the *fourth* degree. Vide *Glanville,*

20

lib. 7, *c.* 18; and *Fleta* gives the reason *why* the heirs do no service till the *fourth* degree, "*ne donatores, vel eorum hæredes per homagii receptionem a reversione repellantur,*" i. e. "lest the donors or their heirs should be expelled from the reversion by acceptance of the homage ;" and *why*, in the *fourth* degree, and downwards, they *shall* do services to the donor, "*quia in quarto gradu vehementer præsumitur quod terra est pro defectu hæredum donatorum reversura,*" i. e. "because in the fourth degree it is very strongly presumed that the land is come back for want of heirs of the donors." *Fleta, lib.* 3, *c.* 11. Vid. *Bract. lib.* 2, *c.* 7.

LIBRÆ, ARSÆ, ET PENSATÆ ; ET AD NUMERUM.—A phrase often occurring in *Domesday's Register*, and some other memorials of that and the next age, as "*Ailesbury,*" in *Buckinghamshire, the King's manor. In totis valentiis reddid* lvi. *lib. arsas et pensatas, et de theolonio* x. *lib. ad numerum,* i. e. "In the whole value it pays fifty-six pounds, burnt and weighed ; and ten pounds by tale." For they sometimes took their money *ad numerum*, by tale, in the current coin, by *consent;* but sometimes they rejected the common coin *by tale;* and money coined elsewhere than at the King's mint, by Bishops, Cities, and Noblemen, who had mints, as of too great alloy ; and would therefore melt it down to take it *by weight*, when purified from the dross, for which purpose they had, in those days, always a fire ready at the *Exchequer* to burn the money, and then weigh it. Vide *Cowell.*

LIGEUS—Is used for "*liege*" lord, sometimes for "*liege*" man ; the word is often used in the ancient law. The feudal system, however violent and fierce, in many of its features, yet was, (perhaps more than is *generally* supposed at the present day,) a kind and enduring tie between the superior *lord*, and the *tenant* or *liege* man, especially when the former was brave and generous, and the latter faithful and courageous. *Liege* lord is he that acknowledges no superior ; and *liege* man is he that oweth obedience to his *liege* lord ; and though we continually read of the tyrannical bearing of the *feudal* Barons, towards their *Vassals*, yet in those rude times, many acts of private benevolence, and noble conduct, no doubt, characterized those chivalrous and large proprietors of land ; their houses were constantly open to the stranger and the distressed ; and thousands found an *Asylum*, who in these days of refinement, wealth and commercial prosperity, would be left destitute. *Skene* says that the word *liege* is derived from the Italian *li'gan*, a bond, a *leaguer;* others derive it from *litis*, or one who is wholly at the command of the Lord, Vide *Blount in loco*. It is probable that *Shakspeare* had in his mind this bond of allegiance, subsisting between the lord and his vassal, when he said,

> "Though perils did
> Abound, as thick as thought could make them, and
> Appear in forms more horrid ; yet my *duty*,
> As doth a rock against the chiding flood,
> Should the approach of this wild river break,
> And stand unshaken *yours*."   King *Henry* VIII.

LINGUA PEREGRINA.—When the pleadings and judgments of the courts, and many of the law treatises were in *Norman French*, and the most barbarous *Latin* imaginable, the difficulty of the study of the law, in order to arrive at any eminence in it, was considerably greater than at the present day. We find a student making an almost inconsolable and whining complaint in these words: "*Emisit me mater Londinum, juris nostri capessendi gratia ; cujus cum vestibulum salutassem, reperissemque linguam peregrinam, dialectum barbarum, methodum inconcinnum, molem non ingentem solum, sed perpetuis humeris sustinendam, excidit mihi fateor ânimus,*" &c., i. e. "My mother sent me to London, for the purpose of entering upon the study of our law; when I had even entered its threshold, I discovered a foreign language, a barbarous dialect, an unhandsome method, an encumbrance not only prodigious, but to be perpetually supported on my shoulders, I confess my mind shuddered," &c.

LITE DIJUDICATA.—Among the *Romans*, after Judgment was given, and the lawsuit determined, (*lite dijudicatâ*,) the conquered party was obliged to do or pay what was decreed, (*judicatum facere*, vel *solvere ;*) and if he failed, or did not find securities, (*sponsores* vel *vindices*,) within thirty days, he was given up (*Judicatus*, i. e. *damnatus et addictus est*) by the *Prætor* to his adversary, (to which custom *Hor.* alludes, *Ode* iii. 3, 23,) and led away by him to servitude. *Cic. Flacc.* 19, *Liv.* vi. 14, 34. These thirty days are called the Twelve Tables, "*dies justi*," i. e. Days of grace: "*rebus jure judicatis*, XXX. *dies justi sunto, post deinde manus injectio esto, in jus ducito*," i. e. "the lawsuit being finished, thirty days' grace are given, after which let him be taken and brought before the court." After sentence was passed the matter could not be altered; hence the term "*agere actum*," to labor in vain. Vid. *Cic. Amic.* 22, *Attic.* ix. 18. *Actum est—acta est res—perii*—i. e. "all is over—I am undone." Vid. *Ter. Andr.* iii. 1, 7. *Adelph.* iii. 2, 7. In certain cases, however, when any mistake or fraud had been committed, the *Prætor* reversed the sentence of the Judges, *rem judicatum rescidit*, (i. e. he annulled the sentence,) in which case he was said, "*damnatos in integrum restituere*," (i. e. he entirely restored the condemned.) *Cic. Verr.* v. 6; or "*Judicia restituere*," ("to restore the decree.") After the cause was decided, the defendant, when acquitted, might bring an action against the plaintiff for a false accusation (*actionem calumniæ postulare*). Vide *Cic. Pro. Cluent.* 31. Hence, "*calumniæ litium*," i. e. *lites per calumniam intentæ*, or unjust lawsuits. Vid. *Cic. Mil.* 27.

LITEM SUAM FACERE.—If a Judge, among the *Romans*, either from partiality or enmity (*gratiâ* vel *immicitiâ*), evidently favored either of the parties, he was said, "*litem suam facere*," to make it his own suit. Vid. *Ulpian Gell.* x. 1. *Cicero* applies this phrase to an advocate too keenly interested for his client, *de Orat.* ii. 75. If *Cicero* meant this in a disgraceful sense, it would appear to have done him no credit, for the most worthy men in all ages accounted it their greatest honor and consolation to use every honest exertion and fair means for the service of those who, perhaps, have placed their lives and fortunes in the hands of their advocates; their duties are extremely responsible; and frequently everything dear to man is in their power. By the *Roman* law, if a Judge was suspected of having taken money from either of the parties, or to have *wilfully* given a wrong judgment, an action lay against him. By the Law of the Twelve Tables, corruption in a Judge was punished with death; but afterwards, *as* a crime of extortion. In the time of King *Alfred*, corrupt administration was a cause of capital punishment. It is reported that this King hanged forty-four unjust Judges in one year. Vide *Mirror des Justices, c.* 2.

LITERA.—From the *Fr.* "*litiere*"—Lat. "*lectum*." Litter. This word was anciently used for *straw* for a bed; even the "King's bed." In our law books this word is often used for the article called litter, now used in stables among horses, &c. Rushes and straw generally composed the material for the sleeping places of our martial ancestors, and occupied the place where feathers and down are now substituted; and many allusions to the flag and rush are to be found scattered in the ancient writings. It appears that the practice of sleeping on rushes was customary so late as the time of *Henry* IV., as *Shakspeare*, speaking of a husband, sung to sleep by his wife, says:

"She bids you
Upon the wanton *rushes* lay you down,
And rest your gentle head upon her lap,
And she will sing the song that pleaseth you."
King *Henry* IV.

Rushes composed the beds upon which the chivalrous sons and fair damsels of the *feudal* ages reposed. The word *litera*, however, seems to have been generally used in *Law* Books for what is now usually called *litter*, for horses, &c., for we read "*tres carectatas* literæ." Vide *Mon. Ang.*, tom. 2.

LITERÆ.—This word often occurs in ancient authors: it not only meant "*Letters,*" but *all* kinds of writings were called "*Literæ.*" Cic. *passim.* Hence, "*quam vellem nescire literas.*" I wish I could not write. Vide *Suet. Ner.* 10. *Senec. Clem.*—but *literæ* is most frequently applied to *epistolary* writings (*Epistolæ vel chartæ epistolares.*) Cic. *Epistolæ* were always sent to those who were absent. (Cic.) *Codicilli* were given to those present. (*Tacit.*) The *Romans*, at least in the time of *Cicero*, divided their letters, if long, into pages, and folded them in the form of a little book; and tied them around with a thread (*lino obligabant*), the knot was covered with wax, or with a kind of chalk, and then sealed, generally with a ring, or some impression thereon. If any small postscript remained, after the page was completed, it was written crosswise (*transversim*) on the margin. Vid. *Cic. Att.* v. 1.

In writing letters, the *Romans* always put their own name *first;* and then that of the person to whom they wrote, *Auson. Ep.* 20: sometimes with the addition of "*Suo,*" as a mark of familiarity or kindness. If he was invested with an office, *that* likewise was added, but no epithets, (as among us,) unless to particular friends, whom they sometimes called "*Humanissimi;*" "*Optimi;*" "*Dulcissimi;*" "*Animæ suæ;*" &c. Vide *Cic.* et *Plin. passim.* They always annexed the letter S for "*Salutem,*" sc. "*wishes health.*" Hence, "*salutem alicui mittere,*" "to send health to any one." Vid. *Plaut.*

They used anciently to begin "*Si vales, bene est,*" i. e. if you are in health, it is well: "*vel, gaudeo;*" "*ego valeo.*" "I am glad;" "I am well." Vide *Senec. Ep.* i. 15, &c. They ended with "*Vale,*" "Farewell." *Ov. Trist.* v. 13, 33. Sometimes they wrote "*Ave,*" "Adieu;" or "*Salve,*" "Save you," to a near relation, with this addition, "*Mi anime,*" "My soul;" "*Mi suavissime,*" "My dearest," &c. They never subscribed their names as we do; but sometimes added a prayer for the prosperity of the person to whom they wrote, as "*Deos obsecro ut te conservent,*" "I pray the Gods save you." *Suet. Tib.* 21; which was always done to the Emperors. Letters were sent by a messenger, commonly a slave, called "*Tabellarius,*" for the *Romans* had no established post. There sometimes was an inscription on the outside of a Letter: sometimes not. When *Decimus Brutus* was besieged by *Antony,* at Mutina, *Hirtius* and *Octavius* wrote letters on thin plates of lead, which, it is said, they sent to him by means of divers (*urinatores*,) and so received his answers. Vid. *Dio.* xlvi. *Frontin* iii. 13, 7. Appian describes letters on leaden bullets, and thrown by a *sling* into a besieged city, or camp.

Julius Cæsar, when he wrote to any one what he wished to keep secret, always made use of the fourth letter *after* that which he ought to have used, as D for A, &c. Vide *Suet. Cæs.* 56. Augustus used the letter *following,* as B for A. The *Romans* had slaves, or freedmen, who wrote their letters (called "*ab epistolis;*") persons who transcribed their books were called "*librarii;*" those who glued them, "*glutinatores:*" some polished them with pumice stone, and anointed them with the juice of cedar, to preserve them from the moths and rottenness. Hence we read of "*carmina cedro linenda,*" "worthy of immortality." *Hor. Art. p.* 232. The titles and *indices* were often marked with vermilion, purple, red earth, or red ochre.

LUXURIA.—There were many laws formerly made to restrain excess in *apparel;* but they are repealed by *stat.* 1, *Jac.* 1, *c.* 25. But as to excess in *diet,* there *still* remains one ancient statute unrepealed, viz.: 10 *Edwd.* 3*d stat.* 3, which ordains "that no man shall be served at dinner with more than *two* courses, except in some great holiday, therein specified, on which he may be served with *three.*" Black. Com. 170, 171.

M.

MACEGRIEFS.——Persons who dealt in stolen flesh.

MACHINANS absque probabili causa.——Plotting without a probable cause.

MACHOLUM.——A granary without roof.

MACREMIUM.——Ship or house timber.

MAGBOTE, or MÆGBOTE.——From the Sax. "*Mæg.*" i. e. a kinsman, and "*bote,*" a compensation. This means compensation for murdering one's kinsman in ancient times, when corporeal punishments for murder were often commuted into pecuniary fines, if the friends or relatives of the party killed were so satisfied. Vide *Leg. Canuti,* c. 2.

MAGIS proprie dici poterit *wrectum,* si navis frangatur, &c., nisi ita sit quod verus dominus aliunde veniens, per certa indicia et signa docuerit res ipse suas; ut si canis vivus inveniatur, &c., et eodem modo, si certa signa apposita fuerint mercibus et aliis rebus.——It may therefore more properly be called a *wreck,* if the vessel be broken to pieces, &c., unless it happen, that the true owner appearing, learn, by certain marks and signs, that the goods are his, as if a live dog be found, &c., and, in the same manner, if certain marks were placed on the wares and other things.

MAGISTRALIA brevia.——Magisterial writs.

MAGNA assisa.——"The great assize." The assize in which the jurors were knights

MAGNA Charta.——The great Charter; the bulwark of *English* liberty. *Vide note.*

MAGNA componere parvis.——To compare great things with small.

MAGNA precaria.——A general reaping day.

MAGNATES graves ultiones fecerunt, et districtiones quos-que redemptiones receperunt ad voluntatem suam.——The nobles committed grievous injuries and took arbitrary distresses until they were redeemed.

MAGNATES regni.——The great men of the realm: the nobles.

MAGNITUDINE laborant sua.——They totter under their own weight.

MAGNOPERE providendum est.——Great care must be taken.

MAGNUM Cape ad valentiam.——" The great *Cape* to the value." *Cape* is a judicial writ touching a plea of lands or tenements, and is divisible into *Cape magnum*, and *Cape parvum*.

MAGNUM Consilium.——The great Council.

MAHEME.——See MAIHEM.

MAHLBRIEF.——The name of the contract between the builder and owner of a vessel, in which the size and class of the vessel is specified, as also the time of building her, and the terms of payment. *Maritime law.*

MAIHEM, MAYHEM, MAIM.——In law, the depriving another of his limbs or eyes by violence; thus weakening him for self-defence. *Vide note.*

MAILLE.——A half-penny ; a tribute.

MAINBOUR.——A surety.

MAINOUR, or MANOUR, or MEINOUR.——From the Fr. "*Manier*," i. e. "*manu tractare*." In a legal sense this denotes the thing taken away, found in the *hand* of the thief who stole it. Thus, to be taken with the "*mainour*," is to be taken with the thing stolen about him. Formerly, in these cases there appears to have been one mode of prosecution by the common law, (without any previous finding by a jury,) as when a thief was taken with the mainour, "*in manu,*" he might, when so detected, "*flagrante delicto,*" be brought into court, arraigned, and tried *without* indictment.

MAINOVRE.——Hand labor.

MAINPERNABLE.——That may be admitted to bail.

MAINPERNORS.——"Manucaptors," are those persons to whom a man is delivered out of custody or prison, on their becoming bound for his appearance ; because they do, as it were, "*manu capere,*" *et ducere captivum, é custodia,* i. e. "take by the hand," and lead the prisoner out of custody.

MAINPRIZE—*Manucaptio.*——From the Fr. "*main,*" i. e. a hand, and "*pris,*" taken. The taking, or receiving a person into friendly custody, who otherwise might be committed to prison, upon security given that he shall be forthcoming at a time and place assigned.

MAINSWORN.——Perjured.

MAINTIEN le droit.——Maintain the right.

MAIS il faut que ces choses la soient veritablement au pouvoir de l'enemie, et conduites en lieu du sureté.——But it is necessary that these things should be really in the power of the enemy, and conveyed to a place of safety.

MAJOR annus.——The bissextile year, or 366 days.

MAJORA regalia.——The greater rights of the crown.

MAJORA regalia imperii præeminentiam spectant, minora vero ad commodum pecuniarum immediate attinent, et hæc proprie, fiscalia sunt, et ad jus fisci pertinent.——The greater rights of the crown regard the regal preëminence, but the lesser directly pertain to pecuniary emolument, and these are properly of the Exchequer, and belong to revenue rights.

MAJORI summæ minor inest.——The lesser goes with the greater.

MAJUS jus.——The greater right.

MALA fide possessio.——An occupation (or holding) in bad faith (or illegally).

Mala grammatica non vitiat chartam.——Bad grammar does not invalidate the deed.

Mala-in-se.——Wrong in itself.

Malam cerevisiam faciens in cathedra ponebatur stercoris.——He who made bad ale was placed in a cart of dung.

Mala-praxis.——Mal-practice.

Mala prohibita.——Wrongs forbidden (by common law).

Maledicta expositio quæ corrumpit textum.——A vicious interpretation which spoils the text.

Maletolt.——An overcharged tax or toll.

Malfeazance.——Doing wrong: a bad act.

Malitia præcognita.——Malice aforethought or prepense.

Malitia supplet ætatem.——Malice supplies the want of age.

Mallobergium.——A public meeting.

Mallum.——A superior court: an assembly.

Malo animo.——With a bad intent.

Malograto.——"In spite: unwillingly." Hence, probably, the Fr. "*malgre*," and the old English word "*maugre*."

Malum animum.——An evil intent.

Malum in se.——Bad in itself: wrong in its own nature.

Malum prohibitum.——A prohibited offence.

Malum veniendi.——Mishap or sickness in coming.

Malus usus abolendus est.—A bad custom should be abolished.

Malveilles.——Offences.

Malversation.——Misconduct.

Managium.——A dwelling.

Manbote.——The Saxon fine paid to a lord for killing his vassal.

Manceps.——A buyer who took in his *hand* the purchased article.

Mancipatio, or mancipium.——This was one of the

modes of transferring property among the *Romans.* Vide *Cic. Off.* iii. 16, *de Orat.* i. 30.

MANCIPII, quasi manu capti.——Slaves, as if taken by the hand (or made captives in war): a slave. *Vide note.*

MANCIPIUM.——Property: right of perpetual possession.

MANCUS.——A Saxon coin of thirty pence.

MANDAVI balivo.——I have commanded the bailiff.

MANDAVI balivo, qui nullum dedit responsum.——I have commanded the bailiff, who has made no return (or answer).

MANENS.——One class of tenants.

MANENT pro defectu emptorum.——"(The goods) remain for want of buyers." A return to a writ of execution.

MANERIUM.——"(A manendo," from residing): a manor (or royalty).

MANIFESTA disseizina.——An open disseizin.

MANSE.——A parsonage.　MANSELLUM.——A small manse.

MANSUETÆ naturæ.——Of a tame kind, or nature.

MANSUETÆ, quasi manui assuetæ.——Tamed, as though used to the hand: domesticated.

MANSUM capitale.——The manor house, or manse: or court of the lord. *Kennet's Antiq.*

MANTHEOF.——From the Latin "*mannus,*" a nag, and "*theoff,*" a thief—a horse stealer. *Ll. Alfred.*

MANU brevi.——Shortly.

MANUCAPTIO.——Mainprize.

MANU forti.——With a strong hand: by violence.

MANU longa.——Indirectly.

MANUMISSIO.——Manumission: setting slaves at liberty. *Vide note.*

MANUOPERA.——Things stolen found upon the thief. Vide MAINOUR.

MANUPASTUS.——A family.

MANUPES.——A foot of measurement.

MANUS.——Anciently used for the person taking an oath. *Vide note.*

MANUS mortua.——Mortmain.

MANU tenere.——To hold in hand: to occupy.

MARA, maras.——Moor: bog.

MARASTRE.——A step-mother.

MARCA.——Sax. "*Mearc.*" A Mark of silver: it was, when in use, thirteen shillings and four pence sterling; though in the reign of *Henry* the First, it was only six shillings and a penny in weight: some were coined, and some only cut in small pieces; but those that were coined were worth something more than the others. In former times, money was paid, and things often valued, and fines assessed, by the *Mark.* Vide *Stow. Ann.* 32.

MARE apertum.——The open (or high) sea.

MARESCALLUS.——"A Marshal." It would appear to signify as much as "*Tribunis militum*" with the ancient *Romans.* It has been derived from the *German,* "*Marschalk,*" i. e. "*Equitum Magister,*" which "*Hotoman,* in his feuds *sub verb.* "*Marschalcus,*" derives from the old word "*March,*" which signifies a horse: others make it of the Saxon, "*Mar,*" i. e. a horse, and "*Scalch,*" a master.

MARESCHANCIE.——The jurisdiction of a marshal.

MARETTUM.——A piece of land which is at times overflowed by the sea.

MARISCUS.——A marsh.

MARITAGIUM.——That portion which is given a daughter in marriage. Vide *Glanville, lib.* 2, c. 18. As a fruit of tenure, under which "*Maritagium*" is strictly taken, is that right which the lord of the fee formerly had to dispose of the daughters of his vassals in marriage.

MARITAGIUM debet esse liberum.——Marriage ought to be free.

MARITARE.——To marry; to provide a husband.

MARITIMA Angliæ.——The ancient revenues from the sea.

MARITIMA incrementa.——Increase of land by the retiring of the sea.

MARKET zeld.——The ancient toll for a market.

MARQUE de division de Partage de terres: ce mot vient du Latin *dividere*.——Notice the division of the allotment of the lands; this word is derived from the Latin *dividere*.

MARTE suo decurrere.——To run by its own force.

MATERIA non est corpus, neque per formam corporalitatis, neque per simplicem essentiam, est tamen ens et quidem substantia, licet incompleta; habetque actum ex se entitativum, et simul est potentia subjectiva.——The first material is not a body, neither by its shape nor by its simple essence; it is, however, a being, and, indeed, a substance, although incomplete; and it has a living action, derived from itself, although it be, at the same time, a subjective power.

MATERIA prima.——The first matter.

MATERTERA.——An aunt by the mother's side.

MAXIMA illecebra est peccandi impunitatis spes.——The greatest incitement to guilt is the hope of sinning with impunity.

MEDFEE.——A reward.

MEDIANTE patre.——With the father's acquiescence.

MEDIETAS.——The moiety. Fr. " *Moitie*," i. e. *cœqua media pars*. The half of any thing; and to hold *by moieties* is often used in the law books in cases of joint tenants. Vide *Litt.* 125.

MEDIETAS linguæ.——"Half tongue." Used where a jury is composed half of aliens and half of natives. *Vide note*.

MEDIETAS terræ.——A moiety of the land.

MEDIOLANI non obtinet.——It did not prevail at *Milan*.

MEDIUM hæreditatis.——Common heirship.

MEEN.——Mesne.

MEINDRE age.——Minority.

MELDFEOH.——Sax. The recompense due and given to him who made discovery of any breach of the penal laws.

MELIOR est conditio defendentis.——The defendant's condition is preferable.

MELIOR est conditio possidentis.——The condition of the possesser is the better one.

MELIUS et tutius, si non festines.——Better and safer, if you do not hurry.

MELIUS inquirendum.——To make a better search; to inquire further.

MEMBRA dividentia.——Parts which are divisible.

MEMBRUM pro membro.——"Limb for Limb." The law of retaliation.

MENDACIUM sibi ipsi imponere.——To take back the lie upon himself.

MENSURA domini regis.——The royal measure.

MENSURA juris vis erat.——And power was the (only) measure of right.

MEPRIS.——Neglect: contempt.

MERCATOR.——Trader; a buyer.

MERCEN-LEGE.——The *Mercian* law under the Heptarchy.

MERCES.——The wages for labor.

MERCIMONIA.——The wares of a *mercator*.

MERCIMONIATUS Angliæ.——Ancient English tax upon merchandise.

MERE.——Mother.

MERENNIUM, Merisme.——Timber.

MERGER——Is where a greater and less estate coincide, and meet in one person, without any *intermediate* estate; in which case, the lesser estate is immediately *annihilated;* or in the law phrase *merged,* that is *sunk* or *drowned* in the greater; as if the *fee* come to tenant for life, or years, these particular estates are merged in the fee. Vide 2 *Rep.* 60, 61. 3 *Lev.* 437. 2 *Plowd.* 418. *Cro. Car.* 275. *Co. Litt.* 338.

MER, or Mere.——Words applicable to location, which *begin or end* with either of these syllables, generally denote fenny, or watery places. *Cowell.*

Merx est quicquid vendi potest.——Merchandise is whatever can be sold.

Mesaventure.——An accident.

Mesne.——"Middle: intervening." The middle between two extremes, and that either in time, or dignity.

Mesne lord.——A middle lord; one between the chief lord and his tenant.

Mesprendre.——To behave amiss.

Mess Brief.——A ship's certificate of admeasurement granted by authority. *Danish Sea Law.*

Mes semble que tiel legal notice n'est sufficient a faire un criminal, coment soit sufficient a rendre luy responsible in matter civil: coment est doubt in ceo: il n'est accessary sans actual notice.——But it appears that a like legal notice is not sufficient to make him criminal; but it may be sufficient to make him responsible in a civil affair: although there is doubt in this: he is not accessary without actual notice.

Mes, si la pleynt soit faite de fême, qu'avera tolle a home ses membres, en tiel case perdra la fême l'une meyn par jugment, come le membre dont elle avera trespasse.—— But if the plaint be made of a woman, who has deprived a man of his limbs, in such case the woman shall be adjudged to lose one hand, as the member with which she offended.

Messoinger.——Falsehoods.

Messuagium sive tenementum.——A messuage or tenement.

Mestier.——Affairs; business.

Meta.——Limit, or bounds: the goal of an ancient racecourse.

Metallum.——A Roman punishment for criminals, which sentenced them to labor in the mines.

Mettre a large——Is, generally, "to set or put at liberty." And there is *Mettre le estats*, and *Mettre le droit*, mentioned by *Littleton* in cases of releases of lands by joint tenants, &c., which may sometimes pass a fee without words of inheritance, 1 *Inst.*, 273, 4.

METUS in constantem virum, vel fœminam potest cadere. ——" That fear which may fall on a firm (or courageous) man or woman." By the Canon law, a marriage contracted under such a fear was void.

MEU.——Moved. MEULX.——Better.

MEYN.——Hand.

MEYNOVERER.——The occupying: to manure.

MEYNPAST.——A household.

MEYNPERNOUR.——A surety, or bail for a prisoner.

MEYNS sachants.——Unlearned.

MICHEL Gemote, or Micel Gemote, or Micel Synod.—— The great meeting. The great councils, in the *Saxon* times, of king and nobles were called "*Wittena Gemotes*," afterwards "*Micel Synods*," or "*Michel Synoth*," and "*Micel Gemotes*." Vide note to "*Wittenagemote*."

MIELS.——Best.

MILES.——A knight: a soldier. *Vide note.*

MILES justitiæ.——A knight of justice. *Vide note.*

MILLENA.——A thousand.

MINISTRO curiæ.——By an officer of the court.

MINORA crimina.——Lesser crimes: misdemeanors.

MINORA regalia.——The lesser rights of the crown.

MINUS sufficiens in literatura.——Deficient in literature.

MINUTE.——From *mi*, middle, and *nuyt*, night. Midnight.

MISE, *Fr.*—Lat. *Missum*—Misa.——Costs or charges. *Vide note.*

MISERA est servitus, ubi jus est vagum, aut incognitum. ——That servitude is miserable, where the law is either uncertain or unknown.

MISERERE.——Have mercy.

MISERICORDIA.——" Mercy." Sometimes is used for an arbitrary or discretionary amerciament.

MISFEAZANCE.——A misdeed.

MISHERSING.——Being free of fines in any court for complaints irregularly made.

MISKENNING.——Irregular in a summons or action.

MISLIER.——To mislead.

MISPRISIO.——Fr. "*Mepris*".‚ A contempt. *Vide note.*

MISSATICUM.——A message.

MISSUS.——A messenger.

MISSUS dominicus.——A king's justice.

MISSUS regalis.——The legate, or commissioner of the crown.

MISTERIUM.——Something hidden.

MISUSER.——"In abuse of any liberty," or benefit; as "he shall make a fine for his *misuser.*" Vide *Old Nat. Brev.*, 149. By misuser, the charter of a corporation, &c., may be forfeited; as also an office.

MITIORI sensu.——In a milder sense: by a more favorable exposition.

MITTERE in confusam.——To put in hotchpot.

MITTERE in confusam cum sororibus quantum pater aut frater ei dederit, quando ambulaverit ad maritum.——To cast into a mixed fund with her sisters whatever her father or brother gave her on her marriage.

MITTER le droit.——To pass the right.

MITTER le estate.——To pass the estate.

MITTIMUS.——"We send." The name of a commitment to prison.

MITTITUR adversarius in possessionem bonorum ejus. ——The opponent is put into the possession of his effects.

MITTOMUS.——Suppose now.

MOBILIA personam sequuntur; immobilia situm.—— Things movable go with the person; immovables belong to the place.

MODIUS.——An ancient measure.

MODO et forma.——In manner and form. *Vide note.*

MODUAM castigationem adhibere.——To chastise with moderation.

MODUS decimandi.——A Modus, or composition in lieu of tithes.

MODUS de non decimando non prævalet.——A custom of being tithe free does not avail.

MODUS et conventus vincunt legem.——The custom and agreements supersede the law.

MODUS faciendum homagium et fidelitatem.——The manner of doing homage and fealty.

MODUS legem dat donationi.——Custom gives law to the gift (or grant).

MODUS levandi fines.——The manner of levying fines.

MOERDA.——Sax. Murder.

MOERYER.——To die.

MOHATRA.——A kind of usurious contract.

MOLENDINUM.——A mill.

MOLITURA.——A toll at a mill; a multure.

MOLLITER manus imposuit.——"He gently laid hands on him." This phrase is used in a defence set up against an action or indictment for an assault. He but "gently laid hands" on the plaintiff or prosecutor for the purpose of expelling him out of his (defendant's) house, &c.

MOLUTUS.——Ground, as weapons sharpened by grinding.

MOLYN ventresse.——

MONATH.——Sax. A month.

MONEIA.——Old English form of spelling money.

MONIALA.——A nun.

MONIER, moneyer.——One who coined money.

MONOMACHIA.——Single combat.

MONS sacer.——"The sacred mount." A place of appearance for litigating persons among the *Romans*.

MONSTRANS de compoto.——Showing the account.

MONSTRANS de droit.——Showing the right.

MONSTRANS de droits, ou records.——Showing the deeds, or records.

MONSTRANS de faits, ou records.——"The showing the

deeds or records." The difference between "*monstrans de faits*" and "*oyer de faits,*" is this; he that pleads the deed or record, or declares upon it, ought to show the same; and the other, against whom such deed or record is pleaded, may demand "*oyer.*" *Cowell.*

MONSTRAVIT.——He hath showed.

MOOT.——Doubtful: a term anciently much used in the Inns of Court.

MOOT, or MUTE HILL.——Anciently, a hill or elevation where public meetings were held in Great Britain.

MORGANGIVA.——The wedding gift. *Vide note.*

MORS.——" Death." There is in law a civil and also a natural death. *Vide note.*

MORT d'ancestor.——" The ancestor's decease." The name of a writ. *Vide note.*

MORTGAGIUM.——A dead pledge. *Vide note.*

MORTMAIN—*Manus mortua.*——A dead hand, or an unchangeable possession. *Vide note.*

MORTUARY.——A gift to the church on the decease of a parishoner. *Vide note.*

MORTUUM vadium.——A dead pledge, or mortgage. Vide note to " *Mortgagium.*"

Mos pro lege.——" Custom for law." Long-established usage in many cases, as in case of a fixed *modus* for tithes, &c., &c. shall stand in the place of law.

MOTS d'usage.——" Words of usage." Phrases in common use.

MULIER.——" A woman." Generally applied to married women. *Vide note.*

MULIER nunquam cum masculo partem capit in aliqua hæreditate.——" A woman never takes part in an inheritance with a man." This refers to the feudal law of descents.

MULIER puisne.——The eldest illegitimate son of a woman, who, before her marriage, was illicitly connected with the father.

MULTA Episcopi.——A fine paid by a bishop to the king for certain legal privileges.

MULTO fortiori, or "*a minori ad majus.*"——Is an argument often used by *Littleton,* and is framed thus : " If it be so in a feoffment passing a *new* right, much *more* it is for the restitution of an *ancient* right." Vide *Co. Litt.* 253, &c. 260, *a.*

MULTUM depreciati, et deteriorati devenerunt pro defectu emptorum, ex causa prædicta, sic impediditorum.——" (The goods) being much depreciated and injured, were reduced in value for want of buyers, who, for that reason, were prevented from purchasing." This was the return of the sheriff, in some cases, to a writ of execution.

MULTUM possessionis, et multum juris.——Much possession, and much right.

MULTUM possessionis, sed nihil juris.——Much possession, but no right.

MULTURE.——A toll for grinding at a mill; also a fine for going to another's mill instead of that upon the barony. Vide note to *Astrict.*

MUNDBRICE.——Sax. Violation or breach of the king's protection.

MUNDEBURDE.——From *mund,* protection ; and *bord,* a pledge.

MUNICIPIUM.——A free city or town.

MURDRAVIT.——"He murdered." Sometimes this word means "*he concealed.*"

MURDRUM.——"Murder": concealment: also a fine paid by the hundred wherein the crime was committed. *Murdre,* in the old statutes, signified any kind of concealment, or stifling.

MUTARI viagium tunc dicitur, quando primum principalem destinationem magister navis non sequitur, ut pote, quod navis cum onere, et cum primis vecturis, ad locum destinatum amplius non ire, nec eat.——The voyage is said to be changed, when the master of a ship does not follow

the first destination; as, for example, when a vessel, loaded with its first freight, does not proceed further towards
its appointed place, and (in fact) does not go.

MUTATO nomine de te fabula narratur.——Changing the
name, the fable concerns yourself.

MUTUATUS.——"Borrowed." A phrase sometimes inserted in warrants of attorney to confess judgment.

NOTES TO M.

MAGNA CHARTA.—The great *Palladium* of English liberty. A copy was
sent to different Cathedrals in England. One is to be seen, in most excellent preservation, in the *British Museum*. It is beautifully written in *Latin*,
in the old court-hand, then in use. Dr. *Goldsmith*, in his abridgment of the
History of *England*, says, "The Barons had long been forming a confederacy
against King *John;* but their union was broken, or their aims disappointed,
by various and unforeseen accidents. At length, however, they assembled a
large body of men at *Stamford*, and from thence, elated with their power,
they marched to *Brackley*, about fifteen miles from *Oxford*, the place where
the court then resided. *John*, hearing of their approach, sent the Archbishop of *Canterbury*, the Earl of *Pembroke*, and others of the Council, to
know the *particulars* of their request; and what those liberties were, which
they so earnestly importuned him to grant. The Barons delivered a schedule
containing the chief articles of their demands; and of which the former
Charters of *Henry* and *Edward* formed the ground-work. No sooner were
these shown to the King, than he burst into a furious passion, and asked why
the Barons did not also demand his kingdom; swearing that he *never* would
comply with such exorbitant demands! But the confederacy was now too
strong to fear much from the consequences of his resentment. They chose
Robert Fitzwalter for their General, whom they dignified with the title of
"MARESCHAL of the army of God, and of the Holy Church," and proceeded
without further ceremony to make war upon the King. They besieged
Northampton; they took Bedford, and were joyfully received in *London*.
They wrote circular letters to all the Nobility and Gentlemen, who had not
yet declared in their favor, and menaced their estates with devastation, in
case of refusal or delay.

John, struck with terror, first offered to refer all differences to the Pope
alone, or to eight Barons, four to be chosen by himself, and four by the con-
federates. This the Barons scornfully rejected. He then assured them that
he would submit at discretion; and that it was his supreme pleasure to
grant all their demands; a conference was accordingly appointed, and all
things adjusted for this most important treaty.

The ground, where the King's commissioners met the Barons, was between
Staines and *Windsor*, at a place called *Runimede*, still held in reverence by
posterity, as the spot where the standard of freedom was first erected in
England. Fathers even now exultingly show this spot to their children;
and the very sight of it warms the heart of every *Englishman*, who has one
drop of blood which revolts against *tyranny* and *oppression!* "There the
Barons appeared with a vast number of knights and warriors, on the fifteenth day of June, while those on the King's part came a day or two after.

.Both sides encamped apart like open enemies. The debates between power and precedence are generally but of short continuance. The Barons, on carrying their arms, would admit of few abatements; and the King's agents, being, for the most part, in their interests, few debates ensued. After some days, the King, with a facility that was somewhat suspicious, signed and sealed the Charter required of him; a Charter which continues in force to this day, and is the famous BULWARK OF ENGLISH LIBERTY, which now goes by the name of MAGNA CHARTA. This famous deed either granted or secured freedom to those orders of the kingdom that were already possessed of freedom, namely, to the Clergy, the Barons and the Gentlemen; as for the inferior, and the greatest part of the people, they were as yet held as slaves; and it was long before they could come to a participation of legal protection."

MANCIPII—(*quasi manu capti.*)—Men became slaves, among the *Romans*, by being taken in *war;* by sale; by way of *punishment;* or by being born in a state of servitude; and it may not be improper to mention some particulars of these *Roman* slaves to show how far their condition was similar to the slaves, and ADSCRIPTI GLÆBÆ, under the *English* and other *European* feudal laws. Enemies, who *voluntarily* laid down their arms, and surrendered themselves, retained their rights of freedom; and were called "DE-DITITII." *Liv.* vii. 31. But those taken in the field, or in the storming of cities, were sold by auction ("SUB CORONA") as it was termed, (*Liv.* v. 22, &c.) because they wore a *crown* when sold; or ("SUB HASTA") because a *spear* was set up where the crier, or auctioneer stood.

There was a continual market for slaves at *Rome.* Those who were in that trade, brought them there from various countries. The seller was bound to promise for the soundness of the slave; and not to conceal his faults. Vide *Hor. Sat.* ii. 3. 285. Hence, they were usually exposed to sale *naked;* and they carried a scroll (*titulus* vel *inscriptio*) hanging at their necks, on which their good and bad qualities were specified. Vide *Gell.* iv. 2. If the seller gave a false account, he was bound to make up the loss, vide *Cic. Off.* iii. 16 and 17; or in some cases to take back the slave. *Ibid.* 23. Those whom the seller would not warrant, were sold with a kind of cap on their heads, (*pileati.*) Vide *Gell.* vii. 4.

It was unlawful for free born citizens among the *Romans,* as among other nations, to sell *themselves* for slaves. Much less was it allowed any *other* person to sell a Freeman. But as this gave occasion to certain frauds, it was ordained by a decree of the Senate, that those who allowed themselves to be sold, for the sake of sharing the price, should *remain* in slavery. Fathers might, indeed, sell their children for slaves; but these did not, on that account, entirely lose the rights of citizens; for, when freed from their slavery, they were held as "*Ingenui,*" not "*Libertini.*" The same appears to have been the case with insolvent debtors, who were given up as slaves to their creditors, "*in servitutem creditoribus addicti,*" (i. e. bound in servitude to their creditors.) Vide *Quinct.* vi. 3, 26, v. 10, 60.

Criminals were often reduced to slavery, by way of punishment. Thus, those who had neglected to get themselves enrolled in the *Censor's* books; or who refused to enlist, had their goods confiscated; and, after being scourged, were sent beyond the *Tiber.* Vide *Cic. pro Cæcin.* 24. Those condemned to the mines or to fight with wild beasts, or to any extreme punishment, were first deprived of liberty, and, by a fiction of law, termed "slaves of punishment," (*servi pœnæ fingebantur.*)

The children of any female slave, became the slaves of her master. There appears to have been no regular marriage among slaves; but their connection was called "*Contubernium,*" and themselves "*Contubernales.*" Those slaves, who were born in the house of their master, were called "*Vernæ,*" or "*Vernaculi,*" hence the expression, "*lingua vernacula,*" (one's mother-tongue.)

These slaves were more petulant than others, because they were more indulged. Vide *Hor. Sat.* ii. 6, 66. Slaves not only did all domestic services, but were likewise employed in various trades and manufactures. Such as had a genius for it were sometimes instructed in literature, and the liberal arts; *artibus ingeniis, liberalibus, vel honestis*—i. e. "in ingenious, liberal, and honorable science." Vide *Cic.* Some of these were sold at a great price. Vide *Plin.* vii. 39. s. 40. Hence arose a principal part of the immense wealth of *Crassus.* Vide *Plutarch "in vita ejus."* Slaves were frequently promoted, according to their behavior, as from being a drudge, or mean slave in town, to be an overseer in the country. Vide *Hor. Ep.*

The country farms of the wealthy *Romans,* in latter times, were cultivated chiefly by slaves. Vide *Plin.* xviii. 3. But there were also free men who wrought for hire, as with us.

Among the *Romans,* masters had, at one time, an *absolute* power over their slaves; they might scourge or put them to *death* at pleasure. Vide *Juv. Sat.* vi. 219. This right was sometimes exercised with so great cruelty, that, especially in the corrupt ages of the republic, laws were made at different times to restrain it. The assertion of *Juvenal* proves that, even where great civilization and refinement reign, and even where men are far removed from a state of nature, they may become tyrants. These facts also teach Legislatures that as little *arbitrary* power as *possible* should be left in the *discretion* (as it is foolishly termed) of any weak and fallible individual.

The *lash* was the common punishment of slaves; but for certain crimes they were branded in the forehead, and sometimes forced to carry a piece of wood wherever they went, which was called *"Furca;"* and whoever had been subjected to this punishment was ever afterwards called *"Furcifer."* Slaves, also, by way of punishment, were often shut up in a house or bridewell, where they were obliged to turn a mill for grinding corn. Vide *Plaut. et Ter. passim.* When slaves were beaten, they used to be suspended with a weight tied to their feet, that they might not move them. Vide *Plaut. Asin.* ii. 2, 34, &c. To deter slaves from offending, a thong (HABENA) or a lash was commonly hung on the staircase, (*in scalis.*) Vide *Hor. Ep.* ii. 2, 15; but this was, it is said, generally applied to younger slaves, *"Impuberes habend,* vel *ferulâ plectebantur,"* i. e. "The youngsters were flogged with a whip or rod." Vide *Ulpian.* Slaves, when punished capitally, were commonly crucified. Vide *Juv.* vi. 219. *Cic. in Verr.* v. 3, 64, &c.; but this punishment (which was a most horrible one, leaving the criminal sometimes for days in extreme agony) was prohibited under *Constantine.* If a master of a family was slain at his own house, and the murderer not discovered, *all* his domestic slaves were liable to be put to death. Hence, we find no less than *four hundred* in one family put to death on this account. Vide *Tacit. Ann.* xiv. 43. How far tyranny and revenge will go when left to the passions of the injured parties!

Slaves were not esteemed as *persons,* but as *chattels;* and might be transferred from one to another like any other effects. Slaves could not testify in a court of justice. Vide *Ter. Phorm.* ii. 1, 62; nor make a will. *Plin. Ep.* viii. 16; nor inherit anything, *idem.* iv. 11; but gentle masters allowed them to make a kind of a will (*quasi testamentum facere*). Vide *Plin. Ep.* viii. 16; nor could slaves serve as soldiers, *Id.* x. 39, unless first made free, except in the time of *Hannibal,* when, after the battle of *Cannæ,* eight thousand slaves were armed without being freed. Vide *Liv.* xxii. 57. These were called *"Volones,"* because they enlisted voluntarily. Vide *Festus:* these afterwards obtained their freedom for their bravery. (*Liv.* xxiv. 16.) Slaves sometimes saved money out of their allowances, which, with their masters' permission, they laid out at interest, or purchased with it a slave for themselves, from whose labors they might make profit. *Cicero* says that sober and industrious slaves, at least such as became slaves from being captives in war, seldom remained in servitude above six years. (*Phill.* viii. 11.) At certain times

slaves were obliged to make presents to their masters out of their poor sav-
ings—"*ex eo quod de dimenso suo unciatim comparserint*,"—i. e. "out of that
which they saved by little and little from their allowance." Vide *Terent.*
There was sometimes an agreement between master and slave, that, when
the latter should pay a certain sum, the master should be *obliged* to give him
his liberty. Vide *Plaut. Aul.* v. 3, &c., *Cæsin.* ii. 5, 6 Although the state
of slaves, in point of *right*, was the same, yet their condition in families was
very different, according to the caprice and pleasure of their masters, and
their various employments; some served in chains, as *Janitors*, and door-
keepers; and some in the country, "*catenati cultores*," i. e. "chained hus-
bandmen." Vide *Flor.* iii. 19. "Vincti fossores" (chained ditchers or dig-
gers). Vide *Luc.* vii. 402; others were confined in work-houses, below
ground (*in ergastulis subterraneis*). So *Pliny*, "*Vincti pedes, damnatæ manus,
inscriptique vultus, arva exercent,*" xviii. 3—i. e. "with chained feet, manacled
hands, and branded countenance, they cultivate the fields."

MANUMISSIO.—As the inhabitants of many towns, during the long continuance of the Feudal system, had gained their freedom and independence by
charters of communities being granted them, the enfranchisement of bondmen or slaves became gradually more frequent; and when "Charters of liberty," or "Manumission," were granted to such persons, they contained *four*
concessions, corresponding to the four capital grievances to which men in a
state of servitude were subject. 1st. The right of disposing of their persons
by sale, or grant, was relinquished. 2. Power was given them of bequeathing, or conveying their property or effects, by will, or any other legal deed;
or if they happened to die intestate, it was provided that their effects should
go to their lawful heirs in the manner as the property of other persons. 3d.
The services and taxes which they owed to their superior, or liege lord,
which were formerly *arbitrary*, were *precisely* ascertained. 4th. They were
allowed the liberty of marrying according to their own inclinations; formerly they could contract no marriage without their lord's permission; and,
it is said, with no person but with one of *his* slaves. All these circumstances
are found in the Charter granted *Habitoribus Montis Britonis*, A. D. 1376.
Many circumstances concurred which produced deliverance from this wretched
state. The gentle spirit of the Christian religion; the doctrines which it
teaches concerning the equality of man, and the mutual charity or good will
we should bear to *all mankind;* its tenets with respect to the Divine Government; and the impartial eye with which the Almighty regards men of
every condition, and admits them to a participation of his benefits, "without
respect of persons," are all inconsistent with, and militate against servitude.
The benign doctrines of Christianity struggled *long* but steadily with worldly
interest; and, establishing generous and equitable maxims, contributed more
than *every* other circumstance to introduce the practice of "*Manumission.*".
When Pope *Gregory* the Great, who flourished towards the end of the sixth
century, granted liberty to one of his slaves, he gives this reason for it:
"*Cum Redemptor noster, totius Conditor naturæ, ad hoc propitiatus humanum
carnem voluerit assumere, ut divinitatis suæ gratia, dirempto (quo tenebamur
captivi) vinculo, pristinæ nos, restituerit libertati; salubriter agitur, si homines,
quos ab initio liberos natura protulit, et jus gentium jugo substituit servitutis, in
ea qua nati fuerant, manumittentis, beneficio, libertate reddantur*"—i. e. "Seeing
that our Redeemer, the Creator of all things, as a propitiation, assumed a
human body, that, by the merit of his divinity, the chain being broken (by
which we were enthralled), he might restore us to liberty. So we act properly, if by the kindness of our manumission, those whom nature ordained
free from the first, but whom the law of nations hath subjected to slavery,
are restored by us to their birth-right of freedom." And a great part of the
charters of "Manumission," previously to the reign of *Louis* the Tenth, are
granted "*pro amore Dei,*" "*pro remedio animæ,*" et "*pro mercede animæ*"....

i. e. "for the love of God," "for the cure of the soul," and "for the welfare of the soul." Vide *Du Cange, voc. "Manumissio."* The formality of Manumission was performed in a church, with great solemnity as a *religious* ceremony; the person to be manumitted was led round the great altar, with a torch in his hand; he took hold of the horns of the altar, and there the solemn words conferring liberty were pronounced. *Ibid.* vol. iv. 467. Manumission was also frequently granted on a death-bed; or by will. Another mode of obtaining Manumission was by entering into Holy Orders; but so many slaves escaped by this mode out of the hands of their masters, that the practice was at last prohibited by almost all the nations of *Europe.*

The genius of the *English* constitution seems early to have favored Manumission generally; yet, in some parts of *England,* personal service continued to a late period. In the year 1514, we find a charter of *Henry* the Eighth, enfranchising two slaves belonging to one of his manors; and so late as the year 1574, there is a commission from Queen *Elizabeth,* with respect to the Manumission of certain bondmen, belonging to her.

Manumission was formerly performed several ways. Some were manumitted by delivery to the sheriff, and proclamation in the county, &c.: others by charter. One way of manumission was, for the lord to take the bondman by the head, and say, "I will that this man may be free"—and then shoving him forward, "out of his hand," (*è manu suo.*) There was also a Manumission *implied,* when the lord made an obligation for payment of money to the bondman—or sued him where he might enter without suit, &c. The form of manumitting in the time of *William* the Conqueror is thus recorded: "*Si quis servum suum liberum facere, tradat eum vicecomiti per manum dextram, in plenu comitatu, et quietum illum clamare debet a jugo servitutis suæ per Manumissionem, et ostendat ei liberas portas; et tradat ei libera arma, scilicet, lanceam et gladium; et inde* LIBER HOMO *efficitur."* Vide *Lamb Archai.* 126—i. e. "If any person desires to make his slave free, he may deliver him to the sheriff, by the right hand, in full County Court, and he should declare that he was discharged by Manumission, from his servitude, and show him the opened doors, and deliver to him free arms, viz., a lance and sword, and thenceforth he becomes a FREEMAN."

MANUS.—In ancient records, this word is frequently used for *the person* taking an oath. "*Tertia, quaria, &c.,* manu *jurare"*—i. e. "the party was to bring so many to swear with him, that *they* believed what he vouched was true." And in case of a woman accused of adultery, "*mulieri hoc neganti purgatio sexta* manu *extitit indicta"*—i. e. "she was to vindicate her reputation upon the testimony of six Compurgators." Vide *Reg. Eccl. Christ. Cant.* The use of the word, in the sense here alluded to, probably came from laying the *hand* on the Scriptures when the oath was taken.

MAYHEM—or *Maihem.*—These words mean a wound, or corporal hurt, by which a man loses the use of any member, *proper* for his defence or fight: as if a man's skull be broke; or any other bone broken, in any other part of the body; a foot, hand, finger, or joint of a foot; or any member be cut off; if by any wound the sinews be made to shrink; or where any one is castrated; or if an eye be put out, or any *foretooth* broke, &c. But the cutting off an ear, or nose, the breaking of the *hinder teeth,* and such like, was held by the Common Law to be *no Mayhem;* as they were not weakening the person's strength, but only a disfiguring, or deforming the body. Vide *Gland.* lib. 4, c. 7. *Bract.* lib. 3, *tract* 2. At one time, by the ancient law of *England,* he that maimed any one, whereby he lost any part of his body, was sentenced to lose the like part, "*membrum pro membro,"* (limb for limb.) Vide 3 *Inst.* 118.

MEDIETAS LINGUÆ.—In petit treason, murder and felony, "*medietas linguæ,*" is allowed by the English law. But in high treason it is otherwise; and we read that *Solomon de Standford,* a Jew, had a cause tried before the Sheriff of *Norwich,* by a jury, who were "*sex probos et legales homines; et sex legales Judæos excivitate Norwici,*" &c.—i. e. "six good and lawful men, and six Jews of the same description, (taken) from the city of Norwich."

MILES, among the *Latins,* signified a Soldier; but in law books it generally signifies a *Knight;* which *Camden* says is derived from the Saxon, *Gnite,* or *Cnight.* The Heralds inform us of several orders of Knights. A Knight, at this day, is, and anciently hath been, reputed and taken for one who, by his valor and prowess, or other services performed for the benefit of the commonwealth, has, by the King, or his sufficient deputy, been advanced above, or separated from the common sort of gentlemen. The *Romans* called Knights, *Celeres,* and sometimes *Equites,* from the performance of those services upon horseback; and among them, there was an order called "*Ordo Equestris,*" but distinguished from those called *Celeres.* The *Spaniards* called them *Cavelleros,* the *French, Chevaliers,* and the *Germans, Rieters:* all which appellations evidently appear to proceed from the *Horse,* which is a great proof of the manner of the execution of their warlike exercises.

MILES JUSTICIÆ.—As soon as the science of law (by the introduction of the *Roman* Civil Code, &c.) became a laborious study, and the practice of it a *separate* profession, such persons as rose to eminence in it obtained honors, which had been theretofore appropriated to *soldiers.* Knighthood was the most remarkable distinction during several ages, and conferred privileges, to which rank and birth alone were not entitled. To this high dignity, persons eminent for their knowledge in the law were advanced; and thereby placed on a level with those whom their military talents had rendered conspicuous. *Matthew Paris* mentions such Knights as early as A. D. 1251. If a Judge obtained a certain rank in the courts of justice, *that* alone gave him the right to the honor of Knighthood; and "*Miles Justiciæ,*" and "*Miles Literatus,*" became common titles. Vide *Pasquier Reserches, liv.* 11, c. 16, p. 130. A profession which led to offices, and ennobled the persons who held them, grew into credit; and the people of *Europe* became accustomed to see men rise to eminence, by *civil,* as well as *military* talents and bravery.

MISE.—This is a law term signifying *expenses;* and was formerly used in the entries of judgments, in personal actions; as where the plaintiff recovers, the judgment is "*quod recuperet damna sua,*" (i. e. that he recover his damages) to such a value, and "*pro misis et custagiis,*" (for costs and charges) so much, &c. This word has also another signification in law, which is, where it is taken for a word of *art,* appropriated to a writ of *Right,* so called because both parties have put themselves upon the *mere right:* so that what, in other actions, is called an *issue,* in a writ of Right is called a "*Mise;*" but if, in a writ of Right, a *collateral* point be tried, *that* is called an *issue.* Vide 1*st Inst.* 294, and 37 *Edward 3d,* c. 16.

MISPRISIO.—A neglect, oversight, or contempt. As, for example, *Misprision* of treason, is a negligence in not revealing treason, where a person knows it to have been committed—so of felony. In a larger sense, *Misprision* is taken for many great offences, which are neither treason nor felony, nor capital, but *very near* them; and, it is said, that every great misdemeanor, which hath no certain name appointed by the law, is generally called *Misprision.* Vide 3 *Inst.* 36. *H. P. C.* 127. *Wood,* 406, 408.

MODO ET FORMA.—Words of art in law pleadings, &c.; and particularly used in the answer of a defendant, whereby he denies the thing laid to his charge, (*modo et forma declarata*) "in manner and form as laid" by the plaintiff. Vide *Kitch.* 232.

MORGANGIVA—or *Morgangina*, from the *Sax.* "*morgen*," the morning, and "*giftan*," to give. These words signify the wedding-day's gift—*dower*, or rather *dowry*, "*Si sponsio virum suum supervixerit, dotem et maritationem suam, cartarum instrumentis, vel testium exhibitionibus et traditam perpetualiter habeat, et* morganginam *suam*," L. L. *Hen.* 1. c. 11.—i. c. "If the wife survive her husband, she shall have her dower and marriage portion, always delivered (or assigned) to her by deeds, or the producing of witnesses, and also the *wedding-morning's gift*." Vide, also, *Du Cange, in verb,* "Morganegiba." There is a custom at present in *Wales*, for the friends and neighbors of a new married couple to make them presents on their wedding day.

MORT D'ANCESTOR.—This is a writ which lay where a man's father, mother, brother, sister, uncle, aunt, &c., died seized of lands, tenements, rents, &c. that were held in fee, and after their death, a stranger abated. Vide *Reg. Orig.* 223. It is used as well against the abator, as any other in possession of the land; but it lies not against the brothers or sisters, &c., where there is a privity of blood between the person prosecuting, and them. *Co. Litt.* 242. And it must be brought within the time limited by the statute of limitations. (3 *Comm.* 189.) If tenant by the curtesy, alien his wife's inheritance and die, the heir of the wife may have an *assize of mort d'ancestor*, if he have not assets by descent from the tenant by the curtesy; and the same shall be as well where the wife was not seized of land the day of her death, as where she was seized thereof. *New Nat. Br.* 489.

MONS—Death. By the *Roman* laws, (affecting freemen,) only the most heinous crimes were punished by a violent death. In ancient times it seems to have been not unusual to hang the malefactors, "*infelici arbore suspendere*," (i. e. to hang them on an accursed tree). Vide *Liv.* i. 26. Afterwards, to scourge (*virgis cædere*), and behead them (*securi percutere*). Vide *Liv.* iii. 5. vii. 19. xxvi. 15. To throw from the *Tarpeian Rock*, (*de saxo Tarpeio dejicere;*) Ib. vi. 20. or from that place in the prison called *Robur.* Vide *Festus Vit. Max.* vi. 31. Also to strangle them, (*lacqueo gulam, guttur, vel cervicem*, i. e. "to break the wind-pipe, the throat, or the neck with a rope,") in prison. *Id.* v. 4, 7. Vide *Sallust, Cat.* 55, &c. The bodies of criminals, when executed, were not burnt, or buried; but exposed before the prison, (usually a certain stairs called *Gemoniæ*,) and thence dragged with a hook, and thrown into the Tiber. Vide *Suet. Tib.* 53; and *Juv.* x. 66. Sometimes, however, their friends purchased the right of burying them. Under the Emperors, several new and more severe punishments were contrived; as, exposure to wild beasts, (*ad bestias damnatio;*) burning alive, (*vivicomburium*,) &c. When criminals were burnt, they were dressed in a tunic, besmeared with pitch, and other combustible matter, called "*tunica molesta.*" Vide *Senec. Ep.* 14. *Juv.* viii. 235. Pitch is mentioned among the instruments of torture in more ancient times. *Plaut. Capt.* iii. 4, 65. Sometimes persons were condemned to the public works; to engage with wild beasts; or fight as Gladiators. Vide *Plin. Ep.* x. 40; or were employed as slaves, in attending on the public baths; in cleansing common sewers; or repairing the streets and highways. *Id.* Slaves, after being scourged, were crucified, usually with a label, or inscription on their breasts, intimating their crime, or the cause of their punishment, *Dio.* liv. 3, as was commonly done to other criminals, when executed. *Suet. Cal.* 32. *Dom.* 10. Thus *Pilate* put a title or superscription on the cross of our Saviour. Vide *Matt.* xxvii. 37. The form of the cross is described by *Dionysius*, vii. 69. Vedius Polio, one of the friends of *Augustus*, devised a new species of cruelty to slaves, throwing them into a fish-pond to be devoured by lampreys. Vide *Plin.* ix. 23. s. 39. *Dio.* liv. 23. A person guilty of parricide, or even murdering a near relation, after being severely scourged, was sewed up in a sack, (*culeo insatus*), with a dog, a cock, a viper, and an ape, and then thrown into the sea, or a deep river. *Cic. pro Rosc. Amer.* ii. 25, 26. *Senec. Clem.* i. 23.

MORTGAGIUM, *vel mortuum vadium*, from "*mort*," *mortuus*, and "*gage*," a pledge. Generally meaning a pledge of lands or tenements. We read of Mortgage in the *Grand Custumary of Normandy*, c. 313. Glanville (*lib.* 1. c. 13) defines it thus, "*Mortuum vadium dicitur illud, cujus fructus, vel redditus, interim percepti in nullo se acquietant*"—i. e. "That is called a dead pledge, whose profit or income does in no way, in the meantime, defray the debt." So that it is called a "*dead gage*," because whatever profit it yieldeth, yet it redeemeth not itself by yielding such profit, except the whole sum borrowed be paid at that day.

The notion of mortgaging and redemption appears to be of *Jewish* extraction; and most probably from them it descended to the *Greeks* and *Romans*. The plan of the *Mosaic* law constitutes a just and equal *Agrarian* law, that the lands might continue in the same tribes and families; therefore, whoever was compelled by poverty to sell, could transfer no estate in the lands, further than to the then *next general Jubilee*, which returned once in every *fifty* years; therefore it was computed by the purchaser, that he could only hold *till* that Jubilee arrived. Vide *Levit.* xxv, 13 *et seq.* ; but it has been said that the vendor had power at *any time* to redeem, paying the value of the lands to the *next Jubilee;* but though he did not redeem them, yet *at* the Jubilee, the lands came back free to the vendor, or his heirs.

MORTMAIN—*manus mortua*, from the Fr. "*mort*," mors; and "*maine*," manus. This word means an alienation of lands to any corporation, guild, or fraternity, and their successors: as bishops, parsons, vicars, &c. The reason of the name "*Mortmain*," may probably be derived from hence, because the services, and other profits of the land, as *Escheats*, &c., should not come into a *dead hand*, or into such a hand as might be called *dead to the world*, so as to be abstractedly different from other lands, &c., and never could, by any defect of the heirs of the donee, &c., return to the donor; or to any *temporal* or common use. *Polydore Virgil* in the seventh book of the Chronicles mentions this law, and gives the reason of the name, "*Et legem hanc manum mortuum vocarunt, quod res semel datæ collegiis sacerdotum, non utique rursus venderentur, velut mortuæ, hoc est, usui aliorum mortalium in perpetuum adeptæ essent. Lex diligenter servatur, sic, ut nihil possessionum ordini sacerdotali a quoquam detur, nisi regis permissu*"—i. e. "And this law they called Mortmain, because estates once given to societies of priests, could not afterwards be sold (they might be accounted) as things without life; that is, they were obtained for the use of other persons, in *perpetuity.* The laws thus carefully observed that nothing be given to the sacerdotal order by any person, without the King's consent." *William* the Conqueror demanded the cause why he conquered *England* in *one* battle, which the *Danes* could not do by *many.* Frederick, the then Abbot of *St. Albans*, answered, that the reason was, because the land, which *was* the maintenance of *martial* men, had been given and consecrated to pious purposes; and for the maintenance of holy votaries. To this the Conqueror said, that if the clergy were so *strong*, that the realm was *enfeebled* of men of war, and subject by it to foreign invasion, he would assist it, and thereupon he took away many of the revenues of the Abbot, and of others also. Vide *Speed.* 418.

MORTUARY.—A gift, or payment to the church on a person's demise. *Selden* says that the usage was to bring the *Mortuary* along with the corpse, when it came to be buried; and to offer it to the church, as a satisfaction for the supposed negligence and omissions the deceased had been guilty of, in not paying his *personal* tithes: from thence it was called "*a corse present.*"

MULIER.—It has been said that this word, used in the *law*, seems to be a word corrupted from *melior*, or the Fr. *meilleur*, and signifies the lawful issue born *in* wedlock, preferred before an elder brother, born *out* of matrimony.

Vide *Stat.* 6, *Hen.* 6, c. 11. But by *Glanville,* lawful issue are said to be *mulier,* not from *melior,* but because begotten "*é muliere,*" and not "*ex concubina :*" for he calls such issue "*filios mulieratos,*" opposing them to Bastards. Vide *Glanv., lib* 7, c. 1. It appears to be thus used in *Scotland* also. *Skene* says "*mulieratus filius,* is a lawful son born of a lawful wife." It, however, is often used in the sense we usually apply to it. Women have held in *England* various offices. *Ann,* Countess of *Pembroke, Dorset,* and *Montgomery,* held the office of Hereditary Sheriff of *Westmoreland,* and exercised it in *person ;* at the Assizes at *Appleby,* she sat with the judges on the bench. Vide *Harg. n. Co. Litt.* 326, *a.* A woman may also be a Marshal, Great Chamberlain, and Constable of *England,* the Champion of *England,* Commissioner of Sewers, Governor of a Work-house, Sexton, Keeper of the Prison of the Gatehouse of the Dean and Chapter of *Westminster,* Returning Officer of Members of Parliament, and Constable. Vide *Rex* v. *Stubbs,* 2 *Burr. Rep.*

N.

NAIF.——A slave by birth.

NAM adipiscimur possessionem corpore et animo : neque per se corpore, neque per se animo. Non autem ita accipiendum est, ut qui fundum possidere, velit *omnes* glebas circumambulet; sed sufficit quamlibet partem ejus fundi introire.——For we obtain possession by body and intendment, not by body alone, nor by intent alone. For it is not to be understood that he who is about to take possession of a farm should walk over the *whole* of the land; but it is sufficient that he enter into what part of the farm he pleases.

NAMARE.——To distrain.

NAM cum navis divertat ad extraneos actus, dicitur mutasse iter, et plura viagia fecisse, et primum dicitur mutatum et amplior rata hoc procedere, etiamsi fuit cæpitum secundum viagium, licet non completum; nam cum fuerit deventum ad actum proximum, destinatio habetur pro profecto ; cum potentia proquinqua actui habeatur pro actu, limita tamen si mutetur ex justa causa, &c.——For when a ship alters her course to transact business foreign to the voyage, she is said to have changed her course, and to have made more voyages, and the first voyage is said to be altered, and a higher rate is taken for this, although the second voyage was begun, but not completed : for when the vessel had performed its first business, its destination shall be considered as completed ; for the immediate power of acting shall be accounted for the act itself ; but if it change its destination for a just cause, &c.

NAM de minimis non curat lex.——For the law takes no notice of mere trifles.

NAM et commodum ejus esse debet, cujus periculum est. ——For he who is liable to the risk should have the advantage.

NAM ex antecedentibus, et consequentibus, fit optima interpretatio.——Because the best meaning consists in that which precedes, and follows.

NAM exemplo perniciosum est, ut ei scripturæ credatur qua unusquisque sibi adnotatione propria debitorem constituit.——For it is a very injurious rule that a writing should have that credit, in which any person, by his own memorandum, may constitute another his debtor.

NAM feudum sine investitura nullo modo constitui'potuit. ——For a fee cannot in any manner be made without (giving) possession.

NAMIUM.——A taking of goods or chattels by way of distress.

NAM leges vigilantibus, non dormientibus subveniunt. ——For the laws assist the watchful, (but) not the slothful.

NAM nemo est hæres viventis.——For no one is the heir of a living person.

NAM omne crimen ebrietas, et incendit, et detegit.—— For drunkenness aggravates, and also discovers every crime.

NAM omne testamentum morte consummatum est, et voluntas testatoris est ambulatoria usque ad mortem.—— For every will is consummated (or perfected) by death ; and, until that event, the testator's will is *ambulatory* (or liable to be altered).

NAM qui facit per alium, facit per se.——For he who acts by another acts by himself. *Vide note.*

NAM qui hæret in litera, hæret in cortice.——"For he who adheres to the (very) letter sticks (only) in the bark;" [he does not reach the substance.]

NAM quilibet potest renunciare juri pro se introducto. ——"For any one may renounce a law (or right) brought in for himself," (i. e. which is raised for his own advantage).

NAM qui non prohibit, cum prohibere possit, jubet.—— For he who forbids not, when he may, orders (the thing to be done). *Vide note.*

NAM quod remedio destituitur, ipsa re valet, si culpa absit.——For that which is without remedy, assists the thing itself, if no fault exists.

NAM quod semel meum est, amplius meum esse non potest.——For that which is once my own, cannot be more strongly (or fully) mine.

NAM si cum gente aliqua neque amicitiam, neque hos- pitium, neque fœdus amicitiæ causa factum habemus, hi hostes non sunt. Quod autem e nostro ad eos pervenit, illorum fit; et liber homo noster ab eis captus, servus fit, et eorum idemque si ab illis ad nos aliquid perveniat.—— For although with any nation we have no league, nor friend ship, nor alliance made, yet they are not enemies. Never- theless, what effects of ours may chance to come into their possession become their property; and our free subject captured by them becomes their slave; and so of their property, if it come to our hands.

NAM silent leges inter arma.——For during (the rage of) war, laws are disregarded.

NAM verba debent intelligi cum effectu, ut res magis valeat quam pereat.——For language should be understood with that intent, that the matter may rather be effected than rendered nugatory.

NASTRE.——Born.

NATIVA.——A female slave.

NATURALIS affectio.——Natural affection. *Vide note.*

NATUS ante maritagium.——Born before wedlock.

NAUCLERUS.——The master of a merchant ship.

NAUFRAGE.——Shipwreck.

NAUFRAGIO facto, exercitor naula restituit, quæ ad manum præceperat, ut qui non trajecerit.——In case of shipwreck, the master restores the freight which comes to his possession, inasmuch as he has not thrown it overboard.

NAULUM.——The passage or freight money on a vessel.

NAUTÆ, Caupones, Stabularii, ut recepta restituerunt ——Mariners, Innkeepers, Ostlers (are bound) to return things as left in their charge.

NAUTÆ pro damno conferre.——The sailors ought to contribute to the loss.

NAUTICO fœnore.——By nautical interest: by bottomry.

NAVARCHUS.——The captain or commander of a vessel.

NAVIS bona.——A good ship.

NE admittas.——A writ for non-admittance of some party during the progress of a suit.

NE ætas quidem distinguebatur, quum prima juventa consulata ac dictaturas inirent.——For the age was not nicely distinguished when the principal youth entered on the consul or dictatorship.

NE aliquid de suo honorabili contenemento amittat.—— Lest he lose any part of his respectable appearance.

NE aliquis scholas regens de legibus in eadem civitate, de cætero ibidem leges doceat.——That no person keeping schools in the same city (for the study) of the laws should from thenceforth teach such laws there.

NE baila pas.——A plea made by a defendant in the action of detinue, in which he denied that the thing sued for was delivered.

NEC erit alia lex *Romæ*, alia *Athænis;* alia nunc, alia posthac; sed et omnes gentes, et omni tempore una lex, et sempiterna, et immortalis, continebit.——Neither shall there be one law at *Rome*, another at *Athens;* one now, another in future; but to all nations and all times one perpetual and fixed rule shall remain.

NECESSITAS culpabilis.——"A blamable necessity:" such a necessity which, though deserving reprobation, yet could not have been avoided.

NECESSITAS inducit privilegium quoad jura privata.—— Necessity gives a privilege like private rights.

NECESSITAS non habet legem.——Necessity has no law.

NEC in papyris, nec in verbis.——Neither written, nor oral. *Vide note.*

NEC in sacerdotis, nec in sacris. Neither in the priesthood nor in holy matters.

NEC fuit electus major.——He was not elected mayor.

NEC magis est contra naturum morbus, egestas, aut aliquid hujusmodi quam appetitio vel detractio alieni.——Nor is disease, poverty, or anything of this kind, more against nature than avarice, or the taking away another's property.

NEC præsidens, nec aliquis de collegio prædicto medicorum, nec successores sui, nec eorum aliquis exercet facultatem illam.——That neither the president, nor any other person of the said college of physicians, nor his successors, nor either of them, exercise that profession.

NEC regibus infinita, aut libera potestas.——Nor is power which is given to kings, either unbounded or at will.

NEC tali auxilio nec defensoribus istis tempus eget.—— The time requires no such aid; no such defenders.

NEC vero me fugit quam sit acerbum, parentum scelera filiorum pœnis luunter: sed hoc preclare legibus comparatum est, ut caritas liberorum amiciores parentes reipublicæ redderet.——Nor, indeed, have I been unconcious how severe it must be that the crimes of the parents should be expiated by the punishment of the children; but this has been clearly ordained by the laws, that love for the children might render parents more friendly towards the republic.

NEC videtur incongruum mulieres habere peritiam juris. Legitur enim de uxore *Johannis Andriæ* glossatoris, quod tantam peritiam in utroque jure habuit, ut publice in scholis legere ausa fit.——Nor does it seem inconsistent that women should be skilful in the law. For it is written that the wife of *John Andrea*, the Interpreter, was so learned in both laws, (i. e. the civil and common law,) that she had enterprise sufficient to lecture publicly in the schools.

NE deficiat justitia.——Lest justice be defeated.

NE disseizé pas.——Not ejected.

NE done pas.——No gift at all.

NE episcopi sæcularium placitorum officium suscipiant. ——That the Bishops do not usurp the office of secular pleas.

NE exeat.——That he depart not.

NE exeat Regno.——That he leave not the realm.

NE faciat vastum, vel estrepementum pendente placito dicto indiscusso.——That he commit no waste, or spoil, whilst the said plea (or suit) is pending.

NEGARE.——To deny.

NEGOTIORUM gestor.——A person who voluntarily assumes the care of another's affairs during the absence of the latter, and without his authority.

NE injuste vexes.——"That you do not unjustly oppress (or harass)." There was formerly a writ so called.

NEMBDA.——Sax. A jury.

NEMINE contradicente.——No one opposing.

NEMINEM voluerunt majores nostri, non modo de existimatione cujusquam, sed ne pecuniaria quidem de re minima, esse judicem: nec nisi qui inter adversarios convenisset.——Our ancestors required that no one, even if influenced by the opinion of any person, or by the most trifling sum of money, should be a judge; nor unless he would (impartially) decide between the parties in dispute.

NEMO ad Regem appellat pro aliqua lite nisi jus domi consequi non possit. Si jus nimis severum sit, allevatio deinde quæratur apud regem. That no person appeal to the King on any suit, unless he cannot proceed at law at home. If the law be too severe, then his Majesty may be applied to for relief. *Vide note.*

NEMO allegans suam turpitudinem audiendus est.——No man setting forth his own depravity is to be heard.

NEMO beneficium suum perdat, nisi secundum consuctu-dinem antecessorum nostrorum, et per judicium parium suorum.——That no man lose his benefice, unless accord-ing to the custom of our ancestors; and by the judgment of his peers, (or equals.) Vide note to " *Beneficia.*"

NEMO bis punitur pro eodem delicto.——No one is pun-ished twice for the same offence, (or crime.)

NEMO debet bis vexari pro eadem causa.——No one ought to be twice harassed for the same cause.

NEMO debet locupletari aliena jactura.——No one ought to grow rich by the misfortune of another.

NEMO est hæres viventis.——No one is the heir of a liv-ing person.

NEMO ex consilio obligatur.——No one is bound by counsel.

NEMO ex proprio dolo consequitur actionem.——No one can bring an action arising from his own deceit.

NEMO in propria causa testis esse debet.——No one should be a witness in his own cause.

NEMO invitus compellitur ad communionem.——No person, against his will, is forced into a copartnership.

NEMO miles adimatur de possessione sui beneficii, nisi convictâ culpâ, quæ sit laudanda per judicium parium suorum.——That no Knight be deprived of the possession of his benefice, unless convicted of a crime, which (con-viction) has been approved by the judgment of his peers (or equals). Vide note to " *Beneficia.*"

NEMO patriam in qua natus est exuere, nec ligeantiam

debitam ejurare possit.——No person can leave the country in which he was born, nor forswear the allegiance which is due.

NEMO plus juris in alium transferre potest quam ipse habet.——No person can transfer to another a greater power than he himself possesses.

NEMO potest esse hæres et dominus.——No one (at the same time) can be both heir and lord.

NEMO potest facere per alium quod per se non potest. ——No one can do an act by deputy which he cannot do of himself.

NEMO punitur pro alieno delicto.——No one is punishable for another's crime (or offence).

NEMO punitur sine injuria, facto seu defalta.——No man is punished except for some offence, wrong or default.

NEMO remotâ causâ, sed proximâ spectetur.——No one is concerned in a remote, but in an immediate cause.

NEMO reus nisi mens sit rea.——No one is guilty, unless he has a guilty intention.

NEMO tenebatur prodere se ipsum.——No man is bound to criminate himself.

NEMO tenetur informare qui nescit, sed quisquis scire quod informat.——No one is expected to instruct others upon a subject about which he is ignorant, but every one is supposed to be conversant with what he undertakes to explain.

NE nulles autres engynnes pur prendre ou destruire savaquire, leveres, ne conilles, nautre desduit des gentils, sur peine d'emprisonment d' un an.——No other engines, to take or destroy deer, hares, or rabbits, which nature has given to gentlemen (for the purpose of sport), under pain of a year's imprisonment.

NE per scripturam aliqua fiat in posterum dubitatio, jubemus non per signorum captiones et compendiosa enigmata ejusdem codicis textum conscribi; sed per literarum consequentiam explanari concedimus.——That no doubt may hereafter arise as to writing, we command that the text (or composition) of any such book be not written by cavilling notes, and condensed enigmas; but we permit them to be explained by the sequel (order or course) of the letters. *Vide note.*

NEQUE quid, neque quantum, neque quale, neque aliquid eorum quibus ens determinatur.——Neither what, nor how much, nor what kind, nor any of those things by which being is defined.

NEQUE quisquam agri modum certum, aut fines proprios habet; sed magistratus et principes, in annos singulos, gentibus, et cognationibus hominum qui una coierunt, quantum eis et quo loco visum est attribuunt agri, atque anno post alium transire cogunt.——Nor has any person a certain quantity of land, or any particular boundaries; but the magistrates and chiefs annually apportion such a quantity of land, and in such a situation, as they shall see fit, to the people, and kindred of those men, who have assembled together; and then oblige them to depart the year following.

NEQUE societas, neque collegium, neque hujusmodi corpus passim omnibus habere conceditur; nam et legibus et senatus consultis, et principalibus constitutionibus, ea res coercetur.——Nor is a society, or college, (or convention,) nor a body (or corporation) of this kind, allowed every where to meet on all occasions, for that matter is restrained both by the laws and decrees of the Senate, and the ordinances of the governors.

NEQUE testamentum recte factum, neque ullum aliud negotium recte gestum, postea furor interveniens perimit.——And lunacy subsequently recurring, does not break the will that was duly made; nor dissolve any proper previous contract.

NE quid detrimenti Respublica capiat.——" Lest the commonwealth receive an injury." This was the injunction given by the *Romans*, on investing the Dictator with supreme power.

NE quis invitus civitate mutetur, neve in civitate maneat invitus. Hæc sunt enim fundamenta firmissima nostræ libertatis, sui quemque juris et retinendi et dimittendi esse dominum.——Let no man against his will change his state (or country), nor let him, contrary to inclination, remain in the same. These are the most stable foundations of our liberty, that every one is lord in his own right of retaining, or renouncing his privilege (of citizenship).

NE quis plus donasse presumatur quam in donatione expresserit.——Lest any one be presumed to have given more than he expressed in the gift (or grant).

NE recipiatur.——"That it be not received." Words of caution given to a Law officer, not to receive the next proceeding of an opponent.

NE relessé pas.——Not released.

NE se volent acquitter.——They are unwilling to discharge.

NE te ipsum præcipites in 'discriminem.——Judge not too hastily.

NE unques accouplé.——Never married.

NE unques accouplé in loyal matrimonie.——He was not united in lawful wedlock.

NE unques executor.——He was not an executor.

NE unques receiver.——He was not a receiver.

NE unques seise que dower.——Never seised (or possessed) of dower.

NE unques seisie.——Never seised.

NEXI, obærati, et addicti.——Bound, overwhelmed in debt, and condemned. *Vide note.*

NIEFE.——A bondwoman. Vide note to "*Manumission.*"

NIENT cul'.——Not guilty.

NIENT culpable.——Not guilty.

NIENT de dire.——He says nothing (or makes default).

NIHIL ad rem accrevit.——He added nothing to the matter.

NIHIL aliud quam jus prosequendi in judicio quod sibi debetur.——Nothing further than the right of suing at law for what is due to him.

NIHIL debet.——He is not indebted.

NIHIL de fine quia pardonatur.——Nothing for a fine, because he is pardoned.

NIHIL de fine, quia remittitur per statutum.——Nothing on account of a fine, because it is remitted by statute.

NIHIL de jure facere potest quis quod vertat ad exhære-dationem domini sui.——A person cannot legally do any-thing which may tend to the disinheriting his lord.

NIHIL de re accrescit ei, qui nihil in re quando jus accres-ceret habet.——No advantage accrues to him who has no interest in the estate, when the right increased.

NIHIL dicit.——He says nothing.

NIHIL dicit ad rem.——He says nothing to the matter.

NIHIL habes in tenementis.——You have no interest in the tenements (or estates). *Vide note.*

NIHIL habes in terra.——You have no interest in the estate.

NIHIL habes in terra petita, quia bastardus.——You have no interest in the land sought after, because you are ille-gitimate.

NIHIL magis consentaneum est, quam ut iisdem modis res dissolvatur, quibus constituitur.——Nothing is more reasonable than that a thing should be dissolved by the same means by which it was framed.

NIHIL operantur quæ tacite insunt.——Those things therein tacitly comprised, are inefficacious.

NIHIL possumus contra veritatem.——We can do no-thing against truth.

NIHIL præscribitur, nisi quod possidetur.——Nothing is prescribed but what is possessed.

NIHIL profuerint signasse tabulas si mentem matrimonii non fuisse constabit. Nuptias, non concubitus, sed con-sensus, facit.——It was of no advantage to sign the contract, if it appear that the intent of marriage was wanting. Not cohabitation, but consent, ratifies the marriage.

NIHIL sanctius, nihil antiquius fuit; perinde ac si in ipso hoc numero, secreta quædam esset religio.——" Nothing (was considered) more sacred; nothing more venerable, as though some secret religion was (comprised) in this number." This is supposed to mean the number *Twelve. Vide note.*

NIHIL simile est idem.——Nothing which is like, is the same thing; similarity is not identity.

NIHIL simul inventum est et perfectum.——Nothing is at the same time invented, and also (made) perfect.

NIHIL tam conveniens est naturali æquitati unum quodque dissolvi eo ligamine, quo ligatum.——Nothing is so agreeable to natural justice, as that everything should be dissolved (or released) by the same tie by which it was bound.

NIHIL tam naturale quam quidlibet dissolvi eo modo quo ligatur.——Nothing is more natural than this, that anything may be dissolved in the same manner as the obligation is imposed.

NIL capiat per breve.——That he take nothing by the writ.

NIL debet.——" He owes nothing." The usual plea in an action of debt.

NIL debet in assumpsit.——He is not indebted in (the action of) assumpsit.

NIL dicit.——He says nothing.

NIL facit error nominis, cum de corpore constat.——An error in the name is of no consequence when it is consistent with the substance.

NIL habet in ballivia mea per quod summoneri potest. ——He possesses no property in my bailiwick by which he can be summoned.

NIL habuit in tenementis.——He had no (interest) in the tenements.

NISI ad hoc admissus sit.——Unless he be admitted to this.

NISI captus est per speciale preceptum nostrum, vel capitalis judiciarii nostri, vel pro morte hominis, vel pro foresta nostra, vel pro aliquo crimine, quare secundum consuetudinem *Angliæ* non sit replegiabilis.——Unless he be taken by our special order, or that of our chief justice: or for the death of a man; or trespassing on our forest, or for some other crime, which, according to the custom of *England*, is not bailable.——*Vide note.*

NISI convenissent in manum viri.——Except they come into the husband's possession.

NISI indictatus, vel appellatus fuit coram justiciariis, ultimis itinerantibus.——Unless he were indicted, or appealed before our Justices at their last circuit.

NISI per legale judicium parium suorum vel per legem terræ.——Unless by the lawful judgment of his peers (or equals), or by the law of the land.

NISI prius.——"Unless before." These words generally designate the proceedings before a Judge and Jury in a suit at law, either at, or after the sittings of a term, or upon the circuit. *Vide note.*

NISI si quid damno fatali contingit, vel vis major contingerit.——Unless if something occur by an utter loss, or by a greater force (destroying it).

NISI sub scriptura, aut specificatione trium testium quod actionem vellet persequi.——Unless (given) under the writing, or attestation of three witnesses, that he be willing to proceed in the action.

NOBILIORES natalibus, et honorum luce conspicuos, et patrimonio ditiores, perniciosum urbibus mercimonium exercere prohibemus.——We forbid those more noble by birth, and conspicuous by the lustre of their honors, and richer in estates, to exercise destructive traffic in cities. *Vide note.*

NOCEM sibi consciscere.——To do injury to himself.

Nocivus.——Injurious: hurtful.

Noctes et noctem de firma.——*Vide note.*

Nocturna diruptio alicujus habitaculi, vel ecclesiæ, etiam murorum portarumve burgi, ad feloniam perpetran-.dum.——The nightly breaking open of any dwelling or church, also of the walls or gates of a castle, for the purpose of committing a felony.

Nocumentorum aliud, injuriosum et damnosum, et aliud damnosum, et non injuriosum.——One treats of nuisances which are injurious and destructive; the other of those destructive, but not injurious.

Nolle prosequi.——"To be unwilling to proceed." Used in criminal cases when further proceedings are discontinued. *Vide note.*

Nolle prosequi ultra.——To be unwilling to proceed further.

Nolo eundum populum Imperatorem et portitorem esse terrarum.——I do not wish the same people to be (both) lords and servants of the lands.

Nomen collectivum.——A collective name.

Nomen generalissimum.——The most general name (or term).

Nomen hæredis, in prima investitura expressum, tantum ad descendentes ex corpore primi vassalli extenditur, et non ad collateres, nisi ex corpore primi vassalli, sive stipitis descendant.——The name of the heir mentioned in the first investiture extends only to the descendants from the body of the first vassal, and not the collateral kindred, unless they are the issue from the body of the first vassal, or from his stock or lineage.

Nomina sunt symbola rerum.——Names are the symbols of things.

Nominatim vel innominatim.——Named or unnamed.

Nomine districtionis.——In name (or in the manner) of a distress.

Nomine pœnæ.——By way of penalty (or punishment).

Nomotheta.——One who gave laws to a nation.

Non accrevit infra sex annos.——It did not accrue within six years.

Nonæ.——Nones. *Vide note.*

Non alienavit modo et forma.——He has not alienated in manner and form.

Non assumpsit infra sex annos.——He hath not undertook within six years.

Non assumpsit infra sex annos ante diem exitus brevis.——He did not undertake within six years before the day of issuing the writ.

Non assumpsit simul cum.——He did not undertake with another (person).

Non autem deperditæ dicuntur, si postea recuperantur.——But they cannot be said to be lost, if they are afterwards recovered.

Non cepit modo et forma, &c.——He did not take in manner and form, &c.

Non compos mentis.——Not of sound mind; in a state of lunacy.

Non compotes.——Idiots: madmen.

Non concubitus, sed consensus facit matrimonium.——Not the consummation, but the consent, ratifies the marriage.

Non constat.——It does not appear; it does not follow.

Non culpabilis.——Not guilty; (frequently abbreviated, as "*non culp*')."

Non culpavit.——He has not offended; he is not guilty.

Non culp' infra sex annos.——Not guilty within six years.

Non damnificatus.——Not damnified; not injured.

Non dat, quod non habet.——He does not give that which he does not possess.

Non debent reparare.——They ought not to repair.

Non debet fieri; sed factum valet.——It ought not to have been done; but (being done) it is efficacious.

Non decimando.——Not titheable.

Nom decipitur qui scit se decipi.——A man is not deceived when he knows himself to be deceived.

Non defuit illis operæ et laboris pretium ; semper enim ab ejusmodi judicio aliquid lucri sacerdotibus obveniebat.
——Nor was there wanting a recompense for their work and labor, as some profit always came to the priests at an ordeal of this kind. *Vide note.*

Non demisit.——He hath not demised or leased.

Non detinet.——He does not retain.

Non diutius remanebit in officio, &c., quam infra burgum prædictum, vel libertatem, et franchesias inde cum tota familia inhabitabit, &c.——He shall not remain longer in office or enjoy its liberties and franchises than during the time he shall live in .the said borough, with his whole family.

Non enim sufficit simpliciter proponere intentionem suam (by which word the count is meant) sic dicendo, " Peto tantam terram ut *jus meum,*" nisi sic illam fundaverit, quod doceat ad ipsum *jus* pertinere, et *per quam viam*, et per *quos gradus jus ad ipsum debeat descendere.*   Item cum agat per breve de recto ad utrumque jus consequendum (s. s.) tam jus possessionis quam proprietatis de seisina talis antecessoris : non sufficit, si dicat, quod talis antecessor suus fuit seisitus in dominico suo ut de libero tenemento tantum, " *vel in dominico suo ut de feodo tantum*" nisi doceat quod in dominico suo ut de feodo, quod sub se continet liberum tenementum, et totum jus possessionis ; dicat, et adjiciat, *et jure,* quod sub se continet *jus proprietatis.*——For it is not enough merely to set forth his charge (by which word the count is meant) by declaring, " I sue for so much land as *my right,*" unless he shall have so laid it (the count), that he can show that the *right* belongs to him, and by *what way,* and by what gradation the same ought to descend to him.   Also when he sues by writ of right, making use of either title (to wit), as well the right of possession, as the right of seisin of such an ancestor; it is not sufficient if he declare that such an ancestor was seised in his demesne as of a free tenement only, "*or only in his own demesne,*" as of fee, unless he show (or prove) that it is in his own demesne as of fee, which in itself comprises a free tenement and the whole right of possession; he should (also) say, and add thereto, *and by right,* which in itself comprises the right of property.

NON enim tam auctoritatis in disputando, rationis momenta quærenda sunt.——In every argument we should have respect more to the weight of reason, than of authority.

NON erit onerabilis et taxabilis pro peculiis, *Anglicè* stock: et quod artifex (*Anglicè, a tradesman*) est onerabilis, et taxabilis pro peculiis (*Anglicè,* stock) in arte.——He shall not be charged and taxable for his cattle, in *English* (his) stock; but an artificer (*in English, a tradesman*) is chargeable and rateable for his effects (in *English,* his stock) in trade.

NON est factum.——It *is* not his deed.

NON est inventus.——" He is not found." The return made by a sheriff when the defendant is not found in his county.

NON facias malum, ut inde fiat bonum.——We are not to do evil, in order that good may come from it.

NON-FEAZANCE.——Non-performance.

NON fecit vastum contra prohibitionem.——He did not commit waste contrary to the prohibition.

NON fuit culpabilis.——He was not guilty.

NON fuit electus major.——He was not elected mayor.

NON habeat potestatem alienandi tenementa.——He cannot possess the power of transferring the estates.

NON habuit ingressum nisi per *Gulielmum,* qui se in illud intrusit, et illud tenenti dimisit.——He had no entry except by *William,* who intruded therein himself, and demised it to the tenant.

NON habuit ingressum, nisi per intrusionem quam ipse fecit.——He had no entry, but by the intrusion which he (himself) made.

NON habuit ingressum, nisi post intrusionem quam *Gulielmus* in illud fecit.——He had no entry, except after the intrusion which *William* made therein.

NON hæc in fœdera veni.——I have not consented to these obligations.

NON inde est culpabilis, et pro bono et malo ponit se super patriam.——Therefore he is not guilty, and, whether to gain or lose, he puts himself upon the country.

NON infregit conventionem.——He has not broken the covenant (or agreement).

NON injuria sua propria absque tali causa.——Not by his own injury without a like cause.

NON in regno *Angliæ* providetur, vel est aliqua securitas major vel solemnior, per quam aliquis statum certiorem habere possit; neque ad statum suum verificandum aliquod solemnius testimonium producere, quam finem in curia domini regis levatum; qui quidem finis sic vocatur, eo quod finis et consummatio omnium placitorum esse debet; et hac de causa providebatur.——There is not in the realm of *England*, nor is there a greater or more solemn security provided by which any one can have a more certain estate; nor can he produce any evidence more solemn to verify his case, than a fine levied in the King's court: it is indeed called a *fine*, because it should be the end and consummation of all suits; and was provided for this purpose. *Vide note.*

NON jus, sed seisina facit stirpem.——It is not the right but seisin (or possession) that makes the stock (or root).

NON licet alicui de cætero, dare terram suam, alicui domui religiosæ, ita quod illam resumat tenendam de eadem domo; nec liceat alicui domui religiosæ terram alicujus sic accipere, quod tradat illam ei a quo ipsam recepit, tenendum. Si qui autem de cætero terram suam domui religiosæ sic dederit, ut super hoc convincatur, donum suum penitus cassetur, ut terra illo domino suo illius feodi incurratur.——It is not lawful that any one, from henceforth, give his estate to any religious house, so that he may resume the same, to hold of such house; nor is it lawful for any religious house so to receive the estate from any one, in order to redeliver it to the person from whom it was received, to be holden (of them). Also, if any person hereafter give his estate to a religious house, and he be thereof convicted, his gift shall be entirely void; and the estate be restored to the lord of the fee. *Vide note.*

Non liquet.——An answer made by the judges among the Romans when they were at a loss how to decide a cause. It signifies, "not clear."

Non misit breve.——He has not sent the writ.

Non nostrum tantas componere lites.——It is not our business to settle such disputes.

Non numero hæc judicantur, sed pondere.——These matters are not judged of by their number, but by their credit. *Vide note.*

Non nunc agitur de vectigalibus, non de sociorum injuriis: libertas, et anima nostra in dubio est.——The question is not at present as to our revenues, or the injuries done to our companions; our very life and liberty are at stake.

Non obstante aliquo statuto in contrarium.——Notwithstanding any statute to the contrary.

Non obstante veredicto.——Notwithstanding the verdict.

Non omittas.——"That you omit not." The name of a writ.

Non omittas capias ad respondendum.——That you omit not to take (the person) to answer.

Non omittas Ca. Sa.——That you fail not (to arrest the defendant) to make satisfaction.

Non omittas propter aliquam libertatem.——That you omit not on account of any liberty (or privilege).

Non omnium, quæ a majoribus nostris constituta sunt, ratio reddi potest; et ideo rationes earum, quæ constituuntur, inquiri non oportet: alioquin multa ex his, quæ certa sunt, subvertuntur.——A reason cannot be given for all those laws which have been made by our ancestors; and therefore the reasons for those (laws) which are in force ought not to be demanded, otherwise many of those which are established would be overthrown.

Non poterit Rex gratiam facere cum injuria et damno aliorum; quod enim alienum est dare non potest per suam gratiam.——The King cannot be bountiful to the injury and damage of other persons; for he cannot grant favors with what is not his own.

Non potest facere per se, sed potest per alium; non per directum, sed per obliquum. He is incapable to do this by himself, but may do it by another; not directly, but indirectly.

Non probe petat aliquid.——He seeks for nothing honestly.

Non pros'.——He will not prosecute. *Vide note.*

Non prosequitur breve, vel sectam.——He does not proceed with his writ or suit.

Non quo, sed quomodo.——Not by whom, but in what manner.

Non quod dictum est, sed quod factum est inspicitur.——It is not what is said that is regarded, but what is done.

Non sequitur.——It does not follow : it is not a matter of course: it is an unwarrantable conclusion.

Non sequitur clamorem suum.——He does not pursue his claim (or suit).

Non sine magna juris consultorum perturbatione.——Not without a great confusion among the lawyers.

Non sum informatus.——I am not informed: I am ignorant.

NON suspicio cujuslibet vani et meticulosi hominis; sed talis quæ possit cadere in virum constantem; talis enim debet esse metus, qui in se contineat vitæ periculum, aut corporis cruciatum.——Not a suspicion sufficient to affright a foolish and timid man, but such as might fall upon one who is resolute; for the fear should be of that description which carries in itself the loss of life or maim of body.

NON tenent insimul.——They do not jointly occupy.

NON tenuit.——He did not occupy (or hold).

NON ullam habebant episcopi auctoritatem præterea quam a rege acceptam referebant. Jus testamenti probandi non habebant; administrationis potestatem cuique delegare non poterant.——The Bishops had no authority except that which they derived (as) received from the King. They had not the power of proving a will; nor could they delegate the right of administration to any person.

NON usurpavit libertates, nec earam aliquam prædictam.——He did not seize the said liberties, nor any of them.

NON videtur concessum retinuisse, si quis ex præscripto minantis aliquid immutavit.——If a man changes any contract by an order enforced by threats, he does not appear to have retained the right which had been granted him.

NORMANNI chirographorum confectionem, cum crucibus aureis, aliisque signaculis sacris, in *Anglia* firmari solitam in ceram impressam mutant: modumque scribendi anglicum rejiciunt.——The *Normans* change the making up (or finishing) deeds with golden crosses, and other sacred marks (or signs), which was formerly the established custom in *England*, into a wax impression; and they reject the *English* manner of writing.

Nos *A. B.*, &c., debitam et festinam justitiam in hac parte fieri volumus, ut est justum.——We, *A. B.*, &c., are willing to do right and speedy justice in this matter, as it is equitable.

NOSAUNCE.——A nuisance.

NOSCITUR a sociis.——He is known by his companions: it is discoverable by what precedes and follows.

Nos divini juris rigorem moderantes.——We, moderating the rigor of the divine law.

NOSME.——A name.

NOTA est sponsio judicalis. "Spondesne quingentos, si meum sit?" "Spondeo, si tuum sit:" "Et tu quoque spondesne quingentos, ni tuum sit?" "Spondeo, ni meum sit." ——The legal undertaking is marked down. "Are you not responsible for five hundred if it be mine?" "I am if it be yours." "And are you not also responsible for five hundred, unless it be yours?" "I am so unless it be mine." *Vide note.*

NOTHUS.——An illegitimate child.

NOTITIA.——Notice.

NOVA constitutio futuris formam debet imponere, non præteritis.——The new constitution should enjoin a form in law for future transactions, but not for those already finished.

NOVÆ narrationes.——New counts.

NOVALE.——New land under cultivation.

NOVA promissio.——"A new promise." One sufficient to take the case out of the statute of limitations.

NOVEL assignment.——"A new assignment:" used in actions of trespass.

NOVEL disseisin.——Recent disseisin: a new entry and ouster.

NOVERINT universi per præsentes, &c., me remisse, relaxasse, et omnino de me, et hæredibus meis quietum clamasse totum jus, titulum, et clameum, quæ habui, et habeo, &c.——"Know all men by these presents, &c., that I have remised, released, and altogether quitted claim, from myself and my heirs, all my right, title and demand which I have had, and now have, &c." These words often occur in ancient releases of lands.

NOVIGILD.——The Saxon fine for an injury committed being of nine times the value of the article for which it compensates.

NOVI operis nunciatio.——To protest against a new work, as a building which might injure another's right.

NOVIS injuriis emersis nova constituere remedia.——To enact new remedies for offences recently arisen.

NOVISSIMA recopilacion.——A collection of Spanish law.

NOVITAS incognita disciplinæ, ut solita armis discerni jure terminarentur.——It was considered a strange innovation of manners, that those matters which were usually decided by arms should be determined by the law. *Vide note to "Jus Civile,"* &c.

NOVITER ad notitiam perventa.——It is newly come to notice.

NOVUM opus.——A new work.

NOXALIS actio.——An action brought against the owner of a slave, when the latter has committed some offence, or in any way damaged another.

NUCES colligere.——"To gather nuts." This was formerly one of the *base services* imposed by lords upon their inferior tenants during the feudal system. Vide *Paroch. Antiq.*

NUDA et firmata.——"Open and determined (or fixed)." These words were applied where some *earnest* or pledge was given, as a ring, &c.; or an oath taken.

NUDA et simplicia.——"Open and sincere." The Civilians applied these words, where a *promise* of espousals was formally made.

NUDA possessio.——"A naked possession:" a bare tenure without a shade of title: as that of a *squatter* (as generally termed) on the wild lands of America.

NUDA promissio.——A naked (or void) promise: one made without any consideration.

NUDUM pactum.——A bare (or naked) contract: one not binding in law.

NUDUM pactum ex quo non oritur actio.——A bare agreement (only), from which no action arises.

NUDUS executor.——A bare executor: one who has no interest in the goods.

NUL agard.——No award.

NUL assets ultra.——No further effects.

NUL autre verbe in nostre ley.——No other word in our law.

NUL disseisin.——A plea in *real* actions, that there was no disseisin; and is a species of the general issue.

NULLA bona habet.——He (or she) has no effects.

NULLA bona testatoris, nec propria.——(That he has) none of the testator's goods, nor of his own.

NULLA bona, ultra, &c.——No goods, besides, &c.

NULLA bona, vel catalla ad valorem, &c.——No goods, or chattels, to the value of, &c.

NULLA electio prælatorum (" sunt verba *Ingulphi*") erat merè libera, et canonica; sed omnes dignitates, tam episcorum, quam abbatum, per *annulum* et *baculum*, regis curia, pro sua complacentia conferebat. Penes clericos, et monachos fuit electio, sed electum a rege postulabant.——No election of the prelates was purely free, and canonical, (" are the words of *Ingulphus;*") but the King's court, in its benevolence, conferred all the dignities (or offices), as well those of the Bishops as the Abbots, by the *ring* and *crosier*. The election was in the power of the clergy and monks, but they required the person elected to be approved of by the King.

NULLÆ ripariæ defendantur de cætero, nisi illæ quæ fuerunt in defenso tempore *Henrici* Regis, avi nostri, et per eadem loca, et eosdem terminos, sicut esse consueverunt tempore suo. *Mag. Ch.*——No rivers shall henceforth be enclosed but such as were so in the time of King *Henry*, our ancestor, (and then) at such places, and by the like bounds, as they were accustomed to be in his time.

NULLA falsa doctrina est quæ non permisceat aliquid veri-tatis.——" No doctrine is so false, but it may be mixed up with some truth." Thus, the person who commits perjury may in *some* parts relate facts, which make his evidence the more dangerous.

NULLAM habeo talem personam in custodia mea, nec habui die impetrationis hujus brevis, vel unquam postea. ——I have not had any such person in my custody, nor had when the writ issued, nor at any time since.

NULLAM veritatem celabo, nec celari permittam, nec mur-drari.——I will not conceal the truth, nor permit it to be concealed nor stifled.

NULLA prædictarum misericordiarum ponatur, nisi per sacramenta proborum et legalium hominum de vicineto. Comites autem et barones non amercientur, nisi per pares suos; et non nisi modum delicti.——Nothing shall be sub-ject to such fines unless imposed by the oath of good and lawful men of the neighborhood. The Earls and Barons shall not be fined, except by their own peers or equals; and (then) only according to the nature of the offence.

NULLA tenementa manerii erunt partabilia, nec inter hæredes masculos nec femellas.——No manorial tenures shall be divisable, neither among the male or female heirs.

NULLA villa, nec liber homo distringatur facere pontes. ——That no vill, or any freeman be distrained to erect bridges.

NULLI liceat feudum vendere vel pignorare sine permis-sione illius domini.——It cannot be lawful for any one to sell or mortgage (his) fee (or estate) without the permission of his lord.

NULLI negabimus, nulli differemus justitiam.——We will not refuse or delay (to do) justice to any person. *Mag. Ch.*

NULLIS in bonis.——No property in the goods.

NULLIUS filius.——An illegitimate son.

NULLI vendemus, nulli negabimus, aut differemus rectum vel justitiam. *Mag. Ch.*——We neither sell, nor deny, nor delay to any person, equity or justice.

NULLUM arbitramentum.——"No award." A plea used by a defendant sued on an arbitration bond for not abiding by an award, "that there is no such award."

NULLUM commodum capere potest de injuria sua propria.——No man can take advantage of his own wrong.

NULLUM iniquum in jure præsumendum est.——Nothing unjust is to be presumed in the law.

NULLUM scutagium ponatur in regno nostro nisi per commune consilium regni nostri.——That no escuage (a fine paid to be excused performing Knights' service) be imposed in our realm, unless by the common council of the nation.

NULLUM simile est idem.——Nothing which is like is the same thing: similarity is not identity.

NULLUM tempus occurit regi.——"No time runs against (the claim of) the King." In the case of a prosecution for murder, theft, &c., no time prevents putting the criminal on his trial.

NULLUS bailivus de cætero ponat aliquem ad legem manifestam, nec ad juramentum simplice loquela sua, sine testibus fidelibus ad hoc inductis.——That no bailiff shall in future put a person upon his wager of battle, nor to his wager of law, on his own single complaint, without producing credible witnesses in support of the same. Vide *note*, and also note to " *Compurgatores.*"

NULLUS clericus, nisi causidicus.——"No clerk unless he be a lawyer." Most of the persons in the high offices of the law were formerly in holy orders.

NULLUS dicitur felo principalis, nisi actor, aut qui præsens est "*abettans*," aut auxilians actorem ad feloniam facere eandem.——No one is said to be the principal felon except he who actually commits the deed, or the person who is present, "*abetting,*" or assisting the actor to perpetrate the felony.

NULLUS episcopus vel archidiacanus de legibus episcopalibus amplius in hundredo placita teneant, nec causam quæ ad regimen animarum pertinet, ad judicium secularium hominum adducat; sed quicunque secundum episcopales leges, de quacunque causa vel culpa interpellatus fuerit, ad locum quem adhoc episcopus elegerit et nominaverit, veniat; ibique de causa sua respondeat; et non secundum hundret, sed secundum canones et episcopales leges, rectum Deo et episcopo suo faciat.——That no Bishop or Archdeacon, on account of his legal spiritualities, shall any longer hold pleas in the Hundred Court, nor hold any plea concerning the welfare of souls, which may lead to a judgment or sentence against laymen; but whosoever shall be summoned agreeably to the spiritual laws respecting any cause or offence, shall come to the place which the Bishop has nominated or appointed; where he shall answer to the complaint, not according to the laws of the Hundred Court, but according to the Canon and Episcopal laws, doing what is just in respect to God and to the Bishop.

NULLUS idoneus testis in re sua intelligitur.——No person is understood to testify properly in his own cause.

NULLUS justiciarius vel minister regis ingredi potest ad aliquod officium exercendum.——No justice or minister of the King can enter to exercise any official duty.

NULLUS liber homo, &c., disseiseitur de libero tenemento vel libertatibus, vel liberis consuetudinibus suis, &c.—— That no freeman be dispossessed of his freehold, or free customs, &c. Vide *Magna Charta.*

NULLUS liber homo aliquo modo destruatur nisi per legale judicium parium suorum, aut per legem terræ.—— That no freeman be in manner destroyed, unless by the lawful judgment of his equals, or by the law of the land. Vide *Magna Charta.*

NULLUS liber homo capiatur, vel imprisonetur, aut disseisietur de libero tenemento suo, vel libertatibus, vel liberis consuetudinibus suis, &c., nisi per legale judicium

parium suorum, vel per legem terræ.——That no freeman
shall be arrested or imprisoned, or turned out of his freehold, or lose his free customs, &c., unless by the legal judgment of his peers (or equals), or by the law of the land.
Vide *Magna Charta.*

Nullus liber homo capiatur, vel imprisonetur, aut ex-
ulet, aut aliquo alio modo destruatur, nisi per legale judicium parium suorum, vel per legem terræ.——That no
freeman be taken, or imprisoned, or exiled, or in any other
manner destroyed, unless by the lawful judgment of his
peers (or equals), or by the law of the land. Vide *Magna
Charta.*

Nullus liber homo disseisietur de libero tenemento suo,
nisi per legale judicium parium suorum, vel per legem terræ.——That no freeman shall be dispossessed of his freehold, unless by the lawful judgment of his peers (or equals),
or by the law of the land.

Nullus venit ex parte defendentis ad ostendum bona et
catella.——No person comes, on the part of the defendant,
to show the goods and chattels.

Nul tiel corporation.——No such corporation.

Nul tiel record.——"No such record." This is part of
the plaintiff's rejoinder, that there is no such record, where
the defendant alleges matter of record in bar of the plaintiff's action.

Nul tort.——"No wrong." A plea in a real action,
that *no wrong* was done, and is a species of the general issue.

Nul tort; nul disseisin.——No wrong; no dispossession.

Numerate pecunia.——Counted money.

Numerum liberorum finire, aut quidam ex agnatis necare,
flagitium habetur: plusque ibi boni mores valent, quam
alibi bonæ leges.——It was accounted an aggravated crime
to limit the number of children, or kill any of their kindred. So that good morals were more prevalent there than
good laws elsewhere.

NUMERUS certus pro incerto ponitur.——A certain number is used for one which is uncertain.

NUMMULARIUS.——A dealer in money; a banker.

NUNCIUS.——"A nuncio." A messenger or servant. The Pope's nuncio was termed "*Legatus Pontificis,*" a Legate of the Pontiff.

NUNC pro tunc.——"Now for that time." These words are frequently used in legal or equitable proceedings, where something is permitted to be done "*eo instanti,*" which should have been performed some time before.

NUNCUPARE.——Words spoken.

NUNDINÆ.——An English fair.

NUNNA.——"A Nun." A consecrated virgin, or woman, who, by vow, hath bound herself to a chaste life, in some place or company of other women devoted to the service of God by prayer, fasting, and such exercises. Saint *Jerome* says it is an *Egyptian* word.

NUNQ' seisie de dower, et de hoc, &c.——Never seised of dower, and of this, &c.

NUNQUAM custodia alicujus de jure alicui remanet, de quo habeatur suspicio, quod possit, vel velit aliquod jus in ipsa hæreditate clamare.——The custody (of a ward) never legally continues with a person, of whom there is entertained any suspicion that he could, or would, claim any right in the inheritance.

NUNQUAM indebitatus.——Never indebted.

NUPER obiit.——"She lately died." The name of a writ which lies for a sister co-heir, dispossessed by her co-parcener of lands, whereof their father, brother, or any common ancestor died seized in fee.

NUPTIÆ secundæ.——"Second nuptials." This was formerly sufficient ground to deprive a man from receiving holy orders. Nor could any benediction be pronounced, or any priest be present at such marriages.

NOTES TO N.

NAM QUI FACIT, &c.—As if a man gives another a power of attorney, or appoints him, verbally, to buy or sell goods, the act of such agent, within the authority given, is as valid as if done by the principal himself.

NAM QUI NON PROHIBET, &c.—If a man consciously, although silently, permits his servant in his business to act injuriously to the property of another, and he (the master) does not prevent it, the law will intend that the master commanded the thing to be done, and he will be answerable.

NATURALIS AFFECTIO.—Natural affection. This is a good consideration in a deed; and if a person, without expressing *any* consideration, covenants to stand seized to the use of his wife, child, brother, &c., here the *naming* of them to be of kin *implies* the consideration of natural affection, whereupon such a use will arise. Vide *Cart.* 138.

NEC IN PAPYRIS, &c.—History informs us that the first manufactured paper, of which we have any record, is the celebrated *Papyrus*, made of a species of reed, growing in Egypt, on the banks of the *Nile*, (*Papyrum nascitur in palustribus Egyptii, aut quiescentibus Nili aquis.* Vide *Plin.*) According to a passage in *Lucan*, which is likewise corroborated by other authorities, this paper was first manufactured at *Memphis*, but it has been a matter of much controversy to fix the precise period of its invention. The *Papyrus* formed, without doubt, at an early period, an important branch of commerce to the *Egyptians*, and was one of the manufactures carried on by that people at *Alexandria.* It obtained an increasing importance among the *Romans*, as literature became more valued and diffused; and in the *Augustan* age, it grew into very extensive demand. We are told in the reign of *Tiberius*, of a popular commotion, which arose in consequence of a scarcity of this valuable material. The commerce in *Papyrus* continued to flourish during a long period, the supply being generally less than the demand. It is said that its value was so great towards the end of the third century, that when *Firmus*, a rich and ambitious merchant, striving at empire, conquered for a brief period the city of *Alexandria*, he boasted that he had seized as much paper and size as would support his whole army.

Papyrus was much used in the time of St. *Jerome*, who wrote at the latter end of the fourth century. An article of so much importance in commerce, contributed largely to the revenues of the *Roman* Empire; and fresh imposts were laid on it under successive rulers, until the duty on its importation at length became oppressive. This was abolished by *Theodoric*, the first King of the *Goths*, in *Italy*, at the end of the fifth, or beginning of the sixth century. *Cassidorus* records the gracious act in the thirty-eighth letter of his eleventh book, in which he takes occasion to congratulate "the whole world on the repeal of an impost upon an article so essentially necessary to the human race," the general use of which, as *Pliny* remarks, "polishes and immortalizes man." The roots of the *Papyrus* are tortuous, the stem triangular, rising to the height of twenty feet, tapering gradually towards the extremity, which is surmounted by a flowering plume. It has been stated, in a note to "*Chartæ*," &c., that "the membranes of the *Papyrus*, being moistened with the muddy waters of the *Nile*, served instead of glue;" but *Bruce*, the celebrated traveller, affirms that there was no foundation for this supposition; and that the turbid fluid of the *Nile* has, in reality, no adhesive quality. This traveller made several pieces of *Papyrus* paper, both in *Abyssinia* and in *Egypt*, and fully ascertained that the saccharine juice, with which the plant is replete, causes the adhesion of the parts together; the water being only of use to promote the solution of the juice, and its equal diffusion over the whole. Sufficient evidence of the abundant use of the *Papyrus* is to be found in the fact that nearly eighteen hundred manuscripts, written on paper of this description, have been found in the ruins of *Herculaneum.*

Paper made of cotton entirely superseded the *Papyrus,* in the course of time, as being much more durable, and better calculated for all the purposes to which paper is ordinarily applied. This new substance was called *Charta bombycina.* It cannot, perhaps, be exactly ascertained when this manufacture was first introduced. *Montfaucon* fixes the time as being the end of the ninth, or beginning of the tenth century, a period when the scarcity of parchment, and the failure in the supply of *Papyrus,* called forth the powers of invention, to supply some adequate substitute. It was about this time that the dearth of writing materials caused the almost sacrilegious practice of erasing many valuable writings of ancient authors, that the parchment on which they were written might be again used. This is much to be deplored.

The paper produced from cotton is not so well adapted for writing upon, nor so durable, as that made from linen. It was probably not very long after the general use of cotton for paper, that linen rags were discovered to be a still better material.

NEMO AD REGEM, &c.—The Barons, at one time, under the Feudal system, engrossed to themselves the trials of all suits, and all offenders; and, no doubt, considerable injustice was often committed by them with impunity; to say nothing of the money which each suitor paid for the trial of his cause. Various expedients were, at different times, resorted to, in order to limit their jurisdiction. At first, the Sovereign endeavored to circumscribe the jurisdiction of the Barons, by contending that they ought to take cognizance *only* of small offences, reserving those of *greater* moment, under the appellation of "*Pleas* of the Crown, and *Royal* Causes," to be tried in the King's Courts. This, however, affected only the Barons of *inferior* note; the more powerful nobles scorned such a distinction; and not only claimed unlimited jurisdiction, but many of them obliged their Sovereigns to grant them "*Charters,*" conveying, or recognizing this privilege, in the most ample form. The attempt was, however, productive of some good consequences, and paved the way for more. It turned the attention of the people to a jurisdiction *distinct* from that of the Barons, whose vassals they were; it gave them a clear idea of the superiority which the Crown claimed over territorial Judges; and taught them, when oppressed by their *own* superior lord, to look up to the Sovereign as their protector. This facilitated the introduction of appeals from the Barons' judgments; and brought them under the review of the Royal Judges, and sometimes of the King himself, who sat with them, when he thought proper.

NEXI OBÆRATI ET ADDICTI.—By the law of the Twelve Tables, it was ordained, that insolvent debtors should be given (*addicerentur*) to their creditors, to be bound in fetters and cords (*compedibus et nervis*), whence such debtors were called "*Nexi obærati, et addicti.*" Debtors were often treated with great severity, though they did not entirely lose the rights of Freemen.

NIHIL HABES IN TENEMENTIS.—This was formerly a plea, pleaded in an action of debt, brought by a lessor against a lessee for years, or at will, without deed. Vide 2 *Lil. Abr.* 214. In debt for rent, upon an indenture of lease, *nil habuit in tenementis,* might not be pleaded, because it is an *estoppel;* and a general demurrer will serve.

NIHIL SANCTIUS.—The ancients were very superstitious about certain numbers:

"*Terna tibi hæc primum* triplici *diversa colore*
Licia circumdo; terque *hæc altaria circum*
Effigiem duco: numero *Deus impare gaudet.*"
Virg. *Eclog.* viii. 73.

"Around his waxen image first I wind
Three woollen fillets, of *three* colors joined;
Thrice bind around his *thrice*-devoted head,
Which round the sacred altar *thrice* is led:
Unequal numbers please the Gods."   *Dryd.*

NISI CAPTUS, &c.—The *Norman* Kings, and their followers, were passionately fond of hunting; and, soon after the Conquest, they appropriated considerable tracts of land for the preservation of deer, hares, and other game;
and enacted very severe and barbarous laws for their protection; and the
infringement of the forest laws was, at one time, considered so henious an
offence, that no bail could be taken for it. Some idea may be formed, from
various authors, of the mode of hunting adopted by the polished, or civilized
nations of antiquity; but we look in vain for any record of the manner in
which the inhabitants of *Britain*, at the period of *Julius Cæsar's* invasion,
followed the chase. However, the following note, as to the savage laws
which were anciently made respecting the game, and the manners of our ancestors relating to the sports of the field, may not be unacceptable.

In the time of the *Saxons*, there is every reason to believe that the pursuit of the stag, the wild boar, the wolf, &c., constituted the whole, or nearly
so, of the field diversions of that period. When *William* the Conqueror
gained the battle of *Hastings*, and became the iron-hearted ruler of the
country, he introduced, among a number of despotic regulations, laws for the
protection of beasts of the chase; some of which are amusing enough to us
at this period. It is true, the *Anglo-Saxons* enacted laws for the regulation
of the chase, but these were of a milder description than those which followed. *Canute*, the Dane, appears to have been the first that instituted the
Forest Laws, which were not only confirmed by *William* the *Norman*, but
rendered by him intolerably oppressive. This monarch is accused of having
devastated the southern part of *Hampshire*, and driving away the poor peas-
antry, in order to accommodate those animals which constituted the object
of the chase, to which *William* and his nobility were so passionately attached.

The game laws of this period were in strict unison with the tempers of
the framers, and characterized by all that overbearing ferocity of disposition,
which, it is said, so conspicuously distinguished *William* the First, and his immediate successors; and offer to our contemplation nothing in the shape of
humanity, or which could in any way harmonize with the better sense, and
better feelings of modern times. For instance, if a poor cottager happened
to be pestered with a wild boar, which, after ravaging, had made its lair in
his garden, he was *at liberty* to drive it away; yet, in so doing, he must be
careful not only to inflict no wound upon the animal, but, in ridding himself
of so unwelcome a visitor, the laws forbade his using any degree of violence.
Moreover, if, by any accident, a peasant happened to lame a stag, or a boar,
he was punished; if he was unfortunate enough to kill one of these animals,
though by mere accident, he was liable to have one of his eyes put out; or
he was otherwise miserably mutilated. In case a man killed one of these
beasts of chase, *wilfully*, he was liable to suffer death, by one of the laws of
King *Rufus*, made by his own authority. Under this law he seized many
great and noble personages, and confined them for years, without bringing them to trial, until he forced them to give up the greater part of their
estates.

William was usually accompanied by a large train of nobility and huntsmen, most of whom appeared to be equally attached to the chase; and on many of whom he lavished, with an unsparing hand, the most princely donations. To *Waleran*, his huntsman, he gave no less than fifteen manors in *Wiltshire*, eight in *Dorsetshire*, and several in *Hampshire;* and his name appears in the list of tenants *in capite* (in Domesday-book) in other counties. In the same book may also be found records of the extensive possessions of other huntsmen of *Groc, Godwin,* &c.

The following remarks may be found in an ancient writer: "In these days our nobility esteem the sports of hunting and hawking as the most honorable employments; the most exalted virtues; and these amusements they account the summit of human happiness. They prepare for a hunt with more trouble, anxiety and cost, than they would for a battle; and follow the beasts of the forest with more fury than they pursue their enemies; by being constantly engaged in this savage sport, they contract habits of barbarity; lose, in a great measure, their feelings of humanity; and become nearly as ferocious as the beasts they pursue. The husbandman is driven, together with his innocent flocks and herds, from his fertile fields, his meadows and pastures, that beasts may roam there in their stead. Should one of these potent and merciless sportsmen pass your door, place before him, in a moment, *all the refreshments* your habitation affords, or that can be *purchased* or *borrowed* in your neighborhood, that you may not be utterly ruined, or perchance, *accused of treason.*"

The *Clergy*, at this period, were the most *ardent* of those who followed the chase; and even *Ladies* caught the predominant passion, and eagerly partook of the sports of the field. The superior clergy, in the olden time, might be said to stand pre-eminent in respect to hunting and field sports: for we find that *Walterus*, Archbishop of *Canterbury*, (who was promoted to the See of *Rochester*, 1447,) neglected the duties of his sacred profession, and devoted himself entirely to field sports. At the age of *eighty*, he followed the chase with the alacrity of youth, and died at a much more advanced period. *Reginald Brian*, Bishop of *Worcester*, in 1352, was distinguished for his attachment to field sports; and in an epistle to the Bishop of Saint *David's*, he reminds him of a promise to send him *"six couples of hounds."* After declaring that "his heart languishes for their arrival," he adds, "Let them come, oh! reverend father! without delay; let my woods re-echo with the *music* of their cry, and the cheerful notes of the horn; and let the walls of my palace be decorated with the trophies of the chase." The cowl was frequently laid aside for the pleasures of the chase: and the monasteries produced some men remarkable at once for their *piety* and for their skill in the field. *William de Clowne*, who is celebrated as one of the most amiable Ecclesiastics of his time, and who filled the Abbacy of St. *Mary*, in *Leicestershire*, was equally distinguished for his excellent qualities as a *huntsman;* and, that his kennel might be well supplied with hounds, the King granted him the privilege of "holding a market for the *sole* purpose of dealing in dogs." There is every reason to believe that the *Anglo-Saxons* pursued the wolf, and wild boar, &c., *on foot:* horses, however, were used by the *Normans*, who appear to have surpassed their predecessors in the knowledge of the chase. They directed their attention, for the most part, to the pursuit of the stag, the roe-buck, fox, hare, &c., and did not depend altogether on their hounds, as they are said to have been excellent marksmen, and the object of the chase was frequently killed by an arrow.

In the laws of King *Edgar* is the following prohibition against *priests* following the chase: " *We lœrath that* preost *ne bestes huntœ ne hafecere ne tœflere; ac plegge on his bocum swa his hade gebirath*"—i. e. "We order that a *priest* be not a hunter, nor a hawker, nor gamester; but that he attend to his books, as becometh his order."

NISI PRIUS, &c.—Upon the trial of causes, especially in *London* and *West-*

minster, if now points arise, they are generally reported and published in books, called "*Nisi Prius Reports;*" but, as many of the verdicts given at those trials are set aside, either from the misdirection of the judges to the jury, on points of law; or where verdicts are obtained by surprise, or contrary to the weight of evidence; and from other causes, (as where the judges are dissatisfied with the verdict; &c.,) these *Nisi Prius* Reports are, by the *experienced* lawyer, held in as little estimation as they deserve. It is a question whether the student should even read such Reports, because he sometimes treasures up points of law which are very frequently overturned, or much shaken, when they are argued in a higher tribunal, where the judges have more time to examine the law of the cases, than they have in the hurry of a *Nisi Prius* trial.

NOBILIORES, NATALIBUS, &c.—The cities of *Italy* were the first who shook off the yoke of the insolent Barons; and established among themselves such a free and easy government, as would render property secure, and industry flourishing. About the beginning of the eleventh century, some of the *Italian* cities began to assume new privileges, and to unite themselves more closely. The great increase of wealth, which the *Crusades* to the Holy Wars brought into *Italy*, (which was a kind of rendezvous for the soldiers of the Cross,) caused a new fermentation and activity in the minds of the public; and, before the conclusion of the last Crusade, all the considerable cities in that country had either purchased, or extorted, large immunities from their Sovereigns. Vide *Murat. Antiq. Ital.* vol. 4. The great Barons in *England*, as well as throughout all *Europe*, many of whom had wasted large sums of money in the Holy Land, were eager to lay hold of a new expedient to raise money by the sale of "*Charters of Liberty;*" and, though the institutions of communities were as repugnant to their maxims of policy, as it was adverse to their power, they disregarded *remote* consequences, in order to obtain *present* relief. Notwithstanding the immense fortunes which were made, and the many honorable men who embarked in trade, many ages elapsed, after granting these Charters of Liberty, and Enfranchisements, before the deep-rooted prejudices against traffic subsided among the Baronial Landholders, (and it is far from being eradicated even at this present day;) nor could they be brought to consider the condition of a *merchant* to be respectable. If nothing else were wanting to convince us of this, the words of the text show with what contempt, men, who prided themselves on birth and dignity, considered those who followed commercial pursuits.

NOCTES, ET NOCTEM DE FIRMA.—In *Domesday* we often find with "*Tot noctes de firma*, or *firma tot noctium*," which is understood of entertainment of meat and drink for as many nights: for, in the time of the *English Saxons*, time was computed not by *days*, but *nights;* and so it continued until the time of *Henry* the First, as appears by his laws; and hence it is usual, especially in *England*, to say "*a seven night*," i. e. *septem noctes*, for a week.

NOLLE PROSEQUI.—This is an acknowledgment, or agreement, by the plaintiff, that he will *not further prosecute* his suit, as to the whole or a part of the cause of action; or where there are several defendants, against some or one of them; and it is in the nature of a *Retraxit*, operating as a release, or perpetual bar. Vide *Tidd's Pract. K. B.*, who cites *Cro. Car.* 239, 243. 2 *Roll's Abr.* 100. 8 *Co.* 58. *Cro. Jac.* 21, sed vide *Raym.* 559, where they may be *other* defendants.

NONÆ.—Nones, so called from their beginning the *ninth* day before the *Ides;* the seventh days of March, May, July, and October, and the fifth of all the other months. By the *Roman* account, the Nones in the aforesaid months are the six days next following the first day, or the Calends; and of others, the four days next after the first, according to these verses,

"Sex nonas, Maius, October, Julius et Mars,
Quatuor at reliqui," &c.

i. e. May, October, July and March have six nones, the others four.

Though the last of these days is properly called *Nones,* for the remainder is reckoned backwards, as distant from them, and accounted the third, fourth, or fifth *None.*

Non DEFUIT, &c.—At the ordeal by the "CORSNED," and probably at other kinds of ordeal, money was paid to the priests for their attendance and services.

Non IN REGNO, &c.—The levying of fines, and suffering recoveries, to enable landholders to alienate their estates, were encouraged by some of the *English* Kings, as having a tendency to check the overgrown power of the Barons; and has been considered one of the reasons why the *English,* at an early period, obtained considerable commerce. It also tended to weaken the unnatural and unjust law of primogeniture; as many landholders sold or mortgaged their estates, the produce of which was generally divided in an equitable manner.

Non LICET, &c.—Many persons, during the middle ages, had been in the habit of transferring their estates to Religious Houses, with the *understanding* of receiving them again, and holding them of such houses; by which means the services of the lords of the fee became impaired.

Non NUMERO, &c.—Evidence is not to be considered as the strongest on account of the *number* of the witnesses for either of the contending parties; but from their credibility, judging from all the circumstances of the case. The *Romans* understood this matter extremely well; and there are expressions to be found in their writings which are forcible, and very pertinent on this point. There is every reason to believe that our ancestors required the *jury* to come (*de viceneto*) from the neighborhood, in order that they might the better judge of the *credibility* of the witnesses produced by the litigating parties, and it was a great mark of their sagacity. In many instances, witnesses have been well clothed by one of the contending parties, in order to appear respectable before a court and jury, whose oath in their *own* neighborhood would not be credited on the most trifling occasion.

Non PROS'.—When a plaintiff on a trial at common law has not produced sufficient evidence to enable him to go to the jury; or where he has mistaken his proper form of action; or where he has no count in his declaration applicable to his case. In these instances the plaintiff usually elects to be "non-prossed;" as in that case he can begin *de novo* (or anew).

NOTA EST SPONSIO, &c.—Agreements of any magnitude were generally, in the Feudal ages, taken down by a third person, or notary. The *Romans* generally adopted the same course; but this extract very probably refers to the language of persons who were about to enter into a suit at law. Vide "*Sacramentum,*" and note.

NULLUS BAILIVUS.—When wager of law became prevalent, unprincipled debtors took advantage of *this mode* of paying their debts; but at length it became so *common,* that no wager of law was permitted to any one, unless he brought credible persons to vouch that they believed what was sworn to to be the fact. Vide note to "*Compurgatores.*"

O.

OB aliquam sui corporis turpitudinem.——"On account of some bodily uncleanness (or loathsome disease)." When a woman was separated from her husband on this account, she could not formerly claim her dower.

OB causam aliquam a re maritima ortam.——On account of some maritime business.

OB continentiam delicti.——On account of the moderation of the offence.

OBERATUS.——One indebted to another, and obliged to serve him till the debt is discharged.

OBIIT nuper.——He lately died.

OBITER.——By the way: loosely: unauthoritatively.

OBITER dicta.——Loose sayings: words spoken by the bye, or on the spur of the occasion.

OB jus quod in eos habet princeps, vel civitas.——On account of the right which the Emperor, or the State has therein.

OBLATI.——In feudal law, persons who placed themselves voluntarily under the authority of ecclesiastical institutions.

OBOLATA terræ.——A measure of land.

OBREPERE.——To creep upon.

OBRUAT illud male partum, male retentum, male gestum imperium.——Perish that thing which is wickedly acquired, disgracefully retained, and improperly used.

OBSTA principiis.——Oppose (adverse) beginnings.

OBTEMPER.——To obey.

OBTULIT se in propria persona.——He appeared in his own person.

OCCASIONE damnorum.——By reason of the damages.

OCCASIONE detentionis debiti.——By reason of detaining the debt.

OCCISION.——Killing. OCCYS.——Killed.

OCCUPAVIT.——An ancient writ of ejectment.

OCTO tales.——The name of an ancient writ which required the sheriff to make up a deficiency of jurors by summoning "eight such" as had been upon the first panel.

OEPS.——Use.

OFFA execrata.——"The execrable (or accursed) mouthful." A method of trial among the *Saxons* by swallowing, or endeavoring to swallow, a mouthful of bread. Vide note to "*Tenetur se purgare*," &c.

OFFICINA brevium.——The depository for writs.

OFFICINA gentium.——The storehouse of the nations. *Vide note.*

OLERON, laws of.——An ancient collection of maritime laws.

OLIM a prælatis, cum approbatione regis, et baronum, dicitur emanasse.——It is said to have formerly issued from the Prelates, with the consent of the King and the Barons.

OLIM in vita sua contradicere non potest.——Formerly in her lifetime, which cannot be disproved.

OLYMPIAS.——An Olympiad. *Vide note.*

OMISSIS omnibus aliis negotiis.——All other matters being omitted: all other proceedings being laid aside.

OMISSUS casus.——An omitted case: one unprovided for.

OMNE actum ab agentis intentione est judicandum.—— Every act is to be judged by the agent's intention.

OMNE æs alienum quod manente societate contractum est, de communi solvendum est, licet posteaquam societas distracta solutum sit: sed nec æs alienum, nisi quod ex quæstu pendebit veniet in rationem societatis. Jure societatis, per socium ære alieno, socius non obligatur; nisi in communem arcam pecuniæ versæ sunt.——Every debt which has been contracted during the continuance of a copartnership, must be paid off by the firm generally, not-withstanding it be afterwards dissolved; but no debt, except that which depends upon profit, shall come to the account of the firm. One partner is not bound by the law of copartnership for the debt of the other, unless the cash be appropriated to the common stock.

OMNE majus in se minus complectitur.——Every greater embraces in itself a lesser.

OMNE principale trahit ad se accessorium.——Every principal draws to itself its accessory.

OMNE privilegio clericali nudati, et coercioni fori secula-ris addicti.——Stripped of all benefit of clergy, and con-demned to the coercion of a lay jurisdiction. *Vide note.*

OMNES comites, et barones, et milites, et servientes, et universi liberi homines totius regni nostri prædicti, habe-ant et teneant se semper bene in armis, et in equis, ut decet et oportet, et sint semper prompti et bene parati ad servitium suum integrum, nobis explendum, et peragen-dum, cum opus fuerit; secundum quod nobis debent de feodis et tenentibus suis de jure facere, et sicut illis statui-mus per commune concilium totius regni nostri prædicti. ——That all Earls, and Barons, and Knights, and Free-men, and Tenants of our said realm, have and hold them-selves well equipped in arms and horses, as it becomes and behooves them; and that they be always ready and well prepared to perform and fulfil their entire services to us, as occasion requires, according to what they owe us in respect of their fees (or lands) and tenements, and as we have appointed to them at the general council of the whole of our said realm.

OMNES Comites et Barones, una voce responderunt, "QUOD NOLUINT LEGES ANGLIÆ MUTARI, QUÆ SECUSQUE, USITATÆ SUNT ET APPROBATÆ."——All the Earls and Barons unanimously answered, "THAT THEY WOULD NOT CHANGE THE ENGLISH LAWS, WHICH HAVE HITHERTO BEEN USED AND APPROVED."

OMNES homines ejusdem facultatis.——All persons of the same profession.

OMNES longo post se intervallo reliquerit.——He left them all at a great distance behind.

OMNES occupatores.——All the tenants.

OMNES prædia tenentes quotquot essent notæ melioris per totam *Angliam*, ejus homines facti sunt; et omnes se illi subdidere, ejusque facti sunt vassalli; ac ei fidelitatis juramenta præstiterunt se contra alios quoscunque illi fidos futuros.——All those holding farms of the better sort, throughout all *England*, became his subjects; and submitted themselves to him, and became his vassals; and took the oath of allegiance to him to be faithful to him against all other persons whomsoever.

OMNES res suas liberas et quietas haberet.——That he should have all his effects free and unmolested.

OMNIA bona et catalla, tam viva, quam mortua.——All his goods and chattels, as well animate as inanimate.

OMNIA catalla cedant defuncti; salvis uxori ipsius et pueris suis rationabilibus partibus suis.——They deliver up all the effects of the deceased, saving to his wife and children their just and reasonable proportions.

OMNIA libere et legaliter facienda.——All things should be done freely and legally.

OMNIA præsumuntur in odium spoliatoris.——Every thing is presumed against the despoiler.

OMNIA præsumuntur solemniter esse pacta.——All things are presumed to be solemnly done.

OMNIA quæ movent ad mortem sunt Deodanda.——All things which cause death while they are in motion become Deodands.

OMNIA quæ nunc vetustissima creduntur, nova fuere; et quod hodie exemplis tuemur, inter exempla erit.——All that we now imagine to be ancient, was at one time new; and what we respect as examples to-day, will, at some future time, be considered as precedents.

24

OMNIBUS ad quos præsentes literæ pervenerint, salutem.——To all to whom the present letters shall come, greeting.

OMNIBUS privilegiis militaribus gaudet.——He delights in all military privileges.

OMNIBUS qui reipublicæ præsunt etiam, atque etiam, mando, ut omnibus æquos se prebeant judices, perinde ac in judicali libro, *Saxonice* DOMBEC, scriptum habetur; nec quicquam formident, quin jus commune, *Saxonice* FOLC-RIGHTE, audacter libereque dicant.——Again, and again, I command, all who hold authority in the commonwealth, that they prove themselves upright Judges to all, like as it is written in the judicial book, called in *Saxon* DOMBEC; nor shall they fear anything; but boldly and freely declare the common law, called in *Saxon* FOLK-RIGHT.

OMNI exceptione majores.——Above all exception.

OMNI quoque corporali cruciatu semoto, inhumanum erat spoliatum fortunis suis in solidum damnare.——All corporeal torture being likewise removed, it was cruel to fine a person who was deprived of all his property.

OMNIS corporalis pœna, quamvis minima major est omni pœna pecuniari quamvis maxima.——Every bodily punishment, although ever so trifling, is heavier than the greatest pecuniary penalty.

OMNIS disseizina est transgressio; sed omnis trangressio non est disseizina.——Every disseisin is a trespass; but every trespass is not a disseisin.

OMNIS innovatio plus novitate perturbat quam utilitate prodest.——Every innovation injures more by its novelty than benefits by its utility.

OMNIS privatio præsupponit habitam.——Every privation is founded upon the supposition of previous enjoyment.

OMNIS prohibitio mandato equiparatur.——Every prohibition is equal to a command.

OMNIUM gravissima censetur vis facta ab incolis in patriam; subditis in regem; liberis in parentes; maritis in uxores; (et vice versa), servis in dominos; aut etiam ab homine in semet ipsum.——Of all others, *that* is considered the most grievous violence, which is committed by inhabitants against their own country; subjects against their king; children against their parents; and husbands against their wives: and so, on the other hand, by vassals against their lords; and even by man against himself.

OMNIUM rerum immunitas.——A privilege (or community) of everything.

ONERA emergentia et contigentia.——Growing and contingent charges.

ONERANDO pro rata proportionis.——"By charging according to the proportion (or quantity)." A writ that lies for a joint tenant, or tenant in common, who has been distrained upon for more rent than his proportion of the land amounts to. Vid. *Reg. Org.* 182.

ONERARI non debet.——He ought not to be charged.

ONUS probandi.——The obligation of proving.

OPORTET.——It is necessary.

OPTIMA evidentia rei prævalebit.——The best evidence of the matter will prevail (*or* be more efficacious).

OPTIMUS interpres rerum usus.——Custom (or use) is the best interpreter.

OPUSCULUM de jure occidendi, vendendi, et exponendi liberos apud veteres *Romanos.*——The small treatise, concerning the law of killing, selling and exposing children among the ancient *Romans.*

ORA.——A Saxon coin worth 16d.

ORARE.——To petition. ORATOR.——Petitioner.

ORDO excipiendi.——The order of pleading.

ORE tenus, et non aliter.——Verbally, and in no other manner.

ORFGILD.——Saxon payment for a beast.

ORFEURE.——A worker in gold.

ORIGO familiarum.——The genealogy of families.

OSTENSUR' Quare conspiratione inter eos præhabita, præ-fat *A* de, &c., indictari, et ipsum, ea occasione, capi, &c., falso et maliciose procuraverunt ad &c., et contra, &c.——It is to be shown why in the previous conspiracy between them, the said *A* of, &c., was indicted, and why, on that occasion, they falsely and maliciously caused him to be arrested, &c., to, &c., and against, &c.

OUSTER.——A dispossession.

OUSTERLEMAIN.——To remove the hand: liberty for an adult to demand his property from his guardian, &c.

OUTFANG-THIEF.——A thief caught beyond the bounds of the manor, and taken for trial to the lord's court.

OVERHERNISSA.——Sax. Contempt.

OVERSMAN.——Scotch for a mediator or umpire.

OVERT.——Open : public.

OWEL.——Equal.

OYER de records et de faits.——To hear the records and deeds.

OYER et terminer.——To hear and determine.

NOTES TO O.

OFFICINA GENTIUM.—This alludes to the prodigious swarms of Barbarians, which, from the beginning of the fourth, to the final extinction of the *Roman* power, poured into the *Roman* empire; these words, " *Officina gentium,*" gave rise to the opinion, that the countries whence they issued were *crowded* with inhabitants; and various theories have been formed by different authors to account for such an extraordinary degree of population among the wild forests of northern *Europe.* But if we consider, that although the countries possessed by the people who invaded the Empire were of vast extent, yet that the most considerable of the barbarous nations subsisted entirely by hunting or pasturage; in which state of society *large* tracts of land are required for maintaining a *few* inhabitants; and that all of them were strangers to the arts of industry, without which population cannot extend to any *great* degree, we must conclude that the countries could not be so populous in ancient times as they are at present.

OLYMPIAS.—An account of time among the *Greeks*, consisting of four complete years, having its name from the *Olympic* games, which were kept there in honor of *Jupiter Olympius*, near the city of *Olympia*, when they entered the names of the conquerors upon public records. The first *Olympiad* began in the year 3938 of the *Julian period*; about fifty years after the taking of *Troy*; 776 years before the birth of *Christ*; and twenty-four years before the founding of *Rome.* Ethelred, the *English Saxon* King, computed his reign by *Olympiads.*   :

OMNE PRIVILEGIO, &c.—The time cannot easily be fixed in which Ecclesiastics *first* began to claim exemption from the civil jurisdiction. It is certain that during the early and purest ages of the church they pretended to no such immunity. The authority of the civil magistrate extended to *all* persons, and to *all* causes. This fact has not only been established by *Protestant* authors, but is admitted by many *Roman Catholics* of eminence, and particularly by the writers in defence of the *Gallican* church. There are several original papers, published by *Muratori,* which show that in the ninth and tenth centuries causes of the greatest importance relating to Ecclesiastics were still determined by the civil judges. Vide *Antiq. Ital.* vol. v. *Dissert.* lxx. Ecclesiastics did not shake off all at once their subjection to the civil courts. The privilege was acquired slowly, and step by step. This exemption seems at first to have been merely an act of complaisance, flowing from veneration for their character. Thus, from a charter of *Charlemagne* in favor of the church of *Mons,* A. D. 796, that monarch directs his judges, if any differences should arise between the administrators of the revenues of the church, and any person whatever, not to summon the administrators to appear "*in mallo publico,*" but first of all to meet with them, and to endeavor to accommodate the difference in an amicable manner. This indulgence was in process of time improved into a *legal* exemption, which was founded on the same respect of the Laity for the clerical character and function. A remarkable instance of this occurs in a charter of *Frederic Barbarossa,* A. D. 1172, to the monastery of *Altenburg.* He grants them "*Judicium non tantum sanguinolentæ plagæ, sed vitæ et mortis*"—i. e. "Not only jurisdiction (to inflict) bloody wounds, but (also) of life and death." He prohibits any of the royal judges from disturbing their jurisdiction; and the reason which he gives for this ample concession is, "*Nam quorum Dei ex gratiâ, ratione divini ministerii onus leve est, et jugum suave, nos penitus nolumus illos oppressionis contumeliâ vel in manu laica fatigari*"—i. e. "For we wish that the burthen of those who, by God's grace, and by his divine purpose, minister to us should be light, and their yoke pleasant, and we particularly desire that they should not be vexed with the haughty language of oppression, or harassed by the hand of the Laity.". Vide *Mencken Script. Rer. Germ.* vol. iii. p. 1067.

P.

PACTA conventa.——Covenants (or conditions) agreed upon.

PACTUM est quod inter aliquos convenit.——That becomes an agreement between those who assented to it.

PAIS.——The country.

PALAM populo.——In presence of the people.

PALATIUM.——A Roman name for palace.

PALICEA.——Anciently, a paled fence.

PALMATA.——That quantity which may be held in the hand.

PANDECTS.——Digests of Roman law, being selections from the writings of ancient authors upon jurisprudence.

PANDOXARE.——To brew.

PANEL.——In England, the names of jurors which the sheriff returns for the trial of a cause, are written on an oblong scrip of parchment, and joined to the jury process.

PANNAGE.——That food which in England the swine feed upon in the forests; such, for instance, as *acorns*, etc.

PARAGE.——(In old English law.) Equality of blood or position. As equality between the elder son, with a large portion, and the younger son with a smaller one.

PARAPHERNALIA.——"The wife's apparel and ornaments." Those goods which a wife is entitled to, over and above her dower and jointure. *Vide note.*

PARATUM habeo.——I have him ready.

PARATUS est verificare per chartam et recordum.——He is ready to prove by the deed and record.

PARATUS sum verificare.——I am ready to prove.

PARAVAIL.——Tenant paravail: a tenant of the fee: or he who is the immediate tenant to one who holds of another; and he is called "*Tenant paravail,*" because it is presumed he hath profit, and *avail* of the land. 2 *Inst.* 296.

PARAVEREDUS.——(In old Continental law.) A post-horse furnished for the service of the king.

PARCELLA areæ: parcella pomarii.——Part of an area: parcel of an orchard.

PARCENER.——One who holds property with another. So called *parceners,* because they may be compelled, or wish to partition.

PARCHEMIN.——Parchment.

PARCUS.——An enclosed spot of land in which to confine stray cattle.

PARENTUM virtus dos est maxima.——The parents' virtue is the most valuable portion.

PARES.——Equals: freeholders.

PARES curiæ.——Equals (or freeholders) of the court.

PARES debent interesse investituræ feudi, et non alii.——
Freeholders should be present at the investiture of a fee,
and none others.

PARES regni.——Peers of the realm.

PARFOURNY.——Finished.

PARIA sint suffragia.——The votes may be equal.

PARICLA.——A duplicate.

PARI delicto.——In a similar offence (or crime).

PARI delicto, potior et defendens.——The defendant is
the better off in the like offence.

PARI materia.——In the like matter, or concern.

PARI passu.——By the same gradation.

PARI ratione.——By a similar reason.

PARIUM judicium.——Trial by jury.

PARLE-HILL, or PARLINGE-HILL.——Anciently, a hill on
which courts were held.

PARLIAMENTUM indoctum.——Entitled by Lord *Coke*,
"*the lack-learning Parliament.*"

PARNER.——To take.

PAROCHE.——A parish.

PAROLE.——Verbally.

PARS antecessoris.——The ancestor's share (or portion).

PARS enitia.——The portion of the eldest child.

PARS illa communis accrescit superstitibus de persona in
personam, usque ad ultimam superstitem.——The common part (or that part which is uncontrolled) accrues to
the survivors from one to another, even unto the last survivor.

PARS mulctæ regi, vel civitati; pars ipsi qui vindicatur,
vel propinquis ejus exsolvitur.——Part of this fine is paid
to the King, or to the State; part to him who is aggrieved,
or to his relations.

PARS pro toto.——A part for the whole.

PARS rationabilis.——" A reasonable part." Formerly when a husband endowed his wife with *personality* only, he said in the marriage ceremony, " with all my worldly goods, I thee endow ;" which entitled the wife to her thirds, or "*pars rationabilis*" of his personal estate.

PARTES finis nihil habuerint.——" The parties to the fine had no interest" (in the lands). Words of exception against the validity of a fine.

PARTICIPES criminis.——Partners in crime : accessories.

PARTITIONE facienda.——By making a division.

PARTUS sequitur ventrem.——The issue belongs to the mother.

PARUM cavisse videter.——He appears not to have taken care.

PARUM proficit scire quid fieri debet, si non cognoscas quomodo sit facturum.——It profits little to know what ought to be done, if one knows not how to do it.

PARVA proditio.——Petit treason.

PARVUM cape ad valentiam.——" The small (writ of) Cape to the value." The writ of *Cape* is a judicial writ, touching a plea of lands, &c., and is divisible into *Cape magnum*, and *Cape parvum*.

PARVUM servitium regis.——The King's petit serjeantry.

PASCHA.——Easter.

PASCUAGIUM.——Anciently, the pasturing of cattle.

PASSAGIUM.——A voyage.

PASTITIUM.——Ground used for the pasturing of cattle.

PASTURA.——" The pasture." Sometimes this word means the land itself, in opposition to "*herbagium*," the herbage, and "*pascium*," the food. Vide *Durnford* and *East's Reports*. Vide, also, *Co. Lit.* 4, *b*.

PATEAT universis per præsentis.——Know all men by these presents.

PATENS.——Lying open : plain : manifest.

PATER, credens filium suum esse mortuum, alterum instituit hæredem; filio domi redeunte hujus institutionis vis est nulla.——A father, believing that his son was dead, appointed another to be the heir; on the return of the son, this appointment is of no effect.

PATER cunctos filios adultos a se pellebat, præter unum quem hæredem sui juris relinquebat.——The father expelled all his adult sons, except one, whom he left heir of his right.

PATER est quem nuptiæ demonstrant.——He is the father whom the marriage designates (to be so).

PATER et mater defuncti, filio, non filiæ hæreditatem relinquent. Qui defunctus non filios sed filias reliquerit, ad eas omnis hæreditas pertineat.——The father and mother being dead, they leave the estate to the son, not to the daughter. A person dying, without sons, but leaving daughters, the whole estate belongs to them.

PATERFAMILIAS ob alterius culpam tenetur sive servi, sive liberi.——"The master of the family is held responsible for the misconduct of another, whether he be a slave or child." Alluding to the *Saxon* law.

PATERNICUM.——In old law, that part of a person's estate which came from the father's side.

PATER patriæ.——The Father of the country: as a President may be called.

PATRIA potestas in pietate debet, non in atrocitate consistere.——Paternal authority should consist in affection, not in barbarity.

PATRIMUS.——In civil law, a person whose father is living.

PATRINUS.——In ancient ecclesiastical law, a godfather.

PATROCINIUM.——(In Roman law.) Patronage.

PATRUELES.——Cousin-germans by the father's side.

PATRUUS.——A father's brother.

PAUMER.——To handle or touch with the hand.

PAUSARE.——To lay down.

PAX ecclesiæ.——The peace of the church.

PAX regia.——" The royal peace." The privilege of the King's peace. By the ancient *Saxon* constitution, this privilege extended from the King's palace gate to the distance of three miles, three furlongs, and a little more, even decending to feet, palms, and barley-corns.

PECCATA suos teneant auctores, nec ulterius progrediatur metus cuam reperiatur delictum.——Let offences bind the transgressors (only): nor let fear proceed further than the crime be discovered (to extend).

PECCATUM illud horribile, inter Christianos non nominandum.——That horrible crime, not (even) to be named amongst Christians.

PECCULATUS.——The act of embezzling public money.

PECHE.——An offence.

PECIA.——Anciently, a word used in records signifying *a piece;* as, *pecia terræ,* a piece of land.

PECULIARI pœna judicem puniunt; peculiari testes quorum fides judicem seduxit; peculiari denique et maxima auctorem ut homicidam.——They punish the judge by a peculiar punishment; the witnesses whose credit misled the judge; (finally), the author, as a person guilty of homicide, by a remarkable, and by the greatest punishment of all.

PECULIUM.——Stock: estate: property. So called *peculium* from the Latin word *Pecus,* that being the chief, and, in many cases, the only property, during the pastoral ages: wealth being estimated by the number of the flocks. Vide *Job,* i. v. 3.

PECULIUM castrense.——In Roman law, that species of property which the son has gained while in the camp, or during war.

PECUNIA.——Properly money; but anciently used for cattle; and sometimes for other property, as well as money. We often find in *Domesday,* " *Pastura ibidem ad* pecuniam *villæ* "—i. e. Pasture ground for the cattle of the village. *Cowell.*

PECUNIA signata.——Coin: money stamped. *Vide note.*

PECUNIA trajectitia.——Money taken over the sea. Maritime interest.

PECUS vagans, quod nullus petit, sequitur, vel advocat. ——Cattle straying, which no person seeks after, follows, or claims.

PEDAGIUM.——In European law, money given for journeying through the country, either on foot or horse.

PEDANEUS.——At the foot: an humble position.

PEDIS abscissio.——"Cutting off the foot." A punishment inflicted formerly on criminals in *England,* instead of death. Vide *L. L. Will. Congr.*

PEDIS possessio.——A foothold: a trespasser: what is termed "*a squatter.*"

PEE.——Foot.

PEINE forte et dure.——"A violent and severe punishment." *Formerly,* where a culprit refused to plead to the indictment, he was placed under heavy weights, and fed with bread and water till he died. This was called "*Peine forte et dure.*" It is reported, that to prevent his estates from being sequestered, a father once bore this dreadful punishment, rather than that his children should be involved in poverty.

PEISIBLE.——Peaceable.

PEISON.——Mast: nuts and other parts of trees.

PELLETUM.——A bullet.

PENDENTE bello.——While the war is raging.

PENDENTE brevi.——Pending the writ (or bill).

PENDENTE lite.——Whilst the contest (or suit) is depending.

PENDENTE placito.——Whilst the action (or plea) is depending.

PENES auctorem.——In the author's possession.

PENIG.——Sax. "A penny." An ancient current silver coin, though now made of copper. The *Saxons,* it is said, had no other sort of silver coin; five made one shilling, thirty made a mark, which was called "*mancus.*"

PENSA.——A weight.

PEONIA.——A spot of ground fifty feet front and one hundred feet deep.

PER æs et libram.——By money and weight. Vide note to "*Hæredes,*" &c.

PER annulum et baculum.——By the ring and staff, (or crosier.)

PER annum: per diem.——By the year: by the day.

PER antiquum relevium, et secundum consuetudinem antiquam feodorum.——By an ancient relief, and according to the ancient custom of fees.

PER attornatem suum venit hic in curiam, et fatetur se nolle ulterius prosequi; ideo consideratum est, quod defendens eat inde sine die.——He comes into court by his attorney, and confesses that he will not further prosecute; therefore it is considered that the defendant go thenceforth without day (or be discharged).

PER autre vie.——For the life of another.

PER breve de privato sigillo.——By writ of privy seal.

PER brevia nostra de cancellaria *Scotiæ.*——By our writ from the (court) of Chancery of *Scotland.*

PER bucellum deglutiendum abjuravit.——He abjured it by the ordeal of swallowing the mouthful. Vide note to "*Teneter se purgare,*" &c.

PER capita.——"By the heads or polls:" a division share and share alike.

PER catalla ad valentiam £10.——By chattels (or cattle) to the value of ten pounds.

PERCEPTURA.——A wear: a place prepared in a river with dams, &c., in which to take fish.

PER clerum et populum.——By the clergy and the people.

PER copiam rotulorum et secundum consuetudinem

mánerii.——By copy of court roll, and according to the custom of the manor.

PER corpus talis hominis.——By the body of such a man.

PER corruptam accomodationem.——By a corrupt agreement.

PER curiam non allocatur.——It is not mentioned by the court.

PER cursum Scaccarii.——By the course of the Exchequer.

PERCUTERE.——To strike.

PER defaltam.——By default.

PERDERE potest quis propter defaltam, lucrari vero nemo potest omnino absens.——Whoever might lose because of the default, yet no one can gain any thing who is absent.

PERDUELLIO.——Hostility against the state or king.

PER duellum.——By single combat. *Vide note,* and also note to "*Est autem magna,*" &c.

PER dures.——By imprisonment.

PEREGRINI.——Strangers: foreigners. *Vide note.*

PEREGRINOS et extraneos Anglicè.——In English, (as to) strangers and foreigners.

PER emendationem.——By an amendment.

PER fas et nefas.——"By wright and wrong." Endeavoring to perform an act by lawful or unlawful means.

PER formam doni.——By the manner of the gift (or grant).

PER fraudem et negligentiam.——By fraud and negligence.

PER guardianum.——By guardian.

PERICULOSUS.——Perilous.

PERIIT per cultellum.——He destroyed himself with a knife.

PER il suo contrario.——By its reverse, or opposite.

PER industriam, propter impotentiam, vel, propter privilegium.——By industry, because of incapacity, or on account of privilege.

PER infortunium.——By misfortune, or ill chance.

PER inquisitionem.——By an inquisition.

PER judicium coronotorum.——By the judgment of the coroners.

PER judicium recordatoris.——By the judgment of the recorder.

PER juramentum legalium hominum.——By the oath of good (or lawful) men.

PER juratum patriæ.——By a jury of the country.

PER juratum vicini.——By a jury of the neighborhood.

PERJURII pœna divina exitium; humana dedecus.—— "The crime of perjury is punished by heaven with perdition; by man, with disgrace." Part of the *Twelve Tables*.

PER laudamentum, sive judicium parium suorum.—— By an acquittal, or condemnation of his equals.

PER legale judicium.——By a legal judgment.

PER legem apparentem.——By a known law.

PER magnum servitium.——(Tenancy) by grand serjeautry.

PER manifestam legem.——By clear (or manifest) law. Vide note to " *Nullus balivus*."

PER meditatatem linguæ.——" By a moiety of speech:" alluding to the trial of an alien, by a jury of natives and foreigners. Vide note to " *Medietas linguæ*."

PER metas et bundas.——By metes and bounds.

PER minas.——By threats.

PER multos annos retroactos.——For many years past.

PER my et per tout.——In part and entirely.

PERNANCY.——Taking: as taking the rents of an estate.

PER nomen generalissimum.——By the most general name.

PER omnia terras et catalla.——By all the lands and goods.

PER ostia aperta.——Through open doors.

PER pais.——By the country.

PER pares curtis.——By the peers (or equals) of the court.

PERPETUI usus causa.——On account of the continual occupancy.

PER proprium visum et auditum, vel per verba patrum suorum; et per talia quibus fidem teneantur habere ut propria.——On a proper view and hearing, or by the testimony of their fathers; and by such other means whereby truth can be obtained, they are decreed to enjoy this property as their own. *Vide note.*

PER quæ servitia ignorant.——By what services they know not.

PER querulam.——By complaint.

PERQUIRERE.——To gain by an act of one's own.

PERQUISITIO.——A purchase: self-acquirement.

PER quod actio accrevit.——Whereby an action hath accrued.

PER quod consortium amisit.——Whereby he lost her society.

PER quod consortium, vel servitium amisit.——Whereby he lost her society or service.

PER quod fuit impeditus in viagio.——Whereby he was hindered in his voyage.

PER quod proficium communiæ suæ habere non potuit. ——By which he could not have the benefit of his common.

PER rationabilem partem.——By a reasonable share.

PER rationabile pretium et extentum.——By a reasonable price and extent.

PER rationabile pretium et extentum habendum.——To take at a reasonable price and extent.

PER responsalem loco suo ad lucrandum vel perdendum; verum opportet eum præsentem in curia qui responsalem ita in loco suo ponit. Et nota differentiam inter responsalem et attornatum.——By a person responsibly (appointed) in his stead to gain or lose; but it is necessary that this person be in court who thus deputes the person appointed. And mark the difference between an appointee and an attorney.

PER sacramentum legale.——By a lawful oath.

PER saltum.——" By a leap." Passing over intermediate objects.

PER scelera semper sceleribus certum est iter.——The sure road to crime is always through iniquity.

PER sectam sufficientem.——By a suitable action.

PERSEQUI.——To pursue.

PER servitium militare.——By knight's service.

PER se, vel deputatum suum.——By himself or his deputy.

PER solam occupationem dominium prædæ hostibus acquiri.——By possession alone the property of the spoils are acquired by the enemy.

PERSONÆ conjunctio æquiparatur interesse proprio.—— The joinder of persons is equalled (by regard) to their personal interests.

PERSONA ecclesiæ.——A parson or rector of a church.

PERSONA impersonata.——A parson impropriate.

PERSONA mixta.——" A secular monk." Probably, also, meaning a person not in holy orders, possessing a Lay impropriation.

PERSONA proposita.——The person intended.

PERSONA standi in judicio.——Capacity to sue.

PERSONE.——A parson.

PER stirpes.——By stock: by lineage.

PER talem personam alicui personæ vel aliquibus personis quibuscunque, sic ut prefertur venditi, vel in burgo prædicto veniendi induct', &c.——By the same person to any other person or persons whomsoever, so that it be offered for sale or brought into the said borough, &c.

PERSPICUA vera non sunt probanda.——" Plain truths do not require to be proved."

PER terminum 12 annorum, si tam diu vixerit; et si

obierit infra predictum terminum, tunc, &c.——For the term of twelve years, if he should so long live; and if he die within the said term, then, &c.

PER testamentum.——"By will." One of the ancient modes of freeing a slave. *Vide note.*

PER testatorem nominati.——Those appointed by the testator.

PER testatos nominatos in obligatione.——By the witnesses named in the bond.

PER testem idoneum: per duellum: vel per chartam.—— By a sufficient witness: by single combat: or by the deed. Vide note to "*Est autem magna,*" &c.

PER testes, et per patriam.——By witnesses, and by the country.

PERTICA.——A perch.

PER titulum doni, vel alterius donationis.——By right of the gift, or of some other donation.

PER totum curiam.——By the whole court.

PER totum regnum et potestatem nostram in terra, et potestate nostra.——By the whole kingdom and our power therein, and by our authority.

PER totum tempus prædictum.——Through the whole of the said time.

PER totum trienium.——For three whole years.

PER tout, et non per my.——By the whole, and not by a part.

PER transgressum districtionis.——By a removal of the distress.

PER universitatem.——In general.

PER usucaptionem.——By possession: by taking the profits.

PER vadium.——By gage.

PER verba de futuro.——By words of future accepta-tion.

PER verba de præsenti.——By words of the present time.

PER viam ellemosynæ.——By way of charity, or alms.

PER vindictam.——One of the ancient modes of freeing a slave. *Vide note.*

PER vinum delapsis capitalis pœna remittitur.——The capital punishment is remitted to those overcome by wine.

PERVISE.——The porch of a church.

PER visum Ecclesiæ.——Under the inspection of the Church.

PER visum juratorum.——By a view of the jury.

PER vitium scriptoris.——Through the fault of the writer (or transcriber).

PERTE.——Part.

PESCHER.——To fish.

PESTOUR.——A baker.

PETERE.——To pray: in civil law, a word made use of in proceedings to recover anything.

PETIT cape.——"Small cape." A writ against a person in possession of lands, to answer for a default.

PETIT serjeanty.——A right to hold lands, upon the condition of rendering annually to the king some imple-ment of war, however small: as a *flag*, a sword, a lance. The Dukes of Wellington and Marlborough held their estates by this tenure, each sending annually to Windsor Castle a small flag, to be there deposited.

PETITIO consilii.——Application for leave to imparle.

PETITION de droit.——A petition of right.

PETITIO principii.——A begging the question.

PETIT judicium.——He prays judgment.

PETO.——I demand.

PETUNT judicium, si curia ulterius vult.——They pray judgment, if the court will proceed further.

PICCAGE.——To pick.

PIE poudre.——The pie powder court. This is a court held at some of the great fairs, in *England*, where justice is administered *instantly*, even whilst the *dust is fresh upon the feet* of the suitors. *Vide note.*

PIGHTEL.——A small enclosure of land.

PIGNORI acceptum.——A bailment by way of pledge.

PIGNORIS appellatione eam proprie rem contineri dicimus quæ simul etiam traditur creditori. At eam, quæ sine traditione nuda conventione tenetur, proprie *hypothecæ* appellatione contineri dicimus.——We correctly call by the term of pledge, such property as is at the same time delivered to the creditor. But we properly designate by the term *mortgage*, that property which is held by bare covenant, without a delivery.

PIGNUS.——A pledge : a security.

PILLERIE, or pilleurie.——Plunder : extortion.

PILLEUR.——A plunderer.

PILORI.——A pillory.

PINNAS bibere.——To drink to the pin (or mark). *Vide note.*

PIRATI in alto mare, more bellico, dictas naves aggressi sunt, et per vim et violentiam ceperunt.——Pirates on the high sea, in a hostile manner, attacked the said ships, and by force and violence captured them.

PIX.——A means of trying the purity of coin.

PLACITA.——Pleas.

PLACITATOR.——A pleader : a counsel. *Vide note.*

PLACITO debiti.——In a plea of debt.

PLAGA.——A wound.

PLAGIARII.——Stealers of men and children; or those who enticed them away.

PLAGIUM.——Man-stealing; or enticing away men and children.

PLAID.——Anciently, a convention of the chief men of a kingdom.

PLATEA.——An open plot of land.

PLEBISCITA.——Laws, decrees, or orders, made by the joint consent of the *Roman* people.

PLEGII ad prosequendum.——Pledges to prosecute.

PLEGIOS de retorno habendo.——Pledges to obtain a return.

PLEIDEOIR.——One who pleads.

PLENA curia illud recordari facias.——That you cause it to be recorded in full court.

PLENA fides.——Full credit.

PLENA probatio.——" Full proof : sufficient evidence " —in opposition to " semi-probatio."

PLENA seizina.——Full possession.

PLENARIA seizina.——Full possession, or seisin.

PLENE administravit.——He (or she) has fully administered.

PLENE administravit, præter, &c.——He has fully administered, except, &c.

PLENE administravit, præter de bonis propriis.——He fully administered, except as to his own goods.

PLENUM dominium.——A fee simple : a full ownership.

PLENUM dominium in omnibus terris.——A complete seignorship in all the lands.

PLEYN.——Full.

PLEYNTE.——A plaint.

PLURIES.——" Very often."   Also the name of a third writ, after two have issued against a defendant.

PLURIME ad rem loquitur.——He speaks very much to the purpose.

PLURIS est oculatus testis unus quam auriti decem.—— One eye-witness is of more weight, than ten who give hearsay evidence.

PLURIES quod averia elongata sunt.——As often as the cattle are eloigned.

PLUS possessionis et multum juris.——More of possession, and much of right.

PLUS valet unus oculatus testis quam auriti decem.—— " One eye-witness is worth more than ten who speak from nearsay."

PLUSORS.——Many.

POER.——Authority.

PŒNA viginti aureorum statuitur adversus eum qui contra annonam fecerit; societatemve coieret quo annona carior fiat.——A penalty of twenty pieces of gold is inflicted on him who shall do anything injurious to the market; or who joins a society whereby the market price may become higher.

POI.——A little.

POINDING.——"Taking goods in execution, or by way of distress." This is a *Scotch* term, and defined to be the diligence (process) which the law has devised for transferring the property of the debtor to the creditor, in. payment of debts.

POLLARDS.——A small coin.

POMARIUM.——An orchard.

PONE.——"Put." The name of a writ or process in replevin.

PONE per vadios et salvos plegios.——Put by gages and safe pledges.

PONTAGE.——Toll for crossing a bridge.

PORRO autem quum maritus sine lite et contraversia sedem incoluerit, eam conjux et proles sine contraversia possidento; si qua lis fuerit illata videntem eam, hæredes ad se (perinde atque is vivus) accipiunto.——Moreover, when the husband, without suit or controversy, shall occupy a place, let the wife and children inhabit it without dispute: if there be any action brought concerning the same, let the heirs defend it (as if he were living).

PORTGREVE.——The highest officer of a port.

PORTMOTE.——An assembly.

PORTORIUM.——In ancient law. A tax taken at the city gates to defray the cost of repairing the roads.

PORTUS.——In civil law. A protected station, or warehouse, in which imported goods are placed, and from whence those to be exported are removed.

POSITIVI juris.——Of positive law or right.

POSSE.——This is the infinitive mood, but used substantively to signify a possibility—such a thing is said to be "*in posse,*" i. e. such a thing may *possibly be;* but of a thing *in being,* we say it is "*in esse.*"

POSSE COMITATUS.——"The power of the county," which the sheriff is authorized to call out, whenever an opposition is made to his writ, or to the execution of justice.

POSSESSIO bonorum.——The possession of goods.

POSSESSIO fratris facit sororem esse hæredem.——The brother's possession makes the sister the heiress.

POSSESSIONES in jurisdictionalibus non aliter apprehendi posse, quam per attournances et avirances, ut loqui solent; cum vassallus, ejurato prioris domini obsequio et fide, novo se sacramento novo item domino acquirenti obstringebat; idque jussu auctoris.——Possessions cannot lawfully be taken in any other manner than by attornments and averments, as they used to call them; for the vassal having renounced homage and fealty to his former lord, also bound himself by a new oath to the present lord, who purchased the seignory, which was done by the direction of the first proprietor. *Vide note.*

POSSESSIO quæ nuda est omino, et sine aliqua investitura, quæ dicitur intrusio.——A possession, which is altogether naked, and without any investiture, is called an intrusion.

POSSE vicinum impediri, ne in suo solo, sine alia causa suaque evidenti utilitate munimentum nobis proquinquum extruat; aut aliud quid faciat, unde justa formido periculi oriatur.——A neighbor can be prevented from raising upon his own ground any building close to another's unless from evident utility; nor can he do anything by which reasonable danger may be apprehended.

POSSUMUS.——To be able.

POSTEA.——"Afterwards." The name given to the endorsement of the verdict made on the record.

POSTEA continuato processu præd' inter partes præd' per jur' ponit inde inter eos in respectu huic usq. ad tunc diem,

scil' in octab. Sancti Trinitat' nisi justiciar' prius, &c.———
Afterwards by continuing the said process between the
parties aforesaid by oath therefor taken between them in
this respect, until which day, viz., in eight days of the Holy
Trinity, unless the judges first, &c.

POSTEA convertit.———He afterwards converted it (or ap-
applied it to his own use).

POST funera natus.———A posthumous child.

POSTLIMINIUM.———A reprisal; a recovery.

POSTLIMINIUM fingit eum qui captus est, in civitate semper fuisse.———The return (or reprisal) supposes the person
who was captured (or seized) to have always been in the
state (city or country).

POST litem motam.———After the suit is moved (in
court).

POST nati.———After-born.

POST obit bond.———After death.

POST regulam peremptoriam quatuor dies ad placitandam,
non est recto sed ex gratia, curia semper existens, interro-
gata quando dies appunctuatur ut curiæ placet.———After a
peremptory rule the four days (are given) to plead, not (as
a matter) of right, but of favor; the court sitting, from
time to time, on being asked, appoints as many days as he
pleases.

POST terminum.———After the term.

POSTULATA.———" Things required." Things demanded
before the main argument be entered upon.

POST ultimam continuationem.———After the last coninu-
ance.

POST ultimum tempus legitimum muliuribus pariendi
constitutum.———After the farthest legal period allowed for
women to have issue.

POST urnam permittitur accusatori, ac reo, ut ex illo
numero rejiciant quos putaverint sibi, aut inimicos, aut ex
aliqua re incommodos fore.———After (the names of the
judges were deposited) in the urn, the accuser and the ac-

cused were permitted to reject from that number those whom they should either suspect to be enemies, or who on any account might be unfriendly.

POTENTIA non est nisi ad bonum.——Power is not conferred, but for the public good.

POTENTIA proquinqua.——A probable possibility : an interest near at hand.

POTENTIA remotissma.——A most improbable possibility : an interest very remote.

POTIOR est conditio defendentus.——The defendant's condition is the more preferable.

POUR autre vie.——For another's life.

POUR mon compte seul.——On my account alone.

POUR seisir terres.——A power possessed by the king to seize the dower of a tenant's widow, if she married without his permission.

POURPARTY.——Division.

POURPRESTURE.——The unlawful appropriation of anything which ought to be for the benefit of all, as enclosing the public street, or building upon it, etc.

POUR tout ce qui concerne l'ordre (judicare, or form of action) ou doit suivre l'usage de lieu on l'on plainte ; mais pour ce qui est de la decision du droit (on the merits) on doi suivre le regla generale lex loix du lien ou le contrat a eté passé ex consuetudine ejus regionis in quo negotium gestum.——In everything relating to the form of the action we must observe the custom of the place where the action is pending ; but in all those things which concern the merits, we must follow the general laws of the place where the contract was made, according to the custom of the country where the transaction occurred.

POURVEYOR.——A person in the employ of royal or great families who provided articles of food for their use.

POVERS.——Indigent persons.

PRÆCIPE.——Command.

PRÆCIPE in capite.——A writ of Right, so called.

PRÆCIPE, quia dominus remisit curiam.——Command, as the lord has adjourned the court.

PRÆCIPE quod reddat locum tenens, &c.——Command that the deputy restore, &c.

PRÆCO.——A herald.

PRÆCLUDI non.——Not to be stopped, or debarred.

PRÆDIA libera.——Free farms: not subject to services. *Vide note.*

PRÆDIA volantia.——Estates quickly passing away.

PRÆDICTUS defendens capiatur.——That the said defendant be arrested.

PRÆDIUM Domini Regis est directum Dominicum, cujus nullus author est nisi Deus.——The estate of the Lord the King is a direct (or absolute) sovereignty, of which no one is the author except God.

PRÆFATUS.——Aforesaid; a word often used in entries, sometimes written *præfat* or *p'fat'.*

PRÆMISSA.——Premises.

PRÆNOMEN.——First name.

PRÆFECTUS urbis.——The Prefect (or Governor) of the city.

PRÆMUNIRE.——" To forewarn." A writ so called, by which certain offenders are put out of the protection of the law. *Vide note.*

PRÆMUNIRE execrabile illud statutum.——That execrable statute *præmunire.*

PRÆPOSITUS ad quartum circiter septimanam frequentem populi concionem celebrato; cuique just dicito, litesque singulas dirimito.——Let the sheriff, about every fourth week, hold a full assembly of the people: let him expound the law to every one, and decide their several suits.

PRÆSCRIPTIO annalis, quæ currit adversus actorem, si de homicida ei non constet intra annum a cæde facta; nec quenquam interea arguet et accusat.——The annual prescription which runs against a prosecutor, if he do not know of the murder within a year after it is committed, nor in the mean time accuse and impeach any person.

PRÆSENTIA corporis tollit errorem nominis; veritas nominis tollit errorem demonstrationis.——The presence of the person removes any error of the name; and the truth of the name removes any error in the proof.

PRÆSIDIUM.——A protection.

PRÆSUMITUR.——The presumption is.

PRÆSUMPTIO juris.——A presumption of law.

PRÆSTARE tenetur quodcunque damnum obveniens in mari.——He is bound to pay whatever loss (or damage) happens upon the sea.

PRÆTEREA autem concedo ut in propriis quisque tam in agris, et in sylvis, excitet, agitetque feras.——But I also grant that every person, in his own fields and woods, may start and chase wild animals.

PRÆTER scriptionem et collectionem.——Besides the writing and collecting.

PRÆTOR.——A Magistrate : a Judge among the ancient *Romans*. *Vide note*.

PRÆTOR fidei commissarius.——The Judge, among the ancient *Romans*, who compelled the performance of trusts; and who appears to have had, in this respect, a similar office to our Chancellors.

PRÆTORITORUM memoria eventorum.——The remembrance of past events.

PRATUM.——Meadow.

PRAVA consuetudo.——An illegal custom.

PRECARIÆ, or PRECES.——In old law. Day's labor required from the tenants of some estates for the lord during harvest time.

PRECE partium.——"At the request of the parties." As where the suit is continued on the prayer or agreement of the plaintiff and defendant.

PREDIAL.——Whatever comes from the land.

PRENDRE.——To take.

PRES.——Near.

PRESTATION.——A payment.

PRESUMPTIO juris, et de jure.——Presumption of right, and according to law.

PRETIUM affectionis.——The reward of affection.

PREUE.——Good.

PRIMÆ impressionis.——On the first impression or view : a novelty.

PRIMAGE.——A sum of money paid to the captain of a ship by the owner of the goods, over and above the freightage for his trouble concerning them.

PRIMARIÆ ecclesiæ.——To the Diocesan church : also the first fruits belonging to the church.

PRIMARIÆ preces.——The principal requests.

PRIMA seisina.——The original seisin, or possession.

PRIMA tonsura.——The first crop or shear.

PRIMER fine.——The first fine.

PRIMITIÆ.——First fruits.

PRIMOGENITURA.——"Primogeniture." The title of an elder son or brother, in *right of his birth.* The reason of which Lord *Coke* curiously says is, "*qui prior est tempore, potior est jure;*" "who is first in point of time, is superior in point of right;" affirming, moreover, that in King *Alfred's* time, Knights' Fees descended to the eldest son, *because,* by the division of such fees between males, the defence of the realm would be endangered.

PRIMUM, coram comitibus et viatoribus obviis, deinde, in proxima villa vel pago ; postremo, coram ecclesia vel judicio.——First, (to be proclaimed) in the presence of the officers and travellers passing by; then, in the next village or street; and, last of all, in the church or in court.

PRIMUM patris feudum.——The first (or principal) fee, or inheritance of the father.

PRIMUM patris fuedum primogenitus filius habeat. Emptiones vero vel deinceps acquisitiones suas, det cui magis velit.——The eldest son shall have the principal feud (or land originally granted). But the father may give his purchased or after-acquired estates to whom he pleases.

PRIMUS inter pares.——The first among his equals: a President.

PRINCIPIA.——Maxims.

PRINCIPES regionum atque pagorum inter suos jus dicunt, contraversiasque minuunt.——The lords of hundreds and districts expound the law and settle disputes.

PRINCIPIIS obsta.——Meet first beginnings: oppose obstacles instantly.

PRISAGE.——The King's right to take two tons of wine from every ship importing to England twenty tons.

PRISO.——Prisoner.

PRISAL in autre lieu.——Taking in another place.

PRISONE forte et dure.——Strong and close confinement.

PRIUS autem intellige, et deinde ad opus accede.——But first understand, and afterwards proceed with the business.

PRIVEMENT enciente.——Privily pregnant.

PRIVIGNUS.——A step-son.

PRIVILEGIUM clericale.——The benefit of clergy.

PRIVITY.——Connection of interest.

PROAMITA.——The sister of a great-grandfather.

PROAVUNCULUS.——The brother of a great-grandfather.

PROAVUS.——A father's grandfather.

PROBATA.——Things proved: proofs.

PROBATIO.——" Proof." Showing the truth of any matter alleged. *Vide note.*

PROBATOR.——An approver.

PRO bono et malo.——Whether for gain or loss.

PROBUS et legalis homo.——A good and true man.

PROCEDENDO ad judicium.——In proceeding to judgment.

PROCES verbal.——Process verbal.

PROCHEIN ami.——The next friend.

PRO confesso.——As confessed: as if conceded: taken for granted.

Pro consilio impendendo.——For counsel to be given.

Pro corpore comitatus.——For the body of the county.

Pro correctione et salute animæ.——For amendment, and the welfare of the soul.

Pro crimine falsi.——For the crime of forgery.

Procul dubio quod alterum libertas, alterum necessitas impelleret.——It was liberty, beyond all doubt, that compelled the one, necessity the other.

Procurator ad agendum.——An Agent, Proctor, or Attorney.

Procuratoribus, qui in aliquibus partibus attornati nuncupantur.——By proctors, who, in some places, are called attorneys.

Pro custode pacis et bono regimine et gubernatione eorum ibidem.——For keeping of the peace, and good rule and government of the people there.

Pro custodio terræ et hæredis.——For the possession of the land, and of the heir.

Pro cursu scaccarii.——By course of the Exchequer.

Pro damno fatali.——For a total loss.

Pro damnis suis occasione detentionis debiti.——For their damages by reason of detaining the debt.

Pro defectu bonæ custodiæ ipsius defendentis, et servientium suorum perdita et amissa fuerunt.——For want of safe custody of the defendant and his servants (the goods) were lost and destroyed.

Pro defectu exitus.——For default of issue.

Pro defectu emptorum.——For the want of purchasers.

Pro defectu hæredis.——For want of an heir.

Pro defectu juratorem.——For want of jurors.

Pro defectu juris.——For want of right.

Pro defectu jurisdictionis.——For want (or in defect) of jurisdiction.

Pro defectu jurisdictionis, et pro defectu triationis.——For want of the jurisdiction and a trial

Pro defectu placiti.——For want of a plea.

PRO defectu tenentis.——For default (or want) of a tenant.

PRO delibero tenemento.——For exonerating (or discharging) the tenement or land.

PRODES homes.——Anciently a title bestowed upon peers or military men who were summoned to the King's council.

PRO digna laborum multorumpque ad inventionem remunerationem.——For a suitable remuneration of the many labors of discovery.

Προδοσια.——Treachery: treason.

PRODITIORE, et contra ligeantiæ suæ debitum.——Treasonable, and against the bond of his allegiance.

PRO domino.——As master.

PRO eo quod leges quibus utuntur Hybernici Deo detestabiles existunt, et omni jure dissonant, adeo quod leges censeri non debeant; nobis, et consilio nostro satis videtur expediens eis utendas concedare leges Anglicanas.——Inasmuch as the laws which the *Irish* people use are odious in the sight of God, and at variance with all justice, so that (in fact) they ought not to be accounted as laws; it appears expedient to us and to our council that the *English* laws should be substituted in their place.

PRO et durante termino vitarum suarum, et hæredum et assignatorum prædictorum *Valentini et Aliciæ*, et pro defectu talium hæredum de prædicto *Valentino et Aliciæ*, &c.—— For and during the term of their lives, and the heirs and assigns of the said *Valentine* and *Alice*, and in default of such heirs of the said *Valentine* and *Alice*, &c.

PRO expensis litis.——For costs of suit.

PRO falso clamore suo.——For his unjust claim (or suit).

PRO feodo militari reputatur.——It is accounted as a Knight's fee.

PROFERENDO hic in curiam.——By offering it here in court.

PROFERT ad curiam.——He tenders (or shows) to the court.

PROGRESSUM est ut ad filios deveniret, in quem scilicet dominus hoc vellet beneficium confirmare.——It is decided that it should descend to the sons ; that is to say, on him to whom the Lord was willing to confer this benefit.

PRO hac vice——"For this turn" (an alternate right of presentation, when alluding to a church living).

PROHÆREDES.——Those who act for heirs.

PROHIBEMUS ne quisquam, &c.——We forbid that any one, &c.

PROHIBETUR ne quis faciat in suo quod nocere possit in alieno ; et sit utere tuo ut alienum non lædas.——It is forbidden that any one should do that in his own (property) which may injure another ; wherefore so use your own that you do no damage to others.

PRO homagis, et servitis.——For homage and service.

PRO indivisio.——For an undivided (part).

PRO instanti.——For the instant : for the present time.

PRO interesse suo.——For his own interest, or on his own account.

PRO jure alicujus murdriendo.——For the concealment (or destruction) of any person's right.

PRO læsione fidei.——On account of an injury to his faith (or fealty).

PROLES.——Children of a legal marriage.

PROLETARIUS.——In Roman law. Of a low condition : plebeians.

PRO libertate patriæ.——For the liberty of the country.

PRO majori cautela.——For greater caution.

PRO misis et custagiis.——For (his) charges.

PROMATERTERA.——In Roman law. The sister of a great grandmother.

PRO necessario victu et apparatu ad manutentionem familiæ suæ.——For necessary food and apparel for the sustenance of his family.

PRONEPOS.——The son of a grandchild.

PRONEPTIS.——The daughter of a grandchild.

PRO non bene utendo facultate medicinæ.——For improperly using the faculty of medicine.

PRO omni transgressione, licet minima, ubi quis ad pacem domini regis vocatus, venire recusaverit; et hoc propter contumaciam.——For every default, even the least, where any one has been called to preserve the peace of our lord the King, and has refused to come; and this because (of his) contumacy.

PRO opere et labore.——For work and labor.

PRO pastura centum ovium.——For the pasture of a hundred sheep.

PROPE altam viam regiam.——Near the King's highway.

PROPINQUI et consanguinei.——Neighbors and relations.

PROPINQUIOR excludit propinquum: propinquus remotum; remotior remotissimum.——He that is nearer, excludes one that is near; he that is near, one that is remote; and one that is remote, the most distant.

PROPIOR sobrino, propior sobrina.——A great uncle or aunt's son or daughter.

PRO placito dicit, &c.——He says for a plea, &c.

PRO placito et monstratione juris dicit.——He says as (or for) a plea, and the showing of right.

PROPORCITAS.——Anciently, the purport of a matter.

PRO præmio.——For a reward.

PROPRIA manu.——With his own hand.

PROPRIA manu pro ignorantia literarum signum sanctæ crucis expressi et subscripsi.——By reason of my ignorance of letters, I have marked and subscribed with my own hand the sign of the holy cross. *Vide note.*

PROPRIA persona, sedente curia.——In proper person, during the sitting of the court.

PROPRIETATE probanda.——By proving property; or the right.

Pro prima tonsura.——For the spring grass; or first shear.

Proprio jure.——In its proper right.

Proprio vigore.——In full force (or effect).

Proprium est quod quis libra mercatur et ære.——"For it is proper that every one should purchase by money weighed." Vide note to "*Hæredes, successoresque.*"

Propter adulterium.——On account of adultery.

Propter adulterium, propter furorem, propter heresiam, propter sævitiam.——"On account of adultery, rage (or madness), heresy, or cruelty." These were at one time causes of divorce from bed and board; but not "*a vinculo matrimonii*" (from the bond of marriage).

Propter affectionem.——On account of partiality.

Propter capitales inimicitias.——On acount of deadly feuds.

Propter defectum.——On account of some defect (as age, &c.)

Propter defectum: propter delictum.——Because of the default: because of the offence (or crime).

Propter defectum sanguinis.——On failure of issue.

Propter delictum.——Because of an offence (or crime).

Propter delictum tenentis.——For the offence (or crime) of the occupier.

Propter donum et feoffamentum.——By reason of the gift and feoffment.

Propter honoris respectum.——In regard to rank (or dignity).

Propter honoris respectum; propter affectum; vel propter delictum.——On account of (his) rank; because of partiality; or for crime.

Propter impotentiam.——By reason of impotency.

Propter longissimum ingressum.——By reason of the antiquity of the entry.

Propter odium delicti.——On account of turpitude of the crime.

PROPTER privilegium.——By reason of privilege.

PROPTER sævitiam aut adulterium.——Because of cruelty or adultery.

PROPTER transgressionem.——On account of trespass or injury.

PROPTER visum et auditum.——By reason of the view and hearing.

PRO querula.——On account of a complaint.

PRO querente.——For the plaintiff.

PRO quodam valario.——For some voluntary consideration.

PRO rata itineris.——At the rate of the voyage or journey.

PRO rata itineris peracti.——At the rate of the journey performed.

PRO rationabile dotagio.——For a reasonable dowry.

PRO re nata.——"For the existing occasion;" for a special business ; or on an emergency.

PRO rotorno habendo.——For a return to be had.

PRO salute animæ.——For the welfare of the soul.

PRO salute animæ ejus ecclesiæ consilio.——For the welfare of his soul, by the advice of the church.

PROTECTIO trahit subjectionem, et subjectio protectionem.——"Protection draws (or implies) allegiance, and allegiance (should ensure) protection." This was one of the greatest principles of the *feudal* law.

PRO tempore existente.——Existing for the time being.

PRO tempore, pro spe, pro commodo minuitur eorum pretium atque auget.——The value of those things is lessened, or increased, according to time, expectation, or profit.

PRO termino vitarum suarum.——During their lives.

PROTHONOTARY.——One of the highest clerks in the courts of King's Bench.

PRO turpi causa.——For a dishonest purpose.

PRO usu et usurpatione.——For the use (or occupation) and usurpation.

PROUT constat nobis per recordum.——As appears to us by the record.

PROUT debuit.——As he stood indebted.

PROUT eis visum fuerit, ad honorem coronæ et utilitatem regni.——As it shall appear to them for the honor of the crown and service of the realm.

PROUT ei bene licet.——As it was very lawful for him.

PROUT in indictamento supponitur.——As is supposed in the indictment.

PROUT lex postulat.——According as the law requires.

PROUT patet per recordum.——As appears by the record.

PRO vero et justo debito.——For a true and just debt.

PROVISIONE viri.——As a provision (or support) for the husband.

PROWE.——Advantage.

PROXENETA.——A negotiator.

PROXIMUS hæres.——The next heir.

PUBLICA judicia.——Criminal trials. *Vide note.*

PUBLICUM bonum est privato præferendem.——Public good is to be preferred to private interest.

PUBLICUM jus.——Law which relates to the condition of the state.

PUDZELD.——In ancient law. A release from paying the tax of money for getting wood from a forest.

PUIS darien continuance.——Since the last continuance (or adjournment).

PUISNE.——Younger: subordinate. *Vide note.*

PUISSE porter brefe de novele disseisine, aux sicum de frank tenement.——They may bring a writ of novel disseisin; as if they were tenants of the freehold.

PULSARE.——To charge or accuse.

PUNCTUM temporis.——The shortest possible space of time.

PUNDBRECH.——The taking cattle, unlawfully, from a pound.

PUNDFULDA.——A pound.

PUR autre vie.——For the life of another.

PUR cause de vicinage.——By reason of vicinage or neighborhood.

PUR ceo que.——Because, forasmuch: a phrase common in old books.

PUR le pais.——By the country.

PUR murdre le droit.——For concealment of the right.

PURALLE, puraille, pœal.——The edges of a forest or park.

PURPARS.——One part of an estate after it has been divided.

PURPRESTURE.——The erection of a house, &c., or an inclosure made upon any part of the king's demesnes, or upon a highway, common, street, or public water, is called a "*Purpresture.*"

PURUM villenagium.——A pure villenage.

PUR usage de pais.——By the custom of the country.

PUTATIO.——The act of pruning trees.

PUTATIVE.——Supposed.

NOTES TO P.

PARAPHERNALIA.——It is not improbable that the *Romans* took their custom of the *Paraphernalia* from the *Orientals.* The weight and value of the ornaments put upon *Rebecca* appear to us, at this day, very extraordinary. But *Chardin* assures us that even heavier were worn by the women of the *East,* when he was there. He says that the women wear rings and bracelets of as great weight as this, and even heavier, throughout all *Asia.* They are rather manacles than bracelets. They wear several of them, one above another, in such a manner as sometimes to have the arm covered with them from the wrist to the elbow. Poor people wear as many of glass, or horn. They hardly ever take them off; they are their riches. Vide *Harmer's Observations,* vol. ii. p. 500. Among the several ornaments which *Abraham* sent by his servant, whom he employed to search out a wife for his son *Isaac,* were jewels of silver and jewels of gold, exclusive of raiment, which probably was very rich and valuable for the age in which *Abraham* lived. Rich and splendid apparel, such as was usually adorned with gold, was general in the *Eastern* nations, from the earliest ages; and the fashions and customs of the Orientals are not subject to much variation. We find that the propensity for golden ornaments prevails even in the present age, among the females of the countries bordering on *Judea. Mungo Park,* in his "Travels in *Africa,*" mentions the following singular circumstance respecting the ornamental dress of an *African* lady: "It is evident, on account of the process by which negroes obtain gold in *Manding,* that the country contains a considerable portion of the precious metal. A great part is converted into ornaments for the *women;* and when a lady of consequence is in full dress, the gold about her person may be worth, altogether, from *fifty* to *eighty* pounds (sterling.)" We find that the same disposition for rich ornamental apparel prevailed in the time of the Apostles; for St. *Peter* cautioned the females of quality, in the first ages of Christianity, when they adorned themselves, not to have it consist in the outward adorning of plaiting the hair, and wearing gold, or of putting on apparel. Vide 1 *Pet.* iii. 3. "Upon thy right hand did stand the Queen in *gold* of *Ophir.* Her clothing is of wrought *gold.*" Vide *Psalms,* xlv. 9, 14.

PECUNIA SIGNATA.—The *Romans,* like other ancient nations, (vide *Strab.* iii. 155,) at first had no coined money, (*pecunia signata,*) but either exchanged commodities, as is at present usual in many of the western parts of *North America,* (and in other parts of the world,) or used a certain weight of uncoined brass (*aes rude*) or other metal. Hence the various *names of money,* also denotes *weight;* the Latin word "*pendere,*" to weigh, is sometimes put as a synonymous word for "*solvere,*" to pay. So *stipendum (a stipe pendenda),* soldiers' pay, (*Festus,*) because at *first* it appears to have been *weighed,* not counted. Vide also *Genesis,* xxiii. 16. Thus, *talentum* and *mina,* among the *Greeks,* and *shekel* among the *Hebrews;* and from the custom of weighing, comes the word *pound* with us. Several *Greek* words are supposed to allude to the ancient custom of exchanging commodities: thus *arnoomai,* (to exchange or purchase, by giving a lamb ;) *arnos,* (a lamb ;) *oneomai,* (by giving an ass;) *onos,* (an ass;) *poleo,* (by giving a foal;) *polos,* (a foul or the young of any animal.)

It is said that *Servius Tullius* first stamped pieces of brass with the image of cattle, oxen, swine, &c., *pecudes,* (cattle,) whence, it is said, comes the word "*pecunia,*" (money.) Vide *Ov. Fast.* v. 284. *Servius, Rex, ovium boumque effigio primus aes signavit,* vide *Plin.* xxxii. 3.—i. e. "Servius, the King, first coined money, with the likeness of sheep and oxen," (stamped thereon.) Silver, it is said, was first coined A. U. 484, or, according to others, A. U. 498; and gold, sixty-two years after. Vide *Plin.* xxxiii. s. 40. *Liv. Ep.* xv. Silver coins, however, seem to have been in use in *Rome,* before that time, but of foreign coinage. Vide *Liv.* viii. 11. Hence we find that *Æs,* or *Æra,* is put for money in general. Vide *Hor. Art. P.* 345—*æs alienum,* a debt; annua *aera,* yearly pay. Vide *Liv.* v. 4.

Money was likewise called *stips,* (a *stipando,*) from being crammed in a cell, that it might occupy less room. *Varr. L. L.* iv. 36. But this word is usually put for a small coin, as we say a *cent,* or half cent, offered to the gods at games or the like, *Cic. leg.* ii. 16, or given as alms to a beggar, or to any one as a New-Year's gift, (*strena,*) or by way of contribution for a public purpose. *Plin.* xxxiii. 10. s. 48.

The first brass coin, (*nummus* vel *numus æris,*) was called AS, (anciently *assis,* from *æs;*) of a pound weight, (*liberalis.*) It appears that the highest valuation of fortune, (*census maximus,*) under *Servius,* was 100,000 pounds' weight of brass. Vide *Liv.* i. 43.

The other brass coins, besides the *as,* were *semisses, trientas, quadrantes,* and *sextantes.* These coins at first had the full weight, which their names imported; hence in later times called *æs grave.* Vide *Plin.* xxxiii. 3. s. 13.

The silver coins were *denarius,* the value of which was ten *asses,* or ten pounds of brass, marked with the letter X ; *Quinarius,* five *asses,* marked V ; and *Sestertius,* two *asses* and a half. The impression on silver coins was usually on one side, carriages drawn by two or four beasts; and on the reverse the head of *Roma,* with a helmet. On some silver coins was marked the figure of Victory ; hence called *Victoriati.*

From every pound weight of silver were coined 100 *denarii,* so that at first a pound of silver was equal in value to a thousand pounds of brass.

Whence we may judge of the scarcity of silver at that time in *Rome*. But afterwards the case was altered. For when the weight of the *as* was diminished, it bore the same proportion to the *denarius* as before, until it was reduced to one ounce; and then a *denarius* passed for sixteen *asses*, (except in the military pay, in which it continued to pass for ten *asses*, at least under the Republic, *Plin.* xxxiii. 3; for in the time of *Tiberius*, it appears no such exception was made, vide *Tacit. Ann.* i. 17,) a *quinarius* for eight *asses*, and a *sestertius*, for four; which proportion continued when the *as* was reduced to half an ounce. *Plin. ibid.* But the weight of silver money also varied, and was different under the Emperors from what it had been under the Republic.

Varro mentions silver coins of less value; *Libella*, worth an *as*, or the tenth part of a *denarius*; *Sembella*, worth a half pound of brass; and *Teruncius*, the fortieth part of a *denarius*.

A golden coin was first struck at *Rome*, in the second Punic war, in the Consulship of *C. Claudius Nero*, and *M. Livius Salinator*, A. U. 546, called *Aureus*, or *aureus nummus*, equal in weight to two *denarii* and a *quinarius*, and in value to twenty-five *denarii*, or one hundred *sestertii.* Vide *Suet. Oth.* 4. Hence the fee allowed to be taken by a lawyer is called by Tacitus, "*dena sestertia.*" Vide *Ann.* xi. 7. The common rate of gold to silver under the Republic was tenfold. But *Julius Cæsar* obtained so much by plundering, that he exchanged it for 3000 *sestertii*, or 750 *denarii* the pound; i. e, a pound of gold for seven pounds and a half of silver. Vide *Suet. Cæs.* 54.

PER DUELLUM.—It appears probable, from a law quoted by *Jo. O. Stiern-höök*, "*de jure Sueonum et Gothorum vetusto*," that judicial combat was *originally* permitted, in order to determine points respecting the *personal* character or reputation of individuals, and was afterwards extended not only to criminal cases, but to questions concerning *property.* The words of the law are, "If any man shall say to another these reproachful words, 'You are not a man equal to other men,' or, 'You have not the heart of a man;' and the other shall reply, 'I am as good a man as you;' let them meet on the highway. If he, who first gave offence, appear, and the person offended absent himself, let the latter be deemed a worse man even than he was called; let him not be admitted to give evidence in judgment, either for man or woman, and let him not have the privilege of making a testament. If he, who gave the offence, be absent, and only the person offended, appear, let him call upon the other *thrice*, with a loud voice; and make a *mark* upon the earth; and then let him who absented himself be deemed infamous, because he uttered words which he durst not support. If both shall appear, properly armed, and the person offended shall fall in the combat, let a half compensation be paid for his death. But if the person who gave the offence shall fall, let it be imputed to his own rashness. The petulance of his tongue hath been fatal to him. Let him lie in the field without any compensation being demanded for his death." Vide *Lex Uplandica ap. Stiern.* p. 76.

Martial people were extremely delicate, with respect to everything that affected their reputation as soldiers. By the laws of the *Salians*, if any person called another a *Hare*, or accused him of having left his shield on the field of battle, he was ordained to pay a large fine. Vide *Leg. Sal. tit.* xxxii. § 4, 6. By the law of the *Lombards*, if any one called another *Arga*, i. e. "a good for nothing fellow," he might *immediately* challenge him to combat. Vide *Leg. Longob. lib.* i. *tit.* v. § 1. By the law of the *Salians*, if one called another *Cenitus*, a term of reproach equivalent to *Arga*, he was bound to pay a very high fine. *Tit.* xxxii. § 1. Thus the ideas concerning the point of honor, which we are apt to consider as a modern refinement, as well as the practice of duelling, to which it gave rise, are derived from the notions of our ancestors, while in a state of society very little improved.

The northern nations of *Europe* held, above every other consideration, their courage and acts of valor. We find the following passages in *Ossian's* Poems, among innumerable others in various authors (*Ossian*, it is generally supposed, lived in the early ages of Christianity:) "My fathers, *Ossian*, trace my steps; my deeds are pleasant to their eyes. Wherever I come forth to battle, on my field are their columns of mist. But mine arm rescued the feeble! the haughty found my rage was fire. Never over the fallen did mine eye rejoice. For this my fathers shall meet me at the gates of their airy halls, tall with robes of light, with mildly kindled eyes. But to the proud in arms, they are darkened moons in heaven, which send the fire of night red-wandering over their face." And again:

"Father of Heroes, *Trenmor*, dweller of eddying winds! I give thy spear to *Ossian*, let thine eye rejoice. Thee have I seen, at times, bright from between thy clouds; so appear to my son, when he is to lift the spear; then shall he remember thy mighty deeds, though thou art now but a blast."

PEREGRINI.—Strangers—Foreigners. With the ancient *Romans*, those who were not citizens were called foreigners (PEREGRINI), wherever they lived, whether in the city or elsewhere; but after *Caracalla* granted the freedom of the city to *all* freeborn men in the *Roman* world, and when *Justinian* sometime after granted it also to *freedmen*, the name of *foreigners* fell into disuse; and the inhabitants of the whole world were divided into *Romans* and *Barbarians*. The whole *Roman* Empire itself was called "ROMANIA," which name is sometimes now given to *Thrace*, as being the last province which was retained by the *Romans*, until the time of the taking of *Constantinople*, by the Turks, A. D. 1453. While *Rome* was free, the condition of foreigners was very disagreeable. They might, indeed, *live* in the city; but they enjoyed none of the privileges of citizens. They were also subject to a peculiar jurisdiction; and sometimes were expelled from the city, at the pleasure of the magistrates. Thus *M. Junius Pennus*, A. U. 627, and *C. Papius Celsus*, A. U. 688, both *Tribunes* of the people, passed a law, ordering foreigners to leave the city. Vide *Cic. Off.* iii. 11. *Brut.* 8. So Augustus, *Suet. Aug.* 42. But afterwards, an immense number of foreigners flocked to *Rome*, from all parts. Vide *Juv. Sat.* iii. 58. So that the greatest part of the common people consisted of them; hence *Rome* was said to be "*mundi fæce repleta*," i. e., "full of the world's dregs." Vide *Luc.* vii. 405. Foreigners were neither permitted to use the *Roman* dress, (*Suet. Claud.* 25,) nor had they the right of legal property; or of making a will. When a foreigner died, his goods were reduced into the treasury, as having no heir, (*quasi bona vacantia;*) but if he had attached himself to any person, as his *patron*, that person succeeded to his effects, (*jure applicationis.*) Vide *Cic. de Orat.* i. 39. But in process of time these inconveniences were removed; and foreigners were not only advanced to the highest honors, but some of them even made Emperors.

PER PROPRIUM, VISUM, &c.—Anciently, when any controversy arose respecting lands, or their boundaries, there was generally no other mode of settling the dispute, except by a VIEW on the spot; and the *evidence* and *hearsay* testimony of aged persons. Deeds or conveyances of land were made but seldom; they were very concise, and the boundaries given in a general manner, and frequently not given in any definite mode, further than mentioning the number of towns, vills, &c.

About the time of the Conquest, very large estates were granted on pieces of parchment, not exceeding in size a sheet of common writing paper. Some of these grants are now extant, as legible as when first written.

PER TESTAMENTUM.—This was one of the ancient modes of *freeing a slave* (by giving him his liberty) *by will.* If this was done in express words, (*verbis directis*), as, for example, "DAVUS, SERVUS MEUS, LIBER ESTO," i. e., "Da-

vus, my servant, be thou free," such freedmen were called "ORCINI," or
"*Charonitœ*," because it was said they had no patron, but in the *infernal* regions. In allusion to which, those unworthy persons who got admission
into the Senante, after the death of *Cæsar*, were by the vulgar called "SENA-
TORES ORCINI." Vide *Suet. Aug.* 35. But if the testator signified his desire,
by way of request (*verbis precativis*), the heir (*hæres fiduciarius*) retained the
right of *patronage*. When a person had his freedom given him at his master's death, he was called "ORCINUS LIBERTUS."

PER VINDICTAM.—This was another of the ancient modes of freeing a
slave; when the master, going with the slave in his hand to the *Prætor* or
Consul, and in the Provinces to the *Proconsul* or *Proprætor*, said, "I desire
that this man be free according to the custom *or* law of the Romans," ("HUNC
HOMINEM LIBERUM ESSE VOLO MORE, vel JURE, QUIRITIUM,") and the *Prætor*, if
he approved, putting a rod on the head of the slave, (*Hor. Sat.* ii. 7, 76.)
"I WILL THAT THIS MAN BE FREE AFTER THE MANNER OF THE ROMANS."
Whereupon the *Lictor*, or the Master, turning him (the slave) *round in a
circle*, (which is called) " *Vertigo*," (Pers. *Sat.* v. 75,) and giving him a blow
on the cheek, (*alapa*,) vide *Isidor.* ix. 4, (whence, *multo majoris alapæ mecum
veneunt*, Liberty is sold, &c. *Phæd.* ii. 5, 22), let him go (*é manu emittebat*),
signifying that leave was granted him to go where he pleased. The rod,
with which the slave was struck, was called " *Vindicta*," as some think from
Vindicius, or *Vindex*, a slave of the *Vitelii*, who informed the Senate of the
conspiracy of the sons of *Brutus*, and others, to restore the *Tarquins;* and
who is said to have been first freed in this manner, vide *Liv.* ii. 5, whence
also, perhaps, "*vindicare in libertatem*," "to free." " *Mulier modo quam* vindicta *remedit*," a woman lately freed. Vide *Ov. Art. Am.* iii. 615.

PIE POUDRE COURT.—" *Curia pedis pulverizati;*" from the Fr. "*pied*," pes;
and " *poudreux*," pulverulentus. *Skene* (*de verbo signif. verbo* "Pes pulve-
rosi") says the word signifies a vagabond, especially a pedler, who had no
dwelling, therefore must have justice *summarily* administered to him, viz.
within three ebbings and flowings of the sea. *Bracton* calls it "*justitia pre-
poudrous*." This court, among the old *Saxons*, was called *ceapung-gemot*,
i. e. a court of merchandise; or handling matters of buying and selling.

PINNAS BIBERE, or "*ad pinnas bibere*." The old custom of drinking,
(brought in by the *Danes*,) was to fix *a pin* on the side of the vessel, or
Wassail bowl, and to drink exactly *to the pin*. This sort of drunkenness was
forbid by the clergy in the council of *London*, Anno 1102. Vide *Cowell*. It
is probable that many, when thirsty, forgot the pin, and drank a little lower.
The *Romans* used to drink to one another, thus, "*bene vobis*, &c." i. e.
"health to you, &c." *Plaut. Pers.* v. i. 20. Sometimes, in honor of a friend,
or mistress. Vide *Ibid.* and *Hor. Od.* i. 27, 9; and they used to take as
many *cyathi*, or cups, as there were letters in the lady's name (*Tibull.* ii. 1,
31 ;) or as they wished years to her ; hence they were said, "*ad numerum
bibere*, (to drink to the number.) Vide *Ov. Fast.* iii. 531. A frequent number was *three*, in honor of the Graces; and *nine*, of the Muses. Vide *Hor.
Od.* iii. 19, 11. The *Greeks* drank first in honor of their Gods, and then of
their friends; hence " *Greco more bibere*," (i. e. to drink after the Grecian
custom.) *Cic. Verr.* i. 26. They began with small cups, and ended with
larger, which is usually the consequence in modern times. A skeleton was
sometimes introduced at feasts in the time of drinking; or at least the representation of one (*larva argentea*), vide *Petron.* 34, in imitation of the *Egyptians*, vide *Herodot.* ii. 78, s. 74, upon which the master of the feast, looking
at it, used to say, VIVAMUS, DUM LICET ESSE BENE. Vide *Petron*, 34.

PLACITATOR.—We find it recorded that *Ralf Flambard*, was "*totius regni*

Placitator," i. e. "Pleader for the whole realm," *temp. Will.* 2. It would appear at this day, that if *Ralf* were pleader for the *whole* kingdom, his time must have been pretty well employed, if law suits were brought for such trifles as is customary in modern days.

POSSESSIONES, &c.—It was formerly the custom, much more than at present, when a purchase was made of estates, in the occupation of tenants, to procure them to *attorn,* by signing an acknowledgment, that they from *thenceforth* considered themselves as holding their lands of the purchaser.

PRÆDIA LIBERA.—Farms not liable to any servitude were, among the *Romans,* called *Prædia libera,* (i. e. free farms;) *optimo jure,* vel *conditione optimâ,* (i. e. in the greatest right, or most perfect condition;) others, "*quæ serviebant; servitutem debebant,* vel *servituti erant obnoxia,*" (i. e. those under servitude; who owed service, *or* were liable to perform duties,) were called "*Prædia Serva,*" (i. e. servile farms.) Vide *Cic. in Rull.* iii. 2. Buildings in the city were called "*Prædia urbana*" (city farms), and were reckoned "*res mancipi,*" only by accession (*jure fundi*), i. e. by farm right; for all buildings and lands were called *Fundi;* but usually buildings in the city were called *Ædes;* in the country *Villæ.* A place in the city without buildings was called *Area;* in the country, *Ager.* A field with buildings was properly called *Fundus.*

PRÆMUNIRE.—We often find this writ mentioned in the old law; it was probably corrupted from "*Præmoneri,*" to be forewarned. Vide *Du Cange in verb.* The offence for which this writ was granted was of a nature *highly* criminal, though not capital. The first words of the writ are, "*Præmunire facias* A. B.," &c., i. e. "Cause A. B. to be forewarned," &c. It took its origin from the exorbitant power claimed and exercised in *England* by the *Pope;* and was originally ranked as an offence immediately against the King, or his prerogative; because it consisted in introducing a foreign power into the land, and thus creating "*imperium in imperio,*" by paying that obedience to papal process which constitutionally belonged to the King. The penalties of a *Præmunire* are mentioned by a great many statutes; yet prosecutions upon a Præmunire are scarcely, if ever, heard of in the *English* courts.

The *Pope* of Rome, at one time, took upon himself to bestow most of the Ecclesiastical livings of any worth in *England,* by *Mandates,* before they were void; pretending therein great care to see the Church provided with a successor before it needed—whence these mandates, or bulls, were called "*gratiæ expectativæ,* or *provisiones,*" i. e. expected rewards, *or* provisions. Vide *Duaremus* de Beneficiis, lib. 3, c. 1. These *provisiones* were at length so common that it became necessary to restrain them by law, vide *Stat.* 35, *Edw.* the First, and subsequent statutes for the punishment inflicted for this offence, which was severe.

PRÆTOR.—"*Is qui præit jure, et exercitu,*" i. e. "he who is first in the law, and the army." This word appears to have been anciently common to all magistrates. Vide *Liv.* iii. 55. Thus the *Dictator* is called "*Prætor Maximus.*" *Liv.* vii. 3. But when the *Consuls,* being engaged in almost continual wars, could not attend to the administration of justice, a magistrate was created for that purpose, A. U. 389, to whom the name of PRÆTOR was thenceforth appropriated. He was at first created only from the *Patricians,* as a kind of compensation for the Consulship being communicated to the *Plebeians;* but afterwards, A. U. 418, also from the *Plebeians.* Vide *Liv.* viii. 15. The *Prætor* was next in dignity to the *Consuls;* and was created at the *Comitia Centuriata,* with the same *auspices* as the *Consuls;* whence he was called their colleague. *Liv.* vii. 1; viii. 32. The first *Prætor* was *Sp. Furius Camillus,* son of the great *M. Furius Camillus,* who died the year the son was

Prætor. When one *Prætor* was insufficient, on account of the number of foreigners who flocked to *Rome,* another *Prætor* was added, A. U. 510, to administer justice to them; or between the citizens and them, *qui inter cives Romanos et peregrinos jus diceret.* Liv. Ep. xix.; xxii. 35, i. e. "who should declare (or pronounce) the law between the *Roman* citizens and strangers; hence called "PRÆTOR PEREGRINUS." The power of the *Prætor* in the administration of justice was expressed in these words, "DO, DICO, ADDICO," i. e. "I ordain, I pronounce, I condemn." *Prætor dabet actionem et judicem,* (the *Prætor* may give the law and judgment;) he gave the form of the writ for trying and redressing a particular wrong complained of; and appointed judges, or a jury, to judge in the cause; DICEBAT JUS, i. e. "he pronounced the law (or sentence;)" ADDICEBAT BONA vel DAMNA, i. e. "adjudged the goods, *or* awarded the damages.

PROBATIO.—Proof. *Bracton* says there is *"probatio duplex,"* i. e. "a double proof," viz., *"viva voce,"* by witnesses; and *"probatio mortua,"* by deeds, writings, &c. Proof, according to *Lilly,* is either giving evidence to a jury on a trial, or else on interrogatories; or by copies of record, or exemplification of them. 2 *Lil. Ab.* 393. Though where a man speaks generally of proof, it shall be *intended* of proof given to a jury, which, in the strict signification, is legal proof. Vide *Bulst.* 56.

PROPRIA MANU, &c.—The barbarous nations who prostrated the *Roman* Empire were *not only* illiterate, but treated literature with great *contempt.* The swarms of invaders found the inhabitants of most of the provinces which they conquered sunk in effeminacy and averse to war. "When we would brand an enemy," says *Lituprandus,* "with the most disgraceful and contumelious appellations, we call him '*a Roman;*' *hoc solo, id est Romani nomine, quicquid, nobilitatis; quicquid timidatis, quicquid aversatiæ, quicquid luxuriæ, quicquid mendacii, immo quicquid vitiorum est comprehendes,"* i. e. "In this thing alone, that is, in the name of *Roman,* there is not only whatever is haughty; but also everything cowardly, of abhorrence, of effeminacy, of lying, yea, all that you can consider disgraceful. Vide *Legatio apud Murat. Scriptor, Ital. vol.* 2, *pars.* 1. p. 481.

This degeneracy illiterate barbarians attributed to the *love* of learning. And, after they had settled in the countries they had conquered, they would not permit even their *children* to be instructed in any literary science, "for," said they, "instruction in the sciences tends to corrupt, enervate and oppress the mind, and he who has been accustomed to *tremble* under the rod of a *pedagogue,* will never look on a sword or spear with an *undaunted* eye." Vide *Procop. de bello Gothor. lib.* 1, p. 4, *ap. Scrip. Byz. edit. Venet. vol.* 1. What a specious argument for ignorance! A considerable number of years elapsed before nations so rude, and so unwilling to learn, could produce historians capable of recording their transactions, or describing their manners and institutions. By that time the memory of their *ancient* condition was, in some measure, lost; and few monuments remain to guide their first writers to any certain knowledge of them. Traditions then supplied the place of truth, and distorted facts a thousand different ways.

If we expect to receive any satisfactory account of the laws and manners of the *Goths, Lombards,* and *Franks,* during their residence in those countries where they were *originally* settled, from *Jornandes, Paulus, Warnefridus,* or *Gregory* of *Tours,* the earliest and most authentic historians of those people, we shall be disappointed. Whatever imperfect knowledge has been conveyed to us of the ancient state of those fierce northern tribes, we owe it, not to their own writers, but to the *Greek* and *Roman* historians.

PUBLICA JUDICIA.—Criminal trials among the *Romans* were at first held (*exercebantur*) by their kings, (*Dyonys.* ii. 14,) with the assistance of a council, (*cum consilio*). Liv. i. 49. The King judged of great crimes himself; and left smaller crimes to the judgment of the Senators.

Tullius Hostilius appointed two persons (DUUMVIRI) to try *Horatius* for killing his sister, and allowed an appeal from their sentence to the people. *Liv.* i. 26. *Tarquinus Superbus* judged of capital crimes by himself alone, without any counsellors, *Liv.* 1, 49. After the expulsion of *Tarquin*, the *Consuls*, at first, judged and punished capital crimes, (*Liv.* ii. 5. *Dyonys.* x. 1.) But after the law of *Popliocola*, concerning the liberty of appeal, the people either judged themselves, in capital affairs, or appointed certain persons for that purpose, with the concurrence of the Senate, who were called " *Quæsitores*," or " *Quæsitores paricidii*," (judges of parricide), whose authority, it appears, lasted only until the trial was over. Sometimes the *Consuls* were appointed. Vide *Liv.* iv. 51. Sometimes a *Dictator*, and *Master of the Horse,* Liv. ix. 26, who were then called QUÆSITORES. The Senators also judged in capital affairs. Vide *Sallust. Cat.* 51, 52, or appointed persons to do so. *Liv.* ix. 26.

PUISNE.—All the judges in *England* are called *puisne* judges, except the Chief Justice of the Courts of *King's Bench*, and *Common Pleas*, and Chief Baron of the *Exchequer*.

———————•◆•———————

Q.

Q'D. CAPIAT in custod' suam omnes prisonar' qui sunt ad largum, extra prisonam.——That he take into his custody all the prisoners who are at large, beyond (the walls) of the prison.

Q'D. CAPIAT in custod' suam omnes prisonar' qui sunt in regulis.——That he take into his custody all the prisoners, who are in the rules (or on the limits).

QUACAMQUE via data.——In every point of view.

QUADRUPLATOR.——An informer: an accuser. *Vide note.*

QUADRENNIUM utile.——The four years permitted in Scotch law to a minor, after he comes of age, to annul, if he can, any deed done to his injury during his minority.

QUÆ ab hostibus capiuntur, statim capientium fient.—— Those things which are taken from an enemy belong, after the battle is over, to the captor.

QUÆ admoneas.——Which things you warn (or admonish) of.

QUÆ ad manus *Martini* executoris postea devinirent,

&c.——Which subsequently came to the hands of *Martin*, the executor.

QUÆ ad omnes pertinent, omnes debent tractare.—— Those things which concern every one, should be exercised by all.

QUÆ ad terram. Which (relate) to the land.

QUÆ ad unem finem loquanta sunt non debent ad alium detorqueri.——What is spoken with one meaning should not be perverted to another.

QUÆ coram nobis resident.——Which things remain before us.

QUÆDAM nuda possessio.——A certain naked (or bare) tenure.

QUÆDAM nuda possessio, absque minima possessione, et nihilo juris.——"A certain bare occupancy, without the the least possession, and no manner of right." A squatter's title.

QUÆDAM præstatio loco relevii in recognitionem domini. ——A certain performance, instead of a relief, in acknowledgment of the lord (or fee).

QUÆ enim res in tempestate, levandæ navis causa, ejiciuntur, hæ dominorum permanent. Quia palam est, eos non eo animo ejici, quod quis habere velit.——Those goods which are thrown overboard in a storm, for the purpose of easing the ship, remain the property of the owners. Because it is evident that those articles are not wilfully cast away, which every one desires to preserve.

QUÆ enim proxima locis obessis deprehendantur non alia ratione publicantur, quam quod ex facto tacite ad hostem comeandi propositum colligantur.——Those things, which are taken adjacent to besieged places, are not confiscated on any other account, than that they are privately intended, as collected, to be consumed by the enemy.

QUÆ est eadem.——Which is the same.

QUÆ fuit uxor.——Who was the wife.

QUÆ in summis tribunalibus multi é legum canone decernunt Judices, solus (si res exigerit) cohibet Cancellarius ex arbitrio ; nec aliter decretis tenetur suæ curiæ, vel sui ipsius, quin, elucente nova ratione, recognoscat quæ voluerit, mutet, et deleat prout suæ videbitur prudentiæ.——The Chancellor, alone, in his discretion, restrains those decisions (if the case so requires) which many of the Judges in the Supreme Courts decide according to the Canon law ; nor is he otherwise bound to the decrees of his own court, or (to those decided by) himself; but that on a new reason appearing he may reconsider, alter, or expunge those things, as he thinks proper, or as it shall appear to him to be prudent.

Quæ ipso usu consumuntur.——Those things which are consumed by the (very) use (or wear) of them.

Quæ libet concessio fortissime contra donatorem interpretenda est.——Every person's grant is to be expounded most strongly against himself.

Quæ minimis non curat.——Which does not regard mere trifles.

Quæ neque tangi, nec videri possint.——Those things which can neither be felt, nor seen.

Quæ nihil frustra.——Which requires nothing vainly.

Quæ plura.——What more.

Quærens in misericordia.——(Let the) plaintiff be in mercy (be liable to punishment or fine), &c.

Quæ relicta sunt et tradita.——Which things are left and delivered (us).

Quærens nil capiat per breve.——That the plaintiff take nothing by his writ.

Quærens non invenit plegium.——The plaintiff did not find a pledge.

Quæstor.——A Roman officer who collected the public revenues.

Quæ secundum Canones et Episcopales leges ad regimen animarum pertinuit.——Which, according to the Canons and Episcopal Laws, appertain to the cure of souls.

Quæstio fit de legibus, non de personis.——The ques tion is as to the laws, not (in respect) of the persons.

Quæstiones publici juris.——Questions of the public right (or law).

Quæ uxor habet.——Which the wife retains.

Qua executrix.——As an executrix.

Quale jus.——What right.

Qualitas delicti.——The nature of the offence (or crime).

Qualitas delinquentis.——The rank (or standing) of the delinquent.

Quam angusta innocentia est ad legem bonum esse?"——"How pitiful is that innocency which restricts itself to the (mere *letter* of the) law!" How many screen themselves under the *literal* words of a statute; who, if *all* circumstances were known, deserve severe punishment. That man's morality is very limited, which is confined to the strict letter of the law.

Quam clamat esse rationabilem.——Which he (or she) claims to be reasonable.

Quamdiu bene administrat.——So long as he (or she) faithfully administers (the deceased's effects).

Quamdiu bene se gesserint.——"As long as they conduct themselves properly." This language was formerly used in the Letters Patent granted to the Chief Baron. All the English Judges now hold their offices by this tenure—formerly they were enjoyed "*durante bene placito*," during pleasure.

Quam legem exteri nobis posuere, eandem illis ponemus. ——The same law which foreign powers have shown to us, we should observe to them.

Quam propé ad crimen sine crimine?——"How near (may one approach) to crime without being guilty?" Centuries since, this was a mooted question. Some reasoned on the different gradations of crime, until, in their *own* opinions, they almost reasoned away the crime *itself*.

QUAMVIS autem nulla specialis sit commerciorum prohibitio, ipso tamen jure belli commercia esse vetita; ipsæ indicationes bellorum satis declarant; quisque enim subditus jubetur alterius principis subditos, eorum bona aggredi, occupari, et quomodocumque iis nocere.——Although no special prohibition to commerce be made, yet, according to the law of war, it is forbidden; (and) these appearances of hostility are sufficient of themselves; for every subject of one belligerent power is commanded to attack the subjects of the other, and seize upon and injure their property in every possible manner.

QUAMVIS quis pro contumacia et fuga utlagetur, non propter hoc convictus est de facto principali.——Although a person may be outlawed for contempt and flight, he is not on this account (alone) convicted of the principal fact.

QUAND il'y a prisi d'amis ou d'ennemis, ou autre tel destoubier en la navigation.——When it is seized either by friends or enemies, or meets with any other such interruption on the voyage.

QUANDO acciderint.——When they may happen.

QUANDO aliquid mandatur, mandatur et omne per quod pervenitur ad illud.——When a thing is commanded to be done, everything necessary to its accomplishment is also commanded.

QUANDO aliquid prohibetur, prohibetur et omne per quod devenitur ad illud.——When a thing is forbidden to be done, everything having a tendency towards its taking effect is also forbidden.

QUANDO aliquis aliquid concedit, concedere videtur et id, sine quo res uti non potest.——When a person grants something, it will appear *that* is also conceded without which the thing cannot be enjoyed.

QUANDO de una et eadem re duo onerabiles existunt, unus, pro insufficientia alterius de integro onerabitur.——When two persons are liable for one and the same thing, one, in case of the other's default, is chargeable with the whole.

QUANDO hasta, vel aliud corporeum quid libet porrigitur â domino, se investituram facere dicente; quæ saltem coram duobus vassallis solemniter fieri debet.——When a spear, or any other selected corporeal thing, is held out by the lord (of the fee), declaring that he invests them with possession, which should be solemnly performed before two vassals at least. *Vide note.*

QUANDO jus domini regis et subditi insimul concurrunt, jus regis præferri debet.——When the right of the lord the king, and the subject meet together (or are similar), the king's right should be preferred.

QUANDO lex aliquid concedit, concedere videtur et id per quod devenitur ad illud.——When the law grants anything, it would also appear to concede that (right) by which it may be accessible.

QUANDO non valet quod ago, valeat quantum valere potest.——When that which I do is of no utility, let it be as efficacious as possible.

QUANDO plus fit quam fieri debet, videtur etiam illud fieri quod faciendum est.——When more is done than ought to be performed, it seems that sufficient is (actually) accomplished.

QUANDO principes inter partes loquuntur, et jus dicunt.——When the Emperors pronounce between the (litigating) parties, and declare the law (of the case).

QUANDO quod ago non valet ut agam, valeat quantum valere potest.——When that which I do is inefficacious in the mode I intend it, let it avail as much as possible.

QUAND un Seigneur de Parlement serra arrien de treason, ou felony, le Roy par ses lettres patents fera un grand et sage Seigneur d'estre le grand Seneschal d'Angleterre; qui doit faire un precept per faire venir xx. Seigneurs, ou xxviii., &c.——When a Peer of a Parliament shall be arraigned for treason or felony, the King by his letters patent suall make a noble and intelligent Peer High Steward of *England*, who is to issue a precept to cause twenty, or twenty-eight Peers to come, &c.

QUA non deliberetur sine speciali præcepto domini regis. .——From which he cannot be discharged without the King's special precept.

QUANTA esse debeat per nullam assizam generalem determinatum est, sed pro consuetudine singulorum comitatuum debeter.——The quantity should not be determined by any general assize, but be due according to the custom of the several counties.

QUANT bestes sauvages le Roy aler hors del forrest, le properté est hors del Roy; silz sount hors del parke capienti conceditur.——When the King's wild beasts go from the forest, the property ceases to be in him; (but) if they go out of the park, (then) they become the property of the captor.

QUANTO gradu unusquisque eorum distat stirpite, eodem distat inter se.——In so great a degree as each person is removed from the stock, in the same relationship they stand distant among themselves.

QUANT' testes?——How many witnesses?

QUANTUM damnificatus.——How much injured (or damaged).

QUANTUM homo debet domino ex homagio, tantum illi debet dominus ex dominio (præter solam reverentiam).—— As much as a man owes to the lord by homage, so much the lord owes him, from (his) seignorship (fealty only excepted).

QUANTUM inde Regi dare valeat per annum, salva sustentatione sua et uxoris, et liberorum suorum.——How much from thence he be able to pay the King annually, having besides a maintenance for himself, his wife and children.

QUANTUM meruit pro rata.——As much as he deserved for the proportion.

QUANTUM valebat.——As much as it was worth.

27

QUA placitum, &c., materiaque in eodum contenta, minus sufficiens in lege existet, &c.; unde pro defectu sufficientis placiti, &c., petit judicium.——By which the plea, &c., and the matter therein contained, are not sufficient in law, &c.; wherefore, on account of the want of a sufficient plea, &c., he prays judgment.

QUARE clausum et domum fregit?——Wherefore (or why) did he break the close and house?

QUARE clausum fregit?——Wherefore (or why) did he break the close?

QUARE clausum fregit et blada asportavit?——Wherefore (or why) did he break (or enter) the field, and carry away the herbage?

QUARE clausum suum fregit, et centum cuniculos suos tunc et ibidem inventos venatus fuit, occidit, cepit, et asportavit?——Wherefore (or why) did he break his close, and hunt, kill, and carry away one hundred of his rabbits, then and there found?

QUARE clausum quærentis fregit?——Wherefore (or why) did he break the plaintiff's close?

QUARE domum fregit?——Wherefore (or why) did he break the house?

QUARE domum ipsius A. apud W. (in qua idem A. quidam H. Scotum, per ipsum A. in guerra captam tanquam captivum suum, quousque sibi de centum libris, per quas idem H. redemptionem suam cum præfato A. pro vita sua salvanda fecerat satisfactum foret detinere), fregit, et ipsum H. cepit, et abduxit, vel quo voluit abire permissit, &c.?
——Wherefore (or why) did he break the house of him A. at W. (in which the said A. kept H., a certain Scotchman, whom A. had taken as his prisoner of war, until one hundred pounds should be paid him by the said H., in redemption to the said A. for saving his life), and he took the said H. and led him away, or permitted him to depart where he pleased?   Vide note.

QUARE ducentos cuniculos suos pretii cepit, &c.?——

Wherefore (or why) did he take two hundred rabbits of his, of the value, &c.?

QUARE ejecit infra terminum?——Wherefore (or why) did he eject within the term?

QUARE impedit?——"Wherefore (or why) did he hinder, or disturb?" The name of a writ, which lies for many purposes.

QUARE impedit infra semestre?——Wherefore (or why) did he disturb within half a year?

QUARE incumbravit?——Wherefore (or why) has he incumbered?

QUARE non admisit?——Why does he not admit?

QUARENTENA.——Quarantine: also a furlong, or forty perches.

QUARE obstruxit?——Why has he obstructed?

QUARE vi et armis?——Wherefore (or why) with force and arms?

QUARE vi et armis clausum ipsus A. apud B. fregit, et blada ipsius A. ad valentiam centum solidorum ibidem nuper crescentia, cum quibusdam averiis depastus fuit, conculcavit, et consumpsit, &c.?——Wherefore (or why) with force and arms did he break into the close of the said A. at B., and with certain cattle which he depastured, trod down and consumed the grass (or herbage) of the said A. lately growing there, to the value of one hundred shillings, &c.?

QUARTALIS.——A quart.

QUARTO die post.——On the fourth day afterwards.

QUASI agnum committere lupo ad devorandum.—— "Like putting the lamb with the wolf to be devoured." When a wardship was given to the heir of the infant, which was formerly the case, this expression was used to mark the impropriety of the custom; and the ancient *Romans* entertained the same opinion. *Vide Hor. Sat.* ii. 5; *Juv. Sat.* vi. 38.

QUASI contractus.——As though by way of agreement.

QUASI designata persona.——As if the person had been (specially) described.

QUASI ex contractu.——In nature of a contract.

QUASI ex delicto.——As an offence or crime.

QUASI inchoatum.——As though it were already begun, (or imperfect.)

QUASI in custodia legis.——As though (he were) in the custody of the law.

QUATENUS sine prejudicio indulgenter fieri potest.—— That it ought so far to be done graciously and without prejudice.

QUATUOR pedibus.——"On all fours;" i. e., perfectly agreeing together: frequently used when a case quoted meets the very *point* in argument.

QUE estate.——Whose (or which) estate.

QUELQUE chose que vous demandex aux lois *Romaines*, elles vous en fournissent la response.——Whatever thing you seek after in the *Roman* laws, they will furnish you with an answer.

QUEMADMODUM theatrum, cum commune sit, rectè tamen dici potest, ejus esse cum locum quem quisque occupavit. ——Like a theatre, which, although it is public, still it may be correctly said that the place which each person has occupied is his own.

QUEM magis utilem de duobus intellexerit.——Whom he may have considered the more useful of the two.

QUE peut achetur ou vendre.——Who may either buy or sell.

QUERENS.——A plaintiff.

QUERULA inofficiosi testamenti.——These words mean a complaint against a testamentary disposition which disinherited the heirs. Vide note to "*Inofficiosum testamentum.*"

QUERULATUS autem postea tenetur respondere, et habebit, licentiam consulendi, si requirat; habito autem consilio, debet factum negare quo accusatus est.——For the plain-

tiff is often bound to reply, and he shall have an imparlance, if he request it; but having obtained time to plead,
he should deny the fact with which he is accused.

QUESTUS est nobis.——Hath complained to us.

QUIA caret forma.——Because it is defective in form.

QUIA delegatus non potest delegare.——Because one
who is elected (a deputy) cannot depute.

QUIA dominus remisit curiam.——Because the lord
hath adjourned the court.

QUIA dom' rem' cur'.——*Vide last extract.*

QUIA duplex est, et caret forma. "Because it is double
(or ambiguous) and informal." Often formerly applied to
a plea filed for delay.

QUIA emptores terrarum.——"Because the purchasers
of lands." An ancient statute so called.

QUIA emptores terrarum de feoffatoribus et hæredibus
suis, et non de capitalibus dominis feodorum.——Because
the purchasers of lands (who bought) from feoffors and
their heirs, and not from the chief lords of the fee.

QUIA eronice emanavit.——Because it issued erro-
neously.

QUIA fortis est legis operatio.——Because the operation
of the law is powerful.

QUIA id commune est, nostrum esse dicitur.——Because
that which is common (to all), is said to be our own.

QUIA impedit?——"Why·does he disturb (or impede)?"
The name of a writ which lies for the patron of a living
against the person who has disturbed his right of presenta·
tion.

QUIA improvide emanavit.——Because it issued impru-
dently.

QUIA interest reipublicæ, ut sit finis litium.——Because
it concerns the republic that there should be an end of
litigation.

QUIA juris civilis studiosos decet haud imperitos esse
juris municipalis; et differentias exteri, patriique, juris

notas habere.——Because it is indecorous that the students of the civil law should be unskilful in the municipal law; and they should also understand the difference between foreign laws and those of their own country.

QUI alienum fundum ingreditur, potest, à domino, si is præviderit, prohiberi ne ingrediatur.——He who is entering upon another's estate, may be prohibited by the owner, if he has foreseen his purpose.

QUI alienum fundum ingreditur, venandi, aut aucupandi gratiâ, potest à domino prohiberi ne ingrediatur.——He who is entering upon another's estate for the purpose of hunting or fowling, may be prevented by the owner.

QUIA non refert an quis intentionem suam declaret verbis, an rebus, vel factis.——Because it is immaterial whether he shows his intention by language, things or deeds.

QUIA non sua culpa, sed parentum, id commisisse cognoscitur.——Because it is known that she did it not by her own fault, but that of her parents.

QUIA particeps criminis.——Because he is a partaker of the crime.

QUIA placitum, &c., materiaque in eodum contenta, minus sufficiens in lege existet, &c.: unde pro defectu sufficientis placitæ, &c., petit judicium, &c.——Because the plea, &c., and the matter therein contained, are insufficient in law, &c., and therefore, for want of a sufficient plea, &c., he prays judgment, &c.

QUIA quicunque aliquid statuerit, parte inaudita alterâ, æquum licet statuerit, haud æquus fuerit.——Because whoever shall adjudge a case, either of the parties being unheard, although he may determine correctly, yet he is by no means an impartial judge.

QUIA res cum onere transit ad quemcunque, &c.——Because the estate with its charge passes to whomsoever, &c.

QUI arma gerit.——Who bears (a coat) of arms.

QUIA tollit atque eximit causam é curia Baronum.——

Because it removes and discharges the action from the Barons' court.

QUI bene interrogat, bene docet.——He who interrogates well, teaches well.

QUIBUS scriptis plenam fidem adhiberi volumus.——To which writings we are willing to give full credit.

QUIBUS lectis et auditis.——Which being read and heard.

QUIBUS major reverentia et securitas debeter, ut templa, et judicia, quæ sanctæ habebuntur; arces et aula Regis; denique, locus quilibit præsente, aut adventante Rege.—— As temples and courts of justice are places in which the greatest reverence and security should be observed, are accounted sacred; so are the palaces and courts of the King; lastly, every place in which the King is present, or to which he is coming.

QUI cadere possit in virum constantem, non timidum et meticulosum.——Which (fear) might fall on a resolute man; not on one who is timid and cowardly.

QUI contra formam humani generis converso more procreatur, ut si mulier monstrosum vel prodigiosum enixa sit, inter liberos non computenter. Partus tamen, cui natura aliquantulum addiderit, vel diminuerit; ut si sex, vel tantum quatuor digitos habuerit, bene debet inter liberos connumeratus; et si membra sint inutilia aut tortuosa, non tamen est partus monstrosus.——An offspring procreated in an unnatural manner, different in shape from the human race; as if a woman produce a monstrous or unnatural (creature), it is not reckoned as one of the children. But a child to whom nature has added a little, or deprived of something (natural); as if it has six, or only four fingers, it is certainly accounted as one of the children; and, although the limbs are useless, or crooked, yet the offspring is not unnatural.

QUICQUID autem ceperis, eousque tuum esse intelligitur, donec tua custodia coercetur; cum vero tuam evaserit cus-

todiam, et in libertatem naturalem esse reciperit, tuum esse
desinet, et rursus occupantis fit.——But whatsoever you
capture is consequently understood to be yours, while it is
retained in your possession; but when it shall have escaped from thence, and regained its natural liberty, it
ceases to be yours, and again becomes the property of the
(next) captor.

QUICQUID per servum acquiritur id domino acquiritur.
——Whatever is obtained by the slave belongs to the lord
(or master). *Vide note.*

QUICQUID solvitur, solvetur secundum modum solventis.
——Whatever is paid, let it be discharged agreeably to the
(general) mode of payment.

QUI cum aliter tueri se non possunt, damni culpam dede-
rint, inoxii sunt.——They are guiltless of homicide, who
cannot otherwise defend themselves.

QUICUNQUE hospiti venienti lectum aut focum negaverit,
trium solidorum in latione.——Whoever shall deny a
traveller a bed or a fire, shall be fined three shillings. · Vide
note to " *Si quis homini.*"

" QUID adhuc desideramus testimonium? Reus est mortis."——" Why should we desire further evidence? He
deserves to die." These were the Chancellor's words on
the trial of Sir *Thomas More.*

QUIDDAM honorarium.——A certain honorary fee.

QUID emptionem, venditionemque recipit, etiam pignara-
tionem recipere potest.——Whatever a person has bought
or sold, that he may also take by way of a pledge.

QUI de nece virorum illustrium, qui consiliis et consis-
torio nostro intersunt, senatorum etiam, (nam et ipsi pars
corporis nostri sunt,) vel cujus libet prostremo qui militat
nobiscum, cogitaverit; (eadem enim severitate voluntatem
sceleris, qua effectum, puniri jura voluerint), ipse quidem,
ut pote majestatis reus, gladio seriatur, bonis ejus omnibus
fisco nostro addictis.——He who shall have devised the
death of the illustrious men, who are present at our coun-

cils and assembly, also of our senators (for they are part of ourself), or lastly, of any other person who fights for us, (for the laws will punish with the same severity the disposition to crime, as if it were committed;) the same person shall be devoted to the sword as guilty of high treason, and all his goods confiscated to our treasury.

QUID enim sanctius, quod omni religione munitius, quam domus uniuscujusque civium?——For what is more sacred, more defended by every religious obligation, than the house of each of the citizens?

QUI destruit medium, destruit finem.——He who destroys the means, destroys the end.

QUID juris clamat.——"Which he claims of right." The name of an ancient form of action.

QUIDQUID multis pecatur inultum est.——"The crime which is committed by the multitude (or mob) must pass with impunity."——In every government it is sometimes politic, if criminals are *very* numerous, to grant a pardon.

QUID si in ejusmodi cera centum sigilla hoc annulo impressero?——"Suppose I shall have put on this kind of wax one hundred impressions with my ring?" It was customary anciently to seal with impressions set in *rings*. There are many grants now extant devoid of any subscription by the grantors. *Vide note.*

QUID sit in misericordia.——That he be in mercy.

QUID tibi fieri non vis, alteri ne feceris.——Do not to another what you would not wish he should do to yourself.

QUIETA non movere.——Not to disturb things at rest (or decided cases).

QUIETI Reditus.——"Quit Rents;" payable out of lands, generally to the superior lord of the fee, where the tenant goes *free* of all other services.

QUIETUM clamavi, remisi, relaxavi, &c.——"I have quitted claim, remised, released," &c. These were words used formerly in deeds of releases of lands.

QUIETUS, recipit; et quærens est in misericordia pro falso clamore.——Being satisfied, he obtains (an acquittal;) and the plaintiff is in mercy for his unjust complaint—i. e. he is liable to fine or imprisonment, &c.

QUI ex damnato coitu nascuntur, inter liberos non computantur.——Those who are born from an illicit connec- tion, are not reckoned among the children.

QUI facit per alium, facit per se.——He who acts for another, does it himself.

QUI guadet lucidis intervallis.——Who is happy in his lucid intervals.

QUI hæret in litera, hæret in cortice.——Commonly translated, "He who sticks to the letter, sticks to the bark;" but it implies more properly one who *stops* or goes no further than the *letter* of an instrument, to the neglect of its intention or meaning.

QUI illi de temporalibus; episcopo de spiritualibus de- beat respondere.——Who ought to answer to him in tem- poral, and to the Bishop in spiritual concerns.

QUI improbe coeunt in alienam litem ut quicquid ex con- demnatione in rem ipsius redactum fuerit inter eos com- municaretur, lege *Julia*, de vi privata tenentur.——Those who dishonestly join in another's suit, that whatsoever be obtained from the judgment should be divided between them, such agreements are considered by the *Julian* law of no effect. Vide note to " *Campi Partitio.*"

QUI inquisitionem petit de vita vel membris.——Who seeks (or holds) an inquest of life or limb.

QUI in utero sunt, in jure civili intelliguntur in rerum natura esse cum de eorum commodo agatur.——In the na- ture of things, those who are in the womb are understood, by the civil law, to be in existence when a thing is done for their benefit.

QUI ire poterant quo volebant.——Who may have pow- er to go where they please.

QUI jussu judicis aliquod fecerit, non videtur dolo malo

fecisse, quia parere necesse est.——He who shall have performed anything, by order of a Judge, does not appear to have acted with any bad intention, as it was necessary to obey (his order).

QUILIBET homo dignus venatione sua in sylva et in agris sibi propriis, et in dominio suo.——Every man has a right to hunt in his own wood and fields, and in his own demesne.

QUILIBET totum tenet et nihil tenet; scilicet, totum in communi, et nihil separatim per se.——Every one holds all, and holds nothing; viz., he holds all in common, and nothing by himself, separately.

————"QUINETIAM lex

Pœnaque lata, malo quæ nollet carmine quenquam
Describi.   Vertere modum formidine fustis."

"Moreover, it is an extensive law and punishment which will not permit a person to be described in doggerel verse. To change the *style* for fear of a club." *Horace* here wittily alludes to the *Roman* law for the punishment of libel.

QUINDENA.——The fifteenth day after a festival.

QUI nolunt inter se contendere, solent per mentium rem emere in commune; quod a societate longum remotum. ——Those who have not desired to manage business for themselves, are accustomed mutually to purchase a thing in common; which is very different from a copartnership.

QUI non habet in crumena, luat in corpore.——He who has nothing in his purse, must suffer in his person.

QUINQUE portus.——The Cinque Ports.

QUINTO exactus.——The fifth exaction.

QUI principi placuit, legis habet rigorem.——He who has pleased the Emperor, has the power of the law. `

QUI prior est tempore, potior est jure.——He who is first in (point of) time, is the stronger in the law.

QUI pro Domino Rege quam pro se ipso sequitur.—— Who sues as well for the King, as for himself.

QUI scit se decipi, non decipiatur.——"He who knows

he is deceived, is not deceived." A remark frequently made where a person purchases an article knowing its defects.

QUI sentit commodum, sentire debet et onus.——He ought to bear the burden who would derive the advantage.

QUI sequitur tam pro pauperibus, quam pro se ipso.—— Who sues as well for the poor, as for himself.

QUISQUIS potest renunciare juri suo per se introducto? ——Who can protest against his own law brought in by himself?

QUI statuit aliquid, parte inauditâ altera, æquum licet statuerit, haud æquus fuit.——He who has decided any matter without having heard both sides of the question, although he shall have determined impartially, it was unfair.

QUI tacet consentire videtur.——"He who is silent appears to consent:" or, as the old adage observes, "Silence gives consent."

QUI tam pro domino Rege, quam pro se ipso in hac parte sequitur.——"Who sues as well for the King, as for himself in this matter." This is an extract from an ancient declaration, where an informer sued for a penalty, part of which would belong to the King, and part to the plaintiff.

QUI tollit atque eximit causam ó curia Baronum.—— Because it removes and discharges the cause from the Barons' Court.

QUI vi rapuit, fur improbior esse videtur.——He who robs by violence, appears to be the greater thief.

Q'UN un'q' prist meason des enemies quel avoit prise devant d'un' Englishe, que il averoit come ceo chose gaigne en batel, &c. Et nemy le Roy ne l'Admiral, ne le partie a qui le propertie fuit devant, &c., pur ceo q' le partie ne vient freshment, mesme le jour q' il fuit prise de luy, et ante occasum solis, et claime ceo.——Spoil which any one takes from the enemy, and which had before been taken from the *English*, let him have as anything gained in battle,

&c. And neither the King, nor the Admiral, nor the party to whom the property before belonged, nor he who possessed it on the very day that it was taken from him, and before sunset, may lay claim to it.

QUOAD hoc casus omissus.——As to this, it is an omitted case.

QUOAD scriptionem et collectionem libellorum in indictamento nominat' tantum, quod defendens est culpabilis; et quoad totum residuum in eodem indictamento content' quod defendens non est inde culpabilis.——That as respects the writing and collecting the libels named in the indictment, the defendant is guilty; but as to the entire residue contained in the same indictment, the defendant is not guilty.

QUOAD vinculum.——Whilst the bond (continued.)

QUO animo?——With what intent?

QUOCUNQUE modo volit; quocunque modo possit.——In what manner he would; in what manner he could.

QUOD ab ædibus non facile revellitur.——Which cannot be easily torn from the house.

QUOD ab initio non valet, tractu temporis convalescere non potest.——That which had no force in the beginning, cannot acquire strength by the lapse of time.

QUOD ab initio vitiosum est, tractu temporis non convalescit.——What is illegal in the beginning, will obtain no validity by the length of its duration.

QUOD accedas ad curiam.——That you go to the court.

QUOD actionem ulterius maintineri non debet.——That he ought not further to maintain the suit.

Quod adest consulito.——Consult the present good.

QUOD ad hostes attinet, cum iis omne cessare solet commercium, nec fieri profecto potest: at cum illis negotiemur quibus cum bellum gerimus; quum nec illis ad nos, nec nobis ad illos tutus accesus sit, et personis captivitas, rebus publicis imminet, si in hostes deprehendantur.——What belongs to the enemy, when all commerce with them has ceased, nor can with certainty be renewed : and when we negotiate with those with whom we are at war; since there is no safe access from them to us, nor from us to them, and their persons and property are in danger of being captured, if they be discovered with the enemy.

QUOD adhuc detinet.——Which he yet detains.

QUOD adhuc remittitur.——Which he remits up to this time.

QUOD ad warrenam pertinet.——" Which belongs to a warren." A warren (or, as it is more commonly called, a *free* warren) is a right of sporting over other persons' lands; but very few if any such warrens are supposed to be now in existence. Vide *Black. Com.*

QUOD a gleba amoveri non poterint, quamdiu solvere possunt debitas et pensiones.——That they cannot be removed from the land, so long as they are able to pay their debts and fees (or duties).

QUOD *A.* injuste levavit tale nocumentum.——That *A.* unjustly made such a nuisance.

QUOD alias bonum et justum est, si per vim, aut fraudem, petatur, malum et injustum est.——What otherwise is fair and honest, if sought for by violence or fraud, it then be-becomes wicked and illegal.

QUOD ante exhibitionem informationis, scilicet, termino Sancti *Michaelis.*——That prior to presenting (or perhaps filing) the information to wit, in *Michaelmas* term.

QUOD breve cassetur.——That the writ be quashed.

QUOD caperet *I. G.* ad satisfaciendum.——That he should take *I. G.* to make satisfaction.

QUOD capiatur.——That he be taken.

QUOD cepit corpus prædicti *I. S.* cujus corpus *A. B.* (ballivus) coram justiciariis domini regis, ad diem et locum infra contentum paratum habebit.——That he took the body of the said *I. S.,* which *A. B.* (the bailiff) will have ready before the King's justices, at the day and place within contained.

Quod cepit damas suas ad valentiam tantum, &c.——That he took his deer to the value of so much, &c.

Quod cepit et asportavit.——Which he took and carried away. .

Quod certa res in judicium possit deduci.——That a certain affair may be brought under consideration (or judgment).

Quod clerici scribunt judicia correcte.——That the clerks transcribe the judgments correctly. *Vide note.*

Quod cognitio causæ captionis et detentionis prædicti *Johannis Paty* non pertinet ad curiam dictæ dominæ reginæ coram ipsa regina, ideo idem *Johannis* remittitur.——Because the question as to the cause of the caption and detention of the said *John Paty*, does not belong to the court of our said Lady, the Queen, before the Queen herself, therefore the said *John* is discharged.

Quod computet.——That he account.

Quod constat curiæ, opere testium non indiget.——What appears to the court, needs not the aid of witnesses.

Quod conditio indebiti non datur ultra quam locupletior factus est qui accepit.——That the situation of the debtor is in no wise different, except that it has made the person richer, who has received it; (meaning the receipt of the article for which he stands indebted.)

Quod convictus est, et forisfaciat.——That he is convicted, and outlawed.

Quod corpus prædicti *A.*, si Laicus sit, capias, et in prisona nostra salvo custodiri facias quosque de prædicto debito satisfecerit.——" That you take the body of the said *A.*, if he be layman, and him in our prison safely keep, until he satisfy the said debt." Words used in a writ sued out upon a forfeited recognizance.

Quod corrupte aggreatum fuit.——Which was corruptly agreed.

Quod cum defendens apud *London*, &c., per scriptum, &c., concessit se teneri.——That whereas the defendant, at

London, &c., by (his) writing, &c., acknowledged himself to be bound.

QUOD cum per consuetudinem totius regni *Angliæ*, hactenus usitatam et approbatam, uxores debent, et solent, a tempore, &c., habere suam rationabilem partem bonorum maritorum suorum; ita videlicet, quod si nullos habuerint liberos, tunc mediatatem, et si habuerint, tunc tertiam partem, &c.——That whereas by the custom of the whole kingdom of *England*, hitherto used and approved, wives ought, and are accustomed from time, &c., to possess a reasonable part of their husbands' effects; in this manner, that if they have no children, they take half; and if they have children, then a third part.

QUOD cur' concessit.——Which the court agreed to.

QUOD custos sustenet parcos, vivaria, &c.——That the keeper preserve the parks, fish-ponds, &c.

QUOD de cætero liceat unicuique libero homini terras suas, seu tenementa seu partem, inde ad voluntatem suam vendere; ita tamen quod Feoffatus teneat terram seu tenementum illud de capitali domino feodi illius, ferendum servitia et consuetudines per quæ Feoffator suus illa prius de eo tenuit. Que estate fuit fait (as saith one) pur l'advantage d'Seigneur.——That from henceforth it be lawful for every freeman to sell his lands or tenements, or part thereof, in what way he please; so that the Feoffee hold the same of the chief lord of the fee, to perform the services and customs by which his Feoffor held the same of him (the lord) prior to that time: which tenure was made (says one) for the advantage of the chief lord (of the fee).

QUOD defendat se duodecima manu.——That he defend himself by twelve compurgators. Vide note to " *Compurgatores.*"

QUOD defendens capiatur pro fine.——That the defendant be arrested for a fine.

QUOD defendens eat sine die.——That the defendant be discharged.

QUOD defendens sit in misericordia, &c.——"That the defendant be in mercy," &c., i. e. subject to fine, imprisonment, &c.

QUOD de quo, vel de quibus, tenementa prædicta tenentur, juratores prædicti ignorant.——Because the jurors know not from, or by whom the said tenements are held.

QUOD detinuit.——Which he (or she) detains.

QUOD distributio rerum quæ in testamento relinquntur, autoritate ecclesiæ fiet.——That the distribution of the effects which are left in a will be made by the authority of the church.

QUOD dolosus versatur in generalibus.——That a deceitful person is skilled in general matters.

QUOD dotat eam de tali manerio cum pertinentiis, &c. ——That he endow her of such a manor with the appurtenances, &c.

QUODDUM scriptum *Anglice.*——A certain writing in *English.*

QUOD durum videbatur circumstantibus.——Which appeared severe to the bystanders.

QUOD eat consultatio.——That the consultation should proceed.

QUOD ei deforceat.——These words, joined with some others, mean that he restore the possession "*which he has unjustly taken.*"

QUOD eligitis et juratis majorem, &c., secundum auctoritatem vestram.——That you elect and swear the mayor, &c., agreeably to your authority.

QUOD elegit sibi executionem fieri de omnibus catallis et medietate terræ.——That he chose to have execution of all the chattels, and a moiety of the land.

QUOD enim jus habet fiscus in aliena calamitate, ut de re tam luctosa compendium sectetur?——For what right has the treasury, in another person's adversity, to derive advantage from such a distressing occurrence?

28

Quod enim si quod fuit in agro pretiosissimum, hoc evictum est, aut quod fuit in agro viliocissimum æstimabile loci qualitas, et sic est ingressus.——Therefore if any very valuable thing, or even of no value at all, was in the field, this is proved, and (thus) its quality and the entry to the same may be ascertained.

Quod Episcopus vel Archdiaconus placita in hundredo non teneat.——That neither the Bishop nor the Archdeacon may hold pleas in the Hundred (Court).

Quod est inconveniens et contra rationem, non est permissum in lege.——That which is incongruous and contrary to reason is not allowed in the law.

Quod faciat tenementum.——That he should raise up (or build) the edifice.

Quod faciat tenementum reseisiri de catallis.——That he cause the tenement to be dispossessed of the goods.

Quod fato contingit, cuivis diligentissimo possit contingere.——That which is accidental may happen to the most careful person.

Quod fato contingit, et cuivis paterfamiliæ, quamvis diligentissimo, possit contingere.——That which occurs by accident, and may happen to any father of a family, however careful he may be.

Quod fieri faciat de bonis.——That he cause to be made of the goods.

Quod fieri non debet, factum valet.——Which ought not to be done, yet being done, is efficacious.

Quod firmarius non erit onerabilis et taxabilis ad ratas pauperum pro peculiis; et quod artifex est onerabilis et taxabilis pro peculiis in arte.——That a farmer shall not be chargeable and taxable to the poor's rates for his stock; but that the artificer (or tradesman) be chargeable and taxable for his stock in trade.

Quod fuit concessum.——Which was agreed.

Quod fuit concessum per cur'.——Which the court consented to.

Quod fuit concessum per plusieurs.——Which was agreed to by many persons.

Quod fuit negatum.——Which was denied.

Quod habeant et teneant se semper in armis et equis, ut decet et oportet: et quod semper sint prompti et parati ad servitium suum integrum nobis explendum et peragendum, cum opus adfuerit, secundum quod debent de feodis, et tenementis suis, de jure nobis facere.——That they keep and continue themselves always (equipped) with arms and horses, as it becomes and belongs to them; and that they be always ready to fulfil and perform to us their entire service, whenever occasion requires, according as they ought by law to do for us on account of their fees and tenures. *Vide note.*

Quod habeat executionem.——That he may have execution.

Quod habetur tale recordum.——That such a record may be had.

Quod ibi semper debet triatio, ubi juratores meliorem possunt habere notitiam.——That there should always be a (new) trial, where the jury may obtain a better knowledge (of the facts).

Quod impedit decies tantum.——That he disturbed ten times only.

Quod in disjunctivis sufficit alteram partem esse veram. ——Which being in the disjunctive, it is (still) sufficient (if) the other part be true.

Quod initio non valet, tractu temporis non convalescet. ——That which is unlawful in the beginning will acquire no validity by the lapse of time.

Quod in majore non valet, nec valet in minore.—— That which does not avail in the greater, does not in the less.

Quod ipse, et hæredes sui, habeant liberam warrenam in omnibus dominicis sui in *N.* in Com' *B.* dum tamen færæ illæ non sint infra metas forrestæ nostræ, ita quod nullus

intret terras illas ad fugandam in eis, vel aliquod capiend'
quod ad warrenam pertinet.——That he and his heirs have
free warren in all his demesnes in *N.* in the county of *B.*
only while those wild animals are not within the bounds
of our forest; so that he enter not into any of those lands
to hunt over them, or take anything which belongs to (free)
warren.

QUOD ipsi, omnesque homines ejusdem facultatis.——
That these and all other persons of the like profession.

QUOD jus cogit, id voluntate impetrato.——What the
law insists upon, allow voluntarily.

QUOD juste et sine dilatione habere faciat tale rationabile
auxilium de militibus libere tenentis suis in bailiva sua.
——"That justly and without delay he cause to be taken
(or levied) such a reasonable aid from Knights, who hold
lands in free tenure in his bailiwick." This was part of
the precept to the sheriff directing him to raise money for
the use of the chief lords of the fee.

QUOD legis constructio non facit injuriam.——That the
construction of law worketh no injury.

QUOD libera sit cujuscunque ultima voluntas.——That
every person's last will be uncontrolled.

QUOD liber traditur defendenti per ordinar'; sed non al-
locat'.——For which purpose the book is given to the defendant by the ordinary; but he is not spoken to.

QUOD licete barganizavit.——Which he lawfully agreed
for.

QUOD licitum sit donatori rem datum dare vel vendere
cui voluerit, exceptis viris religiosis.——That it be lawful
for the donor to give (or devise) the estate which had been
given him, or to sell it to whom he pleased, except to men
in holy orders (or to those holding religious houses, as
monasteries, &c).

QUOD literatura non facit clericum, nisi habet sacram
tonsuram.——That learning does not make a clergyman,
unless he obtain the sacred tonsure.

Quod mandavit ballivo de *D.*, qui respondit quod cepit corpus.——That he had commanded the bailiff of *D.*, who returned that he had taken the body.

Quod manum suorom amoverunt omnino.——That they totally relinquish the possession.

Quod manus domini regis amoveantur, et possessio restituatur petenti, salvo jure domini regis.——That the King's hands may be removed, and the possession restored to the petitioner, saving the King's right.

Quod moderate castigavit.——That he moderately chastised.

Quod naturalis ratio inter omnes homines constituit, vocatur jus gentium.——*That* natural reason which is established among all men, is called the law of nations.

Quod nemo allegans suam turpitudinem audiendus.—— That no person, admitting his own depravity, should be (allowed to be) heard.

Quod nemo ejusdem tenementi simul potest hæres, et dominus.——That no one can be the heir and lord of such tenement at the same time.

Quod nil capiat per breve.——That he take nothing by the writ.

Quod nocumentum amoveatur.——That the nuisance may be abated.

"Quod nolunt leges *Angliæ* mutare, quæ huc usitatæ sunt et approbatæ."——"Because they are unwilling to change the laws of *England,* which hitherto have been used and approved." The language of the ancient *English* Barons.

Quod non apparet, non est.——"That which does not appear, has no existence;" i. e. facts which do not appear in evidence ought not to be taken into consideration.

Quod non corrupte aggreatum fuit.——Which was not corruptly agreed upon.

Quod non est factum suum.——Which is not his deed.

Quod non est justum aliquem post mortem fuisse bastardum.——That it is not right that any one after death (be deemed) to have been illegitimate.

QUOD non fuerunt debito modo electi.——That they were not elected in a legal manner.

QUOD non fuit electus.— —That he was not chosen.

QUOD non habuit.——Which he has not held (or occupied).

QUOD non habuit nec tenuit firmam contra formam statuti.——That he has not held or occupied the estate against the form of the statute.

QUOD non omittas propter, &c.——That you do not omit on account of, &c.

QUOD non omitteret propter libertatem talem, quia, &c. ——That he should not omit by reason of such liberty (or privilege), because, &c.

QUOD non solvit secundum formam et effectum conditionis.——Which he has not paid according to the manner and effect of the condition.

QUOD nullius est, id ratione naturali occupanti conceditur.——What is the property of no one, that, by natural reason, belongs to the occupier.

QUOD nullius est fit occupantis.——That which is no one's property, belongs to the person who has possession of it.

QUOD nullus episcopus vel infra impositus die Dominico causas adjudicare præsumat.——That no bishop or any under him presume to adjudge causes on the Lord's day. Vide note to "*Dies Dominicus*," &c.

QUOD nullus justiciarius vel minister regis insulam illam ingredi potest ad aliquam jurat', extra, &c.——That no justice or minister of the King can enter the island to make oath to anything, besides, &c.

QUOD obstruxit, et obstipavit.——That he obstructed, and hindered.

QUOD officiarius et assistentes sui, &c., consueverunt capere ex quolibet modio grani, per aliquam personam, in burgo prædicto venditi, vel vendendi induct' vicessimam partem cujus libet modii.——That the officer and his assistants, &c., have been accustomed, by some person, to take from every measure of grain sold, or brought to be sold, in the said borough, the twentieth part thereof.

QUOD omnes justiciarii concesserant quad hoc.——That, as to this, all the Judges had agreed.

QUOD ordinarii, hujusmodi bona nomine ecclesiæ occupantes, nullam (vel saltem) indebitam faciunt distributionem.——That the ordinaries, taking possession of effects of this kind, in name of the church, do not make any (or at least) due distribution. *Vide note.*

QUOD partes finis nihil habuerint, et de hoc ponit se super patriam, &c.——That the parties to the fine had no interest (in the land), and of this he puts himself upon the country, &c.

QUOD partes replacitent.——That the parties replead.

QUOD partitio fiat.——That a division be made.

QUOD partitio sit firma et stabilis.——That the division may be firm and sure.

QUOD permittat habere rationabiles divisas.——That he permit (him or her) to possess reasonable shares.

QUOD permittat prosternare.——That he give leave to demolish.

QUOD placita de catallis, debitis, &c., quæ summam quadraginta solidorum attingunt, vel eam excedunt, secundum legem et consuetudinem *Angliæ*, sine brevi regis placitari non debent.——That pleas of goods, debts, &c., which amount to forty shillings, or more, according to the law and custom of *England*, ought not to be sued for without the King's writ.

QUOD pœnam imprisonamenti subire non potest.—— That he cannot undergo the punishment of confinement.

QUOD populus postremum jussit, id jus ratum esto.—— Let that be considered the law which the people last decreed.

Quod prædictæ literæ patentes Domini Regis revocentur, adnullentur, et vacuæ et invalidiæ pro nullo penitus habeantur et teneantur; ac etiam quod rotulamentum eorundem cancelletur, cassetur et adnihiletur.——That the said letters patent of the King be revoked, made void, invalidated and of no effect, and be held and thoroughly accounted of no utility; and that the same roll be cancelled, avoided and destroyed.

Quod præd' quer' solverit præd' def' præd' £300.—— That the said plaintiff shall pay the said defendant the said £300.

Quod pregnantis mulieris damnatæ pœna differatur, quoad pariat.——That the punishment of a condemned pregnant woman be deferred until she be delivered.

Quod principi placuit legis habet vigorem, cum populus ei, et in eum, omne suum imperium et potestatem conferat. ——That which has received the Emperor's consent possesses the force of law, because the people yield up to and for him, all authority and power.

Quod publica sunt omnia fluvia et portus; ideoque jus piscandi omnibus commune est in portu, et in fluminibus. Riparum etiam nusus publicus jure gentium, sicut ipsius fluminis..——That all rivers and ports are public; therefore the right of fishing in ports and in rivers is common to all. So, also, by the law of nations, the public use of streams is similar to that of the river.

Quod quærens action' non.——That the plaintiff has no (cause of) action.

Quod quærens nil capiat per billam.——That the plaintiff take nothing by his bill.

Quod quandoque majus, quandoque minus cassetur.—— That when the principal (is extinct) the accessory also ceases.

Quod recapiat omnes prisonar' qui fecerunt escap' a prison' Mar', et non legitime exonerenter a prisona præd', et ducat eos in prisonam prædict'.——That he retake all

prisoners who have escaped from the prison of the Mar-
shalsea, and who could not be legally discharged from the
said prison, and conduct them into the prison aforesaid.

QUOD recuperet debitum cum damnis.——That he recover his debt with damages (or costs).

QUOD recuperet dotem suam.——That she recover her
dower.

QUOD recuperet terminum suum.——That he recover his
term.

QUOD redeat inde quietus in perpetuum; et quærens in
misericordia.——" That he depart thence forever discharged; and the plaintiff be in mercy," i. e. subject to
fine, imprisonment, &c.

QUOD relatur ad personam, intelligi debet de conditione
personæ.——That which relates to a person, should be understood of his rank (or condition).

QUOD respondeat ouster.——That he answer over (or
again).

QUOD R. S. dedit J. R. et M. uxori ejus, et hæredibus
de corpore ipsius M. procederent, &c.——Which R. S. gave
to J. R., and M. his wife, and the heirs of the body of the
same M.

QUOD sibi erit fidelis, ad ultimum diem vitæ, contra om-
nem hominem (excepto rege) et quod credentiam sibi commissum non manifestabit.——That he shall be faithful to
him to the last day of his life, against every man, (the King
excepted,) and that he shall not divulge the trust (or confidence) committed to his charge.

QUOD sit in misericordia.——" That he be in mercy," i. e.
subject to fine, imprisonment, &c.

QUOD stet prohibitio.——That the prohibition may
stand.

QUOD talem eligi faciat, qui melius et sciat et velit, et
possit, officio illo intendere.——That he cause such a person to be elected, who more fully understands, and is willing and able to perform that duty.

QUOD taliter processum fuit, &c.——That there was such a process, &c.

QUOD tenementum faciat esse in pace.——That he cause the tenement (or holding) to remain unmolested.

QUOD tenementum faciat reseisire de catallis.——That he cause the tenement to be dispossessed of the goods.

QUOD terræ et tenementa de tenura de *Gavelkind* de tempore, &c., inter hæredes masculos partabilia, et partita fuerunt.——Because the lands and tenements of *Gavelkind* tenure, from the time, &c., were divided and shared among the male heirs.

QUOD ultima voluntas esset libera.——That the last will be uncontrolled.

QUOD vendidi, non aliter fit accipientis quam si aut pretium nobis solutum sit, aut satis eo nomine datum; vel etiam fidem habuerimus, sine ulla satisfactione.——What I have sold does not become the property of the purchaser, except there be either a price paid to us, or sufficient given by way of payment; or we obtain a promise (or perhaps a *surety*); or without some other satisfaction.

QUOD vero naturalis ratio inter omnes homines constituit, id apud omnes gentes parque custoditur, vocaturque jus gentium, quasi quo jure omnes gentes utantur.——But that which natural reason has established among men, and is alike observed among all people, is called the law of nations, as though all nations were conversant with such law.

QUOD vidua remanet duodecem menses in domo sua.——That the widow remain twelve months in her house. *Vide note.*

QUO jure.——By what right?

QUO minus.——The name given to a writ issuing from the *Exchequer* court. In this writ it is suggested that the plaintiff owes the King a debt, by which fiction he is considered capable of suing in the court of *Exchequer*. Vide "*Scaccarium.*"

'Quo minus sufficiens existit.——Whereby he is the less able.

Quoniam attachiamenta.——The title of an old Scotch law book.

Quorum unum esse volumus.——"One of whom we desire to be present." A person is said to be of the "*Quorum*," when the writ or *Dedimus* contains the following, or similar words; "*Quorum* aliquem vestrum *A. B. C. D.* &c., unum esse volumus."

Quot generationes numerantur, tot enumerantur gradus dempto stirpite.——As many generations as there are counted, so many degrees are reckoned, taking them from the stock (or root).

Quoties bella non ineunt, multum venando, plus per otium, transigunt.——When wars do not interpose, they pass much (of their time) in hunting; more in idleness. *Vide note.*

Quoties dubia interpretatio libertatis, secundum libertatem respondendum est.——As often as the interpretation of liberty be doubtful, let it be decided in its favor.

Quoties in verbis nulla est ambiguatas, ibi nulla expositio contra verba fienda est.——Where there is no ambiguity in the words, there can be no interpretation made to the contrary.

Quoto gradu unusquisque eorum distat a stirpite, eodem distat inter se.——In the same degree that each person is distant from the stock, so far is each removed among themselves.

Quotuplex.——Of how many kinds?

Quousque debitum satisfactum fuerit.——Until the debt be satisfied.

Quo warranto.——"By what authority?" The name of a writ against a person who has usurped a franchise, or an office.

Quum bellum civitas aut illatum, defendit aut infert, magistratus qui ei bello præsint deliguntur.——When a state defends or goes to war, the magistrates who preside over it are chosen to command.

Quum duæ inter se repugnantia reperiantur in testamento, ultima ratæ est.——When there are two repugnant (clauses) in a will, the last (clause) is established. [*Sed. qu.*]

Quyke.——Quick: living.

NOTES TO Q.

Quadruplator.—The rewards, proposed by the *Roman* laws to the informer, were sometimes a fourth part of the criminal's goods; and sometimes only an eighth part, as *Spurnheim* assures us from *Suetonius* and *Tacitus.*

Quando hasta, &c.—The investiture of possession, during the middle ages, was generally, or perhaps invariably, performed upon the premises, by the delivery of a spear, bow, key, or some other thing, accompanied with such words, in the presence of witnesses, particularly designating the mode by which the donee or grantee was to possess the land. The transferring of houses and lands in *England*, even at present, is sometimes effected by *Feoffment*, where the vendor directs every person to remove from the house or land sold, and delivers the purchaser a key, twig, or turf, whilst he remains on the premises sold; and this mode of conveyancing has its peculiar benefit; for, in *some* cases, it has the same effect as a fine levied, to say nothing of its notoriety. The *Jews* anciently had a mode something similar. Vide *Ruth*, c. vi. 7.

Quare domum, &c.—When wars between the barons were permitted to be carried on, with little or no restraint, there is no doubt considerable sums of money were frequently obtained for the *ransom* of prisoners of war. Nothing can more clearly show the turbulent and disgraceful state of society which existed in those days, almost through the whole of *Europe.* It appears that an action on the case lay against a person who released a prisoner from the custody of a *private* captor. What an inducement did such a state of society as this hold out for bringing into action the worst passions of human nature—cruelty and covetousness!

There is no custom in the middle ages more singular than that of *private* war. It was a right of so great importance, and prevailed so universally, that the regulations concerning it occupy a considerable place in the system of legislation during the middle ages. Among the ancient *Germans*, as well as other nations in a similar state of society, the *right* of avenging injuries was a *private* and *personal* right, exercised by force of arms, without any reference to an umpire, or any appeal to a magistrate for decision. This practice was established among the barbarous nations (after their settlement in the provinces of the empire, which they conquered); for as the causes of disunion among them multiplied, so their family feuds and *private* wars became more frequent. Proofs of this occur in their early historians, vide *Greg. Turon. Hist. lib.* vii. c. 2. *lib.* viii. c. 18. *lib.* x. c. 27; and likewise in the codes of their laws. It was not only *allowable* for the relations to avenge the injuries of their families, but it was *incumbent* on them so to do. Thus, by the laws of the *Angli* and *Wereni*, " *Ad quemcunque hæreditas terræ pervenerit, ad illum vestis bellica, id est, lorica et ultio proximi, et solatio læsi, debet pertinere.*" Vide *Leg. Longob. lib.* ii. *tit.* 14, § 10.—i. e. "Such person to whom the inheritance of the land descends, to him also should belong the war robe; that is, the avenging his nearest relative, the coat of mail, and the comforting of the wounded." None but gentlemen, or persons of noble birth, had the right of waging *private* war. All disputes between the slaves, (*villani,*) the inhabitants of towns, and freemen of inferior condition, were decided in the courts of justice. The right of *private* war supposed nobility of birth, and equality of rank in *both* the contending parties. Vide *Beaumanoir Coustumes de Beauv. c.* lix. p. 300.

The dignified ecclesiastics likewise claimed and exercised the right of private war; but as it was not altogether decent for them to prosecute quarrels in person, *Advocati,* or *Vidames,* were chosen by the several monasteries and bishoprics. These were commonly men of high rank and reputation, who became the protectors of churches and convents which they erected; espoused their quarrels, and fought their battles. Vide *Brussel* Usages Des Fiefs, *tom.* i. p. 144, and *Du Cange, Voc* " Advocatius." On many occasions the martial ideas, to which ecclesiastics of noble birth were accustomed, made them forget the pacific spirit of their profession, and led them into the field in person, at the head of their vassals, " *flamma, ferro, cæde, possessiones Ecclesiarum prelati defendebant.*" Vide *Guido Abbas, ap. Du Cange, ib.* p. 179.—i. e. " The prelates of churches defended their possessions with fire, sword, and slaughter." It was not every injury or trespass, that gave a gentleman a title to make war upon his adversary. Atrocious acts of violence, insults and affronts publicly committed, were legal and permitted motives for taking arms against the authors of them. Such crimes as are now punished *capitally* in civilized nations, at that time justified private hostilities. Vide *Beauman. c.* lix. *Du Cange Dissert.* xxix. sur *Joinville,* p. 331. But though the avenging of flagrant injuries was the only motive that could lawfully authorize a *private* war, yet we find that disputes concerning civil property, (and frequently the most unbounded avarice,) often gave rise to hostilities, and were terminated by the sword. Vide *Du Cange Dissert.* p. 332.

All persons present when any quarrel arose, or any act of violence was committed, were included in the war which it occasioned; for it was supposed impossible for any man in such a situation to remain neuter, without taking side with one or the other of the contending parties. Vide *Beauman.* p. 300. All the kindred of the two principals in the war were included in it, and were obliged to espouse the quarrel of the chieftain with whom they were connected. Vide *Du Cange Dissert.* 332. This was founded on the maxim of the ancient Germans, " *suscipere tam inimicitas, seu patris seu propinqui quam amicitias necesse est,*"—i. e. " that it is as proper to avenge the wrongs of the father and kinsmen, as to have their friendship." A maxim, *perhaps* natural to all rude nations, among which the form of society and political union strengthen such a sentiment. This obligation was enforced by legal authority. If a person refused to take part in the quarrel with his kinsman, and to aid him against his adversary, he was deemed to have renounced all the rights and privileges of kindredship, and became incapable of succeeding to any of his relations, or of deriving any benefit from any civil right of property belonging to them. Vide *Du Cange Dissert.* 333.

The method of ascertaining the degree of affinity, which *obliged* a person to take a part in the quarrel of a kinsman, was curious. While the church prohibited the marriage of persons within the *seven* degrees of affinity, the vengeance of private war extended so far as this prohibition; and all who had such a remote connection with any of the principals were involved in the calamities of war. But when the church relaxed somewhat of its rigor, and did not extend its prohibition of marrying beyond the *fourth* degree of affinity, the *same* restriction took place in the conduct of *private* war. Vide

Beauman. 303. *Du Cange Dissert.* 333 A *private* war could not be carried on between two *full* brothers, because both have the same common kindred, and consequently neither had any persons *bound* to stand by him against the other in the contest; but two brothers of the *half* blood might wage war, because each of them was said to have a distinct kindred. Vide *Beauman.* p. 299. The vassals of each principal, in any private war, were involved in the contest, because, by the feudal maxims, they were bound to take arms in the name of the chieftain of whom they held their land, and to assist him in every quarrel. As soon, therefore, as feudal tenures were introduced, and this artificial connection was established between vassals and the Baron, of whom they held, vassals came to be considered as in the same state with relations. Vide *Beauman.* 303.

Private wars were very frequent for several centuries. Nothing contributed more to encourage those disorders in government and ferocity of manners which reduced the nations of *Europe* to that wretched state which distinguished them during the middle ages; nothing was a greater obstacle to the introduction of a regular administration of justice; nothing could more effectually discourage industry, or retard the progress and cultivation of the arts of peace. Private wars were carried on with all the destructive rage which is to be dreaded from violent resentment, when armed with force, and *authorized* by law. It appears by the statutes, prohibiting or restraining the exercise of private hostilities, that the invasion of the most barbarous enemy could not be more desolating to a country, or more fatal to its inhabitants, than those intestine wars. Vide *Ordom. tom.* i. p. 701. *tom.* ii. 395. 408. 507, &c. The contemporary historians describe the excesses committed in the prosecution of these quarrels in such terms as to excite astonishment and horror: "*Erat eo tempore maximus ad invicem hostilitatibus, totius Francorum regni facta turbatio; crebra ubique latrocinia, viarum obsessio audiebantur passim, imo fiebant incendia infinita nullis præter sola et indomita cupiditate existentibus causis extruebantur prælia; et ut brevi totam claudem, quicquid obtutibus cupidorum subjiciebant, nusquam attendiebant cujus esset, prædæ patebant.*" Vide *Gesta Dei per Francos*, vol. i. p. 482. i. e. "At that time turbulence reigned very extensively in the kingdom of France; everywhere robberies and lying in wait in the highways were heard of; conflagrations became excessive; hostility was enkindled for no other cause than from ungovernable avarice; and, in fine, the defenceless were subjected to entire ruin; the robbers never cared whose property they preyed upon, if it were only accessible to their cupidity."

QUICQUID PER SERVUM, &c.—During the state of vassalage, what the servant obtained, by any mode whatever, either in money or goods, belonged to the lord of the fee, who might, "*vi et armis*," take possession of it whenever he pleased.

QUID SI IN EJUSMODI, &c.—The seal is either *taken* for the wax impressed with a device, and attached to deeds, &c., or for the *instrument* with which the seal is impressed. In law, the former is the most usual sense. It is said that the first sealed charter we find extant in *England* is that of Edward the *Confessor*, upon his founding *Westminster* Abbey. Yet, we read of a *seal* in the MS. History of *Offa*, King of the *Mercians;* and that seals were in use in the time of the *Saxons*, vide *Taylor's Hist. of Gavelk.* fol. 73. It was usual, in the time of *Henry* the Second, and prior to that time, to seal all grants with the sign of the *Cross*, made in gold, on the parchment. Vide *Monast.* 111. fol. 7. et *Ordoricus Vitalis.* lib. 4. That most of the charters of the *English Saxon* Kings were thus signed, appears by *Ingulphus*, and in the *Monasticon*. But it was not so much used after the Conquest. Vide *Cowell*. Coats of arms on seals were introduced about the year 1218. We read of a charter sealed with the *Royal tooth*, called the "*Wang-tooth*," (*wang*—the jaw, *Sax.*); and it is said that one of the *English Saxon* King's Grants has these remarkable words, (which show the state of literature in those days,) " *Pro ignorantia literarum apposui sigillum meum*"—i. e. " on account of my ignorance of letters, I have placed my seal." Vide *Daniel*, vi. 17, as to the antiquity of signets.

QUOD CLERICI, &c.—The student will find the following Chronological List of *Contemporary* Reporters in the English Courts, to be correct, down to the reign of William IV.

HENRY III. commencing 1216.

Jenkins, 4, 19, 21.

EDWARD I.—1272.

Jenkins, EX. 18, 34	Year Book (Maynard) part 1, KB. CP.
Keilwey, KB. & CP. 6	& EX. 1 to 29

EDWARD II.—1307.

Jenkins, EX. 5, 15, 18	Year Book (Maynard) part 1, KB. CP. EX. 1 to 19

EDWARD III.—1326.

Benloe, KB. CP. 32	Year Book, part 3, KB. & CP. 17, 18,
Jenkins, EX. 1 to 47	21, to 30, 38, 39
Keilwey, KB. CP. 1 to 47	Year Book, part 4, KB. & CP. 40 to 50
Year Book, part 2, KB. CP. 1 to 10	Year Book, part 5, Liber Assisarum, 1 to 50

RICHARD II.—1377.

Bellewe, KB. & CP. 1 to 22	Jenkins, EX. 1 to 22

HENRY IV.—1399.

Jenkins, EX. 1 to 14	Year Book, part 6, KB. & CB. 1 to 14

HENRY V.—1413.

Jenkins, EX. 1 to 10	Year Book, part 6, KB. & CP. 1, 2, 5, 7 to 9

HENRY VI.—1422.

Benloe, KB. CP. 2, 18	Year Book, part 7, KB. CP. 1 to 4, 7 to
Jenkins, EX. 1 to 39	12, 14, 18 to 20—part 8—21, 22, 27, 28, 30 to 39

EDWARD IV.—1461.

Jenkins, EX. 1 to 22	Year Book, part 10, KB. CP. & EX. 5
Year Book, part 9, KB. CP. 1 to 22	

EDWARD· V.—1483.

Jenkins, EX.	Year Book, part 11, KB. & CP.

RICHARD III.—1483.

Jenkins, EX. 1 to 2	Year Book, part 11, KB. CP. 1 to 2

HENRY VII.—1485.

Benloe, KB. CP. 1	Moore, KB. CP. 1 to 37
Jenkins, EX. 1 to 24	Year Book, part 11, KB. CP. 1 to 16,
Keilwey, KB. CP. 12, 13, 17 to 24	20, 21

HENRY VIII.—1509.

Anderson, CP. 25, &c.
Benloe, CP. 1 to 38
N. Bendloe, KB. CP. 22, &c.
Bendloe, Keilwey and Ashe, KB. CP.
EX.
Brooke's new Cases, KB. CP. EX.
Dalison, CP. 38

Dyer, KB. CP. EX. CH. 4, &c.
Jenkins, EX. 1 to 38
Keilwey, KB. CP. 1 to 11, and 21
Moore, KB. CP. EX. CH. 3
Year Book, part 11, KB. CP. 12, 13,
14, 18, 19, 26, 27

EDWARD VI.—1547.

Anderson, CP, 1 to 6
Benloe and Dalison, CP. 2.
Brooke's new Cases, KB. CP. EX.
N. Bendloe, KB. CP. EX. 1 to 6

Dyer, KB. CP. EX. CH. 1 to 6
Jenkins, EX. 1 to 6
Moore, KB. CP. EX. CH. 1 to 6
Plowden, KB. CP. EX. 4 to 6

MARY—1553.

Anderson, CP. 1 to 6
Benloe and Dalison, CP. 1 to 5
Benloe in Keilwey and Ashe, KB. CP.
EX. 1 to 5
N. Bendloe, KB. CP. EX. 1 to 5
Brooke's new Cases, KB. CP. EX. 1 to 5
Cary, CH. 5
Dyer, KB. CP. EX. CH. 1 to 5

Dalison in Keilwey and Ashe, CP. 1,
4, 5
Jenkins, EX. 1 to 5
Leonard, KD. CP. 1 to 5
Moore, KB. CP. EX. CH. 1 to 5
Owen, KB. CP. 4 to 5
Plowden, KB. CP. EX. 1 to 5

ELIZABETH—1558.

Anderson, CP. 1 to 45
Benloe in Keilwey and Ashe, KB. CP.
EX. 2 to 20
Benloe, KB. CP. EX. 1 to 21
Bendloe, KB. CP. EX. 1 to 17
Brownlow and Gouldesborough, CP.
11 to 45
Cary, CH. 1 to 45
Coke, KB. CP. EX. CH. 14 to 45
Croke, KB. CP. 24 to 45
Dalison, CP. 1 to 16
Dalison in Keilwey and Ashe, CP. 2
to 7
Dickins, CH. a few Cases
Dyer, KB. CP. 1 to 23

Godbolt, KB. CP. EX. CH. 17 to 45
Gouldesborough, KB. CH. EX. CH. 28
to 31, 39 to 43
Hobart, KB. a few Cases
Hutton, CP. 26 to 38
Jenkins, EX. 1 to 45
Leonard, KB. CP. EX. 1 to 45
Moore, KB. CP. EX. 1 to 45
Noy, KB. CP. 1 to 45
Owen, KB. CP. 1 to 45
Plowden, KB. CP. EX. 1 to 21
Popham, KB. CP. CH. 34 to 39
Saville, CP. EX. 22 to 36
Tothill, CH. 1 to 45
Yelverton, KB. 44, 45

JAMES I.—1603.

Anderson, CP. 1
Bendloe, KB. CP. EX. 19 to 23
Bridgman, CP. 12 to 19
Brownlow and Gouldesborough, CP. 1
to 23
Bulstrode, KB. 7 to 15
Cary, CH. 1
Coke, KB. CP. EX. CH. 1 to 13
Croke, KB. CP. 1 to 23
Davis, KD. CP. EX. 2 to 9
Godbolt, KB. CP. EX. CH. 1 to 23
Hobart, KB. CP. EX. CH. 1 to 23
Hutton, CP. 10 to 23
Jenkins, EX. 1 to 21

William Jones, KB. CP. 18 to 23
Lane, EX. 3 to 9
Leonard, KB. CP. EX. 1 to 12
Ley, KB. CP. EX. 6 to 23
Moore, KB. CP. EX. CH. 1 to 18
Noy, KB. & CP. 1 to 23
Owen, KB. CP. 1 to 12
Palmer, KB. 17 to 23
Popham, KB. CP. CH. 15 to 23
Reports in Chancery, 13
Rolle, KB. 12 to 22
Tothill, CH. 1 to 23
Winch, CP. 19 to 23
Yelverton, KB. 1 to 10

CHARLES I.—1625.

Alleyn, KB. 22 to 24
Bendloe, KB. CP. 1 to 14
Bulstrode, KB. 1 to 14
Clayton, Pl. Ass. York, 7 to 24
Croke, KB. CP. 1 to 16
Godbolt, KB. CP. EX. CH. 1 to 13
Hetley, CP. 3 to 7
Hutton, CP. 1 to 14
Wm. Jones, KB. CP. 1 to 16
Latch, KB. 1 to 3

Ley, KB. CP. EX. 1 to 4
Littleton, CP. EX. 2 to 7
March, KB. CP. 15 to 18
Nelson, CH. 1 to 24
Noy, KB. CP. 1 to 24
Palmer, KB. CP. 1 to 4
Popham, KB. CP. CH. 1 to 2
Reports in Chancery, 1 to 24
Style, KB. 21 to 24
Tothill, CH. 1 to 21

CHARLES II.—1660.

Carter, CP. 16 to 27
Cases in Chancery, part 1—12 to 30.
Cases in Chancery, part 2—26 to 37
Clayton, Pl. Ass. York, 1 to 2
Dickins, CH. *a few Cases*
Finch, CH. 25 to 32
Freeman, KB. CP. EX. CH. 22 to 37
Hardres, EX. 7 to 21
Thos. Jones, KB. CP. 19 to 37
Keble, KB. 13 to 30
Kelynge, KB. 14 to 20
Levinz, KB. CP. 12 to 37
Lutwyche, CP. 34 to 37
Modern, vol. 1, 2, KB. CP. EX. CH. 1 to 29
Modern, vol. 2, KB. CP. EX. CH. 26 to 30

Modern, vol. 3, KB. CP. EX. CH. 34 to 37
Nelson, CH. 1 to 37
Parker, EX. 30
Pollexfen, KB. CP. EX. CH. 22 to 37
T. Raymond, KB. CP. EX. 12 to 35
Reports in Chancery, 1 to 37
Saunders, KB. 18 to 24
Select Cases in Chancery, 33
Shower, KB. 30 to 37
Siderfin, KB. CP. EX. 9 to 22
Skinner, KB. 33 to 37
Style, KB. 1 to 7
Vaughan, CP. 17 to 25
Ventris, KB. CP. EX. CH. 20 to 37
Vernon, CH. 32 to 37

JAMES II.—1685.

Carthew, KB. 2 to 4
Cases in Chancery, part 2—1 to 3
Cases of Settlement, KB. 2 to 4
Comberbach, KB. 1 to 4
Freeman, KB. CP. EX. CH. 1 to 4
Levinz, KB. CP. 1 to 2
Lutwyche, CP. 1 to 4

Modern, vol. 3, KB. CP. EX. CH. 1 to 4
Parker, EX. 3 to 4
Reports in Chancery, 1 to 3
Shower, KB. 1 to 4
Skinner, KB. 1 to 4
Ventris, KB. CP. EX. CH. 1 to 4.
Vernon, CH. 1 to 4

WILLIAM III.—1689.

Carthew, KB. 1 to 12
Cases concerning Settlements, KB. 1 to 14
Colles, Parl. Ca. 9 to 14
Comberbach, KB. 1 to 10
Comyns, KB. CP. EX. CH. 7 to 14
Fortescue, KB. CP. EX. CH. 7 to 14
Freeman, KB. CP. EX. CH. 1 to 14
Kelynge, Cr. Ca. KB. 8 to 13
Levinz, KB. CP. 1 to 8
Lutwyche, CP. 1 to 14
Modern, vol. 3, KB. CP. EX. CH. 1 to 2
Modern, vol. 4, KB. CP. EX. CH. 3 to 7
Modern, vol. 5, KB. CP. EX. CH. 5 to 11

Modern, vol. 12, KB. CP. EX. CH. 2 to 14
Parker, EX. 4 to 13
Precedents in Chancery, 1 to 4
Lord Raymond, KB. & CP. 4 to 14
Reports in Chancery, vol. 2—6
Reports temp. Holt, KB. CP. EX. CH. 1 to 14
Salkeld, KB. CP. EX. CH. 1 to 14
Select Cases in Chancery, 5, 9
Shower, KB. 1 to 6
Skinner, KB. 1 to 9
Ventris, KB. CP. EX. CH. 1 to 2
Vernon, CH. 1 to 14
Peere Williams, CH. & KB. 7 to 14

ANNE.—1702.

Brown, Parl. Cases, 1 to 13

Modern, vol. 7, KB. CH. EX. CH. 1

29

Bunbury, EX. 12 to 13
Cases concerning Settlements, KB. 1 to 13
Cases of Practice, CP. 5 to 13
Colles, Parl. Ca. 1 to 8
Comyns, KB. CP. EX. CH. 1 to 13
Dickins, CH. *a few Cases*
Fortesque, KB. CP. EX. CH. 1 to 13
Freeman, KB. CP. EX. CH. 1 to 5
Gilbert, Cases in Law and Equity, 12 to 13
Gilbert, KB. CH. & EX. 4 to 13
Kelyng, Sir J. KB.
Lutwyche, CP. 1 to 2
Modern, vol. 6, KB. CP. EX. CH. 2 to 3

Modern, vol. 10, KB. CP. EX. CH. 8 to 13
Modern, vol. 11, KB. CP. EX. CH. 4 to 8
Parker, EX. 6 to 12
Peere Williams, CH. & KB. 1 to 13
Practical Register, CP. 3 to 13
Precedents in Chancery, 1 to 13
Lord Raymond, KB. CP. 1 to 13
Reports in Chancery, 4 to 8
Reports temp. Holt, 1 to 9
Salkeld, KB. CP. EX. CH. 1 to 10
Sessions Cases, KB. 9 to 13
Vernon, CH. 1 to 13

GEORGE I.—1714.

Barnardiston, KB. 11 to 12
Brown, Cases in Parl. 1 to 13
Bunbury, EX. 1 to 13
Cases concerning Settlements, KB. 1 to 13 ·.
Cases of Practice, CP. 1 to 13
Comyns, KB. CP. EX. CH. 1 to 13
Dickins, CH. 1 to 13
Fortescue, KB. CP. EX. CH. 1 to 13
Gilbert, KB. EX. CH. 1 to 12
Modern, vol. 8 & 9, KB. CP. EX. CH. 8 to 12
Modern, vol. 10, KB. CP. CH. EX. 1 to 11

Mosely, CH. 12 to 13
Parker, EX. 4
Practical Regis. CP. 1 to 13
Precedents in Chancery, 1 to 8
Lord Raymond, KB. & CP. 1 & 10 to 13
Robertson's Appeal Cases, 1 to 13
Select Cases in Chancery, 10 to 12
Sessions Cases, KB. 1 to 13.
Strange, KB. CP. CH. EX. 2 to 13
Vernon, CH. 1 to 5
Peere Williams, CH. & KB. 1 to 13

GEORGE II.—1727.

Ambler, CH. EX. 11 to 34
Andrews, KB. 11 to 12
Atkyns, CH. 9 to 27
Barnardiston, KB. 1 to 7
Barnardiston, Chancery, 13 to 14
Barnes, CP. 5 to 34
Belt's Supp. Vesey, CH. 20 to 28
Wm. Blackstone, KB. CP. 20 to 24, 30 to 34
Brown, Parl. Cases, 1 to 34
Bunbury, EX. 1 to 14
Burrow, KB. 30 to 34
Burrow, Sett. Cases, KB. 5 to 34
Cases of Settlement, KB. 1 to 5
Cases of Practice, CP. 1 to 20
Cases temp. Talbot, CH. KB. CP. 7, 10
Comyns, CH. EX. 1 to 13
Cunningham, KB. 7, 8
Dickins, CH. 1 to 34
Fitzgibbon, KB. CP. CH. EX. 1 to 5.
Fortescue, all the Courts, 1 to 10

Foster, Cr. Ca. 16 to 34
Kelynge, KB. 4 to 8
Kenyon, KB. 26 to 30
Leach's Crown Law, 4 to 34
Mosely, CH. 1 to 3
Northington, 30 to 34
Parker, EX. 16 to 34
Peere Williams, CH. KB. 1 to 8
Practical Register, 1 to 15
Lord Raymond, KB. 1 to 6
Reports temp. Hardwicke, KB. 7
Robertson's Appeal Ca.
Sayer, KB. 25 to 29
Select Cases in Chancery, 1 to 6
Session Cases, KB. 1 to 20
Strange, KB. CP. EX. CH. 1 to 21
Vesey (sen.) CH. 20 to 28
Willes, CP. EX. CH. H. of L. 11 to 32
Wilson, KB. 16 to 26
Wilson, CP. 26 to 34

GEORGE III.—1760.

Acton, Prize Causes, 49 to 50
Ambler, CH. EX. 1 to 24
Anstruther, EX. 32 to 37

Barnewall & Alderson, KB. 58
Blackstone, (Sir Wm.) KB. CP. 1 to 20
Blackstone, (H.) CP. EX. 28 to 36

Bligh, Parl. Cases, 59 & 60
Bosanquet & Puller, CP. EX. 37 to 44
Bosanquet and Puller, New Rep. CP.
   44 to 47
Bott. Sett. Ca. 1 to 60
Broderip & Bingham, CP. 59 & 60
Brown, Parl. Cases, 1 to 40
Brown, Chancery, 18 to 34
Buck, Bankruptcy, 57 to 60
Burrow, KB. 1 to 12
Burrow, Settl. Cases, 1 to 16
Caldecott, Settl. Cases, 17 to 26
Campbell, NP. 48 to 56
Cases of Prac. KB. 1 to 14
Chitty, KB. 47 to 60
Cooper, Chancery, 55
Corbet & Dan. El. Ca.
Cowper, KB. 14 to 18
Cox, Chancery, 23 to 36
Daniel, Excheq. 57, 58
Dickins, Chancery, 1 to 38
Dodson, Admiralty, 51 to 55
Douglass, KB. 19 to 22
Dow, Parl. Cases, 53 to 58
Durnford and East, KB. 26 to 40
East, KB. 41 to 53
Eden, Chancery, 1 to 7
Edwards, Admiralty, 48 to 50
Espinasse, NP. KB. CP. 33 to 47
Forrest, EX. 41
Frazer, Elect. 32
Gow, NP. CP. 59 & 60
Haggard, Consistory Court, 29 to 60
Hall & Beattie, CH. 47 to 51

Holt, NP. CP. 55 to 58
Jacob & Walker, CH. 59 & 60
Kenyon, KB.
Leach, Crown Law, 1 to 55
Lofft, KB. CP. CH. 12 to 14
Luder, Elect. Ca. 25, 30
Maddock, Chanc. 55 to 60
Marriott, Ad. 16 to 19
Marshall, CP. 54 to 56
Maule & Selwyn, KB. 54 to 57
Merivale, Chancery, 56, 57
Moore, CP. 57 to 60
Nolan, Settl. Ca. 32 to 34
Northington, CH. 1 to 5
Parker, EX. 1 to 6
Peake, NP. 30 to 35
Peckwell, Elect. Ca. 45, 46
Philimore, Eccl. Courts, 49 to 60
Price, EX. 54 to 60
Robinson, Admiralty, 39 to 48
Rose, Bankruptcy, 50 to 56
Russel & Ryan, Cr. Ca. 39, &c.
Schoales and Lefroy, Chancery, 42 to
   46
Smith, KB. 44 to 46
Starkie, NP. 55 to 60
Swanston, CH. 58 to 60
Taunton, CP. 48 to 58
Vesey, Chancery, 29 to 52.
Vesey & Beames, Chancery, 52 to 54
Wightwicke, EX. 50 to 51
Wilson, KB. CP. 1 to 14
Wilson, EX. 57
Wilson, EX. & CH. 58 to 60

GEORGE IV.—1820.

Addams, Eccl. 2 to 6
Barnewall & Alderson, KB. 1 to 3
Barnewall & Creswell, KB. 3 to 10
Barnewall & Adolphus, KB. 10 & 11
Bingham, CP. 3 to 11
Bligh, H. of L. 1 to
Bott, Sett. Ca. 1 to 7
Broderip & Bingham, CP. 1 to 3
Carrington & Payne, NP. 4 to 11
Chitty, KB. 1 to 3
Creswell, Insol. 7 to 9
Crompton & Jervis, EX. 11
Daniel, EX. 1
Danson & Lloyd, Merc. Ca. 8, 9
Dow & Clarke, H. of L. 7 to 11
Dowling & Ryland, KB. 2 to 8
Glynn & Jameson, Bankr.
Haggard, Eccles. 7 to 10
Jacob & Walker, CH. 1, 2
Jacob, CH. 2, 3
Lloyd & Welsby, Merc. Cases, 10 & 11
Maddock, Vice Ch. 1 to 2

Manning & Ryland, KB. 7 to 9
M'Cleland, EX. 4, 5
M'Cleland & Younge, EX. 5, 6
Montagu & Macarthur, Bankr. 10, 11
Moody & Malkin, NP. 7
Moore & Payne, CP. 7
Phillimore, Eccl. 1, 2
Price, EX. 1
Russell & Ryan, Crown Ca. 1 to 8
Russell, Chancery, 6 to
Russell & Mylne, 9 to
Ryan & Moody, NP. 4 to 7
Ryan & Moody, Cr. Ca. 4 to 10
Shaw, H. of L.
Simons & Stuart, Vice Ch. 2 to 7
Simons, Vice Ch. 7 to 11
Starkie, NP. 1 to
Turner, CH. 3 to
Wilson, CH. 1
Wilson & Shaw, H. of L.
Young & Jervis, EX. 7 to
Younge, EX. EQ. 11

WILLIAM IV.—1830.

Barnewall & Adolphus, KB. 1 to	Bligh, H. of L. 1 to
Bingham, CP, 1 to	Clark & Finnelley, H. of L. 3 to
Carrington & Payne. NP. 1 to	Moody & Malkin, NP. 1 to
Crompton & Jervis, EX. 1 to	Moore & Payne, CP. 1 to
Deacon & Chitty, Bankr. 2 to	Russell & Mylne, CH. 1 to
Dow & Clarke, H. of L. 1 to 3	Simons, Vice Chan. 1 to
Dowling, Pract. 1 to	Tamlyn, Rolls, 1 to
Haggard, Eccl. 1 to	Tyrwhitt, EX. 1 to
Knapp, Appeal Cases, 1 to	Wilson & Shaw, H. of L. 1 to
Manning & Ryland, KB. 1 to	Younge, EQ. EX. 1 to
Montagu & Bligh, Bankr. 1 to	

QUOD HABEANT, &c.—Military service was frequently the *only* condition upon which the tenant received a grant, and held his lands: and the person possessing such grant was exonerated from every other burden : *that* tenure among a warlike nation, was not honorable, but easy. The King, or General, who led his troops to conquest, continuing still to be the head of the colony, had the largest portion assigned to him. Having thus acquired the means of rewarding past services, as well as of gaining new adherents, he parcelled out his lands with this view; binding those, on whom they were bestowed, to resort to his standard, with a number of men, in proportion to the extent of the territory they had received. The chief officers, imitating the example of their sovereign and leaders, distributed portions of their lands among *their* dependents, annexing a Feudal condition to the grant: thus a Feudal kingdom resembled a *Military* establishment, rather than a *Civil* Constitution: the victorious troops, being cantoned out in the country, which they had seized, continued therein to occupy such lands, ranged under their proper officers, and were subordinate to military command. The name of a soldier, and "*Liber homo*," were, in those days, almost synonymous. Vide *Du Cange Gloss. voc.* "Miles." An indolent and unwarlike life was held in extreme contempt. And whatever the philosopher may say in praise of quiet and retirement (his *otium cum dignatate*), it has been justly remarked, that, in many respects, such a situation weakens and debases the human mind. When the faculties of the soul are not exerted, they lose their vigor, and low and circumscribed notions take the place of noble and enlarged ideas. Action, on the contrary, and the *vicissitudes* of fortune, which attend it, call forth, by turns, all the powers of the mind, and, by exercising, *strengthen* them. These vicissitudes are often "blessings in disguise." Hence it is, that in great and wealthy states, when property and indolence are perfectly secured to individuals, we seldom meet with that strength of mind, and resolution of action, so common in a nation not far advanced in civilization. It is a curious, but correct, observation, that opulent kingdoms seldom produce very great characters; which must be altogether attributed to that indolence and dissipation, which are the inseparable companions of affluence and security. The beloved *Washington* might have lived and died, "unwept, unhonored, and unsung," had not the critical situation of this country brought his extraordinary abilities and virtues into action.

Rome, it is certain, had more *real* great men within it, when its power was confined within the narrow bounds of *Latium*, than when its dominion extended over nearly all the then known world: and one petty state of the *Saxon* Heptarchy, had, perhaps, as much genuine spirit in it, as the British kingdoms united. As a state, *England* is much more powerful than it was five hundred years since; but it would lose by comparing *individuals* with some of our ancestors. The noble passions of the mind never shoot forth more free and unrestrained than in times which "try men's souls," and in those we call barbarous. That irregular manner of life, and those manly pursuits, from which barbarity often takes its name, are highly favorable to the strength, and peculiar force of mind, dormant, or at least unexercised, in times we call "*polished*." In advanced society the characters of men are more uniform and disguised. The human passions (as well the virtuous as the base) often lie concealed behind forms and *artificial* manners, unknown in the early ages; and the powers of the soul, without opportunities of exerting them, lose their vigor by the want of great stimulants to action. Vide *Macpherson's Notes to Ossian* and *Dissertation.*

These remarks are not made, as by any means countenancing the sanguinary and cruel contests between the powerful Barons, which often were waged on trifling occasions, and were disgraceful to society; but as an incentive to activity and perseverance, without which, *whatever* be man's pursuit in life, he will never arrive at the temple of *true* honor, nor be of any signal service to his fellow man.

QUOD ORDINARII, &c.—The complaint in the text was a most violent encroachment made use of by the Clergy, who, it appears, under the pretence of making a fair distribution of the deceased's property, frequently seized on his effects, and either made no distribution of them at all, or divided them in an arbitrary and capricious manner.

QUOD VIDUA REMANET, &c.—It is said, that anciently, if a man died, and his widow soon afterwards married again; and a child was born within such a time as, by the course of nature, *it might* have been the child of *either* husband; in this case it was said, the child was more than ordinarily legitimate: for he might, when arrived to years of discretion, choose *which* of the fathers he pleased.   Vide 1. *Inst.* 8.   For this reason, by the ancient *Saxon* laws, in imitation of the Civil Law, a woman was "forbidden to marry until a twelve month after her husband's decease."   Vide *Ll. Ethel. A. D.* 1008. *Ll. Canuti.* c. 71, et 1*st. Inst.* 8 *a. in notis* 7, where it is said, "*Brooke* questions this doctrine, from which it seems, as if he thought it reasonable that the *circumstances* of the case, instead of the *choice* of the issue, should determine who is the father.   Vide *Bro. Abr. Bastardy*, p. 18.   *Palm.* 10. 1 *Inst.* 123, *b. in notis* 1, where additional cases are cited to decide on the question according to the woman's condition, &c.

QUOTIES BELLA, &c.—The state of society among the ancient *Germans*, was of the rudest and most simple form. They subsisted entirely by hunting, or by pasture. Vide *Cæs. lib.* 6, c. 21. They neglected agriculture, and lived chiefly on milk, cheese, and flesh. *Ibid.* c. 22. *Tacitus* agrees with *Cæsar* in most of these points. Vide *Tac. de mor. Ger.* c. 14, 15, 23. The *Goths* were equally negligent of agriculture. Vide *Prisc. Rhet. ap. Byz. Script.* v. 1, p. 31. Society was in the same state among the *Huns*, who never ploughed their lands. Vide *Amm. Marcel. lib.* 10, 475. The manners of the *Alans* were similar. *Ib.* p. 447. While society remained in this simple state, men, by uniting together, scarcely lost any part of their natural independence. Accordingly, we are informed, that the authority of civil government was extremely limited among the *Germans*. During the times of peace, they had no common or fixed magistrate; but the chief men of every district dispensed justice, and accommodated differences. Vide *Cæs. lib.* 6, c. 23. Their kings had not absolute or unbounded power; their authority consisted rather in the privilege of *advising*, than in the power of *commanding*. Matters of minor concern were determined by the *chief* men: affairs of importance by the *whole* community. Vide *Tacit.* c. 7, 11. The *Huns*, in like manner, deliberated in common concerning every affair of importance in the society, and were not subject to the rigor of regal authority. Vide *Amm. Marcel. lib.* 31, c. 474. The student will, no doubt, perceive by these extracts, the probability that the WITTENA-GEMOTE, or great assembly, among our *Saxon* ancestors, where weighty affairs, and those of general concern, were transacted, had its origin from a custom implanted among those fierce barbarians who devastated the *Roman* provinces. Every individual, among the ancient *Germans*, was left at liberty to choose whether he would share in any warlike enterprise or not: there seems to have been no *obligation* to engage in it imposed on him by public authority. When any of the chiefs proposed an expedition, such as approved of the cause, and of the leader, rose up, and declared their intent of following him: after coming under this engagement, those who did not fulfil it were considered as deserters and traitors, and looked upon as infamous." Vide *Cæs. lib.* 6, c. 23. Tacitus points at the same custom, though in an obscure manner. *Tac.* c. 11, 4.

R.

RABULA.——A barrator: a pettifogger.

RACHATER.——To buy back.

RADECHENISTRES.——Freemen.

RADERE nomen.——To erase the name.

RAN.——In Saxon law. Stealing.

RANGER.——In forest law. One who has charge of the forest.

RAPTUS mulieris.——Rape.

RAPUIT.——He took violently : he ravished.

RAPUIT, et carnaliter cognovit.——He ravished and carnally knew. *Vide note.*

RATIONABILE maritagium.——A suitable marriage.

RATIONABILIS dos.——A reasonable dowry.

RATIONALIS divisio.——A reasonable partition.

RATIONE contractus.——On account of contract.

RATIONE detentione debitus.——By reason of withholding the debt.

RATIONE doni proprii.——On account of a proper gift (or grant).

RATIONEM ponere.——To arraign.

RATIONE privilegii.——By reason of privilege.

RATIONE rei, aut ratione personarum.——By reason of the thing, or on account of the parties.

RATIONE soli.——On account of the soil.

RATIONE tenuræ.——On account of the tenure.

RATUM maritagium, et non legitimum.——These words signify, " A marriage among Christians, without canonical solemnization."

RE.——King.

RECEIPTMENT.——In old European law. The receiving one who has committed a felony, knowing him to have done so.

RECENS insecutio.——Fresh suit (or pursuit). *Vide note.*

RECEPTIO literarum est actus positivus.——The receipt of letters is a decisive act.

RECESSIT et officium suum relinquit.——He withdrew and left his office.

RECETOUR.——One who harbored and secreted a felon.

RECOGNITIO de novel disseizina.——An acknowledg- ment (or recognition) of a new disseisin.

RECOGNITIO duodecim legalium hominum.——The re- cognition (or acknowledgment) of twelve lawful men.

RECONCILIATIO litis non refrigeranda.——The agreement of a suit is not to be broken.

RECONQUIS.——To obtain again.

RECONUSTRE.——To recognize.

RECORDARE.——To remember (to record).

RECORDARI facias loquelam.——That you cause the plaint to be recorded.

RECORDARI facias loquelam, audita querula, accedas ad curiam, capius si laicus.——That you cause the complaint to be recorded, and when heard that you go to the court, and you take him, if he be a layman.

RECTUS in curia.——" Untainted in court." With clean hands.

RECUSATIO judicia.——The Judge's refusal.

RECUSATIO testis.——The refusing of a witness for the reason of his incapacity.

REDDENDUM.——To pay: to yield: to render: the reservation of rent, &c., in a deed.

REDEUNDO ab terra sancta, legis actionem suam protulit.——He brought his action, on his return from the *Crusades*. *Vide note.*

REDDIDT se.——He surrendered himself.

REDDITUM in invitum.——Rendered against his will.

REDISPOSSESSIO.——A repossessing: taking again.

REDITUS.——A rent: a return. *Vide note.*

REDITUS albæ firmæ.——"Rents of white farm." In *Scotland* this kind of small payment is called "*Blanch-holding.*"

REDITUS albi.——White rents.

REDITUS capitales.——"Chief Rents." Rents paid to the superior lord of the fee.

REDITUS mobiles.——Farm rents (for life, years, &c.): those rents which are variable.

REDITUS nigri.——"Black rents." Black cattle, as *Scotch* steers.

REDITUS siccus.——"Barren (or dry) rent." "Rent seck." Rent payable in corn, &c.; reserved by deed without any clause of distress. These several rents were anciently payable for lands.

REDHIBITION.——The taking back of an article to the one who sold it, on account of some fault discovered in it after the purchase.

REDIMERE.——To pay a ransom.

REEVE.——In old English law. An official in court; sometimes a collector of public dues.

RE. fa. lo.——An abbreviation. "That you cause the complaint to be recorded." A writ so called.

REFERENDARY.——Saxon. A servant of the crown to whom are referred the many requests made to the King.

REFFARE.——To plunder.

REGALIA.——Crown rights (or royalties).

REGALIS potestas in omnibus.——The royal authority in all things.

REGE inconsulto.——Without consulting the King.

REGES ex nobilitate; duces ex virtute, sumunt.——
Kings take title from their dignity; dukes from deeds of
valor. *Vide note.*

REGIA prohibitione non obstante.——Notwithstanding
the King's prohibition.

REGIDOR.——Spanish. A member of a town assembly.

REGIMINI sui ipsius, et bonorum et terrarum suarum
minime sufficit.——It is sufficient to have a small portion
of his goods and lands for his support.

REGIS et principis factum enumeratur inter causas for-
tuitas, ideo si rex et princeps retineant navem oneratam
frumenta ex causa penuriæ, quapropter navis non potuerit
frumenta exportare ad locum destinationis, tenenter assecu-
tores.——The act of the King and Prince may be reckoned
among accidental causes; as if the King and Prince detain
a vessel laden with corn on account of scarcity, whereby
it should not transport the grain to its destined place, (in
this case) the assurers are held liable.

REGISTRUM.——A registry: a place for depositing wills,
deeds, &c.

REGISTRUM omnium brevium.——The registry of all the
writs.

REGNI Angliæ, quod nobis jure competit hæreditario.
——Of the kingdom of *England*, which devolved to us by
hereditary right.

REGRATER.——In old law. A retailer.

REIF.——Scotch.

REI judicatæ.——Of the matter adjudged.

RE infectâ.——The business not having been accomplished.

RE integrâ.——"The thing being unfinished." When
a matter was under debate in the Senante, the *Romans* said
it was "*rê integrâ.*"

REISA.——Sax. A sudden sally of soldiers.

REI vindicatio.——A vindication of the matter.

REJECTIONE celebrata, in eorum locum qui rejecti fu-

erunt, sortiebatur *Prœtor* alios, quibus ille judicium legitimus numerus compleretur.——The rejection being ended,
the *Prœtor* chose others by lot from whom the legal number of the judges was completed (for the trial).

RELAXATIO.——A deed by which one person releases
to another his right in anything.

RELEVIUM.——"A relief:" a fine paid to the feudal
lord for the tenant's entering upon the estate which was
lapsed or fallen in by the death of his ancestor.

RELICTA per mare.——Left by the sea.

RELICTA verificatione.——The plea being abandoned.

RELICTA verificatione, cognovit actionem.——Having
abandoned the plea, he confessed the action.

REMALLARE.——To re-summon.

REMANET causa.——The cause remains (or stands
over).

REM in bonis nostris habere intelligimur, quoties ad re-
cuperandam eam actionem habeamus.——We are considered to have an interest in our own effects, so often as we
are entitled to an action to recover them.

REMISIT curiam.——He adjourned the court.

REMISSUM magis specie quam vi; quia cum venditor
pendere juberetur, in partem pretii emptoribus accrecebat.
——It was abated more in appearance than in reality; because when the seller was directed to weigh (in order that
the toll or tribute might be taken), he, in part, increased
the price to the purchasers.

REMITTER.——To restore (or send back). *Vide note.*

REMITTIT damna.——He remits the damages.

REMITTITUR.——It is remitted: forgiven.

REMITTITUR de damnis.——The damages are remitted
(or forgiven).

REMUE.——Remote.

RENEEZ.——Anciently, an apostate from Christ's faith.

REM tantam agere tam negligenter.——To transact so
important an affair so negligently.

REOFFERE.——A robber.

REPARATIONE facienda.——A writ for making repairs.

REPETUNDARUM crimen.——In Roman law. Dishonest or extortionate practices in a public officer.

REPLEGIARE est rem apud alium detentum, cautione legitima interposita, redimere.——To replevy, is to redeem a thing detained by another person, legal security being given.

REPLEGIARI facias.——That you cause to be replevied.

REPLEVIUM.——A relief: a replevy.

REPREHENSAILLES.——Seizures.

REPRENDRE.——To take back: to replevy.

REPSILVER.——In ancient law. The fee paid by tenants to release them from reaping for the baron.

REQUISITUM autem corporalis quædam possessio ad dominium adipiscendum; atque ideo vulnerasse non sufficit.——But it is requisite that a certain corporeal possession to the fee be acquired; and therefore it is not sufficient to have been interrupted (or injured).

RES angustæ domi.——The distress of the family.

RES caduca.——An escheated thing.

RES controversa.——A point in controversy.

RES corporales sunt quæ sua natura tangi possunt, veluti fundus: incorporales sunt quæ tangi non possunt, et in jure consistunt, sicut usus fructus, usus, &c.——Things corporeal are those which in their own nature can be touched (or handled), as a farm: incorporeal (things) are those which cannot be handled, although they subsist in law, as the enjoyment of the profit, interest (or service), &c.

RES ecclesiæ temporales.——The temporal affairs of the church.

RES gestæ.——The subject matter: things done.

RESCOURER.——To recover.

RESCOUS.——A rescue.

RESCYT.——Receipt.

RESEAUNT.——Residing.

RESEISER: reseisire.——" The taking lands back." Generally applied to the taking lands into the King's hands, where a general livery, or *ouster le maine*, was formerly mis used, contrary to the order of the law.

RESEISIN.——Restoration to possession.

RESIDUUM.——"The remainder." Frequently applied to that part of the testator's estate not specially disposed of.

RESILIRE.——To break off from a bargain before it was made binding.

RES immobiles.——Immovables.

RES integra.——An entire (new, or untouched) matter.

RES inter alios acta, aliis nec prodest, nec nocet.——A transaction between other parties neither benefits nor injures those not interested.

RES judicatæ pro veritate accipiuntur.——Adjudged matters shall be taken as indisputable.

RES mancipi.——Things which may be alienated. *Vide note.*

RES-MOBILES.——Such articles as are capable of a change of place.

RES nova.——A new matter: a new case.

RESPI.——Putting off.

RESPONDEAT ouster.——That he answer over.

RESPONDEAT superior.——"Let the principal be answerable." Often applied in those civil matters where the owner or master is responsible for the act of his agent or servant.

RESPONDENTIA.——Bottomry.

RESPONDERE non debet.——He ought not to answer.

RESPONDRA à touts; mes nul respondra à luy.——He shall answer to every one; but none shall answer to him.

RESPONSALIS ad lucrandum, non perdendum.——Answerable for profit, not for loss.

REPONSA prudentum.——The opinions of learned men.

RESPONSIO unius non omnino andiatur.——The answer of one witness shall not be heard at all.

RESPUBLICA est cœtus multitudinis juris consensu, et utilitatis communione.——A commonwealth is the assemblage of a multitude, by a legal agreement, with a mutual participation of advantage.

RES quotidianæ.——Every-day questions : familiar matters.

RES ratione regenda.——The matter is to be governed by reason.

RES religiosæ.——Religious matters.

RES sacræ.——Articles dedicated to the service of God, as sacred buildings, etc.

RES unius ætatis.——"A thing only of one age." Civilians frequently make use of this phrase to denote *that* legal provision which is confined to the present generation.

RES universitatis.——Things belonging to society in general, as theatres, race-courses.

RETARE.——To accuse with crime.

RETORNA brevium.——The return of writs.

RETORN' habend'.——That a return be had.

RETORNA habenda elongata.——Having a return of what has been eloigned.

RETRACTUS aquæ.——The ebb or return of the tide.

RETRAHERE.——To withdraw.

RETRAXIT.——" He has recalled, or revoked." *Vide note.*

RETROFEODUM.——A rere fief.

RETTE.——A charge.

REUS.——" A guilty person." Sometimes meaning a defendant.

REVE or GREVE.——A collector of public taxes.

REVELAND.——Sax. Land over which the sheriff has authority.

REVENONS à nos moutons.——" Let us return to our

sheep." It is said that a *French* lawyer whose client had lost some sheep, argued before the court and jury upon *every* subject except the matter in question: at length his client said very wittily "*Revenons à nos moutons.*"

REVERSETUR.——Let it be reversed.

REVERSO intuitu.——By a retrospective view.

REVERTENDI animum videntur desinere habere tunc, cum revertendi consuetudinem deseruerent.——The disposition to come back appears to cease, when they leave off the habit of returning (home).

REX allegavit quod ipse omnes libertates haberet in regno suo, quas Imperator vindicabat.——The King stated that he should enjoy all the liberties (or privileges) in his kingdom which an Emperor claims in his dominion.

REX datur propter regnum; non regnum propter Regem. ——A King is given for the realm; not the realm for the King.

REX debet esse sub lege, quia lex facit Regem.——The King ought to be subject to the law, because the law makes the King.

REX est vicarius, et minister Dei, in terra; omnis quidem sub eo est, et ipse sub nullo, nisi tantum sub Deo.——The King is the deputy and servant of God on earth; for every one is subject to him, and he to no one, God only excepted.

REX non potest peccare.——(An ancient maxim.) "The king can do no wrong."

REX nunquam moritur.——"The king never dies."

REX, &c. salutem. Scribatis Episcopo *Karl*, quod *Roberto de Icard* pensionem suam, quam ad preces Regis prædicto *Roberto* concessit, de cætero solvat; et de proxima ecclesiæ vacutura de collatione prædicti episcopi, quam ipse *Robertus* acceptaverit, respiciat.——The King, &c., greeting. Inform Bishop *Karl*, that he henceforth pay to *Robert* of *Icard* his pension (or salary) which at the request of his Majesty he granted to the said *Robert;* and that he be appointed to the next church vacant in the collation of the said Bishop, which the said *Robert* shall accept.

REX tenuit magnum concilium, et graves sermones habuit cum suis proceribus de hac terra, quo modo incoloretur, et a quibus hominibus.——The King held a great assembly (or council), and solemnly advised with his nobles concerning this land, in what manner and by whom it should be inhabited.

REX vicecomiti salutem, &c. Si *A.* fecerit te securum de clamore suo prosequendo, tunc pone per vadium et salvos plegios *B.* quod sit coram justiciariis nostris apud *Westmonasterium* in octavis Sancti *Michaelis,* ostensurus quare cum idem *B.,* ad dextrum oculum ipsius *A.* casaliter læsum, bene et computentur curandum apud *S.* pro quadam pecuniæ summa præ manibus soluta assumpsisset idem *B.* curam suam circa oculum prædictum tam negligentur, et improvide apposuit, quod idem *A.* defectu ipsius *B.* visum oculi prædicti totaliter amisit; ad damnum ipsius *A.,* viginti librarum ut dicit. Et habeas ibi nomina plegiorum, et hoc breve. Teste meipso apud *Westmonasterium,* &c. ——"The King to the Sheriff greeting. If *A.* has made you secure to prosecute his complaint (or suit) then put by gage and safe sureties *B.* that he be before our Justices at *Westminster* in eight days of Saint *Michael,* to show (cause) why the same *B.* at *S.,* for a certain sum of money before then paid into his hands, had undertaken well and sufficiently to cure the right eye of the said *A.,* which was casually hurt, the said *B.* so negligently and heedlessly applied his remedy about the said eye that the said *A.,* through the unskilfulness of the said *B.,* lost altogether the sight of the said eye; to the loss of the said *A.,* of twenty pounds, as he says. And have there the names of the pledges and this writ. Witness myself at *Westminster,* &c." This was one of the ancient forms of an original writ in an action on the case.

REX vicecomiti salutem.——Præcipio tibi quod juste et

sine dilatione, facias stare rationabilem divisam *N.* sicut rationabile monstrare poterit, quod eam fecerit, et quod ipsa stare debeat, &c.——" The King to the Sheriff, greeting. I command you that justly, and without delay, you cause to be made a reasonable division as *N.* can fairly show ought to be made her, and which she ought to have, &c." This was part of the ancient writ of dower.

Rex vicecomiti *Wigorniæ,* salutem. Præcipimus tibi, quod sine dilatione clamari facias et firmiter prohiberi ex parte nostra, ut nullus de cætero eat ad riviandum in ripariis nostris in balliva tua, quæ in defenso fuerunt tempore *Henrici* Regis avi nostri; et scire facias omnibus de comitatu tuo, qui ab antiquo facere debent pontes et riparias illas, quod provideant sibi de pontibus illis, ita quod prompti sint et pariti in adventu nostro, quando eis scire faciemus.——The King to the Sheriff of *Worcester,* greeting. We command you to make proclamation without delay, and strictly forbid on our part, that no person from henceforth shall go out to row upon our banks, in your bailiwick, which were in defence (or enclosure), during the reign of King *Henry,* our ancestor; and that you give notice to all the persons of your county, who formerly constructed bridges and embankments, to take care of those bridges, so that they may be ready and in order on our approach, when we give due notice of the same.

RIBAUD.——A vagabond.

RICARDO et uxori suæ, et hæredibus suis, qui de ea veniunt.——" To *Richard* and his wife, and the heirs from her issuing." These were words used in ancient settlements of lands.

RICOHOME.——A lord.

RIDER, or RIDDER ROLL.——A small piece of parchment with a new clause upon it, tacked to a bill or record.

RIENS in arrière.——Nothing in arrear.

RIENS lour deust.——Not their debt.

RIENS passa per le fait.——Nothing passed by the deed.

RIENS per devise.——Nothing by gift.

RIENS per discent.——Nothing by descent.

RIENS per discent al' temps d'el original.——Nothing by descent to the time of (issuing) the original (writ).

RIENS per discent al' temps d'el writ.——Nothing by descent to the time of the writ.

RIENS per discent, præter, &c.——Nothing by descent, except, &c.

RIENS præter.——Nothing except.

RIFFLURA.——To disarrange.

RIFLETUM.——Anciently. A thicket.

RIGA.——A kind of tribute rendered by tenants cultivating the ground, to their lords.

RINGA.——In old law. A sword-belt.

RIPA.——A river's bank.

RIPARUM usus publicus est; littorum usus publicus est jure gentium.——The enjoyment of rivers is public: the use of the shores (or the sea shores) is (also) public by the law of nations.

RISCUS.——A trunk.

RIXA.——A contention.

RIXATRIX.——In old law. A scold.

ROBARIA.——Originally the robbing of a garment or robe.

ROBERDSMEN.——In old English law. Men who were guilty of great violations of peace on the English and Scottish borders.

RODKNIGHTS.——In old English law. Mounted tenants, whose duty it was to ride with the baron.

ROFFURE.——A plunderer: a robber.

ROGATIO ad populum.——An appeal to the people. Vide note to " *Judicia ad populum.*"

ROGAVERUNT omnes episcopi magnates, ut consentirent quod nati ante matrimonium essent legitimi, sicut illi qui nati sunt post matrimonium, quia ecclesia tales habet pro legitimis. Et omnes comites, et barones una voce responderunt "Quod nolunt leges Angliæ mutare quæ hucusque usitatæ sunt et approbatæ."———All the Bishops asked the noblemen, that they would consent that those born before marriage should be legitimate, as well as those born afterwards, because the church held them to be so. And all the Earls and Barons unanimously replied that "they would not change the laws of England which were hitherto used and approved."

Rogo te per salutem: per fortunam *Augusti*, &c.——— I entreat you by your life (or safety): by the fortune of *Augustus*, &c.

Role d'equipage.———Bill of lading: list of the crew.

Romanorum leges.———The Roman (or Civil) Law; the code of *Justiniän. Vide note.*

Romescot.———Peterpence.

Rother beasts.———Animals with horns.

Rotulus.———A register on a roll of parchment.

Royme.———Queen.

Routte.———A route, i. e. a company or number. *Vide note.*

Rumpere.———To revoke.

Runcaria.———Ground on which bramble-bushes grow.

Rupta.———Soldiers.

Ruptura.———Ploughed ground.

Ryche.———Rich.

Ryvire.———River.

NOTES TO R.

Rapuit, &c.—Lord *Coke* says that this crime was anciently punished with death; a severity which coincides with the rules of the old *Gothic* and *Scandinavian* constitutions. The penalty was mitigated, or rather altered, into a deprivation of sight, as well as of the offending members, by *William* the Conqueror, from *Normandy*. It seems, however, that the female upon whom the injury had been committed, had it in her power to save the criminal from this terrible sentence by accepting him as her husband. Vide 2 *Inst.* 180. *Hawkins*, 6. 1. c. 41. s. 11.

RECENS INSECUTIO.—This means such a quick and earnest following of an offender, where a robbery was committed, as never ceased from the time of the offence done, or discovered, until he was apprehended. And the benefit of the pursuit of such a felon was, that the party pursuing had his goods restored to him, which, had no such pursuit been made, would have been forfeited to the King. Vide *Staundf. Pla. Cor. lib.* 3, c. 10, *et* 12.

REDITUS.—Probably this word is from "*à reddendo*," from being rendered; and is not only a sum of money, but some other consideration (which was frequently the case formerly), paid by the tenant for lands held under lease, or demise. It must, it is said, be a profit to the land proprietor; but there is no occasion for it to be, as it usually is, at this day, a sum of *money;* for corn, spears, capons, spurs, and a variety of other matters, may be rendered, and frequently are rendered, by way of rent. Vide *Co. Litt.* 142. And, in former times, it often consisted of services done, or manual occupations performed to the lord, as to plough so many acres of land; to procure firewood; to attend the king or the lord to the wars, &c.: but, it has been said, that rent must be *certain:* or that which may be *reduced* to a *certainty:* and that it should issue *yearly*, though it would seem there is no *absolute* occasion for it to issue every *successive* year; for it may be reserved every second, third, or fourth year.

REDDEUNDO, &c.—It is almost impossible, at the present day, to conceive how such a wild scheme as the *Crusades* could have been undertaken. It appears that the first efforts to rouse Christendom to the subject was made by Pope *Sylvester* the Second, who, in the *tenth* century, addressed an epistle to the Church universal, as from the oppressed church in *Jerusalem*, calling for immediate relief. But little, however, was effected until the close of the *eleventh* century. About that time *Peter*, a hermit, who had been in military life, and had seen the miseries of the Christians in the East, wrapt in a coarse garment, his head bare, his feet naked, rode through Europe on an ass, bearing a weighty crucifix, and a letter which he affirmed was written in heaven; and, preaching to immense crowds in streets and churches, roused the nations to a holy war. The Popes used every artifice to increase the excitement made by the hermit, and augment the number of spiritual soldiers. A plenary indulgence, and absolution of their sins, were granted to all who should enlist. Amazing were the results. An immense multitude, computed at not less than *eight hundred thousand*, from the various nations of *Europe*, under illustrious commanders, set forth in the year 1096, to recover *Jerusalem* from the hands of the infidels. It was a motley assemblage of nobles, soldiers, monks, nuns, artists, laborers, boys and girls, pressing forward; some from pious motives, some from the hope of gaining heaven (for all who fell in battle were assured of a high seat in the regions of bliss), and many from the prospect of making their fortunes in the rich fields of *Asia*. Never was such enthusiasm felt on any subject. But a miserable fatality awaited the greatest part of these adventurers; for, acting more like an undisciplined band of robbers than Christians, they incensed against them the nations through which they marched, and were amazingly wasted away by famine, sword and pestilence, before they reached the *Saracen* dominions. Such of the rabble as passed into *Asia*, under *Peter* the hermit, were cut to pieces by *Solyman*. The disciplined soldiers, however, were more successful, and in the year 1099 became masters of the Holy City, under *Godfrey* of *Bouillon*, who immediately laid the foundations of a new kingdom. Such was the termination of the first Crusade, or *Croisade*, as it was called in the *French* language, because its object was to extend the triumph of the Cross; and every soldier wore a consecrated cross of various colors upon his right shoulder.

No sooner, however, had the vast multitude returned to *Europe* than the *Saracens* fell upon the new kingdom at *Jerusalem*, threatening it with an utter extermination. A new Crusade was demanded to support the tottering empire; and, in the year 1147 another torrent was seen pouring into the plains of *Asia*. This was headed by the two powerful monarchs, *Conrad* the Third, Emperor of *Germany*, and *Lewis* the Seventh, King of *France;* but it was wholly unsuccessful. By sword, by famine, by shipwreck, and the perfidy of the *Greeks*, they were wasted away, and the next year a miserable handful were seen retreating into *Europe*. The *Saracens* took courage, and, in the year 1187, recaptured *Jerusalem*, with horrible carnage and desolation. Vide *Marsh's Epit. Gen. Ecc. Hist. p.* 219, 220.

REGES EX NOBILITATE, DUCES, &c.—As every individual among the ancient *Germans* was almost independent, and master, in a great degree, of his own actions, it became, in consequence, the great object among those who aimed at being *Leaders* to gain adherents, and attach them to their persons and interests. These adherents *Cæsar* calls "AMBACTI and CLIENTES," i. e. Retainers and Clients. *Tacitus* calls them "COMITES," or Companions. The chief distinction, and power of the leaders, consisted in being attended by a numerous band of chosen youth; this was their pride as well as ornament during peace; and their defence in war. The leaders gained or preserved the favor of these retainers by presents of armor or of horses; or by the profuse, though inelegant hospitalities with which in those times they entertained them. Vide *Tac. c.* 14, 15, 5.

REMITTER.—This means an operation in law, upon the meeting of an ancient right, *remediable*, and a latter *defeasible* estate in the *same* person (the latter being cast upon him *by law*), whereby the ancient right is restored and set up again; and the new *defeasible* estate ceases: and thus he is in of his first or better estate. Vide 1 *Inst* 347, *b. Litt.* § 659. Those who desire to enter into distinctions, almost without a difference; and subtleties, fine as the web of *Arachne*, on this, and similar subjects, may peruse *Preston, Sugden, Saunders, Fearne,* and *Barton.*

RES MANCIPI.—These were things among the *Romans* which might be sold and alienated, or the property of them transferred from one person to another, by a certain right used among *Roman* citizens only, so that the purchaser might take them, as it were, *with his hand* (*manû caperet*); whence he was called "MANCEPS;" and the things "RES MANCIPI," vel *Mancûpi,* contracted "*Mancipii.*" And it behooved the seller to be answerable for them to the purchaser, and to secure the possession (*periculum judicii*, vel *auctoritatem*, vel *evictionem præstare, &c.*), i. e. the danger of a judgment or the title, or be answerable for the loss of the thing sold, &c. Vide *Cic. pro Murena,* 2.

NEC MANCIPI RES, were those things which could not thus be transferred: whence also the risk of the thing lay on the purchaser, (as is often the case in our laws). Vide *Plaut. Pers.* iv. 3, 55, &c. Thus *mancipium* and *usus* are distinguished; *Vitaque mancipio nulli datur,* in property or perpetuity, *omnibus usu.* Vide *Lucret.* iii. 985. So *mancipium,* and *fructus.* Vide *Cic. Epist. Fam.* vii. 29, 30.

RETRAXIT.—This is a term used when a defendant has withdrawn his plea. A plaintiff might formerly come into the court, where the action was brought, and declare that he would not proceed further. This was called a "*Retraxit:*" that being the emphatical word when the Law Entries were in Latin.

ROMANORUM LEGES.—The *Roman* Laws. The rapidity with which the study and knowledge of the *Roman Law* spread over *Europe*, is amazing. A copy of the *Pandects* was found at *Amalfi*, A. D. 1137. *Irnerius* opened a College of Civil Law at *Bologna*, a few years afterwards. Vide *Gian. Hist.*

lib. xi. c. 2. It began to be taught, as a part of academical learning, in different parts of *France,* before the middle of the twelfth century. *Vicarius* gave lectures on the Civil Law at *Oxford,* as early as the year 1147.

A regular system of feudal law, formed in imitation of the *Roman* Code, was composed by two *Milanese* Lawyers, about the year 1150. *Gratian* published the Code of *Canon* Law, with large editions and emendations, about the same time. The earliest collection of these customs, which served as the rules of decision in the courts of justice, is the *"Assizes de Jerusalem."* They were compiled in the year 1099; and are called *"Jus consuetudinum, quo regebatur regnum orientale,"*—i. e. "the law of customs under which the eastern kingdom was governed." But peculiar circumstances gave rise to this early compilation. Those of the Crusaders who were victorious, settled as a colony, in a foreign country; and adventurers from most of the different nations of *Europe* composed this new society. It was necessary, on that account, to ascertain the laws, and customs, which were to regulate the transactions of business, and the administration of justice amongst them. But in no country of *Europe* was there at that time any collection of customs; nor had any attempt been made to render the law fixed and permanent. The first undertaking of that kind was by *Glanville,* Lord Chief Justice of *England,* in his *"Tractatus de legibus, et consuetudinibus Angliæ,"* i. e. "A Treatise on the laws and customs of *England,"* composed about the year 1181. The *"Regiam Majestatem,"* in *Scotland,* ascribed to *David* the First, seems to be an imitation, and a servile one, of *Glanville.* Several Scotish Antiquarians, under the influence of that pious credulity, which disposes men frequently to assent without due examination, to whatever they deem honorable for their native country, contend zealously, that the *"Regium Majestatem,"* is a production *prior* to the treatise of *Glanville;* and some have brought themselves to believe that a nation, in a superior state of improvement, borrowed its laws and institutions from one considerably less advanced in its political and judicial progress. *Pierre de Fontainé,* who tells us that he was the first who had attempted such a work in *France,* composed his *" Conseil,"* which contains an account of the customs of the country of *Vernandois,* in the reign of *St. Louis,* which began A. D. 1226. *Beaumonoir,* the author of the *"Coustumes de Beauvoisis,"* lived about the same time. The establishments of *St. Louis,* containing a large collection of the customs which prevailed within the royal domains, were published by the authority of that Monarch. As soon as men became acquainted with the advantages of having *written* customs and laws, to which they could have recourse on every occasion, the practice of collecting them became common. *Charles* the Seventh of *France,* by an *ordinance,* A. D. 1453, appointed the customary laws in every province of *France,* to be collected and arranged. Vide *Velley* and *Villaret, Histoire,* tom. xvi. p. 113. His successor, *Louis* the Eleventh, renewed the injunction; but this salutary undertaking was not fully executed; so that the jurisprudence of the *French* nation remained more obscure and uncertain, than it would have been, if these prudent regulations of their monarchs, had taken effect. A mode of judicial determination was established in the middle ages, which affords the clearest proof that judges, whilst they had no other rule to direct their decrees, but unwritten and traditionary customs, were often at a loss how to ascertain the *principles* on which they were bound to decide; they were obliged, in dubious cases, to call in a certain number of *old* men, before whom they laid the case, that they might inform them what was the practice or custom, with regard to the point. This was called *"Enqueste par tourbe."* From the above it will appear, that the knowledge of the *"Leges Romanorum,"* was not so *entirely* lost, during the Middle Ages, as many persons believe. That the Civil Law is intimately connected with the Municipal Jurisprudence, in several countries of *Europe,* is a fact so well known, that it requires no illustration. Even in *England,* where the common law has been, by many, supposed to form a system, perfectly distinct from the *Roman* Code:

and although such as apply in that country, to the study of the Common Law, have often boasted of this distinction, it is evident that many of the ideas and maxims of the Civil Law are incorporated into the *English* jurisprudence. This is well illustrated by the ingenious author of "Observations on the Statutes, chiefly the more Ancient," 3*d edit.* p. 76; which the student will do well carefully to peruse.

ROUTTE.—In a legal sense, this word signifies an assembly of persons going forcibly to commit an unlawful act, though they may *not* do it. A Rout is the same which the *Germans* call *Rot*, meaning a band, or great company of men gathered together, and going to execute, or indeed executing, any riot or unlawful act.

S.

SA ET LA.——Here and there.

SAC. SACHA.——A cause: prosecution.

SACCABOR.——One from whom a thing was stolen, and who pursued the thief.

SACCUS cum brochia. A sack with a lance.

SACERDOS interroget dotem mulieris, et si terra ei in dotem detur, tunc dicatur Psalmus iste.——"The priest may inquire respecting the woman's dowry, and if land be given her in dower, then let the Psalm be sung." The Psalm referred to is cxxviii. In some cases formerly, the woman was endowed at the church, and at the church-door.

SACERDOTES a regibus honorandi sunt; non judicandi. ——The priests are to be reverenced by kings; not judged (by them).

SACHENT a touts ceux que icy sount, et a touts ceux que avener sount.——Know all those who are here, and all those who are to come. An ancient form of commencing deeds.

SACIRE.——To seize.

SACQUIER.——One who was appointed in the ancient maritime law of the French, to load and unload vessels whose cargoes consisted of corn, fish or salt; for the prevention of fraud on the part of the crew.

SACRAMENTUM.——An oath: a gage in money formerly

deposited by the litigating parties among the Romans; and by persons who agreed to buy or sell; also, the oath taken by soldiers to their general. *Vide note.*

SACRAMENTUM decisionis.——The oath of decision: the oath formerly taken by a party who *waged* his law in an action of debt. Vide note to "*Sacramentum.*"

SACRAMENTUM domini Regis fregisse.——To have broken the oath of the lord the King.

SACRARE.——To outlaw.

SACRARIUM.——A vestry: the place where the priest's robes are kept.

SACRILEGII instar est rescriptum principis obviare.—— It is like sacrilege to oppose the order of the Emperor.

SACRILEGIUM.——Sacrilege. Also any detestible or odious crime.

SÆPE quæsitum est, an comitum numero et jure habendi sunt, qui legatum comitantur, non ut instructior fiat legatio, sed unice ut lucro suo consulant, institores forte et mercatores. Et quamvis hos sæpe defenderint et comitum loco habere voluerint legati, apparet tamen satis eo non pertinere, qui in legati legationisve officio non sunt. Quam autem ea res nonnunquam turbas dederit, optimo exemplo, in quibusdam aulis, olim receptum fuit, ut legati tenerentur exhibere nomenclaturam comitum suorum.——It has often been inquired, whether those who accompany an ambassador (or legate) are properly reckoned in the number of his companions, not that the embassy may be better equipped, but are probably merchants and factors, who only consult their own profit. And although ambassadors have often maintained and desired to have them as companions, nevertheless, it is sufficiently clear, that they who are not in the service of the ambassador or embassy do not belong to the same. But as the matter has sometimes caused disputes, it was formerly received as the best rule, in some courts, that ambassadors should be obliged to produce a list of their companions (or suite).

Sæpius requisitus.——Oftentimes requested.

———————————"Sævior armis

Luxuria incubuit victam ulciscitur orbem."

"Luxury, more destructive than arms, hovers over, and revenges itself upon a vanquished world."

Sagibaro.——A judge.

Sala.——A hall.

Salarium nautæ debeter, quando navis magister ante tempus conventionis completum, licentiam ei dederit, aut eum in terram reliquerit, ut per eum servire non steterit. Item debetur nautæ salarium conventum, cum magister navis non naviget, ex causa fortuitu, et sine culpa ipsius magistri; licet nautæ non serviat, dummodo ipse nauta, absque licentia magistri, navem non derelinquerit.——The wages are due to the mariner, when the master of the vessel, before the time of the agreement be completed, shall give him liberty (to depart), or leave him on shore, so that he cannot remain to serve him. Also the wages, agreed upon, are due to the mariner, when the master does not sail, from any accidental cause, and without his own default; it is (then) lawful for the mariner not to serve, if he may not have left the ship without the master's consent.

Salic or Salique law.——A code of law compiled in the fifth century by the Salian Franks in Gaul.

Salicetum.——A willow wood.

Salus populi suprema lex est.——The welfare of the people is the paramount law.

Salus ubi multi consiliarii.——Among many counsellors there is safety.

Salva fide et ligeantia domino.——Saving fealty and allegiance to the lord (of the fee).

Salvis exceptionibus tam ad breve, quam ad narrationem.——Saving exceptions as well to the writ, as to the declaration.

Salvis omnibus exceptionibus, advantagiis quibuscunque.——Saving all exceptions, and every advantage.

SALVO contenemento suo.——Saving his appearance: or those things which render him respectable in life. *Vide note.*

SALVO jure petentis.——Saving the right of the petitioner (or plaintiff).

SALVO meo, et hæredibus meis.——Saving my own right, and that of my heirs.

SALVO pudore.——Saving modesty.

SANCTA absolutio.——The holy remission (or pardon). *Vide note.*

SANCTIO justa, jubens honesta, et prohibens contraria. ——A just ordinance, directing what is honorable, and forbidding what is wrong.

SANS ceo.——Without this.

SANS issue.——Without children.

SANS nombre.——Without number: without limit.

SAPIENTES, fideles, et animosi.——Wise, faithful, and courageous.

SAUCES del mer.——Creeks of the sea.

SAUNKE.——Blood.

SC.——Abbreviated from *scilicet.* To wit.

SCACCARIUM.——" The Exchequer:" one of the courts of Common Law in *England.* *Vide note.*

SCANDALUM magnatum.——The scandal against the peerage. *Vide note.*

SCELUS intra se tacitum qui cogitat ullum, facti crimen habet.——He who secretly meditates the commission of a crime, is guilty of the deed.

SCHETES.——Usury.

SCHISMATICUS inveteratus.——A confirmed schismatic.

SCIANT præsentes et futuri, quod ego *Johannes* Constubularius *Cestriæ,* dedi et concessi, et hac præsenti charta mea, confirmavi, *Hugoni* de *Dutton,* hæredibus suis, magistratum omnium leccatorium et meretricium totius *Cestershiræ,* sicut liberius illum magistratum teneo de comite. ——Know all men present, and to come, That I, *John,*

the constable of *Chester*, have given and granted, and, by
this my present deed, have confirmed, to *Hugh* de *Dutton*,
and his heirs, the magistracy over all debauchees and
harlots, throughout *Cheshire*, as freely as I hold that office
of the Earl.

SCIENDUM et feudum, sine investitura, nullo modo, constitui posse.——And be it known, that a fee, without
(giving) possession, cannot in any manner be made.

SCIENDUM tamen, quod in hoc placito, non solet accusatus per plegios dimitti, nisi ex regiæ potestatis beneficio.
——Be it known, however, that on this plea, a person
accused is not usually discharged on bail, unless by favor
of the royal authority.

SCIENTER.——Knowingly: wilfully.

SCIENTIA enim utrinque per, pares facit contrahentes.
——For knowledge on the part of each, places contracting
parties on an equal footing.

SCI' fa. quare executionem non.——That you give notice
why execution be not issued.

SCILICET—per quas feudum amittitur—Si domino deservire noluerit; si per annum, et diem cessaverit in
petenda investituræ; si dominum ejuravit, id est, negavit
se à domino feudum habere; si à domino in jus cum
vocante (ter citatus), non comparuerit.——That is to say—
by what acts a fee is fortified.   If (the vassal) be unwilling
to serve his lord; if he neglect to seek after his possession
for a year and a day; if he has forsworn (or renounced)
his lord, that is, denied that he holds the fee of him; (or)
if being called into court by the lord, (being three times
cited,) he may not have appeared.

SCINTILLA juris.——A spark of right.

SCINTILLA juris et tituli.——A shadow (or spark) of
right and title.

SCIRE facias.——That you make known.   *Vide note.*

SCIRE facias ad audiendum errores.——That you give
notice to hear errors.

SCIRE facias ad computandum.——That you give notice to account.

SCIRE facias ad computandum, et rehabendam terram.——That you give notice to account, and re-occupy the land.

SCIRE facias ad rehabendam terram.——That you make known as to re-possessing the lands.

SCIRE facias quare consultatio non debet concedi post prohibitionem.——That you give notice why a consultation should not be granted after the prohibition.

SCIRE facias quare executionem non.——That you cause it to be understood why he does not (obtain) execution.

SCIRE feci.——I have made known.

SCIRE fieri.——To be informed.

SCOTIÆ leges dantur.——Laws are given to *Scotland*. *Vide note.*

SCRIBÆ conventionem faciunt.——Notaries (or clerks) make the contract. *Vide note.*

SCRIBERE est agere.——To write is to perform.

SCRIPSIT, fecit, et publicavit; seu scribi fecit, et publicari causavit.——He wrote, made and published; or caused to be written, made and published.

SCULDASIUS.——An assistant to a judge.

SCUTAGIUM.——"Scutage;" also a sum formerly paid to be excused performing knights' service: a tenure by which considerable land in *England* was once holden.

SCUTAGIUM (or Scutum) non adimit hæreditatem.——(Escuage or shield-service) does not take away the inheritance.

SCUTO magis quam gladio opus est.——"It is used rather as a shield than a sword." As by the English law, an old mortgage term, regularly assigned, from time to time, protects against dower, and subsequent latent incumbrances: this may be in some respects a new doctrine—but see *Preston, Sugden,* &c.

SCYRAN.——To divide.

Scyre-gerafa.——A sheriff.

Secta.——A suit: litigation: also the pledges produced that the plaintiff should prosecute his claim.

Secta ad furnum; secta ad torrale; et ad omnia alia hujusmodi.——Suit (or service) at the oven (or bakehouse); also at the kiln; and to all other things of this sort.

Secta ad molendinam.——Suit (or service) at the mill. Some lands were formerly held by performing such services as these.

Secundum absolutam probatam.——According to absolute proof.

Secundum æquum et bonum.——According to what is just and right.

Secundum allegata et probata.——As alleged and proved.

Secundum conditionem personarum.——According to the rank (or situation) of the parties.

Secundum consuetudinem husbandriæ.——According to the custom of husbandry (or tillage).

Secundum consuetudinem manerii.——According to the custom of the manor. *Vide note.*

Secundum discretionem boni viri.——According to the judgment of an honest man.

Secundum formam chartæ.——According to the import of the deed (or writing).

Secundum formam doni.——According to the form (or manner) of the gift.

Secundum legem et consuetudinem *Angliæ.*——According to the law and custom of *England.*

Secundum legem et consuetudinem parliamenti.——According to the law and usage of parliament.

Secundum legem et consuetudinem regni.——According to the law and custom of the realm.

Secundum legem terræ.——According to the law of the land.

SECUNDUM potestatem ordinatam.——According to set-tled authority.

SECUNDUM subjectam materiam.——According to the subject-matter.

SECURITAS legatorum, utilitati quæ ex pœna est prepon-derat.——The safety of ambassadors, which outweighs the expediency of the punishment.

SE defendendo.——In his own defence.

SEDENTE curia.——During the sitting of the court.

SEDITIO regni, vel exercitus.——The sedition of the realm or of the army.

SED non allocatur.——But it is not discussed (or con-sidered).

SED nonnunquam aliter est.——But sometimes it is otherwise.

SED non valet confirmatio nisi ille qui confirmat sit in possessione rei vel juris unde fieri debet confirmatio ; et eodem modo nisi ille cui confirmatio fit sit in possessione. ——But the confirmation is inefficacious, unless he who makes it is in the possession, or has the right of the proper-ty under which the confirmation ought to be performed, and in like manner, unless he, to whom the confirmation is made, be in possession.

SED per curiam.——But by the court.

SED recentiori jure gentium, inter *Europæos* populos in-troductum videmus, ut talia capta censeantur, ubi per horas viginti quatuor in potestate hostium fuerint.——But we observe by the more recent law of nations, introduced among *Europeans*, that such things were considered cap-tured, where they were twenty-four hours in the enemy's possession.

SED secundum earundem plenitudinem, judicenter.—— Let them be judged of according to their magnitude.

SED si non prosunt singula, juncta juvant.——But if they do not assist separately, taken together they are ad-vantageous.

SEGNITER irritant animos demissa per aurem, quam quæ sunt oculis subjectæ fidelibus.——What we hear produces a slight impression, when compared with that which is presented to the eye.

SEISE quousque, &c.——Seised (or possessed) until, &c.

SEISINA facit stirpitem.——Seisin makes the Root (or Stock).

SELECTI judices de decuria senatoria conscribuntur, in urnam sortito mittuntur, ut de pluribus necessarius numerus confici possit: post, urna permittitur accusatori ac reo, ut ex illo numero rejiciant quos putaverint sibi, aut inimicos, aut ex aliqua re incommodos fore; rejectione celebrata, in eorum locum qui rejecti fuerunt subsortiebatur *Prætor* alios, quibus ille judicium legitimus numerus compleretur; his perfectis, jurabunt in leges judices ut obstructi religione, judicarent.——The (names of) select judges are written down from the senatorial roll, (and) are thrown by lot into an urn, that out of many the requisite number may be procured; afterwards, the urn is sent to the accuser, and to the criminal, that they may reject from that number those whom they consider would be unfriendly (to them) or improper on some other account; the rejection being declared the *Prætor* chooses by lot others in the stead of those who have been rejected, with whom he completes the legal number of Judges; these things being finished, the Judges swore upon the laws that they would decide under the obligation of their oath. *Vide note.*

SEMBLE.——It seems.

SEMIPLENA probatio.——"Half full proof." Proof insufficient to convict.

SEMPER animo, et intentione prosequendi.——Always with the desire and intention to proceed.

SEMPER dabitur dies partibus ab justiciariis de banco, sub tali conditione, "nisi justiciarii *itinerantes* prius venerint ad partes illas.——"A day shall always be allowed to the parties by the Judges of the Bench under such condition, 'unless the Judges in *Eyre* sooner come into those parts.' " The Judges in *Eyre* meant those who went the circuit in *England*.

SEMPER levi nota adspersi fuisse videntur.——They appear to have been always published with some trifling remark.

SEMPER paratus.——Always ready.

SENATUS consulta.——"Decrees of the *Roman* senate." These related to the people at large. *Vide note.*

SENATUS consultum Tertullianum.——The Tertullian decrees.

SENATUS consultum ultimæ necessitatis.——A decree made on extreme necessity. *Vide note.*

SENATUS decreta.——"The decrees of the senate." These related to private matters.

SENSUS verborum ex causa dicendi accipiendus est.—— The meaning of the words is to be taken from the subject upon which they are spoken.

SENTENTIA lata cum eo cujus principaliter interest et à quo alii jus habent consecutum, jus facit quoad omnes, etiam non intervenientes, et non citatos.——A sentence (or decree) given against him who is principally concerned, and from whom others have a derivative title, becomes a law as to all persons, notwithstanding they do not attend, or have not been summoned.

SENTENTIA rerum divinarum, humano sensu excogitata, palam docta, et pertinaciter defensa.——An opinion of things divine, devised by human reason, publicly taught, and obstinately defended.

SEQUATUR sub suo periculo.——Let him follow at his peril.

SEQUESTRARI facias.——That you cause to be sequestered.

SEQUESTRARI feci.——I have caused to be sequestered.

SERIATIM.——In regular order: in succession.

SERMO relatus ad personam et intelligi debet conditioni personæ.——The discourse refers to the person, and it should be understood according to the situation (condition or rank) of the party.

SERVATO juris ordine.——The order (or form) of law being preserved.

SERVI aut fiunt, aut nascuntur; fiunt jure gentium, aut jure civili: nascuntur ex ancilliis nostris.——Slaves are made so, or they are born so: they are made slaves by the law of nations, or by the civil law: they are born (slaves) from our bondwomen. *Vide note.*

SERVICE de Chevalier.——Knight's service.

SERVIENTES ad legem.——Serjeants at law.

SERVI nascuntur.——They are born slaves. *Vide note.*

SERVITIA servientium, et stipendia famulorum.——The services of those employed, and wages of servants.

SERVITII adscriptitii glebæ.——"Slaves attached to the soil." Those who were bought and sold with the land.

SERVITIO obnoxium.——Liable to perform service.

SERVITIUM militaire.——Military service.

SERVITIUM scuti.——Knight's service.

SERVITIUM sokæ.——"Socage service." A considerable part of the lands in *England* were formerly held by these services.

SERVITUS est jus, quo res mea, alterius rei vel personæ servit.——Bondage is a law by which my property is subject to the circumstances or person of another. *Vide note.*

SERVUS facit, ut herus det.——The servant performs (the work) that the master may pay him.

SI á domino ter citatus non comparuerit.——"If being summoned thrice by the lord, he has not appeared." This was one of the causes by which the tenant forfeited his land.

SI aliquid ex solennibus deficiat, cum equitas poscit, subveniendum est.——If anything customarily appointed is wanting, which equity requires, it should be supplied.

SI aliquis mulierum pregnantem percusserit, vel ei vene-
num dederit, per quod fecerit abortivam, si puerperium jam
formatum fuerit, et maxime si fuerit animatum, facit homicidium.——If any one strike a pregnant woman; or give
her poison by which she miscarry; if the embryo has been
already formed, and particularly if it has quickened, he is
guilty of murder.

SI aliquis per superbiam elatus, ad justitiam Episcopalem
venire noluerit, vocetur semel, secundo, et tertio; quod si
nec ad emendationem venerit, excommunicetur, et si opus
fuerit ad hoc vindicandum, fortitudo et justitia Regis, sive
Vicecomitis, adhibeatur.——If any person, elated by pride,
will not come (or submit) to Episcopal justice, let him be
called once, twice, thrice; but if, after this, he do not submit to correction, let him be excommunicated; and if occasion require, let the power and justice of the King, or
the Sheriff, be used to vindicate this act.

SI antiquitatem spectes, est vetustissima; si dignitatem,
est honoratissima; si jurisdictionem, est capacissima.——If
you look at its antiquity, it is most venerable; if at its dignity, it is very honorable; if at its jurisdiction, it is extremely extensive.

SI autem in narratione facienda aliquis articulorum prædictorum omittatur, et narratio a petente advocetur, ita
quod error revocari non possit; et petens clameum suum
pro se, et hæredibus suis amittet in perpetuum.——But if
in making the declaration (or count), either of the said
articles (conditions, or things) are omitted, and the count
be pleaded by the plaintiff, so that such error cannot be
recalled, the plaintiff will lose his claim for himself, and
his heirs forever.

SI autem villanus sockmannus villanum soccagium ad
alium transferre voluerit, prius illud restituat domino, (vel
servienti, si dominus præsens non fuerit); et de manibus
ipsius fiat translatio ad alium, tenendum libere, vel in soccagio, secundum quod domino placuerit; quia ille villanus

31

sockmannus non habet potestatem transferrendi, cum liberum tenementum non habet.——Therefore if a villain in
socage desires to transfer his socage land to another person, he must first restore it to the lord, (or to his attorney,
if the lord shall not be present;) and the transfer may be
made from his hands to the other person, to hold in fee, or
in socage, as the lord may please; for the villain in socage
has not a power of transferring (the possession), because he
has not the fee.

SIBYLLINA.——The Sibylline books.   *Vide note.*

SI certa signa apposita fuere mercibus et aliis rebus.——
If certain marks were set to the merchandise, and the
other things.

SIC enim debet quis meliorem agrum suum facere, ne
vicini deteriorem faciat.——For, although a person desires
to improve his estate, yet he should do no injury to his
neighbor.

SI constare poterit.——If it shall be made to appear.

SI curia cognoscere velit.——If the court wish to certify
(or take cognizance).

SICUT alias præcipimus.——As we have otherwise commanded.

SICUT pluries præcipimus.——As we have many times
commanded.

SIC utere tuo, ut alienum non lædas.——So use your
own that you injure not another's property.

SICUT si talibus circumstantibus, quæ timorem, credulitatem, aut errorem, capitani excusare possint.——Such as, if
under similar circumstances, may be sufficient to excuse
the captain's fear, credulity, or mistake.

SIC volo, sic jubeo, stet pro ratione voluntas.——So I
will, so I order, and let my will stand in the place of
reason.

SI debeat respondere, quousque, &c.——If he should
answer, until, &c.

SI decedens plura habuerit animalia, optima cui de jure

fuerit debitum reservato Ecclesiæ suo sine dolo, fraude, seu contradictione qualibet, pro recompensatione substractionis decimarum personalium, necnon et oblationum : secundum melius animal reservetur, post obitum, pro salute animæ suæ.——If a person dying has several animals, the best is kept for whom it legally belongs, which is to his church, without any guile, fraud, or objection whatever, as a recompense for withholding his personal tithes, and oblations : that the second best animal be reserved, after his death, for the welfare of his soul.

SI dominum cucurbitaverit, id est cum uxore ejus concubuerit.——"If he has cuckolded his lord, that is, if he has committed adultery with his wife." This appears to have caused a forfeiture of the tenant's feud.

SI dominum deservire noluerit.——If he be unwilling to serve his lord.

SI dominum ejuravit, id est, negavit se á domino feudum habere.——If he has forsworn his lord; that is, if he has denied that he holds the fee of him.

SI dominus commisit feloniam, per quam vassallus amit teret feudum, si eam commiserit in dominum; feudi proprietatem etiam dominus perdere debet.——If the lord commit a felony, for which a vassal would lose his fee, had he committed such an offence against the lord, the lord ought also (in such a case) to lose his seigniorship in the fee.

SI dominus feodi negat hæredibus defuncti seisinam, justiciarii domini regis faciunt inde fieri recognitionem per duodecim legales homines qualem seisinam defunctus inde habuit die qua fuit vivus, et mortuus; et sicut recognitum fuerit, ita hæredibus ejus restituant.——If the lord of the fee refuse (to give) possession to the heirs of the deceased, the justices of the lord the King shall thereupon cause recognition to be made by twelve lawful men, as to what seisin (or possession) the deceased had therein, on the day on which he was alive, and at the (very) time he died;

and according as that recognition shall be, so shall they restore the possession to the heirs. *Vide note.*

Sɪ enim ipsi raptores metu, vel atrocitate pœnæ, ab hujusmodi facinore se temporaverint, nullæ mulieri, sive volenti, sive nolenti, peccandi locus relinquetur; quia hoc *velle* mulieris, ab insidiis nequissimi hominis, qui meditatur rapinam, inducitur. Nisi etenim, eam solicitaverit, nisi odiosis artibus circumveniret non faciet eam velle in tantum dedecus sese prodere.——For even supposing that these violators, through fear, or the severity of the punishment, abstain from a foul deed of this kind, yet the opportunity of acting wickedly to any woman will not be lost, whether she would or would not; because this same *will* of the woman is led astray by the subtleties of a most debauched man, who meditates seduction. For, unless he solicit her, and, by his odious devices, beguile her, he will not prevail on the female to be willing to give herself up to so great a disgrace.

Sɪ eo nomine, forte ingrediatur fundum alienum, non quoad sibi usurpet tenementum, vel jura; non facit disseisinam, sed transgressionem, &c.; querendum est a judice quo animo hoc fecit.——If, on that account, he accidentally enters upon another's fee, he does not therefore usurp to himself the tenure or the rights; he does not make a disseisin, but a trespass, &c.: it is to be inquired of by the judge with what intention he did this.

Sɪ equam meam equus tuus prægnantem fecerit, non est tuum, sed meum, quod natum est.——If my mare be in foal by your horse, it is not your foal but mine.

Sɪ fecerit feloniam, dominum forte cucurbitando.——If he shall commit felony, (as) perhaps by cuckolding his lord.

Sɪ fecerit te securum, pone per vadios et salvos plegios. ——If he make you secure, put by gages and safe pledges.

Sɪ *Friscus*, cum patris filia, se conferat in *Brabantiam* ibique nuptias celebret; huc reversus, non videtur toleran-

dus: quia sic jus nostrum pessimis exemplis eluderetur.——
If a *Friscian* go with his sister into *Brabant,* and there marry her, his return hither does not appear to be allowed; if
so, our law might be evaded by the most disgraceful examples.

SIGILLUM est cera impressa, quia cera sine impressione
non est sigillum.——"A seal is impressed on wax; for wax,
without an impression, is not a seal." Signets and rings
have been used from very ancient times, and are mentioned
by many sacred and profane authors. Vide *Daniel,* vi. 17.

SIGNUM crucis imposui.——I have placed the sign of the
cross. *Vide note.*

Si home aint feoffées à son use devant le statt. de 27 Hen.
VIII. eu devise la terre al auter, et puis les feoffées sont
feoffment del terre use del devisor; et puis le statut, le devisor morust, la terre passera per le devise, car aprés le feoffment, le devisor avoit mesme l'use que il avoit. devant.——
If a man having feoffees to his use, before the statute 27
Hen. VIII. had devised the land to another, and then the
feoffees make feoffment of the land to the use of the devisor, and after that statute the devisor died, the land shall
pass by the devise; for, after the feoffment, the devisor had
the same use which he had before.

SI home port ejection firmæ, le plaintiff recovera son
terme qui est arrere, si bien come in "quare ejecit infra terminum;" et si nul soit arrere, donques tout in damages.——
If a man bring an ejectment for a farm, the plaintiff shall
recover his term which is in arrear, as well as he would in
an action, "wherefore he ejected within the term;" and if
none (meaning no term) remain, he shall have all in damages.

SI imperialis majestas causam cognitionaliter examina-
verit, et partibus cominus constitutis, sententiam dixerit,
omnes omnino judices, qui sub nostro imperio sunt, sciant
hanc esse legem, non solam illi causæ pro qua producta est,
sed et in omnibus similibus.——If his Imperial Majesty has

thoroughly examined a cause, and thereupon the matters being determined, he has made his judgment or (decree), surely all the judges who are under our authority may understand that this is the law, not only for that cause, which occasioned the judgment, but also in all similar cases.

Si in chartis membranisve tuis carmen, vel historiam, vel orationem, *Titius* scripserit, hujus corporis non *Titius*, sed tu dominus esse videris.——If *Titius* write a song, history, or oration on your papers or parchments, you will be considered the owner of the material, (on which the writing was made,) and not *Titius.* Vide note to " *Chartæ,*" &c.

Si in confiniis hostium deprehendantur, præsumantur hostibus advehi.——If effects are taken in the enemies' precints, they are considered to have been carried away by the enemy.

Si ita sit, tunc sigilla vestra.——If so then set your seals.

Si iter mutaverit ex aliqua justa, et necessaria causa, puta, ex causa refectionis, vel ad evitandum maris tempestatum, vel ne inciderit in hostes; si quidem in istis casibus, mutato itinere, tenetur accecurator.——Suppose a vessel shall alter her course on account of any just and necessary purpose, either for (the purpose of) refreshment; to avoid the tempest of the sea, or falling in with the enemy; if this be the case, although the course be changed, yet in these instances the assurer is bound.

Si jeo mist mon clothes al un taylor à faire, il peut eux conserver tanque satisfaction par le fesans : mes si jeo contract oue un taylor, que il avera tant per le fesans de mon appareil, il ne peut eux conserver tanque satisfaction pur le fesans.——If I send my clothes to a tailor to make, he may keep them until he be paid for the making: but if I contract with him that he shall have a certain sum for making my apparel, he cannot keep the same until he be paid for the making.

Si judicium redditum sit.——If judgment be given.

SI juratores erraverint, et justiciarii secundum eorum dictum, judicium pronuntiaverint, falsam faciunt pronuntiationem, et ideo sequi non debent eorum dictum; sed illud emendare tenenter per diligentem examinationem. Si autem dijudicare nesciant, recurrendum erit ad majus judicium.——If the jurors mistake, and the judges give judgment according to the verdict, they pass an erroneous sentence, and therefore ought not to follow up their verdict; but are bound to amend it by a diligent examination, (or inquiry.) But if they are unable to decide it, recourse shall be had to a higher tribunal.

SI le capitaine a fuilli en sa premiere qualitié; comme s'il a dérouté, &c., les assureurs qui se sont renders garans de la barraterie du patron, en sont responsables, mais malgré ladite clause, ils ne sont pas tenue des fautes que le capitaine commet en sa qualitié de facteur.——If the captain has acted improperly in his chief capacity; as if he has changed his route, &c., the assurers, who have guaranteed against the barratry of the owner, are responsible for it; but, notwithstanding the said clause, they are not bound for any offences which the captain has committed in his capacity of factor.

SILENT leges inter arma.——There is a suspension of law amidst the din of arms.

SI le prince arrest le navire comme s'il s'en voulait servir, s'il avoit affaire de portion ou de toute la marchandize, s'il ne veut permettre aux navires de sortir, qu'en flotte ou redoublement d'equipage; ou s'il prevoyoit à plus grand danger les arrestans pour quelque tems, l'assureur n'est en acune indemnité quand telle chose advient *dedans le meme* port, pour ce que ce sont des dangers de la terre procedans du volonte du prince.——If the vessel be detained by the prince, for his use, or if he has any claim on a portion or the whole of the merchandise; or if he (the prince) will not permit vessels to sail except in fleets, or without increasing the equipage, (i. e. the crew); or if he by any means expose those thus detained to great danger, the assurer has no risk, when such a thing occurs *within the same* port, (i. e. where the insurance was made,) because these are land risks, and proceed from the (paramount) will of the prince.

SI malgré l'interdiction de commerce, qu'emporte toujours tout declaration de guerre, les sujets du roi ne font point commerce avec les ennemis d l'etat, ou avec des amis ou alliés, par l'interposition desquels on feroit passer aux enemis des munitions de guerre et de bouche, ou de autres effets prohibies; car tout cela etant come prejudiceable à l'etat, seroit sujet à confiscation, et à être declaré de bonne prise, etant trouvé soit, sur les navires de la nation, soit sur ceux des amis et alliés.——If, contrary to the prohibition of commerce, which, at all times, is the consequence of a declaration of war, the subjects of the King carry on trade with the enemies of the nation, or with friends or allies, by whose interposition they forward to the enemy military stores, provisions or other prohibited articles; this being all prejudicial to the interests of the nation, should be subject to confiscation, and declared a lawful prize, whether found in vessels of the nation, or in those of friends and allies.

SI mercatum aliquid levatum sit, ad nocumentum vicini mercati.——If any merchandise be placed there, to the injury of a neighboring market.

SIMILITER.——"In like manner." A word used in making up the issue, when it is said the "*similiter*" is added.

SI milites quid in clypeo literis sanguine suo rutilantibus adnotaverint; aut in pulvere inscripserint gladio suo, ipso tempore, quo in prœlio, vitæ sortem derelinquunt, hujusmodi voluntatem stabilem esse oportet.——If soldiers write anything upon their shields, in letters glaring red with their own blood; or make marks in the dust with their sword, at the time they die in battle, a testament of this kind ought to be considered valid. *Vide note.*

SI modo postea nascatur, tunc enim fictione juris nativitas retrotrahitur.——If the child be born subsequently, then, by a fiction of law, the birth shall have a retrospective construction.

SIMONIA.——Simony. *Vide note.*

SI mortuo viro, uxor ejus remanserit, et sine liberis fuerit, dotem suam habedit; si vero uxor cum liberis remanserit, dotem quidem habebit, dum corpus suum legitime survaverit.——If at a man's decease, his wife survive, and there be no issue, she shall have her dower; but if she survive with children, she shall have her dower so long as she conducts herself chastely. *Vide note.*

SIMPLICITAS est legibus amica, et nimia subtilitas in jure reprobatur.——Simplicity is a favorite of the laws, and too much subtlety is reprobated in law.

SIMPLEX loquela.——A single plea, or plaint.

SIMUL cum aliis.——Together with other persons.

SIMUL cum quodam *I. S.* clausum suum fregit.——He broke the close in company with a certain (person named) *I. S.*

SIMUL et semel.——At once and together.

SIMUL et vicissim.——Together, and at different times.

SI navis mutaverit iter vel ceperit secundum viagium; vel conveniret asportare alias merces in alium locum; vel alias assecurationes fecerit pro dicto secundo viagio, tunc in casibus prædictis assecuratores pro primo viago, not amplius tenentur: nam cum navis diverterit ad extraneos actus, dicitur mutasse iter, et plura viagia fecisse, et primum dicitur mutatum; limita tamen mutatur in justa causa. Periculum intelligitur solum currere assecuratori pro *illo* itinere convento, et non pro alio; nam si navis mutaverit iter, vel a via recta illius itineris diverterit, non tenetur amplius assecurator; non vero limita si iter mutaverit ex aliqua et necessaria causa.——If a vessel shall have changed her course, or have taken a second voyage; or has agreed to carry more merchandise into another place; or made more insurances for the said second voyage; then, in the said cases, the insurers for the first voyage are no longer bound; for when a vessel diverts for purposes foreign to her voyage, the voyage shall be said to be changed, and (it shall be considered) that she has made more (or other) voyages; and the first shall be said to be altered; yet, for a proper cause she may change her destination. The risk is understood to arise to the insurer only for *that* voyage agreed upon, and not for any other: for if the vessel shall have changed her voyage, or deviated from the direct course, the assurer is no longer bound; nor is he (bound) if the voyage be changed from another and necessary cause.

SINE aliqua causa.——Without any cause.

SINE aliquo vestimento.——Without being clothed: (without any title.)

SINE assensu capituli.——Without the consent of the chapter.

SINE calumnia verborum non observata illa dura consuetudine, "qui cadit à syllaba, cadit à totâ causâ."—— Without a false construction of the words, that usual severity not being attended to, "that he who mistakes in one syllable, loses his cause altogether."

SINE DIE.——" Without day"—as, the Court adjourned "*sine die*"—no day being mentioned for sitting again.

SINE judicio parium, vel per legem terræ.——Without the judgment of his peers (or equals), or by the law of the land.

SINE hoc quod.——Without this that.

SINE prejudicio melioris sententiæ.——Without prejudice of a milder (or more favorable) judgment.

SINE qua non.——An indispensable condition.

SINE suo suorumque prejudicio.——Without prejudice to him or from them.

SI non adest risicum assecuratio non valet; nam non est materia in qua forma posset fundari.——If there be no risk the insurance is invalid; for it is immaterial in what form it be recorded.

Sɪ non omnes qui rem communem habent, sed certi ex his dividere desiderant; hoc judicium inter eos accipi potest.——If all who hold an estate in common do not wish to divide it, but only some of them, that consideration must be regulated among themselves.

Sɪ non sequatur ipsius vadii traditio, curia domini regis hujusmodi privatas conventiones tueri non solet.——If the delivery of the pledge do not follow, the King's court does not usually sanction private agreements of this sort.

Sɪ pares veritatem noverint, et dicant se nescire cum sciant.——If the jury know the truth, and say that they are ignorant when they understand it.

Sɪ paret.——If it appears.

Sɪ partes alium in contrahendo locum respexerunt.—— If the parties, making the agreement, have regard to another place.

Sɪ per annum et diem cessaverit in petenda investitura. ——If he shall have neglected to claim possession for a year and a day.

Sɪ petens sectam produxerit, et concordes inveniantur, tunc reus poterit vadiare legem suam contra petentem, et contra sectam suam prolatam; sed si secta variabilis inveniatur, ex tunc non tenebitur legem vadiare contra sectam illam.——If the plaintiff shall have preferred his suit, and the sureties he produced, then the defendant may wage his law against the plaintiff, and against the suit preferred: but if the suit be found variable (that is, debt and trover together, &c.), in that case he will not (as) against such suit be bound to wage his law. *Vide note.*

Sɪ plura sint debita, vel plus legatum fuerit, ad quæ catallæ defuncti non sufficiant, fiat ubique defalcatio,·excepto regis privilegio.——If there be more debts or legacies which the goods of the deceased are insufficient to discharge, let there be a general deduction (or a deduction by each legatee), the King's privilege excepted.

Sɪ questum tantum habuerit is, qui partem terræ suæ do·

nare voluerit, tunc quidem hoc ei licet; sed non totum
questum, quia non potest filium suum hæredem exhære-
dere.——If a person, who has nothing more than an acquired estate, would dispose of part of his land, this is
lawful for him to do; but he cannot give away the whole
of such property, because he cannot disinherit his son, the
heir.

SI quid misericordia causa ei fuerit relictum, puta, men-
struum, vel annum alimentorum nomine, non oportet,
propter hoc, bona ejus iterato venundari; nec enim frau-
dandus est alimentis quotidianis.——If anything be left
to a person for the sake of charity, suppose by way of a
monthly or yearly allowance for provisions, it is not
proper that, on this account, his property should be sold a
second time; for he ought not to be defrauded of his daily
support.

SI quid singuli temporibus adduci hosti promiserint, est
in eo fides conservanda.——If they have promised that
any particular thing should be conveyed in the time of
war to the enemy, it should be rigidly observed.

SI quid universitati debetur, singulis non debetur; nec
quod debet universitas, singuli debent.——If anything be
due to a society (at large), it is not due to the individuals;
nor do those individuals stand indebted for what the society owe in its corporate capacity.

SI quis ad battalia curte sua exierit.——"If any one
should go out of court to battle." Meaning his right to
the decision by single combat, which was at one time a
common mode of settling disputes. Vide note to "*Est
autem*," &c.

SI quis aliquid dixerit contra testamentum, placitum
illud in curia Christianitatis audiri debet, et terminari.
——If a person allege any matter against a will, that plea
ought to be heard and determined in the Ecclesiastical
court.

SI quis baronum, seu hominum meorum, pecuniam suam

noń dederit, vel dare disposuerit, uxor sua, sive liberi, aut parentes et legitimi homines ejus, eam pro anima ejus dividant, sicut eis melius visum fuerit.——If any of my barons, or subjects, should not give or dispose of his money, his wife, or children, or else his parents, and next of kin, may divide it for (the peace of) his soul, as may appear to them to be most proper.

Si quis famosum libellum ignarus repererit, et corrupat priusquam alter inveniat, aut nulli confiteatur inventum. Si vero non statim easdem chartulas corruperit, vel igne consumperit, sed earum vim manifestaverit, sciat se quod auctorem hujus modi delicti capitali sententiæ subjugandum.——If any ignorant person has found an infamous libel, and destroys it before another may find it, or does not confess to any one that he has found it. Certainly, if he has not immediately torn (or defaced it), or burnt it up, but has made known its contents to any one, let him understand that he has subjected himself to as heavy a sentence for this offence, as if he were the author.

Si quis famosum libellum sive domû, sive in publico, vel in quocum loco ignarus invenit, aut discerpat priusquam alter inveniat, aut nulli confiteatur inventum. Nam quicunque obtulerit inventum, certum est ipsum reum ex lege retinendum, nisi prodiderit auctorem; nec evasuram pœnas hujusmodi criminis constitutas, si proditus fuerit cuiquam retulisse quod legerit.——If any ignorant person shall find an infamous libel either at home or in public, or in any other place, or shall destroy it before another has found it, or does not confess that he has found it. For it is certain that whoever shall expose the same when found, shall be guilty in law of retaining it, unless he produce the author; nor shall he evade the punishment appointed for a crime of this nature, if it be discovered that he has taken it to any one to be perused.

Si quis felem (horrei regii custodem) occiderit, vel furto abstulerit, felis summa cauda suspendatur, capite aream at-

tingente; et in eam grana tritici effundantur, usquedum
summitas caudæ tritico cooperiatur.——"If any one kill
or steal a cat (the keeper of the king's granary), let the cat
be suspended by the end of the tail, its head touching the
floor, and grains of wheat be poured upon it, until the tip
of the tail be covered with the wheat." This was the fine
formerly payable by the person who killed or stole the
king's cat. Vide *Black. Com.*

Si quis homini aliqui pergenti in itinere mansionem
vetaverit, sexaginta solidos componat in publico.——If
any person refuse to entertain a traveller, he shall be fined
sixty shillings for the public use. *Vide note.*

Si quis impatientia doloris, aut tædio vitæ, aut morbo,
aut furore, aut pudore, mori voluit, non animadvertatur in
eum.——If any person from insupportable grief, or from
weariness of life, from disease, or madness, or shame, has
desired him to die, it (that crime) shall not be chargeable
upon him.

Si quis intestatus obierit, liberi ejus hæreditatem equali-
ter dividant, &c.——If any person die intestate, his children divide the inheritance equally, &c.

Si quis me nesciente, quocunque meo telo vel instru-
mento in perniciem suam abutatur; vel ex ædibus meis
cadat; vel incidat in puteum meum, quantumvis tectum et
munitum; vel in cataractum, et sub molendino meo con-
fringatur, ipse aliqua mulcta plectar; ut in parte infelicita-
tis meæ numeretur, habuisse, vel ædificasse aliquod quo
homo periret.——If any person, without my knowledge,
be in any manner whatever destroyed by my weapon or
implement, or fall from my house, or into my well, although
covered and secured; or into my waterfall, and be broken
to pieces under my mill, yet I shall be punished with some
fine; as it may be considered in part of my misfortune to
have possessed, or erected anything by which a person
could have perished.

Si quis sine liberis decesserit, pater, aut mater ejus in

hæreditatem succedat, vel frater et soror, si pater et mater
desint; si nec hos habeat, soror patris vel matris, et deinceps qui propinquiores in patrua fuerint; et dum· virilis
sexus extiterit, et hæreditas ab inde sit, fœmina non hæredi-
tet.——If any one die without children, the father or
mother succeed in his inheritance, or the brother and sister,
if the father and mother be dead; if there be none of
these, (then) the sister of the father or mother, and afterwards they who shall be nearer of kin on the father's side;
and while any of the male sex remain, from whom the estate descended, no female shall inherit.

SI quis terram hæreditariam habeat, eam non vendat à
cognatis hæredibus suis; si illi viro prohibitum sit, qui eam
ab initio acquisivit, ut ita facere nequeat.——If any person
possess hereditary land, he cannot sell it from his kindred
heirs; if it were prohibited to that person, who originally
obtained it, that he should not do so.

SI quum aurum tibi promissem, tibi ignoranti, quasi
aurum æs solverim, non liberabor.——If I have promised
you gold, and in the stead, owing to your ignorance, pay
brass, I shall not be discharged (from the debt).

SI rector petat versus parochianos oblationes et decimas
debitas et consuetas.——If a rector require from his pa-
rishioners the offerings and tithes due and accustomed.

SI recupaverit tenementa de quibus vir obiit seisitus, tenens reddat damna, videlicet, valorem dotis, tempore mortis viri, usque ad diem, quo per judicium curiæ seisinam
suam recuperaverit.——If she shall have recovered the
tenements of which her husband died seised, let the tenant
pay the damages, that is to say, the value of the dower
from the time of the death of the husband, until the day
on which she recovered her possession by the judgment of
the court.

SI super hoc convictus fuerit, feudum de jure amittet.
——If he shall be convicted of this crime (or offence), he
shall, by law, lose his fee.

SI tamen ad deprivationem aut inhabilitatem rectoris, aut expulsionem scholaris alicujus per episcopum vel ejus commissarium agatur; dummodo ad ejus expulsionem concurrat consensus rectoris et trium de septem maxime senioribus scholaribus.——If it be done to the deprivation or disqualifying of the rector, or the expulsion of any scholar by the bishop or his commissary; provided that the consent of the rector, and three (out) of seven of the senior scholars be obtained for his expulsion.

SI tamen evidenti argumento falsum jurasse convincantur (in quod superius judicium cognoscere debet) mulctantur in bonis, de cætero perjuri et intestabiles.——If, however, they are proved, by clear evidence, to have sworn falsely (of which a higher court should take cognizance) a fine is levied on their goods, and thenceforth, because of the perjury, they are incapable of giving evidence.

SI te fecerit securum.——If he shall have made you secure.

SI tenens injuste, et sine judicio disseisiverit ipsum quærentem de libero tenemento.——If the tenant has illegally, and without (any) judgment, ejected the plaintiff from his freehold.

SIT in misericordia pro falso clamore suo.——Let him be in mercy for his false suit.

SIT omnis vidua sine marito duodecim menses.——That every widow remain without a husband twelve months. Vide note to " *Quod vidua,*" &c.

SIT quilibet homo dignus venatione sua, in sylvis, et in agris sibi propriis, et 'in domino suo; et abstineat omnis homo á venariis regiis ubicunque pacem eis habere voluerit.——That every man be entitled to his hunting, in the woods, and in the fields, of which he is the proprietor; and in his own domain: and that every one abstain from the royal hunting grounds, wheresoever he (the King) desire they should be unmolested.

SI universitas ad unam redit, et stet nomen universitatis.

——If the university (or corporation) be reduced to one, even then the name of the corporation continues.

SI un soit mise en le panel et denomination d'un partie, tout l'array est quassable: quod conceditur per omnes justiciarios.——If there be a charge in the panel, and the description of a party, all the proceedings are liable to be quashed: which was agreed to by all the judges.

SI uxor possit dotem promeri, et virum sustinere.——If the wife may deserve her dower, and support the husband.

SI vassallus feudum dissipaverit, aut insigni detrimento deterius fecerit, privabitur.——If a vassal has wasted the fee, (or estate,) or done any notorious injury thereto, he shall be ejected (or deprived thereof).

SIVE plus, sive minus.——Whether more, or less.

SIVE sit masculus, sive fœmina.——Whether male or female.

SIVE quis incuria, sive mort repentinâ fuerit intestatus mortuus, dominus tamen nullam verum suarum partem (præter eam quæ jure debetur herioti nomine) sibi assumito. Verum possessiones uxori, liberis, it cognationibus proximis, pro suo cuique jure, distribuantur.——If any person die intestate, by a neglect or sudden death, yet the lord shall take to himself no part of his effects (except that which is legally due, in name of a heriot). But his property shall be distributed among his wife, children, and next relations, according to their several rights.

SIVE volentibus, sive nolentibus mulieribus, tale facinus fuerit perpetratum.——Such a disgraceful deed will be committed, whether the women are willing or not.

SOCCAGIUM.——" Socage." This was a tenure by which many estates were held under the feudal system. The tenants performed husbandry, &c., for the superior lord of the fee.

SOCIETAS jus quomodo fraternitatis in se habet.——A society contains in itself, in a certain degree, a law (or tie) of brotherhood.

32

SOCIETAS Leonina.——" The copartnership with the lion." Alluding to the well-known fable, when the lion appropriated all the prey to himself.

SOCII, communitas, collegium, societas et collegæ.—— The companions, community, college, society and fellows.

SODALES legem quam volent, dum ne quid ex publica lege corrumpant, sibi ferunto.——That the fellows (of colleges) make for themselves such a law as they please, if they do not violate any public law.

SOIENT mis en la prisone fort et dure.——Let them be be put in strong and close confinement.

SOIT baile aux commons.——Let it be delivered to the commons.

SOIT baile aux seigneurs.——Let it be delivered to the lords.

SOIT droit fait al partie.——Let right be done to the party.

SOIT fait comme il est desiré.——Let it be done, as it is requested.

SOIT mis et demeerge.——Let it be fixed and remain.

SOKEMANRIES.——" Copyhold tenures." Estates held by copy of court roll, upon the devise or alienation of which, a fine is generally payable to the lord. In many parts of *England*, lands are now held by copy of court roll, which is frequently as good, or nearly so, as freehold.

SOKEMANS.——Copyhold tenants.

SOLA, quæ de hostibus capta sunt, limitaneis ducibus, et militibus donavit; ita ut eorum essent, si hæredes illorum militarent, nec unquam ad privatos pertinerent; dicens attentius illos militaturos, si etaim sua rura defenderent. Addedit sane his et animalia, et servos ut possent colere quod acceperant; ne per inopiam hominum, vel per senectutem, desererentur rura vicina barbariæ, quod turpissimum ille ducebat.——Those lands which were taken from the enemy, he gave to the Generals of the Marches (or Borders), and to the soldiers, in order that they should be their own (property), if their heirs performed military service, nor should (such lands) ever belong to those in private life; remarking, that they would fight the more earnestly, if they defended their own lands. He also judiciously added to these lands, cattle and slaves, that they might cultivate what they had received; lest for want of men, or because of their old age, the neighboring fields (meaning the boundaries of the realm) might be deserted to the barbarian, which he considered most disgraceful.

SOLEMPRE crie.——Solemn proclamation.

SOLENT fœminarum ductu bellare, et sexum in imperiis non discernere.——The women were accustomed to be led to war, and their sex did not impede their succession to empire.

SOLENT Prætores, si talem hominem invenerint, qui neque tempus, neque finem expensarum habet, sed bona sua dilacerando, et dissipando, profundit, curatorem ei dare, exemplo furiosi; et tamdiu erunt *ambo* in curatione, quamdiu vel furiosus sanitatem, vel ille bonos mores, receperit.——"Should the Prætors find such a man, (meaning a profligate,) who has neither end nor limit to his expenses; but who extravagantly spends his property in waste and dissipation, they appoint a guardian for him, as though he were a mad man, and *both* shall remain so long under the guardianship, until the mad man recover his senses, or he (the profligate) recover his good morals." This was a judicious proceeding under the *Roman* laws, and described with considerable ingenuity.

SOLERE aiunt barbaros reges *Persarum*, ac *Syrorum*, uxoribus civitates attribuere hoc modo; *hæc* civitas mulieri redimiculum, præbeat; *hæc* in collum; *hæc* in crines, &c.——They inform us that the barbarous kings of *Persia* and *Syria* assigned provinces (or states) to their wives, in this way: *this* province should provide the lady's attire; *that* for her neck; *another* for her hair, &c.

SOLIDI legales.——Lawful shillings.

SOLIS die, quem "dominicum" recte dixere majores, omnium omnino litium, et negociarum finis esset intentio. ——On Sunday, which the elders properly call "the Lord's day," it was the intention that all manner of lawsuits and business should entirely cease.

SOLUTIO pretii emptionis loco habetur.——By payment of the purchase money, he stands in the place of the vendor.

SOLVENDUM in futuro.——"To be paid at a future time."

SOLVIT ad diem.——"He paid at the day."

SOLVIT ad, aut post diem.——"He paid at or after the day." These were pleas to an action of debt, on bond, or penal bill.

SOLVIT residuum mihi.——He paid the residue to me.

SOLVIT residuum per me.——He paid the residue by me.

SOLVUNTUR tabulæ.——"The proceedings are discharged." This was a phrase in use among the ancient *Romans,* on the acquittal of a prisoner. *Vide note.*

SON assault.——His own assault.

SON assault demesne.——"His own first assault." The name of a plea, whereby the defendant insists that the plaintiff was the first aggressor.

SOULSE.——A shilling.

SPARSIM.——Scattered about : in several places.

SPE pacis.——"With a desire for peace." (With the hope of terminating the suit).

SPE recuperandi.——With the hope of recovering.

SPES accrescendi.——The expectation of increase.

SPOLIATUS debet ante omnia restitui.——One who is robbed, should, before all things, be restored (to his property).

SPONDET peritiam artis.——He pledges the skill of his craft.

SPONSALIA.——Marriage contracts. *Vide note.*

SPONSIO judicialis.——A judicial agreement.

SPONTE facta.——Things voluntarily done.

SPORTULA.——A largess: a present.

SPUILSIE.——The taking away of an owner's effects without his consent.

STABITUR huic præsumptioni donec probetur in contrarium.——It will stand (agreeably) to this presumption, until the contrary be proved.

STARE decisis.——"To abide by decisions:" to rest on decided cases.

STARE decisis, et non quieta movere.——To adhere to decided cases, and not agitate matters which have been established.

STARRUM.——A deed or contract. *Vide note.*

> " Stat fortuna improba nocte
> Arridens nudis infantibus. Hos fovet omnes,
> Involvitque sinu."

> " Dame Fortune stands by night, and smiling bland,
> To helpless children reaches forth her hand;
> Her fostering care such infants still engage,
> She feels their wants, and knows their tender age."

STAT pro ratione voluntas.——"My will stands in the place of reason." Applied to a tyrant who governs capriciously.

STATUIMUS ut omnes liberi homines fœdere et sacramento affirment, quod intra et extra universum regnum *Angliæ Wilhelmo* Regi domino suo fideles esse volunt; terras et honores illius omni fidelitate ubique servare cum eo, et contra inimicos et alienigenos defendere.——"We ordain that all freemen affirm by league and oath, that they will be faithful to King *William* their Lord, as well within as without the whole realm of *England;* and that they will every where preserve, with all fidelity, his lands and honors, and defend him against enemies and foreigners." This was the feudal oath of fidelity, or fealty, taken to *William* the Conqueror.

STATUS.——The state : circumstance : condition : also the interest in lands.

STATUTA pro publico commodo late interpretantur.—— The statutes are expounded liberally for the public advantage.

STATUTUM de cibariis utendis.——The statute for the regulation of provisions.

STATUTUM de finibus levandis.——The statute relating to the levying of fines.

STATUTUM de malefactoribus in parcis.——The statute relating to such as commit crimes in parks.

STATUTUM de moneta.——The act relating to the coin.

STERLINGUM.——Sterling.　*Vide note.*

STET processus.——Let the process be stayed.

STET prohibitio.——Let the prohibition stand.

STET rei agendi potestas.——Let the ability of performing the thing remain.

STILLICIDIUM.——The dripping of water from the eaves of a house.

STIRPS.——The stock : lineage : race.

STOWE.——A valley.

STRENUO opponente.——By a vigorous opposition.

STRICTA et coarcta.——Compressed and concise : " *multum in parvo.*"

STRICTI juris.——Of strict right (or law).

STRICTI sensus.——Of a precise meaning.

STRICTISSIMI juris.——Of most rigid right (or law).

STRICTO jure.——In strict law (or right).

SUAPTE natura.——In its own nature.

SUAVITER in modo, fortiter in re.——Gentle in the manner, but vigorous in the execution.

SUB-BOSCUS.——Underwood.

SUB chartæ expositione.——Under the declaration of the charter (or deed).

SUBINFEUDATIONES.——" Sub-Feuds." Feuds given or

granted by a donor or feoffor who held from a superior proprietor.

SUB feudi interpositione.——Under the interposition of the fee.

SUBHASTATIO.——An auction sale among the Romans, where a spear was set up to denote the place of sale.

SUBITA radicê retenta est; stipitê crurâ teneri.——"While the root is secure, the trunk is secure:" or "the root is held by its shoots, as the branch is held by the trunk."

SUBLATA causa, tollitur effectus.——The cause being removed, the effect ceases.

SUB manu congruere.——To bargain by a shake of the hand. *Vide note.*

SUB modo.——Under a condition : within bounds.

SUB pede sigilli.——At the foot of the seal.

SUB plegiorum datione.——Under the giving of pledges (or security): under bail.

SUBPŒNA ad faciend' atornat'.——A subpœna to make an attorney.

SUBPŒNA ad testificandum.——A subpœna to give evidence.

SUBPŒNA duces tecum.——"Bring with you under a penalty."——The name of a writ by which a witness is commanded to produce something in his possession, to be given in evidence.

SUB potestate curiæ.——Under the protection (or custody) of the court.

SUB potestate parentis.——Under the authority of the parent.

SUB potestat eviri.——Under the control of the husband.

SUB privilegio manerii.——Under the privilege (or custom) of the manor. *Vide note.*

SUBSCRIPTIONE testium, non edicto Prætoris, signacula testamenti imponerentur.——By the subscription of the witnesses, and not by the Prætor's edict, signets are affixed to wills. *Vide note.*

SUBSELLIA.——Lower seats or benches for inferior magistrates.

SUBSIDIUM justitiæ.——An aid to justice.

SUB spe reconciliationis.——In the hope of reconciliation.

SUBSTANTIA prior et dignior est accidente.——" The substance (should be considered) as prior to, and of more worth than the accident." This has reference to pleadings, &c., in courts of law: but judgments cannot now, so easily as formerly, be arrested for a defect in point of form.

SUBSTRATUM.——The foundation: the subject matter.

SUBTILITATE juris.——By an evasion (or quirk) of law.

SUB tutela et cura.——Under wardship and protection.

SUB vadimonii positione.——Under a given pledge.

SUB-vicecomes.——Under-sheriff.

SUCCESSIONES feudi talis est natura, quod ascendentes non succedant.——"The nature of the succession to a fee is such, that the ascendants, (i. e. fathers and grandfathers, &c.,) do not succeed thereto." The reason for this was founded on the feudal principle, that lands should not be held by aged persons, who might be incapable of accompanying the King, or superior lord into the field; or to perform the other services under which the tenants held their estates. *Vide note.*

SUFFICIT semel extitisse conditionem; ad beneficium assecuratoris de amissione navis, etiam quod postea sequeretur recuperatio : nam per talem recuperationem non poterit præjudicari assecuratori.——It is sufficient if the condition once existed, although afterwards a recovery might be the consequence for the benefit of the assured, as to the loss of the vessel : for such a recovery cannot tend to his prejudice.

SUGGESTIO falsi.——A suggestion (or incitement) to falsehood, or wrong.

SUGGESTIO falsi suppressio veri.——A false suggestion is a suppression of truth.

SUI et necessarii hæredes.——His own and proper heirs.

SUI generis.——"Of its own kind." Not to be classed under any ordinary description.

SUI juris.——Of his own right.

SUMMA de laudibus Christi feræ virginis (divinum magis quam humanum opus) Qu. 43, § 5. Item quod jura civilia, et leges, et decreta scivit in summo, probatur hoc modo ; sapientia advocati manifestatur in tribus ; unum, quod obtineat omnia contra judicem justum, et sapientem ; secundo, quod contra adversarium astutum et sagacem ; tertio, quod in causa desperata ; sed beatissima virgo contra judicem sapientissimum dominum; contra adversarium calidissimum diabolum, in causa nostra desperata, sententiam oblatam obtinuit.——The consummation of the praise of the uneducated virgin (mother) of Christ (a divine, rather than a human work) Qu. 43, § 5, (is this,) that she knew perfectly the civil, and the statute law, and the decrees, (or ordinances,) is proved in this manner : the wisdom of an advocate is shown in three particulars, first that he obtain all things against a wise and just judge ; secondly, against a subtle and sagacious opponent ; thirdly, in a desperate cause ; but the blessed virgin procured a decisive judgment from the wisest judge, the Lord, against the most crafty opponent, the devil, in our hopeless cause." This is one, of many, of the innumerable specimens of the superstition of some of the writers in the middle ages.

SUMMA et maxima securitas, per quam omnes statu firmissimo sustinentur, quæ hoc modo fiebat, "quod sub decennali fidejussione debebant esse universi," &c.——The principal and highest assurance, by which all are kept in the safest condition, which was effected in this manner : that "all should be bound under a suretyship of ten years," &c.

SUMMONEAS ad auxiliandum.——That you summon to assist.

Summoneas ad jungandum auxilium.——That you summon to lend assistance.

Summoneas ad warrantizandum.——That you summon to warranty.

Summum jus, summa injuria.——" Rigid law is the greatest injustice." A too strict interpretation of the law is frequently productive of the greatest injustice ; or, as pointedly expressed, " Apices juris non sunt jus;" i. e. "The extremity of justice is injustice ;" or " Right too rigid hardens into wrong."

Sunt jura, sunt formulæ, de omnibus rebus constitutæ, ne quis aut in genere injuriæ, aut in ratione actionis, errare possit. Expressæ enim sunt ex uniuscujusque damno, dolore, incommodo, calamitate, injuria, publicæ à *Prætore* formulæ, ad quas privata lis accommodatur.——There are laws and forms appointed for all affairs, lest any one should err, either respecting the nature of the injury, or the cause of action. Because these public forms, for which a private suit is adjusted by the *Prætor*, are expressed (or defined) according to the loss, suffering, inconvenience, calamity, or injury of every person. *Vide* note to "*Actionis Compositæ*," &c

Sunt quædam brevia formata super certis casibus de cursu, et de communi consili totius regni approbata et concessa, quæ quidem nullatenus mutari poterint, absque consensu, et voluntate eorum.——There are some writs framed upon certain particular cases (as a matter) of course, and agreed upon and conceded to by the general assembly of the whole kingdom, which in no case can be altered without their consent and approbation.

Super altum mare.——Upon the ocean.

Super breve illud.——Upon that writ.

Superoneravit.——He surcharged.

Supersedeas.——" You may remove or set aside." A writ so called to stay proceedings.

Supersedeas, quia improvide emanavit.——That it be superseded, because it improvidently issued.

SUPER se susceperunt.——They took upon themselves.

SUPER subjectam materiam.——" On the matter submitted." Thus, it is said a lawyer is not responsible for his opinion, when it is given "*super subjectam materiam*," on the circumstances as laid before him by his client.

SUPER visum corporis.——On view of the body.

SUPER visum vulneris.——On view of the wound.

SUPPRESSIO falsi, suppressio veri.——A suppression of falsehood is a suppression of truth itself.

SUPRA protest.——An acceptance of a bill after protest.

SUPRA subjectam materiam.——Upon the matter submitted.

SUR cognizance de droit, come ceo, que il a de son done. ——Upon acknowledgment of right, as that which he has of his own gift.

SUR cognizance de droit tantum.——Upon an acknowledgment of right only.

SUR concesserunt.——" Upon their yielding up."

SUR conusans de droit, come ceo, &c.——" Upon acknowledgment of right, as this," &c.

SUR done, grant et render.——" Upon gift, grant, and render" (or yielding up). These five last extracts refer to several kinds of fines levied for various purposes as occasion required. Vide *Black. Comm.*

SURDRE.——To arise.

SURDUS.——Deaf.

SUR la pie.——At the foot.

SUR rebut.——Upon rebutter.

SUR rejoin.——Upon rejoinder.

SURSUM redditio.——A surrender: a yielding back.

SUR trover, et conversion.——Upon trover, and conversion.

SUSCEPTIO super se.——A taking on himself.

SUSCEPTO super se onere testamenti.——Having taking upon himself to discharge the obligation of the will.

SUSPENDATUR per collum.——" That he be hanged by

the neck." These words were abbreviated by the clerk of assize in *England*, and formerly inserted in the margin of the calendar of the prisoners against the names of such who were to be hung: and it has been said that it was the only order to the sheriff for the execution of the criminal. *Vide note.*

SUUM cuique incommodum ferendum est, potius quam de alterius commodis detrahendum.——Every man should bear his own inconvenience rather than diminish the comforts of another.

SUUM cuique tribuere.——To give each his own.

SUUS hæres.——A proper heir.

SUUS judex.——A proper judge.

SUZEREIN.——A crown vassal.

SWAIN mote.——A court which inquired into offences or grievances committed by officers of the forest, etc.

SWOLING.——A plough land.

SYB and SOM.——Sax. Peace and security.

SYLVÆ cæduæ.——"Cutable woods." Woods which being felled at certain stated times are titheable; and said to include every sort of wood, except gross wood of the age of twenty years. Vid. *Bac. Abr. tit. Tithes, c. n.* 4. Gross wood does not mean high and large wood, but such wood as is generally used as timber; and all such wood, if twenty years old, is, by the *English* law, exempted from tithe. Vide 2 *Inst.* 462.

SYLVESTRES.——Living in woods.

SYNGRAPHÆ.——Certain deeds and bonds used by the ancients. *Vide note.*

SYNOTH.——Title of Saxon national council.

NOTES TO S.

SACRAMENTUM.—When the ancient *Romans* engaged in a law suit, a sum of money used to be deposited by *both* parties, called SACRAMENTUM, which fell to the successful party after the cause was determined. Vide *Festus. Varro de Lat. ling.* iv. 36: or a stipulation was made about the payment of a certain sum, called SPONSIO. The plaintiff said, "QUANDO NEGAS HUNC FUNDUM ESSE MEUM? SACRAMENTO TE QUINQUAGENARIO PROVOCO;" i. e. "Why do you deny that this field belongs to me; I pledge you to prove it, by depositing fifty pieces" (of money). SPONDESNE QUINGENTOS, sc. *nnmmos* vel *asses*, SI MEUS SIT? i. e. *si meum esse probavero.* The defendant said, "SPONDEO QUINGENTOS SI TUUS SIT?" Then the defendant required a correspondent stipulation from the plaintiff, thus, "ET TU SPONDESNE QUINGENTOS, NI TUUS SIT?" i. e. *si probavero tuum non esse.* Then the plaintiff said, "SPONDEO, NI MEUS SIT." *Vide* translation at p. 283. Either party lost his cause, if he refused to give this promise, or to deposit the money required.

Festus says this money was called *Sacramentum*, because it used to be expended on sacred rites; but others, because it served as an oath, "*quod instar sacramenti*, vel *jurisjurandi esset*," to convince the judges that the law suit was not undertaken without a cause; and this, in many instances, checked wanton litigation. But this condition, however reasonable it may appear, must have borne hard upon the poor man, who, notwithstanding he had a good cause of action, could not always find a friend who was willing to enable him to fulfil the *Sacramentum*.

Sacramentum is sometimes put for the suit or cause itself (*pro ipsâ petitione*), vide *Cic. pro Cæcin.* 33. So SPONSIONEM FACERE, to institute a law suit. Vide *Cic. Quinct.* viii. 26. The plaintiff was said "*Sacramento* vel *sponsione provocare*," &c. The defendant, "*Contendere ex provocatione*," &c. Vide *Cic. pro Rosc. Com.*, 13, &c.

The same form was used in claiming an inheritance (IN HÆREDITATIS PETITIONE); in claiming servitudes, &c. But in the *last*, the action might be expressed both affirmatively and negatively, thus: "AIO JUS ESSE VEL NON ESSE;" i. e. "I demand whether it be law or not."

SALVO CONTENEMENTO SUO.—Lord *Coke* says that "Contenement," signifieth his "Countenance;" as the armor of a soldier is *his* Countenance; the books of a scholar are *his* Countenance, and the like. 2 *Inst.* 88. He also adds that "the *Wainagium* is the Countenance of the villain; and there was a great reason to save his wainage, for otherwise the miserable creature must carry the burden on his back." *Ibid.*

SANCTA ABSOLUTIO.—The holy absolution given by the Pope, or Romish Catholic Clergy. The humiliating posture in which a great Emperor implored absolution is an event so singular, that the words in which *Gregory* himself describes it, convey a striking picture of the pontifical power of those days; and to us would appear fabulous unless the facts were indubitable: the words are these, "*Per triduum ante portam castri, deposito omni regio cultu, miserabiliter, utpote discalceatus, et laneis indutus; peristens non prius cum multu fletu apostolicæ miserationis auxilium, et consolationem imploranti destitit, quam omnes qui ibi aderant, et ad quos rumor ille pervenit, ad tantam pietatem, compassionem et misericordiam movit, ut pro eo multis precibus et lachrymis intercedentes; omnes quidam insolitam nostræ mentis duritiem mirarentur: nonnulli vero in nobis non apostolicæ sedis gravitatem, sed quasi tyrannicæ feritatis credulitatem esse clamârunt.*" Epist. Greg. ap. Memoire della Contessa Matilda da Fran. Mar. Florentine, Lucca, 1756, vol. i. p. 174— i. e. "He continued for three days before the castle door, stripped of his royal robes, in a suppliant posture, barefooted, and clothed in a woollen garment; and, continuing in great lamentation, received not the aid and comfort of apostolical commiseration, until all who were present, and even those who heard of the same, were moved with pity and compassion for such piety; and became intercessors for him, with many prayers and tears, wondering at the unusual severity of our judgment. Even some exclaimed that it more resembled the cruelty of a tyrannous proceeding than the dignity of the Apostolical chair."

For sanctioning, as was supposed, the violent death of *Thomas à Becket*, Archbishop of *Canterbury*, a man who had acquired, by his pretended sanctity, an amazing power, *Henry* the Second, King of *England*, was compelled by Pope *Alexander*, to walk barefoot over three miles of flinty road, with only a coarse cloth over his shoulders, to the shrine of the murdered saint; where eighty monks, four bishops, abbots and other clergy, who were present, whipped his bare back with a knotted cord; compelled him to drink water, mingled with *Becket's* blood; and to give forty pounds *per annum* for tapers, to burn perpetually before the martyr's tomb.

For opposing him in the appointment of an Archbishop of *Canterbury*, Pope *Innocent* the Third, in the commencement of the thirteenth century, excommunicated *John*, King of *England*, forbidding all persons to eat, drink, or converse with him, or do him service; absolving all his subjects from their allegiance; ordering the other monarchs of *Europe* to kill him; and laid the whole kingdom under an interdict, so that every religious privilege was taken away; every church was shut; no bell was heard; no taper lighted; no divine service performed; no sacrament administered; no priest was present; no funeral solemnities were allowed at the burial of the dead: and no place of interment was permitted but the highways. Vide *Marsh's Epit. Gen. Ecc. Hist.*

SCACCARIUM—From the *Fr.* "Exchequer," i. e. *Abacus, Tabula Lusoria;* or possibly from the *Germ.* "*Scatz*," viz.: *Thesaurus.* This was an ancient Court of Record, whereunto all causes relating to the revenues, and rights of the crown, were reserved. *Camden*, in his *Britan.* p. 113, says, "This court took its name, '*a tabula ad quam assidebant*,' (i. e. "from the table where they sat:") the cloth covering it being checkered. The *English* had it (the court) from the *Normans*, as appears by the *Grand Customary*, c. 56, where it is described to be an assembly of *High Justiciers*, to which it appertained to amend that which the inferior *Justiciers* had misdone and unadvisedly judged; and to do right to all, as from the Prince's mouth." And this seems the origin of the Court of "*Exchequer Chamber.*" This court is of considerable antiquity, being a Court of Record, set up by *William* the Conqueror, as a part of the *Aula Regia*, though regulated and reduced to its present order by *Edward* the First: and was intended principally to manage the crown revenues, and recover the King's debts and duties: though for many years last past, by a fiction of law, any person may sue for a private personal debt, by *suggesting* in the declaration that he (the plaintiff) is the *King's* debtor; and *that* on account of the defendant not paying the demand due to the plaintiff, *he* is the *less* able to pay his Majesty. A writ issues called a "*Quo Minus*," and the defendant is arrested, or served with process. Some have said that this court is called the Exchequer, "*Scaccarium*," from the *checkered* cloth, resembling a *chess* board, which was mentioned before, and covers the large table immediately beneath the judge's seat; and on which, formerly, when certain of the King's accounts were made up, it is said, that the sums were marked and *scored* with counters. This court consists of two divisions: the receipt of the Exchequer, which manages the royal revenues; and the court, or *judicial* part of it; which latter is again divided into a court of *Equity*, and a court of *Common Law*. The court of Equity is held in the Exchequer Chamber, before the Lord Treasurer, the Chancellor of the Exchequer, the Chief Baron, and three puisne Barons. The common law suits are tried in a similar manner to those of the King's Bench, and Common Pleas. The Exchequer Court is inferior in rank, not only to the Court of King's Bench, but also to that of the Common Pleas. The judges of this court go the circuit as the other judges; but when *Exchequer* causes are tried at the *Assizes*, motions for new trials, and for judgment, as in case of non-suit, &c., must be heard before the Barons of the *Exchequer*, upon consultation with the judge who tried the cause in the county, who gives them his evidence (or a copy) taken at the trial. Until very lately, few attorneys were allowed to practice in the Exchequer Court, but a very considerable alteration, in this respect, has been made within a few years past.

SCANDALUM MAGNATUM.—A statute made in the reign of *Richard* the Second, was called by this name, by which punishment was to be inflicted on those who uttered scandal, or libelled any noble personage.

SCIRE FACIAS.—This is the name of a writ for many purposes, commanding the defendant to show cause why a certain specific thing should not be done; as why execution should not issue on an old judgment, &c., &c.

SCOTIÆ LEGES, &c.—In former days the laws in the *Highlands* of *Scotland*, must have been extremely defective, and arbitrarily administered. Force probably was the arbitrator in most cases. We find it recorded, that when individuals were oppressed, they throw themselves into the arms of a neighboring clan, assumed a *new* name, and were encouraged and protected: but the fear of this desertion had its beneficial effects; as no doubt it made the chiefs cautious in their government; and as their consequence in the eyes of others was in proportion to the number of their people, they usually took care to avoid everything that ended to diminish it.

It has not been many years that the authority of any regular laws extended to the *Highlands*. Before that time, the clans were governed in their civil affairs, not by the verbal commands of their chief, but by what was called CLECHDA, or the traditional precedents of their ancestors. When differences happened between individuals, some of the oldest men in the tribe were chosen umpires. The chief interposed his authority, and invariably enforced the decision. In their wars, which were frequent, on account of family feuds, the chief was less reserved in the execution of his authority; but even then he seldom extended it to the taking the *life* of any of his tribe. No crime was capital except murder; and that was very unfrequent in the *Highlands*. It was seldom that any *corporal* punishment whatever was inflicted. The memory of an affront of *this sort* would remain for ages in a family; and a blow, or personal chastisement, was considered an indelible disgrace; and they would seize every opportunity to be revenged, unless it came immediately from the hands of the chief himself; in that case, it was taken rather as a *fatherly* correction, than a legal punishment for offences.

SCRIBÆ.—Notaries, or Clerks. The *Scribæ* among the ancient *Romans*, wrote out all the public accounts; the laws and all the proceedings (*acta*) of the magistrates. Those who exercised that office, were said *"scriptum facere."* Vide *Liv.* xi. 46. They were denominated from the magistrates whom they attended, thus, " *Scrib Questorii*," " *Ædilitii*," &c., and were divided into different " *Decuriæ*," whence *decuriam emere*, for *munus scribæ emere*. Cic. Verr. iii. 79. This office was more honorable among the *Greeks*, than the *Romans*. Vide *Nep. Eum*. 1. The *Scribæ* at *Rome*, however, were generally composed of freeborn citizens; and they became so respectable, that their order is called by *Cicero*, " *Honestus*," *quod eorum fidei tabulæ publicæ, periculaque magistratuum committuntur*. Cic. Verr. iii. 79—i. e. " Honorable," because the public acts, and the trials of the magistrates were committed to their care."

There were also *Actuarii*, or *Notarii*, who took down in short hand, what

was said or done, (*notis excipiebant.*) Vide *Suet. Jul.* 55. These were different from the *Scribœ*; and were commonly slaves, or freedmen. Vide *Dio.*
lv. 7. The *Scribœ* were also called "*Librarii.*" Vide *Festus.* But *Librarii*
is usually put for those who transcribe books, (*Cic. Att.* xii. 6;) for which
purpose those wealthy *Romans* who had a taste for literature, sometimes
kept several slaves. Vide *Nep. Att.* 13.

The method of writing short hand is said to have been invented by
Mœcenas, vide *Dio.* lv. 7; but according to *Isidore*, by *Tiro*, the favorite slave
and freedman of *Cicero.* Vide *Isid.* i. 22. *Senec. Ep.* 90.

SECUNDUM CONSUETUDINEM MANERII.—The custom of many manors in
England were extremely peculiar; some even ridiculous; for which, at the
present day, we are unable to account; the reasons for establishing them
being lost. The following curious custom is extracted from Dr. *Plot's* Natural
History of *Staffordshire:*

"Sir Philip de Somerville held the manors of Whichenovre, Scirescot,
Ridware, Netherton, and Cowlee, all in the county of Stafford, of the Earls
of Lancaster, by this memorable service. The said Sir Philip shall find,
maintain, and sustain, one bacon-flitch, hanging in his hall at Whichenovre,
ready arrayed all times of the year, but in Lent, to be given to every man or
woman married, after the day and year of their marriage be past, in form
following :*

"Whensoever that any such before named will come to inquire for the
bacon, in their own person, they shall come to the bailiff, or to the porter
of the lordship of Whichenovre, and shall say to them in the manner as en-
sueth :

"'Bailiff, or porter, I do you to know, that I am come for myself to demand
one baconflyke hanging in the hall of the lord of Whichenovre, after the
form thereunto belonging.'

"After which relation, the bailiff or porter shall assign a day to him, upon
promise by his faith to return, and with him to bring twain of his neighbors.
And in the mean time, the said bailiff shall take with him twain of the freeholders of the lordship of Whichenovre, and they three shall go to the manor
of Rudlow, belonging to Robert Knightleye, and there shall summon the
aforesaid Knightleye, or his bailiff, commanding him to be ready at Whichenovre, the day appointed, at prime of day, with his carriage, that is to say,
a horse and a saddle, a sack and a pryke, for to convey the said bacon and
corn a journey, out of the county of Stafford, at his costages. And then the
said bailiff shall, with the said freeholders, summon all the tenants of the
said manor, to be ready at the day appointed at Whichenovre, for to do and
perform the services which they owe to the bacon. And at the day assigned,
all such as owe services to the bacon shall be ready at the gate of the manor
of Whichenovre, from the sun-rising to noon, attending and awaiting for the
coming of him who fetcheth the bacon. And when he is come, there shall
be delivered to him and his fellows, chapelets, and to all those which shall
be there to do their services due to the bacon. And they shall lead the said
demandant with trumps and tabors, and other manner of minstrelsy, to the
hall door, where he shall find the lord of Whichenovre, or his steward, ready
to deliver the bacon, in this manner :

"He shall inquire of him which demandeth the bacon, if he have brought
twain of his neighbors with him; which must answer, 'they be here ready.'
And then the steward shall cause these two neighbors to swear, if the said
demandant be a wedded man, or have been a man wedded; and if since his
marriage, one year and a day be past; and if he be a freeman or a villain.†

---

*There was a similar institution at Dunmow, in Essex, for an account of
which see Leland's Itinerary.

†Villain, in the language of the time, signified a servant, or bondman.

And if his said neighbors make oath, that he hath for him all these three points rehearsed, then shall the bacon be taken down and brought to the hall door, and shall there be laid upon one half quarter of wheat, and upon one other of rye. And he that demandeth the bacon shall kneel upon his knee, and shall hold his right hand upon a book, which book shall be laid upon the bacon and the corn, and shall make oath in this manner :

"'Hear ye, Sir Philip de Somerville, lord of Whichenovre, mayntener and gyver of this baconne; that I, A., sithe I wedded B. my wife, and sithe I had hyr in my kepying, and at my wylle, by a year and a day after our marriage, I would not have chaunged for none other; farer ne fowler; richer ne pourer; ne for none other descended of greater lynage ; sleepyng ne waking, at noo time. And if the seyd B. were sole, and I sole, I would take her to be my wife before all the wymen of the world, of what condiciones soever they be, good or evylle; as help me God and his seyntes; and this flesh and all fleshes.'

"And his neighbors shall make oath, that they trust verily he hath said truly. And if it be found by his neighbors before named, that he be a freeman, there shall be delivered to him half a quarter of wheat and a cheese; and if he be a villain, he shall have half a quarter of rye without cheese. And then shall Knightleye, the lord of Rudlow, be called for to carry all these things tofore rehearsed; and the said corn shall be laid on one horse, and the bacon above it: and he to whom the bacon appertaineth shall ascend upon his horse, and shall take the cheese before him, if he have a horse. And if he have none, the lord of Whichenovre shall cause him to have one horse and saddle, to such time as he be passed his lordship: and so shall they depart the manor of Whichenovre with the corn and the bacon tofore him that hath won it, with trumpets, taborets, and other manner of minstrelsy. And all the free tenants of Whichenovre shall conduct him to be passed the lordship of Whichenovre. And then shall they all return except him to whom appertaineth to make the carriage and journey, without the county of Stafford, at the costs of his lord of Whichenovre."

SELECTI JUDICES, &c.—Certain persons under the *Roman* laws could not be selected *Judices;* either from some natural defect, as the *deaf, dumb,* &c; or by custom, as *women* and *slaves;* or by law, as those condemned upon trial of some *infamous* crime, *turpi et famoso judicio,* e. g. *calumniæ, prævaricationis, furti, vi bonorum raptorum, injuriarium de dolo malo pro socio, mandati, tutelæ, depositi, &c.,* i. e. "of a disgraceful and infamous judgment (or sentence), viz. of slander, prevarication, (or injuring a client's cause,) theft, robbery of goods, deceitful injuries relating to, or on account of partnership, commission, title, deposit, (or bailment)," &c.; and by the *Julian* law, those who had been degraded from being senators; which was not the case formerly. Vide *Cic. Cluent.* 43. By the *Pompeian* law, the *Judices* were chosen from persons of the highest fortune.

The *Judices* were annually chosen by the Prætor, "*Urbanus,*" or "*Peregrinus;*" according to *Dio. Cassius,* by the *Questors,* vide xxxix. 7; and their names written down in a list (*in* ALBUM RELATA, vel *Albo descripta*). They swore to the laws: and that they would judge uprightly, according to the best of their knowledge," (*de animi sententiâ*). The *Judices* were prohibited by *Augustus* from entering the house of any one. Vide *Dio.* liv. 18. They sat by the *Prætor,* on benches; whence they were called his *Assessors,* or *Consilium.* Vide *Cic. Act. Ver.* 10; and *Consessores* to one another. *Cic. fin.* ii. 19. *Sen. de Benif.* iii. 7.

They were divided into DECURIÆ, according to the different orders; thus, "*Decuria senatoria judicium,*" &c., Cic. pro Cluent. 37. *Augustus* added a fourth *Decuria,* (because there were three before, either by the law of *Antony,* or of *Cotta*), consisting of persons of an inferior fortune, who were called "DUCENARII," because they had only two hundred thousand *cesterses,* the half of an estate of an *Eques*, and judged in lesser causes. *Caligula* added a fifth *Decuria*. (Suet. 16). *Galba* refused to add a sixth *Decuria*; although strongly urged by many to do it. (*Suet.* 14.)

The office of a *Judex* was attended with trouble, *Cic. in Verr.* i. 8; and therefore in the time of *Augustus*, people declined that honor; but not so afterwards, when their number was greatly increased. Vide *Suet.* et *Plin.*

SENATUS CONSULTA.—When several opinions had been offered, and each supported by a number of Senators, the Consul or Magistrate presiding might first put to the vote which question he pleased, (*sententiam primam pronunciare, ut in eam discessio fieret,*) vide *Cic. Ep. Fam.* i. 2, x. 12; or suppress altogether (*negare se pronunciaturum*) what he disapproved. Vide *Cœs. de Bell. Civili.* i. 1; and herein consisted the chief power of the *Consul* in the Senate. A decree of the Senate was made by "a separation" (*per discessionem*) of the Senators to different parts of the house. He, who presided, said, QUI HOC CENSETIS, ILLUC TRANSITE. QUI ALIA OMNIA, IN HANC PARTEM—i. e. "Let those who are of such an opinion, pass over to that side; those who think differently to this."

The phrase "QUI ALIA OMNIA," was used instead of "QUI NON CENSETIS," sc. *hoc,* from a motive of superstition, (*ominis causâ.*) Vide *Festus.* He who had proposed the opinion, *qui sententiam senatui præstitisset,* (Cic. in Pis. 32,) or who had been the principal speaker in favor of it, the *Consul,* or whoever he was, (PRINCEPS vel AUCTOR *Sententiæ,* Ov. Pont. ii. 3, 31) first passed; and those who agreed with him, followed. (*Plin. Ep.* ii. 11). Those who dissented went into a different part of the house; and into whatever part the majority of the senators went, the *Consul* said of it, "HÆC PARS MAJOR VIDETUR," (i. e. this appears to be the majority.) Then a decree of the Senate was made, according to their opinion, vide *Plin. Ep.* ii. 12; and the names of those who had been the most keen for the decree were usually prefixed to it. When a decree of the Senate was made, without any opinions being asked, or given, the Fathers were said, "*Pedibus ferre sententiam,*" i. e. "to pass the decree with the feet;" and such decree was called "SENATUS CONSULTUM PER DISCESSIONEM"—i. e. a decree made by vote. Vide *A. Gell.* xiv. 7. But when the *opinion* of the Senators was asked, it was simply called "SENATUS CONSULTUM." Vide *Cic. in Pis.* 8; although it was then made, *per discessionem;* and if the Senate was unanimous, the *discessio* was said to be "*sine ulla varietate,*"—i. e. without any difference of opinion. Vide *Cic. pro Sext.* 34; if the contrary, it was to be "*in magna varietate sententiarum,*"— i. e. with considerable difference of opinion. *Ib.* Sometimes the Consul brought *from home,* in writing, the decree which he wished to be passed; and the Senate, (at certain times of the republic,) readily agreed to it. Vide *Cic. Phil.* i. 1.

When secrecy was necessary, the clerks and other attendants were not admitted; but what passed was written out by some of the Senators, (*Cic. pro Cyll.* 14.) A decree made in this manner was called "TACITUM." Some think the "*Senatores pedarii,*" were then likewise excluded. Vide *Valer. Max.* ii. 2.

Julius Cæsar, when *Consul,* directed what was to be done in the Senate, (DIURNA ACTA,) to be published, (*Suet. Jul.* 20,) which also appears to have been done formerly. (*Cic. pro Cyll.* 14.) But this was prohibited by *Augustus.* Vide *Suet. Aug.* 36. An account of their proceedings, however, was always made out; and under the succeeding Emperors, we find some Senator chosen for that purpose. Vide *Tac. Ann.* v. 4.

Public registers (ACTA, i. e. *tabulæ* vel *commentarii*) were also kept of what was to be done in the assemblies of the people, and by courts of justice; also of births and funerals, of marriages and divorces, &c., which served as a fund of information for historians; hence DIURNA URBIS ACTA, (i. e. the daily acts relating to the city.) Vide *Tacit. Annal.* xiii. 31. ACTA POPULI. Vide

Suet. Jul. 20. ACTA PUBLICA. Tacit. Ann. xii. 24. UBBANA. *Plin. Ep.* ix. 15, usually called by the simple name "ACTA." The decrees of the Senate concerning the honors conferred on *Cæsar*, were inscribed in golden letters, on columns of silver. Vide *Dio.* xliv. 7. Several decrees of the Senate still exist, engraven on tables of brass; particularly that recorded, *Liv.* xxxix. 19.

Decrees of the Senate were rarely reversed. When a question was under debate, (*ré integrâ*,) every one was at liberty to express his dissent, (*contradicere*, vel *dissentire*;) but when it was once determined, (*ré peractâ*,) it was looked upon as the common concern of each member, to support the opinion of the majority, *quod pluribus placuisset, cunctis tuendum,*—(i. e. "what pleased the majority must be supported by all.") Vide *Plin. Ep.* vi. 13 After every thing was finished, the magistrate presiding dismissed the Senate by a set form, "NON AMPLIUS VOS MORAMUR," (i. e. ye need not tarry longer;) or "NEMO VOS TENET," (i. e. no one detains you), &c. Vide *Plin. Ep.* ix. 13.

SENATUS CONSULTUM ULTIMÆ NECESSITATIS.—The power of the *Roman* Senate was chiefly conspicuous in civil dissensions, or dangerous tumults within the city, in which that solemn decree used to be passed, "UT CONSULES DARENT OPERAM, NE QUID DETRIMENTI RESPUBLICA CAPERET," (i. e. "that the *Consuls* should take care that the commonwealth receive no harm.") By which decree an absolute power was granted to the *Consuls*, to punish, and even to put to death, whom they pleased, without a trial; to raise forces, and carry on war, without the order of the people. Vide *Sallust. de bello Cat.* 29. This decree was called "ULTIMUM," or "EXTREMUM," Vide *Cæs. de bell. Civ.* i. 4. and *Formam* Scti *ultimæ necessitatis.* Vide *Liv.* iii. 4. By this the republic was said to be intrusted to the Consuls, (*permitti* vel *commendari consulibus, ut rempublicam defenderent.*)

SERVI AUT FIUNT, &c.—There were also other kinds of slaves, under the Feudal system, besides those mentioned in the text. The "OBLATI" were *voluntary* slaves of churches, and were very numerous; and may be divided into three different classes. The first were such as put themselves, and their effects, under the protection of a particular church, or monastery, binding themselves to protect its privilege and property against every aggressor. These were prompted to do so, not merely by devotion, but in order to obtain that security which arose from the *protection* of the Church. They were rather vassals than slaves; and many persons of noble birth, in the boisterous times of the Middle Ages, found it prudent to secure the protection of the Church in this extraordinary manner. Persons of the second class bound themselves to pay an annual tax, or quit-rent, out of their estates, to some church, or monastery. Besides this, they sometimes engaged to perform certain services. They were called "CENSUALES." The last class consisted of such as *actually* renounced their liberty, and became slaves, in the strict and proper sense of the word. These were called "MINISTERIALES," and enslaved their bodies, as some of the charters bear evidence, that they might preserve the liberty of their souls. Vide *Potgiesserus*, "*de statu servorum*," *lib.* 1. How zealous the clergy were to encourage the opinion which led to this practice, will appear in a clause of a charter, by which a person gave himself up as a *slave* to a monastery: "*Cum sit omni carnali ingenuitate generosius, extremum quodcumque Dei servitium, scilicet, quod terrena nobilitas multos plerumq; vitiorum servos facit; servitus vero Christi nobiles virtutibus reddit; nemo autem sani capitis virtutibus vitia comparaverit, claret pro certo eum esse generosiorem, qui se Dei servitio præbuerit proniorem. Quod ego* Ragnaldus, *intelligens*," &c.—i. e. "The lowest service of the Deity is more noble than all worldly distinction; because earthly grandeur makes men too frequently the slaves of sin; but the service of Christ exalts us in moral worth; and as no man of sound judgment compares vice with virtue, therefore it is perfectly evident that he is the most exalted who hath humbled himself to the service of God. Which I, *Ragnaldus*, (well) knowing," &c. Another charta is expressed in the following words: "*Eligens majus esse servum Dei quam libertus seculi, firmiter credens, et sciens, quod servire Deo, regnare est, summaque ingenuitas sit in qua servitus comparabatur Christi*," &c. Vide *Du Cange, voc.* "Oblatus," vol. iv. 1286, 1287. *Mabillon de re diplomat.* lib. vi. 632—i. e. "Choosing rather to be the bondsman of God than the freedman of the world, (well) knowing, and firmly believing, that to serve God, is to reign; and that the greatest freedom is to be acquired by submitting to the service of Christ," &c.

SERVI NASCUNTUR, &c.—Under the feudal system, from the seventh to the eleventh century, these "SERVI," or slaves to the great landholders, seem to have been the most numerous class, and consisted either of slaves taken in war; or of persons, the property in whom was acquired by some of the various methods enumerated by *Du Cange, voc.* "Servus," vol. vi. p. 447. The wretched condition of this numerous set of men will appear from several circumstances; 1st. Their masters had absolute dominion over their persons. They had the power of punishing their slaves *capitally*, without the intervention of any judge. This dangerous right they possessed, not only in the more early periods, when their manners were fierce; but it continued as late as the twelfth century. Vide Joach. Potgiesserus, *de statu servorum Lemgor.* 1737, 4. to *lib.* 3. c. 1. sec. 4, 10, 13, 24. Even after the jurisdiction of masters was restrained, the life of a slave was deemed to be of so little value that a very slight compensation atoned for taking it away. *Idem,* lib. 3. c. 6.

When masters had power over the lives of their slaves, it is evident that no bounds were set to the rigor of the punishments which the unprincipled and violent frequently inflicted upon them. The codes of ancient laws, it is true, prescribed punishments for the crimes of slaves; but they were very different from those inflicted on freemen. The latter paid, generally, only a *fine*, or compensation; the former were subject to *corporal* punishments: the severity of these were, in many instances, excessive. Slaves might be put to the rack on very slight occasions. The laws, with respect to these points, are to be found in *Potgiers.* lib. 3, c. 7; and are shocking to humanity. 2dly. If the dominion of masters over the lives and persons of their slaves was thus extensive, it was no less so over their actions and property. Male and female slaves were allowed, and even encouraged, to cohabit together: but this union was not considered as a *marriage*; it was called "CONTUBERNIUM," (which see and the note) not "NUPTIÆ," or "MATRIMONIUM." This notion was so much established, that during several centuries *after* the barbarous nations had embraced Christianity, slaves, who lived as husband and wife, were not joined together by any religious ceremony, and did not receive the nuptial benediction of the Priest. When this conjunction between slaves came to be considered as a lawful marriage, still they were not permitted to marry in *form* without the consent of their master; and such as ventured to do so without receiving that sanction, were liable to be punished with great severity; and sometimes were punished with death. Vide *Potgiers.* lib. 2. & 3. When the manners of the *European* nations became more gentle, and their ideas more liberal, slaves, who married without their master's consent, were subject only to a fine. 3dly. All the children of slaves were in the same condition with their parents; and became the property of their masters. Vide *Du Cange Gloss. voce* "Servus," vol. vi. 450. Slaves were so entirely the property of their masters, that they could sell them at pleasure; and, of course, could sell the husband from the wife, and the child from the parent. While domestic slavery continued, property in the slave was sold in the same manner as that which a person had in any other movable. Afterwards slaves became "ADSCRIPTI GLEBÆ;" and were conveyed by sale, together with the farm or estate to which they belonged.

Slavery, at no distant period after the flood, prevailed, perhaps, in almost every region of the globe. (In *Germany*, and in other countries of *Europe*, slaves were generally attached to the soil, till later times, and, probably, some are even at the present day.) They were usually employed in conducting the business of agriculture, and, on every occasion, in the most degrading labor, which a freeman would not do. Among the ancient *Germans*, according to *Tacitus*, it was not uncommon for an ardent gamester to stake even his *personal* liberty, and become a slave in a moment by an unlucky throw of the dice. In *England*, now so tenacious of the rights of man, that the moment a slave touches its shores, he is as "*free as the air he breathes,*" a species of slavery, similar to that among the ancient *Germans*, subsisted, even to the end of the sixteenth century, as appears from a commission issued by Queen *Elizabeth*, 1574. Vide *Rymer Ob. Stat.* 251.

SERVITUS EST JUS, &c.—Slaves had a title to nothing but subsistence and clothes from their master: all the profits of their labor accrued to him. If the master, from indulgence, gave his slaves any "*Peculium,*" or fixed allowance, for their subsistence, they even had no right of property in what they saved out of such *Peculium:* all they accumulated belonged to their owners. Vide *Potgiers.* lib. 2, cap. 10. *Murat. Antiq. Ital.* vol. i. p. 768. Consequently, all the effects of the slaves belonged to their masters at their death: and they could not dispose of them by testament. *Idem.* lib. 2, c. 11. Slaves were distinguished from freemen by a peculiar dress. Among all the barbarous nations, long hair was a mark of dignity and freedom; slaves were, for that reason, obliged to shave their heads; and by this distinction, how indifferent soever it may be in its own nature, they were reminded every moment of the inferiority of their condition. *Idem.* lib. 3, c. 4. For various reasons, it was enacted, in almost all the nations of *Europe*, that no slave should be permitted to give evidence against a freeman in a court of justice. *Du Cange voce* "Servus," vol. vi. p. 451.

SIBYLLINA.—Certain persons called *Quindecemviri*, had the charge of the SIBYLLINE books; inspected them by the appointment of the Senate, in dangerous junctures; and performed the sacrifices which they enjoined. It belonged to them, in particular, to celebrate the secular games. Vide *Horat. de Carm, Sæc.* 72. *Tacit. Annal.* ii. 11. vi. 12; and those of *Apollo.* Vide *Dio.* liv. 19. They are said to have been instituted on the following occasion. A certain woman called *Amalthea*, from a foreign country, is said to have come to *Tarquinius Superbus*, wishing to sell *nine* books of *Sibylline*, or prophetic oracles. But upon *Tarquin's* refusal to give her the price she asked, she went away, and burnt three of them. Returning soon after, she demanded the same price for the remaining *six.* Whereupon, being ridiculed by the King, as a senseless old woman, she went away and burnt the other *three;* and coming back, still demanded the *same* price for the *three* which remained. (*Gellius* says the books were burnt in the King's presence. Vide *Gell.* i. 19.) Tarquin, surprised at the strange conduct of the woman, consulted the augurs what to do. They, regretting the loss of the books which had been destroyed, advised the King to give the price required. The woman, therefore, having delivered the books, and having desired them to be carefully kept, disappeared, and was never afterwards seen. Vide *Dionys.* iv. 62. *Lactant.* i. 6. *Gell.* i. 19. Pliny, however, says she burnt *two* books, and only preserved one. Vide *Plin.* xiii. 13. s. 27. Tarquin committed the care of these books, called LIBRI SIBYLLINA, (*ibid.*) or VERSUS, (vide *Horat. Carm. Sæc.* 5. *Cic. Verr.* iv. 49) to two men, (DUUMVIRI) of illustrious birth, one of whom, *Attilius* or *Tullius*, is said to have been punished by *Tarquin* for being unfaithful to his trust, by ordering him to be sewed up alive in a sack, *in culeum insui*, and thrown into the sea; (the punishment afterwards inflicted on parricides. In the year 387, ten men (*Decemviri*) were appointed for this purpose; five Patricians, and five Plebeians. Vide *Liv.* vi. 37, 42; afterwards fifteen, as it is thought, by *Sylla.* Vide *Serv. in Virg. Æn.* vi. 73. *Julius Cæsar* made them sixteen, *Dio.* xlii. 51—xliii. 51.

These Sibylline books were supposed to contain the fate of the *Roman* empire, vide *Liv.* xxxviii. 45; and, therefore, in public danger or calamity, the keepers were frequently ordered by the Senate to inspect them. Vide *Liv.* iii. 10. v. 13, &c. They were kept in a stone chest, below ground, in the temple of *Jupiter Capitolanus.* But the Capitol being burnt in the *Marsic* war, the Sibylline books were destroyed together with it, A. U. 670. Whereupon ambassadors were sent everywhere to collect the oracles of the Sibyls. Vide *Tacit. Annal.* vi. 12. For there were other prophetic women, besides the one who came to *Tarquin.* Vide *Pausan.* x. 12. *Lactantius,* from *Varro,* mentions ten, *Ælian* four. *Pliny* says there were statues of three Sibyls, near the *Rostra,* in the *Forum,* vide xxxiv. 5. s. 10. The chief was the Sibyl of *Cumæ,* whom *Æneas* was supposed to have consulted; called by *Virgil,* Deiphobe, *Æn.* vi. 36, 98, from her age, *longæva vivax* 321. Vide *Ov. Met.* xiv. 104; and the Sibyl of *Erythræ,* a city of *Ionia,* (vide *Cic. divin.* i. 18), who used to utter her oracles with such ambiguity, that whatever happened, she might seem to have predicted it, (*Id.* ii. 54); as the priestess of *Apollo* at *Delphi,* (*Pausan.* iv. 12, &c.) The verses, however, were so contrived, that the first letters of them, joined together, made *some* sense, hence called ACROSTICHIS, or in the plural ACROSTICHIDES, vide *Dionys.* iv. 62. Christian writers often quote the Sibylline verses in support of Christianity; as *Lactantius,* i. 6. ii. 11. 12, iv. 6; but these appear to have been fabricated. From the various Sibylline verses thus collected, the *Quindecemviri* made out new books; which *Augustus,* (after having burnt all other prophetic books, *fatidici libri*), both Greek and Latin, above two thousand, deposited them in two gilt cases, (*forulis auratis*) under the base of the statue of *Apollo,* in the temple consecrated to him, on the *Palatine* hill, vide *Suet. Aug.* 31, to which *Virgil* alludes, *Æn.* vi. 69, &c., having first caused the priests to write over, with their own hands, a new copy of them, because the former books, were fading with age. Vide *Dio.* liv. 17.

SI DOMINUS FŒDI, &c.—As Fees, in process of time, became *hereditary,* the superior lord could not dispossess the heir, on his father's death; and, if he attempted to do so, a remedy was provided, as appears by the language of the text.

SIGNUM CRUCIS, &c.—From these words is derived the phrase to *sign* a paper or deed, instead of "to *subscribe.*" In the ninth century *Herebaud, Comes Palati,* though the *supreme Judge* of the Empire, (by virtue of his office), could not subscribe his name. Vide *Nouveau Traite de diplomatique par deux Benedictins,* 4to. tom, 2. p. 422. As late as the fourteenth century *Du Gueslin,* Constable of *France,* the greatest man in the state, could neither read nor write. Vide *St. Palaye Memoires sur l'ancienne Chevalerie,* tit. 2. p. 82. Nor was this ignorance confined to laymen; the greater part of the clergy were not many degrees superior to them in science. Many dignified Ecclesiastics could not subscribe the Canons of those councils, in which they sat as members. Vide *Nouv. traite de diplom.* tom. 2. p. 424. One of the questions appointed by the *Canons,* to be put to the candidates for holy orders, was this, "Can you read the Gospels and Epistles, and explain the sense of them, at least literally?" Vide *Regino Prumiensis ap. Bruck. His. Philos.* v. 3. 631. *Alfred* the Great complained that from the Humber to the Thames, there was not a Priest who understood the liturgy in his mother tongue; or who could translate the easiest piece of *Latin:* and that from the Thames to the sea, the Ecclesiastics were still more ignorant. Vide *Asserius de rebus gest. Alfredi, ap. Camd. Anglica,* &c., p. 25 The ignorance of the clergy is ludicrously enough described by an author of the dark ages. "*Potius dediti* gulæ *quam* glossæ ; *potius colligunt* libras, *quam legunt* libros; *libentius intuentur* Martha, *quam* Marcum ; *malunt legere in* Salmone, *quam in* Solomone." Vide *Alanus de arte predic. ap. Leberif. dissert.* tom. 2. 21—i. e. "They were more given to gluttony, than to their commentary ; they would rather collect money, than read books; they would rather ogle *Martha* than pore over *Mark;* and would rather read in *Salmone,* than peruse the book of *Solomon.*" To the obvious causes of such universal ignorance, arising from the state of government and manners, from the seventh to the eleventh century, we may reckon the scarcity of books during that period. The *Romans* wrote those books which they wished to endure, either on parchment, vellum, or on paper made of the Egyptian *Papyrus.* The latter, being the cheapest, was most commonly used. But after the *Saracens* conquered *Egypt,* in the seventh century, the communication between that country and the people settled in *Italy,* and in other parts of *Europe,* was almost entirely obstructed, and the *Papyrus* was no longer in use amongst them. They were, therefore, obliged, on that account, to write their books on parchment, or vellum ; and as the price of that was high, books became extremely rare, and of great value. We may judge of the scarcity of the materials for writting them, from one circumstance: there still remain several MSS. of the eighth, ninth, tenth, and following centuries, written on parchment, from which former writings had been erased, in order to substitute a new composition, perhaps not worth a dollar. In this manner, it is not improbable that many valuable books of the ancients *perished,* through the ignorance of the Monks, and others, who were not acquainted with their real worth. A book of *Livy, Virgil* or *Tacitus,* might have been erased to make room for the legendary account of a pretended Saint; or some worthless tale. Vide *Murat. Antiq. Ital.* 3. 833. P. de Montfaucon affirms that the greater part of the MSS. which he had seen (those of a later date excepted) were written on parchment, from which some former writing had been erased. Vide *Mem. de l'Acad. des Inscript.* tom. 9, 325. Many of these are to be seen at the *Radcliffe* Library, *Oxford.* It has, however, been lately stated, that a method of restoring the erased letters to that degree, that they may be legible, has been discovered, by an application of *ammonia.*

As the want of the materials for writing is a great reason why so many of the works of the ancients have perished, it accounts likewise for the small number of MSS. of any kind *previous* to the eleventh century, when they began to multiply, from a cause which shall presently be mentioned. Many circumstances prove the scarcity of books during these ages. Private persons seldom possessed any books whatever. Even monasteries, of considerable note, had only one missal. Vide *Murat's Antiq.* vol. 9, 789. *Lupus,* Abbot of *Ferieres,* in a letter to the Pope, A. D. 855, beseeches him to lend him a copy of *Cicero de Oratore,* and *Quintilian's* Institution; "for," says he, "although we have *parts* of these books, there is no *complete* copy of them in all *France.*" *Ibid.* vol. 3, 385. The price of books became so high, that persons of a moderate fortune could not afford to purchase them. The Countess of *Anjou* paid for a copy of the *Homilies* of *Haimon,* Bishop of *Albérstadt,* two hundred sheep, five quarters of wheat, and the same quantity of rye and millet. Vide *Histoire Liter. de France, par des Religieux Benedictins,* tom. 7, p. 3. Even so late as the year 1471, *Louis* the Eleventh borrowed the works of *Rasis,* the *Arabian* physician, from the Faculty of Medicine, in *Paris;* and he not only deposited in *pledge,* a considerable quantity of plate, but was obliged to procure a nobleman to join with him, as surety in a deed, binding himself, under a considerable penalty, to restore it. Vide *Gabr. Naude. Addit. a l'Histoire de Louis XI., par Comines, edit. de Fresnoy,* tom. 4, p. 281.

Anthony Panormita offered to sell an *estate* that he might be enabled to purchase a copy of *Livy.* Of this circumstance we have a curious account, in a letter written by *Panormita* himself, to *Alphonsus,* King of *Naples,* to whom he was Secretary: "Sire—You have informed me from *Florence,* that the books of *Livy,* written in a fair hand, are to be sold, and that they ask for them one hundred crowns. I beseech your Majesty to cause to be sent to me this king of books, and I will not fail to send the money for it. I beseech your prudence to let me know, whether *Poggius,* or I, do better—*he,* who to purchase a farm near *Florence,* sells *Livy ;* or I, to purchase this *book,* sell my land? Your goodness and modesty induce me to put this familiar question to you. Farewell and triumph." History does not record the fact, but it is sincerely hoped that the King sent him *Livy,* without subjecting the scholar to sell his land.

Many charters, granted by persons of the highest rank, are preserved, and are very legible; from which it appears that the grantors could not subscribe their names. It was usual for persons who could not write, to make the sign of the Cross, in confirmation of a charter or deed. Several of these now remain, where kings and persons of great eminence, instead of writing their names, affix the sign of the Cross. *Du Cange voc* "Crux," vol. iii. p. 1191. From this circumstance, it is usual to say, "I signed" the bond, &c. This being the state of literature, the memory of past transactions was in a great degree lost, or preserved in annals filled with trifling accounts or legendary tales. Even the codes of laws, published by the several nations, which established themselves in different countries of *Europe,* fell into disuse; while in their place, customs vague and capricious were substituted. The human mind, neglected, uncultivated, and depressed, continued in the most profound ignorance. *Europe,* during four centuries, produced but few authors who deserve to be read, either on account of the elegance of their composition, or the propriety and value of their sentiments. There are few inventions, useful or ornamental to society, of which that long period can boast.

Many curious circumstances with regard to the high price of books, are collected by *Gabr. Naude,* to whom the reader is referred, should he consider this branch of literary history a curiosity. When any person made a present of a book to a church or a monastery, in which were the only libraries, or nearly so, for many ages, it was deemed a donative of such value, that he offered on the altar " *pro remedio animæ suæ,*" i. e. "in order to obtain forgiveness for his sins." Vide *Murat.* vol. 3, p. 836. *Hist. Lit. de France,* tom. 6, p. 6. (Many books, even at this day, are to be seen chained in ancient churches in *England.*)

In the eleventh century, the art of making paper was invented, by which not only the number of MSS. increased, but the study of the sciences was wonderfully facilitated. It may be here remarked that numerous valuable paper MSS. are now decaying, whilst those on parchment endure for many ages. With respect to the material, which ought to be used on the transfer of landed property, parchment should be considered the most advisable article, and it is much to be regretted that it is not more generally used.

SI MILITES, &c.—It is not improbable that some warriors may have written their intentions in this manner; but however this be, the testament of a soldier, just about to engage, was said to be made "*in procinctu,*" when in the camp, while he was girding himself, or preparing for battle, in the presence of his fellow-soldiers, where, *without* writing, he named his heir, (*nuncupavit*) vide *Cic. de nat. D.* ii. 3, (from this word "*nuncupavit,*" it is evident we apply the word "*nuncupative*" to a verbal testament.)

SIMONIA—Simony. " *Venditor rei sacræ,*" so called, it is said, from the resemblance it bears to the sin of *Simon Magus.* Though the *purchasing* of holy orders seems to approach near to this offence.

SI MORTUO, &c.—In *Cowell's* Interpreter, we find the following to be one of the customs of our ancestors. in relation to the state of widowhood. At

East and *West Enborne* in *Berkshire*, *(England,)* if a customary tenant of the manor dies, the widow shall have what the law calls her free bench, in all his copyhold lands, *dum sola et casta fuerit,* i. e. "whilst she lives single and chaste:" but if she commits incontinency, she forfeits her estate; yet if she will come into court riding backwards upon a black ram, with the tail in her hand, and repeat certain words, the Steward is bound by the *custom* to re-admit her to her free bench.

SI PETENS, &c.—After the trial by battle had, in a considerable degree, de-clined, *wager of law* became a very common mode of deciding controversies between parties; but if the plaintiff's suit consisted of separate and distinct counts, the defendant, in this case, was not bound to "*wage his law.*" It is very probable that this custom was the *origin* of prohibiting demands of a *distinct* nature being included in the *same* declaration; whether such a rule should be now·so strictly observed, requires the consideration of the judicious and enlightened lawyer.

SI QUIS HOMINI, &c.—Hospitality was so absolutely necessary in the state of society prevalent during the Middle Ages, that it was not then considered as one of those virtues which men *may* practice *or not,* according to their own caprice and disposition. Hospitality was *enforced* by statutes, and such as neglected this duty were liable to punishment. The student is referred to laws of the same import collected by *Jo. Fred. Polac. Systema Jurisprud. Germanicæ. Lips.* 1733, p. 75. The laws of the *Sclavi* were more rigorous than any that he mentions; they ordained "that the movables of an *inhos-pitable* person should be confiscated, and his house burnt." They were even so solicitous for the entertainment of strangers, that they permitted the mas-ter of the house to *steal,* for the support of his guests. "*Quod noctu furatus fueris, cras appone hospitibus,*" i. e. "What you steal at night set before your guests on the morrow." Vide *Rerum Meclesburg, lib.* viii. *a Mat. Jo. Beehr. Lips.* 1751, p. 50. In consequence of these laws, or of the state of society which rendered it proper to enact them, hospitality abounded while the in-tercourse among men was inconsiderable, and secured the stranger a kind reception under every roof, where he chose to take shelter.

No nation in the world carried hospitality to a greater length than the ancient *Scots.* It was even *infamous,* for many ages, in a man of condition, to have the door of his house shut at all, "*lest,*" as the bards used to express it, "THE STRANGER SHOULD COME AND BEHOLD HIS CONTRACTED SOUL." Some of the Chiefs were possessed of this hospitable disposition to an extravagant degree; and the bards, perhaps, on a private account, never failed to recom-mend it in their eulogiums. "CEAN UIA NA DAI," or "*the point to which all the roads of strangers lead,*" was an invariable epithet given by them to their Chiefs; on the contrary, they distinguished the inhospitable by the title of "THE CLOUD WHICH THE STRANGERS SHUN." These last, however, were so un-common, that *Macpherson* says, "In all the old poems I have ever met with, I found but *one* man branded with this ignominious appellation, and that, perhaps, only founded upon a *private* quarrel, which subsisted between him and the patron of the bard who wrote the poem." Vide translation of *Os-sian's* poems by *Macpherson,* vol. ii. 9 *in notis.*

SOLVUNTUR TABULÆ.—By the word "*Tabulæ,*" writings of every kind were called which could be of use to prove the charge in court, particularly ac-count books, *(tabulæ accepti, et expensi,)* letters, bills or bonds, *(syngraphæ,)* &c. In a trial among the *Romans* for extortion, the account books of the person accused were commonly sealed up, and afterwards, at the trial, de-livered to the judges for their inspection. Vide *Cic. Verr.* i. 23, 61, *Balb.* 5. The *Romans* were accustomed to make out their private accounts, *tabulas, sc. accepti et expensi conficere,* vel *domesticas rationes scribere,* i. e. "to finish their accounts of debts and credits, or write out their domestic concerns," and keep them with great care; many of them marked down the occurrences of *each* day, first in a note book, and then transcribed them into what we call a ledger (*codex* vel *tabulæ*) which was preserved. Vide *Cic. Quint.* 2. But many disused this custom *after* the law had commanded a man's papers to be *sealed* up when accused of certain crimes, and produced in courts as evidence against him. Vide *Cic. Verr.* i. 23, 29. *Rosc. Com.* 2, &c. The prosecutor having produced these different kinds of evidence, explained and enforced them in a speech, sometimes in two or more speeches. Vide *Cic. in Verr.* Then the advocates of the criminal replied, and their defence sometimes lasted for several days. Vide *Ascon. in Cic. pro Cornel.* In the end of their speeches, *epilogo*, vel *peroratione*, i. e. "in the end, or beginning of their speech, they tried to move the compassion of the JUDICES; and for that purpose often introduced the *children* of the criminal." Vide *Cic. pro Sext* 69. This was done with great effect, in a trial some years since in *England* by Lord *Erskine*, when at the bar. In ancient times only *one* counsel was allowed on each side. Vide *Plin. Ep.* i. 20. In certain cases persons were brought to attest the character of the accused, called "LAUDATORES." If the accused could not produce at least ten of these, it was thought most prudent to produce none, *quàm illum quasi legitimum numerum consuetudinis non explere*, i. e. "than not to obtain the legal customary number." Vide *Cic. Verr.* v. 22. Each orator when he had finished, said, "DIXI," i. e. "I have spoken;" and when all the pleadings were sealed, a herald cried out, "DIXERUNT," vel "DIXERE," i. e. "they have spoken. Vide *Ascon. in Cic.* &c. Then the *Prætor* sent the *Judices* to give their verdict, (*in consilium mittebat ut sententiam ferrent* vel *dicerent.*) Cic. Verr. i. 9, upon which they went to deliberate among themselves. Sometimes they passed sentence in open court, but usually by ballot. The *Prætor* gave to each *Judex* three tablets; on one was written the letter C. for *condemno*, I condemn; on another, the letter A. for *absolvo*, I acquit; and on the third N. L. for *Non liquit*, sc. *mihi*, I am not clear. *Cæs.* B. *Civ.* iii. 83. Each of the *Judices* threw which of the tablets he thought proper into an urn. There was an urn for each order of the Judges: one for the Senators, another for the *Equites*, and a third for the *tribuni ærrarii*, Cic. ad. Q. Fratr. ii. 6.

The *Prætor*, after the ballots were given, having taken out and counted them, pronounced sentence, according to the opinion of the majority, (*ex plurimum sententiâ*,) in a certain form: if the majority gave in the letter C. the *Prætor* said, "VIDETUR FECISSE, " i. e. "Guilty." *Cic. Verr.* v. 6. If the letter A. "NON VIDETUR FECISSE," "Not guilty." If N. L. the cause was deferred, (*causa ampliata est.*) Ascon. in Cic.

SPONSALIA.—*Augustus* ordained that no nuptial engagement should be valid, which was made more than *two* years before the celebration of the marriage, that is below ten years of age, (girls having been allowed to marry at twelve.) Vide *Dio. Liv.* 16. This, however, was not always observed. No young man or woman was allowed to marry, without the consent of parents or guardians. *Cic. Flacc.* 35. Hence, a father was said "*spondere*" vel *despondere filiam* aut *filium*, (i. e. to promise or betroth his daughter or son.) Vide *Cic. Att.* i. 3. *Ter. And.* i. 1, 175. *Tacit. Agric.* 9, adding these words, "QUÆ RES RECTI VERTAT;" or "DII BENE VERTANT." Vide (*Plaut. Aul.* ii. 2, 41, and 49, &c.,) i. e. "may this matter turn out prosperous," or "may the Gods order this well."

There was a meeting of friends, usually at the house of the woman's father or nearest relation, to settle the articles of the marriage contract, which was written on tables ("*legitimæ tabellæ*,") and sealed. Vide *Juv.* ii. 119, vi. 25, 119, x. 336. This contract was called SPONSALIA. (Espousals.) The contract was made in the form of a stipulation. *An Spondes?* "Do you agree ?' *Spondeo*, "I do agree." Then likewise the dowry was promised.

(*Plaut. Trin.* v. 2. 34,) to be paid on the marriage day, (*Suet. Cl.* 26. *Juv.* x. 335,) or afterwards; usually at three separate payments, (*tribus pensionibus*). Vide *Cic. Att.* xi. 4. 23 *et ult.* On this occasion there was commonly a feast; and the man gave the woman a ring (*annulus pronubus*) by way of pledge, vide *Juv.* vi. 27, which she put on her left hand on the finger next the least; because it was believed a nerve reached from thence to the heart. Vide *Macrob. Sat.* vii. 15.

There was a day fixed for the marriage. Vide *Ter. And.* i. 1. 75. Certain days were reckoned unfortunate, as the Calends, Nones, and Ides; and the days which followed them, particularly the whole month of May, MENSE MALUM MAJO NUBERE VULGUS AIT. Vide *Ovid. Fast.* v. 490. *Plut.* 2. *Rom.* 85. And those days which were called ATRI, (marked in the calendar with black;) also certain festivals, as that of the *Salii, Parentalia,* &c. Vide *Macrob. Sat.* i. 15. But widows might marry on those days. *Ibid. Plut.* 2. *Rom.* 103. The most fortunate time was the middle of the month of June. Vide *Ovid. Fast.* vi. 221.

If, after the espousals, either of the parties wished to retract, (*sponsalia dissolvere, infirmare* vel *infringere*), which they expressed thus, "CONDITIONE TUA NON UTOR," (I do not use or depend on your contract,) it was called RE-PUDIUM. Hence *Repudiatus repetor,* "after being rejected, I am sought back." Vide *Ter. And.* i. 5. 15; and when a man or woman, after signing the contract, sent notice that they wished to break off the match, they were said "*Repudium ei,* vel *amicis ejus mittere, remittere* vel *renunciare,*" i. e. "to send him or his friends a rejection, to disclaim or renounce." Vide *Ter. Phorm.* iv. 3. 72. v. 6. 35. But *Repudiare* also signifies to divorce either a *wife,* (Suet. Cæs. 1.) or a *husband,* (Quint. vii. 8. 2.)

On the wedding day, the bride was dressed in a long white robe, bordered with a purple fringe, or embroidered ribbons, (*segmenta et longi habitus, Juv.* ii. 124), thought to be the same with TUNICA RECTA (the straight Tunick), *Plin.* viii. 48, bound with a *girdle,* (*Lucan.* ii. 362,) made of wool, *Zona* vel *cingulum laneum,* tied in a *knot,* called "*Nodos Herculeus,*" which the husband untied (*solvebat*). Vide *Ov. Ep.* ii. 116. Her face was covered (*nubebatur*) with a red or flame-colored veil (*luteum flammeum*), to denote her modesty. Vide *Lucan.* ii. 361. *Juv.* ii. 124, vi. 224, &c.; hence "*Nubere,*" sc. "*se viro,*" to marry a husband. Her hair was divided into six locks with the point of a spear, *Plut. in Romul. et Quæst.* 86 vel 87. *Ovid. Fast.* ii. 560, and crowned with flowers, *Catul.* lix. 6. Her shoes were of the same color with her vail (*lutei socci*).

No marriage, it is said, was celebrated without consulting the auspices or soothsayers, vide *Juv.* x. 336, &c, and offering sacrifices to the gods, espe-cially to *Juno,* the goddess of marriage. Vide *Virg. Æn.* iv. 59. Anciently, a hog was sacrificed. *Varro R. R.* ii. 4. The gall of the victim was always taken out, and thrown away, to signify the removal of all bitterness from marriage. Vide *Plut. Præcep. Conjug.* The marriage ceremony was per-formed at the house of the bride's father, or nearest relation. In the evening the bride was conducted (*ducebatur*) to her husband's house. She was taken (apparently) by force (*abripiebatur*), from the arms of her mother, or the nearest relation, in memory of the violence used to the *Sabine* women. Three boys whose parents were alive, attended her, two of them supporting her by the arm; and the third bearing a flambeau of pine or thorn before (*tæda pinea* vel *spinea*). Vide *Festus Catul.* lix. 15, &c. There were five other torches carried before her, called *Faces Nuptiales* (nuptial torches). *Cic. Cluent.* 6. Hence *Tæda* is sometimes put for marriage. Vide *Virg. Æn.* iv. 18. *Ov. Met.* iv. 60.

Maid servants followed with a distaff, a spindle, and wool, *colus compta, et fusus cum stamine,* (i e. a neat or adorned distaff, and spindle with flax,) in-timating that she was to labor at spinning, as the *Roman* matrons did of old, vide *Plin.* viii. 48, s. 74; and as some of the most illustrious did in later

times. *Augustus* is said to have seldom worn anything but the manufacture
of his wife, sister, daughter and nieces; at least for his domestic robes. A
great number of friends and relations attended the nuptial procession, *pom-
pam nuptialem ducebant* (i. e. led the nuptial show), which was called *officium*.
Vide *Juv.* ii. 132. The boys repeated jests and railleries (*sales et convicia*) as
she passed along. *Lucan.* ii. 369, &c.

The door posts of the bridegroom's house were adorned with leaves and
flowers, and frequently the rooms with tapestry. Vide *Juv.* vi. 51, 79 and
226.

When the bride came home, being asked who she was, she answered, "UBI
TU CAIUS, IBI EGO CAIA," i. e. " *Ubi tu Dominus et paterfamilias, ibi ego Domina et materfamilias*," (i. e. "Where you are the Lord and Master of the
family, there I will be the Lady and Mistress of the family.") A new married woman was called "CAIA," from *Caia Cæcilia*, or *Tanaquil*, the wife of
Tarquinius Priscus, who is said to have been an excellent spinster (*lanifica*)
and housewife. *Cic. Mur.* 12, &c. Her spindle and distaff were kept in the
temple of *Sangus*, or Hercules. *Plin.* vii. 48, s. 74. There is no doubt but
the appellation of *spinster*, very common in ancient deeds, originated from
the good old custom of spinning wool in the house by the maidens for domestic garments. Vide *Proverbs* xxxi. 13.

The bride bound the door-posts of her husband with woollen fillets. Vide
Plin. xxix. 2, s. 9. *Lucan.* ii. 355, &c., and anointed (*unguebat*) them with
the fat of swine or wolves, to avert fascination, or enchantments; whence
she was called UXOR, quasi UNXOR. Vide *Serv. in Virg. Æn.* iv. 458. *Plin.*
xxviii. 9, s. 37.

She was *lifted* over the threshold (*Lucan.* ii. 355), or gently stepped over
it. (*Plaut. Cas.* iv. 4.) It was thought ominous to touch it with her feet,
because the threshold was sacred to *Vesta*, the goddess of virgins. *Serv. in
Virg. Eccl.* viii. 28. The husband, on this occasion, gave a great feast (CŒNA
NUPTIALIS) to his relations and friends; and to those of the bride and her
attendants. *Plaut. Curc.* v. 2, 62, &c. This appears also to have been the
custom with the Jews. Vide ST. *John*, c. xi.

Musicians attended, who sang the nuptial song (*Epithalamium*.) They
often repeated *Io Hymen Hymenæe!* Plaut. Cas. iv. 3. These words used
also to be resounded by the bride's attendants, on the way to her husband's
house. Vide *Mart.* xiii. 42, 5. *Ovid. Ep.* xii. 143, &c. Hence, "*Hymenæos
canere*," to sing the nuptial hymn or song. *Virg. Æn.* vii. 398. After supper the bride was conducted to her husband's bed-chamber (*in thalamum*) by
matrons who had been married only to *one* husband; and laid (*collocabatur*)
in the nuptial couch, which was frequently magnificently adorned. This
was placed in the hall, vide *Hor. Ep.* i. 1, 87, opposite the door, and covered
with flowers. *Cic. Cluent.* 5. *Catull.* lix. 192, &c. Nuptial songs were
sung before the door, by young women, until midnight, *Ov. Fast.* iii. 675,
695, hence called *Epithalamia.* The husband scattered nuts among the boys,
Plin. xv. 22, intimating that he dropped his boyish amusements, and thenceforth was to act as a man. Hence, "*nuces relinquere*," to leave trifles and
mind serious business. *Pers.* i. 10; or from boys playing with nuts, in the
time of the *Saturnalia*, which at other times was forbidden. Young women
when they married, consecrated their *play* things and dolls, or babies (*Pupæ*)
to Venus *Pers.* ii. 70. The guests were dismissed with small presents.
Mart. xiv. 1. *Juv.* vi. 202.

Next day another entertainment was given by the husband, when presents were sent to the bride, by her friends and relations, and she began to
act as mistress of the family, by performing sacred rites. *Macrob. Sat.* i. 15.

It does not appear that the *Romans* had, at one time, more than one wife;
but it appears to have been an immemorial custom among the *Jews*, and
their forefathers, the patriarchs, to have sometimes more than one at the
same time; and that this polygamy was not directly forbidden by the law

of *Moses*, is evident. But that even polygamy was ever properly and distinctly permitted in that law, does not appear. And what our Saviour says about the common *Jewish* divorces, which may lay a much greater claim to such a permission than polygamy, seems to be true in this case also: that *Moses*, for the hardness of their hearts, suffered them to have several wives, at the same time, but from the beginning it was not so. *Matt.* xix. 8. *Mark*, x. 5. Vide *Burder's Notes to Joseph. Antiq.*

STARRUM.—Star—from the Hebrew "*Shetar.*"—A Deed or Contract. All the deeds and obligations of the *Jews* were, in *England*, anciently called "*Stars;*" and written for the most part in *Hebrew* alone; or in *Hebrew* and *Latin*, one of which yet remains in the Treasury of the *Exchequer*, written in *Hebrew*, without points; the substance of which is expressed in *Latin*, immediately under it, like a condition under a *Latin* obligation of a bond. This bears date in the reign of King *John:* and many *Stars*, as well of Grant and Release, as obligatory, and by way of Mortgage, are pleaded and recited at large in the ancient Plea Rolls. Vido *Pasch. 9th. Edw. 1st.* In one of the statutes of *Cambridge* University, the antiquity of which is unknown, the word *Starrum* is twice used for an inventory or schedule.

STERLINGUM.—Sterling. This was the epithet for silver money, current in *England*, and it took its name from this, that there was a pure coin stamped in *England*, by the *Easterlings*, or merchants of *East Germany;* and *Hoveden* writes it "*Easterling.*"

SUB MANUM CONGRUERE.—The joining of the right hand was esteemed among the *Persians* and *Parthians*, in particular, a most inviolable obligation to fidelity; so Doctor *Hudson* observes, and refers to the Commentary on *Justin* xi. 15, for its confirmation. We often find the like use of it in *Josephus*. Vide *Burder's* notes to *Josephus*.

SUB PRIVILEGIO MANERII.—The customs of manors are, in many cases, extremely singular; frequently whimsical. A curious feudal privilege appears in *Du Cange;* that of the lord being *entitled* to the table cloth, &c., of the house where he dined. It seems that table cloths were made for the nobility and opulent gentry, of great value; some would formerly cost eighteen pounds sterling. Damask table cloths are of great antiquity. *La Brocquere* thus described some used abroad. "They are (says he) four feet in diameter, and round, having strings attached to them, so that they may be drawn up like a purse. When they are used, they are spread out; and, when the meal is over, they are drawn up; so that all which remains, even to a crum, is preserved." Vide *Fosbrook's* Antiquities.

SUBSCRIPTIONE TESTIUM.—Amongst the *Romans*, wills were subscribed by the Testator, and usually by the witnesses; and sealed with their scals or rings, (vide *Cic. pro Cluent.* 13, 14) and also with the scals of others. (*Cic. Att.* vii. 2.)

SUSPENDATUR PER COLLUM.—When the proceedings of the courts were in *Latin*, the execution of the criminal was directed by the words "*suspendatur per collum*," written against his name in the Calendar prepared for that purpose. And in *England*, even at the present day, it is true that the marginal note of a calendar, signed by the Judge, appears to be the only warrant that the Sheriff has for the execution of a convict, yet a late respectable author informs us that it is made with more caution and solemnity than is represented by *Blackstone*. When the assizes are finished, the *Clerk* of the Assize makes out in writing *four* lists of all the prisoners, with separate columns containing their crimes, verdicts and sentences: leaving a blank column, in

which, if the judge has reason to vary the course of the law, he writes opposite the names of the capital convicts, " to be reprieved," "respited," " transported," &c. These four calendars, being first *carefully* compared together
by the Judge and Clerk of Assize, are signed by them; and one is given to
the Sheriff, one to the Jailer, and the Judge and Clerk of Assize each keeps
another.   If the Sheriff receive afterwards no special order from the Judge,
he executes the sentence of the law, in the usual manner, agreeably to the
directions of his calendar.   In every county this important subject is settled
with great deliberation by the Judge, assisted by the Clerk of Assize, before
the Judge leaves the Assize-town; but, probably, in different counties, with
some slight variation; as in *Lancashire,* no calendar is left with the jailer,
but one is sent to the Secretary of State. If the Judge thinks proper to
reprieve a capital convict, he sends a memorial or certificate to the King,
directed to the Secretary of State's office, stating that from favorable circumstances appearing at the trial, (or as the case may be,) he recommends him
to his Majesty's mercy, and to a pardon, upon condition of transportation, or
other punishment. This recommendation is always attended to. Vide *notes
to Black. Comm. by Christian.*

SUCCESSIONES FEUDI.—Wills are of very considerable antiquity: the disposal of estates no doubt existed among the ancient *Hebrews,* and probably
other nations of high antiquity; but there is much variety of opinion how
far the right of disposal, by will, existed among the *Romans,* prior to the
law of the Twelve Tables.

In *England,* the right of disposal of land has been more or less restrained
at various times.   Considerable difficulties attended the disposal of landed
property, under the Feudal system: and it was attended with great opposition when the landed proprietors gave way to the intelligence of the age,
which was enlightening mankind, by the extension of literature, upon the
invention of printing.

SYNGRAPHÆ.—By this name bonds were anciently called, which being
formally written out, signed, and sealed, were then *mutually* exchanged
between the parties.   Thus, *Augustus* and *Antony* ratified their agreement
about the partition of the *Roman* provinces, after the overthrow of *Brutus*
and *Cassius,* at *Philippi,* by giving and taking, reciprocally, written obligations, (*Syngraphæ*).   Vide *Dio.* xlviii. 2, 11.   A difference having afterwards arisen between *Cæsar* and *Fulvia,* the wife of *Antony,* and *Lucius,* his
brother, who managed the affairs of *Antony* in *Italy,* an appeal was made
by *Cæsar* to the disbanded veterans: who, having assembled in the *Capitol,*
constituted themselves judges in the cause; and appointed a day for determining it at *Gabii.*   *Augustus* appeared in his defence, but *Fulvia* and *L.
Antonius* having failed to come, although they had promised, were condemned
in their absence: and, in confirmation of the sentence, war was declared
against them, which terminated in their defeat, and finally, in the destruction
of *Antony.* Vide *Dio.* xlvii. 12, &c.   In like manner the articles or agreement between *Augustus, Antony,* and *Sex. Pompeius* were written out, in the
form of a contract, and committed to the charge of the *Vestal Virgins.* Vide
Dio. xlviii. 37.   They were further confirmed by the parties joining their
right hands, and embracing one another.   But *Augustus* (says *Dio.*) observed
this agreement no longer than to the time he found a pretext for violating
it.   Certain deeds were also called *Syngraphæ* by the Canonists, when
two parts were written on the same piece of parchment, with some word
or letters written *between* such deeds, *through* which the parchment was
cut, either in a straight or indented line, most frequently the latter, in such
a manner as to leave half the word or letters on each part.

T.

TABERNA.——A wine shop.

TABULA in naufragio.——A plank in the shipwreck.

TABULA rasa.——"A smoothed tablet." The ancient *Romans* used tables covered with wax, on which they wrote with a sharp instrument called *Stylus;* with the flattened end they could easily erase what they had written, and use the wax again. *Horace* alludes to the *Stylus.* Vide note to "*Literæ,*" &c.

TACITO et illiterato hominum consensu et moribus expressum.——Acknowledged by the tacit and ignorant consent and usage of the people.

TACTIS sacrosanctis scripturis.——"Laying hands on the Holy Scriptures." A method formerly used by laymen on taking an oath.

TÆCAN (Sax.)——To take.

TAILSIE.——An entail.

TALARE.——To carry away.

TALES de circumstantibus.——"Such persons who are standing round." Those in court who frequently made up a jury, in default of summoned jurors in attendance.

TALIBUS oratis dictis, aram tenebat.——Having said these prayers, he caught hold of the altar. *Vide note.*

TALI et hæredibus suis, vel cui terram illam dare, vel assignare voluerit.——"To such person and his heirs, or to whom he would give or assign the land." These were words used in ancient gifts and grants, where the donees and feoffees had full power to sell their estates.

TALI et uxori suæ.——To such person and his wife.

TALIO.——A punishment under the *Roman* law. *Vide note.*

TALIS.——Such: as follows.

TALIS loco suo ponit talem attornatum.——Such person appoints in his place a certain attorney.

TALIS qui ita convictus fuerit, dupliciter delinquit contra regem, quai facit disseisinam et roberiam *contra pacem suam*, et etiam ausu temerario irritabilia facit ea, quæ in curia domini regis rite acta sunt, et propter duplicem delictum, merito sustinere debet pœnam duplicatam.——Such person who was thus convicted, doubly offends against the king, because he commits a disseisin, and a robbery, *against his peace,* and also by a daring temerity supposes those things offensive, which were correctly transacted in the king's court; and because of this double offence, he deserves to bear a double punishment. *Vide note.*

TALITER in eadem curia nostra processum fuit, quod prædictus *A.* recuperet, &c.——And the process was in such manner obtained in our same court, that the said *A.* recover, &c.

TALI viro et uxori suæ, et eorum hæredibus; vel alicui mulieri ad se maritandum.——To such a man and his wife, and their heirs; or to such woman as he should marry.

TALLY.——A piece of wood cut with notches into two corresponding parts; the creditor kept one, the debtor the other, to show the account between them.

TAM ad triandum, quam ad inquirendum.——As well to try, as to inquire.

TAM amplo modo non habere potuit, sed proficium suum inde per totum tempus amisit.——He could not enjoy it in so ample a manner, but lost his profit for the whole time.

TAM aquæ quam soli.——As well of the water as of the soil.

TAMEN clamorem emittere debet, sive masculus, sive fœmina.——"Whether male or female, yet the child should cry." This was supposed to have been *necessary*, where the husband claimed to be tenant "by courtesy." The expectation of the infant's *crying* was thrown by the lawyers of former days into a singular verse.

"Nam dicunt *E.*, vel *A.*, quotquot nascuntur ab *Eva.*"
Long since translated as follows:

"If boy the baby chance to be,
He cries, *O, A;* if girl, *O, E:*
Oh Eve! exclaimeth little madam,
Whilst little master cries, Oh Adam!"

TAMEN illa tormenta gubernat dolor, moderatur naturâ
cu jusque tum animi, tum corporis, regit Quæsitor; flecit
libido; corrumpit spes, infirmat metus, ut in tot rerum an-
gustiis nihil veritati loci relinquatur.——Notwithstanding
pain governs those tortures, the Quæstor rules and regulates
as well the mind as the body of every one; desire inclines;
hope bribes; fear enfeebles; so that in such a distressed
state of things, no room is left for the truth. *Vide
note.*

TAM immensus aliarum super alias acervatarum legum
cumulus.——"Such an immense pile of laws, heaped upon
one another." The lawyers of the feudal ages were aston-
ished at the multiplicity and finely-spun distinctions between right and wrong introduced by *Justinian's* code.
Vide note to "*Lingua peregrina.*"

TAM in personam, quam in rem.——"As well against
the person as the property." These words allude to a
mixed action, or an action as well against the person as to
recover the property.

TAM in redditione judicii, quam in adjudicatione executionis.——As well in rendering the judgment as in award-
ing the execution.

TAM pro domino, quam pro se ipso.——As well for the
lord as for himself.

TAMQUAM certorum corporum.——As well as of particular (or distinct) bodies.

TANQUAM falsarii.——As though they were forgers.

TANQUAM testamentum inofficiosum.——"As though it
were an unkind will." Among the *Romans*, a will was
called "*inofficiosum*," which excluded the children or rela-

tions from the inheritance.   Vide *Plin. Ep.* v. 1.   *Cic. pro Cluent.*

TANTA vis probitatis, ut eam in hoste etiam diligamus. ——So noble is the power of virtue, that we respect it even in our enemy.

TEINDS.——Tithes.

TEKNA.——Gr.   Children.

TELLIGRAPHUM.——A land-writing.

TELONIUM.——A place where toll is received.

TELUM.——A weapon.

TEMERE jurandum.——To swear rashly.

TEMPORA quibus causæ forenses dijudicantur.——(Law) terms when litigated causes are tried.   *Vide note.*

TEMPORE confectionis statuti; et non pro tempore futuro.——At the time of the passing the act; and not for the future.

TEMPORE pacis.——In the time of peace.

TENANT pur copie.——Tenant by copyhold.

TENEMENTORUM: aliud liberum; aliud villenagium. Item liberorum, aliud tenetur libere pro homagio, et servitio militari; aliud in libero soccagio cum fidelitate tantum.——Of tenures: the one is free, the other is a villenage.   Also of free tenures, the one is held freely by homage, and Knight's service; the other in free socage, with fealty only.

TENENDUM.——"To hold."   That clause in a deed wherein the tenure of the land is created and limited.

TENENDUM per servitium militare.——To hold by Knight's service   *Vide note.*

TENENDUM per servitium militare, in burgagio, in libero soccagio.——To hold by Knight's service, in burgage, in free socage.   *Vide note.*

TENENDUM sibi et hæredibus suis, quos de carne suo, et uxore sibi procreatos habuerit.——To hold to him and his heirs, born of the body of himself and wife.

TENENDUM sibi et hæredibus suis, si hæredes habuerit

de' corpore suo procreatos.——"To hold to him and his heirs, if he should have heirs born of his body." The words in the two last extracts were formerly used in many ancient settlements of estates.

TENENDUM tibi, et hæredibus tuis, vel cui dare, vel assignare in vita; vel in morte legari volueris.——To hold to you and your heirs, or to whom you may desire to give or assign (the estate) in your lifetime; or leave it at your decease.

TENERE placita.——To hold pleas: to try civil actions.

TENETUR se purgare is qui accusatur "*per Dei judicium,*" scilicet, per calidum ferrum, vel per aquam, pro deversitate conditionis hominum; per ferrum calidum, si fuerit homo liber; per aquam, si fuit rusticus.——He who is accused of a crime is bound to acquit himself "by the judgment of God;" that is, by hot iron, or by water, according to the different conditions of men; by hot iron, if he be a freeman; by water, if he be a peasant. *Vide note.*

TENHENED.——In Saxon law. The head of a deconnery.

TENIR en frank fee.——To hold in frank fee.

TENOREM et effectum sequentem.——To the tenor and effect following.

TENOR est qui legem dat feudo.——"The mode (custom or manner used) is that which gives the law (or rule) to the fee." The customary manner in which the estate had been held for many years shows the nature of the tenure.

"TER centum, ter virginti, cum quinque diebus

Sex horas, neque plus, neque minus, integer annus habet." The year consists of three hundred and sixty-five days and six hours, neither more nor less.

TERME de grace, est terme de grace que de nom, parce que c'est humilitatis ratione qu'elle l'accorde, et pour le distinguer de celui parte par la lettre; il est re'element

terme de droit, puisque c'est la loi que le done.——A
period (days) of grace is nominally such; it is only given
because it is supposed to be granted on petition, and in
order to distinguish it from the period fixed by the bill
itself; for it is, in fact, a period of right, since it is the law
which gives it.

TERMES de la ley.——Terms of the law.

TERMINUM suum prædictum.——His aforesaid term.

TERMINUS.——The end, limit, or boundary: sometimes
it means the stock or root to which, by reference, the future
succession is to be regulated.

TERMINUS ad quem.——The bound (or place) to
which.

TERMINUS a quo.——The place from which.

TERMINUS juris.——The period of one or two years allowed for the determining of appeals.

TERMINUS hominis.——A similar period to *terminus
juris*, but shorter.

TERRÆ dominicales.——Demesne lands.

TERRÆ dominicales regis.——The King's demesne
lands.

TERRA fertilis et fecunda.——Land fertile and abound-
ing.

TERRAM tenens per arcum et sagittam.——Holding the
estate by the bow and arrow. *Vide note.*

TERRA *Walliæ*, cum incolis suis, prius Regi jure feodali
subjecta, jam in proprietatis dominium totaliter et cum in-
tegritate conversa est, et coronæ regni *Angliæ* tanquam pars
corporis ejusdem annexa et unita.——The territory of *Wales*,
with its inhabitants, before subject to the King by the feudal law, is now altogether, and wholly converted into a
princedom, annexed and united to the crown of *England*,
as though it were a part thereof.

TERRE tenant.——The tenant who occupies the land:
he who has the actual possession.

TESTAMENTA rumpiuntur agnatione posthumi.——Wills

are invalidated by posthumous kindred on the father's side.

TESTAMENTI executores esse debent ii quos testator ad hoc elegerit, et quibus curam ipse commiserit; si vero testator nullos ad hoc nominaverit, possunt propinqui, et consanguinei ipsius defuncti ad id faciendum se ingerere.——Those should be the executors of a will whom the testator has chosen, and to whose care he has committed it; but if the testator has nominated no persons for this purpose, the relations and kindred of the deceased may take that duty on themselves and perform it. *Vide note.*

TESTAMENTUM est suprema contestatio in ea solemniter facta, ut quem volumus post mortem nostram habeamus hæredem.——A will is the strongest (or best) proof, solemnly made in that matter, respecting that person, who, after our decease, should be the heir.

TESTAMENTUM est voluntatis nostræ justa sententia de eo quod quis post mortem suam fieri velit.——A testament is the perfect deliberation of our desire respecting that which every one wishes should be performed after his death. *Vide note.*

TESTATIO mentis.——A testament: a will.

TESTATUM capias.——That you take the person testified (or to have been proceeded against elsewhere).

TESTATUM capias ad respondendum.——That you take the person testified (before) to make answer.

TESTATUM capias ad satisfaciendum.——That you take the person testified to make satisfaction.

TESTATUM est quod latitat et discurrit.——"It is testified that he lurks and wanders:" words used formerly in writs to hold to bail.

TESTATUM existit.——It is attested.

TESTATUM fieri facias.——That you cause the testified writ to be executed.

TESTATUM pluries.——A testified process issued more than twice.

TESTES.——Witnesses. *Vide note.*

TESTE meipso.——Witness ourself.

TESTIS unius inhabilis et defectus suppletur ex fide et habilitate alterius.——The incapable and defective testimony of one person is supplied by the integrity, and ability of another.

THASSARE.——To put grain or hay into a stack, &c.

THEADA.——A nation or people.

THEFT-BOTE.——Sax. " A compromise of felony." Among the *Saxons,* during the *Heptarchy,* a theft was commuted by a pecuniary fine.

THESAURUS inventus.——Treasure discovered: treasure trove.

THIA.——An aunt.

THINGUS.——A knight: a thane.

THRAVE.——A measure of grain or corn.

THRIMSA.——A Saxon coin.

TINET.——Materials for fencing and hedging.

TITIA divortium a *Seio* fecit. *Mœvia Titio* repudium misit.——" *Titia* obtained a divorce from *Seius. Mœvia* sent a retraction to *Titius.*" For the difference between *Divortium* and *Repudium, vide Ter. And.* i. 5, 15. *Ter. Phorm.* iv. 3, 72, v. 6, 35. *Plaut. Aul.* iv. 10, 69. But *Suet. Cœs.* appears to have used *Divortium* and *Repudium* synonymously. Vide *Quintil.* vii. 8, 2. *Vide note.*

TITULUS est justa causa possidendi id quod nostrum est. ——Title is a just cause of possessing that which is our own.

TOLL and TEAM.——A Saxon expression used to imply certain privileges.

TOLLUTUS.——Taken away.

TOLNETUM.——Toll: stallage.

TOLT.——A removal: a taking away.

TONODERACH.——Scotch. A thief-taker.

TORCENOUSE.——Injurious: wrongful.

TORRALE.——A drying place for grain or malt.

TORI et mensæ participatione mutuo cohabitaverunt usque ad mortem.——They lived together, even until death, in the mutual participation of bed and board.

TORT.——A wrong: an injury.

TORT-FEASOR.——A wrong-doer: a trespasser.

TOSCHEODORACH.——Scotch. Serjeant-at-arms.

TOTALITER expunxit et delevit.——He expunged and defaced it altogether.

TOT a primer.——Immediately.

TOT en tot.——Entirely.

TOTIDEM verbis.——In so many words.

TOTIES quoties.——As often as: so many times.

TOTUM statum suum.——His whole estate: his whole interest.

TOUS par avail.——The under tenants, who are supposed to make "*avail*" or profit of the land.

TOUT ensemble. The whole altogether.

TOUT fuit en luy, et vient de luy al commencement.—— All originated in him and comes of him from the commencement.

TOUT les judges ont opine chacun selon leurs luminores. ——Every judge voted according to his own opinion.

TOUT temps prist.——Ready at all times.

TRADAS in ballium.——You deliver to bail.

TRADIT fidejussores de pace et legalitate tuenda.——That he give sureties for keeping the peace, and good behavior.

TRADITIO.——A delivery: a livery of seisin.

TRADITIONE, cantilenis, aut verbis. By tradition, by songs, or verbally. *Vide note.*

TRADITIONE cartæ.——By delivery of the deed, (or writing.)

TRADITIONIBUS dominia rerum, non nudis pactis, transferentur.——That the ownership of estates be transferred by deliveries, and not by bare (or naked) agreements (or covenants).

TRADITIO nihil aliud est quam rei corporalis de persona in personam, de manu in manum translatio, aut in possessionem inductio: sed res incorporales, quæ sunt ipsum jus rei vel corpori inhærens, traditionem non patiuntur.——A delivery is nothing else than a transfer, or the induction into possession of a corporal thing from person to person, from hand to hand; but (as to) incorporal things in which there is an inherent right itself to the property or substance, those do not bear delivery (or livery). *Vide note.*

TRAHENS.——One who draws a bill.

TRAHIR.——To betray.

TRAHISON.——Treason : treachery.

TRAITE de droit de propriete.——A mark (or indication) of the right of ownership.

TRANSEAT in exemplum.——Let it become a precedent.

TRANSFRETARE.——To cross a strait.

TRANSIT in rem judicatam.——It passes into a matter adjudged: or into an adjudged case.

TRANSITUS.——A passage : a change, or transit (of a thing) from one place to another.

TRASSARE.——To draw.

TREBUCHET.——A tumbrel : a place of castigation.

TRESAYLE.——Of the grandfather's grandfather.

TRES faciunt collegium.——Three make a society (or college).

TRESOR trouvé.—— "Treasure trove, or found." Money or property found, of which no person makes a claim within a year and a day; it then belongs to the king, or the lord of the manor.

TRESPASS, quare clausum fregit.——Trespass, wherefore he broke the close.

TRESPASS vi et armis, de filio, vel filia, rapto vel abducto.——Trespass with force and arms concerning a son or daughter, taken or carried away.

TRESPASS vi et armis, de uxore rapta et abducta.——Trespass with force and arms, concerning a wife taken or carried away.

TRESTORNARE.——To turn aside.

TREUGA.——Truce.

TRIA admonitia.——Three warnings: the third summons.

TRIBUTA reddere——To pay tribute.

TRIENS.——A third part: an ancient term for dower.

TRINA admonitio.——The third summons.

TRINODA necessitas.——The threefold necessity: the three-knotted obligation. *Vide next extract.*

TRINODA necessitas, scilicet, pontis reparatio; arcis constructio, et expeditio contra hostem.——The threefold obligation, to wit, the reparation of a bridge; the erecting a fort or castle; and an expedition against an enemy.

TRIUM noctium hospes.——A three-night guest. *Vide note.*

TU ab servitio militare spoliabis.——You will be deprived of your tenure by Knight's service. Vide note to " *Tenendum per,*" &c.

TUA omnia uni nunquam navi credito.——" Never trust all your property in one ship:" or, as Lord *Eldon* used facetiously to remark, " Carry not all your eggs in one basket." He alluded to the improper mode of lending all a man was worth upon one security.

TUAS res tibi habeto.——Have your things to yourself.

TU dominum pernegas servare.——" Thou refusest to serve thy lord," (meaning that person who granted the estates under the feudal law.) *Vide note.*

TUITISCUS.——Of the people.

TU magis scire potes quanta fides sit habenda testibus; qui et cujus dignitatis, et cujus æstimationis sint, et qui simpliciter visi sint dicere: utrum unum eundemque meditatem sermonem attulerint, an ad ea quæ interroganeras ex tempore verisimilia responderint.——" You should the more fully understand (or learn) how much faith may be placed in witnesses; those who (show) themselves of dignity and consequence; and who appear to speak plainly (or sincerely); whether they have spoken the same pre-meditated speech, or have immediately answered what is credible to those things which you have asked them." The character and condition of witnesses were particularly attended to under the *Roman* jurisprudence (*diligentiâ expendebantur*). Vide *Cic. pro Flacc.* 5.

TUNC enim desperari incipit recuperatio, &c.——For then the recovery began to be despaired of.

TURBA.——The aged men to whom in the early times cases were sometimes submitted. Also, *turf.*

TURPE est patricio et nobili et causa oranti, jus in quo versaretur ignorare.——That it is disgraceful for a patrician, nobleman and orator, to be ignorant of that law in which he should be conversant. *Vide note.*

TURPE reos empta miseros defendere lingua.——It is shameful to defend the distressed for hired pay. *Vide note.*

TURPIS contractus.——A base or unfair agreement.

TUTELA legitima.——Legal wardship. *Vide note.*

TUTIUS erratur ex parte mitiori.——It is safer to err on the mild side.

TU vis solare inopem et succurre relicta.——You are desirous to relieve the needy and assist the destitute.

TUZ ceux.——All those.

TWA night gest.——The old Saxon phrase respecting one who is entertained the second night, and thereby entitled to be called a *guest*

TWELFHENDE.——Twelve hundred.

TYHTLAN.—An accusation.

TYMBORELLA.——The tumbrel: or ducking-stool. *Vide note.*

NOTES TO T.

TALIBUS, &c.—During the dark ages of Christianity, it was customary for murderers to consider themselves safe by flying to the altar of a religious house, or monastery.

TALIO—(*similitudo supplicii* vel *vindictæ hostimentum*, i. e. a similar pun‑ ishment, or a requital of vengeance).—A punishment *similar* to the injury, "an eye for an eye, a limb for a limb," &c.; but this punishment, though mentioned in the Twelve Tables, seems very rarely to have been inflicted, because the removal of it could be purchased by a *pecuniary* compensation; in this respect it was similar to the law of the *Saxons*.

TALISQUE ITA CONVICTUS, &c.—During the continual wars among the Barons of *Europe*, it was the interest of every sovereign to abolish or to check a practice which almost annihilated his authority. *Charlemagne* pro‑ hibited it by an express law, as "an invention of the devil to destroy the happiness and order of society." Vide *Capitul.*, A. D. 801. *Edit. Baluz.* vol. i. p. 371. Some Kings declared it unlawful for any person to commence war until he had sent a formal defiance to the kindred and dependants of his adversary; they ordained, that after the commission of the trespass or crime, which gave rise to a *private* war, that *forty* days must elapse before the person injured should attack the vassals of his adversary; they also en‑ joined all persons to *suspend* their *private* animosities, and to cease from hostilities when the King was at war. When, therefore, men broke the peace at *this* time, they were said to have broken the "*peace of our lord the King*," and this form is even yet stated in an indictment, when a person is tried for an offence at common law; and probably the origin of the words "*against the peace*" is derived from the custom before alluded to.

TAMEN ILLA TORMENTA, &c.—By the *Roman* laws, the slaves of the de‑ fendant could be demanded by the prosecutor to be examined *by torture* in several trials, chiefly for murder and violence. But slaves could not be ex‑ amined in this manner against their *master's* life (*in caput domini*), except in case of incest, or a conspiracy against the state. *Cic. Topic.* 34. *Mill.* 22. Augustus, in order to elude the law and subject the slaves of the criminal to torture, ordered that they should be sold to the public or to himself, *Dio. Liv.* 5. Tiberius ordered them to be sold to the public prosecutor (*mancipari publico actori jubet*). Vide *Tacit. Ann.* ii. 30, iii. 67; but the ancient law was afterwards restored by *Adrian*, and the *Antonines*, vide *D.* xlviii. 18, *de quest.* The slaves of *others* were sometimes demanded to be examined by torture, but not without the consent of their master; and the accuser giving security that if they were *killed or maimed* during the torture, he would make up the *damage. Ibid.* When slaves were examined by torture, they were stretched on a machine called "*Eculeus*," or "*Equuleus*," having their legs and arms tied to it with ropes (*fidiculis*), vide *Suet. Tib.* 62, and being raised upright as if suspended by a cross, their members were distended by means of screws (*per cochleas*), sometimes till they were dislocated, *ut ossium com‑ pago resolveretur*," i. e. "that the joint of the bones might be separated," hence "*Eculeo longior factus*," (i. e. making the criminal longer than the *Ecu‑ leus.*) Vide *Senec. Ep.* 8. To increase the pain, sometimes plates of red hot iron (*laminæ candentes*), pincers, burning pitch, &c., were applied to them. But some authors give a different account of this matter; but however this may be, the torture of the rack must have been so severe that humanity shrinks at the idea of its infliction.

The confessions of slaves extorted by the rack were written down on tables, which were *sealed* up till they were produced in court. *Cic. Mill.* 22. Private persons also sometimes examined their slaves by torture. Vide *Cic. pro Cluent.* 63, 66. It is matter of astonishment that a people so enlightened as the *Romans* were, did not perceive the futility of this mode of punishment to draw out the truth from the wretched sufferers; it is strange that by a *few years'* trial, the many false accusations made by the sufferers to mitigate their own dreadful pains, did not teach the government the uncertainty of obtaining the truth from men whose souls were pierced with anguish, and who were often willing to say or do anything, ever so *wicked*, to obtain a little respite from the "*Eculeus*," and burning iron plates.

TEMPORA QUIBUS, &c.—Terms are those spaces of time wherein the Courts of Justice are open for all that complain of wrongs or injuries, and seek their rights by course of law or action in order to their redress. During the *English* terms, the courts at *Westminster* Hall sit and give judgments, &c.; but the High Court of Parliament, the Chancery, and inferior courts do not observe the terms, only the courts of King's Bench, Common Pleas and Exchequer, the highest courts at common law. Of these terms, there are four in every year, viz., *Hilary* term, which begins the 23d of January, and ends the 12th of February, unless on Sundays, and then the day after; *Easter* term, which begins the Wednesday fortnight after Easter day, and ends the Monday next after Ascension day; *Trinity* term, which begins on the Friday after Trinity Sunday, and ends the Wednesday fortnight after; and *Michaelmus* term, which begins the 6th and ends the 28th of November.

TENENDUM PER SERVITIUM MILITARE.—Knighthood, *Military*, is that of ancient Knights, who acquired it by high feats of arms.

These were called *Milites* in ancient charters and titles, by which they were distinguished from mere *Bachelors*, &c. These Knights were girt with a sword, and a pair of gilt spurs; whence they were called *Equites aurati*.

Knighthood is not hereditary, but acquired. It does not come into the world with a man like nobility; nor can it be revoked. The sons of Kings, and Kings themselves, with other sovereigns, heretofore had Knighthood conferred upon them as a mark of honor. They were usually knighted at their baptism or marriage.

Between the age of *Charlemagne* and that of the *Crusades*, the service of the infantry was degraded to the Plebeians:. the cavalry formed the strength of the armies, and the honorable name of MILES, or soldier, was confined to the gentleman who served on horseback, and was invested with the character of Knighthood. The Dukes and Counts who usurped the rights of sovereignty, divided the provinces among their faithful Barons; the Barons distributed among their vassals the fiefs or benefices of their jurisdiction; and these military tenants, the peers of each order, and of their lord, composed the noble or Equestrian order, which disdained to conceive the peasant or burgher as of the same species with themelves. The dignity of their birth was preserved by pure and equal alliances; and their sons alone, who could produce four quarters or lines of ancestry, without spot or reproach, might legally pretend to the order of Knighthood; but a valiant Plebeian was sometimes enriched and ennobled by the sword, and became the father of a new race. A simple Knight could impart, according to his judgment, the character which he received: and the warlike sovereigns of *Europe* derived more glory from this personal distinction than from the lustre of their diadem. This ceremony, of which some traces can be found in *Tacitus*, and the woods of *Germany*, was, in its origin, simple and profane; the candidate, after some previous trial, was invested with the sword and spurs; and his cheek or shoulder was touched with a slight blow, as an emblem of the *last affront* which it was lawful for him to endure. But superstition mingled in many public and private actions of life: in the holy wars it sanctified the profession of arms; and the order of chivalry was assimilated in its rights and privileges to the sacred orders of Priesthood.

The bath and white garment of the novice was an indecent copy of the regeneration of baptism: his sword, which he offered on the altar, was blessed by the ministers of religion: his solemn reception was preceded by fasts and vigils: and he was created a Knight, in the name of God, of St. George, and of St. Michael, the Archangel. He swore to accomplish the duties of his profession; and education, example, and the public opinion, were the inviolable guardians of the oath. He devoted himself to speak the truth;

to maintain the right; to protect the distressed; to practice courtesy—a virtue' less familiar to the ancients; to pursue the infidels; to despise the allurements of ease and safety; and to vindicate, in every perilous adventure, the honor of his character. The *abuse* of the same spirit provoked the illiterate Knight to disdain the arts of industry and peace; to esteem himself the sole judge and avenger of his own injuries; and proudly to neglect the laws of civil society, and military discipline. Yet the benefits of this institution, to refine the temper of barbarians, and to infuse some principles of faith, justice and humanity, were strongly felt, and have been often observed. The asperity of national prejudice was softened; the community of religion and arms spread a similar color and generous emulations over the face of Christendom. Abroad, in enterprise and pilgrimage; at home, in martial exercise, the Knights of every country were perpetually associated; and impartial taste must prefer a Gothic tournament to the Olympic games of classic antiquity.

The lance was the proper and peculiar weapon of the Knight; his horse was of a large and heavy breed; but this charger, till he was roused by the approaching danger, was usually led by the attendant, and he quietly rode a pad or palfrey, of a more easy pace. His helmet and sword, his greaves and buckler, it is unnecessary to describe in this place; but at the period of the Crusades the armor was less ponderous than in later times; and instead of a massy cuirass, his breast was defended by a hauberk, or coat of mail. Each Knight was attended to the field by his faithful Squire, a youth of equal birth, and similar hopes; he was followed by his archers, and men at arms, and four, or five, or six soldiers, were computed as the furniture of a complete "Lance."

In the expeditions to the neighboring kingdoms, or the Holy Land, the duties of the Feudal tenure no longer subsisted; the voluntary service of the Knights and their followers was prompted by zeal or attachment, or purchased with rewards and promises; and the number of each squadron was measured by the power, the wealth, and the fame of each independent chieftain. They were distinguished by his banner, his armorial coat, and his cry of war; and the most ancient families of Europe must seek in these achievements the origin and proof of their nobility. Vide *Gibbon's Decl. and Fall of the Rom. Emp.*

The services, both of Chivalry and of Grand Serjeantry, were all personal; and as to their quantity or duration, uncertain. But personal attendance in Knight-service being found inconvenient and troublesome, the tenants sometimes found means of compounding for it; first, by finding others to serve in their stead; and, in process of time, by making a pecuniary satisfaction to the lords in lieu of it. When Knight-service, or personal military duty, degenerated into escuage, or pecuniary assessments, all the advantages (promised or real) of the feudal constitution, were destroyed, and nothing but the hardships remained. These hardships, which were numerous and grievous, were from time to time palliated by successive acts of Parliament, until at length King *James* the First consented, in consideration of a proper equivalent, to abolish them all, upon a plan similar to that which he had formed, and begun to put in execution, for removing the feudal grievances of heritable jurisdiction in *Scotland.* At length, the military tenures, with all their heavy appendages (which during the usurpation had been discontinued) were totally destroyed by the statute, 12 *Car.* ii. c. 24. Vide *Black. Comm.* vol. 2.

TENENDUM PER SERVITIUM MILITARE IN LIBERO SOCCAGIO.—By the ancient *English* constitution, the King had the power of compelling his vassals to be knighted. In all ages, however, whether of the high power, or on the decline of Chivalry, many persons, considering the duties and charges of the honor, had been wont to commute it by a fine; and this custom had often whetted the avarice of monarchs. *Elizabeth* was the last of the *English* sovereigns who enriched her Exchequer by receiving these commutations. *Charles* the First endeavored to augment his revenue by similar means; but the spirit of the age was hostile to his claim; and, certainly, as the military system had changed, it was absurd and unjust that the burden should survive the benefit of the ancient system. The people triumphed, and *Charles* conceded a prerogative, which was generally known at that time as a means of public oppression. By a statute passed in the sixteenth year of his reign, (c. 20.) the right of compelling men to receive Knighthood was abolished. Vide *Mills' Hist. Chiv.*

Knighthood was an institution perfectly peculiar to the military and social state of our ancestors. There seems to have been no analogy between the Knights of Chivalry, and the *Equites* of *Rome*; for pecuniary estate was absolutely necessary for the latter; whereas, though the *European* Cavalier was generally a man of some possessions, yet he was often promoted into the order of Chivalry, solely as a reward for his redoubted behavior in battle. The *Roman Equites* discharged civil functions, regarding the administration of justice, and the farming of the public revenues: but the Chivalry of the Middle Ages had no such duties to perform. Knighthood was also distinct from nobility; for the nobility of *Europe* were the governors and lords of particular districts of country; and although they originally ought to hold their dignities only for life, yet their titles soon became hereditary. But Knighthood was always a *personal* distinction. A man's chivalry died with him. It was conferred upon noblemen and kings; not being, like their other honors, the subject of inheritance. It was not absorbed in any other title of rank, and the common form of address to Royalty, *Sir King*, shows its high consideration. Vide *Mills' Hist. Chiv.*

The *English* customs regarding the degradation of Knights are minutely stated by *Stowe*, in the case of an *English* Knight, Sir *Andrew Harclay*, Earl of *Carlisle*, who, in the time of *Edward* the Second, was deprived of his Knighthood, previously to his suffering the penalties of the law, for a treasonable correspondence with *Robert Bruce*. He was led to the bar as an Earl, worthily apparelled, with his sword girt about him, horsed, booted and spurred, and unto him Sir *Anthony Lucy* (his judge) spoke in this manner: "Sir *Andrew*," quoth he, "the King for thy valiant service hath done thee great honor, and made thee Earl of *Carlisle*, since which time, thou, as a traitor to thy lord the King, led his people, that should have helped him at the battle of *Heighland*, away by the county of *Copland*, and through the Earldom of *Lancaster*, by which means our lord the King was discomfited there of the *Scots*, through thy treason and falseness; whereas, if thou haddest come betimes, he hadde had the victory; and this treason thou committed for the great sum of gold and silver that thou received of JAMES DOUGLAS, a *Scot*, the King's enemy. Our Lord the King wills, therefore, that the order of Knighthood, by the which thou received all the honor and worship upon thy body, be brought to naught, and thy state undone, that other Knights of lower degree may after thee beware, and take example truly to serve." Then commanded he the officers to hew his spurs from his heels; then to break his sword over his head, which the King had given him to keep and defend his land therewith, when he made him Earl. After this, he let unclothe him of his furred tabard, and of his hood, and of his coat of arms, as also of his girdle; and when this was done, Sir *Anthony* said unto him, "Andrew," quoth he, "now thou art no Knight, but a knave; and for thy treason, the King wills that thou shalt be hanged and drawn, and thy head smitten off from thy body, and burned, and thy body quartered, and thy head being smitten off, afterwards to be set upon *London* bridge, and thy four quarters shall be sent into four good towns of *England*, that all others may beware by thee." And as Sir *Anthony Lucy* had said, so was it done in all things, on the last day of October. Vide *Mills' Hist. Chiv.*

TENETUR SE PURGARE, &c.—It would be tedious to enumerate the various modes of appealing to the justice of God, which superstition introduced during the ages of ignorance. In the year 775, a contest arose between the Bishop of *Paris*, and the Abbot of *St. Denys*, concerning the property of a small abbey. Each of them exhibited deeds and records. Instead of trying the authenticity of these, the cause was referred to the "*Judicium crucis*," (the trial of the cross:) Each produced a person, who, during the celebration of Mass, stood before the cross, with his arms extended; and he, whose representative *first* became weary, and altered his posture, was to lose the cause. The person employed by the Bishop on this occasion had less strength than his adversary; and the question was decided in favor of the Abbot. *Mabillon de re diplomat.* lib. 6, 498. The Emperor *Charlemagne* was present; and if a prince so enlightened as he was, *countenanced* such an absurd mode of decision, it is no wonder that other monarchs should have tolerated it so long. When the prohibition to the mode of trial by single combat was promulgated, this new method of appeal was made to Heaven, as an infallible method of discovering truth; the person accused, in order to prove his innocence, submitted to trial in certain cases, either by swallowing (or endeavoring to swallow) a piece of bread, called the "*Corsned*;" plunging his arm in boiling water; lifting a red-hot iron with his naked hand; or by walking barefoot over (or perhaps rather *among*) burning ploughshares; or by other experiments equally presumptuous and perilous. All these forms of trial were conducted with devout ceremonies; the ministers of religion were employed; the Almighty was called upon for the manifestation of guilt, or for the protection of innocence; and whoever escaped unhurt, or came off victorious, was pronounced to be acquitted "by the judgment of God." Vide *Murat. dissertatio. de judiciis Dei, Antiq. Ital.* vol. 3, p. 612.

TERRAM TENENS PER ARCUM ET SAGITTAM.—Lands were sometimes holden in *England* by paying yearly a bow and arrows, spear, &c.

The *Normans* introduced into *England* the use of the longbow; it had been characterized by them, and been mainly instrumental in winning for them the battle of *Hastings*. It was afterwards used by the small land-holder, the tenant in socage and the general mass of the people; while the lance was the weapon of the lord and knight. The bow was the emblem of freedom, and the preëminence of the *English* archers shows that the political condition of *England* was superior in the fourteenth century to that of any continental nation.

> "——————these gallant yeomen,
> *England's* peculiar and appropriate sons,
> Known in no other land. Each boasts his hearth
> And field as free as the best lord his barony,
> Owing subjection to no human vassalage,
> Save to the King and law. Hence are they resolute,
> Leading the van in every day of battle,
> As men who know the blessings they defend.
> Hence are they frank and generous in peace,
> As men who have their portion in its plenty;
> No other kingdom shows such worth and hapiness,
> Vailed in such low estate."
>
> *Halidon Hill, Act.* iii. sc. 2.

The arrow was of the remarkable length of a "cloth-yard." The expression in the old ballad of *Chevy-Chase*,

> "An arrow of a *cloth-yard* long
> Up to the head drew he"—

marks the usage of our early ancestors: and that sentence of *Lear* in *Shakspeare's* play, "Draw me a clothier's yard," shows that in the sixteenth century the national character had not been lost. It was fostered by every proper means: by royal command, archery was practiced in towns on holidays, after church; while coits, cock-fighting and amusements with the ball were strictly prohibited. Other nations drew the bow with strength of arm, but Englishmen with their whole vigor; "they laid their body on the bow,"* as an old writer has forcibly expressed the usage; and when in amusement they were exercising their skill, eleven score yards was the *least* distance at which the mark was set up. No one could better shoot an arrow than a yeoman, in the days of Edward III.: they were the most powerful attendants Knights could boast of.

> "A yeoman had he, and servants no mo,
> At that time for him lust to ride so;
> And he was clad in coat and hood of green,
> A sheaf of peacock's arwes bright and keen,
> Under his belt he bare full thriftily.
> Well could he dress his takel yeomanly.
> His arwes dropped not with feathers lowe,
> And in his hand he bare a mighty bowe.
> A not head† had he with a brown visage,
> Of wood-craft could he well all the usage.
> Upon his arm he bore a gay bracer,
> And by his side a sword and bokeler;
> And on the other side a gay dagger,
> Harnessed well, and sharp as point of spear;
> A Cristofere on his breast of silver shone;
> An horn he bare, the baudrick was of green.
> A forester was he, soothly as I guess."‡

The reader scarcely needs to be informed that the loss of the battle of *Cressy* by the French began with the confusion among the *Genoese* cross-bow men. The *English* archers then stepped forward one pace, and, as *Froisart* says, "Let fly their arrows so wholly, and so thick, that it seemed snow was piercing through heads, arms and breasts. The *French* cavaliers rushed in to slay the *Genoese* for their cowardice, but the sharp arrows of the *English* slew them and their horses too. The chivalry of the Black Prince decided the victory. The Earls of *Flanders* and *Alençon* broke through the archers, but deeper they could not penetrate; and in the personal conflict of the chivalries of the two nations, the *English* were conquerors." Vide *Froisart,* c. 131.

"At the battle of *Poictiers* the *English* archers threw the *French* cavalry into confusion by slaying the unmailed horses." "True to say," as *Froisart* observes, "the archers did their company that great advantage; for when the Black Prince descended the hill on which he had posted himself, the archers were mingled with his chivalry in true knightly fashion, and shot so closely together that none durst come within danger." Vide *Mills' Hist. Chiv.* vol. ii. p. 13, *et sub.*

TESTAMENTI EXECUTORES, &c.—Among the ancient *Romans* none but a citizen, *sui juris* (of his own right), could make a will; or be a witness to a testament; or inherit anything by testament. *Cic. pro Arch.* 5 *Dom.* 32. Anciently, testaments used to be made *in Comitia Curiata,* vide *Gell.* xv. 37. The testament of a soldier, just about to engage, was said to be made "*in procinctu;*" while in camp, when he was *girding* himself, or preparing for

---

* This national character is alluded to in Latimer's Sermons, folio 69; a work not of very good promise for such matters.

† Hair cut short.

‡ Chaucer's Prologue to the Canterbury tale, line 101.

battle in the presence of his fellow soldiers, without writing he named his heir (*nuncupavit*). Vide *Cic. de Nat. D.* ii. 3, *de Orat.* 153. So *in procinctu carmina facta* (i. e. verses made while girt), written by *Ovid* at *Tomos*, where he was in fear of a continual attack from the *Getæ*. Vide *Pont.* i. 8, 10. But the usual mode of making a will, after the law of the Twelve Tables were enacted, was "*per æs, et libram*" (by money and weight or balance); or "*per familiæ emptionem*" (by friendly purchase), as it was called, wherein, before five witnesses, a *Libripens* and an *Antestatus*, the testator, by an *imaginary sale*, disposed of his family and fortune to one who was called "*familiæ emptore*," who was not the heir as some have thought (vide *Suet. Ner.* 4), but only *admitted*, for the sake of form, that it might appear that the testator had alienated his effects in his *life time*. This act was called "*familia mancipatio*" (a family sale), which, being finished in due form, the testator, holding the testament in his hand, said: "*Hæc, ut in his tabulis cerisve scripta sunt ita do, ita lego, ita testor itaque vos Quirites, testimonium præbitote,*" i. e. "According as these things are written in these tablets or wax, so I give, so I bequeath, so I testify, and approve you, O citizens, to bear witness." Upon which, as was usual in like cases, he gently touched the *tip* of the ears of the witnesses. *Plin.* xi. 45. This act was called "*nuncupatio testamenti*" (a declaring the will). *Plin. Ep.* viii. 18. Hence "*nuncupare hæredem*" (to name the heir), for *nominare, scribere,* vel *facere* (to elect, to write, to make). *Suet. et Plin. passim.* But sometimes this word signifies to name one's heir *viva voce,* without writing, as *Horace,* just before his death, is said to have named *Augustus.* The above-mentioned formalities were not always observed, especially in later times. It was reckoned sufficient if the testator subscribed his will, or even named his heir "*viva voce*" before *seven* witnesses. Something similar to this seems to have prevailed anciently, vide *Cic. Verr.* i. 45. Sometimes the testator wrote his will wholly with his own hand, in which case it was called "*Holographum.*" Sometimes it was written by a friend, or by others. *Plin. Ep.* vi. 26. Thus the testament of *Augustus* was written partly by himself, and partly by two of his freedmen. *Suet. Aug.* 102: but lawyers were *usually* employed in drawing up wills. *Cic. de Orat.* ii. 6. But it was ordained, under *Claudius* or *Nero,* that the writer of another's testament should not mark down any legacy for *himself. Suet. Ner.* 17. This was very proper, and prevented imposition. When a testament was written by another, the testator wrote below that he had dictated and read it over. Testaments were usually written on tables covered with wax, because in them persons could more easily erase what they wished to alter. *Quint.* x. 3, 31. Hence, sometimes, *ceræ* is put for *tabulæ ceratæ* (waxed tables), or *tabulæ testamenti* (testamentary tables). Vide *Juv.* i. 63. But testaments were called "*tabulæ,*" although written on parchment or paper. *Ulpian.* Testaments were subscribed by the testator, and usually by the witnesses; and sealed with their seals or rings, and also with the seals of others. They were likewise tied with a thread. Hence, "*Nec mea subjectâ convicta est gemma tabellâ mendacem linis imposuisse notam,*" "nor is my ring," i. e. "nor am I convicted of having affixed a false mark, or seal, to the thread on a forged deed, or will." Vide *Ovid. Pont.* ii. 9, 69. It was ordained that the thread should be *thrice* drawn through holes and sealed. Vide *Suet. Ner.* 17. Testaments, like all other civil deeds, were written in *Latin.* It is *said* a legacy expressed in *Greek* was invalid. Vide *Ulp. Frag.* xxv. 9. Testaments were usally either deposited privately in the hands of a friend, or in a temple with the keeper of it. Thus *Julius Cæsar* is said to have intrusted his testament to the eldest of the *vestal virgins.* Vide *Suet. Jul.* 83.

TESTAMENTUM EST VOLUNTATIS, &c.—Wills or testaments, says Judge *Blackstone,* are of very high antiquity. We find them among the ancient *Hebrews:* not to mention what *Eusebius* and others have related of Noah's testament, "made in writing, and witnessed under his seal, by which he disposed of the whole world," a more authentic instance of the early use of testaments occurs in the sacred writings (*Gen.* c. xlviii.) in which *Jacob* bequeaths to his son *Joseph* a portion of his inheritance, double to that of his brethren; which will we find executed many hundred years afterwards, when the posterity of *Joseph* were divided into two distinct tribes, those of *Ephraim* and *Manasseh*, and had two several inheritances assigned them; whereas the descendants of each of the other patriarchs formed only a single tribe, and had only one lot of inheritance. *Solon* was the first legislator that introduced wills into *Athens*, but in many other parts of *Greece* they were totally discountenanced. In *Rome*, they were unknown till the laws of the Twelve Tables were compiled, which first gave the right of bequeathing; and among the northern nations, particularly among the *Germans*, testaments were not received into use. Hence it appears that the right of making wills and disposing of property after death, is merely a creature of the civil state, which has permitted it in some countries, and denied it in others; and subjected it to various restrictions and regulations where the law allows it.

In *England*, this power of bequeathing is coeval with the first rudiments of the law; not indeed that it extended originally to all a man's personal estate.

It is also sufficiently clear that before the conquest, lands were devisable by will. But, upon the introduction of the military tenures, the restraint of devising lands naturally took place, as a branch of the feudal doctrine of non-alienation without the consent of the lord. By the common law of *England*, since the conquest, no estate greater than for a term of years, could be disposed of by testament, except only in *Kent*, and in some ancient Burghs, and a few particular manors, where their *Saxon* immunities, by special indulgence, subsisted. But when ecclesiastical ingenuity had invented the doctrine of *Uses* as a thing *distinct* from the land, uses began to be devised very frequently, and the devisee of the use could, in chancery, compel its execution. However, when the statute of uses, viz., 27 *Henry* VIII. cap. 10, had annexed the *possession* of the *use*, these uses being now the *very* land itself, became no longer devisable: whereupon the statute of wills was made, viz., 32 *Hen.* VIII. cap. 1, explained by 34 & 35 *Hen.* VIII. cap. 5, which enacted, that "all persons being seised in fee simple (except *femme* coverts, infants, idiots, and persons of nonsane memory), might by will and testament in writing, devise to any other person, (except to bodies corporate,) two-thirds of their lands, tenements, and hereditaments, held in chivalry, and the whole of those held in socage;" which now, through the alteration of tenure by the statute of *Charles* II. c. 12. *Car.* II. cap. 25, amounts to the whole of their landed property, except their copyhold tenements. As for copyhold and other customary lands, these are devisable or not, according to the customs of the respective manors. And generally, a devise of copyhold will not pass without a surrender to the use of the will. Students who desire further information on this subject will consult *Lovelass, Powell, Roberts, Roper, Swinburne,* &c.

TESTES.—Among the *Romans*, free citizens gave their testimony upon oath (*jurati*). The form of interrogating them was ." *Sexte Tempani, quæro ex te, arbitrisne, C. Sempronium in tempore pugnam inisse?*" i. e. "I ask of you *Sextus Tempanus* whether you think *C. Sempronius* was in the fight at that time?" *Liv.* iv. 40. The witness answered "*Arbitror,*" (I think so,) vel "*non arbitror,*" (I do not think so.) *Cic. Acad.* iv. 47, *pro Font.* 9. Witnesses were either voluntary or involuntary. The prosecutor *only* was allowed to *summon* witnesses against the will. (*Quint.* v. 78), and of these a different number by different laws, usually no more than ten. Witnesses were said "*testimonium dicere, dare, perhibere, præbere,*" also "*pro testimonio audiri.*" "To declare, to give, to produce, to afford testimony, and also to be heard in evidence." *Suet. Claud.* 15. The phrase "*depositiones testium,*" (depositions of the witnesses) is not used by the classics, but only in the *civil* law. Persons might give evidence, although absent, by writing, (*per tabulas*,) but it was necessary that this should be done voluntarily, and before witnesses, (*præsentibus signatoribus.*) Vide *Quint.* v. 7. The character and condition of witnesses, were, by the *Romans, particularly* attended to; and no doubt character should have a great weight with every jury, for better is the evidence of *one* man of tried integrity, than the oath of a thousand of infamous character. No one it appears was obliged to be a witness against a near relation, or friend, by the *Julian* law, vide *l.* 4. *D. de test;* and never, "*more majorum,*" (by custom of the ancients,) in his own cause (*de re sua*). Vide *Cic. Rosc. Am.* 36. The witnesses of each party had particular benches in the *Forum,* on which they sat. Great dexterity was often shown in interrogating witnesses, *Cic. pro Flacc,* 10; but it does not appear that the ancients had that base plan of *confuting* and *confounding* witnesses, upon which many of the modern advocates very wickedly *pride* themselves. Persons of infamous character were not permitted to give evidence, (*testes non adhibiti sunt,*) and therefore were called "*intestabiles,*" (*Plaut.*); as those witnesses were, who being once called as witnesses, *antestati,* vel *in testimonium adhibiti,* (formerly called, or brought to evidence,) afterwards refused to give their testimony. Vide *Gell.* xv. 13. Women, anciently, were not admitted as witnesses, (*Gell.* vi. 7,) but in after times they were. (*Cic. Verr.* i. 37.) A false witness, by the law of the Twelve Tables, was thrown from the *Tarpeian* Rock, (*Gell.* xx. 1;) but afterwards the punishment was arbitrary, except in war, when a false witness was beaten to death by sticks. (Vide *Polyb.* vi. 35.) Jews have been sworn in our courts from the earliest times on the *Pentateuch;* and no distinction appears ever to have been taken between their swearing in a *civil,* or in a *criminal* case. In an old case, where a witness refused to be sworn in the usual form, by laying his right hand on the book and kissing it afterwards, *Glyn,* C. Justice, ruled that he might be sworn by having the book laid *open* before him and holding up the right hand. Vide *Dutton* v. *Colt,* 2 *Sid.* 6. So, on the trial of some rebels at *Carlisle,* in the year 1745, a witness being sworn in the same manner, by holding up his hand, the point was referred to the Judges for their opinion, and they all agreed that the witness was legally sworn. *Mahometans* may be sworn on the *Koran;* and, upon the same principle, all persons, according to the ceremonies of their religion. Whatever may be the form, the meaning of the oath is the same. It is calling upon God to witness what we say, and invoking his vengeance if what we assert be false. Vide *Rex* v. *Gilham,* 1 *Esp.* 285. The ancient mode of administering oaths in *France,* was thus: the witness, if a layman, raised his right hand; or if a priest, placed it upon his breast. The same form, at least the raising the hand, continued after the revolution, and a deposition taken in *France,* and sworn to in this manner, was admitted in evidence by the Supreme Court of *Massachusetts.* 6 *Mass. Rep.* 262.

Atheists, and such infidels as profess not any religion that can bind their conscience to speak the truth, are excluded from being witnesses. Lord *Coke,* indeed, says generally, that an infidel cannot be a witness, in which denomination he intended to comprise Jews as well as Heathens. And Sergeant *Hawkins* thought it a sufficient objection to the competency of a witness, that he believed neither the Old nor the New Testament. Lord *Hale,* however, was of a different opinion, and strongly points out the unreasonableness of indiscriminately excluding all heathens from giving evidence, as well as the inconsistency of compelling them to swear in a *form* which they may possibly not consider binding. "It were a very hard case," he says, "if a murder committed here, in the presence *only* of a *Turk* or a *Jew,* should be dispunishable, because such an oath could not be taken which the witness holds binding; and who possibly might think himself under no obligation, if sworn according to the usual style of the courts of *England.*" All doubts upon this subject, were, however, removed by the case of *Omichund* v. *Barker* before Lord Chancellor *Hardwicke* and others; where it was solemnly decided that the depositions of witnesses professing the *Gentoo* religion, who had been sworn, according to the ceremonies of their religion, ought to be admitted in evidence. And it may now, perhaps, be considered as an established rule, that infidels of any other country, who believe in a God, the avenger of falsehood, may be received as witnesses; but infidels who do not believe that there is a God, or a future state of rewards and punishments, cannot be admitted. The student will find some very excellent observations on such evidence in an extremely well-written treatise on the law of Evidence by *S. M. Phillips.* Vide also *Starkie, Archbold, Bentham* and *Roscoe.*

TITIA, &c.—By the *Roman* law, after the espousals, if either of the parties wished to retract, (*sponsalia dissolvere, infirmare,* vel *infringere,*) which they expressed thus, *conditione tuo non utor,* i. e. "I do not accept your condition," it was called REPUDIUM. Hence, *Repudiatus repetor,* i. e. "after being rejected I am sought back." *Ter. And.* i. 5, 15. And when a man or woman, after signing the contract, sent notice that they wished to break off the match, they were said *Repudium ei,* vel *amicis ejus mittere. Ter. Phorm.* iv. 3, 72: v. 6, 35. But *Repudiare* also signifies to divorce either a wife (*Suet. Cæs.* i.) or a husband. *Quintil.* vii. 8, 2.

TRADITIONE, CANTILENIS AUT VERBIS.—It is generally believed that the use of letters was not known in the north of *Europe* until long after the institution of the Bards: the records of the families of their patrons, their own, and more ancient poems, were handed down by *Tradition.* Their poetical compositions were admirably contrived for that purpose. They were adapted to music; and the most perfect harmony was observed. Each verse was so connected with those which preceded or followed it, that if one line had been remembered in a stanza, it was almost impossible to forget the rest. The cadences followed in so natural a gradation; and the words were so adapted to the common turn of the voice, after it was raised to a certain key, that it was almost impossible, from a similarity of sound, to substitute one word for another. This excellence is said to be peculiar to the *Celtic* tongue, and is, perhaps, to be met with in no other language. The descendants of the *Cellæ,* who inhabited *Britain* and its isles, were not singular in this method of preserving the most precious monuments of their nation, (*traditione, cantilenis aut verbis.*) The ancient laws of the *Greeks* were couched in *verse,* and handed down by *tradition.* The *Spartans,* through a long habit, became so fond of this custom that they never would allow their *Laws* to be committed to writing. The actions of great men and the eulogiums of kings and heroes, were preserved in the same manner. All the historical monuments of the old *Germans* were comprehended in their ancient *songs;* (vide *Tacit. de Mor. Germ.*) and were either hymns to their gods, or elegies in praise of their heroes, and were intended to perpetuate the great events in their nation, which were carefully interwoven with them. This species of composition was not committed to *writing,* but delivered by *oral* tradition. (Vide *Abbe le Bleterie Remarques sur la Germaine.*) The care they took to have their poems taught to their children; the uninterrupted custom of repeating them upon certain occasions; and the happy measure of the verse, served to preserve them for a long time uncorrupted. This oral chronicle of the *Germans* was not forgotten in the eighth century; and probably it would have remained to this day, had not learning, which is too apt to think everything not committed to *writing* fabulous, been introduced. The *Peruvians* had lost all other monuments of their history; and it was from ancient poems which his mother, a princess of the blood of the *Yncas,* taught her son, that he collected the materials for his history. If other nations, then, that have been often overrun by enemies, and had sent abroad and received colonies, could for many ages preserve by oral tradition, their laws and histories uncorrupted, it is much more probable that the ancient inhabitants of the northern parts of *Britain* had the works of the bards handed down with purity: and from part of those it is very probable that some of the maxims of the *English* Common Law had their origin. Vide *Macpherson's Dissert. Concern. the Æra of Ossian.*

TRADITIO NIHIL, &c.—There is no doubt but, anciently, almost all the transfers of landed property were made by giving possession *only ;* but few deeds (and those only of large estates) are to be found more than four or five hundred years old: these ancient deeds are very short and simple,·with warranties; and generally without covenants.

TRIUM NOCTIUM HOSPES.—Anciently called "*Third night awn-hinde.*" By the laws of *Edward* the Confessor, if any man lay a *third* night in an inn, he was called "*third night awn-hinde,*" for whom his host was answerable, if he committed an offence. The first night the guest was called "*forman night,*" or "*uncuth,*" (Sax.) *unknown,* and was reckoned only a stranger: the second night, "*twa-night ;*" and the third an "*agen-hinde,*" or "*awn-hinde,*" viz., a domestic. Vide *Bract.* lib. 3.

TU DOMINUM PERNEGAS SERVARE.—In the history of our *Anglo-Saxon* ancestors, many instances are recorded where vassals refused to survive their lord. *Cyneheard,* brother of the deposed King *Sigebrycht,* slew the usurper *Cynewulf ;* and though he offered freedom to the attendants of the slain, yet they all preferred death to submission to a new chief; and they died in a vain and wild endeavor to revenge him. Immediately afterwards, fortune frowned upon *Cyneheard,* and his eighty-four companions, save one, were slain, though liberty had been offered to them; but declaring that their generosity was not inferior to the generosity of the attendants of *Cynewulf,* they perished in a hopeless battle. The feeling which in chivalric times became designated as the dignity of obedience, may be traced in these circumstances: but it is more clearly shown in a singular record of the domestic manners of ancient *Europe ;* for we learn from *Athenæus,* in his treatise of the Suppers of the *Celts,* that it was the custom of the *Gaulish* youth to stand behind the seats, and to attend upon their fathers, during the principal daily meal.

Here we see the germ, if not of the duties of the Squire to the Knight, yet of the feeling which suggested their performance. The beautiful subordination of Chivalry had its origin in the domestic relations of life; obedience became virtuous when nature sanctioned it, and there would be no loss of personal consideration in a youth performing services which his own father had performed, and which, as years and circumstances advanced, would be rendered to himself. Vide *Mills' Hist. Chiv.*

TURPE EST, &c.—This reproof was applied by *Cicero* to *Q. M. Scævola ;* who, being wounded at the reproach cast upon him, so sedulously applied himself to the study of the law, that in a short time he became (it is said) a greater lawyer and orator than *Cicero* himself.

TURPE REOS EMPTA, &c.—By the *Cincian* law, lawyers among the *Romans* were prohibited from taking fees or presents from those who consulted them, which rendered the science of jurisprudence highly respectable, as being undertaken by men of rank and learning; not from the love of gain, but from a desire of *assisting* their fellow-citizens; and especially the oppressed, and, through their favor, of rising to preferment. *Augustus* enforced this law by ordaining that those who transgressed it should restore fourfold. Vide *Dio.* liv. 18. Under the Emperors, however, lawyers were *permitted* to take fees, (*honorarium: certam, justamque mercedem,*) i. e. "an honorary fee: a fixed and certain reward," *Suet. Ner.* 17, from their clients; but not above a specified sum, (*capiendis pecuniis posuit modum* (sc. Claudius) *uuque ad dena sestertia*) i. e. "Claudius instituted a rule for receiving fees to the amount of ten sesterces," (*Tac. Ann.* xi. 7 ;) and after the business was done, (*paratis negotiis permittebat duntaxat decem millium dare*) i. e. "after the business was performed to give ten thousand." Vide *Plin. Ep.* v. 21. Thus the ancient and friendly connection between patrons and clients fell into disuse, and everything was done for hire: no longer were those honorable and charitable feelings brought into action by the learned, generous, and uninterested lawyer towards the poor and oppressed; but the profession of the law degenerated into a *love of pelf.* This ought not so to be; the lawyer should stand as a guardian angel between the oppressor and him "who is ready to perish." Complaint began to be made that persons of the lowest rank sometimes assumed the profession of lawyers; vide *Juv.* viii. 47;) pleadings became venal, (*venire advocationes;*) advocates made a shameful trade of their function by fomenting lawsuits, (*in lites coïre;*) and instead of honor, which was at one time their only reward, lived upon the *spoils* of their fellow-citizens, from whom they received large and annual salaries. Vide *Plin. Ep.* v. 14. Various edicts (*edicta libri,* vel *libelli*) were published by the Emperors to check this corruption. *Ibid.* Also, decrees of the Senate, *ib.* p. 21, but these were artfully eluded.

Lawyers were consulted, not only by private persons, but also by magistrates and judges (*Cic. Top.* 17. *Muræn.* 13, &c.); and a certain number of them attended attended every *Proconsul* and *Proprætor* to his province. The writings of *several* eminent lawyers came to be almost as much respected in courts of justice (*usi fori*) as the laws themselves (*l.* 2, § 38, *D. de Orig. juris*). But this happened only by tacit consent. Those *laws* only had a binding force, which were solemnly enacted by the whole *Roman* people, assembled in the *Comitia,* or in some other legal manner. The origin of lawyers at *Rome* was derived from the institution of patronage. It was one of the offices of a patron to explain the law to his clients, and to manage their law suits.

Titus Coruncanius, who was the first Plebeian *Pontifex Maximus,* A. U. 500 (*Liv. Epit.* 18), is said to have been the first who gave his advice *freely* to all the citizens without distinction (*l.* 2, § 35 and 38, *D. de orig. jur.*); whom many afterwards imitated, as *Manilius, Crassus, Mucius, Scævola, C. Aquilius, Gallus, Trebatius, Sulpicius,* &c.

Those who professed to give advice to all promiscuously, used to walk across the Forum (*transverso foro*), and were applied to (*ad eos adibatur*) there, or at their own houses. *Cic. Orat.* iii. 333. Such as were celebrated for their knowledge in law, often had their doors beset with clients before daybreak, vide *Hor. Sat.* i. 1, v. 9; their gate was open to all (*cunctis janua patebat*), Tibull. i. 4, 78; and the house of an eminent lawyer was, as it were, the oracle of the whole city. *Cic. de Orat.* i. 45. Hence *Cicero* calls their power *Regnum judicale.* Att. i. 1.

The lawyer gave his answers from an elevated stool (*ex solio, tanquam ex tripode.* Vide *Cic. de Legg.* 1, 3. *Orat.* ii. 33, iii. 33. The client, coming up to him, said: "*Licet consulere?*" (i. e. "Is it proper to consult you?") The lawyer answered, "*Consule*" (consult). Vide *Cic. pro Mur.* 13. Then the matter was proposed, and an answer was returned very shortly, thus: "*Quæro an existimes?* vel, *Id jus est necne?*" (I ask what is your opinion? or, Is that the law or not?) *Secundum ea, quæ proponuntur, existimo; placet; puto* (i. e. According as proposed, I judge; it pleases me; so I think). Vide *Hor. Sat.* ii. 3, 192. Lawyers gave their opinion either *vivâ voce* or in writing: commonly, without any reason annexed. Vide *Senec. Ep.* 94.

Sometimes, in difficult cases, the lawyers used to meet near the Temple of Apollo in the *Forum* (Juv. i. 128), and after deliberating together, which was called "*Disputatio Fori*," they pronounced a joint opinion. Hence what was determined by the lawyers, and adopted by custom, was called *Recepta sententia* (a received opinion); *Receptum jus* (an accepted law); *Receptum mos* (a received custom); *Post multas variationes receptum* (allowed after considerable discussion); and the rules observed in legal transactions, by their consent, were called *Regulæ juris* (the rules of law).

When the laws or edicts of the *Prætor* seemed defective, the lawyers supplied what was wanting in both from natural equity; and their opinions in process of time, some authors assert, obtained the authority of laws. Hence lawyers were not only called "*Interpretes*," but also "*Conditores et Auctores juris*" (the founders and authors of the law). Vide *Digest.*: and their opinions, "*Jus civile*" (the civil law). Vide *Cic. pro Cæcin.* 24, *de Offic.* iii. 16; opposed to "*Leges*" (Cæcin. 26).

TUTELA LEGITIMA.—Any father of a family among the ancient *Romans* might leave whom he pleased as guardians (*tutores*) to his children. *Liv.* i. 34. But if he died intestate, this charge devolved by law upon the nearest relation by the father's side. This law has been generally blamed, as in later times it gave occasion to many frauds in prejudice of wards, vide *Hor. Sat.* ii. 5, and *Juv. Sat.* vi. 38. It was said, "*Quasi agnum committere lupo*" (like giving the care of the lamb to the wolf). Where there was no guardian by testament, nor a legal one, then a guardian was appointed to minors and to women by the *Prætor*, and the majority of the *Tribunes* of the people by the *Atilian* law. But this law was afterwards changed. Among the ancient *Romans*, women could not transact any private business of importance without the concurrence of their parents, husbands, or guardians. *Liv.* xxxiv. 2. And a husband, at his death, might appoint a guardian for his wife, as well as to his daughter; or leave her the choice of her own guardians. *Liv.* xxxix. 9. If any guardian did not discharge his duty properly, or defrauded his pupil, there was an action against him (*judicium tutelæ*). Vide *Cic.* Under the Emperors, guardians were obliged to give security for their proper conduct. The student may find a signal instance of punishment inflicted on a perfidious guardian, recorded in *Suet. Galb.* 9.

TYMBORELLA.—The Tumbrel. This was an article used for punishment by the old *English* law, and inflicted on a woman convicted of being a common scold. She was placed in this engine of correction, which, it appears, consisted of a long beam, or rafter, moving on a *fulcrum*, and extended over a pond, on which end the stool was placed. This disgraceful punishment has long since been disused.

U.

UBERRIMA fides.——A phrase common in Roman law. The most abundant good faith.

UBI diligentissimus præcavisset et providisset non dicitur proprie casus fortuitus.——Where the most cautious person might have anticipated and foreseen (an event), it cannot properly be called an accidental circumstance.

UBI factum, ibi poterit esse forcia quandoque, sed nunquam forcia sine facto, quia ubi principale non consistit,
nec ea quæ sequuntur locum habere debent; sicut dici poterit de præcepto, conspiratione, et consimilibus, quamvis
hujusmodi esse possunt etiam sine facto; et quandoque
puniuntur si factum subsequatur, sed sine facto non, &c.;
nec etiam abesse debent præcepto, &c., nisi factum subsequatur.——When there is an act committed, there, in general, is a force (or violence); but there is never a force
without the act; because where the principal thing does
not exist, those matters which follow are of no consequence;
as may be said of the rule respecting conspiracy, and the
like, although crimes of this nature may arise without any
deed (actually committed), and occasionally are punished
if the act follow; but without the deed, it is otherwise, &c.;
nor should we disregard the rule, &c., except the deed
follow.

UBI jus incertum, ibi jus nullum.——Where the law is
uncertain, there is no law.

UBI major pars est, ibi est totum.——Where the greater
part is, there is the whole.

UBI non apparet dominus rei, quæ olim fuerunt inventoris de jure naturali, jam efficiuntur principis jure gentium.——Where the owner does not appear, those things
which formerly belonged to the finder by the law of nature, now belong to the Emperor by the law of nations.

UBI nullum matrimonium, ibi nulla dos.——Where
there is no marriage, there is no dower.

UBI nullum placitum, ibi nullum essonium.——"Where
there is no plea, there is no essoin." Days of grace were
formerly allowed to defendants after the return of writs,
in order that they might have time to plead, or perhaps to
settle the suit; these were called "*Essoin days,*" or days
of *excuse* from pleading. Vide note to "*Vocatio in jus.*"

UBI quis (cui nullum jus competit in re, nec scintilla

juris) possessionem vacuam ingreditur, quæ nec corpore, nec animo possideantur, sicut hæreditatem jacentem antiquam quæ abdita fuerit ab hærede, vel saltem a domino capitali ratione custodiæ, vel ratione eschetæ, si forte hæredes non existant, &c.——When any one (to whom no right, nor spark of right in the estate belongs,) enters upon a vacant possession, which should not corporeally or virtually be possessed, like an ancient disregarded inheritance, which shall have been taken from the heir, or at least from the chief lord by reason of wardship, or on account of escheat, if it happens there may be no heirs living.

UBI quis uxorem suam dotaverit in generali de omnibus terris et tenementis.——"Where a man shall have endowed his wife generally of all his lands and tenements." In some cases dower was only assigned of a certain part of the freehold. *Vide note.*

UBI revera.——When in truth.

UBI scelus est id, quod non proficit scire, jubemus insurgere leges, armari jura gladio ultore, ut exquisitis pœnis subdantur infames, qui sunt, vel qui futuri sunt rei.—— Where that infamy exists, which ought not to be known, we command the laws to be enforced, (and) that the authorities be armed with the avenging sword, that those infamous wretches may be overwhelmed with the severest punishment, who are, or shall be guilty of this crime.

UBIVIS tutior quam in meo regno essem?——Where should I be safer than in my own kingdom?

UDAL.——Allodial.

UL.——Any one.

ULNAGIUM.——Ell, or yard measure.

ULTERIUS concilium.——Further arguments.

ULTERIUS de eadem dixerit.——He shall further declare concerning the same (thing).

ULTERIUS non vult prosequi.——"He is unwilling to prosecute further." Part of the entry formerly made when the prosecutor wished to stay proceedings.

ULTIMA intentio regis.——The King's final resolve.

ULTIMA ratio spoliata ante omnia restituenda.——It is of the greatest importance that stolen property should be restored before all other things.

ULTIMA voluntas esset libera.——The last will should be made without restraint.

ULTIMUM supplicium.——The last atonement: death. Vide "*Est autem magna assiza.*"

ULTIMUS hæres.——The last heir.   *Vide note.*

ULTRA mare.——Beyond sea.

ULTRA vires.——A term in Scotch law. Beyond the power of.

UNA eademque persona.——One and the same person.

UNA fui; testamentum simul obsignavi cum *Clodio*, testamentum autem palam fecerat, et illum hæredem et me scripserat.——I was of the party. I signed the will with *Clodius*, but that will was made openly, and he had appointed him and myself his heirs.

UNCIA.——In Roman law. An ounce.

UNCORE prêt.——Always ready.

UNDE convictus est.——Wherefore he is convicted.

UNDE deterioratus.——Whereby he is injured.

UNDE nil habet.——From whence he (or she) derives no interest.

UNDE petit judicium.——Whereby he seeks judgment.

UNDE petit remedium.——Whereby he seeks relief.

UNDE statuimus, ut decimas ecclesiasticas omnis populus inferat quibus sacerdotibus, aut in pauperum usum, aut in captivorum redemptionem errogantium; sic suis orationibus, pacem populo et salutem impetrant.——Wherefore we ordain that all persons bring their tithes to some priests, either for the use of the poor, or for the redemption of wandering captives; thus obtaining, by their prayers, peace and safety for the people.

UNDRES.——Persons under age.

UNE disposition á faire une mauvaise chose.——An inclination to do a bad act.

UNG.——One.

UNGELD.——A person out of the protection of the law.

UNICA taxatio.——A single taxation: an assessment or taxation made for each person.

UNIUS responsio testis omnino non audiatur.——That the evidence of one witness be not regarded.

UNIVERSORUM bonorum.——Of all the effects.

UNIVERSORUM, quæ ex questu veniunt.——Of all the goods which accrued by profit.

UNLAGE.——An unjust law.

UNO contextu, uno eodemque tempore.——With one series, and at the same time.

UNO quorum continetur, inter alia, juxta tenorem et ad effectum sequentem.——In one of which is comprised, among other things, nearly to the tenor and effect following.

UNQUES prist.——Always ready.

UNUM qui consilium daret; alterum qui contracteret; tertium qui receptaret et occuleret, pari pœnæ singulos esse obnoxios.——That he who gives counsel; the other who assists; a third who harbors and conceals, are all liable to the same punishment.

UNUSQUISQUE per pares suos judicandus est, et ejusdum provinciæ; peregrina vero judicia modis omnibus submovemus.——Every one is to be tried by his equals (or peers), and of the same province (or county); but we reject by all means strange (or foreign) decisions. *Vide note.*

UPSUN.——Between sunrise and sunset.

URE.——Effect.

USA.——River.

USANCE.——Usury: interest.

USER de action.——Is the pursuing, or bringing an action in the proper county, &c.

USQUE ad filum aquæ.——To the middle of the stream.

USQUE ad inferos.——Even to the lowest depths.

Usucaptio.——A possession by use: a prescription. *Vide note.*

Usufructuarius.——One who has the use, and enjoys profit of the estate.

Usuræ asses.——Pounds of (or for) interest.

Usura centesima.——Usury at one per cent. per month.

Usu rem capere.——To hold any estate by custom: a title by occupancy.

Usuria contra naturam est: quia usuria sua natura est sterilis, nec fructum habet.——"Usury (or interest) is against nature; because interest is in its nature barren and unfruitful." At one time the receiving interest was considered a crime; probably founded on the *Mosaic* law, *see Exod.* c. xxii. 25. *Vide note.*

Usuria dicitur ab "*usu,*" et "*ære,*" quia datur pro "*usu æris.*"——It is called usury, from "*usu,*" (use) and "*ære*" (money), because it is given for the use of money.

Usuria dicitur quasi "ignis urens."——It is called usury, as though it were "a consuming fire." The Hebrew word for *interest* signifies to bite as a snake. *Vide note.*

Usuria maritima.——Maritime interest: bottomry.

Usus fructibus.——"Use by the profits:" the profits or use of the land or money.

Usus fructus rei immobilis, sub conditione fidei; vel jus utendi prædio alieno.——The use is the profit of a thing immovable, under the condition of a trust; or the right of using another person's estate.

Ut ab inde excluditur.——That he be thenceforth excluded.

Ut antiquam.——As ancient; as of ancestry.

Ut billa aut breve cassetur.——That the bill or writ be quashed.

Ut cita mortis periculum sententia sancta eum moderatur.——"As being near the point of death a holy feeling governs him." Thus the last words of a dying man are given in evidence of his murder; and this has been the law for ages.

Ut consanguineo et hæredi.———As to a relation and heir.

Ut currere solebat.———As it was wont to run.

Ut de bonis suis propriis.———As of his own proper goods.

Ut de corona.———As though (held) of the crown.

Ut de feudo.———As concerning the fee.

Ut de vadio.———As concerning a pledge (or mortgage.)

Ut de wardo.———As (relates) to guardianship.

Ut ecce, maritus probatur non concubuisse aliquamdiu cum uxore, infirmitate, (vel) alia causa impeditus: vel erat in ea invaletudine ut generare non possit.———Seeing that it is proved that the husband had no knowledge of the wife for a considerable time, being unable, from infirmity, or some other cause: or he was so sick that he had not the power of procreation.

Ut feudum antiquum.———As an ancient fee.

Ut feudum maternum.———As a maternal fee, or one descended on the mother's side.

Ut feudum paternum.———As a paternal fee, or one descended on the father's side.

Ut feudum stricte novum.———As a fee strictly new: (granted on specific conditions.)

Ut hospites.———As guests.

Uti.———To use.

Utile, per inutile non vitiatur.———That which is serviceable is not (rendered) invalid by what is useless.

Utiles esse opiniones has quis negat cum intelligat quam multa firmentur jurejurando; quantæ salutis sint fœdera religionis; quam multos divini supplicii metus à scelere revocârit; quamque sancta fit societas civium inter ipsos, Diis immortalibus interpositis, tum judicibus, tum testibus? ———Who can deny the advantage of these opinions, when he considers how many things may be established by an oath; how precious are the ties of our religious security; how many has the dread of divine punishment withdrawn from crime; and how sacred is the society of citizens among themselves, the immortal gods being placed as well before the judges, as the witnesses? *Vide note.*

UTILITAS vero mercantium, et quod alter populus alterius rebus indigeat, fere jus belli, quod ad commercia subegit. Hinc in quoque bello aliter atque aliter commercia permittuntur, vetanturque, prout e rea sua subditorumque suorum esse censent principis.——But the convenience of an interchange of those goods, which one country requires from another, the law of war as respects commerce hath almost prohibited. Hence in every war, commerce is allowed or forbidden, as the belligerent powers may conceive to be advantageous, or not.

UTINAM tam facile vera invenire possem, quam falsa convincere.——I wish I could as easily find the truth as I can discover the falsehood.

UTI non potuit.——He was not able to enjoy.

UTI possidetis.——" As you enjoy" (or retain). This is often used where each party is to retain that which he possesses.

UT jus meum possessarium.——As my possessory right.

UTLAGATUS est; quasi extra legem possitus.——He is outlawed; placed, as it were, out of the law's protection

UTLAGHE.——Sax. An outlaw.

UTLEPE.——Sax. Escape.

UT liberum tenementum.——"As a free tenement:" as a freehold not subject to any conditions.

UT martius populus aliquid sibi terræ daret, quasi stipendium; cæterum ut vellet manibus atque armis suis uteretur.——That the warlike people should give him some lands by way of stipend (or salary); but that (as a recompense) he would employ his power and weapons.

UT per aspectum corporis sui constare poterit justiciariis nostris, si prædictus *A.* sit plenæ ætatis, necne.——That on a view of his person it may appear to our Justices, whether the aforesaid *A.* be of full age or not.

UT personaliter, libere et debito modo resignavit.——That he resigned personally, freely, and in legal (or due) form.

UT pœna ad paucos, metus ad omnes, perveniat.——That punishment may come to a few; (but) fear to all.

UT rector prosternat arbores in cœmeterio.——That the rector may cut down trees in the church-yard (or burial-ground).

UT res captæ ab hostibus—efficiatur duo requiruntur. Primum, quod navis capta ducatur ab præsidiis ipsium hostium et ab eorum confinibus. Secundum, quod ita ducta, ut sit in tuto; nec a militibus occurrentibus momento recuperare possit, et penes eos pernoctârit.——With respect to property captured from the enemy—care is taken that two things be required: first, that the ship taken be conducted from the enemies' station, and from their limits; secondly, that she be so brought out as to be in safety, nor can then be retaken by a military force, and remain in their power a whole night.

UT res magis valeat.——That the thing may rather take effect, (or be efficacious.)

UT res magis valeat, quam pereat.——That the matter may be of validity, sooner than be lost.

UTRUM averia carrucæ, captæ in vetito namio sint irre-plegibilia?——Whether beasts of the plough taken in a prohibited place, are irrepleviable?

UTRUM feudum ecclesiasticum, vel laicum.——"Whether it be an ecclesiastical or a lay fee." *Vide note.*

UTRUM relatus est odio vel malitia.—Whether he be accused from hatred or malice.

UT si duos vel tres testes produxerit ad probandum, oportet quod defensio fiat per quatuor, vel per sex; ita quod pro *quolibet* testes *duos* producat juratores, usque ad duodecim.——As if he produced two or three witnesses to give evidence, it behooves that the defence be made by four or six; so that for *every* witness, he produce *two* jurors up to twelve. Vide " *Compurgatores.*"

UT statuta illa, et omnes articulos in eisdem contentos, in singulis locis ubi expedire viderit, publice proclamari; et firmiter teneri; et observari faciat.——That he cause those statutes, and all the articles in them contained, to be publicly proclaimed in all those places where he should see fit; and be firmly held and obeyed.

NOTES TO U.

UBI QUIS UXOREM, &c.—Dower at the common law was more general before the doctrine of Uses and Trusts had deprived many widows of their dower. Terms of years, even when the purposes for which they were raised are *satisfied*, are now sometimes (where regularly assigned in trust to attend the fee) made use of as a protection against dower, although the proprietor has, in all other respects, a clear fee simple. Vide *Sugden, Preston, &c.*

ULTIMUS HÆRES.—The last Heir: he to whom the land comes by escheat, for want of lawful heirs. This is in some cases the lord of whom they are held; but, in others, the King is the *ultimus hæres.* Vide *Bract.* lib vii. c. 17.

UNUSQUISQUE PER PARES, &c.—It was a fundamental principle in the feudal policy, that no freeman could be subjected to new laws, unless by his own consent. In consequence of this, the vassals of every Baron were called to his court, in which there were established, by mutual consent, such regulations as they deemed most beneficial to their small society; and granted their superior such supplies of money as were proportioned to their abilities, or his wants. As the superior lord, according to the original plan of the feudal system, retained the direct or ultimate property of those lands, which he granted in temporary possession to his vassals, the law, even after fiefs became hereditary, still supposed the original practice to exist.

USUCAPTIO, signified in the *Roman* law, when any one obtained the property of a thing, by possessing it for a certain time without interruption, according to the law of the Twelve Tables; for two years, if it were a farm, or immovable; and for one year, if the thing was movable. *Ut usus auctoritas,* i. e. "occupation gives title." *Jus dominii, quod usu paratur fundi biennium, cæterarum rerum annus usus esset,*" i. e. "the right of inheritance which is acquired in a farm by two years' use, and in all other things by one year's possession." Vide *Plin. Ep.* v. i. But this took place only among citizens, for *adversus hostem,* i. e. *peregrinum æterna auctoritas erat,* Cic. Off. i. 12: i. e. "law went against an enemy, i. e. a stranger, as an enduring bar." *Res semper vindicari poterat a peregrino, et nunquam usu capi,* i. e. "things could at all times be taken from a foreigner, and at no time could he gain prescriptive title." Hence, *Cicero* says, " *Nihil mortales a diis usu capere possunt,*" i. e. "men could not hold against the gods by prescriptive title."

If there was any interruption in the possession, it was called "*usurpatio*," which, in country farms, seems to have been by breaking off the shoot of a tree. Vide *Cic. de Orat.* iii. 28. But, afterwards, a longer time was necessary to constitute prescription, especially in the provinces: namely, *ten* years among those who were present; and twenty years among those who were absent; sometimes a length of time was required beyond remembrance. This method of acquired property by possession was called "*longæ possessionis præerogativa*, vel *prescriptio*," (i. e. the prerogative or prescription of long possession). The time necessary to acquire a prescriptive right to real property, at this day, is different in different countries.

USURIA CONTRA NATURAM, &c.—The interest of money was called by the Romans, "*Fœnus*" vel "*Fœnus, Usura,*" "*Merces,*" "*Fructus,*" vel "*Impendium:*" the capital "*Ouput,*" or "*Sors,*" also "*Fœnus,*" which is sometimes put for the *principal* as well as the *interest*. When one *As* was paid monthly, for the use of a hundred, it was called *usura centesima*, because in a hundred months the interest equalled the capital. This we call *twelve per cent. per annum*, as Plin. "*duodenis assibus debere* vel *mutuari,*" (i. e. to owe or borrow at twelve per cent.) *Ep.* x. 62. v. 55. *Centesimus computare. Id.* ix. 28, which was usually the legal interest at *Rome*, at least towards the end of the Republic, and under the first Emperors. Sometimes the double of this was exacted, "*binæ centesimæ,*" twenty-four per cent.; and even forty-eight per cent. Vide *Cic. Verr.* iii. 70. Horace mentions one who demanded *sixty* per cent. "*Quinas hic capiti mercedes exsecat*, i. e. *quintuplices usuras exigit*, vel *quinis centesimis fœnerat*, i. e. "he takes five interests for the capital," or "he exacts quintuple usury or loans at five centages." Vide *Sat.* i. 2, 14. After the death of *Antony* and *Cleopatra*, A. U. 795, the interest of money at *Rome* fell from twelve to four per cent. *Dio.* li. 21.

The *Romans* commonly paid money by the intervention of a banker, "*in foro et de mensæ scriptura, magis quam ex arca domoque vel cista pecunia numerabatur,*" (i. e. at the bank, and by an accountant, more than from the chest, house, or scrutoire), whose account books of debtor and creditor (*tabulæ* vel *codices accepti, et expensi; mensæ rationes*), were kept with great care, hence *acceptum referre*, vide *Cic.*, and amongst later writers, "*acceptum ferre*" (to mark with the debtor as received): "*Expensum ferre*" (to mark down on the creditor side). "*Ratio accepti atque expensi, inter nos convenit,*" (i. e. the sum of debt and credit between us agrees). Vide *Plaut. In rationem inducere* (to state on account).

There appears to have been considerable cruelty exercised towards *Roman* citizens by the race of *usurers;* perhaps more than is practiced at the present day in money matters. The student will observe, on reading *Terence's* Comedies, what odium was attached to usury; but the shafts of ridicule strike with feeble effect on hearts made callous by avarice. *Cato* reprobated usury "*Cum ille, dixisset, Quid fœnerari? Tum Cato, Quid hominem, inquit occidere,*" i. e. "When (the borrower) said, How will you lend at usury? Then *Cato* answered, What, would you kill the man?" Vide *Cic. Off.*

By the law of the Twelve Tables, it was ordained that insolvent debtors should be given up (*addicerentur*) to their creditors, to be bound in fetters and cords (*compedibus et nervis);* whence they were called "*nexi, obœrati, et addicti*" (which see); and though they did not entirely lose the rights of freemen, yet they were in *actual* slavery, and often treated more harshly than even slaves themselves. *Liv.* ii. 23.

If any one was indebted to several persons, and could not find a cautioner (*vindex*, vel *compromissor*), within sixty days, his body, literally, according to some; but, perhaps more probably, according to others, *his effects* might be cut into pieces (*secari*), and divided among his creditors. Vide *A. Gell.* xx. 1. Thus "*Sectio*" is put for the purchase of the *whole booty* of any place, or of the *whole effects* of a proscribed or condemned person, vide *Cic. Phil.* ii.

26; or for the booty or goods themselves. And "*Sectores*" for the purchasers, vide *Ascon. in Cic. Verr.* i. 23; because they made profit by selling them in parts (*a seco*). Hence, "*Sectores collorum et bonorum*, i. e. *qui proscriptos occidebant et bona eorum emebant*" (Cic. Rosc. Am. 29), i. e. "Dividers of neck and goods, i. e. "those who slew proscribed persons, and sold their goods."

To check the cruelty of usurers, a law was made, A. U. 429, whereby it was provided that no debtor should be kept in irons or bonds; that the goods of the debtor, and not his person, should be delivered up to his creditor. Vide *Liv.* viii. 28. But the people not being satisfied with this, often afterwards demanded an *entire* abolition of debts, which they used to call "*New Tables.*" But this does not appear to have been ever granted them. At one time, indeed, by a law passed by *Valerius Flaccus*, silver was paid with brass, as it is expressed, *Sallust. Cat.* 33; that is, the fourth part of the debt only was paid. Vide *Vell.* ii. 23. Julius Cæsar, after his victory in the civil war, enacted something of the same kind. Vide *Cæs. Bell. Civ.* iii. 1.

USURIA DICITUR QUASI IGNIS URENS.—In the Middle Ages, the *Lombards* (a name frequently given to *all* Italian merchants in many parts of *Europe*), engrossed the trade of every kingdom in which they settled; and they became masters of the greater part of its cash. Money, of course, was in their hands not only a sign of the value of all other commodities, but became an object of commerce itself. They dealt largely as bankers. The business of a broker, a person who lent out money at interest, was for many ages considered *detestable*, originating, no doubt, from the strong language of the *Mosaic* law, and some passages in the Psalms of *David.* It is very probable the words in the text had reference to the enormous usury taken in the Middle Ages, which was frequently excessively cruel. In an *Ordonnance*, 1295, we find those brokers or usurers styled "*Mercatores*" and "*Campsores.*" They carried on their commerce with somewhat of that rapacious spirit which is natural to monopolizers, who are not restrained by the competition of rival trades, and are destitute of every honorable principle. The fathers of the Church had preposterously applied the prohibition of usury in the Scripture to the payment of *any* interest; and condemned it as a sin: it is true the *Mosaic* law forbade the taking of usury or interest by one Jew from another; however, the Schoolmen, led on by *Aristotle*, whose sentiments they followed implicitly, and without examination, adopted the same error, and enforced it.

Thus the *Lombards* found themselves engaged in a traffic which was everywhere deemed cruel and odious. They were liable to punishment, if detected, and, consequently, were not satisfied with that moderate premium which they might have honestly claimed, if their trade had been opened and authorized by law. They exacted a sum proportioned to the danger, and also the risk of discovery. Accordingly, we find it was usual for them to demand twenty per cent. for the use of the money in the thirteenth century. Vide *Murat. Antiq. Ital.* vol. i. p. 893. About the beginning of that century the Countess of *Flanders* was obliged to borrow money in order to pay her husband's ransom; she procured the sum necessary, and the lowest usury she paid was twenty per cent.: and some of them exacted nearly thirty per cent. Vide *Marten & Durand. Thesaur. Anecdotorum,* vol. i. 886. In the fourteenth century, A. D. 1311, *Philip* the Fourth fixed the interest which might be legally exacted in the fairs of *Champagne,* at twenty per cent. Vide *Ordon.* tom. i. 484. The interest of money in *Arragon* was somewhat lower. As late as the year 1490, it appears that the interest of money in *Placentia* was at the rate of *forty* per cent. This is the more extraordinary, because at that time the commerce of the *Italian* states was become considerable. *Charles* the Twelfth fixed the interest in the low countries at twelve per cent. It was complained of at that time as having a pernicious effect on agriculture and commerce. The *Lombards* were likewise established in *England*, in the thirteenth century, and a considerable street' in the city of *London* still bears their name. They enjoyed great privileges, and carried on an extensive commerce, particularly as bankers. After the interest of money had for many years fluctuated in *England*, at last it was enacted by a most excellent statute, made in Queen *Anne's* reign, that it should not exceed *five* per cent., which has been the legal interest there ever since, though it is very often lent at a lower rate. This wise law of Queen *Anne* is, however, shamefully evaded by the abominable practice of purchasing *life annuities*, in which there is little risk of losing the principal, while the interest paid is often enormous.

In ancient times, if any one after his death was found to have been a usurer, all his goods and chattels were forfeited to the King.

UTILES ESSE OPINIONES, &c.—Although it would be next to impossible in civil and criminal cases, to dispense with the solemn obligation of an oath, as a general bond to speak the truth, in the presence of an omniscient Creator; yet it has been considered by many reflecting and judicious persons that the multiplication of oaths, which has been so customary during the last century, has rendered them far less sacred in public estimation than formerly: nothing is more pernicious to morals than the too frequent exaction of oaths, which is now usual on the most trifling occasions. Indeed, when we observe how frequently, in every political and civil business, the strongest oath is taken, we cannot but consider that those solemn ideas which every person should feel, when he takes an oath, are gradually weakened, till at length its frequency bids fair to obliterate all consciousness of the obligation. *Livy* informs us that the sanctity of an oath (*fides et jusjurandum*,) had more influence with the ancient *Romans* than the fear of laws and punishments. *Liv.* i. 21. ii. 45. They did not, he says, as in after times, when a neglect of religion prevailed, by interpretations, adapt an oath and the laws to themselves, but every one conformed his own conduct to his oath. *Liv.* iii. 20, ii. 32, &c.

UTRUM FEUDUM, &c.—It sometimes happened that a dispute arose whether lands were subject to tithes, and feudal services, or not; if they belonged to a Church or a Monastery, they were free of tithes; and probably of all other feudal burdens.

V.

VACANTIA bona.——Property in which no one claims an ownership.

VACATUR.——It is set aside: vacated.

VACCILLANTES literatæ.——Letters written with a trembling hand.

VACHIVIA.——Anciently. A dairy.

VADELECT——In old English law. A servant.

VADIATIO duelli.——Wager of battle.

VADIATIO legis.——Wager of law.

VADIMONIUM deserere.——To forfeit his recognizance.

VADIUM mortuum.——A dead pledge: a mortgage. Vide note to "*Mortgagium*."

VADIUM vivum.——A living pledge: as an ox, &c.

VADUM.——A fording-place.

VALEAT quantum valere potest.——"Let it prevail as far as possible." Let the argument pass for what it is worth.

VALIDIORA sunt exempla quam verba, et plenius opere docetur quam voce.——Examples are stronger than arguments; and instruction can be given better by precedent than by language.

VALOR beneficiorum.——The value (or assessment) of the benefices.

VALOR maritagii.——"The value of a marriage." In the feudal times, the Barons often received money on the marriage of their wards. *Vide note.*

VALVASOR.——A vassal occupying the second rank.

VANA est illa potentia quæ nunquam venit in actum. ——That power is useless which never comes into action.

VANA quoque ad veros accessit fama timores.——Idle rumors were often added to well-founded apprehensions.

VARDA.——In old English. Guardianship.

VAS.——A pledge.

VASSALERIA.——The tenure or holding of vassals.

VASSALLUS.——A Tenant: a Vassal: a Feudatory. *Vide note.*

VASSALLUS qui abnegavit feudum, ejusve conditionem, expoliabitur.——A vassal who has disowned his fee, or (denied) his covenant, shall be deprived (of his land). *Vide note.*

VASTUM.——Waste. *Vide note.*

VAVASORS.——An ancient name of dignity next below a peer. *Vide note.*

VEAGE.——Voyage.

VECORIN.——The crime of stopping one upon the wayside.

VEEL.——Old.

VEL causam nobis significes.——Or that you may make known the cause to us.

VEL consuetudines loci.——Or the customs of the place.

VEL ex similibus.——Or of like matters.

VEL extra illud contractum.——Or agreed for besides that.

VENARIA.——In old English law. Animals that were hunted.

VENATIONES, et sylvaticas vagationes, cum canibus, et accipitribus.——Hunting, and wandering in woods with dogs and hawks.

VENDITIONI exponas.——That you expose to sale.

VENDITIO per mutuam manuum complexionem.——A sale by mutual shaking of hands.

VENEFICIA.——Poisonings.

VENELIA.——A narrow, or strait way.

VENIA ætatis.——Privilege of age.

VENIRE ad respondendum.——To come to make answer.

VENIRE de novo.——To come anew.

VENIRE de placito, et ejectione.——To come, concerning the plea and ejectment.

VENIRE facias.——That you cause to come.

VENIRE facias ad respondendum.——That you cause to come to make answer.

VENIRE facias de novo.——That you cause to come anew.

VENIRE tam quam.——To come as well.

· VENIRE tam triandum, quam ad inquirendum.——To come as well to try (the cause) as to make inquisition.

VENIT et defendit vim et injuriam.——He comes and defends the force and injury.

VENIT et defendit vim et injuriam, quando et ubi curia

consideravit; et damna et quicquid quod ipse defendere debet, et dicit, &c.——He comes and defends the force and injury, when and where the court has considered; and the damages, and whatsoever he to ought defend, and says, &c.

VENIT et dicit.——Comes and says.

VENKER.——Vanquished.

VENTRE inspiciendo.——The name of a writ. *Vide note.*

VENUE.——The place from which the jury come.

VERBA attendenda, non os loquitur.——Words are to be attended to more than the orator.

VERBA cartarum fortius accipiuntur contra proferentem.——The language of deeds should be taken forcibly against him who produces them (or gives them in evidence).

VERBA fortius accipiuntur contra proferentem.—— Words are taken more strongly against him who asserts them (as the grantor, feoffer, &c.).

VERBA generalia restringuntur ad aptitudinem rei.—— General words are to be restricted to the fitness of the subject.

VERBA intentione debent inserviri.——Words ought to be governed by the intention.

Verba intentionis, et non contra, debent inservire.—— The meaning of the words, and nothing else, should be regarded.

VERBA ita intelligenda sunt, ut res magis valeat quam pereat.——Words should be so understood that the matter may avail rather than be of no utility.

VERBA precaria.——Words of trust.

VERBIS aut cantilenis.——By words or songs.

VERBUM imperfecti temporis, rem adhuc imperfectam significat.——A word of time imperfect, shows that the matter is incomplete (or unfinished).

VEREBAT.——A ship in which goods are transported.

VEREDICTO non obstante.——Notwithstanding the verdict.

VEREDICTUM, quasi dictum veritatis.——A verdict, as though it were the decision of truth itself.

VERGE.——A staff, or ensign of office.

VERGENS ad inopiam.——In Scotch law. In declining circumstances.

VERITAS nominis tollit errorem demonstrationis.—— The truth of the name removes the error of the description.

VERITAS visû, et morâ: falsa, festinatione et incerta, valescunt.——Truth is strengthened by investigation and delay: falsehood requires haste and uncertainty.

VERITATEM dicere.——To speak the truth.

VERITATIS simplex oratio est.——The language of truth is simple.

VERT.——*Fr. Verth*, i. e. *Viridis*, of a green color, otherwise called "*Greenhue.*" This word signifies everything that beareth a green leaf within a forest that may cover deer; but especially large and thick coverts.

VERUNTAMEN non ita præcise recipiendus est locus in quo contractus est initio, ut si partes in alienum contrahendo locum respexerint. Ille potius considerandus; nam contraxisse unusquisque in eo loco intelligitur in quo sit solviri.——Nevertheless that place is not so especially to be regarded in which the contract originated, but that the parties may consider it to have been made in some other place. That (the place where the payment is to be made) is rather to be regarded; for every person is understood to have contracted where the payment should have been made.

VERUNTATEM, &c., locus in quo contractus, &c., potius considerrand', ubi obligavit.——Truly, &c., the place where the contract was made is rather to be considered as that where he bound himself (to pay).

VESTURA terræ.——The vesture (or crop) of the field.

Vesque.——Bishop.

Vetant leges sacratæ, vetant duodecim tabulæ, leges frangentur privatis hominibus irrogatæ, enim est privilegium. Nemo unquam tulit, nihil est crudelius, nihil perniciosius, nihil quod minus hæc civitas ferre possit.—— The sacred laws forbid, the Twelve Tables forbid, that the laws ordained for private persons should be broken, for that is their privilege (or peculiarity). No one ever suffered it, nothing is more cruel, nothing more injurious, nothing that can be more intolerable in the city than this.

Vetustas semper pro lege habetur.——Antiquity shall always be esteemed as law.

Vetustate temporis, aut justiciari cognitione roborata. ——Confirmed by antiquity, or strengthened by judicial cognizance.

Vexata quæstio.——A mooted point: a disputed question.

Viadatio duelli.——The pledge to fight in single combat.

Via facti.——The bearing (or import) of the deed.

Viagium usque ad finem designatum.——The voyage to the end (or place) appointed (or agreed upon).

Via regia.——The highway, or common road, called the King's way. It is sometimes called "*via militaris*," the military way.

Via trita: via tuta.——The customary way is the safe one: the beaten path is the sure one.

Vi aut clam.——By force or covertly.

Vi bonorum raptorum.——Of goods forcibly taken away.

Vicecomes in propria persona assumptis secum duodecim, &c., accedat ad locum vastatum et inquirat.——The sheriff in his own person, taking with him twelve, &c., proceed to the place wasted, and make inquisition.

Vicecomes non misit breve.——The sheriff has not sent the writ.

VICEM personarum ecclesiæ gerere.——To do the duty as parson of the church.

VICINA.——The neighborhood.

VICINETUM, or visnetum.——" A neighboring place ;" " *Locus quem vicini habitant*," (the place which the neighbors inhabit). The place from whence a jury were to come for the trial of causes. [The reason why jurors were formerly chosen from places adjacent to the litigating parties, was their knowledge of their characters.]

VICONTIEL.——The name of a roll under which the sheriff collects rents.

VICTUS victori in expensis condemnandus est.—— The vanquished is to be condemned in costs to the conqueror.

VIDENDUM est igitur ut ea liberalitate utamur quæ prosit amicis noceat nemini. Nihil enim est liberale quod non idem justum.——Consequently it is to be observed that our liberality which rewards our friends must not injure another. Nothing can (truly) be called liberal that is not (strictly) just.

VIDETUR cognitio requisita in utroque.——It appears that a recognizance is required on both sides.

VIDIMUS.——We have seen.

VIDUA regis.——The widow of a crown vassal who could not marry a second time without the King's consent.

VI et armis.——By force and arms: by unlawful means.

VI et armis, de filio, vel filia, rapto, vel abducto.—— With force and arms, in respect of the son or daughter being taken, or carried away.

VI et armis, de uxore rapta, et abducta.——With force and arms, the wife being taken, and carried away.

VI et armis et contra pacem.——With force and arms, and against the peace.

VI et armis, videlicet, baculis, cultellis, arcubus et sagittis.——With force and arms, (to wit,) with clubs, knives, bows and arrows.

VIGILANTIBUS, et non dormientibus leges subveniunt.
——The laws protect the vigilant, not the slothful.

VIGILANTIBUS, et non dormientibus, servat lex.——The law assists those who watch, and not those who sleep.

VIGILANTIBUS, et non dormientibus succurrant jura.—— The laws assists the vigilant, not the careless.

VIGILANTIBUS jura subveniunt.——Laws assist the vigilant.

VIGILIA.——"A vigil:" the eve, or next day before any solemn feast; because formerly Christians were wont to watch, fast and pray in their churches, preparatory to such solemnities.

VIGINTI annorum lucubrationes.——The studies of twenty years.

VIIS et modis.——By ways and means.

VILLANA faciunt servitia, sed certa et determinata.—— They perform villein services, but they are certain and fixed.

VILLANI.——Villeins: bondmen.

VILLANUM soccagium.——"A villein socàge; a base holding." The tenure at one time of a considerable part of the lands of *England*.

VILLENAGIORUM, aliud purum, aliud privilegiatum. Qui tenet in puro villenagio faciet quicquid ei præceptum fuerit, et semper tenebitur ad incerta. Aliud genus villenagii dicitur villanum soccagium; et hujusmodi villani socmanni villani faciunt servitia, sed certa et determinata.
——Of villeinages, one is pure, the other privileged. He who holds (land) in pure villeinage shall do whatsoever he has been required to perform; and he shall always be held to uncertain services. The other kind of villeinage is called villein socage; and villein sockholders of this description perform villein (or mean) services, but they are certain and determined. Vide *note to* "*Servi*," &c.

VILLENAGIUM privilegiatum.——A privileged villeinage.

VINCULO matrimonii.——In the bond of wedlock.

VINCULUM personarum ab eodem stirpe descendentium. ——A band (or race) of persons descending from the same stock or lineage.

VINCULUM personarum, ab eodem stirpe decendentium, vel ascendentium, carnali propagatione in matrimonio.—— The connection or relation of persons, descending or ascending from the same stock begotten in wedlock.

VINCULUM pacis, et nervus belli.——The bond of peace and strength of war.

VINDICES injuriarum.——The avengers of wrongs.

VIOLATOR legum.——A transgressor of the laws.

VIRGA.——A yard.

VIRGA ferrea.——The iron yard.

VIRI et mulieris conjunctio, individuâ vitæ consuetudine cum divini et humani juris communicatione.——The union of husband and wife according to the inseparable custom for life, partakes both of the divine and human law.

VIRI magnæ dignitatis.——Men of high rank.

VIRI quantas pecunias ab uxoribus dotis nomine acceperunt, tantas ex suis bonis, æstimatione facta, cum dotibus communicant. Hujus omnis pecuniæ conjunctim ratio habetur, fructusque servantur. Uter eorum vita superavit, ad eum pars utriusque cum fructibus superiorum temporum pervenit.——So much money as the husbands receive with their wives by way of (marriage) pórtion, so much of their own goods, upon a valuation being made, is imparted (or conferred) with the dower. The consideration of this whole money is held jointly, and the profit (or interest) is preserved. Should one survive the other, the share of both, with the interest for the time elapsed, accrues to the survivor.

VIRO et uxori et hæredibus suis, (vel) viro et uxori hæredibus comunibus, si tales, vel non existerint, tunc ejus hæredibus qui alium supervixerit.——"To the husband, wife, and their heirs, (or) to the husband and wife, and their common heirs, if such shall exist; then if none remain, then to the heirs of him, or her, who shall survive." These were words of limitation used in some ancient grants of land.

VIRTUTE dimissionis.——By virtue of the demise.

VIRTUTE dimissionis quousque postea, scilicet, 4th September, 2 Jac.——By virtue of the demise until afterwards, to wit, on the 4th September, 2d James.

VIRTUTE ejus hospitalitatis.——On account of his hospitality. *Vide note.*

VIRTUTE officii.——By virtue of the office.

VIS armata.——Armed force.

VIS clandestina.——Clandestine force.

VIS divina.——The act of God.

VIS fluminis.——The force of a stream.

VIS inermis.——Unarmed force.

VIS laica.——Lay force.

VIS major.——A greater force (or power).

VIS major; vel causus fortuitus.——Greater power; or a chance case.

VISNE.——A neighborhood.

VISUS franchi plegii.——View of frank pledge.

VITA omnis in venationibus, atque in studiis rei militaris consistit.——Their whole life consists in hunting, and the study of military affairs.

VITA testatoris.——In the testator's lifetime.

VIVA voce.——Verbally.

VIVEVOYS.——The testimony of a witness.

VIVUM vadium.——A living pledge.

VOBIS præcipimus quod si ita sit, tunc sigilla vestra apponatis.——We command that if it be so, then set your seals.

VOCABULA artis.——Technical terms.

VOCARE in jus.——To summon to court.

VOCATA ad concionem multitudine, quæ coalescere in

populum unius corporis nulla re præterquam legibus poterat.——The multitude, being called to the assembly, which could grow into a people of one community by no operation except by the laws.

VOCATIO in jus.——Summoning to court. *Vide note.*

VOCEM non habere.——A phrase made use of by *Bracton*, signifying an "infamous person;" one who is not admitted to be a witness.

VOCHER.——To vouch.

VŒVE.——Widow.

VOILOIR.——A will.

VOIRE dire.——Witnesses are sometimes examined upon the "*voire dire*," previously to their being examined *in chief;* this is done to ascertain whether they are interested in the cause at issue, or labor under any other incapacity which may render them incompetent to give evidence.

VOLATILIA quæ sunt feræ naturæ, alia sunt regalia, alia communia.——Fowls of the air, which are of a wild nature; some are royal, others are common.

VOLATUS cygnorum, et cygnettorum ferorum vocatus. ——Called a flight of wild swans and cygnets.

VOLENTI non fit injuria.——"An injury cannot be done to a willing person." If a person consent to a wrong, he cannot complain.

VOLENTI non fit injuria, si dolo sit inductus ad consentiendum.——If a person be willingly induced to consent to a fraud, he receives no injury.

VOLO et præcipio ut omnes de comitatu eant ad comitatus et hundreda, sicut fecerint tempore Regis *Edwardi.*—— I will and command that all persons of the county repair to the county and hundred (courts), as they did in the time of King *Edward.*

VOLUIT ligamenta coifæ suæ solvere, ut palam monstrare se tonsuram habere clericalem; sed non est permissus. Satelles vero eum eripiens, non per coifæ ligamina, sed per guttur eum apprehendens, traxit ad carcerem.——

He was desirous to unloose the strings of his cloak (or hood) to show openly that he was shorn for the priesthood; but he was not permitted. For the officers seizing him, not holding him by the strings of the cloak, but by the throat, dragged him to prison.

VOLUIT, sed non dixit.——He was willing, but said nothing.

VOLUNTAS donatoris.——The will of the testator.

VOLUNTAS regis in curia; non in camera.——The will of the King in his court (of law); not in his chamber.

VOLUNTAS reputabatur pro facto.——The will should be taken for the deed.

VOLUNTATIS nostræ justa sententia de eo, quod quis post mortem suam fieri velit.——The true meaning of our will respecting that matter, which every person desires to be performed after his death.

VOTUM castitatis solemne.——"The solemn vow of (perpetual) chastity." This was formerly, by the canon law, considered as an impediment to matrimony.

VOUCHEE.——The person vouched in a writ of right, &c.

VOUCHER.——A word of art when the tenant in a writ of right calls another into the court, who is bound to him to *warranty;* and is either to defend the right against the demandant, or yield him other lands to the value.

VOUS êtes charges de rendre justice aux peuples commencez par la rendre a vous mêsmes.——You are appointed to render justice to the people; begin by doing justice to yourselves.

VULGO quæsiti.——Spurious children.

NOTES TO V.

VALOR MARITAGII.—It is almost impossible to conceive the degradation mankind may submit to without education; or the covetous means men had recourse to where there was no *legal* restraint. We find that even the *marriage* of the tenants' *orphan* daughters furnished occasions for the rapacity of the Barons in the feudal ages.

VASSALUS.—A vassal. This word in ancient writers signifies a *Tenant,* or *Feudatory :* a person who vowed fidelity and homage to a superior, on account of land, &c., held of him. It also sometimes means a *slave,* or servant, and especially a domestic of a prince. Vide *Du Cange.*

VASSALUS QUI ABNEGAVIT, &c.—That was one of the offences by which the Vassal forfeited his Fee, "if he *denied* that he held of his Lord:" he also forfeited it, if he transferred it without the consent of the Lord, by which he might lose his services; or have a tenant imposed upon him unable to go to the wars, when called upon.

VASTUM.—Waste. This word has divers significations; but it is generally appropriated to a spoil in houses, woods, lands, &c., to the prejudice of the heir, or of him entitled to the reversion or remainder. Vide *Kitchen,* fol. 168.

VAVASORS.—The first name of dignity next beneath a peer, was, at one time, that of " *Vidames," " Vicedomini," " Valvasors,"* or " *Vavasors;"* who are mentioned by ancient lawyers as " *Viri magnæ dignitatis,"* (men of exalted rank,) and Sir *Edward Coke* speaks highly of them: yet so mutable is all earthly honor that we now scarcely hear their names; and legal antiquarians are not agreed upon their original or ancient office. Vide *Black. Com.* 1. c. 12. *Bract. lib.* 1. c. 8: also *Spelman.*

VENTRE INSPICIENDO.—*Thomas* de *Aldham* of Surrey, brother of *Adam* de *Aldham, Anno.* 4 *Hen.* III. claimed his brother's estate, but *Joan,* widow of the said *Thomas,* obtained the writ "*De ventre inspiciendo,"* directed to the Sheriff of the county, as follows: " *Quod assumptis tecum discretis, et fidelibus militibus, et discretis et legalibus mulieribus de comitatu tuo in propria persona accedas ad ipsam Johannam, et ipsam, a prædictis mulieribus, coram præfatis militibus videri facias, et diligenter tractari per ubera et ventrem, et inquisitionem factam, certificari facias sub sigillo tuo, et sigillo militum, justiciariis apud Westmin.," &c.* That honorable and trusty Knights with discreet and proper matrons being had from the county, you (the Sheriff) go in person to *Joan,* and cause her to be examined and carefully searched in the abdomen and breasts by the said matrons in presence of the said Knights; and that search so made be certified under your (Sheriff's) seal, and the seal of the Knights, to our court at *Westminster, &c.* In Easter term, 39 *Eliz.,* there is mention of a peculiar case of this nature. A writ was then issued out of Chancery, into the Common Pleas, on the prosecution of *Percival Willoughby,* who had married the eldest of the five daughters of Sir *Francis Willoughby,* who died without any son, but left a widow named *Dorothy,* who, at the time of his death, pretended to be pregnant by *Sir Francis,* and if a son were born all the five sisters would thereby lose the inheritance descended unto them. This writ was directed to the Sheriffs of *London,* and they were commanded to cause the said *Dorothy* to be viewed by "twelve Knights," and searched by "twelve women," in the presence of the twelve Knights, "*ad tractandum per ubera, et ad ventrem inspiciendum,"* i. e. "to handle the breasts and examine the abdomen," whether she were with child or not; and to certify the same to the Court of Common Pleas; and if she were with child, to certify *how long,* in their judgments, "*et quando sit paritura,"* and when likely to be delivered. Upon which the Sheriffs accordingly caused her to be searched; and returned that she was *twenty* weeks gone with child, and that within *twenty* weeks more, "*fuit paritura,"* she was to be delivered. Thereupon another writ issued out of the Common Pleas, requiring the Sheriffs safely to keep her in such a house, and that the doors should be well guarded; and that every day they should cause her to be viewed by some of the women named in the writ; and that when she should be delivered, some of them should be with her, to view the birth, whether it were "*male* or *female*," to the intent that there should be no falsity. And upon this writ the Sheriffs returned, that they had caused her to be kept and viewed: and that on such a day she was delivered of a daughter. The consequence was that the estate descended to the *six* daughters, whereas had a son been born, by the law of the *English* primogeniture, all the five daughters of Sir *Francis* would have had no interest in his landed property. Vide *Cro. Eliz.* 566. *Cro. Jac.* 685. *Moore,* 523. Vide also *Ex parte Ayscough, Peere Will. Trin. Term.* 1731.

VIRTUTE EJUS HOSPITALITATIS.—*Hospitality.* The rites of hospitality were acknowledged and practiced from the earliest antiquity, and in the most barbarous ages. Natural feeling taught men to receive the stranger with kindness, in times when there was no commercial intercourse between different countries, and nothing but necessity could induce an individual to leave his home. We find hospitality enjoined in the *Mosaic* writings; in the poems of *Homer,* as well as among the *Arabs,* the *Germans,* and almost all the nations of antiquity; but different ideas were held in different places as to the degree and extent of the service which was due to the guest. In this respect, no people surpass the *Arabs.* Among them the host receives the stranger who comes to his tent with paternal kindness. If his provisions fail, he conducts his guest to his neighbor, who now entertains them both with equal generosity. This simple custom was consecrated among the *Greeks* by their religion. *Jupiter,* who was hence surnamed "the Hospitable" (*Xenios*), was the guardian of strangers, and the avenger of the injuries offered them. We learn from *Homer* the belief that the immortals sometimes appeared on earth in human shapes, and contributed to the observance of the rites of hospitality. In the early times of *Greece,* when increasing commercial intercourse compelled men to take frequent journeys, individuals entered into agreements to afford each other mutual entertainments, whenever business should bring either of them into the country of the other; and this was promised not only for themselves, but for their children and posterity. In *Homer,* we find this custom spoken of. The visitor was kindly saluted; he was bathed, clothed, entertained, and his conversation listened to with pleasure. After nine days, if the stranger had not previously made himself known, the question might be put to him, "Who, and whence art thou?" If he declared himself to be connected by ancient ties of hospitality between their ancestors, his host was rejoiced to have renewed the ancient bond. Still more welcome was the guest, if he could show half the ring broken between their fathers, in perpetual token of their agreement. The host made presents to his guest at his departure; which was carefully handed down in the family. Vide *Encyclopædia Americana.*

VOCATIO IN JUS.—Or summoning to court. If a person among the ancient *Romans* had a quarrel with any one, he first tried to make it up, *litem componere* vel *dijudicare,* i. e. "to agree or settle the dispute" in private, "*inter parietes,*" i. e. within the walls (or at home). Vide *Cic. pro P. Quint.* v. 11: "*per disceptatores domesticos,* vel *opera amicorum,*" i. e. "by private arbitrators or the intervention of friends." Vide *Cæcin.* 2. If the matter could not be settled in this way (*Liv.* iv. 9), the plaintiff (*actor* vel *petitor*) ordered his adversary to go *with him* before the *Prætor,* "*in jus vocabit*" (he called him into court), by saying to him, "*In jus voco te.*" (I call you to court.) "*In jus eamas.*" (Let us go to court). "*In jus veni*" (come to court). "*Sequere ad tribunal*" (follow to the tribunal). "*In jus ambula*" (walk to the court), or the like. Vide *Ter. Phorm.* v. 7, 43 and 88. If he refused, the prosecutor took some one present to witness, by saying, "*Licet antestari?*" (May I take you to witness?) If the person consented, he offered the *tip of his ear* (*auriculum opponebat*), which the prosecutor touched. Vide *Hor. Sat.* i. 9, 76. Then the plaintiff might drag the accused (*reum*) to court by force (*in jus ra-*

pere), in any way, even by the neck (*obtorto collo*). Vide *Cic. et Plaut. Pœn.* iii. 5, 45. According to the law of the Twelve Tables, "*Si calvitur (moratur) pedumve struit (fugit* vel *fugam adornat) manum eundo jucito (injicito),* i. e. "If he delays, or makes tracks (betakes to flight), arrest him." *Festus.* But worthless persons, as thieves, robbers, &c., might be dragged before a judge without this formality. Vide *Plaut. Pers.* iv. 9, v. 10. By the law of the Twelve Tables, none were excused from appearing in court, even the sick and infirm. If they could not walk, they were furnished with an open carriage (*jumentum,* i. e. *plaustrum,* vel *vectabulum. Gell.* xx). But afterwards this was altered, and various persons exempted, as magistrates; those absent on account of the state; matrons; and boys and girls under age. It was likewise illegal to force any person to court from his own house; because a man's house was esteemed his sanctuary (*tutissimum refugium, et receptaculum*). But if any one lurked at home to elude a prosecution, he was summoned three times, with an interval of ten days between each summons, by the voice of a herald, or by letters, or by the *Prætor's* edict; and if he still did not appear (*si non sisteret*), the prosecutor was put into the possession of his effects. If the person cited found security, he was let go. If he made up the matter by the way (*eundo via*), the process ceased. Hence, perhaps, may be explained the words of our Saviour. *Matt.* v. 25.

W.

WACREOUR.——A worthless fellow.

WACTA.——Watch.

WADIA.——Pledge.

WAFTORES.——The officer whose duty it was to protect the fishermen on the coasts of Suffolk and Norfolk.

WAIVE: WAIF: WAYF.——A stolen article which the thief has thrown aside in his flight for fear of detection.

WAINABLE.——Tillable.

WALAPANG.——In Lombardic law. To disguise one's self in order to commit theft.

WALDA.——Sax. A thicket.

WALLIA: WALLA.——Sax. A wall to protect lands against the sea.

WALLIÆ statutum.——The statute of Wales.

WANNAGIUM.——A certain allowance of land to be apportioned to each plough.

WADSET.——Is a right whereby lands, &c., are pledged as security for a certain sum.

WAPENTAKE.——What is called a *Hundred* is in many places in *England*, called a *Wapentake;* because, it is said, that annually, at public meetings, the people confirmed their union or acquiescence with the Governor by *touching his weapon*, generally a lance.

WARA.——A measure of land.

WARDÆ cancellarii omnes fiunt minores pro defectu parentum, et guardianum.——All minors are made wards of chancery who have neither parents nor guardians.

WARACTIAM.——Fallow land.

WARD-CORN.——In English law. The necessity of keeping guard with a *horn* to use upon times of surprise.

WARD-MOTE.——A court held in each ward in London.

WARD-PENNY.——A fee paid to the sheriff for watching a castle.

WARDEGMOT.——Sax. A court held in a ward.

WARENNA.——A warren.

WARGUS.——An exiled person.

WARNIAMENTUM.——In ancient law. A garment.

WARNISTURA.——Anciently. Furniture.

WARRANTIÆ chartæ.——The warranties of the deed or charter.

WARRANTIZO.——I warrant.

WARRANTO vendidi.——I sold under a warranty.

WARRANTIZANDO vendidit.——He sold under a warranty.

WASTEL.——Bread of the finest kind.

WASTINUM.——Land not under cultivation.

WAVESON.——Goods that float on the water after a wreck.

WEALD.——Sax. A wood.

WEF.—— A waif.

WEHADINC.——Trial by battle.

WEND.——A circuit.

WERE.——Sax. A price.

WEREGILD.——A fine paid in the reign of all the *Saxon*

kings in *England* as a redemption for committing homicide: also an amercement formerly paid to the king, lord of the fee, and relations of the party slain, where a person had committed murder. *Vide note.*

WERPIRE.——To throw away.

WERRA.——War.

WERVAGIUM.——Anciently. Wharfage.

WEYVIARE.——To abandon.

WIC: WIK: WYC.——House.

WIFA.——In old law. A mark.

WIGREVE.——A superintendent of a wood.

WITA.——In Saxon law. A fine paid for an offence.

WITAN.——Sax. Men of learning and wisdom.

WITHERNAM.——A distress unlawfully taken out of the county and another distress made. *Vide note.*

WITTEMON.——Sax. Dower.

WITTENA-GEMOTE.——The annual general council of principal men: held among the *Saxons* prior to the conquest. *Vide note.*

WLADARIUS.——In Polish law. A steward.

WOLFESHEAD.——An outlaw: meaning a person who might be killed with impunity like a wolf.

NOTES TO W.

WEREGILD, or WERGILD.—This fine was paid partly to the King for the loss of a subject, and partly to the next of kin of the person slain. Vide *L. L. Hen.* I. In the *Saxon* laws, particularly in those of King *Athelstan,* the several WEREGILDS for homicides were established in *progressive* order, from the death of the *Ceorl,* or peasant, up to that of the *King* himself. And in the laws of *Henry* the First, there is an account of what other offences were then redeemable by *Weregild,* and what were not so. The *Weregild* of a *Ceorl* was *two hundred and sixty-six thrysma:* that of the King, *thirty thousand;* each *thrysma* was equal to about one shilling sterling. How lowly estimated must have been the heinous crime of murder, when human life could be even *wantonly* taken away, and the punishment due for the offence commuted for money!

WITHERNAM.—From the *Sax.* "*wither,*" i. e. *altera,* or as some say "*contra,*" and "*nam,*" *capio* Where a distress is driven out of the county; and the sheriff, upon replevin, cannot make deliverance to the party distrained upon: in this case the writ of *Withernam* is directed to the sheriff, for the taking of so many of *his* beasts or goods, who did thus unlawfully distrain, into *his* (the sheriff's) keeping, until the party make deliverance of the *first* distress. It is, therefore, "a taking or reprisal of other cattle or goods in lieu of those that were formerly unjustly taken away or eloigned, or otherwise withdrawn." Vide *F. N. B.* 68, 69. 2 *Inst.* 140.

WITTENA-GEMOTE.—When a litigating party considered himself aggrieved by a judgment in an inferior court, or by favor or affection shown at the trial of the cause, there lay an appeal to the King, in the general assembly of the state, called the WITTENA-GEMOTE, which was convened annually, or oftener, where the Sovereign pleased, to consult on public business, to try great offenders, and which, in short, had the highest jurisdiction. To this superior court, as the *English* nation emerged from its state of barbarism, and civilization assumed different pursuits, whereby litigation increased, appeals became frequent, so that the intervention of the *Wittena-gemote* was generally made use of in matters of importance. But, notwithstanding the exercise of this *appellant* jurisdiction consumed a considerable time of the sitting of this Great Assembly, it does not appear that there was any other tribunal erected for the hearing and investigation of appeals from the inferior courts: and such appears to have been the nature of the jurisprudence of the country, until the time of the *Norman* Conquest. Vide note to "*Quoties bella,*" &c., and to "*De minoribus rebus,*" &c.

Y.

YALEMAINES.——However.

YCEMENT.——In a similar way.

YCEUX.——Those or them.

YCONOMIUS.——In ancient records. A patron: defender.

YEME.——In French law. Winter.

YEOVEN: YEVEN.——In old English. Given.

YEULX.——Eyes.

YINGEMAN.——In old law. Englishman.

YVERNAGIUM.——In old law. Winter-seedness.

Z.

ZYGOSTATES.——Gr.-Lat. One appointed to oversee the weighing in a trade between buyer and seller, in order to prevent fraud or quarrels.

www.ingramcontent.com/pod-product-compliance
Lightning Source LLC
Chambersburg PA
CBHW020813270326
41928CB00006B/357